ADMINISTRATIVE LAW IN AOTEAROA NEW ZEALAND

This book on administrative law in Aotearoa New Zealand fills a gap with its fresh scholarly account of the law in this area, focusing on analysis of structures and principles.

It identifies underlying tensions between competing objectives and outlines current trends and debates. It includes chapters on administrative justice, and throughout promotes an awareness of wider administrative law beyond judicial review. Given the recent recognition of tikanga – Māori customary law – as part of the laws of Aotearoa New Zealand, this book also offers tentative explorations of the roles tikanga may come to play in administrative law.

The book is suitable for use in university courses, especially in specialist administrative law courses. It is also addressed to judges, officials and practitioners seeking to deepen their understanding of this area of law; to academic audiences around the common law world; and to policy makers designing or evaluating administrative regimes.

Administrative Law in Aotearoa New Zealand

Hanna Wilberg

•HART•
OXFORD • LONDON • NEW YORK • NEW DELHI • SYDNEY

HART PUBLISHING

Bloomsbury Publishing Plc

Kemp House, Chawley Park, Cumnor Hill, Oxford, OX2 9PH, UK

1385 Broadway, New York, NY 10018, USA

Bloomsbury Publishing Ireland Limited, 29 Earlsfort Terrace, Dublin 2, D02 AY28, Ireland

HART PUBLISHING, the Hart/Stag logo, BLOOMSBURY and the Diana logo are trademarks of Bloomsbury Publishing Plc

First published in Great Britain 2025

1

This book was published with the assistance of

The Law Foundation NEW ZEALAND

A catalogue record for this book is available from the British Library.

A catalogue record for this book is available from the Library of Congress.

Library of Congress Control Number: 2025942504

ISBN: PB: 978-1-50993-090-6
ePDF: 978-1-50993-092-0
ePub: 978-1-50993-091-3

Typeset by Compuscript Ltd, Shannon
Printed and bound in Great Britain by TJ Books, Padstow, Cornwall

MIX
Paper | Supporting responsible forestry
FSC® C013056
FSC www.fsc.org

For product safety related questions contact productsafety@bloomsbury.com

To find out more about our authors and books visit www.hartpublishing.co.uk. Here you will find extracts, author information, details of forthcoming events and the option to sign up for our newsletters.

For Richard

Foreword

I am delighted and honoured that Hanna asked me to write a foreword to *Administrative Law in Aotearoa New Zealand*. The book is a great achievement, a very welcome and important addition to the – now globalised – literature of public law. In my opinion, Hanna has succeeded in all the aims she set for herself (see p xi of her Preface). The book is firmly structured; the reasoning is clear and persuasive; and, just as importantly, the writing style is attractively uncluttered and readable. Although Hanna does not expressly address readers coming to administrative law for the first time, I am sure that many engaged and curious beginners (especially those fortunate enough to be Aotearoa New Zealanders) could benefit greatly from this book. One of Hanna's pervasive themes is that legal rules express and reflect moral and political values. To my mind, this insight is fundamental to understanding law; and, ideally at least, it underpins sound legal education from day one.

Another basic feature of law that Hanna's account brings out is its dimension of time, its dynamism. In my experience, the sort of people who are attracted to the study of law often find law's essential instability (initially, at least) quite challenging – a problem rather than an opportunity, as it were. In fact, it is a social function of legal and other sorts of norms – that is, propositions telling us what we may, must and must not do – to link our social past with the present and adapt it for the future. In Einsteinian terms, time is one of law's dimensions. Administrative law provides an illuminating case-study in this regard because it has developed so fast and changed so much in the past 70 years or so – a feature captured by Hanna in (for instance) the contrast between the 'traditional grounds' and their 'modern extensions' (in Chapters 4 to 7) and in the discussion of the concept of 'jurisdiction' and functional alternatives in Chapter 9.

In the broad sense adopted by Hanna, 'administrative law', in some form or another, is as old as public administration itself – as far as we know, at least 5,000 years. Public administration – 'running the country' – is the first and primary function of human government. Its three classic legal modes are the making of general rules, the application of general rules to individual cases, and resolution of disputes about general rules and their application. In principle, there is no reason why all three legal modes of public administration should not be contemporaneously undertaken by one and the same official or institution, or by a single set of officials or institutions. In practice, however, such concentration of power is apt to generate conflicts of interest and lead to tyranny. In the history of the English legal system (which Aotearoa New Zealand inherited through British imperialism), the idea, that different modes of administration are best allocated to different officials or institutions, bore significant fruit in the late seventeenth and early eighteenth centuries. Making of general rules came to be understood as the characteristic function of the legislature; application of general rules to individual cases as the characteristic function of the 'executive' (originally the monarch); and resolution of disputes as the characteristic function of courts and other tribunals.

The functions are only 'characteristic' because none of the modes is the exclusive (as opposed to the predominant) function of any one of the institutions. In the case of courts, this was obvious from the start: until well into the nineteenth century, general rule-making by courts (incidental to resolution of disputes: 'common law') was at least as significant and important as the legislature's general rule-making. Legislation took over from the common law partly because addressing problems generated by massive and rapid, industrial, social and economic change required (and continues to require) voluminous, large-scale, timely rule-making of a sort that courts were (and are) incapable of providing through adjudication.

As problems and legislative 'solutions' multiplied, so did the apparatus needed successfully to translate the 'laws on the books' into actions and outcomes 'on the ground'. In the West, we live in a world in which 'big government' spends a significant proportion of society's income and employs a sizeable proportion of the working population. In this light, it is, perhaps, somewhat surprising that as a subject of systematic study, public administration and law relating to it did not capture wide and systematic attention of scholars, in places such as Aotearoa New Zealand, Australia and England, until the mid-twentieth century. Compared with systematic private law scholarship, concerted study of administrative is a very recent pursuit. Hanna captures this youthfulness and the potential it provides for teaching and learning more general lessons about the nature and development of law as a social phenomenon.

Hanna locates the focus of her book – on judicial control of public administration – within a wider lens. On the one hand, she stresses that the law of, and law generated by, judicial review is far from the whole of administrative law. On the other hand, she explains that there are very significant avenues for controlling public administration other than judicial review. Further, she gives two, more positive reasons for paying close attention to judicial control of public administration: because 'judicial review norms are generally applicable across all the different regimes that make up the administrative state'; and because 'judicial review decisions create binding precedent' (p 8). As I read it, Hanna's account also illustrates wider constitutional reasons for studying courts, particularly, as controllers of public administration. Furthermore, I think that the governance arrangements of Aoteoroa New Zealand provide a good context in which to explore these issues. Let me explain.

In the early centuries of the English common law, courts and judges were integrated into the system of government by the fact that they were understood to be royal officials performing certain governmental functions on behalf of (and under the ultimate control of) the monarch, albeit not to the exclusion of the monarch's personal performance of those functions when, and to the extent that, the monarch chose. When it was first developed by English courts in the late-sixteenth and early-seventeenth centuries, judicial review was available primarily to control local governmental bodies and other institutions that derived their authority from the monarch, not organs of central (ie the monarch's own) government. In the 'Glorious Revolution' of the late-seventeenth century, the constitutional position of the central courts and their judges was dramatically changed. Judges were no longer to be royal officials who held their positions at the unfettered discretion of the monarch but became effectively answerable only to Parliament and only for serious misconduct in office.

The nineteenth century witnessed various fundamental changes in the shape of English government. Whereas, around 1700, government ministers were still agents of and answerable to the monarch (the chief executive), by the middle of the nineteenth century the ministry had become part of and answerable, instead, to Parliament. The monarch eventually ceased to have any effective role in the day-to-day running of the country. From the early nineteenth century, various major functions formerly performed by local government authorities were taken over by central government (headed by ministers answerable to Parliament), and central government took on many new tasks that had not previously been undertaken at all by governments. As a result, people dissatisfied with government decisions and actions increasingly looked to the judges for redress. To meet this demand, the courts became willing to extend their judicial review activities from subordinate and local government to central government departments and ministers, the inheritors of the monarch's administrative powers. At the same time, government was being democratised. Universal adult suffrage was achieved by the third decade of the twentieth century, and popular election became the basic source of government authority and legitimacy.

Of course, the details of these broad developments differed from one country to another; and Aotearoa New Zealand can tell its own version of the general story. However, for our purposes, the barebones account is sufficient to show that at the very same time as courts were being increasingly asked to exercise control over public administration, their political credentials for doing so began to be weakened because, despite democratisation of the legislature and the executive, the basic qualification for being a judge remained legal experience and expertise – 'merit' – not popular election. Election of judges was adopted in some US states in the nineteenth century and continues to this day. But federal judges in the US have always been appointed and still are. In 2025, Mexico adopted popular election for choosing judges at all levels from the lowest to the highest. However, the move is extremely controversial and, ironically, only 19 per cent of eligible voters took part in the judicial elections. At the same time, even though merit, rather than popular election, remains the most common criterion for judicial appointments, in the face of 'populist' and authoritarian government in recent decades, the judiciary has increasingly come to be seen as an essential element of a 'democratic' system – as witnessed by large-scale protests in Israel in 2023, conducted in the name of 'democracy', against reforms of the country's Supreme Court.

Hanna's account, focusing on judicial control of public administration, provides a case-study of the tensions resulting from the contemporaneous juxtaposition of merit-based appointment and popular election as alternative sources of public authority and governmental legitimacy. For instance, she shows how, in significant ways, modern judicial extensions of the substantive grounds of judicial review have aggravated the tension by enabling courts to exercise more intrusive control over public administration. On the other hand, Chapter 6 explores the ways in which the concept of 'rights' has been deployed in attempts to ease the tension by providing apparently apolitical grounds for juridical intervention; but the account also suggests limits of this legitimisation strategy. One important reaction to the constitutionally compromised position of courts is to remove judicial appointments as far as possible from governmental and political control by establishing 'independent' judicial appointment bodies. In some ways, however, this merely sharpens the dilemmas resulting from our desire for extensive, robust government combined with an equally potent desire to prevent strong governments from becoming tyrannous. A different path, taken in the US, is to substitute overtly political affiliations for legal expertise and merit as the effective criteria for judicial appointment. However, as experience shows, this expedient can also aggravate rather than mitigate the underlying tension. Witness the spectacle of presidential nominees for the US Supreme Court trying to persuade sceptical senators that despite their acknowledged political sympathies and affiliations, on the bench they will apply 'the law' and nothing but the law.

In systems such as that of Aotearoa New Zealand, where appointed judges (and the whole appointments process) are simply assumed to be apolitical, the tension lies largely beneath the surface; but it is there, nonetheless. As Hanna also points out, the position of the judiciary in the Aotearoa New Zealand governmental system is significantly affected by the fact that, unlike its US counterpart (for instance), it has no upper-case-C Constitution. In systems that have, courts can be understood as the ultimate 'guardians' of the provisions of the Constitution, which have higher authority than non-Constitutional laws and, so, lie outside the direct control of the legislature and the executive and can be seen, in that sense, as above democratic politics. Once again, however, this arrangement may aggravate or, at least, not ameliorate the perilous position of courts by causing them to be seen as ultimately supreme over the other branches of government, including the legislature, thus making the task of justifying their authority even more urgent and difficult. Finding a sweet spot between effective judicial control on the one hand, and judicial dominance on the other, is a central challenge for administrative law.

Expertly guided exploration of all these and many other issues await the fortunate readers of this book.

Peter Cane
Sydney, June 2025

Preface and Acknowledgements

The image on the front cover of this book is a painting of North Head or Maungauika by Auckland artist Sarah Langdon.[1] This volcanic cone and promontory marks the entrance to Auckland's Waitematā Harbour. It has been prized by Māori for centuries and was used as a strategic vantage point to guard the harbour during World War II. It was also the subject of the landmark administrative law case of *Ireland v Attorney-General* discussed in Chapter 5, an unsuccessful challenge brought by local resident and poet Kevin Ireland to a decision by the Department of Conservation to use buildings on the reserve for its regional headquarters. It is now maintained and administered by the Tūpuna Maunga Authority, a co-governance entity representing the local council and the several iwi with mana whenua over Auckland maunga. Its connections with administrative law in Aotearoa New Zealand thus are many.

I have been teaching administrative law and writing on it in earnest since at least 2009. I started work on this book in 2019. I am primarily a doctrinal analytical scholar. So I have been wrestling all that time with how to make sense of the subject; of each of its individual parts and how they fit together. By making sense, of course, I do not mean constructing one neat and coherent structure. That would not be an accurate reflection of the complexity that comes from competing principles, concepts, objectives and values, all set in a great variety of public administrative contexts. What I do mean is to identify all those elements and identify the roles they play and how they relate to each other. In this book, I am sharing the fruits of that endeavour.

What kind of book this is, and who might want to read it? It is not a short survey of general principles, but nor does it offer a comprehensive discussion of all the cases. Instead, it offers an in-depth exploration of the principles, concepts, objectives and values and of the relationships between them, through discussion of the main authorities and selected other examples. I have sought to limit footnotes as much as is consistent with that enterprise, while also referring readers to some useful further reading.

My hope is that this book will serve to expose students at the level of elective and postgraduate courses to the complexities. It will be of interest to judges and members of the legal profession who wish to deepen or challenge their understanding of this area, and to academic colleagues who may wish to adopt or debate aspects of my account. It will also hopefully add to the picture of administrative law in Aotearoa New Zealand that is available to international audiences.

Let me turn then to the many acknowledgements that are due. In wrestling with the subject and constructing my account, I have been standing on the shoulders of giants. The major influences on my thinking include my Otago public law lecturers, especially Stuart Anderson and Bruce Harris and also Paul Roth and Grant Liddell.

[1] Entitled 'Above the Waterline', 2017.

They next include Paul Craig who taught me at Oxford. My late, great, and much-missed colleague Mike Taggart was never formally my teacher, but I learnt an immeasurable amount from him. I do not know what intuition prompted me in 2009 to finally make time to sit in on Mike's Administrative Law course. All I know is that I will forever be grateful that I took that opportunity – as it sadly turned out this was his final semester of teaching. Finally, my thinking has, of course, been shaped by many of the books on the subject; and none more so than Peter Cane's *Administrative Law*.

I would also like to acknowledge and thank my administrative law students. Over the years, their questions and comments, and the analysis in their exams and assignments, have inspired many ideas and insights.

The largest debts of gratitude, of course, I incurred in the writing of this book itself.

A very special thanks must go to two colleagues whose generous assistance and support went above and beyond. Matthew Groves encouraged me to undertake this project and supported my proposal to Hart Publishing. He provided detailed and prompt comments on at least three long chapters. He has given me many opportunities outside of this book and suggested some very fruitful projects. Marcelo Rodriguez Ferrere was the most amazing supporter in the final few months. His detailed and insightful comments immeasurably improved four long chapters, and he continuously conveyed such genuine excitement about my project that I could not help but feel buoyed by it. Thank you from the bottom of my heart to both of you.

I am also greatly indebted to Peter Cane for his thoughtful foreword, which places my exploration of modern New Zealand administrative law in its broader historical and international context. I am delighted and honoured to have my book introduced by Peter in this way.

Thank you to the New Zealand colleagues who participated in the Administrative Law workshop in early 2020 at which we workshopped several of my draft chapters, and to attendees at two Auckland law school seminars (especially Anna Hood, Arie Rosen and David V Williams) and at the Society of Legal Scholars Conference in 2020 at which I presented draft chapters.

A great many colleagues generously took time to comment on draft chapters or on papers that ended up feeding into a chapter: Farrah Ahmed, Stephen Bailey, Joanna Bell, Anna Broadmore, Peter Cane, Eddie Clark, Paul Craig, Jodi Gardner, Andrew Geddis, Claudia Geiringer, David Grinlinton, Carol Harlow, Dean Knight, Liz Fisher, Janet McLean, Caroline Morris, Ron Paterson, Ellen Rock, Matthew Smith, Rayner Thwaites, Bridgette Toy-Cronin and Ed Willis. Thank you all.

Thanks also go to my research assistants over the course of this journey: Mikayla Dempsey, Kristian Metzler, Jovana Nedeljkov, Mia Rutledge, Jae Kim and Jack McKenzie. It was great working with you.

The fellows and President of Magdalen College, Oxford, kindly hosted me on a fellowship that gave me space to think and write (and surrounded me with good conversation and with serene beauty) at a crucial point. I am very grateful.

Thank you to the New Zealand Law Foundation and its Director Lynda Hagen who provided generous funding for research assistance in the first two years.

Hart Publishing has been a joy to work with from start to finish. Thank you, Sinead Moloney, for supporting my idea and then accepting my proposal, to Paula Devine for copy-editing, and to Kate Whetter ,Verity Stuart and Linda Goss for patiently shepherding this project through to completion and for your kind help with all my queries and requests.

Finally, thank you to family, friends and colleagues who provided support: to Peter Cane, Jane Kelsey and Janet McLean for mentoring and advice; to Anna, Treasa and Harriet for your friendship and support; to Vernon, Elizabeth, Elaine and Myra for your interest in my project and your regular patient enquiries about my progress as multiple deadlines passed; and to my parents and sisters for waiting when I didn't have time, and for being excited about the book.

To Richard: thank you for your continuing forbearance and generous support, for your pride in my work, but especially for always reminding me what else is important to us.

I have endeavoured to state the law as at 1 July 2024.

Hanna Wilberg
Auckland, January 2025

Contents

PART II
THE GROUNDS OF JUDICIAL REVIEW: NORMS GOVERNING ADMINISTRATION

Table of Cases

Table of Statutes

Table of International Covenants, Conventions or Declarations

Part I

Introduction and Overview

1

Introduction

A. Administrative Law is the Law Governing Public Administration

We all interact with officials and authorities exercising public powers every day, directly or indirectly. On occasion, these interactions are momentous: immigration officials deciding, for instance, whether an overseas-based partner or family member may join us. However, other interactions pervade our lives. We sort our rubbish and register our dogs to comply with bylaws that our council has made. We enjoy clean beaches, parks and streets thanks to council bylaws requiring us to pick up after our dogs and not litter. We look to co-governance authorities representing iwi and local government to guard our cultural heritage and mana whenua.[1] We follow road rules made by officials in Wellington to keep ourselves and others safe. We enjoy safe food and water thanks to regulations made by ministers, take medicines Pharmac has decided to subsidise, and are entitled to send our children to a school within our officially declared zone. Officials – or automated systems employed by authorities – issue our birth certificates, wedding licences, passports and company registrations. Officials, automated systems or contractors engaged by authorities determine how much tax we have to pay,

[1] Mana whenua – customary authority over land; iwi – tribes.

our ACC entitlements to compensation and other assistance when we are injured, and our entitlement to subsidised rest home care in our old age. They grant patents for our inventions, licences required for occupations such as immigration advisers, and clearance for our companies to acquire others. Council officers decide whether to grant building permits and resource consents and, when things go well, that means we can expect the home we buy to be safe and habitable.

For some of us, these interactions are even more pervasive and existential. Prisoners' lives are controlled and constrained by corrections regulations and the prison guards enforcing them. Recipients of social security benefits depend on decisions by Work and Income case managers for their livelihoods. They must reapply for their benefits regularly, apply for one-off grants when those benefits do not cover essential expenses, and show compliance with ongoing obligations to avoid sanctions. In exceptional times of emergency, these interactions become similarly pervasive and existential for all of us. During the Covid-19 pandemic, ministers and officials decided on a daily basis whether and to what extent it was safe for us to leave our homes and congregate with others, and what activities required vaccination to contain the spread of the virus and to protect the most vulnerable.

Administrative law is the law that governs these interactions and these exercises of public powers: the law that governs public administration. Government lawyers apply this law in advising decision-makers on their powers and obligations. We rely on it when challenging exercises of public power. Tribunals and courts apply and develop it when adjudicating on challenges in the form of appeals and judicial review applications. Other institutions devoted to grievance resolution and accountability, such as the Ombudsmen and the Regulations Review Committee, also apply and develop this law.

Legislation is the primary source of administrative law, along with internal guidelines elaborating that legislation. In addition, administrative law comprises the principles developed in judicial review decisions, tribunal decisions and determinations by other grievance and accountability institutions. Judicially developed principles also include principles of private law to the extent that these apply to public authorities and officials.

In short, administrative law comprises two aspects: norms from a range of sources and a range of accountability institutions and mechanisms.

B. Administrative Law in Aotearoa New Zealand

In Aotearoa New Zealand, many of the principles found in judicial decisions started life in the United Kingdom, but the body of principles has long since become autonomous and distinct. Te Tiriti o Waitangi and tikanga Māori play a large and increasing role both in judicially developed principles and in legislation.[2] International law obligations also play a role that is perhaps larger than in some other jurisdictions.

United Kingdom authority is still the most relevant, but it is only ever persuasive. Other common law jurisdictions such as Canada and Australia share the common English heritage but have diverged very significantly; case law from those jurisdictions is of interest, but must be treated with caution.

[2] Te Tiriti o Waitangi – the Treaty of Waitangi; tikanga Māori – Māori customary law.

The large body of legislation is, of course, all made in New Zealand, although much of it has counterparts elsewhere. Some of it is unique to New Zealand, such as the accident compensation scheme, and some of it was pioneered here, such as the Ombudsman institution and the New Zealand Bill of Rights Act 1990.

C. The Scope of this Book

In this book I aim to elucidate the structure and principles of administrative law in Aotearoa New Zealand, as well as current debates and trends. My focus is on principles that apply generally across all areas of public administration rather than on the law governing particular regimes. Many of these general principles are found in judicial review case law rather than legislation or principles developed by other accountability institutions. Much of this book therefore focuses on the principles of judicial review and other judge-made principles.[3] By the structure of administrative law, one of the things I mean is the conceptual structures for these principles and for debates about them.

In addition, by structure, I also mean the institutional structures of public administration. I adopt an understanding of administrative law according to which it has a role in facilitating as well as constraining public administration, and its objectives include promotion of social goals as well as protection of affected individuals.[4] On that view, administrative law includes the full range of sources of law outlined above. It also includes institutions and mechanisms for making decisions, guiding decision-making, resolving grievances and broader accountability.[5] These comprise what we may call the administrative justice system. My account of these institutions and their structure draws on the literature on administrative justice.[6]

The remainder of this introductory chapter provides an introduction to judicial review and further background to administrative law. It first outlines what judicial review is and then how it fits into administrative law. Next it outlines how administrative law relates to constitutional law and to political accountability. The final substantive part introduces the administrative justice literature. The chapter closes with an outline of the plan of this book.

D. What is Judicial Review? Its Nature and Limits

Judicial review of public administrative decisions forms part of administrative law. To avoid confusion we should note that, in Aotearoa, there is no judicial review of primary legislation; we will come to the constitutional reason for this.

The term judicial review refers to two related things, corresponding to the two components of administrative law generally. First, judicial review *proceedings* are an

[3] Parts II–IV.
[4] See Ch 3.A.
[5] See Ch 2.
[6] Part V.

accountability mechanism and, more specifically, an avenue of recourse for aggrieved parties. Secondly, the body of common law principles developed in judicial review is a source of administrative law *norms*.

The norms developed in judicial review, in turn, have two distinct aspects: instructions to public administration and instructions to the reviewing courts themselves. The first aspect is largely found in the grounds of review: these are primarily norms for the conduct of public administration.[7] Failure to comply with those norms constitutes grounds for review. This conduct-guiding aspect of the grounds of review is highlighted by *The Judge Over Your Shoulder*, a guide to public decision-making compliant with the principles of judicial review.[8]

The second aspect of the norms, addressed to judicial review courts themselves, is found throughout the principles of judicial review. The principles concerning the availability of judicial review and the remedies govern the extent and limit of the powers of judicial review courts.[9] The formulations of the grounds of review also have this as a secondary aspect: they set out not only what is expected of public administration but also the limits of the extent to which the courts will intervene on each ground.

The limits of the courts' role are part of the characteristic features of judicial review. We may identify two characteristic features that lead to four characteristic limits. First, the grounds of judicial review express norms that have been developed specifically to constrain the exercise of *public* administrative power. The availability of review, and of the constraints developed in judicial review, is therefore limited to decisions that are of a sufficiently public nature.[10]

The remaining three limits flow from the second characteristic feature. Judicial review is an inherent (common law) jurisdiction as opposed to a statutory jurisdiction. This inherent jurisdiction is of a limited *supervisory* nature: it concerns the legality of administrative decisions and the fairness of administrative procedures. It is to be distinguished from review of the substantive merits. For such merits review, challengers need to resort to tribunals and other accountability institutions.

Flowing from this feature, the second limit of judicial review is that courts will intervene only if there is a suitable legal yardstick that makes the challenge justiciable (suitable for judicial determination).[11] The third limit concerns the grounds of judicial review: to a large extent, these are limited to legal standards governing the required procedure, permissible reasoning and the scope of the power. The fourth and final limit concerns the remedies: with rare exceptions, the courts do not substitute the correct decision. They merely declare the law, quash decisions and remit the question to the decision-maker for reconsideration.[12]

These limits are, however, a site of ongoing contest and debate as to whether and to what extent they should be maintained. The answers turn in part on underlying contests between competing political values. They also turn on the implications of

[7] See Peter Cane, *Administrative Law*, 5th edn (Oxford, Clarendon Press, 2011) at 9, 13–14.

[8] Crown Law, *Te Pouārahi: The Judge Over Your Shoulder*, 3rd edn (Wellington, 2019).

[9] See Chs 8 and 10.

[10] See Ch 11.

[11] See Ch 8.A.

[12] See Ch 10.

constitutional principles such as the rule of law and separation of powers, and the constitutional doctrine of Parliamentary sovereignty, on which more below. Debates about the scope of judicial review are intractable because there is no right answer to the contest between political values, and because the meaning and content of the relevant constitutional principles and doctrines are also highly contested.[13]

Some statutes purport to exclude judicial review by so-called privative clauses. However, courts find ways around this unless they are satisfied that adequate avenues of recourse are available to aggrieved parties.[14]

Let us finish with an outline of the grounds of review. As noted, these are primarily instructions to officials on how (not) to exercise their powers but also incorporate parts of the limits of judicial scrutiny on review.

The three main overarching grounds are procedural unfairness, illegality and unreasonableness. Procedural unfairness in the main takes the forms of breach of the right to a hearing and bias, and also includes failure to consult or give reasons.[15] Illegality can take the forms of acting outside the scope of a power or unlawful delegation or dictation, and also unlawful reasoning: improper purposes, taking account of irrelevant considerations or failing to take account of mandatory relevant considerations.[16] Unreasonableness was traditionally confined to *Wednesbury* unreasonableness: a decision that was so outrageous that no reasonable authority could consider it within its powers.[17]

The modern grounds of judicial review also include reliance on fundamental rights sourced in Te Tiriti, common law, international law and statute, and on other important interests or values such as legitimate expectations and consistency. Decisions infringing such rights or values, or failing to take account of them, may be struck down for illegality, and their reasonableness may be scrutinised more intensively than the traditional *Wednesbury* standard.[18]

E. How Judicial Review Fits into Administrative Law and Reasons for the Common Focus on Judicial Review

Judicial review is the most well-known part of administrative law, at least among lawyers. Often, in fact, the two terms are used as synonyms, as if judicial review was the whole of administrative law. Yet, as we have seen, administrative law encompasses much more than judicial review. It is therefore useful to consider the place of judicial review within administrative law, and the reasons why general accounts of administrative law tend to focus on it.

Judicial review, in the two senses identified earlier, forms part of both aspects of administrative law. Judicial review proceedings are among the accountability

[13] See Ch 3.
[14] See Ch 8.E.
[15] See Ch 4.
[16] See Ch 5.
[17] See Ch 7.
[18] Chs 6–7.

institutions of administrative law, and the common law principles developed in judicial review are among the sources of norms applicable to public administration. Many accounts of administrative law focus on judicial review, particularly in its second aspect, as a source of norms. In this book also, over half of the chapters are devoted to the norms found in the principles of judicial review. There are various reasons for this; let me mention two.

First, a main reason for this focus is that judicial review norms are generally applicable across all the different regimes that make up the administrative state. The bulk of the legislation and other sources of norms are specific to particular regimes, although there is also some general public law legislation and some other sources of general norms. The detail of the regime-specific norms cannot be covered in a general book on administrative law.

Second, it is also important that judicial review decisions create binding precedent. Furthermore, their sources (court decisions) are comprehensively published and reported so as to make them highly accessible. What about the output of other administrative law accountability institutions such as tribunals, the Ombudsman or the Regulations Review Committee? Part of the answer is that many of these are specific to particular regimes. However, even the generally available accountability institutions are not widely relied on as sources of general administrative law norms. The reasons include uncertainty about their status as precedent, and limits to their accessibility, as explored in Chapter 2.

In light of all this, it makes some sense to focus on the principles of judicial review in the discussion of norms applicable to public administration in a general administrative law book. However, it is important to appreciate that, for anyone involved in practice with a particular administrative regime, the significance of judicial review is much more limited. That goes for both the principles of judicial review as a source of norms and for judicial review proceedings as an accountability institution.

For instance, for social security recipients and for case managers who decide on social security benefits, the main sources of norms are the Social Security Act 2018 and delegated legislation made under that Act. The principles of judicial review do apply to those decisions, and arguably more attention should be paid to those principles – such as the right to a hearing – in this context. But these these principles function as part of the background and as a gloss on some features of the governing legislative regime. Turning to accountability institutions, the Act constitutes its own set of institutions and mechanisms to review decisions. Judicial review is also available, but its use is rare, and almost always follows initial recourse to the statutory mechanisms.

Similarly, when we look at regulatory regimes such as the Fisheries Act 1996, the Act is the main source of norms for the fishing industry, regulatory authorities and environmental groups. For accountability, judicial review in this context has a higher profile, being used regularly both by industry and environmental groups. But it still sits alongside other accountability institutions such as the Ombudsman and Parliamentary mechanisms.

Finally, further reasons for the focus on judicial review in many mainstream accounts are found in certain attitudes. For one thing, lawyers have a tendency to focus on courts and the common law. In the administrative law context, that means a focus on judicial review. Furthermore, we can also see the influence of particular political values in the focus on judicial review as a constraint on public power. Alternative values support a broader approach to administrative law, concerned as much with facilitating promotion of the social goals of administrative regimes. From that perspective, other sources of law and other accountability mechanisms are equally worthy of attention. The contest between competing political values, mentioned earlier, is therefore reflected in debates not only about the limits to judicial review but also in divergent approaches to the scope of administrative law.[19]

F. How Administrative Law Relates to Constitutional Law and Political Accountability

Administrative law, as noted above, is the wider law that applies to and governs public administration – all the various sources of norms, and the various accountability institutions and mechanisms. But there is an even broader context. The law that applies to government as a whole includes constitutional law,[20] and the accountability institutions for government include political accountability. Let us briefly consider each of these in turn.

Aotearoa New Zealand does not have a 'written' constitution. That means two things: the constitution is not enshrined in a single canonical instrument and the courts do not have power to enforce the constitution by striking down legislation.[21] Te Tiriti o Waitangi is a founding document and has fundamental constitutional status, but courts cannot enforce it against legislation.[22] However, Aotearoa does have an 'unwritten' constitution: a set of governmental institutions and processes along with a set of constitutional norms, some of which are found in written instruments. Some of those norms, known as constitutional conventions, govern the conduct of the political system and are not legally enforceable.

In addition, there are two types of constitutional norms that have a wider application, including a role in law generally and also in administrative law. The first type includes the principles of democracy, the rule of law and the separation of powers, the doctrine of Parliamentary sovereignty, and the Crown's obligation under te Tiriti o Waitangi to respect Māori authority and to share authority on appropriate terms. These are structural principles concerning the allocation of public powers and structural constraints on such powers. The second type is rights-conferring norms. These include the rights affirmed by the New Zealand Bill of Rights Act 1990 and rights to land, resources and taonga[23] affirmed under te Tiriti.

[19] See Ch 3.A.

[20] For helpful introductions, see Matthew SR Palmer and Dean R Knight, *The Constitution of New Zealand: A Contextual Analysis* (Oxford, Hart Publishing, 2022); Bruce Harris, *New Zealand Constitution: An Analysis in Terms of its Principles* (Wellington, Thomson Reuters, 2018).

[21] Hence the term judicial review refers solely to review of exercises of public administrative power, as noted earlier.

[22] See Ch 6.A for full discussion.

[23] Treasures.

These norms function in at least two ways. The first function applies only to the structural norms. These provide the organising principles of our set of governmental institutions and processes. For instance, democracy is the organising principle for the institution of Parliament and the process of elections. Co-governance authorities are set up in recognition of Māori authority under te Tiriti. Courts are an institution that is necessary for the rule of law.

Secondly, both types of norms play a special role in debates about the exercise of public powers. There is a distinction between legality and constitutionality in this regard. Compliance with most of these norms does not directly affect the legality of exercises of public powers: courts cannot strike down exercises of power for breach of these norms. The exception is the Bill of Rights. Even the other norms may be implied as legal constraints on the exercise of powers. Regardless of the effect on legality, however, non-compliance is unconstitutional in the sense of constitutionally illegitimate. An appeal to these norms thus has a much higher status than an argument that the exercise of power is a bad idea on policy grounds or even that it is unfair.

Such arguments can be made in public and political debates, and they can also be made in court proceedings including judicial review. For instance, the norms are relevant to debates about the limits of judicial review. They affect the constitutional legitimacy of judicial scrutiny and intervention in different types of contexts and on different types of question. Courts take these norms into account accordingly.[24]

How, then, does administrative law relate to constitutional law? Because of our unwritten constitution, there is no clear division between the two. Constitutional law is perhaps broader and certainly overlaps with administrative law. It applies to aspects or parts of government other than public administration that are not the concern of administrative law. For instance, the Bill of Rights Act remedy of a declaration of inconsistency against an Act of Parliament is a matter of constitutional rather than administrative law, as it does not concern an exercise of power by the public administration.[25] However, constitutional law does also apply to the public administration. The impact of constitutional norms on the limits of judicial review is just one example of this.

Political accountability is the other aspect of the broader context of administrative law. Like constitutional law, this overlaps with legal accountability in the form of administrative law but extends beyond it. Ministers are politically accountable for exercises of power that may be beyond the reach of legal accountability via administrative law, such as the conduct of foreign affairs. Parliament is politically accountable, but clearly not legally accountable via administrative law.

However, political accountability also applies to public administration, alongside legal accountability through administrative law. The existence of this parallel form of accountability is relevant to the nature and scope of administrative law. It is therefore worth outlining briefly how political accountability works in this context. Ministers are accountable directly and, at least in theory, the public administration is accountable through its Ministers.

[24] See Ch 3.B.
[25] See *Taylor v Attorney-General* [2018] NZSC 104, [2019] 1 NZLR 213.

Ministers are accountable in two ways. First, they must be Members of Parliament (MPs).[26] As such, they are accountable at the polls either to their constituency or, if they are a list MP, to the electorate as a whole through their party.[27] Secondly, Ministers collectively are accountable via the convention of responsible government.

Responsible government means that the executive government is formed by the party or a group of parties with a majority in the House of Representatives, and its position depends on maintaining the 'confidence' of the majority. That party or group of parties chooses a Prime Minister. The Prime Minister appoints Ministers to head all the departments or ministries from among that group of parties and forms a Cabinet with some of those Ministers to exercise the central executive power. The Ministers collectively are referred to as the Government, and they are collectively responsible to the House or Representatives. If the Government loses on a motion of no confidence or fails to pass its budget, by convention the Prime Minister is obliged to resign and that brings down the entire government.

Turning to the public administration, this is politically accountable via the convention of individual Ministerial responsibility, at least in theory. As already noted, government departments or ministries are headed by a Minister. They are accountable to that Minister and the Minister, in turn, is accountable to the electorate. Ministers' accountability means two things.

First, they are obliged to answer questions in Parliament, and expected to answer questions in public, about the work of their department or ministry.[28] The public and MPs can judge the performance of those departments and ministries and the Ministers' explanations and justifications. These judgments feed into Ministers' direct electoral accountability as MPs, and into the Government's collective responsibility to the House of Representatives.

Secondly, individual Minsters may ultimately be expected to resign if their department or ministry is responsible for a major failure. This happens very rarely and only for truly major failures. For instance, Kate Wilkinson resigned as Minister of Labour after 29 men lost their lives in the Pike River mine explosion in 2010, and Dennis Marshal resigned a year after 14 people were killed when a Department of Conservation viewing platform collapsed at Cave Creek in 1995. A more common alternative to resignation, even for major failures, is for the Minister to take charge of remedying the problems that led to the failure, and to explain and justify those measures. Indeed, both these resignations occurred only after the Ministers involved had at least set in train processes to address the causes of failure.

It will be apparent that political accountability for public administration works at a high systemic level. Front-line administrative decisions register in this system only collectively. For instance, if there is widespread dissatisfaction with ACC's approach to claims, that becomes a political issue. However, accountability for individual decisions normally has to be achieved through administrative law.

[26] Constitution Act 1986, s 6.

[27] List MPs form part of the Mixed Member Proportionate electoral system instituted by the Electoral Act 1993, part 6 (esp ss 127 and 150).

[28] Departments and ministries are also obliged to answer questions directly in Select Committee enquiries of the House.

G. Administrative Justice Debates on Institutional Design and Evaluation

Aside from doctrinal and normative analysis of the law, administrative law scholarship also includes the literature on administrative justice. This literature addresses questions about the design and evaluation of administrative justice systems for making decisions, resolving grievances about them and holding decision-makers accountable more broadly.[29] It reports on empirical work investigating the operation in practice of the existing institutions and mechanisms, identifies a range of possible features of institutions and mechanisms, constructs normative frameworks of objectives and principles for evaluating the options, and debates the application of such frameworks.

There are no easy answers to the questions of design and evaluation, as the relevant objectives tend to compete, and contestable trade-offs are therefore inevitable. In Aotearoa New Zealand, we have tended to take an ad hoc approach and there is very limited local literature. There is much work to be done in exploring the extensive foreign literature on this topic and considering its fit and application to our circumstances.

H. The Structure of this Book

In Part I of the book, this introductory chapter is followed by two further chapters. Chapter 2 offers a tour of administrative law as a whole. It outlines who and what makes up the public administration, the various sources of legally relevant norms that apply to it, and its various accountability institutions and mechanisms. Chapter 3 introduces debates about the shape of administrative law as a whole and about the appropriate scope of judicial review within this. It outlines the influence of competing political values and constitutional norms in those debates.

Parts II and III focus on judicial review in its two broad aspects discussed earlier. Part II concerns the general norms applicable to public administration, as framed by the grounds of judicial review. Part III focuses on judicial review as an avenue of recourse, and explores its limits in that sense. The order in which judicial review topics are discussed in these two parts diverges from the more traditional order. On the traditional approach, judicial review is implicitly presented as both the main legal avenue of recourse for holding public administration to account and the main source of applicable legal norms. The logical place to start on that approach is the availability of review. In this book, I start in Part II with the norms applicable to public administration. The availability of avenues of recourse is addressed in the remaining three parts, starting in Part III with the availability and limits of judicial review.

Part II, then, analyses the administrative law norms found in the grounds of judicial review. Where appropriate, the chapters in this part also reference other sources of similar or related norms, such as statutory appeals and non-judicial accountability mechanisms. The grounds of review discussed this part concern procedural fairness

[29] See Part V of the book.

(Chapter 4), illegality (Chapter 5), modern rights-based review (Chapter 6) and other modern extensions of substantive review (Chapter 7). The latter two – the more modern grounds – involve the extension of judicial scrutiny beyond the traditional constitutional limits of judicial review. For that reason, their scope is unsettled and contentious. Principles governing them include, more prominently than in the traditional grounds, norms addressed to judges about the limits of judicial intervention as well as norms addressed to decision makers.

Part III concerns the availability and limits of judicial review. Chapter 8 examines availability, including justiciability (suitability for judicial determination) and the approach to privative clauses purporting to exclude or restrict access to judicial review. Chapter 9 asks whether we could adopt a better framework for calibrating judicial restraint than the current approach, particularly for questions of law. Remedies are the subject of Chapter 10. This includes judicial review and other public law judicial remedies. The focus is on the characteristic limits of those remedies.

Part IV is concerned with the contested interface between private and public law, and the extent to which the law treats public power differently from private power. Chapter 11 explores the public nature test that determines the extent to which public law constraints apply to partly private decisions or public decisions of partly private bodies. Chapter 12 addresses the converse question: the extent to which private law applies to officials or authorities exercising public powers.

Part V finally explores the administrative justice literature, debating institutional design and evaluation. Chapter 13 introduces the subject, Chapter 14 frontline decision-making, and Chapter 15 examines remedial avenues.

2

Public Administration and its Law

Lawyers may experience administrative law primarily through judicial review proceedings and decisions. That is so especially for litigation lawyers. In the day-to-day life of administrative law, however, the main protagonists are public officials and the public who engage with them. For them and for the lawyers who advise them, administrative law is found at least as much in statutes, regulations and guidelines, and in specialist avenues of grievance resolution and other accountability agencies. Judicial review principles, for officials, feature primarily as part of the rules and guidelines to consider in exercising their powers.

This chapter offers a tour of this wider administrative law landscape. It addresses three questions.[1] First, who and what is the public administration? What types of

[1] The approach to administrative law in this book owes a lot to Peter Cane, *Administrative Law*, 5th edn (Oxford, Clarendon Press, 2011). For the three questions addressed in this chapter, see ibid, ch 1.2.

entities and office holders does it include, and what types of functions and powers do they have? Secondly, what types of legal norms govern public administration? What are the various sources of such law? Third and finally, what accountability institutions and mechanisms exist to ensure that public administration complies with the applicable legal norms? The answers to these questions reveal public administration and administrative law as a wide and greatly varied field in all these respects.

Not all of this wide field can be discussed in any detail in a book on administrative law such as this one. The remainder of this book instead focuses on four aspects of administrative law that apply generally across the field: the generic legal norms that have been developed mainly in judicial review proceedings concerning the exercise of public powers; the limits to judicial scrutiny and supervision in judicial review and other judicial proceedings; the relationship between public and private law and powers; and the principles of administrative justice that are relevant to designing and evaluating regimes for public administrative decision-making and remedial avenues.

However, anyone wishing to practice administrative law effectively, or to write about it in an informed fashion, should have an awareness of this field as a whole, and be skilled at navigating it.[2] They should know how to find the relevant administrative regime for those who are seeking public assistance or are subject to regulation. When engaging with a particular regime, they need to be skilled at navigating the applicable specialist law from the various sources. And they should be aware of the range of options for holding public administration accountable to its legal norms.

A similar broad awareness is also desirable for courts exercising their supervisory jurisdiction in judicial review or other judicial proceedings, in order to understand the choices they make in their full context. They need to develop and apply the substantive principles of judicial review sensitive to the great variety of administrative contexts. Similarly, the appropriate extent and type of judicial restraint depends on the context.[3]

The survey in this chapter is intended to outline the scope of that task. For detailed accounts of much of this wide and varied field, readers will then need to turn to relevant specialist sources, for instance on particular administrative regimes such as immigration or competition law.

A. What and Who is the Public Administration?

Public administration or the 'administrative state' may be understood as comprising the administration of all the regimes by which government intervenes in society and the economy in pursuit of social or other public interest objectives. This administration involves exercises of powers vis-à-vis private individuals and entities, and the discharge of functions and exercise of powers within government. In surveying this field, we can ask what and who forms part of public administration?

Starting with the 'what' question, we can identify various types of objectives, functions and powers. The social or other public interest objectives include promoting

[2] For a detailed guide, see Mai Chen, *Public Law Toolbox: Solving Problems with Government*, 2nd edn (Wellington, LexisNexis, 2012).

[3] See Joanna Bell, *The Anatomy of Administrative Law* (Oxford, Hart Publishing, 2020).

health and safety, national security, economic and social development (wellbeing and prosperity), environmental protection, and the partnership between the Crown and Māori authorities under te Tiriti o Waitangi. A list of examples of regimes created for such objectives can be found in B below.

The primary functions of different regimes may be identified as regulation, redistribution or public provision.[4] Regulatory regimes may intervene in specific activities such as commerce, building, education, employment or immigration; or they may intervene in a broader range of activities to address particular aspects or impacts of those activities, such as competition, environmental impacts or discrimination. Regimes for redistribution include raising revenue by taxes, rates and levies; and providing assistance to those in need by regimes such as accident compensation (known as ACC), social security and social housing. Regimes for public provision include providing infrastructure such as hospitals, roads, railroads, utilities and prisons; and providing public services such as health and education, sporting and cultural facilities and libraries.

Types of powers include issuing licences and permits, often backed up by monitoring and auditing; enforcing and adjudicating prohibitions; levying rates and taxes; issuing financial assistance; determining access to services such as health, education or housing; selecting providers for such services; imposing requirements; and imposing penalties. Other types of tasks include analysing issues and problems; planning responses to these; and deploying public resources and labour power. The types of power exercised by accountability mechanisms and institutions will be covered in Part C.

Turning secondly to the 'who' question, this concerns the types of office or entity. The types include elected Ministers of the Crown in their capacity as heads of government departments and in the exercise of their statutory powers. They further include core public service departments and ministries directly accountable to Ministers;[5] Crown entities that have varying levels of independence from Ministers such as the Accident Compensation Corporation, the Commerce Commission and school boards;[6] independent statutory office holders such as the Legal Services Commissioner;[7] state enterprises;[8] local government;[9] and private entities contracted to carry out public functions. Increasingly, they include co-governance entities involving the Crown or local government and Māori authorities,[10] and Māori authorities exercising devolved powers.[11] They include officials and other authorised employees within all these types of entities. Finally, they also include entities charged with holding the administration accountable and providing redress, such as administrative tribunals.

Where tribunals are concerned, we may also count some party-to-party tribunals as part of public administration. In some statutory regimes regulating private activities,

[4] John Brathwaite, *Regulatory Capitalism: How it Works, Ideas for Making It Work Better* (Cheltenham, Edward Elgar, 2008) at 1.

[5] See the Public Service Act 2020, s 10 and sch 2.

[6] See the Crown Entities Act 2004, s 7 and schs 1 and 2.

[7] Legal Services Act 2011, ss 70–71.

[8] State-Owned Enterprises Act 1986.

[9] Local Government Act 2002, Part 3.

[10] See, eg, Ngā Mana Whenua o Tāmaki Makaurau Collective Redress Act 2014.

[11] Eg the Whānau Ora Commissioning Agencies contracted by Te Puni Kōkiri (Ministry of Māori Development).

such as employment and residential tenancies, most of the regulatory work is done by the legislation itself, redefining the rights, obligations and relationships of the parties so as to redress power imbalances.[12] The same goes for discrimination law in its application to private activity.[13] Such regimes confer only limited powers on public administration. However, they do constitute specialist tribunals to determine disputes about the application of this regulatory law. Those tribunals may be understood as court substitutes, providing private dispute resolution in a more accessible format. Alternatively, however, they may also be understood as regulatory authorities, administering the application of the regulatory regime by exercising powers vis-à-vis private individuals and entities. An indication of this public administrative role is seen in the fact that there has been much judicial review of such tribunals in other jurisdictions.[14] In New Zealand, there has been much less litigation of this kind,[15] but that does not detract from the administrative regulatory function of these tribunals.

Aspects of criminal justice may also be considered part of public administration, although this is usually treated as a separate field. Criminal proceedings are conducted by the general courts. However, police powers, prosecutorial discretion, the corrections system and the Parole Board all belong to public administration as well as to criminal law. Administrative law norms such as the principles of judicial review apply to these powers, albeit courts exercise varying levels of restraint in enforcing those norms in this context.[16]

The extent to which public administration includes private entities exercising public powers or public authorities engaging in private law activities is a contentious question. This is explored in Chapter 11.

In summary, the 'what' and 'who' of public administration cover a great variety of regimes, powers and functions and a wide range of office holders or entities. The next question is what law governs this wide field: what types of norms and from what sources. The variety of regimes, powers and functions calls for much variation in the applicable norms.

B. Legal Norms of Public Administration

Legal norms governing public administration include both positive requirements or expectations and negative constraints or limits.[17] They include not only formal binding law but also norms that guide rather than bind administration, since these are an important part of the legal controls on public administration. Some sets of norms apply generally across public administration as a whole or large parts of it, while

[12] See the Employment Relations Act 2000 and the Residential Tenancies Act 1986.

[13] Human Rights Act 1993.

[14] In Canada, for instance, many of the leading judicial review cases involve review of labour law adjudicators: see, eg, *Dunsmuir v New Brunswick* [2008] SCC 9, [2008] 1 SCR 190.

[15] Some tribunals are protected from judicial review by privative clauses that have generally been upheld as effective by the courts: see Ch 8.E(3).

[16] See Ch 8.A(1)(g).

[17] The inclusion of positive expectations is suggested by a 'green light' lens: see Ch 3A.

others are specific to one regime. The sources of norms include legislation and other general rules, as well as norms developed in the adjudication of disputes or grievances by accountability institutions.

The norms that govern public administrative decisions further vary in that they may concern the substance, the reasoning or the procedure. Substantive norms concern the objectives the administration is required to pursue, what it is expected to achieve, and the scope of its powers: what it may and may not do. Reasoning standards concern what decision-makers must and must not take into account. Procedural standards concern matters such as who must be consulted or heard and by what process, time limits, and review requirements.

(1) Generally Applicable Norms

Let us first consider the range of generally applicable norms, and then turn to the norms that are specific to particular regimes. The generally applicable norms include those that are constitutional. Compliance with these affects constitutional legitimacy but may have only a qualified role in determining legality, as discussed in Chapter 1. Among these are obligations under te Tiriti o Waitangi (the Treaty of Waitangi). Te Tiriti guarantees Māori tino rangatiratanga (authority) and equal citizenship as well as rights to land, natural resources and other taonga (treasures). The Crown's obligations under it include active protection, acting in good faith as a Treaty partner, redress for breaches of Te Tiriti, and a principle of options.[18]

Turning to norms that are generally applicable and binding, these include generally applicable legislation such as the New Zealand Bill of Rights Act 1990, the Official Information Act 1982 and the Public Service Act 2020. These Acts provide both negative constraints and positive requirements. The Bill of Rights Act guarantees most of the major civil and political rights.[19] Those rights operate primarily, though by no means solely, as negative constraints.

The Official Information Act 1982 provides for transparency.[20] It requires official information (defined broadly) to be made available on request unless there is good reason for withholding it.[21] The permissible reasons for withholding information are listed.[22] Some are conclusive reasons, such as where release would threaten national security or the safety of a person. Other reasons, such as protecting personal privacy or trade secrets, must be weighed against considerations in favour of release. There is a right of access to internal policies and to reasons for decisions. Access to a requester's own personal information is provided in similar terms by the Privacy Act 2020. Where information is withheld under the Official Information Act, the requester may complain

[18] See, eg, *New Zealand Maori Council v Attorney-General (Lands)* [1987] 1 NZLR 641 (CA); Waitangi Tribunal, *He Whakaputanga me te Tiriti: The Report on Stage 1 of the Te Paparahi o te Raki Inquiry* (WAI 1040, 2014). See further Ch 6.A.

[19] See Ch 6.D.

[20] Equivalent provisions for local government are found in the Local Government Official Information and Meetings Act 1987.

[21] Official Information Act 1981, ss 5, 12–15.

[22] ibid ss 6 and 9, see also s 18.

to the Ombudsmen. The Ombudsmen's decision is described as a recommendation but becomes binding on the twenty-first working day.[23] The access to information provided by the Act is an important tool for both legal and political accountability.

The Public Service Act 2020 includes large parts that contribute to constituting the public administration. It sets out lines of accountability in the public service, allocation of functions and powers to delegate.[24] In addition, it provides for the public service to support the Crown in its relationships with Māori under te Tiriti o Waitangi, and provides lists of public service purposes, principles and values. The latter include political neutrality, free and frank advice to Ministers, openness, a 'spirit of service to the community', accountability and trustworthiness, respect and responsiveness in dealing with people. It also confers powers to issue minimum standards and guidance on those values.[25] Provisions for the wider public sector beyond the core public service are found in other legislation, especially the Crown Entities Act 2004 and the Local Government Act 2002.

It is also now recognised that alongside state law in the form of common law and legislation, the law of Aotearoa includes tikanga Māori (customary law).[26] Tikanga is recognised in the development of the common law and, as such, can apply to exercises of power by public administration.[27] As an independent source of law it applies most obviously to the work of Māori authorities within Māori communities. The Waitangi Tribunal applies tikanga in dealing with cross-claims by several iwi (tribes) to the same land.[28] While the courts have limited authority and expertise in relation to tikanga,[29] it can be the controlling law in such contexts.[30]

Generally applicable and binding norms also include the grounds of judicial review (norms developed by the courts in judicial review proceedings). These are analysed in detail in Chapters 4 to 7. They have two aspects: instructions to public officials on the lawful exercise of their powers, and instructions to judges on the nature and extent of their supervisory powers. In their first aspect, they are relevant well beyond judicial review proceedings.[31] First, they should be considered by officials and their legal advisers when decisions are made. This point is highlighted and illustrated by *Te Pouārahi: The Judge Over Your Shoulder*, a guide to public officials on making decisions compliant with these principles.[32] Secondly, the norms comprised in the grounds of judicial

[23] Sections 30 and 32. That is unless an Order in Council directing otherwise is promulgated before that date, but no such Order has ever been made. Such an Order would be subject to review by the High Court: s 32B.

[24] Public Service Act 2020, s 10, Parts 2 and 3, and the schedules, esp schs 3 and 6.

[25] ibid ss 11–20.

[26] See esp *Ellis v R* [2022] NZSC 114, [2022] 1 NZLR 239.

[27] See, eg, *Sweeney v The Prison Manager, Spring Hill Corrections Facility* [2021] NZHC 181, [2021] 2 NZLR 27 at [71], [74]–[77]; *Te Pou Matakana Ltd v Attorney-General (No 2)* [2021] NZHC 3319 at [108]–[112]. See, generally, Jayden Houghton, *Tikanga Māori and State Law* (Wellington, Thomson Reuters, forthcoming 2025), esp ch 11.

[28] See *Wairarapa Moana Ki Pouākani Incorporation v Mercury NZ Ltd* [2022] NZSC 142, [2022] 1 NZLR 767.

[29] See also *Ngāti Whātua Ōrākei Trust v Attorney-General (No 4)* [2022] NZHC 843, [2022] 2 NZLR 601.

[30] See *Ellis* (n 26) at [267].

[31] Cane, *Administrative Law* (n 1) at 9 and 13–14.

[32] Crown Law, *Te Pouārahi: The Judge Over Your Shoulder*, 3rd edn (Wellington, 2019).

review can be invoked by and through the full range of administrative grievance resolution and accountability mechanisms.

The norms found in the grounds of judicial review operate primarily as constraints on the exercise of powers. For instance, public officials exercising powers must not decide without giving those affected a fair hearing,[33] must not exceed the scope of their powers and must not decide for improper purposes or take account of irrelevant considerations.

Finally, generally applicable norms are arguably also developed by non-judicial grievance resolution and accountability institutions. Administrative tribunals are primarily concerned with interpreting and applying the particular regime – we will return to that. However, some of their decisions may also contribute to the development of general norms. For instance, the Social Security Appeal Authority ruled that it is a fundamental breach of natural justice for the members of a review body to hide their identity behind pseudonyms.[34] The Ombudsman and the Regulations Review Committee deal with general norms. Both lack a power of binding rulings – they make recommendations. However, those recommendations can serve as a source of guidance to public administration beyond the particular case in which they are made.

For any of these institutions to be effective in this role of contributing to the development of administrative law norms, their output needs to be made accessible. We need reporting systems that identify decisions and findings of wider interest, add keywords and summaries, and disseminate them.[35] Such systems exist to varying extents, but there is room for improvement. For the Regulations Review Committee, a published digest is updated every few years.[36] The Ombudsmen publish brief case notes on their website, but only a very small number every year.[37] They also sometimes issue full opinions on complaints of wider public interest, and reports on systemic investigations. For tribunal decisions, often only minimal summaries are available, if any.

The lack of accessibility helps explain why these sources are rarely appealed to for guidance. Conversely, however, the fact that these sources are not often thought of as legally relevant guidance is among the reasons for the lack of reporting.

The grounds on which these institutions intervene are discussed in detail below in Section C of this chapter. The norms they develop in applying those grounds include constraining norms similar to those developed in judicial review, for instance

[33] I have put this as 'must not decide without' to show that this is a constraint on power. While there is a positive obligation to give a fair hearing, this operates as a constraint on the power to make a decision advancing the regime's purposes. The same goes for mandatory considerations.

[34] *An appeal against a decision of a Benefits Review Committee* [2017] NZSSAA 52. This ruling was affirmed on appeal by the High Court in *Chief Executive of the Ministry of Social Development v L* [2018] NZHC 2528, 2 NZLR 135, but in other cases there may not be an appeal.

[35] See Trevor Buck, 'Precedent in Tribunals and the Development of Principles' (2006) 25 *Civil Justice Quarterly* 458 at 461, 469–76.

[36] See Dean Knight and Edward Clark, *Regulations Review Committee Digest*, 7th edn (Wellington, New Zealand Centre for Public Law, 2020).

[37] For 2022 and 2023, there are 14 and 12 case notes respectively; up to half of those are on Official Information Act complaints rather than on Ombudsman Act complaints.

principles of natural justice.[38] In addition, the norms developed by the Ombudsmen include broader principles of good government, such as deciding without undue delay, communicating with reasonable clarity and treating people with respect. The norms elaborated by the Regulations Review Committee include guidance on constitutional desiderata for delegated legislation, such as what types of matters are best dealt with by primary legislation.

(2) Sources Specific to Particular Regimes

Turning to sources specific to particular regimes, this is where the largest body of administrative law norms is found. Navigating these sources is an essential skill for lawyers practising administrative law.

The main source of binding norms is the legislation (primary and secondary) that constitutes the regime. Norms found in such legislation include both positive obligations and negative constraints. We look there to find everything we need to know about a regime:

- the constitution of agencies and entities to operate the regime,
- the regime's purposes and objectives,
- Treaty of Waitangi obligations (the provisions commonly known as 'Treaty clauses'),
- guiding values,
- powers to make delegated legislation and individual decisions,
- allocation of powers to particular officials within those agencies and entities and powers to delegate,
- obligations and requirements imposed on officials and agencies and on persons or entities who engage with the regime,
- entitlements to benefits or licences,
- liability to penalties, sanctions and other consequences of non-compliance,
- discretions to impose or grant the above,
- criteria for applying all of the above,
- exceptions and qualifications,
- definitions,
- procedures for the exercise of powers,
- provisions for review and appeal, and
- immunities or privative clauses purporting to exclude or limit access to judicial review.

It is easy to miss some of the relevant provisions and thus misunderstand the position.

[38] See, eg, Ron Paterson, *Investigation into SSC conduct of MFAT leaks inquiry* (Ombudsman opinion, June 2016).

The many regimes that make up the administrative state in Aotearoa New Zealand include those instituted by the Immigration Act 2009, Corrections Act 2004, Parole Act 2002, Health and Safety at Work Act 2015, Commerce Act 1986, Conservation Act 1987, Resource Management Act 1991, Building Act 2004, Local Government Act 2002, Pae Ora (Healthy Futures) Act 2022, Education and Training Act 2020, Tax Administration Act 1994, Income Tax Act 2007, Accident Compensation Act 2001, Social Security Act 2018, New Zealand Superannuation and Retirement Income Act 2001, Lawyers and Conveyancers Act 2006, Legal Services Act 2011, the Broadcasting Standards Act 2007, and many more.

In addition, there are large bodies of norms that guide rather than bind. These include most obviously the internal manuals, policies and guidelines issued by agencies. Jerry Mashaw's influential study of the disability insurance programme in the United States further identified standard bureaucratic routines and practices of investigation and decision-making as part of these norms. He argued that, taken together, both the programme's policy guidelines and its routines and practices had generated an internal law of administration. These were largely unaffected by external legal processes and controls and were law in the sense that they were a guide to behaviour integrated into a system of hierarchical control.[39]

Decisions of administrative tribunals are also significant sources of regime-specific norms.[40] They develop interpretations and elaborations of the legislation and guidelines. Their main task is to determine the merits of particular cases and, in doing so, they build a body of illustrative applications and of influential reasoning. Whether their decisions have precedent status is an unsettled question,[41] but they at least represent a source of relevant guidance. Decisions of other institutions such as internal review bodies are not binding but can still provide guidance.

However, there is very limited dissemination of such decisions to facilitate this. Decisions of internal review bodies are not normally published at all. Decisions of external specialist tribunals are often published online, but we have already noted the lack of reporting services.

Administrative lawyers have some acquaintance with many of the statutory regimes listed above, as they will have read judicial review or appeal cases involving those regimes. Some regimes, however, are very rarely litigated in the general courts, and almost never reach the appellate courts. As a result, only a few specialist lawyers have any acquaintance with them. One of those is the regime under the Social Security Act 2018. This therefore provides a useful case study exploring the legal features of a public administrative regime. Of course, one regime cannot be considered representative of all. In particular, regimes of a regulatory nature have some characteristic features that differ from a redistributive regime like this.

[39] Jerry Mashaw, *Bureaucratic Justice: Managing Social Security Disability Claims* (New Haven, Yale University Press, 1983) ch 11.

[40] See Elizabeth Fisher, 'Administrative Tribunals: An Essay about the Legal Imagination of Administrative Law Scholars' in James Goudkamp, Mark Lunney and Leighton McDonald (eds), *Taking Law Seriously: Essays in Honour of Peter Cane* (Oxford, Hart Publishing, 2021) 259 at 274–76.

[41] See Ch 14 for brief discussion.

(3) An Example: The Social Security Act Regime

Let us consider the regime under the Social Security Act 2018[42] as an example of a particular regime of norms.[43] This regime provides for financial assistance for those who, for various reasons, cannot support themselves and their family through paid employment. Other Acts need to be consulted for other parts of social security, such as family tax credits (which make up a significant part of low income families' income),[44] social housing,[45] accident compensation[46] or superannuation.[47] The delegated legislation made under the Social Security Act 2018 includes the Social Security Regulations 2018,[48] Ministerial Directions under s 7 of the Act, and special assistance welfare programmes under s 101 of the Act.

The internal guidelines adopted by Work and Income, the division of the Ministry of Social Development that administers the regime, are known as the Manuals and Procedures (MAP). Much of MAP is available publicly online, but some parts are withheld from publication.[49] The instruments under sections 7 and 101 are designated as secondary legislation and subject to the disallowance regime under the Legislation Act 2019. However, they are published only on the MAP website rather than centrally by the Parliamentary Counsel Office.[50]

The Act sets out the purposes and principles of the regime.[51] These include providing financial support to those in need and alleviating financial hardship but also requiring people as far as possible to find and retain paid employment, and to draw on other resources before seeking assistance under the Act.

The Act has no Treaty clause. However, the obligations under te Tiriti o Waitangi are relevant to the exercise of powers under it. The Welfare Expert Advisory Group pointed out the need to treat people with mana (dignity or respect). Programmes and policies should be responsive to Te Ao Māori (the Māori world view), such as by recognising and building on the strengths and assets of whānau (families). The Ministry should engage in meaningful partnerships with Māori, including in governance, and should work on devolution of service delivery to Māori organisations.[52]

Financial support takes the form of either benefits and other assistance under the Act or special assistance pursuant to a welfare programme made under s 101. There are three tiers of benefits or assistance. Entitlements to 'main benefits' under the Act, such as jobseeker support, are based on specific eligibility conditions.[53] Regular and

[42] SSA 2018.

[43] See, further, Māmari Stephens, *Social Security and Welfare Law in Aotearoa New Zealand* (Wellington, Thomson Reuters, 2019).

[44] Income Tax Act 2007, part M.

[45] Public and Community Housing Management Act 1992.

[46] Accident Compensation Act 2001.

[47] New Zealand Superannuation and Retirement Income Act 2001.

[48] SSR 2018.

[49] See www.workandincome.govt.nz/map.

[50] They fall under s 73 rather than s 69 of the Legislation Act 2019.

[51] SSA 2018, ss 3–4.

[52] Welfare Expert Advisory Group, *Whakamana Tāngata: Restoring Dignity to Social Security in New Zealand* (February 2019) ch 5.

[53] Part 2 of both the SSA and SSR.

ongoing supplementary assistance such as the accommodation supplement and the temporary additional support include both entitlements and discretionary grants, but both again have specific eligibility conditions under the Act.[54] Finally, discretionary safety net assistance includes emergency assistance for some persons who do not meet the normal eligibility criteria,[55] and additional safety net assistance for those who do receive main benefits or equivalent assistance. For instance, one-off emergency grants for essential needs such as food or outstanding rent payments are available either under the Act as advance payments of benefits[56] or under the special needs grants welfare programme.[57]

The entitlements are subject to any disqualifying factors[58] and to compliance with relevant obligations,[59] each set out in their own part of the Act. Disqualifying factors include, for instance, absence overseas.[60] The obligations that attach to jobseeker support are to take reasonable steps to find employment, plan and prepare for employment, attend interviews and accept any offer of suitable employment.[61] MAP elaborates on these obligations; for instance, it provides that persons will be deemed non-compliant with these obligations if they move to a town listed as a 'limited employment location'. Failure to comply with obligations entails sanctions in the form of reduction, suspension or cancellation of benefits.[62] Before such a sanction takes effect, the Act requires a notice setting out various specified details and an invitation to respond within five days.[63]

The Act designates the agency that is to operate the regime, but does so by an unhelpfully circuitous route. The decision-maker is referred to as 'MSD' (short for Ministry of Social Development). That is defined in the Act's extensive 'dictionary' as the chief executive or a delegated employee of the 'responsible department' which, in turn, is defined as the department currently designated as such by the Prime Minister.[64]

The Act provides a long series of specific powers to make regulations by Order in Council,[65] and also a general power to make 'regulations providing for any other matters contemplated by this Act, necessary for its administration, or necessary for giving it full effect'.[66] More remarkable are the powers of the Minister, acting alone rather than by an Order in Council, to give Ministerial Directions under s 7 and to

[54] SSA 2018, ss 65, 96.

[55] Examples include s 63 of the SSA 2018; the Christchurch Mosque Attacks Welfare Programme, cl 11, available at www.workandincome.govt.nz/map/legislation/welfare-programmes.

[56] SSA 2018, s 347; see also SSR 2018, regs 201–204; Ministerial Direction on Advance Payments of Instalments of Benefit, available at www.workandincome.govt.nz/map/legislation/ministerial-directions.

[57] Special Needs Grants Programme, available at www.workandincome.govt.nz/map/legislation/welfare-programmes.

[58] Part 4 of both the SSA and the SSR.

[59] Part 3 of both the SSA and the SSR.

[60] SSA 2018, s 219. The SSR 2018 in part 4, subpart 6 set out limited exceptions applicable to benefits that do not require the person to be looking for work.

[61] SSA 2018, s 144.

[62] Part 5 of both the SSA 2018 and SSR 2018.

[63] SSA 2018, ss 252–256. Strict compliance is required for sanctions to be valid: *An appeal against a decision of a Benefits Review Committee* [2016] NZSSAA 91.

[64] SSA 2018, sch 2.

[65] Part 8.

[66] SSA 2018, s 418(2).

approve welfare programmes under 101. These provisions confer extremely broad discretions. It is notable that non-recoverable one-off hardship grants are provided only by such welfare programmes, not directly by the Act. The criteria for the exercise of broad discretions under the relevant instruments are problematic, as they are contradictory, leaving officers with an unguided choice between two unsatisfactory alternatives.[67]

The Act requires MSD to enquire into claims for benefits and decide whether to grant these, and provides for reviews of such grants. It provides for payment of those benefits and of tax on them, and for deduction of debts from benefit payments.[68] Deduction of debts is further regulated by a Ministerial Direction under s 7 of the Act.[69]

Case law establishes that MSD 'should be proactive in seeing to welfare, and not defensive and bureaucratic'. For instance, if a benefit other than the one applied for would better meet an applicant's need, then MSD should consider granting that benefit.[70] Applicants should be told about options open to them to improve their position.[71] According to the Manuals and Procedures (MAP), the objective is to ensure that clients receive their 'full and correct entitlement'.

Finally, the Act also provides remedial avenues.[72] Recall that the decisions of such bodies are also relevant for elaborating the features of the regime. Applicants may apply for review of decisions by internal Benefits Review Committees and may then appeal to the external Social Security Appeal Authority. From there, further appeals limited to questions of law are available in the general courts. The Ombudsman does not accept complaints about decisions in this regime, given that specialist avenues are available.

The Ombudsman does deal with complaints about the way people have been treated, as distinct from challenges to decisions. For such complaints, MSD also provides an informal avenue of recourse (not provided in the legislation). Its website offers a complaints form and explains the kinds of complaints that will be considered. It does not provide any indication of the process followed in addressing such complaints.

C. Accountability and Grievance Resolution Mechanisms

An integral part of the law that governs public administration, along with the norms surveyed in the previous part, are the institutions and mechanisms that hold the administration to account for its compliance with those norms and address grievances.

[67] See Hanna Wilberg "Forcing people to repay welfare 'loans' traps them in a poverty cycle – where is the policy debate about that?" *The Conversation* (28 September 2023), available at: www.theconversation.com.

[68] Part 6 of both the SSA 2018 and the SSR 2018. Welfare Programmes under s 101 tend to incorporate many of these provisions.

[69] Ministerial Direction on Debt Recovery, available at: www.workandincome.govt.nz/map/legislation/ministerial-directions.

[70] *Hall v Director-General of Social Welfare* [1997] NZFLR 902 (HC) at 912.

[71] *An appeal against a decision of a Benefits Review Committee* [2007] NZSSAA 50. Failure to do so may result in a benefit being backdated to a date before application for it was made: SSA 2018, ss 317–318.

[72] Part 7 of both the SSA 2018 and the SSR 2018, schs 7–9 of the SSA.

Accountability is a complex and contested concept. We might say its core sense involves persons who have entrusted power to others requiring the latter to provide information about their use of that power and to explain and justify it and requiring imposition of remedies or sanctions.[73] Accountability can be political or legal. Our concern here is with legal accountability.

What mechanisms and institutions are used to ensure and to check that public administration complies with the applicable legal norms?[74] The most familiar legal accountability institutions are remedial avenues for individual complaints about decisions: courts, tribunals, Ombudsmen and other grievance resolution bodies.

However, accountability for compliance with legal norms can also take other forms. These vary in several respects. Compliance, broadly conceived, encompasses both the positive and negative aspects of those norms: achieving the statutory objectives of the various regimes (or at least due attention to these and adequate effort in pursuing them), and observing the legal constraints of powers so as to avoid abuse. Accountability can concern conduct other than decisions. It can be systemic and can be demanded on an accountability institution's own motion rather than in response to individual complaints. Remedies or other interventions can be prospective rather than retrospective, and recommendatory rather than binding.

This part of the chapter first explores the range of remedial avenues, and then outlines other forms of accountability to legal norms. Internal management plays a role. External accountability institutions include the Parliamentary process for scrutinising and disallowing delegated legislation, the Auditor-General, public inquiries, and the Ombudsman. The purpose here is to survey these avenues of accountability, and the account is descriptive or taxonomical. An assessment of the effectiveness of different types of avenues, particularly in relation to individual grievances, is found in Chapter 15.

(1) Remedial Avenues for Individual Complaints about Decisions

Remedial avenues for individual complaints – courts, tribunals, the Ombudsmen and other grievance resolution bodies – are the most familiar legal accountability institutions. What these have in common is that they deal with individual complaints that challenge decisions or rules. They usually provide binding remedies with retrospective effect, addressing what has gone wrong for the complainant.

However, there are also significant differences between remedial avenues. They can be specialist or generalist, and internal or external. Their process can be formal and adversarial, or more informal and investigative. They can be focused on negative norms or extend to positive ones. Their jurisdiction can be a limited supervisory jurisdiction or full merits review. Their remedies can be limited to quashing and remitting

[73] See Richard Mulgan, *Holding Power to Account: Accountability in Modern Democracies* (Houndsmills, Palgrave Macmillan, 2003) at 7–14; Mark Bovens, 'Analysing and Assessing Accountability' (2007) 13 *European Law Journal* 44 at 450–452.

[74] For detailed discussion in generic terms (not about a particular jurisdiction), see Mulgan ibid ch 3.

or extend to substituting the correct decision. The Ombudsmen's jurisdiction is recommendatory rather than binding.

(a) Specialist Remedial Regimes

Most administrative regimes include their own specialist remedial regime. The first stage usually comprises an internal review on the merits. This may take the form of informal reconsideration or a dedicated internal review body, or both. For instance, under the Social Security Act 2018, applications for review of decisions are heard by Benefits Review Committees.[75] These are made up of two employees of the Ministry of Social Development and a representative of the 'community's interests' appointed by the Minister of Social Development. As is usual at this first stage, their procedure is informal. They consider the merits of the matter, and they can substitute the correct decision. In addition, before a review application is sent to one of these Committees, the Ministry carries out an informal reconsideration of the challenged decision. This is not provided for in the Act, but there is a general power in the Legislation Act for decision-makers to correct errors in their own decisions.[76]

The second stage is often an appeal on the merits to a specialist tribunal which is external to the decision-making authority or agency. Such tribunals may, however, still be considered part of the public administration.[77]

For instance, under the Social Security Act 2018 there is an appeal on the merits from the decision of a Benefits Review Committee to the Social Security Appeal Authority.[78] The Authority's members are appointed by the Governor-General on the recommendation of the Minister of Social Development, after consultation with the Minister of Justice. Such tribunals are supported by the Ministry of Justice.

The Authority's process is relatively informal and investigative. It has the investigative powers of a Commission of Inquiry at all stages of an appeal. That means it can ask its own questions, can require documents and other information or evidence to be produced, and is not bound by the rules of evidence that apply in the courts. It often holds oral hearings but has a discretion to dispose of appeals on the papers. Appellants may represent themselves or be represented by lawyers or lay advocates. The Authority schedules a telephone conference before each hearing, at which it explains the process to the appellant, seeks to clarify the issues and identifies relevant evidence. These features are fairly typical of specialist administrative tribunals.

(b) Other Tribunals

Some other tribunals also hear complaints against public administration, often at first instance. The Waitangi Tribunal investigates claims of breaches of Te Tiriti o

[75] SSA 2018, ss 390–394 and sch 7; SSR 2018, regs 246–247.

[76] Legislation Act 2019, s 46.

[77] Robert Thomas, *Administrative Law in Action: Immigration Administration* (Oxford, Hart Publishing, 2022) at 4–11.

[78] Social Security Act 2018, ss 395–404 and sch 8; Social Security Regulations 2018, regs 248–256.

Waitangi.[79] The Human Rights Review Tribunal's jurisdiction includes complaints about discrimination by public authorities in the exercise of public powers.[80] From the latter, an appeal is available to the general courts.

(c) Ombudsmen and Other Parliamentary Avenues for Complaints

Individual complaints about public administration can also be brought to the Ombudsmen, who are Officers of Parliament, and through a range of other Parliamentary avenues. These include MPs' constituency clinics, petitions to Parliament, and the Regulations Review Committee. These other complaints avenues are also available for accountability other than responding to individual complaints about decisions. They are therefore discussed further under that heading below.

Here we will consider the Ombudsmen. They are constituted under the Ombudsmen Act 1975 as Officers of Parliament, and as such are independent from executive government. Their role is primarily to address individual complaints, but they can also address broader systemic issues on their own motion. Even when addressing individual complaints, they pay attention to the context and may make recommendations of a systemic nature.

The Ombudsmen have power under several enactments, including two separate complaints jurisdictions. The first, under the Ombudsmen Act itself, concerns any decisions and conduct of central and local government agencies generally. The second concerns compliance with disclosure obligations under the Official Information Act 1982. Only the first of these will be outlined here.

The jurisdiction under the Ombudsmen Act is broad, and the powers are recommendatory. The Ombudsmen can consider 'any matter of administration', 'affecting a person'. There are, however, some important exclusions. First, only the bodies listed in Schedule 1 of the Act can be investigated. These exclude courts and tribunals, ministers of the Crown, elected councils (collectively, as distinct from individual councillors), police[81] and health providers. The last two are excluded because specialist bodies are available for complaints against them: the Independent Police Conduct Authority and the Health and Disability Commissioner.

Secondly, the Ombudsmen are not generally authorised to investigate complaints where a right of appeal, objection or review on the merits is available.[82] That is unless 'by reason of special circumstances it would be unreasonable to expect' the person to resort to that other avenue.[83] This exclusion is otherwise complete: it applies whether or not such a right has been exercised or could still be exercised. Since courts and tribunals are not subject to investigation by the Ombudsman, the outcome of an appeal, objection or review is also not open to investigation. Thus there are many administrative regimes whose individual decisions are never investigated by the Ombudsmen,

[79] Treaty of Waitangi Act 1975.

[80] Human Rights Act 1993, Part 1A and Part 3.

[81] Constables are also specifically excluded by s 13(7)(d) of the Act.

[82] Judicial review is not review on the merits and therefore is not relevant to this.

[83] Ombudsmen Act 1975, s 13(7)(a). In addition, there is a discretion to refuse an investigation if 'the complainant has an adequate remedy or right of appeal': s 17(1)(a).

including the social security, accident compensation and tax regimes. However, the Ombudsmen will still investigate complaints about poor treatment in those contexts.

The Ombudsmen determine their own procedure in carrying out an investigation. They have powers to compel answers and production of evidence, but usually rely on the cooperation of the authority being investigated. The complainant's role is generally limited and passive.

The grounds on which the Ombudsmen can raise concerns are broad. They are set out in sections 22(1) and (2) of the Ombudsmen Act 1975, under the misleading heading 'Procedure after investigation'. They include legal grounds: that a decision or other conduct 'appears to have been contrary to law' or 'based … on a mistake of law', or that the exercise of a discretion was influenced by improper purposes or irrelevant considerations. However, they also extend to finding that that a decision or other conduct was 'unreasonable, unjust or oppressive', that it was based on a mistake of fact, and that it 'was wrong'. While this means the Ombudsmen may intervene on the merits, in practice that is relatively rare.[84]

Where the Ombudsmen do regularly go beyond legal grounds is in considering complaints of maladministration about aspects of official conduct other than decisions. The complaints that Ombudsmen have considered include complaints about delays, failure to apologise, unprofessional behaviour, inadequate advice or explanations, inadequate record keeping, lack of provision for periodic reviews, and staff having inadequate knowledge.[85]

Where an Ombudsman concludes that one or more such concerns are made out, they may report that opinion to the agency involved and recommend appropriate remedies.[86] The available remedies listed in the Act include reconsideration by the agency, cancelling or varying the decision, rectifying omissions, altering a practice, and giving reasons. However, the list is not exhaustive. Other remedies that have been recommended include apologies, providing better information or explanations, and payments of ex gratia compensation. Various systemic changes have also been recommended. These include, eg, reviews or changes to policy, practices and procedures, or training for staff on specified matters.

While Ombudsmen's powers are recommendatory, their recommendations command much respect. There is a strong expectation that they will be adopted, and an established and consistent practice of doing so.[87] This is backed up by the Ombudsmen's powers to ensure attention to their recommendations.[88] They may request an agency to notify them within a set timeframe of the steps the agency proposes to take, and may send a copy of the report to the relevant Minister. Failing an adequate response, they

[84] Ron Paterson, 'A Guardian Illuminated: The Role of New Zealand's Parliamentary Ombudsman in the Health and Disability System' in Matthew Groves and Anita Stuhmcke (eds), *The Ombudsman in the Modern State* (Oxford, Hart Publishing, 2022) 331 at 353.

[85] These can be seen in case notes and Annual Reports on the Ombudsman website, available at: www.ombudsman.parliament.nz/resources.

[86] Ombudsmen Act 1975, s 22(3).

[87] See, for instance, Office of the Ombudsmen, *Report of the Ombudsmen for the year ended 30 June 2008* [2008] AJHR A.3 at 24; Graham DS Taylor, 'May Judicial Review Become a Backwater?' in Michael Taggart (ed), *Judicial Review of Administrative Action in the 1980s: Problems and Prospects* (Auckland, Oxford University Press, 1986) 152 at 173.

[88] Ombudsmen Act 1975, s 22(3)–(4).

may then report the issues to the Prime Minister and to the House of Representatives. Such measures are, however, not commonly necessary.

Indeed, the majority of complaints are resolved without formal investigation and recommendation. It is often enough for the Ombudsmen's office to raise the issue with the agency, and to engage in informal dispute resolution. In the course of their ongoing engagement with agencies, the Ombudsmen build constructive relationships.[89] Agencies are therefore generally receptive to working informally with the Ombudsmen to achieve resolution and to improve their policies and processes.

The Ombudsmen may also criticise empowering legislation, including Acts of Parliament, as 'unreasonable, unjust or oppressive, or improperly discriminatory', and recommend that such legislation be reconsidered.[90] For instance, the Ombudsmen have repeatedly criticised legislation that results in lump sum payments of arrears of ACC or social security benefit entitlements being taxed at an excessive rate.[91] This power is, however, used sparingly in practice. The example just given also suggest that it may not be as effective as other types of recommendations: the legislation in question remained unchanged for decades, despite repeated criticism by the Ombudsman and tribunals.[92]

Decisions of the Ombudsman in this general complaints jurisdiction are protected from judicial review by a privative clause.[93] This has not, to date, been litigated,[94] but arguably deserves to be given effect at least in most contexts.[95] In the UK, in contrast, there have been instances of judicial review of Ombudsmen opinions.[96]

In summary, accountability via the Ombudsmen can be both retrospective and prospective. It is primarily focused on the individual but extends to systemic accountability. It is not solely focused on negative constraints. It extends beyond supervision of legality to the merits and to official conduct other than decisions. The content of recommendations can be substitutionary – recommending what should be done.

(d) Judicial Review

Judicial review proceedings are heard by the High Court and the appellate courts. They are thus an avenue external to the public administration. They are available generally in relation to all parts of public administration. They respond to individual complaints, although those can sometimes raise systemic issues.

[89] Mai Chen, 'New Zealand's Ombudsman Legislation: The Need for Amendments After Almost 50 Years' (2010) 41 *Victoria University of Wellington Law Review* 723.

[90] Ombudsmen Act 1975, s 22(1)(b) and (2)(e).

[91] *2009/2010 Report of the Ombudsmen* (Ombudsmen New Zealand, 2010) at 26, noting that this issue had arisen on a number of occasions in the past. The problem goes back at least as far as 1990.

[92] The issue was finally addressed by a 2024 amendment.

[93] Ombudsmen Act 1975, s 25.

[94] Some case law involving judicial review of Ombudsmen decisions does exist, but it concerns the Ombudsman's powers under the Official Information Act 1981: see, eg, *Wyatt Co (NZ) Ltd v Queenstown-Lakes District Council* [1991] 2 NZLR 180 (HC).

[95] Hanna Wilberg, 'Judicial Review of the Ombuds Office: Good for Administrative Justice?' in Greg Weeks and Mark Aronson (eds), *Controlling the Administrative State: Essays in Honour of Matthew Groves* (Oxford, Hart Publishing, 2025) forthcoming.

[96] See, eg, *R v Parliamentary Commissioner for Administration, ex parte Balchin* [1998] 1 PLR 1; *R v Parliamentary Commissioner for Administration, ex parte Dyer* [1994] 1 WLR 621.

The superior courts' judicial review jurisdiction is an inherent jurisdiction – in other words, it is a jurisdiction which the courts have established for themselves. Courts also regard this jurisdiction as a constitutional fundamental, invoking the rule of law principle. Unlike in the United Kingdom, there is no requirement to seek leave or permission; but claims can be struck out. The grounds of review are developed by judicial decisions.[97] However, the procedure is regulated by legislation. There are two procedural routes into judicial review, but the differences between them are minor: Part 30 of the High Court Rules and the Judicial Review Procedure Act 2016.[98]

The procedure in the courts is adversarial: the courts respond to the arguments and evidence presented to them by the complainant and respondent – they do not take an active role in investigating. Formal rules of evidence determine what types of evidence are admissible. Parties are usually represented (and the procedures are designed on that basis), and only lawyers with practising certificates may appear.

However, the procedure for judicial review differs from trial-style proceedings in either criminal or civil law.[99] It is intended to be 'simple, untechnical and prompt'.[100] The main difference is that evidence is usually by affidavit, as the proceedings do not usually require resolution of factual disputes. Special leave is required to call oral evidence or to cross-examine deponents on their affidavits.[101] Further, formal orders for discovery are also discretionary. There is an expectation that the respondent decision-maker will assist the court by disclosing the relevant information and documents that were before the decision-maker at the time, and if appropriate explaining their process and reasoning at the time. This is sometimes referred to as a 'duty of candour'.[102] Failure to explain may result in the court drawing adverse inferences.[103]

The grounds of review represent negative constraints on the exercise of public powers, as already noted. They do not generally extend to the merits: they are largely confined to concerns about legality and procedure. The remedies are not substitutionary, but they are binding and retrospective.[104]

(e) Other Judicial Proceedings against Public Administration

There are at least three further types of judicial proceeding for challenging decisions of public administration, which are discussed in detail later in the book. One is by way of statutory appeal on questions of law from the decisions of administrative tribunals.[105]

[97] On the debate concerning the foundation of judicial review, see Ch 3.

[98] See further Ch 8.D.

[99] See *McGechan on Procedure* (online looseleaf ed, Thomson Reuters Westlaw) at [HR30.3.02]–[HR30.3.03] and [JR14.05]–[JR14.08]. For more detail, see Graham Taylor, *Judicial Review: A New Zealand Perspective*, 4th edn (Wellington, LexisNexis NZ, 2018), Parts two and three.

[100] *Attorney-General v Dotcom* [2013] NZCA 43, [2013] 2 NZLR 213 at [39].

[101] See *Geary v Psychologists' Board* [2009] NZCA 134, [2009] NZAR 338 (the Supreme Court declined leave to appeal).

[102] See, eg, *Wallace v Chief Executive of the Department of Corrections* [2023] NZHC 2248 at [9]. The duty is more established in the UK; see, eg, *Yilmas v Secretary for the Home Department* [2022] EWCA Civ 300.

[103] *Ririnui v Landcorp Farming Ltd* [2016] NZSC 62, [2016] 1 NZLR 1056 at [105]; stating that the 'duty of candour' means no more than this.

[104] See Ch 10.B.

[105] See Ch 10.D.

The second involves collateral challenges to exercises of public administrative decisions on the grounds of judicial review, in the context of criminal or private law proceedings brought either by the Crown or by the challenger.[106] Finally, complaints against public administration can also be brought as private law claims in tort, contract or restitution without invoking grounds of judicial review.[107]

(2) Accountability Beyond Responding to Individual Complaints about Decisions

This part surveys a variety of accountability mechanisms that do not require complaints to activate them, are available for monitoring conduct beyond decisions, and address systemic rather than only individual issues.

(a) Internal Management Mechanisms for Accountability

The means by which public administration is held accountable to the applicable legal norms include internal management mechanisms such as monitoring and auditing, discussed in Chapter 14. In addition to the internal management within each authority or agency, there is also internal accountability of the core public service as a whole to the Public Service Commissioner.[108] The Commissioner employs public service chief executives, provides leadership and guidance, sets minimum standards, and has powers of inquiry.[109]

(b) Parliamentary Accountability

Parliament has a range of significant functions in holding public administration to account. While some of these are at least partly political, at the same time we can also think of them as forming part of administrative law accountability. The conclusions are usually recommendatory.

As part of systemic accountability, departments, ministries, Crown entities and state enterprises must account annually to Select Committees of Parliament for their performance. This involves a written annual report and then a review hearing at which officials are questioned by the Committee. The Committee's own report on the review is then debated in Parliament.[110]

Two significant accountability mechanisms that are part of Parliament or linked to it call for closer attention and thus are further discussed below. Both are available for general accountability for the discharge of public administrative functions. The first is also available as an avenue for individual complaints. It is Parliament's own mechanism for controlling delegated legislation: the Regulations Review Committee

[106] See Ch 10.E.
[107] See Ch 12.
[108] The public service is defined as the core of central government departments and agencies: Public Service Act 2020, s 10.
[109] ibid, ss 17–20 and 42–46, sch 3.
[110] Standing Orders of the House of Representatives 2023, SOs 353–357.

and Parliament's power to disallow such legislation. The second is a separate institution but is constituted as an Officer of Parliament: the Controller and Auditor-General primarily audits public finances, but also carries out general inquiries.

Further Officers of Parliament are the Ombudsmen, an office we have already considered, and the Parliamentary Commissioner for the Environment. The Ombudsmen primarily investigate individual complaints, but can also carry out inquiries into systemic issues of their own motion under the Ombudsmen Act.[111] Further, they are also the agency charged with monitoring and reporting on conditions in prisons and other places of detention or residential care.[112] The Commissioner for the Environment provides reports and advice drawn from environmental investigations to help maintain or improve the quality of the environment. This office is not further discussed here.

(c) Regulations Review Committee and Parliament's Disallowance Power

One Parliamentary accountability mechanism is devoted entirely to delegated legislation. All new delegated legislation must be presented to Parliament.[113] One of Parliament's standing select committees, the Regulations Review Committee, scrutinises delegated legislation both when it is presented and in response to complaints at any time. It also scrutinises provisions in Bills that grant powers to make delegated legislation. In recognition of this significant scrutiny function, by convention the Committee is chaired by an Opposition Member of Parliament. Its powers are recommendatory. Parliament itself, however, can 'disallow', amend or replace delegated legislation – that is a binding power.[114]

The Committee's functions are set out in the Standing Orders.[115] It can act in response to a complaint, when it receives newly made delegated legislation or bills conferring power to make delegated legislation, and on its own motion. The Committee considers delegated legislation against grounds of concern set out in Standing Orders. Where it identifies such concerns, it reports those concerns to Parliament, and recommends changes that would address those concerns. Government is required to respond to such recommendations. It is not unusual for recommendations to be accepted, but there is no obligation to do so. Where concerns have not been addressed or are too fundamental to be addressed by changes, a member of the Committee may present a motion for disallowance.

Parliament's powers to disallow, amend or replace delegated legislation are found in the Legislation Act 2019.[116] They are exercised by passing a resolution: a majority vote in favour of a motion of disallowance, amendment or replacement.[117] Any member

[111] Ombudsmen Act 1975, s 13(3).

[112] Part 2 of the Crimes of Torture Act 1989, monitoring compliance with the Optional Protocol (adopted in 2002) to the Convention Against Torture, and Other Cruel, Inhuman, or Degrading Treatment or Punishment, adopted by the General Assembly of the United Nations on 10 December 1984.

[113] Legislation Act 2019, s 114.

[114] Further, some delegated legislation requires positive confirmation by statute or by resolution. For a guide to all these processes and powers, see Dean Knight and Edward Clark, *Regulations Review Committee Digest*, 7th edn (Wellington, New Zealand Centre for Public Law, 2020) ch 2.

[115] Standing Orders of the House of Representatives 2023, ch 5, SOs 325A–329.

[116] Legislation Act 2019, Part 5.

[117] ibid ss 116 and 119.

can put such a motion. However, a motion of disallowance put by a member of the Regulations Review Committee has a special status. Disallowance results by default if there is no vote on such a motion within 21 sitting days.[118] Disallowance, whether by resolution or by default, has the effect of revoking the regulation from the date of the resolution, or a later date specified in it.[119] Unlike a court order, therefore, it is not retrospective; it does not invalidate anything that has already been done pursuant to the regulation. The powers to disallow, amend or replace are, in fact, virtually never used.[120] However, the existence of the power provides an additional reason for government to agree to recommended changes to regulations.

These mechanisms help to improve the legitimacy of delegated legislation. As legislation that is not made directly with the consent of elected representatives, it is at least subject to their scrutiny and ultimately can be rejected by them. Further, the Committee's scrutiny of Bills can help avoid the enactment of unduly broad powers to make delegated legislation.

For handling complaints, this avenue is a direct alternative to judicial review of delegated legislation. We have already seen that it differs in terms of the available remedies. Further differences concern the procedure, and the grounds of intervention.

Turning to procedure first, a complainant will be given the opportunity to address the Committee. However, its procedure is not adversarial, unlike that of the courts. That is even more obvious in the case of general inquiries, where the public can make submissions and there is no dispute between two parties.

The grounds on which the Committee can raise concerns are set out in Parliament's Standing Orders.[121] They are grounds of legality or constitutional principle. The Committee does not engage with the merits of the legislative policy. The legality grounds are similar to grounds of review: that the delegated legislation is not in accordance with the empowering legislation's objects and intentions, that it trespasses unduly on rights and liberties, and that it excludes the courts' jurisdiction or is retrospective without express authorisation in the empowering legislation.[122] Beyond that, however, there are three broader grounds reflecting constitutional principle. They are that the delegated legislation appears to make some unusual or unexpected use of the delegated powers, that it unduly makes rights and liberties dependent upon administrative decisions that are not subject to review on the merits by an independent tribunal, and that it contains matter more appropriate for parliamentary enactment.[123]

Let us consider these three broader grounds a little further. First, the concern about unusual or unexpected use is similar to judicial review illegality but has wider application.[124] This can be seen, for instance, in different conclusions reached by the

[118] ibid s 117.

[119] ibid ss 116(2) and 118. Amendments or replacements take effect on the twenty-eighth day after the resolution is published, or a date after that specified in the resolution: s 119(2).

[120] Knight and Clark, *Regulations Review Committee Digest* (n 114) at 22–23 mentions just two instances. In one, automatic disallowance was controversially followed by the promulgation of an identical regulation the next day. Stop press: it was controversially used in 2025 to disallow a regulation adopted by the Council for Legal Education on the teaching of tikanga.

[121] Standing Orders of the House of Representatives 2023, SO 327(2).

[122] ibid paras (a), (b), (e) and (g).

[123] ibid paras (c), (d) and (f).

[124] Knight and Clark, *Regulations Review Committee Digest* (n 114) ch 7.

courts and the Committee on the first set of lockdown orders during the Covid-19 pandemic.[125]

Secondly, the concern that delegated legislation should provide review on the merits by an independent tribunal where it empowers administrative decisions that impact on rights and liberties is very much a matter of degree.[126] Judicial review or similar limited supervision clearly does not amount to review on the substantive merits of the decision. Where review on the merits is available, the degree of required independence depends on the importance of the rights and liberties at stake, and also on the breadth of the discretion conferred on the original administrative decision-maker. Avenues internal to the empowered agency will rarely suffice, but an appeal to the relevant Minister has been considered acceptable in some contexts. Truly independent review is most indispensable where the power has a significant impact on important rights or liberties; and where the regulation fails to provide clear criteria for the exercise of that discretion. The matters considered by the Committee under this heading are among the matters that are also addressed by the literature on administrative justice.[127]

Finally, the concern about regulations containing matter more appropriate for parliamentary enactment most obviously applies to policy choices that are sufficiently contentious to require the direct consent of elected representatives. This was the Committee's view, for instance, where regulations gave staff at children's and young persons' residences search and seizure powers. The merits of such powers were hotly contested, and the Committee concluded that if such powers were to be granted it should be by primary legislation.[128]

In summary, the Regulations Review Committee's scrutiny and its power to recommend changes (backed by the ultimate power of Parliament to disallow, amend or replace) is a significant part of the accountability for delegated legislation. Its procedures are investigatory rather than adversarial. Its jurisdiction concerns legality and broader constitutional principles but does not extend to the merits. It provides prospective accountability. While it can deal with individual complaints, its concerns are of a systemic nature about general rules, and it can act on its own motion. Its powers are recommendatory but backed up at least in theory by binding and substitutionary powers available to Parliament.

(d) Controller and Auditor-General

Public entities are subject to regular oversight of a systemic, prospective and recommendatory nature from the Controller and Auditor-General, an Officer of Parliament constituted under the Public Audit Act 2001. The primary role of this office is to carry out regular audits of public finances.[129]

[125] *Borrowdale v Director-General of Health* [2021] NZCA 520, [2022] 2 NZLR 356; the Committee engaged informally, as Parliament's sittings had been suspended: letter from chairperson of Regulations Review Committee to Director-General of Health, dated 20 April 2020.

[126] Knight and Clark (n 114) ch 8.

[127] See Ch 15. Under the European Convention on Human Rights (entered into force on 3 September 1953) applies, art 6 imposes a similar requirement.

[128] Knight and Clark (n 114) ch 10 (esp at 97–98).

[129] Public Audit Act 2001, s 15.

However, it also carries out two related types of more general scrutiny. First, performance audits concern not only financial probity and prudence but also whether an 'entity is carrying out its activities efficiently and effectively', and its 'compliance with statutory obligations'.[130] Secondly, the office may inquire 'into any matter concerning' an entity's 'use of its resources'.[131] These powers are used when concerns arise about governance, management, organisational or other systemic issues within particular entities or across the public sector. All such reports are published and presented to Parliament.

For instance, in 2014 the Auditor-General inquired into the Accident Compensation Corporation's handling of complaints received from its claimants. The Auditor-General reported problems with low complainant satisfaction, limited organisational learning from complaints, lack of consistency, and lack of knowledge among staff.[132] Another example of a wider inquiry is a recent inquiry into mental health services for young people. This found that such services are fragmented, rather than working collaboratively across agencies and entities. It also raised further concerns about lack of understanding of the specific mental health needs of young people and lack of tailored provision for those needs.[133] A further example is the inquiry into the coordination of the government's response to the Covid-19 pandemic.[134]

It will be noted that these general scrutiny functions very much extend to examining the extent to which the public administration is achieving its mission. They are not limited to scrutinising compliance with negative constraints. They are also not limited to examining decisions.

(e) *Inquiries*

Inquiries are ad hoc bodies for investigating questions of public interest and concern. The impetus for such an investigation is usually one of two kinds. The inquiry may respond to a major failure that might have been prevented by more effective government interventions. For instance, in recent years we have had inquiries into what failings led to the Christchurch mosque shootings, the Pike River mine explosion, the leaky building crisis and the level of damage and loss of life caused by the Canterbury earthquakes. Alternatively, inquiries may respond to more general concerns about how things are currently done in some area of government. For instance, we have had inquiries into ACC's dispute resolution systems and into mental health services. Inquiries tend to report on what went wrong or what shortcomings there are in current systems and practice, and on desirable improvements. Their powers are advisory and recommendatory.

[130] ibid s 16.

[131] ibid s 18.

[132] Controller and Auditor-General, *Accident Compensation Corporation: How it deals with complaints* (Wellington, Office of the Auditor-General, August 2014).

[133] Controller and Auditor-General, *Meeting the mental health needs of young New Zealanders* (Wellington, Office of the Auditor-General, February 2024).

[134] Controller and Auditor-General, *Co-ordination of the all-of-government response to the Covid-19 pandemic in 2020* (Wellington, Office of the Auditor-General, December 2022).

While each inquiry is an ad hoc body, the framework for establishing and conducting inquiries is found in the Inquiries Act 2013. Depending on the level of concern and interest, an inquiry can take one of two forms. A public inquiry is appointed by an Order in Council. It usually is a multi-member body chaired by a respected figure such as a judge (sometimes a retired one). In cases of special prominence, it can take the form of a Royal Commission.[135] A government inquiry is appointed by one or more Ministers. It is usually carried out by a single person, often a King's Counsel. The Act provides for terms of reference to be set out when inquiries are appointed, and for a range of investigatory powers. Inquiries often hold extensive public hearings to gather evidence and to hear a range of views.

Mark Elliott has helpfully explored the many respects in which inquiries are different from legal proceedings, aside from the fact that their powers are recommendatory.[136] Rather than being initiated by an individual complainant, the process is run by the government for the benefit of the public. Inquiries can look at the wider picture – they are concerned with systemic issues. The standards they apply are wider than legal standards: for instance, they can ask about the wisdom of policy choices; they can evaluate both past events and reform proposals 'with regard to a range of more diffuse bureaucratic, financial, institutional, moral and political criteria'. They are often explicitly concerned with learning lessons and with proposals for reform, 'ranging from substantive policy and administrative practice to institutional design and interaction'.[137] Transparency is one of their most important functions – one of their principal virtues is that they augment the democratic process by providing the public with information about what happened. They can also be concerned with attributing responsibility or blame, but according to broader standards than legal liability.

[135] Appointed under prerogative powers, but still regulated by the Inquiries Act 2013.

[136] Mark Elliott, 'Ombudsmen, Tribunals, Inquiries: Re-fashioning Accountability Beyond the Courts' in Nicholas Bamforth and Peter Leyland (eds), *Accountability in the Contemporary Constitution* (Oxford, Oxford University Press, 2013) at 250–55.

[137] ibid at 254 and 255.

3

Introducing Debates: The Role of Political Values and Constitutional Principles

Most of this book is devoted to understanding and evaluating particular doctrines, processes and institutions of administrative law. This chapter is different. It provides some background to the remainder of the book, by introducing debates about the shape of administrative law.

Part A concerns the shape of administrative law as a whole: how far and in what ways does it extend beyond judicial review? The focus in this part is on the influence of competing political value systems on the divergent views in that regard, and on the implications of those value systems for the answers to that question.

Part B concerns debates about the appropriate scope of judicial review: how far should this supervisory jurisdiction extend? That question concerns both the areas that should be subject to the jurisdiction and the standard and intensity of review. This part focuses on constitutional norms. It surveys the relevance of constitutional norms to those debates, sketching a variety of arguments that can be made based on those principles.

The debates introduced here are referenced again at relevant points throughout the book. They are always in the background, even when not expressly mentioned.

A. Divergence on the Purpose and Scope of Administrative Law and the Influence of Competing Political Values

What law governs the exercise of powers within public administration? The relevant body of law is, of course, administrative law, but what should we understand by that? The most well-known part is judicial review, but administrative law includes much more than that, as outlined in Chapter 2. As to what to include, and what purposes should guide that choice, there are divergent approaches. Is administrative law concerned primarily with imposing and enforcing constraints on public power, or does it extend more broadly also to setting public policy goals and facilitating and expecting their achievement? What sources of law or legally relevant norms deserve attention in this context? What accountability institutions and mechanisms should be the concern of administrative law analysis?

(1) Two Broad Groups of Approaches

I will outline two broad groups of approaches to these questions. Mainstream approaches tend to focus relatively narrowly on judicial review and its negative constraints. Alternative approaches involve broader answers to the questions just outlined. In sketching the features of these competing approaches in this chapter, I devote particular attention to the various respects in which alternative approaches can depart from the mainstream. Differences also concern the approach to statutory interpretation and judicial review doctrine, and attitudes to the branches of government.

Few modern authors in Aotearoa New Zealand subscribe to pure versions of either approach. Nonetheless, the current textbook writers – Philip Joseph, Graham Taylor and Matthew Smith – have tended largely to hew to a mainstream approach, at least in terms of their focus and coverage of topics.[1] New Zealand does, however, have a strong tradition of alternative approaches in at least some respects, such as reliance on alternative avenues of recourse. It was the first common law country to adopt an Ombudsman,[2] and introduced a number of administrative appeal tribunals from around the same time. These institutions were promoted and analysed by authors at the time, notably Graham Taylor[3] and Ken Keith.[4] Sir Geoffrey Palmer and Mai Chen somewhat more recently also promoted a broader perspective.[5] The work of

[1] Philip A Joseph, *Constitutional and Administrative Law in New Zealand*, 5th edn (Wellington, Brookers, 2021); Graham Taylor, *Judicial Review: A New Zealand Perspective*, 4th edn (Wellington, LexisNexis NZ, 2018); Matthew Smith, *New Zealand Judicial Review Handbook*, 2nd edn (Wellington, Brookers, 2016).

[2] Parliamentary Commissioner (Ombudsman) Act 1962.

[3] See Graham DS Taylor, 'May Judicial Review Become a Backwater?' in Michael Taggart (ed), *Judicial Review of Administrative Action in the 1980s: Problems and Prospects* (Auckland, Oxford University Press, 1986) 152.

[4] See Kenneth Keith, 'The Ombudsman and "Wrong" Decisions' (1971) 4 *New Zealand Universities Law Review* 361.

[5] Mai Chen and Geoffrey Palmer, *Public Law in New Zealand: Cases, Materials, Commentary and Questions* (Oxford University Press, Auckland, 1993); Mai Chen, *Public Law Toolbox: Solving Problems with Government*, 2nd edn (Wellington, LexisNexis, 2012).

David Mullan[6] and later Mike Taggart[7] was influenced by Canada, where alternative approaches were being mainstreamed.[8] Today, Dean Knight adopts a significantly alternative approach, for instance to the scope of administrative law.[9] There continues to be some work on alternative avenues of recourse.[10] My own aim in this book is to follow an alternative approach, but readers will undoubtedly find many places where I have lapsed into a narrower approach closer to the mainstream.

The divergence of approaches can be traced to a variety of influences. A significant reason for the mainstream narrow focus on judicial review is the lawyerly preoccupation with courts. Judicial reasoning is the most distinctively legal form of reasoning. As such, it is the focus of legal training and of much legal scholarship.

A further significant reason is found in the influence of competing political value systems and the associated attitudes to public administration. As Harlow and Rawlings have put it:[11] 'Behind every theory of administrative law there lies a theory of the state.' A debate in political philosophy that is of particular relevance concerns the proper role, size and shape of government or 'the state'.[12] Two main competing philosophies can be identified in that regard.

Liberal individualist philosophies tend to favour a minimal 'night watchman' state. Their highest value is individual liberty, and they define liberty in negative terms – freedom from government interference. On that basis, state intervention in the economy and in the distribution of wealth and resources should be limited. Towards the other end of the spectrum are social democratic philosophies that place a higher value on the welfare of people and of the community, and on that basis favour a large interventionist welfare state. The liberty that matters on this view is positive liberty – having the means to exercise liberty. Government can be a force for good – it must play an active role in pursuing these large goals. It must regulate, redistribute and provide services. Both philosophies have significant influence in politics in Aotearoa New Zealand; their relative influence fluctuates over time.

Mainstream accounts of administrative law, as in most areas of law, tend to be presented as objective and politically neutral. However, some authors espousing alternative approaches have pointed out that many aspects of mainstream accounts reflect a liberal individualist philosophy. One of the classic works in this alternative tradition

[6] See, eg, David Mullan, 'Substantive Fairness Review: Heed the Amber Light!' (1988) 18 *Victoria University of Wellington Law Review* 293.

[7] See, esp, Michael Taggart, 'The Contribution of Lord Cooke to Scope of Review Doctrine in Administrative Law: A Comparative Common Law Perspective' in Paul Rishworth (ed), *The Struggle for Simplicity in the Law: Essays in Honour of Lord Cooke of Thorndon* (Wellington, Butterworths, 1997) 189.

[8] See Ch 9.C(3).

[9] See Dean Knight, 'Of Wise Decisions, Government Accountability and a Small-ish Democracy' (Inaugural lecture, Wellington, 15 August 2024).

[10] See, eg, Mihiata Pirini, 'The Citizen and Administrative Justice: Reforming Complaint Management in New Zealand' (2010) 8 *New Zealand Journal of Public and International Law* 239; John Hopkins, 'Order from Chaos? Tribunal Reform in New Zealand' (2009) 2 *Journal of Australasian Law Teachers Association* 47.

[11] Carol Harlow and Richard Rawlings, *Law and Administration*, 4th edn (Cambridge, Cambridge University Press, 2021) at 1.

[12] For readers unfamiliar with political philosophy, a useful introduction to the range of theories that are relevant to social policy is to be found in ch 4 of Christine Cheyne, Mike O'Brien and Michael Belgrave, *Social Policy in Aotearoa New Zealand: A Critical Introduction* (Auckland, Auckland University Press, 2005).

is *Law and Administration* by Carol Harlow and Richard Rawlings. They introduced the traffic light metaphor, coining the 'red light' and 'green light' labels for competing approaches influenced respectively by liberal individualist and social democratic values.[13]

In sketching the diverging approaches to administrative law, my focus in this chapter is on the influence of these competing value systems and their implications for the shape of administrative law. This necessarily has an element of caricature, given the multi-dimensional complexity of the full picture.[14] First, political value systems are just one influence on approaches to administrative law, as already noted. Secondly, the two competing philosophies presented here in fact form part of a spectrum, and the account here engages with only some aspects and dimensions of debates in political philosophy. Thirdly, the association with political values is not always clear or conscious and is often not consistently maintained.

(2) The 'Red Light' Influence

Harlow and Rawlings described approaches influenced by liberal individualist values as giving government the 'red light'. What they meant was that these approaches focus on *control* of public power and *constraints* on it. Government has extensive unilateral powers, and the role of administrative law is to protect individuals by limiting and controlling those powers and their exercise. As Wade's leading textbook has put it in many successive editions: 'The powerful engines of authority must be prevented from running amok.'[15] Partly due to this, the focus in many administrative law books and courses is on the part of administrative law that defines and enforces the limits of powers: judicial review. Most of the general principles of judicial review are negative; they are constraints on what government can do and how.[16]

The two diverging approaches, red and green light, have also been associated with contrasting attitudes to the branches of government. However, these are more contingent on the actual role and output of those branches in a given place and period, as we will see.

A more extreme 'red light' approach involves distrust of Parliament and democracy.[17] In particular, legislation providing for redistribution is considered unnecessary and at least potentially inconsistent with the rule of law.[18] Lord Hewart famously attacked the discretionary powers that are an integral part of such legislation, particularly

[13] Harlow and Rawlings (n 11) ch 1. This metaphor has been in use since 1984, when it was introduced in the first edition of this book. For a much more theoretical account, see Martin Loughlin, *Public Law and Political Theory* (Clarendon Press, Oxford, 1992).

[14] For a detailed and nuanced intellectual history of the debate, see Janet McLean, *Searching for the State in British Legal Thought: Competing Conceptions of the Public Sphere* (Cambridge, Cambridge University Press, 2012) ch 6.

[15] HWR Sir William Wade and Christopher Forsyth, *Administrative Law*, 11th edn (Oxford, Oxford University Press, 2014) at 4.

[16] See Peter Cane, *Administrative Law*, 5th edn (Oxford, Clarendon Press, 2011) at 10–11.

[17] As pointed out by Jeremy Waldron, 'The Rule of Law in Public Law' in Mark Elliott and David Feldman (eds), *The Cambridge Companion to Public Law* (Cambridge, Cambridge University Press, 2015) 56.

[18] Friedrich Hayek, *Law, Legislation and Liberty, Vol 1: Rules and Order* (University of Chicago Press, 1973) at 72–73, 124–44.

the extensive powers to make delegated legislation, as contrary to the rule of law.[19] Such attacks have recently resurfaced in the United States.[20] This is not a mainstream position.

Red light adherents do place great trust in the courts as guardians of individual liberty and of the rule of law. Dicey stressed the importance of government being controlled by the general courts, due to the independence those courts have from executive government.[21]

Traditionally, there was also a tendency to interpret statutory powers narrowly so as to protect individual liberty.[22] While the mainstream approach to statutory interpretation has shifted to a purposive approach, that is now subject to a tendency to privilege fundamental rights over legislative purpose.[23] In debates about judicial review doctrine, we may associate red light approaches with approaches that restrict powers as much as possible. These include insistence on requiring specific authority, reading statutory purposes narrowly and restrictively,[24] and limiting the availability of justified limits on rights.[25]

(3) The 'Green Light' Influence

Harlow and Rawlings described alternative approaches influenced by social democratic values as giving government the 'green light'. That was because social democratic values call for a large and positive role for government.[26] From that perspective, which I seek to adopt in this book, the 'red light' objective of controlling and constraining government is still necessary,[27] but is considered very incomplete. Administrative law is the law of public administration. Its role and aims must be as much to *facilitate* the various administrative regimes' promotion of community welfare as to control and constrain public power.[28]

For green lighters, the worry is just as much that government agencies will not do enough to serve community welfare, as that they will abuse their power. For instance, Liz Fisher and Sid Shapiro have argued that administrative law should have something to say when authorities fail to prevent disasters or to respond to them adequately.[29]

[19] Lord Hewart of Bury, *The New Despotism* (London, Ernest Benn Ltd, 1929).

[20] See, eg, Philip Hamburger, *Is Administrative Law Unlawful?* (Chicago, University of Chicago Press, 2014).

[21] Albert V Dicey, *Introduction to the Law of the Constitution* (New York, Oxford University Press, 2013 (first published 1885)), ch IV.

[22] For instance, both criminal and tax statutes received a strict construction: Ross I Carter, *Burrows and Carter Statute Law in New Zealand*, 6th edn (Wellington, LexisNexis NZ Ltd, 2021) at 301.

[23] See Ch 6.E.

[24] See Ch 5.C, especially the discussion of *Attorney-General v Ireland* [2002] 2 NZLR 220 (CA).

[25] See Ch 6.C and D.

[26] That is not to say that everyone committed to social democratic values embraces green light approaches to administrative law.

[27] While public powers are necessary and beneficial, they may be abused.

[28] Harlow and Rawlings (n 11) at 32–37 discuss the work to this effect of James Landis, Louis Jaffé, John Willis, Harold Laski, Ivor Jennings, William Robson, John Griffith and Harry Street.

[29] Elizabeth Fisher and Sidney A Shapiro, *Administrative Competence: Reimagining Administrative Law* (Cambridge, Cambridge University Press, 2020) at 32.

Administrative law analyses should take account of the interests of the community served by regulation as much as of the interests of individuals who are subject to that regulation. As Dean Knight points out:[30]

> While the overt manifestation of administrative law is typically litigation by aggrieved individual litigants, it is important not to forget the countervailing interests of the silent majority that underscore the actions of the administration. Even though usually not represented in these proceedings, the public has an interest in the outcome of challenges to administrative instruments, decisions or actions. Members of the public who share their train carriage with the impenitent smoker have an interest in the validity of the non-smoking bylaw. The citizens of Gore have an interest in the validity of the liquor ban in their main street.

This attention to the policy objectives of each regime and how to promote their achievement is the reason why these approaches are also labelled 'functionalist'.[31] Administrative law scholarship in this tradition includes studies of administrative law 'in context'.[32]

From this perspective, delegation of broad administrative discretion is endorsed as necessary and beneficial.[33] Administrative regimes that are designed to promote social improvement cannot operate by inflexible rules, since it is impossible to predict and provide in advance for the infinite variety of individual circumstances in which they fall to be applied. Delegated legislation, and the discretion that is necessarily involved in making it, is necessary because Parliament does not have the time to pass the volume of legislation required. Much of the detail may also be of insufficiently wide interest to receive meaningful scrutiny and debate in Parliament.[34] Further benefits include flexibility and ability to make adjustments in light of experience. The need for delegated legislation and its legitimacy is generally accepted in the mainstream nowadays.

This green light perspective also supports an expansion in the sources of law and the accountability mechanisms that are considered to be part of administrative law. As we have seen, that is the main point distinguishing alternative approaches. This aspect is not necessarily tied to a green light perspective.

The *sources* of law or legally relevant norms on this view extend well beyond judicial review case law with its largely negative controls. At least as importantly, they extend to sources of positive norms setting out goals and facilitating their achievement. They therefore include the legislation that sets up administrative authorities and confers powers on them.[35] They also include the output of

[30] Dean Knight, 'Ameliorating the Collateral Damage Caused by Collateral Attack in Administrative Law' (2006) 4 *New Zealand Journal of Public and International Law* 117 at 133.

[31] See, eg, Loughlin (n 13).

[32] See, eg, Robert Thomas, *Administrative Law in Action: Immigration Administration* (Oxford, Hart Publishing, 2022).

[33] See, eg, Fisher and Shapiro (n 29) at 279–81.

[34] Eddie Clark argues that better deliberation on detailed local, specialised or technical matters is likely in the context of public participation in rule-making: see Edward Clark, 'Procedural Fairness and Citizen Control: Addressing the Legitimacy Deficit in the Canadian Administrative State' (Doctor of Juridical Science thesis, University of Toronto, 2017) at 35–39.

[35] See, eg, John AG Griffith and Harry Street, *Principles of Administrative Law*, 1st edn (1952).

accountability institutions other than judicial review, such as administrative tribunals[36] or Parliamentary avenues.[37]

The *accountability* mechanisms that are needed from this perspective must serve to hold the administration accountable to the positive goals set out for it, as well as to guard against abuse of its powers. There is a 'learning or regulatory dimension' of accountability.[38] For most green lighters the accountability mechanisms still include judicial review, but from this perspective that can only do a limited part of the job.

For the task of facilitating and promoting pursuit of community welfare objectives, there are better means than the negative controls of judicial review. Good decision-making that is both fair to individuals and faithful to the regime's objectives is best promoted by internal and prospective controls. These include the internal guidelines adopted by authorities[39] and internal management techniques.[40] Griffith and Street likened this to the 'control' of a river by its banks.[41] Administrative justice scholarship inspired by green light commitments therefore includes studies focusing on a regime's 'efficacy … to deliver public services',[42] and studies of front-line administration and its control through internal management.[43]

External and retrospective mechanisms can also make a contribution to promoting pursuit of community welfare objectives. But among the external mechanisms, judicial review is least well suited to that. Alternative avenues such as specialist tribunals and the Ombudsmen are more likely than the courts to have the necessary understanding of the relevant regime's public policy objectives. Partly for this reason, a central part of the green light project is a shift away from reliance on general courts to providing specialist administrative tribunals. Contrast Dicey's conviction that this way lies tyranny!

Dispute resolution in the context of New Zealand's Accident Compensation (ACC) scheme provides an example of this concern about understanding and promoting the regime's public policy objectives. ACC is a no-fault scheme. In place of large tort

[36] See Elizabeth Fisher, 'Administrative Tribunals: An Essay about the Legal Imagination of Administrative Law Scholars' in James Goudkamp, Mark Lunney and Leighton McDonald (eds), *Taking Law Seriously: Essays in Honour of Peter Cane* (Oxford, Hart Publishing, 2021) 259 at 274–76.

[37] The existence of Dean Knight and Edward Clark, *Regulations Review Committee Digest*, 7th edn (Wellington, New Zealand Centre for Public Law, 2020) reflects a view of the Regulations Review Committee's work as a source of legally relevant guidance.

[38] See, eg, Dean Knight, 'Accountability Through Dialogue: New Zealand's Experience During the First Year of the COVID-19 Pandemic' in Joelle Grogan and Alice Donald (eds), *Routledge Handbook on Law and the COVID-19 Pandemic* (Abingdon, Routledge, 2022) 31; Rayner Thwaites and Dean Knight, 'Administrative Law Through a Regulatory Lens: Situating Judicial Adjudication Within a Wider Accountability Framework' in Susy Frankel and Deborah Ryder (eds), *Recalibrating Behaviour: Smarter Regulation in a Global World* (Wellington, LexisNexis, 2013) 529.

[39] See Kenneth C Davis, *Discretionary Justice: A Preliminary Inquiry* (Urbana, IL, University of Illinois Press, 1977).

[40] Jerry Mashaw, 'The Management Side of Due Process: Some Theoretical and Litigation Notes on the Assurance of Accuracy, Fairness, and Timeliness in the Adjudication of Social Welfare Claims' (1973–1974) 59 *Cornell Law Review* 772.

[41] Griffith and Street (n 35) at 24.

[42] Harlow and Rawlings (n 11) at 35. Studies on welfare, housing, and planning law are cited in Carol Harlow and Richard Rawlings, 'Administrative Law in Context: Restoring a Lost Connection' [2014] *Public Law* 28 at 40.

[43] See, eg, Jerry Mashaw, *Bureaucratic Justice: Managing Social Security Disability Claims* (New Haven CT and London, Yale University Press, 1983). See further Ch 14.

damages for the few accident victims lucky enough to win these, it provides a universal entitlement to more limited compensation. The guiding principle of community responsibility for adequate welfare for all accident victims[44] is quintessentially social democratic. However, the administration of ACC tends to become unduly focused on containing cost. Vulnerable claimants can be treated unfairly and unlawfully, and remedies are needed. The question is whether courts are the best avenue of recourse. Will they be faithful to the communitarian bargain with its inherent limits on recovery or will they tend to focus on the needs of the individual before them, and measure the merits of complaints by the standards of the common law of torts? The regime provides specialist remedial avenues and limits access to judicial review.[45]

Finally, when it comes to retrospective accountability for the purpose of grievance resolution, green light accounts consider alternatives to judicial review important for that too. Part of the reason for the shift away from reliance on the courts is that an accountability regime must play a further positive role: it must provide *access to justice*. It must therefore include avenues that are more accessible than judicial review to vulnerable groups with limited resources. Those include administrative tribunals, Ombudsmen and Parliamentary avenues.[46]

This access to justice point has especially broad support extending into the mainstream, more than other aspects of green light approaches. The green light innovations here have gained significant ground in practice: tribunals are now available as part of many regimes. However, these are attended by perennial struggles, such as ensuring that specialist tribunals have the necessary independence to be trusted by the aggrieved (Dicey had at least part of a point there).[47] The scholarship associated with this aspect is the part of the administrative justice literature devoted to evaluating administrative decision-making and grievance resolution regimes, and to designing and promoting better ones.[48]

For these alternative avenues to achieve green light objectives, they must not be (too) readily subject to judicial review, or at least they must not be readily bypassed in favour of judicial review. Privative clauses of various types and strengths are an integral part of the design of many remedial regimes. Green lighters tend to promote and defend such limits to judicial review. However, these remain constitutionally contentious in the mainstream. They have had a mixed reception from the courts: full privative clauses are ignored, but ones that merely substitute alternative avenues of recourse are often given effect.[49]

The implications of green light approaches also extend to statutory interpretation. Statutes should be interpreted to promote the achievement of their policy purposes. The modern purposive approach to statutory interpretation very much reflects the influence of the green light approach in this respect. In debates about judicial review doctrine, we may also associate green-light thinking with approaches that give greater

[44] Sir Owen Woodhouse, *Compensation for Personal Injury in New Zealand: Report of the Royal Commission of Inquiry* (1967) at [55]–[56].

[45] Accident Compensation Act 2001, Part 5. See further Chs 8.E(3) and 9.D(2).

[46] See Ch 2.

[47] See Ch 15.

[48] See Chs 13–15.

[49] See Ch 8.E(3).

weight to the social policy objectives pursued by public administration. These include insistence that limits on rights can be lawful if justified by competing objectives,[50] broader and more permissive interpretations of statutory purposes, and toleration of additional unauthorised purposes as long as they are public purposes and do not compromise the statutory purpose.[51]

A further implication that has not so far been received into the mainstream in New Zealand is that administrative authorities and tribunals with their specialist experience may be better placed than courts to interpret their own empowering statutes. On that basis, it can be argued that courts should sometimes accord a measure of deference to those authorities on questions of statutory interpretation.[52] In New Zealand, that proposal was championed by Mike Taggart.[53] However, except in the United States and Canada, it has so far barely even registered in the mainstream.

The contrasting attitudes to the branches of government that have been associated with the competing approaches are more contingent, as already noted. In the earlier parts of the twentieth century, until about the 1980s, 'green light' approaches tended to look to Parliament for social improvements, and to emphasise Parliament's democratic credentials. Courts, on the other hand, were distrusted. That was partly because courts, being generalists, had an inadequate understanding of particular administrative regimes. It was also partly because of the individualist philosophy of many judges at that time,[54] and because of the individualist slant of common law doctrine and adversarial procedure. Green lighters deplored the courts' use of statutory interpretation to undermine regimes for social improvement.[55] Harlow and Rawlings had this complaint about the mainstream:[56]

> Lawyers … suffer from a professional deformation; they are too easily inclined to assume a judicial answer to every problem. Equally, they show a predisposition to leave the judicial branch of government unexamined.

Some old-school green lighters proposed getting rid of judicial review almost entirely.[57] Most did not go so far, but defended traditional limits of judicial review, resisting the modern tendency to expand legal accountability ever further.[58]

One line of scholarship called for greater reliance on political rather than legal accountability (as well as for the greater use of tribunals, as already noted). John Griffith penned a famous defence of the 'political constitution'.[59] The argument was that the United Kingdom's lack of a written constitution or other protections for

[50] See Ch 6.C and 6.D.

[51] See Ch 5.C, esp the discussion of *Ireland* (n 24).

[52] See Ch 9.

[53] Taggart (n 7); see also John Smillie, 'Judicial Review of Administrative Action – A Pragmatic Approach' (1980) 4 *Otago Law Review* 417.

[54] John AG Griffith, *The Politics of the Judiciary* (Fontana Books, 1977).

[55] Harry W Arthurs, 'Rethinking Administrative Law: A Slightly Dicey Business' (1979) 17 *Osgoode Hall Law Journal* 1 at 17–23.

[56] Harlow and Rawlings, *Law and Administration*, 3rd edn (Cambridge, Cambridge University Press, 2009) at 48. This passage does not seem to appear in the fourth edition.

[57] See, eg, Arthurs, 'Rethinking Administrative Law' (n 55) at 34–46.

[58] See, eg, Taylor (n 3) at 155–59; Mullan (n 6).

[59] John AG Griffith, 'The Political Constitution' (1979) 42 *Modern Law Review* 1.

fundamental rights and its reliance on the principle of responsible government was a strength rather than a weakness. Traditional limits on the scope of judicial review should be maintained, to avoid undermining that political constitution.

Innovation has always been needed here too. Green lighters have not dismissed the concerns raised by proponents of a more legalised constitution about the flaws and limits of our current system of political control. Rather, their view has been that where political accountability is not working well, we should improve it rather than replace it with more legal accountability.[60]

(4) Switching the Traffic Lights

Changes in political context since the 1980s have had a significant impact on this debate about the roles of legal and political accountability.[61] Social democratic commitment to government intervention promoting community welfare has waned among most governments, not just those led by conservative parties. Governments have turned instead towards a greater reliance on markets and individual responsibility, and a greater focus on intervention of the 'law and order' variety. The resulting 'neoliberal' policies of deregulating the economy and 'austerity' in social welfare programmes have undermined green lighters' faith in governments and Parliaments as promoters of community welfare. At the same time, courts have developed greater awareness of social justice and a greater commitment to it. Among the newer tools available to judges for that purpose are modern human rights instruments and an increasing recognition of the Treaty of Waitangi.[62]

In this changed context, the contest between social welfare and individualist values no longer neatly aligns (if it ever did) with trust in Parliament and in the courts respectively. In this particular regard, the traffic lights have, to some extent, been switched.

The successors of the green light tradition are still committed to a broader understanding of the purposes of administrative law and of its sources, and to the call for a wider range of accountability mechanisms. But many who are committed to social justice now place greater faith in courts, embracing the power of courts and human rights to promote welfare by protecting vulnerable individuals.[63] To that extent, we could say they have turned into red lighters, focused on constraining the power of government. We should note too, though, that constraints have always been *part of* the green light project.

This has resulted in a split, as the change in attitude includes by no means all successors of the green light tradition. Other green lighters retain their 'old school' distrust of courts. They also retain a deep scepticism about human rights on various grounds,

[60] See Harlow and Rawlings (n 11) at 32.

[61] For discussion, see Michael Taggart, 'Reinvented Government, Traffic Lights, and the Convergence Between Public and Private Law' [1999] *Public Law* 124 at 125–29, 136.

[62] See Ch 6.

[63] Eg Murray Hunt, *Using Human Rights Law in English Courts* (Oxford, Hart Publishing, 1997); Claudia Geiringer, 'Inaugural Lecture: Mr Bulwark and the Protection of Human Rights' (2014) 45 *Victoria University of Wellington Law Review* 367.

including that these promote individualist values.[64] While courts can use human rights to protect vulnerable individuals, they are not accountable and hence cannot be trusted to do so consistently once we concede to them extensive powers to control government. And the protection of individuals, even if vulnerable, should always be balanced against considerations of community welfare. Courts remain structurally predisposed to prioritising individual interests.

The confusion caused by this split in the former green light camp is compounded by a development at the other end of the political spectrum. The old-school green light court sceptics are now often found on the same side of the debate as some supporters of neo-liberal policies who would have been expected to espouse red light views. Some supporters of neo-liberal policies now call for giving the 'green light' to governments pursuing those neo-liberal policies. When courts intervene in the cause of social justice, these supporters of neo-liberal policies attack courts as improperly 'activist' and adopt the 'green light' preference for political accountability.[65] Advocacy of political constitutionalism is thus now found on both sides of politics.[66]

Where legal avenues for grievance resolution are concerned, there is a similar crossover between the political camps. The green light and social justice preference for tribunals and other forms of alternative dispute-resolution can be co-opted by (neo-)liberal policymakers bent on austerity. The two camps may agree on some of the advantages. Other objectives pursued by the two camps are, however, diametrically opposed. Those committed to social justice value tribunals for their greater accessibility. Accessibility is bound to suffer when tribunals are adopted as the cheaper option. Tribunals then are more likely to represent second-rate justice for the poor.[67]

B. Constitutional Norms Relevant to the Scope of Judicial Review

In this part, our focus narrows to judicial review, but against the background of the broader field of administrative law discussed in the previous part and Chapter 2. This part concerns debates about the scope and limits of judicial review. How far should judicial scrutiny of public administration by the general courts extend?[68] For instance, when and to what extent should courts substitute their view for that of the

[64] See, eg, John AG Griffith, 'The Common Law and the Political Constitution' (2001) 117 *Law Quarterly Review* 42.

[65] See, eg, Roger Partridge, *Who Makes the Law? Reining in the Supreme Court* (Wellington, The New Zealand Initiative, 2024); see also the Judicial Power Project at the Policy Exchange think tank (headed by another New Zealander, Richard Ekins). The author of one of the leading modern defences of the political constitution (Adam Tomkins, *Our Republican Constitution* (Hart, Oxford, 2005)) left little doubt about his politics when he subsequently became a conservative party MP for a term.

[66] Robert Greally, 'Ideologies of Political Constitutionalism' (2024) 44 *Oxford Journal of Legal Studies* 949.

[67] See Ch 15.

[68] The questions discussed here apply not only to judicial review but also to administrative law appeals to the courts that are confined to questions of law.

decision-maker? Conversely, when and to what extent is it appropriate to limit review on account of justiciability concerns, or to give effect to privative clauses in legislation that seek to exclude or restrict access to judicial review? Underlying this is a more fundamental question: Why and on what basis are constraints on public power applied and enforced by the general courts at all – why do we have judicial review?

The scope of review is a perennially unsettled and contentious question, debated in both commentary and judicial decisions. It has expanded greatly in all its different aspects over the past 60 years. There is continuing pressure for further expansion, and continuing resistance to that. The detail of the current answers is explored in Parts II and III of this book concerning the grounds of judicial review and the limits of the jurisdiction respectively.

This part of this chapter introduces the constitutional norms that feature in these debates. These norms are invoked throughout the book. They are democracy, the rule of law, Parliamentary sovereignty and the separation of powers. We need to start by understanding the role and status of these norms. As discussed in Chapter 1, while these are not legally enforceable in our 'unwritten' constitution, they have constitutional effects in two respects. First, they provide the organising principles of our set of governmental institutions and processes. For instance, democracy is the organising principle for the institution of Parliament and the process of elections. Secondly, non-compliance with these norms is unconstitutional in the sense of constitutionally illegitimate. The norms thus affect the constitutional legitimacy of the answers to questions about the scope of judicial review. Courts take these norms into account accordingly.

A crucial point to emphasise about the constitutional norms discussed here is that their meaning and content is itself highly contested. The same principle may be invoked by both sides on any given point of contention. All agree that these are fundamental constitutional norms. Their special status rests in part on that universal agreement. But that agreement does not extend to their meaning and content: the debates about the scope of judicial review are so intractable partly because they flow directly from debates about these norms. These are concerned with both the meaning and content of each principle and how they relate to each other and to other norms and values.

There are several reasons for this level of disagreement about the content of constitutional norms. Some disagreements flow from conceptual debates, such as debates about the nature of law itself. Others flow from political value disagreements. We have already seen – in the previous part – that different approaches to administrative law are influenced by political values or philosophies. These political disagreements also lead to different understandings of constitutional norms which, in turn, are relevant to the scope of judicial review.

This part of the chapter surveys some of this complexity. Taking each of the four constitutional norms in turn, it outlines some of the desiderata that may be encompassed by each principle and identifies some of the points of conflict, where contentious choices or trade-offs are required in answering our questions about the scope of judicial review. In the process, it touches on some of the relevant intersections between constitutional, conceptual and political debates.

(1) Democracy

(a) Content and Meaning

Democracy means rule by the people. However, in practice, we have representative democracy: rule by elected representatives. Such a representative democracy can be rendered more democratic by providing additional opportunities for participation. For instance, both Parliament and local government have procedures inviting people to make submissions on proposed laws before they are passed. Another example is that the political party system allows people to participate by joining parties. Voting systems also vary, and some might be considered more democratic than others.

Democratic systems of government can thus be found in many different versions, and there is much room for debate on the best system. One question concerns whether unqualified adherence to majority rule may be contrary to democracy in some circumstances. For instance, Sir Robin Cooke, in a famous article, argued that observance of certain rights is fundamental to democracy. Parliament's powers should not extend to abolishing the right to vote and to access the courts.[69]

(b) Arguments Concerning the Scope of Review

The principle of democracy gives rise to one of the main arguments for limiting the scope of judicial review. Questions requiring competing interests or values to be weighed should be decided by decision makers who have democratic legitimacy. That may mean that they are elected and therefore directly democratically accountable, or that they have to answer to an elected politician. It may further mean that they follow democratic decision-making procedures, such as majority voting and hearing public submissions. Judges, of course, lack any such democratic legitimacy.

Such questions therefore may not be justiciable – not suitable for judicial determination.[70] If courts do scrutinise decisions on such questions, they should do so with an appropriate measure of respect for the decision-maker's judgement.[71] This argument for limiting or excluding review carries more weight the stronger the primary decision-maker's democratic credentials and the more substantive the value judgements involved in the decision.[72] Generally, courts should confine themselves to interpreting and applying the law, including the empowering law and the legal requirements of procedural fairness.

Debate arises in this regard when there are calls for greater judicial protection of substantive interests such as fundamental rights or legitimate expectations. Such judicial protection requires judges to engage with the justifications for limiting rights or disappointing expectations – and thus to weigh competing interests or values.[73]

Democracy may also be considered the substantive principle underpinning the doctrine of Parliamentary sovereignty. Arguments based on that doctrine are considered under a separate heading below.

[69] Sir Robin Cooke, 'Fundamentals' [1988] *New Zealand Law Journal* 158.
[70] Ch 8.A.
[71] Chs 6–9.
[72] *Wellington City Council v Woolworths New Zealand Ltd (No 2)* [1996] 2 NZLR 537 (CA) at 546, 553.
[73] Chs 6 and 7.

(2) The Rule of Law

(a) Content and Meaning

A central concern of the rule of law is to prevent arbitrary exercise of power.[74] A helpful summary of the largely undisputed core content of the rule of law is provided by Tamanaha:[75]

> The rule of law, at its core, requires that government officials and citizens are bound by and act consistent with the law. This basic requirement entails a set of minimal characteristics: law must be … prospective …, be made public, be general, be clear, be stable and certain, and be applied to everyone according to its terms.

Note that this places requirements on citizens as well as on government officials, and on government officials in all three branches of government. In the administrative law context, however, the focus is on the rule of law as it applies to executive government and administrative officials. The classic source for the list of minimal characteristics set out in the quote above is Fuller's work.[76]

This core definition of the rule of law is 'thin'. That means its content is relatively limited, and involves demands that are largely formal rather than substantive. Beyond this undisputed core, further content of a more substantive nature is ascribed to the rule of law in some 'thicker' and hence more contested definitions. Most commonly, these additional requirements include protection of fundamental human rights.[77] For Bingham, this specifically includes a more demanding form of equality before the law (equal treatment except where objective differences justify different treatment) and fair, lawful and reasonable exercise of public powers.[78] Some other accounts treat the rule of law as inextricably connected with democracy.[79]

An objection to such thicker accounts is that they are simply employing the rhetorical appeal of the rule of law to enhance the separate argument for fundamental rights or democracy. That may rob the principle of any distinct and independent value, turning it into nothing less than a demand for a just society and government.[80]

Another disagreement that underlies the debate between thinner and thicker accounts is conceptual. The competing positions reflect different conceptions of law itself. Thick versions reflect adherence to some form of natural law position. If you think that we all have inherent rights emanating from natural law (that is to say, these rights exist prior to positive law and independently of it), then you will consider that the rule of law requires government to be subject to such rights.[81] Conversely, if you take the positivist view, namely that law is identified by the fact that it emanates from

[74] See, eg, Martin Krygier, 'What's the Point of the Rule of Law?' [2019] 67 *Buffalo Law Review* 743 at 760–68; John Locke, *Second Treatise of Government* (1688).

[75] Brian Z Tamanaha, 'A Concise Guide to the Rule of Law' in Gianluigi Palombella and Neil Walker (eds), *Relocating the Rule of Law* (Oxford, Hart Publishing, 2008) 3 at 3.

[76] Lon L Fuller, *The Morality of Law* (New Haven CT, Yale University Press, 1964).

[77] See, eg, TRS Allan, *Constitutional Justice: A Liberal Theory of the Rule of Law* (Oxford, Oxford University Press, 2001).

[78] Tom Bingham, *The Rule of Law* (London, Allen Lane, 2010), chs 5–7.

[79] See Jürgen Habermas, *Beyond Facts and Norms* (Cambridge, MA, MIT Press, 1996).

[80] Joseph Raz, 'The Rule of Law and its Virtue' (1977) 93 *Law Quarterly Review* 195 at 196.

[81] See, for instance, Ronald Dworkin, *Law's Empire* (Fontana, 1986); Ronald Dworkin, *A Matter of Principle* (Cambridge, MA, Harvard University Press, 1985); Allan (n 77).

one of the sources of law recognised by the prevailing rule of recognition,[82] then you will consider government to be subject to rights only where the sources of law have established such rights.[83] Whether there is anything in the concept of the rule of law itself that requires at least some rights to be so established is then a topic of further debate: certain more process-oriented rights have often been considered inextricably linked to formal rule of law desiderata such as certainty and prospectivity.[84] The debate about the nature of law is a central debate in jurisprudence. This aspect of the debate about the content of the rule of law is so intractable because the debate about the understanding of law is equally intractable.

Thick accounts of the rule of law often further claim that fundamental rights must be enforceable legal limits to Parliament's power.[85] If that is accepted, then the doctrine of Parliamentary sovereignty that forms part of our constitutional system cannot be reconciled with the rule of law. However, this does not necessarily follow, even if we accept fundamental rights as integral to the rule of law. Not all laws need to be enforceable to satisfy the rule of law.[86] It is possible to consider Parliament to be subject to law in the form of human rights and constitutional principles, albeit accountability for its compliance takes forms other than legal enforcement.[87] That may be considered enough for the rule of law.

The lack of enforcement of limits on Parliament's power is not unique to Parliament. A further instance involves the courts themselves. They too exercise public power, which must also be subject to law. However, in the case of final appellate courts, this subjection to law cannot be enforceable. If there was an unlimited right to bring further appeals, courts could no longer play their crucial role of settling authoritatively what the law is: the lack of finality would entail a fundamental lack of certain and settled law.[88] This is a good example of the tensions that can arise between different aspects of the requirements of the rule of law itself.

The rule of law – even in its 'thick' versions – tends to be discussed in negative terms: it constrains the exercise of public power. A useful corrective to this is offered by Krygier. He points out that weak government is as harmful and dangerous as oppressive government, and that rule of law constraints have an enabling role. Public power is more effective, as well as less arbitrary and oppressive, when it is 'tempered' by such constraints.[89] Jeff King has gone further, arguing that the rule of law should be understood to have a social dimension. The arbitrary power that is the central concern of the rule of law should be understood as encompassing private arbitrary power. On that understanding, regulatory regimes that protect against such power are essential for the realisation of the rule of law.[90]

[82] HLA Hart, *The Concept of Law* (1961). According to Hart, this rule of recognition is constituted by the social fact of its acceptance by both officials and citizens.

[83] For instance, Raz (n 80).

[84] See John Hart Ely, *Democracy and Distrust* (Cambridge, MA, Harvard University Press, 1980).

[85] See Tamanaha (n 75) at 4–6, noting also some of difficulties with this claim.

[86] Timothy A O Endicott, *Vagueness in Law* (Oxford, Oxford University Press, 2000).

[87] For an account on which this is the effect of the New Zealand Bill of Rights Act 1990 in relation to Parliament's legislative powers, see Paul Rishworth et al, *The New Zealand Bill of Rights* (2003) at 30–31.

[88] See Endicott (n 86) at 193–195.

[89] Krygier (n 74) at 768–782.

[90] Jeff King, 'The Rule of Law' in Richard Bellamy and Jeff King (eds), *The Cambridge Handbook of Constitutional Theory* (Cambridge, Cambridge University Press, 2025).

Finally, a word is needed on Dicey's account of the rule of law in his classic work on the constitution.[91] His central concern was to maintain the rule of the ordinary law applied by the ordinary courts, as they alone had the necessary independence. This meant three things in particular: avoiding undue official discretion because individuals ought not to be liable other than pursuant to the ordinary law applied by the ordinary courts; equal application of the same ordinary law by ordinary courts to both officials and citizens; and individual constitutional rights taking the form of the ordinary law applied by the ordinary courts.

This account has been widely referenced in administrative law discussions of the rule of law in both English and New Zealand sources. However, it is an account shaped by a red light approach to administrative law, and as such is contentious. We need to be aware of this account, as it has been influential. But support for it now is very much qualified. An insistence on the ordinary courts is not the only way to safeguard independence: few today agree with Dicey's critique, on this ground, of the French system of separate public law courts.[92] But in the mainstream view, statutory tribunals are still considered suspect unless they are subject to the supervision of the ordinary courts.[93] Administrative discretion is now almost universally accepted as necessary and appropriate. The issue is how much discretion is acceptable and appropriate, and what controls and constraints are needed to maintain the rule of law.[94] There is an unavoidable tension between the need for discretion and the need for constraints to avoid arbitrariness.[95] This is an example of the tensions between different aspects of the rule of law and other important values.

(b) Arguments Concerning the Scope of Judicial Review

What, then, are some rule of law arguments concerning the scope of judicial review? The reasons for limiting the scope of review are largely found in the other norms, and also in the green light preference for alternative avenues of accountability. The rule of law question is whether and to what extent such limits can be reconciled with the rule of law. Some limits are consistent with the rule of law on most views. What amounts to excessive limits – or conversely, how much judicial review is required by the rule of law – is the point on which there is much room for debate.

Privative clauses seek to restrict or exclude access to review.[96] Complete exclusion would generally be inconsistent even with the thinnest version of the rule of law, at least unless other legal avenues of recourse are available. Hence the rule of law provides the chief argument against absolute privative clauses. However, case law accepts that the rule of law does not demand unlimited access to judicial review. Where there are

[91] AV Dicey, *Introduction to the Law of the Constitution* (1885), ch IV.

[92] See, eg, HWR Wade and Christopher Forsyth, *Administrative Law*, 11th edn (Oxford, Oxford University Press, 2014) at 17.

[93] See Ch 8.E.

[94] See, eg, Bingham (n 78), ch 4: 'law not discretion' is listed as one of the eight ingredients of the rule of law, but this is qualified in the text as merely requiring discretion to be constrained so as to prevent it being exercised arbitrarily.

[95] For discussion, see Ch 5.A.

[96] See ch 8. E.

alternative statutory avenues of recourse, New Zealand courts have upheld limits on judicial review in favour of those alternatives.[97]

Justiciability limits also can be consistent with the rule of law.[98] Most, if not all, accounts of the rule of law accept that the rule of law does not require law to 'rule everything'. Tamanaha rightly cautions against misinterpreting the rule of law as supporting 'extension of the reach of law ever further into the social, economic and political realms', and turning it into the rule of judges.[99] On this view, it does not offend the rule of law to exclude judicial review of certain issues on grounds of justiciability.

Conversely, the rule of law requires a lot more than just judicial enforcement of law, and there are limits to the contribution judicial review can make. The rule of law also requires that people generally comply with the law and generally believe in, and are committed to, the rule of law.[100] Postema argues that both public office holders and the public at large must accept a responsibility for expecting and demanding adherence to the law of each other.[101] When all of this is lacking, the rule of law is fragile, no matter how comprehensively the law is enforced by the courts.

Whether emergencies serve to modify the demands of the rule of law is a recurring question that arose starkly in the Covid-19 pandemic.[102] How assertively reviewing courts should control exercises of discretion is always a balancing exercise, and that balance may need adjusting in an emergency.[103] Greater judicial restraint was in fact seen in pandemic cases such as the challenge to the first lockdown in *Borrowdale*.[104] The courts applied a generous purposive approach to interpreting the scope of empowering provisions, recognising that the legislation was meant to enable an effective response to an epidemic. And the remedy for the one aspect that was found unlawful was confined to a declaration. These instances of restraint may be seen as compromising the rule of law.[105] Alternatively, they may be seen as reflecting appropriate recognition that the demands of the rule of law are sensitive to context.[106] The necessary accountability may appropriately take a range of forms in this context.[107]

Turning finally to the more fundamental question, why are the legal limits on exercises of public power enforced by the courts, that is by judicial review? The background to this question includes the existence of alternatives to judicial enforcement. As we

[97] See Ch 8.E.

[98] See Ch 8.A.

[99] Tamanaha (n 75), at 4, 6, 14–15.

[100] ibid at 6.

[101] Gerald J Postema, 'Fidelity in Law's Commonwealth', in Dennis Klimchuk (ed), *Private Law and the Rule of Law* (Oxford, Oxford University Press, 2014) 17.

[102] See, generally, Victor V Ramraj (ed), *Emergencies and the Limits of Legality* (Cambridge, Cambridge University Press, 2008).

[103] See Janet McLean et al, 'Legality in Times of Emergency: Assessing NZ's Response to COVID-19' (2021) 51 *Journal of the Royal Society of New Zealand* 197.

[104] *Borrowdale v Director-General of Health* [2021] NZCA 520, [2022] 2 NZLR 356 at [84]–[155], [226].

[105] See, eg, Claudia Geiringer and Andrew Geddis, 'Judicial Deference and Emergency Power: A Perspective on *Borrowdale v Director-General*' (2021) 31 *Public Law Review* 376.

[106] See, eg, Hanna Wilberg, 'Interpreting Pandemic Powers: Qualifications to the Principle of Legality' (2020) 31 *Public Law Review* 384 at 388–89.

[107] Dean Knight, 'Accountability Through Dialogue: New Zealand's Experience during the First Year of the COVID-19 Pandemic' in Joelle Grogan and Alice Donald (eds), *Routledge Handbook on Law and the COVID-19 Pandemic* (Abingdon, Routledge, 2022) 31.

saw in the previous part, green light approaches prefer a focus on those alternatives, and some argue against retaining judicial review at all. Such arguments may be countered by rule of law arguments.

Two related aspects of the rule of law are relevant in this context. First, we saw that the minimal requirements of the rule of law include that government must be subject to law and this must be sufficiently clear and certain. That requires an institution with authority to make binding rulings on what the law is: binding rulings on the interpretation of legislation and on the common law. The courts are such an institution.[108] Secondly, the courts of general jurisdiction are the only institution which is set up to ensure that those binding rulings are of general application and, as far as possible, consistent with each other; these are further requirements of the rule of law.[109] The courts' power to resolve legal disputes – including legal disputes about exercises of public power – is therefore a crucial aspect of the rule of law. That is one reason for at least including the courts in a remedial regime.

(3) Parliamentary Sovereignty

(a) Content and Meaning

Parliamentary sovereignty means that statute law is the supreme source of law. Neither executive government nor the courts have power to change, disapply or disregard the law found in statutes.[110] Nor can Parliament bind its own successors.[111] The possible qualifications include manner and form restrictions: Parliament may be able to require a special majority or other special procedures for amendment or repeal of certain laws.[112] There are also dicta suggesting that, in truly extreme cases, courts may refuse to give effect to legislation that violates constitutional fundamentals,[113] and arguments for an exception in relation to legislation in breach of the Treaty of Waitangi.[114]

(b) Arguments Concerning the Scope of Review

Parliamentary sovereignty gives rise to at least two arguments for limits on the scope of review. First, it requires courts to respect Parliament's allocation of powers. Parliament has granted the powers in question to the decision-maker, not to the courts. The judicial review jurisdiction is not a statutory power: it is an inherent jurisdiction. Hence it

[108] See *R (UNISON) v Lord Chancellor* [2017] UKSC 51, [2017] 3 WLR 409 at [66]–[73], for the importance of courts and tribunals for the rule of law in this regard.

[109] This was a central concern for Lord Carnwath in *R (Privacy International) v Investigatory Powers Tribunal* [2019] UKSC 22, [2020] AC 491 at [138]–[139].

[110] *Fitzgerald v Muldoon* [1976] 2 NZLR 615 (SC) at 622; *Shaw v Commissioner of Inland Revenue* [1999] 3 NZLR 154 (CA).

[111] *Ellen Street Estates Ltd v Minister of Health* [1934] 1 KB 590; *R v Pora* [2001] 2 NZLR 37 (CA) at [110].

[112] *Ngaronoa v Attorney-General* [2018] NZSC 123, [2019] 1 NZLR 289.

[113] See, eg, *Taylor v NZ Poultry Board* [1984] 1 NZLR 394 (CA) at 398; *AXA General Insurance Ltd v HM Advocate* [2011] UKSC 46, [2012] 1 AC 868 at [51]. The Safety of Rwanda (Asylum and Immigration) Act 2004 (UK) was widely thought to raise this prospect, but is now set to be repealed.

[114] Claire Charters, 'Responding to Waldron's Defence of Legislatures: Why New Zealand's Parliament Does Not Protect Rights in Hard Cases' [2006] *New Zealand Law Review* 621.

would be inconsistent with statute, and therefore with Parliamentary sovereignty, for courts on judicial review to re-make the impugned decision of the body empowered by Parliament. At a minimum, this argument calls for a deferential standard of review.

The second argument concerns privative clauses purporting to limit or exclude access to review. As we have seen, such clauses may be in tension with the rule of law. However, when courts ignore such clauses, as they do when the clause purports to exclude review entirely, that is difficult to reconcile with Parliamentary sovereignty.[115]

Turning to the fundamental question as to why limits on public powers are enforced by the courts, there is a protracted debate on this question that is motivated by concern about respecting Parliamentary sovereignty. This is known as the debate on the 'foundations' of judicial review. The two sides are known as the 'ultra vires' school and the 'common law' school of thought.

According to the ultra vires school, the courts' power to review the primary decision-maker's exercise of statutory powers[116] can only derive from their power to interpret legislation so as to give effect to the will of Parliament.[117] The concern that animates this theory is that, in the absence of a basis in statute (either express or implied), judicial imposition of limits or requirements on the exercise of powers granted by statute would be inconsistent with Parliamentary sovereignty. Given that judicial review is by definition not a jurisdiction conferred by statute, this is prima facie problematic.

However, these authors argue that statutory authority for judicial review does exist, much of it implicit rather than explicit, and provides the legitimate foundation for judicial review. The explicit authority is found in the statutory limits on statutory powers: those are standards with clear statutory authority. While those statutes do not explicitly confer jurisdiction on the courts to interpret and enforce those limits, such jurisdiction is said to be implicit in the grant of limited powers: Parliament must have intended that the limits it set would be enforced; and it must have intended that this would be done by the courts, whose constitutional role it is to interpret and apply the law.

A further argument invoking implied authority is relied on as authorising judicial review standards which appear to have their source in common law, such as the requirements of natural justice. The argument is that when Parliament legislates to grant powers, it does so against the background of established standards governing the exercise of such powers. It must have intended those standards to apply unless it has clearly provided otherwise.

The more recent 'modified' version of the 'ultra vires' model acknowledges that the *source* of much of judicial review doctrine is in judicial decisions, but it insists that these principles can have legal *force as limits on statutory powers* only by virtue of Parliament's implicit intention to allow them to have that force in the absence of provision to the contrary.[118] It also acknowledges that this implicit legislative inten-

[115] Chs 8.E and 9.D.

[116] Judicial review of non-statutory powers requires some other justification: Christopher Forsyth, 'Of Fig Leaves and Fairy Tales: The Ultra Vires Doctrine, the Sovereignty of Parliament and Judicial Review' (1996) 55 *Cambridge Law Journal* 122 at 124–27.

[117] Wade and Forsyth, *Administrative Law* (n 92) at 27–28.

[118] Christopher Forsyth and Mark Elliott, 'The Legitimacy of Judicial Review' [2003] PL 286.

tion cannot be very specific, particularly if it is to extend to authorising further developments of judge-made grounds of review that occur after the date of enactment. In this version, Parliament is taken to have intended that the powers it grants will be subject to the requirements of the rule of law, as interpreted and developed by judges from time to time.

The opposing camp in this debate is known as the 'common law' school of thought.[119] Authors on this side reject the reliance on implied legislative intent as artificial and unnecessary. While much of judicial review involves enforcing limits to statutory powers that are set by statute, that is only one part of the picture. The jurisdiction itself, as well as a large part of the standards applied, are both creatures of the common law.

In my view, there is nothing inconsistent with Parliamentary sovereignty in judicial development of the common law, nor in applying established common law requirements to the exercise of statutory powers where statute has not abrogated those requirements. There is therefore no need to justify the common law aspects of judicial review as being implicitly authorised by statute.

The debate flows from disagreement about the meaning and content of Parliamentary sovereignty, and the principles of statutory interpretation that follow from it. The common law school takes Parliamentary sovereignty in this context to mean no more than that statute prevails over common law: statute overrides and abrogates common law to the extent of any inconsistency. That seems the better view.

The ultra vires school takes Parliamentary sovereignty to mean more than that. There are two possible versions of the doctrine that can explain the ultra vires model. In one version, it means that Parliament is the only legitimate source of public power, both for executive government and for the courts.[120] That is why the judicial review jurisdiction must have at least implicit statutory authorisation. The other version is that the imposition of any purely external standards or controls would necessarily be inconsistent with a statutory grant of power to a public body and hence deny the supremacy of statute law: a statutory grant can be subject to limits only to the extent that they are provided by the statute either expressly or implicitly.

Finally, note the existence of a related but significantly different position that is sometimes confused and conflated with the common law model of judicial review. Common law constitutionalism maintains that there is a set of fundamental rights and principles found in the common law which cannot be abrogated by statute. It is the role and responsibility of the courts to act as guardians of those rights and principles by refusing to give effect to statutes that purport to abrogate these.[121] Unlike the common law model of the foundations of judicial review, common law constitutionalism does involve a direct challenge to Parliamentary sovereignty.

[119] Dawn Oliver, 'Is the Ultra Vires Rule the Basis of Judicial Review?' [1987] PL 543; Paul Craig 'Ultra Vires and the Foundations of Judicial Review' [1998] *Cambridge Law Journal* 63.

[120] According to Paul Craig, *Administrative Law*, 9th edn (Thomson Reuters, London, 2021) at [1-004], that was Dicey's view.

[121] See, eg, Sir John Laws, *The Common Law Constitution: Hamlyn Lectures 2013* (Cambridge, Cambridge University Press, 2014). See also Cooke, 'Fundamentals' (n 69).

(4) Separation of Powers

(a) Content and Meaning

Separation of powers refers to separation between different types of government power. Following Montesquieu, the standard division of government powers is into legislative, executive and judicial power.[122] The purpose of this division is to guard against concentration of power, since that invites abuse. There is a variety of different ways in which powers can be separated, and different countries practice different versions.[123]

The most obvious version involves assigning each type of power to a separate branch of government and keeping these branches as separate and independent as possible. A pure version of such strict separation is probably impossible, but several countries have adopted aspects of it. For instance, in the US, the executive and legislature are separately empowered and accountable and are in competition with each other. In France, the executive and the judiciary are strictly separated in the sense that executive government has its own courts, and the ordinary courts have no jurisdiction over the executive.

Aotearoa New Zealand has adopted the Westminster model of government from the United Kingdom, in which there is no such strict separation. This system employs a different version of the principle that is known as 'checks and balances'. The branches of government are defined by their most prominent type of power, but each exercises a combination of all three types of power.[124] What is important in this version is that the branches act as checks on each other, with the purpose of maintaining a balance of power between them.

In the Westminster system, the executive and legislative branches are closely integrated,[125] and the executive has significant control over the legislature.[126] The legislature still acts as a check on the executive, but its power to do so is significantly attenuated. Moreover, Parliamentary sovereignty means that the judiciary does not have a direct power to act as a check on the legislature. As a result, it may be said that the power of the judiciary to check the executive is particularly important, and that judicial independence from the executive therefore assumes critical importance.[127]

(b) Arguments Concerning the Scope of Judicial Review

The need for checks and balances is one of the reasons why the limits on government need to be enforced by judicial review – providing a further answer to our fundamental

[122] Charles Louis de Secondat, Baron de Montesquieu, *L'Esprit des Lois* (1748).

[123] For a comparative study exploring models for distributing and controlling power, covering the US, Australia and the UK, see Peter Cane, *Controlling Administrative Power: An Historical Comparison* (Cambridge, Cambridge University Press, 2016).

[124] See, eg, Cane, *Administrative Law*, 4th edn (Oxford, Clarendon Press, 2011) at 49–54, on the legislative and adjudicatory functions of the executive branch.

[125] This was described as the 'efficient secret' of the constitution by Walter Bagehot, *The English Constitution*, 1st edn (London, Chapman & Hall, 1867).

[126] See Jack Beatson, *Key Ideas in Law: The Rule of Law and the Separation of Powers* (Oxford, Hart Publishing, 2021).

[127] See Cane, *Administrative Law* (n 124) at 45.

question. Courts are the appropriate branch for legal checks because that is where their expertise lies, because of their power to make binding rulings on what the law is and because of their independence.

But how far should judicial review extend – what limits on it are needed and appropriate? In response to arguments for expanding substantive review, the checks-and-balances principle can be seen as one of the reasons for limiting such expansion. The role of judicial review is to keep a check on the executive government to maintain a balance of power. If judges failed to maintain the distinction between checking the legality of exercises of executive power and exercising those powers for themselves, then the balance would collapse.[128]

Justiciability limits to judicial review are also sometimes linked to the separation of powers.[129] The judicial branch is less well placed than the political branches to weigh in on questions of foreign relations, allocation of scarce resources, risk assessments, disputed scientific questions, and contested social and moral questions. Aside from their lack of democratic legitimacy, the reasons also include that courts are distinguished from the political branches by different institutional features, such as their adversarial procedures.[130]

Separation of powers concerns are sometimes raised in relation to a different avenue for scrutinising exercises of public powers. Administrative tribunals are often empowered to review decisions on their substantive merits. The combination of administrative and judicial functions has been criticised as inconsistent with the separation of powers, but that reflects the separate functions model that does not apply in New Zealand. The more substantive concern is about such tribunals' independence. That needs to be managed by striking a balance that is appropriate in the particular context.[131]

Returning to the courts, finally, their independence also means that they are not subject to checks by the other branches except in the extreme case where Parliament will call for a judge's removal.[132] Who, then, guards the guardians? One answer is that despite the absence of direct checks between the courts and Parliament, there is a delicate balance of power between these two institutions. By virtue of Parliamentary sovereignty, judicial rulings can always be overturned by legislation and, in that sense, Parliament has the last word. However, legislation always falls to be interpreted by the courts and, in that sense, the courts have the last word. Courts have occasionally threatened to go further and disapply legislation if it encroaches too severely on fundamental rights or norms, but they have never yet done so. We may say that threatening to do this helps to maintain the balance, but actually doing so would collapse it.[133]

The norms introduced in this part of the chapter appear throughout the book as part of what is at stake in debates about the limits of judicial review. This chapter has provided background on what they are and how contestable they are.

[128] Rayner Thwaites and Dean Knight, 'Review and Appeal of Regulatory Decisons: The Tension Between Supervision and Performance' in Suzy Frankel (ed), *Learning from the Past, Adapting for the Future: Regulatory Reform in New Zealand* (Wellington, LexisNexis, 2011) 215 at 222.

[129] See Beatson (n 126) at 126–29.

[130] See Ch 8.A.

[131] See Ch 15.B(1)(b) and D(1).

[132] Constitution Act 1986, s 23.

[133] This is the implicit suggestion in *Westco Lagan Ltd v Attorney-General* [2001] 1 NZLR 40 at [91].

Part II

The Grounds of Judicial Review: Norms Governing Administration

4

Traditional Grounds of Review: Procedural Fairness

In this chapter, we turn to the grounds of judicial review. As discussed in the Introduction and Chapter 2,[1] the grounds have two aspects: they represent both instructions to officials on how (not) to exercise their powers, and instructions to judges on the nature and extent of their supervisory powers. In their first aspect, as instructions to officials, they are relevant well beyond judicial review proceedings – they should be considered before decisions are made and can be invoked when decisions are challenged by other avenues of recourse. The first set of grounds, which is the subject of this chapter, are known as procedural fairness grounds or natural justice.

There are two main aspects to procedural fairness at common law: the right to a hearing and the rule against bias. The right to a hearing means that the person addressed by a decision (for instance, whether to dismiss[2] or deport[3] them) must be given an opportunity to make their case for a favourable decision. A variant that has much less universal application is a duty to consult groups with a special interest in a decision. The rule against bias means that decision-makers must be impartial and must not appear to be predisposed towards the parties or to have predetermined the issue. In addition, in many cases, decision-makers are required to give reasons for their decision. This is included in this chapter, since it can be thought of as a further aspect of

[1] See Chs 1.D and 2.B(1).

[2] *Ridge v Baldwin* [1964] AC 40 (HL).

[3] *Daganayasi v Minster of Immigration* [1980] 2 NZLR 130 (CA).

procedural fairness. Finally, procedural fairness requirements also include particular statutory requirements beyond those developed by the common law.

The right to natural justice is also affirmed in section 27(1) of the New Zealand Bill of Rights Act 1990.[4] Unlike other grounds of review, therefore, it has the status of a fundamental right. This has a concrete legal effect in several respects. It means that legislation that potentially conflicts with natural justice must be interpreted so as to remove that conflict if possible.[5] If the legislation cannot be interpreted that way, it may be declared to be inconsistent with the Bill of Rights.[6] It also means that so-called *Baigent* damages for breach of the Bill of Rights may be available where no other remedy provides adequate vindication.[7] Courts had long doubted whether this remedy would ever be needed and appropriate for a breach of natural justice.[8] However, the remedy was finally granted for a breach of natural justice in *X v Oranga Tamariki*, as discussed in Chapter 12.[9]

A number of different terms are in use for these grounds. Traditionally, they were known as the principles of natural justice. More modern terms are 'procedural fairness' and 'procedural impropriety'. The 'procedural' qualifier signifies that these grounds do not concern the substantive merits of the decision, as 'fairness' might otherwise suggest. A further label sometimes used for these grounds is simply 'procedural grounds'. However, they must not be confused with illegality grounds that can be described in similar terms: improper purposes, irrelevant considerations and mandatory considerations are also sometimes described as 'procedural'. What is meant in that context is that those grounds concern the reasoning process.

This chapter starts by considering the rationale for procedural fairness requirements (Part A): Why were these requirements developed by the common law, and why are they frequently affirmed, reinforced and expanded by statute – including, but not limited to, the Bill of Rights? Why should we care about them? It then examines the first of the two main requirements, the right to a hearing (Part B), and its variant, the consultation duty (Part D). Legitimate expectations are relevant to both variants; a part on these is therefore inserted between the two variants (Part C). Next comes the second of the main requirements, the rule against bias (Part E), before briefly turning to the duty to give reasons (Part F).

A. Rationales for Procedural Fairness Requirements

There are at least two broad rationales for procedural fairness requirements: one is instrumental and the other intrinsic. As we will see, these may be invoked in debates about the application of principles of fair procedure.

[4] Similarly, see the European Convention on Human Rights, Article 6, effective via the Human Rights Act 1998 (UK).

[5] See, eg, *Drew v Attorney-General* [2002] 2 NZLR 58 (CA) at [67]–[68]. See generally Ch 6.E.

[6] That power was established in *Taylor v Attorney-General* [2018] NZSC 104, [2019] 1 NZLR 213.

[7] *Simpson v Attorney-General* [1994] 3 NZLR 667 (CA) (*Baigent*'s case). See Ch 12.A(3).

[8] *Combined Beneficiaries Union Inc v Auckland City Cogs Committee* [2008] NZCA 423, [2009] 2 NZLR 56 at [65]–[70].

[9] *X and Y v Chief Executive of Oranga Tamariki* [2022] NZCA 622, [2023] 2 NZLR 261; see Ch 12.B.(3).

The instrumental rationale is that procedural fairness leads to better decisions. For the right to a hearing, this is nicely dramatised in the English *John v Rees* decision:[10]

> The path of the law is strewn with examples of open and shut cases which, somehow, were not; of unanswerable charges which, in the event, were completely answered; of inexplicable conduct which was fully explained.

In short, the person affected by a decision will usually have relevant information. Better decisions are likely to be made if that person is given the opportunity to share such information, and to contest information provided by others.[11] Decisions will be 'better' not only for the individual affected but also in terms of achieving the purposes of the governing law.[12] For the rule against bias, the corresponding rationale is that decision-makers' bias is likely to some extent to divert their focus from the merits of the case and from the statutory criteria, thus leading to inferior decisions.[13]

The intrinsic rationale is concerned with dignity.[14] The dignity of persons is respected by giving them the opportunity to participate in decisions about them.[15] Without that, persons are treated as if they were inanimate objects rather than "beings capable of explaining themselves".[16] This is demeaning and will arouse resentment. While judicial review on procedural fairness grounds may be brought in most cases primarily in the hope of changing the outcome, it will also often be motivated by this sense of grievance. In Aotearoa New Zealand, this concern is reinforced by the high value that tikanga places on mana.[17] Turning to bias, subjecting a person to a biased decision-maker, or even one who merely appears to be biased, fails to treat them with respect.[18]

In addition, by virtue of respecting the dignity of persons subject to decisions, procedural fairness also has a legitimising effect. People are more likely to accept decisions affecting them when they feel they have been treated fairly in the process of reaching those decisions.[19] This can serve as a further rationale. It particularly helps to explain why the mere appearance of bias invalidates a decision: justice must not only be done, but must be seen to be done.[20] A version of this legitimacy rationale also

[10] *John v Rees* [1970] 1 Ch 345 at 402 (Megarry J).

[11] *Daganayasi* (n 3) at 143; *R (Osborn) v Parole Board* [2013] UKSC 61, [2014] AC 1115 at [67].

[12] Dennis J Galligan, *Due Process and Fair Procedure: A Study of Administrative Procedures* (Oxford, Clarendon Press, 1996) ch 1.

[13] *Locabail (UK) Ltd v Bayfield Properties Ltd* [2000] QB 451 (CA) at [2]; Paul Daly, *Understanding Administrative Law in the Common Law World* (Oxford, Oxford University Press, 2021) at 34.

[14] TRS Allan, 'Procedural Fairness and the Duty of Respect' (1998) 18 *Oxford Journal of Legal Studies* 497 at 497, 505–06.

[15] *Osborn* (n 11) at [68].

[16] Jeremy Waldron, 'How Law Protects Dignity' (2012) 71 *Cambridge Law Journal* 200 at 201.

[17] See, eg, *Sweeney v The Prison Manager, Spring Hill Corrections Facility* [2021] NZHC 181, [2021] 2 NZLR 27 at [71], [74]–[77]. Tikanga is Māori customary law, and forms part of New Zealand law: see Ch 2.B(1). Mana may be translated as personal status as well as dignity.

[18] Daly, 'Understanding Administrative Law' (n 13) at 34.

[19] Matthew Groves, 'The Unfolding Purpose of Fairness' (2017) 45 *Federal Law Review* 653 at 675–79; Matthew Groves, 'Is There a "Small Town" Exception to the Bias Rule?' (2021) 28 *Australian Journal of Administrative Law* 114 at 115–16.

[20] *R v Sussex Justices, ex parte McCarthy* [1924] 1 KB 256.

applies to duties to consult in relation to decisions on a large scale: democratic participation promotes legitimacy in that context.

The instrumental and intrinsic rationales are related and compatible. However, there can be tensions between them,[21] and opinions can differ as to their relative importance. In some contexts, this leads to divergent views on the application of the principles of fair procedure. A good example is the controversial issue of whether breach of the right to a hearing should invalidate a decision in a case where a hearing would have made no difference. Say, for example, a prisoner is facing disciplinary charges for assault, in circumstances where the assault is clearly recorded on CCTV. Should the law still insist on the prisoner being given an opportunity to respond? Why?

The instrumental rationale may seem to have little purchase in such a scenario: nothing the prisoner could say would make any difference. As a result, it is tempting to conclude that insisting on a hearing would be a waste of scarce resources and would unnecessarily compromise efficient administration and effective discipline.[22] This view occasionally carries the day.[23] There are, however, two possible objections to this.

The first objection is to query the irrelevance of the instrumental rationale. How can we be confident the person affected would have had nothing relevant to say, if we never gave that person the opportunity?[24] Even if persons charged could not possibly exonerate themselves, they may still have something to say by way of mitigation. In *Ridge v Baldwin*, for instance, a Chief Constable's position had been irreparably compromised by adverse judicial comments about him. However, he could have argued that he should have been allowed to resign rather than be dismissed, in which case he would have retained his pension rights.[25]

The second objection is that even if, exceptionally, we can be confident that a hearing would have made no difference to the outcome, the opportunity should still be afforded because of the intrinsic rationale concerned with dignity. In such an exceptional case, everything turns on whether we consider that dignity rationale sufficiently weighty by itself to justify the cost and burden of a hearing.

Thankfully the choice does not have to be as stark as this may suggest. As we will see, the content of procedural fairness beyond a certain core is highly variable depending on the context. Where the instrumental rationale is weak, a better approach is to treat this as a factor for limiting the content of the hearing requirement, rather than asking whether it categorically excludes the right to a hearing. A further option is to declare the breach of the right but exercise the remedial discretion to decline quashing the decision.[26]

[21] Joanna Bell, *The Anatomy of Administrative Law* (Oxford, Hart Publishing, 2020) at 103–09.

[22] See, further, Part B.(3)(f) of this chapter below.

[23] In addition to occasional cases adopting this view, in the United Kingdom it has been enacted as the default rule in the Criminal Justice and Courts Act 2015 (UK), s 84.

[24] For the same reason, courts must not dismiss an appeal as being devoid of merit unless and until the appellant has been given an opportunity to be heard: *R v Taito* [2002] UKPC 15, [2003] 3 NZLR 577 (PC) at [19].

[25] *Ridge* (n 2) at 68.

[26] See Ch 10.C.

B. Right to a Hearing

The old Latin term for the right to a hearing was *audi alteram partem* (hear the other side) – reflecting a connection with adversarial proceedings. The right has two main limbs: affected persons are entitled to adequate notice of the decision to be made and disclosure of the basis for it, and to a reasonably effective opportunity to make their case.[27] Beyond a certain core content, what is required by both aspects is highly variable, depending on the context. As we saw in Chapter 2, the 'what' and 'who' of public administration cover a great variety. Procedures closely modelled on adversarial proceedings are inappropriate for many administrative decisions that do not arise in an adversarial context.[28] In contexts where a decision is not addressed to an individual, the right to a hearing may not apply at all (although the variant requiring consultation will sometimes apply). Courts weigh a range of factors in determining whether the right applies and how much it requires in the circumstances.

The discussion of the right to a hearing below begins by addressing (1) what is meant by this right – the two basic elements and the range of their potential content. The remaining three sections concern (2) when it applies and what factors weigh in favour of a stronger right; (3) when it is excluded and what factors weaken the right; and (4) what limits have been discarded.

(1) Content of the Right to a Hearing: The Two Limbs and their Various Elements

The two main limbs of the right to a hearing are (a) notice and disclosure and (b) an opportunity to respond. We will explore the content of each of these limbs in turn. At the end, we will note (c) the decision-maker's duty to consider the resulting submissions.

(a) Notice and Disclosure

The first limb potentially has a number of elements: beyond prior notice, it includes disclosure of what may be called the 'charge' and may include disclosure of adverse or prejudicial information and a warning of unexpected findings.

(i) Reasonable Amount of Prior Notice

Prior notice is an invariable requirement whenever the right to a hearing applies – no hearing is possible without this. To facilitate a fair opportunity to be heard, the timing of the notice must allow reasonable time for the person to prepare their case. What is 'reasonable' will vary from case to case.[29] The more important the interest affected, the stronger the argument for ample time to respond fully. And the more complex

[27] See *Ridge* (n 2) at 79.
[28] See also Ch 15.D for tension with other aspects of administrative justice.
[29] Relevant contextual factors generally are discussed in Parts (2) and (3) below.

the issues to be determined, the more time is needed for an effective opportunity to respond. For instance, if there is a need to gather evidence or to obtain legal advice, that will require more time. On the other hand, there may be factors militating in favour of shorter notice. The most obvious example is where there is some urgency, such as where there is some danger to be averted by the decision.[30]

(ii) Disclosure of 'the Charge' and the Consequences Faced

Sufficient information about the proposed decision must also be disclosed. At a minimum, persons affected by a decision are entitled to know the decision they face and the legal basis for it; this is sometimes referred to as 'the charge'. For instance, in *Ridge v Baldwin* the Chief Constable should have been told he was facing dismissal on the grounds that he was unfit for the office. The notice must specify the particular complaint relied on.[31] While there is no duty to draw affected persons' attention to the relevant law – knowing the law is their own responsibility – the decision-maker may have to specify which part of the law is being invoked, where that is not obvious.[32] Much of this aspect of disclosure falls away where a decision is made on application by the persons affected and according to criteria that were known to them.

A related unsettled question is whether applicable internal rules or guidelines must be disclosed. There is a general right to request access to such materials under section 22 of the Official Information Act 1982 and, in practice, a large proportion of internal guidelines is now made available online. The Law Commission in 2012 recommended a stronger duty of proactive disclosure.[33] The duty of disclosure as part of the common law right to a hearing does not depend on a request. However, it is not clear when that duty applies to internal rules that are relied on as the basis for a decision.

A clear case was *SmithKline Beecham*, where internal guidelines had been published and an application had been made in reliance on those guidelines. A change to the guidelines could not be applied to that application without first notifying the applicant and providing an opportunity to address the changed guidelines.[34] The courts are increasingly willing to require disclosure beyond this. In *Simes*, a decision-maker who relied on its own prior decisions as precedents, where those decisions were not publicly available, was held to be obliged to disclose those decisions to the affected party.[35]

[30] *Birss v Secretary for Justice* [1984] 1 NZLR 513 (CA) at 517 (Richardson J).

[31] See, eg, *Gibson v New Zealand Search and Rescue Dogs Inc* [2012] NZHC 1320, [2012] NZAR 699 at [42]–[44].

[32] See Ron Paterson, *Investigation into SSC conduct of MFAT leaks inquiry* (Ombudsman opinion, June 2016).

[33] Law Commission, *The Public's Right to Know: Review of the Official Information Legislation* (NZLC R125, 2012).

[34] *Smithkline Beecham (NZ) Ltd v Ministry of Health* [1992] NZAR 357 (HC) at 367–68.

[35] *Secretary for Justice v Simes* [2012] NZCA 459, [2012] NZAR 1044 at [79]–[82]; see also *Secretary for Internal Affairs v Pub Charity* [2013] NZCA 627, [2014] NZAR 177 at [74]–[78].

(iii) Disclosure of Prejudicial Information

Disclosure of prejudicial information is required when applicable. Bare knowledge of the grounds on which the decision-maker will decide is insufficient to enable persons affected to make their case if they do not know the facts that are alleged against them in relation to those grounds. Sometimes, all relevant information is already known to the person affected. For instance, in *Ridge v Baldwin* the reason for dismissing the Chief Constable was that damaging comments had been made about him in a judgment. He would have been well aware of these comments. If he had been given notice that he was facing dismissal on grounds of unfitness, there would have been little need for further disclosure. However, whenever the person affected is unaware of adverse information or allegations that are before the decision-maker, these do need to be disclosed.

This was the central issue in *Daganayasi*.[36] The Minister of Immigration turned down an appeal against a deportation order, deciding that there were no sufficiently exceptional circumstances of a humanitarian nature. Joanna Daganayasi had invoked that ground of appeal based on her young son's serious medical condition and his need for medical supervision that was not available in her family's Fijian village. But the Minister had received two reports from a medical referee engaged by the department that dismissed this need and discredited the boy's doctors who supported her application. These reports were clearly prejudicial: they denied the validity of the grounds on which the application was made. They were also misleading, and Miss Daganayasi could have clarified the situation. Yet they were not disclosed to her or her legal advisers for comment before the decision was made. The Court had little difficulty in holding that the right to a hearing demanded an opportunity to correct or contradict these prejudicial reports.[37]

Issues can arise as to the extent of required disclosure. Usually, it is sufficient to disclose the substance of prejudicial information; disclosure of the full documents and evidence is not necessary.[38] The issue may also concern what classes of information are included.

The English *Bushell* case established one significant exclusion from disclosure: Ministers are not required to disclose the advice on which their decision was based.[39] The collective knowledge, experience and expertise of officials in the Minister's department is treated as the Minister's own for this purpose. This acknowledges that powers are conferred on a Minister not as an individual but as the head of a department, for whose actions and decisions the Minister is accountable to Parliament according to constitutional conventions.[40]

Daganayasi accepted that the *Bushell* exclusion applies in New Zealand. However, this was held not to cover the medical referee's reports.[41] This might seem to be because

[36] *Daganayasi* (n 3).

[37] ibid at 134, 143.

[38] See, eg, *A v Attorney-General* [2013] NZCA 289, [2013] 3 NZLR 630 at [45]–[70].

[39] *Bushell v Secretary of State for the Environment* [1981] AC 75 (HL) at 102.

[40] ibid at 95–96. For discussion of cases where this *Bushell* reasoning – erroneously, I suggest – has been taken as authority that Ministers as decision-makers are not required to be personally aware of mandatory relevant considerations, see Ch 5.C(2)(d).

[41] *Daganayasi* (n 3) at 142–43.

the medical referee was an external consultant rather than an official in the department. However, Cooke J states that the position would 'probably' be the same if the reports had been prepared by an officer of the department, although the point is left open. Instead, the ruling is best understood as resting on a distinction between advisers gathering further information about the case (not excluded from disclosure) and bringing to bear their own knowledge and experience to provide their assessment of the case (excluded).[42]

A further unclear point is whether the *Bushell* exclusion applies outside the context of government ministers receiving advice. The constitutional conventions underpinning the exclusion certainly do not apply to other types of decision-maker. The Court of Appeal in *Simes* unfortunately did not address this issue. This case involved an administrative decision-maker, and the Court found that the exclusion did not apply. However, that was for different reasons.[43]

Disclosure can alternatively also be sought under the Privacy Act 2020, which provides for access to personal information.[44] In that context, there is no equivalent of the *Bushell* exception. Evaluative or opinion material is protected from disclosure only if it was provided by a third party on condition of confidentiality – the protection specifically does not extend to material 'compiled by a person employed or engaged by an agency'.[45] However, remedies under the Act are concerned with ensuring access – they are unlikely to include invalidating a decision made following non-disclosure.[46] To make a difference to a decision, the Act needs to be deployed proactively to seek disclosure of information (for the purpose of commenting on it) prior to the decision being made.

(iv) Warning of Unexpected Findings

The final issue about disclosure is whether and when persons are entitled to be warned of likely findings against them. The short answer is that such warnings are required only where the findings are unexpected.[47]

The notice and disclosure requirement certainly does not go so far as to generally require disclosure of a draft decision to affected persons for their comment.[48] In many contexts, nothing is required beyond notice of the 'charge' and disclosure of prejudicial information.

However, in some circumstances, especially in inquiries, the decision-making process can be iterative, and the role of persons involved can evolve. For instance, those who expected to be mere witnesses may find their own conduct under scrutiny.[49] In such contexts, resulting findings may sometimes be unexpected, and that is when

[42] ibid at 143. The discussion in *Bushell* (n 39) at 95–96, 102 is open to either of the two interpretations.
[43] *Simes* (n 35) at [107]–[108].
[44] Privacy Act 2020, s 22, information privacy principle 6; and part 4, subpart 1.
[45] ibid s 50.
[46] ibid, ss 91–92, 102, 104.
[47] *Khalon v Attorney-General* [1996] 1 NZLR 458 (HC) at 466.
[48] *Hoffmann-La Roche & Co AG v Secretary of State for Trade and Industry* [1975] AC 295 (HL); *Dow v Royal Commission on the Pike River Coal Mine Tragedy* [2012] NZHC 2404.
[49] See, eg, *Carroll v Auckland Coroner's Court* [2013] NZHC 906, [2013] NZAR 650.

fairness requires a warning. Such unexpected findings are also sometimes referred to as 'straying from the charge': without prior notice of the fresh 'charge', no findings should be made on unexpected matters.

The leading New Zealand case on this point is the *Erebus Royal Commission* case, concerning the inquiry into the air disaster on Mt Erebus in Antarctica. As the airline involved, Air New Zealand was, of course, on notice that the inquiry might result in findings of error against it. However, the inquiry report went further, finding that the airline's representatives had done all they could to cover up its shortcomings: there had been 'a predetermined plan of deception' and an 'orchestrated litany of lies'.[50] On judicial review of the report, the Privy Council held that the airline had not been given sufficient notice that it was at risk of such a finding.[51]

Subsequent cases have clarified the basis for this finding. As pointed out in *Khalon*, it would be very unusual for an adverse finding on credibility to be unexpected: in any inquiry to establish facts, witnesses are on notice that their credibility will be assessed. What made the Erebus inquiry's finding unexpected was that it went beyond assessing credibility, and amounted to a finding of conspiracy to perjure.[52] That was a fresh 'charge' that required notice.[53]

(b) Opportunity to Respond

Next, recall that notice and disclosure is only the first of two limbs of the right to hearing. The second limb is that affected persons then need to have a reasonably effective opportunity to put their case to the decision-maker – after all, that is the purpose of notice and disclosure.

Where an adequate opportunity to respond has been provided, but the person has chosen not to take that opportunity, then the decision-maker is entitled to proceed. However, if a court finds that the person was unable to take advantage of the opportunity for good reason, then proceeding without input from the person will be a fundamental breach of natural justice.[54]

The extent of what is required under this heading varies greatly with the circumstances, depending on a range of factors which are discussed below.[55] At a minimum, an opportunity for written submissions is required. Beyond that, one or more elements of court-like procedures are required in some contexts, but certainly not always. These include an oral hearing in person, the opportunity to call witnesses and to cross-examine opposing witnesses, and legal representation. These will be addressed in turn, noting the importance of context: the further removed a process is from adversarial proceedings, the less likely it is that full application of these court-like procedures will be appropriate. We must be wary of judicialising every administrative procedure.[56]

[50] *Re Erebus Royal Commission; Air New Zealand Ltd v Mahon* [1983] NZLR 662 (PC) at 669.

[51] ibid at 671, 676–84.

[52] *Khalon* (n 47) at 464.

[53] See also Gillian Coumbe, 'The "*Erebus* ground" of natural justice' [2014] *New Zealand Law Journal* 151.

[54] See, eg, *H (SC 52/2018) v Refugee and Protection Officer* [2019] NZSC 13, [2019] 1 NZLR 433 at [38]–[39], [64].

[55] Sections (2) and (3) of this part B.

[56] See, eg, *Bushell* (n 39) at 95–97, 101–02. See also Ch 15.D.

(i) Oral Hearing or Written Submissions?

The label 'right to a hearing' is misleading. The essence of the right is an opportunity to make one's case. In a court setting, that does involve an oral hearing.[57] In the administrative context, however, the right will often be satisfied by no more than an opportunity to make written submissions.[58] That is so especially for first instance administrative decisions, but may also apply to administrative review or appeal decisions. For instance, in *Daganayasi* the decision was in the nature of an appeal. But, by implication from the statute, the right was held to be limited to written submissions.[59]

The minimum requirement of an opportunity to make written submissions is in some cases satisfied simply by the person concerned submitting a written application. Where, however, further relevant information is subsequently disclosed to the person, that will then require a further opportunity for written submissions in response.

Where an oral hearing is required, there are further choices to be made. The hearing may take the adversarial form of a court hearing, in which the person concerned, their representative, or both, are present to hear the evidence and arguments against them and have the opportunity to respond. Alternatively, however, an oral hearing may take more limited forms. It may be an inquisitorial hearing that does not involve presentation of opposing arguments and evidence.[60] Or it may simply involve an interview with the decision-maker. That is, for example, the procedure normally followed in determining refugee status claims at first instance.[61]

Whether an oral hearing is required at all depends on at least two questions: first, whether and to what extent this is necessary for an effective hearing in the circumstances and, secondly, the balance of factors for and against a strong right to a hearing.

An effective hearing is, in certain circumstances, difficult to achieve without an oral hearing. These are considered to include cases where facts or credibility are in issue.[62] Credibility is usually considered as almost impossible to assess without a face-to-face exchange.[63] Where credibility is a central issue (as, for instance, in a refugee status claim), only very weighty countervailing factors will outweigh this need for an oral hearing.

There is a wide range of other circumstances that can make an oral hearing at least desirable.[64] An oral hearing is generally considered to be a more effective opportunity to make one's case. Oral submissions may have a greater impact on the decision-maker, and an oral hearing provides an opportunity for gauging the decision-maker's reaction so as to tailor further submissions to this.[65] An oral hearing in the form of a

[57] As reaffirmed in *R v Taito* [2003] 3 NZLR 577 (PC).

[58] *Jeffs v New Zealand Dairy Board* [1967] NZLR 1057 (PC) at 1068.

[59] *Daganayasi* (n 3) at 142.

[60] See, eg, *Sharman v New Zealand Association of Counsellors Inc* [2013] NZHC 3553, [2014] NZAR 638 at [14], [16], [48]–[55].

[61] As permitted by the Immigration Act 2009, s 149(1)(f), and as discussed in *H v Refugee and Protection Officer* (n 54) at [9], [31]–[36].

[62] See, eg, *Lloyd v McMahon* [1987] AC 625 (HL) at 696.

[63] See *H v Refugee and Protection Officer* (n 54) at [14], [75].

[64] For discussion, see *Osborn* [2013] UKSC 61 (n 11) at [80]–[96].

[65] See *R (Smith) v Parole Board* [2005] UKHL 1, [2005] 1 WLR 350.

court-style adversarial hearing also provides the best opportunity for understanding the case against the person and addressing this in response.

We should, however, not overlook that an oral hearing, particularly without representation, also involves risks for the person concerned. It may sometimes result in something closer to an interrogation. The risks also include that the decision-maker may form a negative impression of the person.

Turning to the factors for and against a strong right to a hearing: on the assumption that an oral hearing is generally more effective, it should be available where the right is strong. For instance, it is more likely to be required where important interests at stake.[66] It is less likely to be required for first instance decisions and in other contexts where a particularly high volume of decisions would make it unduly burdensome for the administration.

(ii) Right to Call Witnesses, and to Cross-examine Witnesses for the Other Side?

Only a full court-style oral hearing provides the opportunity to call witnesses and to cross-examine opposing witnesses. The purpose of these procedures is to elicit evidence in support of the person's case, and to test and cast doubt on adverse evidence.

Whether and to what extent this is needed for an effective hearing therefore depends on the nature of the issues.[67] Witnesses can be crucial where there are factual issues to resolve. Cross-examination can be crucial if the resolution of the factual issues turns on the credibility of witnesses, on the reliability of their recollection, or (in the case of expert witnesses) on the reliability of their expertise. For instance, a prison disciplinary hearing about a riot would require cross-examination of any eyewitness whose evidence conflicted with alibi evidence offered for an accused prisoner.[68]

Aside from such situations where it is essential for an effective hearing, it will be rare for cross-examination to be required in first instance administrative decisions: the balance of factors will usually come down against it. Often, alternative procedures will be adequate even in formal hearings such as inquiries. For instance, inquiries may adopt a written version of cross-examination.[69]

Even where it is essential for an effective hearing, cross-examination sometimes is not possible. An example involves evidence against refugee status claimants. The validity of their claim cannot be determined with confidence without an opportunity to test the credibility of the sources of evidence against them. Yet the New Zealand authorities have neither the factual nor the legal power to compel the attendance of witnesses from the country of origin for that purpose. Fair procedure therefore cannot require this; instead, the issue then concerns the weight to be accorded to the untested evidence.[70]

[66] ibid.

[67] For a helpful discussion, see *Badger v Whangarei Refinery Expansion Commission of Inquiry* [1985] 2 NZLR 688.

[68] Obiter dictum in *R v Board of Visitors of Hull Prison, ex parte St Germain (No 2)* [1979] 1 WLR 1401 (QBD).

[69] See, eg, *Dow v Royal Commission on the Pike River Coal Mine Tragedy* [2012] NZHC 2404.

[70] *Q v Attorney-General* [2011] NZAR 625 (HC).

(iii) Legal Representation?

Drew is the leading case on the question of when legal representation is required for a fair hearing. The context was a prison disciplinary hearing. The Court of Appeal held that legal representation is sometimes required in that context, always depending on all the circumstances.[71] On the facts of *Drew* itself, legal representation should have been allowed because the nature of the issues was such that a lay person of average competence would not have been able to effectively represent himself. On a charge of illicit drug use, the prisoner here was faced with expert evidence that appeared conclusive against him unless doubt could be cast on it by cross-examination.[72] A lawyer's skills were needed for effective cross-examination.

The Court set out two lists of factors, one to explain why legal representation is sometimes required in this context and one to determine when this is so.[73] Let me state these factors at a higher level of generality so as to be applicable to the legal representation issue regardless of context.

Legal representation is the more likely to be required the more court-like the decision-maker and the process. The process followed in prison disciplinary proceedings is at the court-like end of the spectrum. Also in favour of legal representation are factors in favour of a strong right to a hearing generally, such as where important interests are severely affected. In the disciplinary context, for instance, the severity of the applicable penalties is a relevant factor. Finally, there is the issue whether a reasonably effective hearing is possible without legal representation. That was the crucial factor in favour of representation in *Drew*, where it turned on the fact that cross-examination was needed. Where complex points of law are involved, that is another feature that makes legal representation necessary for an effective hearing.[74] Also relevant is the person's individual level of competence.[75]

On the other hand, factors that count against legal representation include the need for reasonable speed in making the determination. In the prison context, that can be important for effective discipline.[76] However, unless there is a particular need for speed, this will not outweigh strong factors for legal representation such as existed in *Drew*. Moreover, the Court noted that legal representation may, in fact, expedite matters by facilitating more effective hearings.[77]

Drew finally also illustrates how statute can implicitly support a stronger right to a hearing. Here, the statute expressly provided a right to cross-examine. In order for this to be an effective right, the Court considered that where its use is needed, then legal representation must be allowed.[78]

[71] *Drew* [2002] 2 NZLR 58 (n 5) at [58]–[65]. The Corrections Act 2004, s 135 now provides as much. At the time, the Penal Institutions Act 1954 was silent on the point, and regulations barred legal representation.

[72] *Drew* (n 5) at [60] and [79].

[73] ibid at [64] and [71].

[74] See, eg, *Obiaga v Visiting Justice at Auckland Prison* [2018] NZHC 3095, [2019] NZAR 148 at [28]–[33], concerning an attempt to argue self-defence.

[75] See also *Drew* (n 5) at [50].

[76] See also ibid at [40].

[77] ibid at [75].

[78] ibid at [58].

(iv) Summary

Overall, two considerations determine whether the right to the opportunity to make one's case requires more than an opportunity to make written submissions, such as an oral hearing, witnesses and cross-examination or legal representation. The first is whether and to what extent the feature in question is necessary for a reasonably effective hearing. The second is the balance between factors in favour of a strong right to a hearing and countervailing factors.

(c) Decision-maker Must Consider the Resulting Submissions

The right to a hearing would be pointless if the decision-maker was not required to consider the submissions put forward in the exercise of the right. This duty can be seen as part of the right to a hearing. Alternatively, such submissions are also recognised as mandatory relevant considerations, so that failing to take them into account constitutes illegality.[79]

Further issues arise where decision-makers delegate their powers or duties. The decision itself may be delegated only where this is authorised.[80] Alternatively, however, a designated decision-maker may personally make the decision, but may delegate part of the process of hearing persons concerned. In that situation, the substance of the submissions received must be reported to the decision-maker in sufficient detail: the one who decides must 'hear' those affected at least to that extent.[81] The *Bushell* proposition that the knowledge of departmental officials is imputed to a Minister[82] does not apply to knowledge of submissions received from persons concerned. Such knowledge must actually be imparted to the Minister, if the Minister is personally making the decision.[83] The unacceptable result otherwise is 'a division of labour in which the person with knowledge decides nothing, and the decision is taken by a person without knowledge'.[84]

(2) When does the Right to a Hearing Apply? What Factors Support a Stronger Right?

The modern New Zealand position on the application of the right to a hearing was established in *Daganayasi*. In summary, a person is entitled at least to a limited form of a hearing quite simply whenever a significant decision is made about that person individually.[85] This applies unless there are good reasons to exclude the right.[86] In the absence of any such good reasons, the person to whom a decision is addressed does

[79] *Air Nelson Ltd v Minister of Transport* [2008] NZAR 139 (CA) at [54]–[55] (concerning the duty to consult variant of the right to a hearing). See further Ch 5.C(2).

[80] See Ch 5.B(1).

[81] *Jeffs v New Zealand Dairy Board* [1967] NZLR 1057 (PC) at 1066–1068; *Air Nelson* (n 79) at [53]–[56].

[82] *Bushell* (n 39) at 95.

[83] *Air Nelson* (n 79) at [45].

[84] *R (National Association of Health Stores) v Department of Health* [2005] EWCA Civ 154 at [26].

[85] *Daganayasi* [1980] 2 NZLR 130 (n 3) at 143, 145.

[86] See section (3) of this Part.

not require any further basis for claiming a right at least to the essential features of a hearing – notice and an opportunity to respond.[87]

Where the decision is not addressed to the person in question individually, the right to a hearing does not generally apply to that person, as we will see in section (3). However, a version of the right known as a duty to consult may apply. This is discussed separately in Part D below.

The right to a hearing does not require a positive basis in statute (although statute can affirm, add to, or limit or exclude the right, expressly or by implication). As put in *Daganayasi*, the right applies by way of 'judicial supplementation of the Act when this is necessary to achieve justice without frustrating the apparent purpose of legislation'.[88] This echoed *Cooper v Wandsworth*: 'the justice of the common law will supply the omission of the legislature'.[89] It may be understood as an application of the principle of legality to protect the common law right to a hearing. According to this principle, legislation is read as not abrogating common law rights such as this unless it does so expressly or by necessary implication.[90] Since the New Zealand Bill of Rights Act 1990 now affirms the right to natural justice in section 27(1), this approach to interpreting empowering legislation is further underpinned by the interpretive direction in section 6 of that Act.

In most cases the question is not whether the right applies, but how much is required by way of a hearing – recall that this varies greatly. A range of factors determine both how strong the right to a hearing is (hence how much content it has) and what particular procedures are required.

Two basic factors may support a stronger right to a hearing and hence more content: the importance of the interest at stake and the severity of the impact on it, as seen in *Daganayasi*.[91] In addition, we will see in Part C that where an applicant has a relevant legitimate expectation, this can also be a factor in favour of a stronger right to a hearing.

A right to a particular court-like procedure such as an oral hearing or legal representation can be further supported by factors that are specific to those procedures. Three such factors were identified in *Drew* in relation to legal representation.[92] They can be generalised to apply to other court-like procedures such as an oral hearing. The first factor is that the procedure is necessary in the circumstances for a reasonably effective opportunity to put the applicant's case. The second factor is the extent to which the decision-maker or the process or both are court-like; and the third is any support to be found in the statute. Decisions on review or appeal tend to be more court-like and thus more likely to require court-like procedures.

[87] The decision in *Daganayasi* purports to apply older additional requirements. Properly understood, however, the way these requirements are applied amounts to discarding them: see section (4) of this Part.

[88] *Daganayasi* (n 3) at 141. See also *Genge v Visiting Justice at Christchurch Men's Prison* [2019] NZCA 583, (2019) 24 PRNZ 695 at [15]; *Dotcom v United States of America* [2014] NZSC 24, [2014] 1 NZLR 355 at [119]–[120], [281]; *R (Bourgass) v Secretary of State for Justice* [2015] UKSC 54 at [99]. See further section (3)(a) of this Part.

[89] *Cooper v Wandsworth Board of Works* (1863) 14 CBNS 180 at 194; also *Ridge v Baldwin* (n 2) at 73.

[90] *R v Secretary of State for the Home Department, ex parte Simms* [2000] 2 AC 115 (HL). See further Ch 6.C(2).

[91] *Daganayasi* (n 3) at 144–45.

[92] *Drew* (n 5). See above, section (1)(b)(iii) of this Part.

A question that has not so far received much judicial attention is whether the principles of te Tiriti o Waitangi (the Treaty of Waitangi) and tikanga[93] may support further content for the right to a hearing. Treaty principles may be applicable by virtue of a statutory Treaty clause, or pursuant to the presumption of consistency with te Tiriti.[94] Respect for tikanga is called for by those principles.[95] The principles have long been held to require consultation in appropriate contexts, as we will see in Part D. The less-explored question is whether they also have any effect on the right to a hearing in individual decision-making. *Ngati Apa Ki Te Waipounamu Trust* gave short shrift to such an argument.[96] More recently, *Hart v Department of Corrections* held that the Treaty principles of partnership and good faith required the Crown to be transparent in its dealings with iwi.[97] Applied to the Crown's purported decision settling a dispute between two iwi over whale bone taonga that were held by the Crown as custodian, this simply reinforced the basic requirements of notice and an opportunity to comment before deciding to deliver the taonga to the other iwi.[98] Whether Treaty principles might make more of a difference has been helpfully explored by Mikayla Dempsey. Her suggestions include that in decisions about Māori individuals, an oral hearing will often be more consistent with tikanga, and will better respect the person's mana,[99] thus also making it more consistent with the principles of te Tiriti.[100]

The positive factors discussed above must be weighed against countervailing factors that may limit or exclude the right to a hearing, outlined in the next section.

(3) When does the Right to a Hearing Not Apply? What Factors Exclude or Weaken the Right?

The right to a hearing may not apply at all where, exceptionally, statute excludes it in sufficiently clear terms – as we will see in section (a). Where the decision is not addressed to the individual in question, the right applies only in the form known as the duty to consult: section (b). Beyond these two situations, a variety of features of a case can weigh against the right to a hearing, potentially resulting in a weaker right with less content. These include (c) the impugned decision is preliminary or mere advice, (d) urgency or other need for speed, (e) cost or other administrative burdens, (f) a hearing would have made no difference, and (g) disclosure would risk harm to other important interests.

[93] Māori customary law.

[94] See Ch 6.A.

[95] *Ellis v R* [2022] NZSC 114, [2022] 1 NZLR 239 at [98], [126], [257].

[96] *Ngati Apa Ki Te Waipounamu Trust v Attorney-General* [2004] 1 462 (CA). The Treaty argument did not feature in the unsuccessful appeal to the Privy Council: *Ngati Apa Ki Te Waipounamu Trust v Attorney-General* [2006] UKPC 49, [2007] 2 NZLR 80.

[97] Tribes.

[98] *Hart v Director-General of Conservation* [2023] NZHC 1011, [2023] 3 NZLR 42 at [79]–[83]. Taonga are treasures.

[99] Dignity and status.

[100] Mikayla McKenzie Dempsey, 'Hearing the Māori Voice: The Case for Proper Implementation of Tikanga and Treaty Principles in Natural Justice Analysis' (2021) 27 *Auckland University Law Review* 55, esp at 70, 74, 84.

(a) Statute Expressly or Impliedly Excludes the Right

Mere statutory silence does not exclude the right to a hearing, as already noted.[101] However, statute can exclude or limit the right either expressly or by necessary implication. Let us consider these two possibilities in turn.

An instance of an express exclusion is found in the provision for the Waitangi Tribunal to order 'resumption' by the Crown, for the purposes of settling Treaty claims, of land held by state-owned enterprises.[102] This exceptional power was inserted as a safeguard at the time when large swathes of Crown lands were transferred to the newly created state-owned enterprises: their quasi-private status should not compromise the availability of their land for Treaty settlements.[103] The affected state-owned enterprise expressly has no right to be heard on a resumption application. In *Wairarapa Moana*, the Supreme Court upheld this exclusion. While the operative provision had some ambiguity, the exclusion was put beyond doubt by the preamble of the Amendment Act and by the provision's history.[104]

An implied limit or exclusion may be found where the right to a hearing would frustrate the purpose of the legislation,[105] or would be inconsistent with the scheme of the legislation. Similarly, where the statute makes express provision for procedure, that may be interpreted as an exhaustive code. Courts are slow to find rights abrogated by implication, but instances do exist.

For example, in *Commissioner of Police v G*, the statute provided for New Zealanders convicted in Australia and deported to New Zealand after release from prison to be served with a determination that they were subject to release conditions as 'returning prisoners'. That notice was to be served if practicable on the person's arrival in New Zealand, or as soon thereafter as reasonably practicable. The Court held that a right to be heard before making that determination would have been inconsistent with that scheme.[106]

CREEDNZ concerned the National Development Act 1979, which provided for fast-track planning approvals for large infrastructure projects.[107] The legislation was held to exclude hearing rights at the preliminary stage of deciding whether to apply the fast-track procedure. One of several reasons for this was implication from the statute. The statutory procedures involved limited hearing rights in the Planning Tribunal at a later stage. Those procedures were considered to be an exhaustive code. To imply further hearing rights at other stages of the process would have frustrated the statutory purpose of providing a streamlined procedure.[108]

[101] See section (2) of this part above.

[102] Treaty of Waitangi Act 1975, ss 8A–8C.

[103] This was the solution adopted in response to the successful challenge in *New Zealand Maori Council v Attorney-General* [1987] 1 NZLR 641 (CA) (the *Lands* case).

[104] *Wairarapa Moana Ki Pouākani Incorporation v Mercury NZ Ltd* [2022] NZSC 142 at [143], [153]–[157].

[105] *Daganayasi* (n 3) at 141.

[106] *Commissioner of Police v G* [2023] NZCA 93, [2023] 2 NZLR 107 at [177].

[107] Facilitating Prime Minister Muldoon's 'Think Big' initiatives.

[108] *CREEDNZ v Governor-General* [1981] 1 NZLR 172 (CA) at 177–78, 190–91. Similarly, see *Te Korowai o Ngāruahine Trust v Hiringa Energy Limited and Balance Agri-Nutrients Limited* [2022] NZHC 2810 at [264] (this point was not addressed on appeal). On procedural codes, see also *Furnell v Whangarei High Schools Board* [1973] 2 NZLR 705 (PC).

(b) 'Exercises of Power on a Large Scale': Legislative and/or Policy Decisions

Apart from being excluded in some contexts by statute, the main circumstance in which the right to a hearing does not generally apply is where the decision is not addressed to the person in question as an individual. That encompasses decisions on a large scale that are not addressed to any particular individual but are instead of a legislative or policy nature. It also includes situations where the decision is addressed to an individual, but where the person seeking to invoke the right is a third party to that decision.[109]

Authority for this limit includes *Ridge v Baldwin*, where Lord Reid explained that the right was not normally appropriate for decisions made 'on a large scale' – it applied more naturally to decisions on 'a single isolated case'.[110] In *Daganayasi*, Cooke J explained why the need for the right to a hearing arises where a decision focuses on an individual: it is then that we need a procedure that ensures that this individual's circumstances are fully and fairly assessed.[111]

We will see that the position has been softening in modern law. There are now quite extensive exceptions, where decisions on a large scale attract the variant of the right to a hearing known as the duty to consult.[112] However, a duty to consult requires a specific basis, as discussed in Part D: usually a statutory provision or a legitimate expectation.

As a general rule, the right to a hearing as such does not apply unless the decision is addressed to the person who is seeking to invoke the right. This was affirmed in the *CREEDNZ* case already touched on.[113] The initial decision to fast-track the approval for a new aluminium smelter was made by Order in Council. The nature of the decision-maker and of the power were among several reasons for rejecting the claim to a hearing at the initial stage. The Executive Council is the body at the apex of the political system that deals with major issues in a broad way. It would rarely be required to hear all the individuals affected before making its decision. Further, the legislative form of an Order in Council, while not determinative, reflected a 'judgment that public policy considerations loom very large'.[114] Both points counted against a right to a hearing at this stage.

(c) Preliminary Decisions or Advice

There may be no right to a hearing or only a very weak right where what is challenged is mere advice or only preliminary to a final substantive decision.[115] However, it all depends on whether the decision has real consequences for the affected individual. This can be seen by contrasting *CREEDNZ* and *Wright*.

[109] See, eg, *Wyeth (NZ) Ltd v Ancare New Zealand Ltd* [2010] NZSC 46, [2010] 3 NZLR 569 at [40]–[43].
[110] *Ridge v Baldwin* (n 2) at 72, 76.
[111] *Daganayasi* (n 3) at 143.
[112] This also resonates with the modern liberal approach to standing, which admits claims by parties representing a public interest: see Ch 8.B(1).
[113] *CREEDNZ* (n 108).
[114] ibid at 177–78, 188–89.
[115] On whether judicial review is available in such a context at all, see Ch 8.B(2).

In *CREEDNZ*, the preliminary nature of the decision was a further reason for rejecting a right to a hearing before the decision to apply the fast-track planning procedure. That decision had no real impact on the objectors' interests, since it merely changed the procedure by which they could have input in the decision at a later stage – it did not determine that the project would go ahead.[116]

In the English case of *Wright*, in contrast, there was a strong case for at least some form of hearing – subject to other factors against – before a provisional decision.[117] The applicants were nurses facing complaints about misconduct which placed vulnerable adults in their care at risk of harm. The challenged decision in each case was their provisional inclusion in a list of persons unsuited to working with vulnerable adults. The statutory process included a right to a hearing at the next step, preceding confirmation of the listing. However, it also required suspension of those who were provisionally listed, and that usually resulted in dismissal from the person's current position. The provisional decision therefore had a very real impact on the applicants' current livelihood and probably also on their future career. This meant that fairness did require as much of a hearing as could be reconciled with other factors at play.[118]

The same approach applies where the challenge is to reports of inquiries or investigations that do not go beyond findings and recommendations. While they are, in that sense, merely advisory, adverse findings or comments in such reports still may have a real impact on the interests of the persons concerned – in particular on their reputation and careers. Where that is so, fairness requires notice that the person is at risk of an adverse finding and a fair opportunity to respond.[119]

(d) Urgency or Need for Speedy Resolution

A strong factor weighing against a right to a hearing is where urgent action is needed to ensure the safety of other people. For instance, when an airline's pilots failed the civil aviation authority's exams, the authority was justified in grounding the airline without according it a prior hearing.[120] This was also the strongest factor against a hearing in the *Wright* case introduced earlier: where the nurses were accused of putting vulnerable people in their care at risk of harm, there was a need for urgent action to ensure the safety of those vulnerable people.

However, the need to ensure the safety of others falls to be balanced against the decision's impact on the interests of the person subject to it. In *Wright*, the House of Lords considered that only an immediate risk to safety could justify completely dispensing with a hearing, where important interests such as livelihood were at stake. Some truncated form of urgent hearing will still be required whenever that does not

[116] *CREEDNZ* (n 108) at 189.

[117] *R (Wright) v Secretary of State for Health* [2009] UKHL 3, [2009] 1 AC 739. This was a claim under Art 6 of the European Convention on Human Rights, but the analysis would be the same for the common law right to a hearing.

[118] ibid at [21]–[22], [28]. Contrast the truly preliminary decision in *Vandervis v Dunedin City Council* [2022] NZCA 219 at [43]–[51].

[119] *Re Erebus Royal Commission; Air New Zealand Ltd v Mahon* [1983] NZLR 662 (PC) at 671; *Royal Australasian College of Surgeons v Phipps* [1999] 3 NZLR 1 (CA) at 14–15 (on appeal to the Privy Council, the application of the right to a hearing was no longer in issue).

[120] *R v Secretary of State for Transport ex p Pegasus Holding (London) Ltd* [1988] 1 WLR 990.

unduly compromise safety. Even where urgency does outweigh the need for a prior hearing entirely, the right to a hearing still has some effect. Protecting the interests of the persons subject to the decision, such as the nurses in *Wright*, then requires an urgent hearing very soon after a provisional decision is made, providing an opportunity to reverse the decision before lasting damage is done to the person's interests.[121] In New Zealand, the Court of Appeal appeared to endorse a similar compromise solution as broadly consistent with natural justice in *Commissioner of Police v G*.[122]

This issue arises also in the context of Oranga Tamariki discharging its child protection responsibilities by uplifting newborn babies without notice – frequently involving Māori whānau.[123] The Family Court has the power to grant interim custody orders on an ex parte application without notice to the mother where the child's safety is at sufficiently serious risk. This is justified only where the safety concerns could not be addressed by an urgent hearing on notice.[124] For instance, there was no such justification where an application was made a month before the birth of the child.[125]

The need for speedy resolution can also arise for reasons less pressing than threats to safety. In such cases, it only features as a factor for a weaker right with less content, and can often be outweighed by the importance of the interest affected or other factors in favour. In *Drew*, for instance, the Court accepted that in prison disciplinary proceedings there was a need for reasonable speed: delays might compromise effective discipline and were burdensome in the context of a large volume of hearings.[126] No-one suggested that this excluded the right to a hearing, but it did weigh against allowing legal representation in every instance. Representation was held to be required only where the factors in favour were especially strong.[127]

(e) Cost or Other Administrative Burden

A factor that can sometimes bear some weight against a strong right to a hearing is administrative convenience and cost saving. However, this needs to be approached with great caution: "convenience and justice are often not on speaking terms".[128] A desire for mere convenience and cost saving can be distinguished from more weighty concerns that too much of a hearing may compromise the purpose of the power, such as in the cases discussed under the previous heading where safety or effective discipline are at stake. Mere convenience and cost saving certainly should not be allowed to outweigh strong factors in favour of a hearing.

[121] *Wright* (n 117) at [29].

[122] *Commissioner of Police v G* (n 106) at [178]–[179]. However, the Court did not necessarily accept the need for urgency in that case: see at [180].

[123] See Peter Boshier, *A Matter of Urgency: Investigation Report into policies, practices and procedures for the removal of newborn pēpi by Oranga Tamariki, Ministry for Children* (The Office of the Ombudsman, August 2020). Whānau means family/ies.

[124] *DE v Chief Executive of the Ministry of Social Development* [2007] NZCA 453, [2008] NZAR 226 at [43]–[45], [73]–[76].

[125] *CLM v Chief Executive of the Ministry of Social Development* [2011] NZFLR 11 (HC) at [30]–[48].

[126] *Drew* (n 5) at [71], see also at [40]–[41].

[127] ibid at [60]–[63], [79]. McGrath J, dissenting in part, would have found representation available only in hearings before Visiting Justices (the tier above prison internal hearings).

[128] *General Medical Council v Spackman* [1943] AC 627 (HL) at 638.

A strong reminder is found in *Taito*.[129] This was not an administrative law case. Rather, it concerned the hearing of criminal appeals in the Court of Appeal – a context in which a full right to a hearing would normally be assumed as axiomatic. Yet the Court had adopted a system of disposing of the bulk of such appeals on the papers (whenever legal aid for the appeal had been declined), as a way of dealing with concerns about a flood of unmeritorious appeals due to an automatic right of appeal. The 'practical necessity' argument based on that concern was roundly dismissed by the Privy Council: there was no sufficient reason to exclude the normal requirements of natural justice. A crucial flaw in the argument was that the merits of an appeal could not be assessed with any confidence unless there was a proper hearing.[130]

Considerations of finality may weaken the right to a hearing in circumstances where there have already been several hearings on the same matter. *Burt* is well known as authority for the reviewability of exercises of the prerogative of mercy. But it is also notable for finding only a weak right to a fair hearing in that context, largely because the person had already had a full hearing at trial and on appeal. There was therefore no right to see and comment on a report to the Minister of Justice that recommended declining mercy.[131] Much depends again, however, on the strength of other factors. The Privy Council in *Lewis* came to the opposite conclusion on the same issue, due at least in part to the importance of the interest at stake: the prisoner in *Lewis* was on death row.[132]

One aspect of the law on procedural fairness that may be understood as avoiding undue cost and other administrative burdens is the curing principle. Courts may exercise their remedial discretion to refuse a remedy for a breach of the right to a hearing in a decision at first instance, if that breach has been 'cured' by a full and fair hearing on an appeal from that decision.[133]

(f) A Hearing Could Have Made No Difference

An even more controversial argument that is sometimes invoked against application of the right to a hearing is that in the circumstances of the case, a hearing could have made no difference. The evidence and the applicable law so clearly supported the decision that nothing the person could have said would have changed the outcome.

The reasons why this argument is controversial were discussed in Part A to illustrate the rationales for the right to a hearing. In New Zealand, courts have almost always resisted this argument as a basis for excluding the right.[134] However, the argument may be used as a factor: if the factors for a hearing are weak, and there are other factors against it, then this factor may contribute to finding a limited form of a hearing

[129] *R v Taito* [2003] 3 NZLR 577 (PC).
[130] ibid at [13], [19].
[131] *Burt v Governor General* [1992] 3 NZLR 672 (CA).
[132] *Lewis v Attorney-General of Jamaica* [2001] 2 AC 50 (PC) at 74, 76, 78. See BV Harris, 'Judicial Review, Justiciability and the Prerogative of Mercy' (2003) 62 *Cambridge Law Journal* 631 at 653–54.
[133] See Ch 10.C(3)(f).
[134] See, eg, *Quake Outcasts v Minister for Canterbury Earthquake Recovery* [2015] NZSC 27, [2016] 1 NZLR 1 at [187].

sufficient. The argument may also be relevant to the remedial discretion, helping to support a limited remedy.[135]

(g) Disclosure would Risk Harm to Other Important Interests

A factor that specifically concerns the disclosure requirement is where disclosure of material that is otherwise needed for a fair hearing would risk harm to other important interests. Such cases can raise very intractable issues where important interests are at stake on both sides and there is only limited potential for accommodating both of the competing interests.

Counter-terrorism powers have frequently given rise to this issue. 'Closed materials procedures' provide for terrorism suspects to be deported, detained, or subjected to restrictions such as control orders, all in reliance on classified information that is not disclosed to the person concerned.[136] Disclosure would undermine the relationship with foreign intelligence agencies and the intelligence-sharing arrangements with them. That might compromise national security, including (to put it more concretely) efforts to prevent terrorist attacks.[137] Yet without disclosure, suspects have no real opportunity to meet the case against them, in circumstances where their most important interests may be at stake.

On the traditional approach to matters of national security, courts would have avoided addressing such issues, as national security was simply non-justiciable. In *CCSU*, the House of Lords accepted that a duty to consult had to give way to national security concerns, and that it would be inappropriate for the Court to assess the validity of those concerns.[138] Modern courts no longer accept either of these points. Instead, they have struggled to balance the needs of natural justice against the needs of national security.

Searching for a procedure that offers at least a measure of reconciliation between the two competing interests, courts in cases like *Zaoui* have concluded that at least a summary of the classified information (the 'gist') must be provided to terrorism suspects facing deportation, detention or restrictive orders.[139] Other compromise solutions include the use of 'special advocates' – lawyers with security clearance, assigned to represent the terrorist suspect. The classified information is disclosed to the advocate but not the client, and the advocate is then under severe restrictions in seeking any further instructions from the client.[140]

[135] See, eg, *Poananga v State Services Commission* [1985] 2 NZLR 385 (CA) at 396.

[136] These provisions allow classified information to be provided to courts and tribunals without disclosing them to the person concerned. Contrast public interest immunity, developed at common law and codified in the Evidence Act 2006, s 70 which gives the court discretion to allow the government to withhold information from both the court and its opponents in litigation.

[137] See *R (Binyam Mohamed) v Secretary of State for Foreign and Commonwealth Affairs* [2010] EWCA Civ 65; [2011] QB 218 at [10]. The issue in that case was what information could be published in a judgment.

[138] *Council of Civil Service Unions v Minister for the Civil Service* [1985] 1 AC 374 (HL) at 402, 404–07, 412–13.

[139] *Zaoui v Attorney-General* [2004] 2 NZLR 339 (HC). See also *A v UK* (2009) 49 EHRR 29; adopted (reluctantly) in *Secretary of State for the Home Department v AF (No 3)* [2009] UKHL 28, [2010] 2 AC 269.

[140] Instances of their use include *A v Minister of Internal Affairs* [2018] NZHC 1328.

All these compromises are highly problematic, offering limited protection to terrorism suspects.[141] Moreover, even these limited compromises do not necessarily apply when classified information is relied on against terrorist suspects for purposes other than control orders, detention or deportation.[142]

Similar issues and solutions can be found in a variety of contexts other than counter-terrorism. For instance, in *Roberts*, the House of Lords upheld use of the special advocate procedure, without provision of a summary of the secret information, by the Parole Board in appropriate cases.[143] The safety of prison informants and the public interest in not releasing dangerous prisoners were considered to outweigh prisoners' rights to an effective opportunity of countering allegations against them.[144] In contrast, where the decision about a prisoner concerned prolonged segregation rather than parole, in *Bourgass* the UK Supreme Court held that the prisoner's interest is so important that he must be given sufficient details of allegations to afford him a real opportunity to respond.[145]

As these examples show, such cases always depend on contestable assessments of the strength of the competing interests in the particular context. Whatever solution is adopted in the truly difficult cases will at best partly reconcile the competing important interests.

(4) (Mostly) Discarded Old Limits – Still Worth Knowing About

Some history is relevant to understanding the modern position outlined above. Two old limits to the application of natural justice were discarded in two landmark cases that liberalised the application of natural justice. *Ridge v Baldwin* discarded the requirement of a duty to act judicially.[146] *Daganayasi* abandoned the requirement that the decision must affect an existing right.[147] These old limits, however, still exert some influence at least occasionally. It is therefore worth looking briefly at each of them.

First, the requirement of a duty to act judicially. This had, in the decades prior to *Ridge v Baldwin*, become established as a distinct requirement, turning on a categorical distinction between administrative and judicial (or quasi-judicial) functions. The meaning of 'quasi-judicial' was open to debate, but it included powers to determine disputes between parties or to alter established rights. According to *Nakkuda Ali*, it did not include a discretionary grant or withdrawal of a 'privilege' such as a licence.[148] The challenge in *Ridge* was to the dismissal of the Chief Constable on grounds of

141 See, eg, John Ip, 'Closed Material Procedures and Special Advocates' (2012) 75 *Modern Law Review* 606; Adam Tomkins, 'National Security and the Due Process of Law' (2011) 64 *Current Legal Problems* 215; New Zealand Law Commission, *The Crown in Court: A Review of the Crown Proceedings Act and National Security Information in Proceedings* (NZLC R135, December 2015) part 2.

142 Eg *Home Office v Tariq* [2011] UKSC 35, [2012] 1 AC 452.

143 *Roberts v Parole Board* [2005] UKHL 45, [2005] 2 AC 738.

144 Steyn and Bingham dissented.

145 *R (Bourgass) v Secretary of State for Justice* [2015] UKSC 54.

146 *Ridge v Baldwin* (n 2).

147 *Daganayasi* (n 3).

148 *Nakkuda Ali v Jayaratne* [1951] AC 66 (PC) at 78.

being unfit for the position. The courts below had held there was no right to be heard because this was not a quasi-judicial decision.

Lord Reid discarded the 'duty to act judicially' as a categorical pre-condition for the application of natural justice. That duty was simply another name for the duty to observe natural justice. He went back to older lines of cases in which natural justice extended to three types of decision: dismissal from office unless the office was held 'at pleasure', interference with property and expulsion of members of associations. The principle which Lord Reid distilled from those authorities was that natural justice applied to the exercise of powers to affect existing rights, or powers analogous to imposing penalties, when exercised in a single isolated case, rather than on a large scale.[149]

The discarded 'duty to act judicially' formulation serves to remind us that the paradigm context for the full application of the principles of natural justice is found in adversarial judicial proceedings. That explains why the extent of similarity with judicial proceedings functions as one of the factors relevant to determining the content of the right to a hearing in a particular context.[150] It also helps to explain why, as a general rule, the right to a hearing as such still does not apply to decisions on a large scale.[151] However, *Ridge* recognised that relevant similarity with judicial proceedings is a matter of degree. There is a wide range of contexts that are far removed from judicial proceedings and still call for some form of a hearing.

The other discarded old limit is the requirement that the decision must affect a person's existing rights. This requirement was retained in *Ridge*, but finally discarded in *Daganayasi*.

Until the end of the 1970s, a right to a hearing was still considered inapplicable to persons applying for something which they had no right to claim, such as discretionary licences or immigration permits. One situation that did satisfy this requirement on the old view was where legislation required a favourable decision on satisfaction of a specific and narrow test (in contrast with discretionary benefits).[152]

The first signs of softening were 1970s cases recognising a legitimate expectation arising from an existing licence or permit: first an expectation that this licence or permit would continue for its term, and then also an expectation that it would be renewed on its expiry. Such a legitimate expectation gave rise to a right to a hearing before it could fairly be disappointed, despite the discretionary nature of the power.[153] However, those situations still involved interference with an established position.

The achievement of the New Zealand landmark decision in *Daganayasi* was to quietly consign these requirements to history.[154] The High Court decision and the Minister's argument on appeal largely still reflect the old requirement: the challenge must fail, as only the most limited hearing right was available to an illegal immigrant seeking to avoid deportation.

[149] *Ridge* (n 2) at 65–72.
[150] Section (1)(b) of this part.
[151] See *Daganayasi* (n 3) at 143; and section (3)(b) of this part.
[152] See *Durayappah v Fernando* [1967] 2 AC 337 (PC) at 349–51; *Ridge v Baldwin* (n 2) at 65–66.
[153] See Part C.
[154] See Dean R Knight, 'Simple, Fair and Discretionary Administrative Law' (2008) 39 *Victoria University of Wellington Law Review* 99 at 111.

Cooke J dismissed this approach, without acknowledging that this involved a new departure.[155] He purported to apply the requirement for either a right or a legitimate expectation to be affected. However, his analysis and conclusion emptied these requirements of their established content.

Concerning a right, he said:[156]

> The present is not a case of an entrenched right, but if the Minister decides the specific and quite narrowly-worded question in the appellant's favour and consequently orders that the appellant be not deported, the Act requires him to issue a permit. So it seems to me by no means a distortion of language to say that the Minister is determining a question affecting the rights of an individual.

The two previously established senses of a decision affecting a right are tacitly discarded here. First, as Cooke J acknowledges, there was no existing ('entrenched') right. Secondly, the legislation did not require a permit to be issued on satisfaction of a specific and narrow test, contrary to Cooke J's suggestion. Rather, the test to be applied by the Minister was broad and discretionary: he had to be satisfied that there were exceptional circumstances of a humanitarian nature.[157] This was tacitly disregarded.

Turning to a legitimate expectation, Cooke J considered that this could be said to exist in this case simply because Miss Daganayasi 'had bona fide and substantial grounds for claiming that the statutory test was fulfilled'.[158] No established position was taken away, but tacitly that no longer mattered.

The only real reasons in favour of a right to a hearing in this case were that the decision concerned an individual and would often be of major importance to that individual. That was enough: this represents the modern approach established by *Daganayasi*.[159] The Court also relied on the power being in the nature of an appeal. However, the point was not that this rendered the power 'judicial', but rather that Parliament must have intended the appeal right to be effective, and a hearing was required for that.[160]

Despite having been abandoned several decades ago, the thinking behind the requirement for an existing right or a legitimate expectation arising from an established position still rears its head on occasion. There is a recurring tendency to limit procedural rights where decisions are seen as involving grace and favour, rather than rights. Perhaps the most obvious example is the prerogative of mercy. When the courts moved to treat this as justiciable, they still accepted only a fairly limited right to a hearing.[161] There is good justification for this to some extent, given that the power is a last resort, invoked by persons who have already had the benefit of a trial and a full

[155] He did not cite two recent High Court cases to the contrary, or the English appellate authority relied on in those cases: see KJ Keith, 'Administrative Law Developments in New Zealand as Seen through Immigration Law' in Grant Huscroft and Michael Taggart (eds), *Inside and Outside Canadian Administrative Law: Essays in Honour of David Mullan* (2006) 125 at 138.

[156] *Daganayasi* (n 3) at 144.

[157] Immigration Act 1964, s 20A, quoted in *Daganayasi* (n 3) at 135.

[158] *Daganayasi* (n 3) at 145, also at 143.

[159] ibid at 144–45.

[160] ibid at 142.

[161] *Burt* (n 131).

set of appeal rights.[162] However, the notion that this power involves grace and favour, and hence there is less room for procedural rights, may also have had some unacknowledged influence in this decision.

A more explicit and more surprising temporary throwback to the old requirement occurred in one of the least likely contexts: the Bill of Rights. The right to natural justice is enshrined in section 27(1) of that Act. The wording of that section is reminiscent of the old requirement: the right applies to 'a determination in respect of that person's rights, obligations or interests protected or recognised by law'. Nevertheless, this wording is also open to an interpretation consistent with *Daganayasi*, and in due course that liberal interpretation was adopted in the *Combined Beneficiaries Union* case.[163] However, there was an intervening period when the Court of Appeal in a series of decisions appeared to accept that the scope of section 27 was limited to decisions of an adjudicative nature that affected established rights or similarly protected interests.[164]

C. Legitimate Expectations

We encountered legitimate expectations briefly in the last section. Legitimate expectations can arise in different ways and play different roles. We will look first at their roles and then at what gives rise to them.

(1) The Roles of Legitimate Expectations: A Chameleon Concept

A legitimate expectation today has two potential roles in relation to procedural fairness. First, where an applicant has a legitimate expectation affected by the decision this should be a factor in favour of a stronger right to a hearing – for instance, an oral hearing rather than merely written submissions. Secondly, a legitimate expectation provides the basis for a duty of consultation in relation to a decision made on a large scale, where the right to a hearing as such generally does not apply.[165]

These modern roles represent a shift: in the early authorities that introduced the concept of a legitimate expectation, it played a different role. It was a novel alternative to the old requirement that a right to a hearing applied only to decisions affecting the applicant's existing rights.

Schmidt was the first case to contemplate a right to a hearing for decisions about immigration permits, and this was on the basis of a legitimate expectation.[166]

[162] ibid at 682–83.

[163] *Combined Beneficiaries Union Inc v Auckland City COGS Committee* [2008] NZCA 423, [2009] 2 NZLR 56 at [7]–[51].

[164] See *Minister of Fisheries v Pranfield Holdings Ltd* [2008] 3 NZLR 649 (CA) at [134]–[136]; *Chisholm v Auckland City Council* [2005] NZAR 661 (CA) at [32].

[165] That duty is discussed in Part D.

[166] *Schmidt v Secretary of State for the Home Department* [1969] 2 Ch 149 (CA).

Lord Denning suggested that an immigrant had a legitimate expectation that an immigration permit, once granted, would remain in operation for its stated term. As a result, the holder of the permit had a right to be heard before a decision was made to cancel that permit. The next step in the development was to extend the legitimate expectation to situations where renewal was sought of an existing permit on its expiry.[167] Subsequently, as we have seen, the requirement of an existing right was abandoned in *Daganayasi*.[168] This rendered the alternative of a legitimate expectation redundant. Since then, the concept is instead available in the two roles already mentioned.

One further role remains to be mentioned. As we will see, modern case law has moved some distance towards giving legitimate expectations more substantive effect in certain circumstances, beyond their role in supporting a procedural fairness requirement. But that is a topic for another chapter.[169]

Here, our focus is on the modern role as a factor or basis for procedural fairness requirements. In this role, even an expectation of a substantive benefit (such as continuation or renewal of an immigration permit) gives rise to no more than procedural rights.

(2) What is a Legitimate Expectation? On What Basis can it be Established?

We have already seen that an established position, such as an existing licence or permit, can give rise to a legitimate expectation that it will continue for its term,[170] or even that it will be renewed past that term.[171] The leading authority of *Terminals NZ* confirms that there are at least three ways in which an applicant may acquire a legitimate expectation: a promise or undertaking, an established practice or benefit, and a published internal policy.[172] Let us look at each of these in turn.

A promise or undertaking is the most obvious basis: provided the terms and circumstances were such as to make it reasonable to rely on it, this will give rise to a legitimate expectation.[173] The *Liverpool Taxi* case is the classic authority, concerning an increase in the number of taxi licences that was opposed by the applicant taxi operators' association. A legitimate expectation arose from an undertaking by the defendant council that the increase would not be implemented until legislation had been passed to address another matter of concern to the association. That expectation meant that further consultation was required before the council could act in breach of the undertaking.[174]

[167] *McInnes v Onslow-Fane* [1978] 1 WLR 1520 (Ch).
[168] *Daganayasi* (n 3); see above, Part B.(4).
[169] See Ch 7.C.
[170] *Schmidt* (n 166).
[171] *McInnes* (n 167).
[172] *Comptroller of Customs v Terminals (NZ) Ltd* [2012] NZCA 598, [2014] 2 NZLR 137 at [123]. There was an appeal to the Supreme Court but not on the legitimate expectation issue.
[173] ibid at [124]–[125], [128]–[143].
[174] *R v Liverpool Corporation ex p Liverpool Taxi Fleet Operators' Association* [1972] 2 QB 299 (CA) at 594.

An established practice or benefit was the basis of the legitimate expectation found in the landmark *CCSU* case. Thanks to that legitimate expectation, staff at Government Communication Headquarters (GCHQ) and their unions would have been entitled to consultation before unions were banned from GCHQ (except that the government successfully invoked national security concerns against this, as we saw earlier).[175] There were two different lines of reasoning in support of a duty to consult. Lord Diplock found a legitimate expectation of continuing union membership, on the basis that this was a long-standing benefit.[176] Lord Fraser found a legitimate expectation of consultation on proposed changes in employment conditions, based on a long-standing practice of such consultation.[177] Both emphasised that not every existing benefit or established practice will give rise to a legitimate expectation: it must be so well established that the applicant could reasonably expect it to continue.[178]

A particularly strong basis for expecting continuation of an established benefit was found in *Pascoe Properties*. Nelson inner-city ratepayers had had the benefit of a car park on a particular square for 30 years. More significantly, the establishment of the car park had been funded by a targeted rate imposed on them. This gave rise to a legitimate expectation that they would be consulted on any proposal to change the use of the square.[179]

Finally, a published policy gives rise to a legitimate expectation. Modern case law requires authorities to comply with their published policies unless they have good reasons to depart from them.[180] The longer-standing procedural requirement established in *Khan* is to hear the person concerned before declining an application that meets the criteria set out in a published policy.[181]

A related point is that an authority is free to change published policy, but the new policy can be applied to an application that was made under the old policy only after giving the applicant the opportunity to address the requirements of the new policy.[182] This last point does not depend on a legitimate expectation: without the opportunity to address the requirements of the new policy, the applicant simply will not have had a proper opportunity to make their case, in a context where the right to a hearing applied on the usual basis.

The effect of legitimate expectations acquired in any of these ways, as already noted, is to support a claim to procedural fairness. They function either as a factor for a stronger right to a hearing, or as the basis for a duty of consultation in circumstances where the right to a hearing as such does not apply because the impugned decision is not addressed to the person in question. The duty to consult is explored in in the next Part.

[175] *Council of Civil Service Unions* (n 138) at 402, 404–07, 412–13; see text above at n 138.
[176] ibid at 412. This is essentially an established position, as per *Schmidt* (n 167) and *McInnes* (n 168).
[177] ibid at 401.
[178] ibid at 401, 408.
[179] *Pascoe Properties Ltd v Nelson City Council* [2012] NZRMA 232 (HC) at [9]–[12].
[180] See Ch 7.C and D.
[181] *R v Secretary of State for the Home Department ex p Khan* [1984] 1 WLR 1337 (CA).
[182] *Smithkline Beecham (NZ) Ltd v Ministry of Health* [1992] NZAR 357 (HC) at 375.

D. Duty to Consult

Where some form of a right to a hearing applies, even though the impugned decision is not addressed to the person claiming the right to be heard, it is usually called a duty to consult. The usual context involves decisions of a legislative or general policy nature, affecting the public at large or categories of people. An alternative context is where the decision is individually addressed to someone other than the person claiming the right to be heard. This part examines (1) when a duty to consult applies; (2) how it compares in content to the individual right to be heard; and (3) the rationales for expanding procedural rights in this way.

(1) Scope of the Duty: When does it Apply?

There is no general common law duty to consult those affected by a proposed rule or other decision that is addressed to the public at large,[183] to categories of people, or to an individual third party. Even where the effect of a proposed rule or decision falls mainly on a particular group or category of people, that does not necessarily give rise to a duty to consult representatives of that group.[184] A duty to consult requires a more specific basis. It can arise as a matter of common law, or it can be provided by statute. In Aotearoa NZ, a duty to consult Māori iwi and hapū also forms part of the principles of te Tiriti o Waitangi. Tikanga[185] may also give rise to a duty to consult. Let us consider these sources in turn.

At common law, it is always a question of degree whether the context provides a sufficient basis for a duty to consult. The main basis for a duty to consult is a legitimate expectation of consultation or of a favourable outcome, as we have already seen.[186]

An additional 'residual category of case' giving rise to a common law duty to consult was posited by the High Court in *Nicholls v Health and Disability Commissioner*. This comprises cases 'where the demands of fairness in the particular circumstances clearly require the decision maker to consult either generally or with a particular person or persons'.[187]

This obiter suggestion was applied in *Lower North Island Red Deer Foundation*.[188] The Department of Conservation had enlarged a concession allowing hunting of deer from helicopters in various forest parks. The applicant association, representing ordinary hunters in the most affected parks, had not been consulted. Yet there had been consultation with the competing interest, those engaged in hunting from helicopters. That, along with some additional factors, was held to result in 'undoubtedly a level of

[183] See *CREEDNZ* (n 108) at 177–78, 188–89.

[184] *R (Moseley) v Haringey London Borough Council* [2014] UKSC 56, [2014] 1 WLR 3947 at [35], adopting *R (BAPIO Action Ltd) v Secretary of State for the Home Department* [2007] EWCA Civ 1139 at [43]–[47] (Sedley LJ).

[185] Māori customary law.

[186] See Part C. above.

[187] *Nicholls v Health and Disability Commissioner* [1997] NZAR 351 (HC) at 370.

[188] *Lower North Island Red Deer Foundation Inc v Minister of Conservation* [2017] NZHC 1346, [2017] NZAR 1058 at [49]–[65].

unfairness', turning 'what would otherwise just be desirable and sound practice into a formal obligation'.[189]

A further special situation giving rise to a common law duty to consult was established in *Fowler & Roderique*: where the proposed large-scale decision affects an individual 'in a way that is significantly different from the way in which it affects the public generally'.[190] This case involved a challenge to new regulations imposing a moratorium on new licences for oyster fisheries. The claimants had been applying for a new licence under the old regulations for four years, and the Ministry had kept delaying a decision on their application. The Court of Appeal was inclined to consider that the claimants as a result were sufficiently uniquely affected by the moratorium to give rise to a duty to consult them.[191] This may be seen as a version of legitimate expectation.[192] Alternatively, it may fall into the residual category identified in *Nicholls*, albeit this case was not cited there.[193]

Turning to statutory duties to consult, these are imposed by a wide range of statutes. Notable examples include the Resource Management Act 1991,[194] the Pae Ora (Healthy Futures) Act 2022 and its predecessors, and the Local Government Act 2002. In all of these, the class to be consulted is a wide one, often the public at large.

Finally, consultation with representatives of Māori interests is required in some contexts by the principles of te Tiriti o Waitangi.[195] This turns on two questions: what those principles require in the context, and to what extent they have legal effect in the context.

As to the first question, one of the main principles of te Tiriti is partnership between the Crown and Māori, calling for good faith. Where Māori interests under te Tiriti are affected, this has been held to require the Crown to provide active protection and to exercise its powers sufficiently informed as to the facts and law relating to those interests. That, in turn, requires consultation in some contexts.[196] Beyond that, in many contexts the principles require much more than consultation. This may also be relevant to the content of the duty to consult, as we will see.

As to the second question, the legal effect of these principles is somewhat confined because te Tiriti still does not have legal effect in its own right.[197] The consultation requirement that flows from Treaty principles can be invoked in the courts only

[189] ibid at [59], [63].

[190] *Fowler & Roderique Ltd v Attorney-General* [1987] 2 NZLR 56 (CA) at 74; see also at 77–79.

[191] However, the Court exercised its discretion to grant no remedy due to intervening changes in circumstances.

[192] Only one of the judgments refers to legitimate expectations (at 74), and it is not clear whether that reference is intended to identify a separate additional basis for a duty to consult.

[193] Indeed, as in *Lower North Island Red Deer Foundation* (n 189), one of the features relied on was that the Minister had consulted a representative of competing interests: *Fowler & Roderique* (n 190) at 78.

[194] Slated for replacement at the time of writing.

[195] See, eg, *Te Korowai o Ngāruahine Trust v Hiringa Energy Limited and Balance Agri-Nutrients Limited* [2022] NZHC 2810 at [262]; on the appeal the court did not comment on this argument: *Greenpeace Aotearoa Inc v Hiringa Energy Ltd* [2023] NZCA 672 at [209]–[211].

[196] *New Zealand Maori Council v Attorney-General* [1987] 1 NZLR 641 (CA) (*Lands case*) at 683; *New Zealand Maori Council v Attorney-General* [1989] 2 NZLR 142 (CA) (*Forests case*) at 152.

[197] *Hoani Te Heu Heu Tukino v Aotea District Maori Trust Board* [1941] NZLR 590 (PC).

where a strong Treaty clause requires powers to be exercised consistently with these principles,[198] or pursuant to the presumption of consistency with te Tiriti[199] if the legislation can be read subject to these Treaty principles. In addition, many statutes specifically provide for consultation with representatives of Māori interests.[200] Such provisions may also be read against the background of Treaty principles.

Tikanga has recently been recognised both as forming part of the common law and as continuing to shape and regulate the lives of Māori as a source of law in its own right.[201] In either role, it may give rise or contribute to a duty to consult.[202] In *Raukawa Settlement Trust*, the Court noted that an interested party's right to be heard in the Waitangi Tribunal is 'reinforced by the tikanga of natural justice'.[203]

(2) Content of a Duty to Consult: What is Required?

The different terminology of a 'duty to consult' rather than a 'right to be heard' reflects not only the different basis but also the different content of this procedural fairness requirement. Some differences are due to the size and indeterminacy of the class of persons entitled to be consulted. For instance, where it is the public at large, notice needs to take the form of public notice rather than individual communication. Another reason for differences is that consultation concerns a proposal put forward by the decision-maker. That fact by itself therefore is never sufficient to disqualify the decision-maker on grounds of apparent bias:[204] the decision-maker is 'quite entitled to have a working plan already in mind', but 'must keep its mind open and be ready to change and even start afresh'.[205]

The weaker nature of individual consultees' interest in a decision can also lead to weaker content than the right to a hearing, according to the Supreme Court in *Wyeth v Ancare*. The Court rejected a complaint about inadequate disclosure as part of consultation on an application for approval of a hazardous substance, giving a generous interpretation to statutory reasons for non-disclosure. It reasoned that submitters were not personally affected by an approval decision: they were not facing penalties nor defending a private right, so there was no case for them to answer.

[198] See, eg, State-Owned Enterprises Act 1986, s 9; COVID-19 Recovery (Fast-track Consenting) Act 2020, s 6.

[199] *Trans-Tasman Resources v Taranaki-Whanganui Conservation Board* [2021] NZSC 127, [2021] 1 NZLR 801 at [151]. See Ch 6.A.

[200] See, eg, Resource Management Act 1991, ss 46A, 58D and Sch 1, cll 2(2) and 3.

[201] *Ellis v R* [2022] NZSC 114, [2022] 1 NZLR 239.

[202] See Jayden Houghton, 'Co-governance Design and Implementation: Lessons from *Norman v Tūpuna Maunga o Tāmaki Makaurau Authority*' (2024) 31 *New Zealand Universities Law Review* 263 at 272–76.

[203] *Raukawa Settlement Trust v Waitangi Tribunal* [2019] NZHC 383, [2019] 3 NZLR 722 at [69]. Tikanga might also have been relevant to the unsuccessful consultation challenge in *Tuna v Te Urewera Board* [2023] NZHC 3680, but this is not mentioned.

[204] See below, Part E.(8)(c) and (d).

[205] *Wellington International Airport Ltd v Air New Zealand (No 1)* [1993] 1 NZLR 671 (CA) at 675, quoting McGechan J in the High Court.

While Wyeth was a competitor, any effect of the decision on its business was irrelevant to the decision.[206]

Subject to such modifications, however, the content of a duty to consult broadly corresponds to the right to a hearing, and the courts have never drawn a sharp distinction between the two. As put by the Supreme Court in *New Zealand Pork Industry Board*, affirming the leading authority of *Wellington International Airport*,[207] it is a duty to 'inform, listen and consider'. The decision-maker 'must tell those consulted what is proposed, must give them a fair opportunity to express their views and must consider their views with an open mind'.[208] This corresponds to the two elements of the right to a hearing (notice and opportunity to respond), together with the rule against bias or predetermination.

For both elements, the details vary widely, depending on the context – just as with the right to be heard. For instance, there is often room for argument on which proposals require consultation at all.[209] Where consultation is required, the opportunity to make submissions may or may not need to include a public hearing, and any such hearing may require more or fewer court-like elements.

Issues often arise as to how much information must be disclosed. The party consulted must be 'adequately informed so as to be able to make intelligent and useful responses'.[210] Where a decision-maker is choosing between available alternatives, the consultation materials must acknowledge the existence of those alternatives.[211] In *Wyeth v Ancare*, submitters on an application for approval of a hazardous substance sought disclosure of the chemical composition. This was rejected on the statutory ground of commercial sensitivity.[212] In *Norman v Tupuna Maunga Authority*, a plan to remove all exotic trees from Ōwairaka (Mt Albert), amounting to half of the mature trees on the mountain, was sufficiently significant to require notification as part of the statutory process for adopting a management plan. That had not occurred: the draft plan that was published for consultation only referred vaguely to removal of some inappropriate exotic vegetation and trees. This did not amount to adequate notice of the proposal.[213]

A related requirement may arise where a proposal has been revised following consultation. According to *NZ Pork Industry Board*, further consultation is required if the revised proposal is substantially different from the original one.[214] For instance, in *Jones*, a proposal to require renewal of teachers' registration annually rather than

[206] *Wyeth (NZ) Ltd v Ancare New Zealand Ltd* [2010] NZSC 46, [2010] 3 NZLR 569 at [40]–[43], [48], [55]; citing *Public Disclosure Commission v Isaacs* [1988] 1 WLR 1043 (PC) in support. See also *Moseley* (n 184) at [38].

[207] *Wellington International Airport* (n 205) at 674–76, adopting *Port Louis Corporation v Attorney-General of Mauritius* [1965] AC 1111 (PC) at 1124.

[208] *New Zealand Pork Industry Board v Director-General of the Ministry for Primary Industries* [2013] NZSC 154, [2014] 1 NZLR 477 at [168]. See also *Moseley* (n 184) at [25].

[209] See, eg, *Norman v Tūpuna Maunga o Tāmaki Makaurau Authority* [2022] NZCA 30, [2022] 3 NZLR 175 at [212], discussed below.

[210] *Wellington International Airport* (n 205) at 674–76.

[211] *Moseley* (n 184) at [27]–[31], [39]–[42]. That was found satisfied, eg, in *Save Chamberlain Park Inc v Auckland Council* [2018] NZHC 1462.

[212] *Wyeth v Ancare* (n 206) at [53].

[213] *Norman* (n 209) at [212]–[213].

[214] *New Zealand Pork Industry Board* (n 208) at [172]–[173]. The Court found no breach: at [186]–[189].

every three years was developed only after consultation on a change in registration fees. Further consultation was required.[215] Where the revised proposal is sufficiently different, it may be necessary to start the process afresh.[216]

Consultation also has its limits. In both the leading cases, the Court had to remind applicants that consultation is not the same as negotiation, and there is no requirement to achieve agreement.[217] If, for tactical reasons, the party being consulted chooses not to engage with the process, the decision-maker is free to proceed regardless.[218]

Where the duty to consult is imposed by statute, of course, much turns on the statute, both its express terms and any implications. For instance, the statute may specify whether consultation is to occur on a fully formulated proposal or at an earlier stage.[219] Even in the context of statutory duties to consult, however, common law principles often play a significant role.[220] Where the statute provides no detail other than a requirement to consult, as is often the case, the content will be supplied entirely by the common law.[221] More generally, the content of a statutory requirement may be boosted where the common law might also recognise a legitimate expectation giving rise to a duty to consult. Where there is no such potential common law duty in the background, the content of a statutory consultation requirement is likely to be more limited, as we have seen.[222] A separate and additional common law duty to consult is less likely to be found where there is a detailed statutory code.[223]

Statutory consultation regimes are commonly expressed in discretionary terms. A notable feature of the case law is that courts have not always reviewed the exercise of that discretion on a correctness standard. That is in contrast to the approach to common law requirements of procedural fairness: those are treated as questions of law on which courts will substitute their own view.[224]

The courts' approach to statutory discretion in this area has varied. Some cases have applied a correctness approach, just as with common law procedural requirements.[225] The approach taken by the Supreme Court in *Discount Brands* was less clear.[226] The case concerned the much-litigated obligation to publicly notify consent applications under the Resource Management Act unless satisfied that the effect on the environment will be minor. Keith J appealed to the established correctness standard for

[215] *Jones v Teaching Council of Aotearoa New Zealand* [2021] NZHC 1581 at [90]–[123].

[216] *Muaūpoko Tribal Authority Incorporated v Minister for the Environment* [2023] NZCA 641 at [143] held that consideration should have been given to this possibility.

[217] *New Zealand Pork Industry Board* (n 208) at [168], [187]; *Wellington International Airport* (n 205) at 675–76, 682.

[218] *Wellington International Airport* (n 205) at 683–84.

[219] As noted in *NZ Pork Industry Board* (n 208) at [168].

[220] Pointed out in *Wyeth v Ancare* (n 206) at [40].

[221] See, eg, *Wellington International Airport* (n 205).

[222] *Wyeth v Ancare* [(n 206) at [40]–[43].

[223] *Wellington City Council v Minotaur Custodians Ltd* [2017] NZCA 302, [2017] 3 NZLR 464 at [43]–[48]. Much the same applies to the right to a hearing: see Part B(3)(a).

[224] Affirmed in *R (Osborn) v Parole Board* [2013] UKSC 61, [2014] AC 1115 at [65]. See further Ch 9, introduction and Part A.

[225] Eg *Walsh v Pharmaceutical Management Agency* [2010] NZAR 101 (HC) at [167]–[168], [187]–[191].

[226] The 'lack of methodological clarity' is deplored in Michael Taggart, 'Administrative Law' [2006] *NZ Law Review* 75 at 79; see also at 75–79 and 81–88.

questions of natural justice.[227] Aside from this, all judgments focused on the prior obligation to be satisfied that the Council had adequate information to notify or to decide not to notify. They held either that the Council had not properly understood that requirement, committing an error of law; or that the Council's application of the requirement did not pass the close scrutiny that was appropriate because of the impact on participatory rights.[228]

However, in *Minotaur Custodians* the Court of Appeal interpreted the detailed consultation provisions in the Local Government Act 2002 as deliberately committing the scope of consultation to local authorities' discretion. Review of that discretion was therefore confined to review for irrationality and improper purpose.[229] A suggestion of review on less than a correctness standard, albeit much less explicit, may also be seen in *Wyeth v Ancare*.[230]

(3) Rationale for Broad Duties to Consult the Public

At common law, the applicability of procedural rights turns on the individual impact of the impugned decision. That goes for the right to be heard and the rule against bias but also, generally, for the duty to consult. Both the common law bases on which exercises of power on a large scale may attract a duty to consult (legitimate expectation and the residual category where fairness requires consultation) involve identifying a form of individual impact even though the decision is not addressed to the applicant as an individual. That is consistent with the rationales for procedural fairness requirements, both the instrumental rationale and the intrinsic one based on dignity.

Statutory consultation requirements, by contrast, often apply regardless of individual impact.[231] As noted, it is not uncommon for the class entitled to consultation to be the public at large, or other large and often indeterminate classes of persons. What is the policy behind such statutory requirements for wide participation? Janet McLean has noted that a variety of rationales are at play here, depending on context.[232] While the traditional rationales for the right to a hearing do not apply as such, we can identify a similar mix of instrumental and non-instrumental rationales. Consultation is valuable instrumentally for improving the quality of decisions, and less instrumentally for boosting their legitimacy.[233]

[227] *Discount Brands Ltd v Westfield (New Zealand) Ltd* [2005] NZSC 17, [2005] 2 NZLR 597 (SC) at [54].

[228] ibid at [21]–[29], [43]–[57], [116], [119]–[125], [149]–[151] and [178]. Despite subsequent amendments to the provisions, this approach has been applied in *Wendco (NZ) Ltd v Auckland Council* [2015] NZCA 617 at [46]–[47] and *Norman* (n 209) at [257]–[261], leaving open whether a less-exacting approach might now be appropriate.

[229] *Minotaur* (n 223) at [42], [68]. See also, similarly, *McInnes v Minister of Transport* [2001] 3 NZLR 11 (CA) at [15].

[230] *Wyeth v Ancare* (n 206) at [47], [55] – but cf [56].

[231] That was emphasised by Lord Reed in *Moseley* (n 184) at [37]–[38].

[232] Janet McLean, 'Participation and the Duty to Consult' in James Goudkamp, Mark Lunney and Leighton McDonald (eds), *Taking Law Seriously: Essays in Honour of Peter Cane* (Oxford, Hart Publishing, 2021) 124.

[233] See *Discount Brands* (n 227) at [25], [46]; *Moseley* (n 184) at [24].

Legitimacy has several aspects in this context. In relation to those affected by the decision, it includes the same arguments as for individual decisions: respecting the dignity of those affected and rendering decisions more likely to be accepted by them. This interest representation rationale is important when primary legislation delegates the task of balancing competing interests, as for instance with resource management decisions or gambling rules.[234] Consultation is especially indispensable for legitimacy in this sense in contexts where entities with monopoly position have unilateral power to set access fees, as is the case with airport landing fees.[235]

In relation to the public at large, however, the rationale is the 'democratic principle' of public participation in public decision-making.[236] Eddie Clark has argued that even where citizens will be affected by a measure only as members of the general public, democratic legitimacy requires that obligations should be imposed on them only after giving them all an equal opportunity to be heard and to influence the outcome. Deliberation is also enhanced by such participation.[237]

It might be objected that the legitimacy of public rule-making in this democratic sense is assured by our Parliamentary democracy: officials and Ministers are indirectly and directly accountable to Parliament, which is accountable at the ballot box. However, electoral accountability provides only a bare minimum of legitimacy.[238] Even Acts of Parliament obtain greater legitimacy by public consultation on most Bills via the Select Committee process.[239] Administrative rule-makers are in much greater need of added legitimacy, given that their electoral accountability is only indirect.

The experience of United States Administrative Law is instructive in this context. A requirement of participatory procedures in rulemaking is particularly fully developed there; and this may be traced to the fact that electoral accountability is very attenuated for executive agencies in the United States system.[240] In the modern New Zealand system, some rule-making entities similarly enjoy a relatively independent position,[241] making consultation especially important for the legitimacy of their rules.

Consultation with representatives of Māori interests has a further distinct form of legitimacy rationale. Exercises of public power lack legitimacy to the extent that they fail to respect obligations under te Tiriti, as discussed in the Introduction and Chapter 6.[242] As we saw in section (1), those obligations include consultation in some contexts.

[234] See McLean (n 232) at 132–33.

[235] Airport Authorities Act 1966, ss 4A and 4B. This has been litigated extensively; see, esp, *Wellington International Airport* (n 205). See McLean (n 232) at 135–37.

[236] See *Discount Brands* (n 227) at [46]; *Moseley* (n 184) at [24], [38].

[237] Edward Clark, *Procedural Fairness and Citizen Control: Addressing the Legitimacy Deficit in the Canadian Administrative State* (Doctor of Juridical Science thesis, University of Toronto 2017), ch II, drawing on the republican theory of Phillip Pettit and Henry Richardson.

[238] See Michael Taggart, 'From 'Parliamentary Powers' to Privatization: The Chequered History of Delegated Legislation in the Twentieth Century' (2005) 55 *University of Toronto Law Journal* 575 at 626.

[239] For this practice, see M Harris and D Wilson (eds), *McGee: Parliamentary Practice in New Zealand*, 4th edn (Auckland, Oratia Books, 2017) at 405–407.

[240] See Peter Cane, *Controlling Administrative Power: An Historical Comparison* (Cambridge, Cambridge University Press, 2016); Paul Craig, *Public Law and Democracy in the United Kingdom and the United States of America* (Oxford, Clarendon Press, 1990); Taggart (n 239) at 608–13.

[241] See Crown Entities Act 2004.

[242] Chs 1.F, 6.A.

The Treaty basis for consultation could also give rise to stronger obligations. The interests guaranteed by te Tiriti go beyond property interests – they include a measure of shared authority, or at least of self-government. The Waitangi Tribunal considers that 'where the authority of the Crown to make law and the right of Māori to exercise autonomy overlap', the Treaty partnership calls for 'consultation and cooperation, possibly even negotiation towards obtaining Māori agreement',[243] and for the Crown to be 'in continuing dialogue with Māori'.[244] Case law has not developed much in this direction – the groundbreaking early *Lands* case expressly held to the contrary.[245] Measures designed for these purposes do exist, but they are created by mutual agreement and often also by statute.[246] One instance of judicial recognition is found in *Ngāti Whātua Ōrakei*, concerning Treaty settlements in the context of cross claims. The High Court held that the Crown in this context has a Treaty duty to take reasonable steps to understand, recognise and respect the applicable tikanga, and to actively protect iwi and hapū's ability to pursue resolution through tikanga processes.[247]

Turning finally to the rationale of improving the quality of rule-making, it is not difficult to see how consultation can help with this. Unlike with individual decisions, we cannot usually say that the applicant is in the best position to provide relevant information because the decision is about the applicant. However, the challenge in making good rules of broad application arises from the very fact that the task is polycentric: it is to be adequately informed of the wide variety of impacts and implications the rule may have. Inviting input from all who might conceivably be affected will clearly assist with this task. Consultation also allows the agency to draw on a greater pool of expertise and experience than is available among its own staff.[248]

Indeed, where the rule-making involves regulation of some activity in the broader public interest, it is particularly important not to confine input to those who will be most directly affected, namely those subject to the regulation. That would deprive the agency of the benefit of perspectives representing the public interest to be served by the regulation. For instance, in setting fishing quota, it would be contrary to the purpose of the regime to consult only fishing interests: representatives of environmental interests provide an essential competing perspective on this regime.

The desirability of drawing on a wider pool of expertise and experience also helps explain why consultation often includes those with interests that are expressly declared irrelevant to the decision-making process – for instance, competitors of businesses seeking approval under resource management or hazardous substances legislation. While their interest as competitor is irrelevant,[249] that interest provides them with an

[243] Waitangi Tribunal, *Whaia te Mana Motuhake: Report on the Māori Community Development Act Claim* (WAI 2417, 2015) at 42.

[244] Waitangi Tribunal, *Tu Mai te Rangi! Report on the Crown and Disproportionate Reoffending Rates* (WAI 2540, 2017) at 47.

[245] *New Zealand Maori Council v Attorney-General (Lands)* [1987] 1 NZLR 641 (CA) at 683.

[246] See, eg, the Māori Advisory Committee constituted by the Environmental Protection Authority Act 2011, ss 18–21; and the Tupuna Maunga Authority under the Ngā Mana Whenua o Tāmaki Makaurau Collective Redress Act 2014.

[247] *Ngāti Whātua Ōrākei Trust v Attorney-General (No 4)* [2022] NZHC 843 at [66]–[67], [579]–[588].

[248] See *Wyeth v Ancare* (n 206) at [43]; *NZ Pork Industry Board* [2013] NZSC 154 (n 208) at [9].

[249] See, eg, *Wyeth v Ancare* (n 206) at [43]; Resource Management Act 1991, s 104(3)(a)(i) concerning resource consents, and several similar provisions in relation to plans.

incentive to engage in the process that others may lack, and they often have relevant expertise and access to information. The extent to which such conflicted consultees are likely to assist in promoting the regulatory regime's objectives is, nevertheless, debatable.

E. The Rule against Bias

The old Latin maxim for the rule against bias was *nemo iudex in sua causa* (no one should be a judge in their own cause). As with the Latin term for the right to a hearing, this reflects a connection of natural justice principles with adversarial proceedings and thus with courts. How and to what extent the same principles apply to decision-makers other than courts is a matter of debate. The leading authority on the test for bias is the Supreme Court's decision in *Saxmere*, which concerned judicial bias.[250] Sometimes this test is said to be inapplicable to administrative or executive decision-makers, and sometimes it is treated as merely needing to be applied in a context-sensitive fashion. The choice between these approaches is rarely acknowledged.

This part of the chapter begins by (1) introducing apparent bias. The subsequent sections address (2) the rationales of the apparent bias rule and tensions with competing considerations, (3) the *Saxmere* test and how this is to be understood in light of those tensions, and (4) what types of situations give rise to a bias concern. The next two parts explore doubts about two categorical approaches: (5) questioning presumptive bias arising from a financial interest, and (6) questioning predetermination by administrative decision-makers as a separate category. A better approach is set out in the next two sections, (7) outlining the contextual factors that determine the expected standard of impartiality and (8) exploring the variability of the standard of impartiality in each of the different types of situation that can give rise to bias concerns. A final brief section (9) covers waiver of the right to object on grounds of bias.

(1) Apparent Bias is Enough for Disqualification: No Need to Show Actual Bias

Actual bias involves allowing personal interests, preferences or predispositions to influence a decision. Those are irrelevant and improper considerations: decisions ought to be made on the merits according to the empowering statute. Actual bias, therefore, impacts the public interest in serving the statutory purpose and the affected party's interest in a fair chance to obtain a favourable decision. It involves bad faith and is also unlawful on the separate ground of improper purpose.[251]

Actual bias is rarely made out. One of the few examples of a finding that a public decision-maker acted for a self-interested motive is found in *Porter v Magill*. Conservative councillors had exercised their power to sell council housing for the

[250] *Saxmere Co Ltd v Wool Board Disestablishment Co Ltd* [2009] NZSC 72, [2010] 1 NZLR 35.
[251] See Ch 5.

improper purpose of manipulating the composition of the electorate in marginal wards (home owners were thought more likely to vote conservative than council housing tenants).[252]

The rule against bias, however, goes further than prohibiting actual bias. It is a rule against *apparent* bias, disqualifying decision-makers based on circumstances that raise concerns about impartiality. There is no need to show that the judge or other decision-maker actually allowed such irrelevant and improper matters to influence the decision.[253]

(2) The Rationales of the Apparent Bias Rule, and the Tension with Competing Considerations

The advantages of not requiring actual bias include that it avoids a difficulty: actual bias is usually difficult to prove.[254] Alleging such bad faith is also an unnecessarily antagonistic complaint, especially if the parties are in an ongoing relationship. More fundamentally, the rationale for disqualifying decision-makers on grounds of the mere appearance of bias is the need to maintain public confidence in impartial decision-making. It is important that 'justice should not only be done but should manifestly and undoubtedly be seen to be done'.[255]

This rationale is in tension, however, with a pragmatic recognition that an unrealistically high standard of impartiality will disqualify far too many. No-one can claim to occupy an entirely neutral position in relation to any matter for decision. Every individual has a personal background, interests, perspectives, and connections that may indirectly influence their decisions. If all such factors led to disqualification, very few people would be available to make decisions on any matter. The likelihood of connections may be especially high in Aotearoa New Zealand, given our small population and professional community.[256] Aside from the impossibility of finding entirely neutral decision-makers, it would not even be desirable: such decision-makers would lack the necessary humanity.[257]

Decision-makers therefore must, to some extent, be expected and trusted to do the best they humanly can to put any irrelevant inclinations aside. Judges are bound to do so by their oath of office,[258] and are equipped to do so by their training and experience.[259] A similar expectation must apply to public officials.

Moreover, disqualifying too many decision-makers might actually compromise impartial decision-making because it might encourage 'judge-shopping':[260] finding

[252] *Porter v Magill* [2001] UKHL 67, [2002] 2 AC 357 (HL).
[253] *Saxmere* (n 250) at [3].
[254] *Locabail (UK) Ltd v Bayfield Properties Ltd* [2000] QB 451 (CA) at [3].
[255] *R v Sussex Justices, ex parte McCarthy* [1924] 1 KB 256 at 259.
[256] See *Saxmere* (n 250) at [101]. See also Groves (n 19) at 114.
[257] See William Lucy, 'The Possibility of Impartiality' (2005) *Oxford Journal of Legal Studies* 3 at 14.
[258] *Saxmere* (n 250) at [8].
[259] *Locabail* (n 254) at [21].
[260] See Groves (n 19) at 117.

grounds to question the impartiality of all decision-makers except those whom applicants expect to be friendly to their cause.[261]

A balance has to be struck between these competing considerations. That is the point of the *Saxmere* test, as I will explain.

(3) The *Saxmere* Test: Balancing these Conflicting Concerns

On the *Saxmere* test for apparent bias, a judge is disqualified if a 'fair-minded' and fully informed lay observer would have a 'reasonable apprehension' (or would consider it a 'real possibility') that the judge might not bring an impartial mind to the resolution of the question, and might therefore not decide it on its merits.[262] This test addresses two questions: how strong does the concern about impartiality need to be before it disqualifies a decision-maker, and from whose perspective is this to be judged?

The required degree of concern, a 'reasonable apprehension' or a 'real possibility', represents the middle of the available spectrum: greater than mere suspicion, but not as much as probability.[263] The perspective from which this is to be judged is similarly a compromise between two opposing stronger options. If it was the perspective of an ordinary or average lay observer, an appearance of bias might be too readily found, since the lay observer may not fully appreciate that it is necessary and reasonable to expect judges and other public decision-makers to put aside irrelevant considerations. If, on the other hand, the perspective was that of the court,[264] an even greater proportion of cases would pass the test. While it might indeed be reasonable to trust more decision-makers to put irrelevant considerations aside, public confidence might suffer unduly. That is why this approach was discarded in favour of the intermediate approach, positing a lay observer, but one who is fair-minded and fully informed.[265]

While this is an artificial and awkward construct, its point is to take account of both of the competing considerations set out in the previous section. Taking the middle ground on the required degree of concern serves the same purpose. Both elements of the *Saxmere* test, then, are best understood as an instruction to strike a balance between these two competing considerations: on the one hand the need to maintain public confidence and, on the other hand, the need for a dose of realism about the level of detachment that is practicable and desirable.

(4) What Types of Situations Give Rise to a Bias Concern? The Two-stage Test

The Supreme Court in *Saxmere* adopted a two-stage approach for establishing an appearance of bias. First, there must be a factual basis for the concern. Secondly, the

[261] See *Saxmere* (n 250) at [8], [88].

[262] ibid at [3]–[5], [37], [89], [127].

[263] ibid at [4].

[264] That was the position maintained in *Auckland Casino Ltd v Casino Control Authority* [1995] 1 NZLR 142 (CA) at 149, following *R v Gough* [1993] AC 646 (HL).

[265] *Saxmere* (n 250) at [3]–[5] adopted this approach from *Porter v Magill* (n 252) at [102]–[103] and *Ebner v Official Trustee in Bankruptcy* (2000) 205 CLR 337 at [6].

party alleging apparent bias must articulate a 'logical connection' between that situation 'and the feared deviation from the course of deciding the case on its merits'.[266]

What types of situations, then, provide the necessary factual basis for an appearance of bias? There are at least four: cases where decision-makers have a financial interest in the outcome; where they have a relationship (family, friendship or enmity) with a party or a witness; where they have a relevant predisposition (either based on their background and position in life, or revealed in statements or conduct); and where they also hold another incompatible role (especially where a person acting as judge is also acting as prosecutor). Multi-member authorities can be disqualified by such an appearance of bias in relation to one or more of their members.[267]

Each of the four types of situations must be evaluated in the particular case to decide on which side of the line it falls. This is very much a question of degree, calling for a contestable exercise of judgement in each case.

There has, however, been a tendency to think about the situations that give rise to an appearance of bias in categorical terms. Two of the above situations have been treated in some case law and commentary as distinct and separate categories: financial interest and predetermination. As discussed in sections (5) and (6) below, such approaches are open to doubt.

The better view is that a spectrum of variable standards applies across all four situations. The standard of impartiality that is expected of a decision-maker, and perhaps also the level of concern that will disqualify, varies according to the circumstances, as discussed below in section (7). Further, the four different situations overlap, and the distinctions between them are often more a matter of degree. As we will see in section (8), the spectrum of variable standards applies across all four situations.

(5) Questioning Presumptive Bias as a Separate Category

The separate doctrine of presumptive bias represents one long-standing categorical distinction. According to this doctrine, a direct financial interest automatically disqualifies a decision-maker. There is no need to evaluate whether a sufficient appearance of bias arises.[268] In *Pinochet*, the House of Lords controversially expanded this category of automatic disqualification to include any direct personal interest in the matter for decision.[269]

However, this separate doctrine is now very much in doubt. It has been abandoned in Australia,[270] and in Aotearoa New Zealand it has been doubted by the Court of Appeal in *Muir*[271] and disapproved in dicta of the Supreme Court in *Saxmere*.[272] There is arguably no need for a separate doctrine, because the *Saxmere* test of apparent bias

[266] *Saxmere* (n 250) at [4], quoting *Ebner* (n 265) at [8].
[267] *Auckland Casino* (n 264) at 149.
[268] *Dimes v Grand Junction Canal (Proprietors of)* (1852) 3 HL Cas 756, 10 ER 301 (HL); *Auckland Casino* (n 264) at 148–49.
[269] *R v Bow Street Metropolitan Stipendiary Magistrate Ex p Pinochet Ugarte (No 2)* [2000] 1 AC 119 (HL).
[270] *Ebner* (n 265) at [54]–[55].
[271] *Muir v Commissioner of Inland Revenue* [2007] NZCA 334, [2007] 3 NZLR 495 at [42].
[272] *Saxmere* (n 250) at [42], also at [89].

will almost certainly be satisfied in cases that would otherwise attract the presumptive bias rule.[273] Furthermore, even the supposedly automatic disqualification rule is hedged about with several qualifications: it is subject to a de minimis rule, it applies only to a sufficiently direct interest, and it does not apply if the decision-maker was unaware of the interest.[274] These qualifications can all be explained on the basis of the apparent bias test: the financial interest would not give rise to a sufficient appearance of bias in such cases.

(6) Questioning Predetermination by Administrative Decision-makers as a Separate Category

Presenting predetermination as a separate category is the second categorical approach that is open to doubt. There is uncertainty on two connected issues. One is the approach to bias allegations against public administrative or executive decision-makers, and the other is the place of predetermination.

The content of the apparent bias rule varies according to context.[275] The bias rule shares this contextual variability with the other main element of natural justice, the hearing rule. There is no dispute about this variability. The point on which there is some divergence is whether all of this variability can be accommodated within one test, the *Saxmere* test for apparent bias. The better view is that it can. As regards different types of decision-maker, the fullest, strongest version of the test applies to judges presiding in court proceedings. For administrative or executive decision-makers, the expectation of impartiality varies greatly.[276]

Concerning predetermination, case law establishes a 'closed mind' test as the appropriate test for allegations of predetermination against some types of executive or administrative decision-makers.[277] As I will explain below, this can be understood as one end of a spectrum of varying applications of the *Saxmere* test.

In some cases, however, it has been presented as a separate and distinct test that applies in contexts where the *Saxmere* test is inappropriate and unworkable.[278] On this view, bias is said to refer to a conflict of interest:[279] it involves some form of personal interest, which is a 'peculiarly toxic' influence on public decision-making, and even the appearance of this can never be allowed.[280] Predetermination, in contrast, is said to refer to policy commitments. These are permissible to some extent for administrative or executive decisions in which policy is a relevant consideration.

[273] *Muir* (n 272) at [42]; *Ebner* (n 265) at [54].

[274] *Auckland Casino* (n 264) at 148.

[275] *Man O'War Station Ltd v Auckland City Council* [2002] 3 NZLR 577 (PC) at [11].

[276] See *McGrath v Minister of Justice* [2014] NZHC 3279, [2015] NZAR 122 at [15]–[17].

[277] *CREEDNZ* (n 108) at 179, 192–94, 214.

[278] *Enterprise Miramar Inc v Wellington City Council* [2018] NZCA 541, [2019] 2 NZLR 501 at [74]–[77]; also *CREEDNZ* (n 108) at 179.

[279] Eg Philip Havers QC and Alasdair Henderson, 'Recent Developments (and Problems) in the Law on Bias' [2011] *Judicial Review* 80 at [22]–[34].

[280] Mark Elliott and Jason NE Varuhas, *Administrative Law: Text and Materials*, 5th edn (Oxford, Oxford University Press, 2017) at 341–43.

The *Saxmere* test for apparent bias is said to be a test for bias only. On this view it applies to judges and to administrative decision-makers exercising powers similar to those of judges. It also applies to allegations of an improper personal interest even in the context of policy decisions.[281] Conversely, allegations of predetermination against judges do attract the *Saxmere* test of apparent bias.[282] However, that test is considered inappropriate for allegations of predetermination against administrative or executive decision-makers in contexts where policy is a relevant consideration.[283] Where predetermination by policy makers is at issue, it is said, the mere appearance of it does not disqualify.[284]

I agree that it is helpful to recognise that the degree of concern inherently arising from each of the different types of situation varies. However, it is less helpful to present these as strictly separate categories, and to treat the *Saxmere* test for apparent bias as applicable to only some of them.

The better view is that predetermination is one of the forms of apparent bias.[285] It was treated as such by the Court of Appeal in *Riverside Casino v Moxon*.[286] Cases of bias or predetermination vary on several dimensions.[287] None of these involve a simple binary choice, as we will see next and further in section (8) below.

The structure of the *Saxmere* test is capable of accommodating that variability, by adjusting the content of the test according to context.[288] Indeed, this is clear from *Porter v Magill*, which adopted this test for the United Kingdom. That case involved a complaint of predetermination against an auditor discharging an inquisitorial function.[289]

The first dimension that varies in the administrative law context is the standard of impartiality expected of a decision-maker. This depends on the nature of the decision-maker and of the power exercised. Those features do not fall into two sharply distinguished categories, judges and policymakers. Rather, these are two ends of a spectrum. The expected standard of impartiality varies along that spectrum, ranging from strict judicial impartiality to a bare requirement not to have an entirely closed mind. Where on the spectrum a particular power falls is determined by a range of contextual factors discussed in section (7) below.

Secondly, it may be that the degree of concern that must be shown to disqualify a decision-maker also varies along a spectrum. If it is true that in some contexts, nothing short of actual bias will disqualify, then that represents the extreme end of the spectrum. In most circumstances, apparent bias will be sufficient to disqualify even

[281] ibid at 341.

[282] *Newton v Family Court* [2022] NZCA 648, [2022] 3 NZLR 846 at [253]–[254]; Havers and Henderson (n 279) at 90.

[283] See esp *Enterprise Miramar* (n 278) at [74]–[77].

[284] See *Travis Holdings Ltd v Christchurch City Council* [1993] 3 NZLR 32 (HC) at 46–47; *Save Chamberlain Park Inc v Auckland Council* [2018] NZHC 1462 at [175].

[285] For this view see, eg, *Manawa Energy Ltd v Electricity Authority* [2022] NZHC 1444 at [92]–[93].

[286] *Riverside Casino Ltd v Moxon* [2001] 2 NZLR 78 (CA) at [26]–[35], and see the heading before [36].

[287] See Fisher J in *Moxon & Ors v Casino Control Authority* HC Hamilton M324/99, 24 May 2000 at [35].

[288] For recognition of this point, see *Ebner* (n 265) at [4].

[289] *Porter v Magill* (n 252) at [103] (test), [105] (complaint), and [89]–[92] (nature of the function).

administrative decision-makers exercising policy-driven powers on a large scale.[290] However, the level of concern may need to rise above a 'real possibility' that the applicable standard of impartiality has not been met. This point is rarely addressed, because it is often overlooked that the level of concern and the standard of impartiality are two separate questions.[291]

Finally, the types of situation that can give rise to an appearance of bias are greatly varied: they cannot be reduced to a simple choice between conflict of interest and predetermination. We have already seen that at least four different types of situation can be identified, and we will see in section (8) below that there is further variation within those types. In addition, that variability intersects with the varying standards of impartiality and varying required levels of concern. For instance, different levels of predisposition are permissible in different contexts. And while self-interest is always toxic, conflicts of interest can take other forms, and some forms are permissible in some contexts.

(7) Contextual Factors

When dealing with administrative decisions, a set of contextual factors determines the standard of impartiality expected of a decision-maker (and arguably also the level of concern required for disqualification) in any particular context. These factors concern the degree to which an impartial decision-maker is needed and is appropriate to expect in the circumstances. They are largely the same factors that also determine the strength of the right to a hearing: they include the nature of the decision-maker and of the power (how similar to judicial power); whether the decision directly concerns an individual; the importance of the interest affected; the severity of the impact on that interest; and any other circumstances that make an impartial hearing especially necessary (such as where the person's credibility is at issue).[292] The stronger these factors are, the more difficult it is to defend any lack of impartiality.

Two considerations may cut across some of these factors. The first is that statute may evince an intention to provide for less than impartial decision-making, even where some of the factors favour a high standard of impartiality. For instance, the statute may designate a type of decision-maker who cannot be expected to be impartial;[293] or it may assign conflicting roles to a decision-maker.[294] The second countervailing consideration is necessity: in some circumstances, it may be necessary to tolerate a less than fully impartial decision-maker because no other decision-maker is realistically available.[295]

[290] See, eg, *Riverside Casino Ltd v Moxon* (n 286) at [31]; *R (Condron) v National Assembly for Wales* [2006] EWCA Civ 1573.

[291] The distinction is acknowledged by Fisher J in *Moxon* (n 287) at [35] and the Court of Appeal in *Riverside Casino v Moxon* (n 286) at [32]–[33].

[292] For examples of these factors at play, see section (8) below.

[293] See, eg, *CREEDNZ* (n 108) at 179.

[294] See, eg, *Enterprise Miramar* (n 278) at [75]–[77].

[295] See, eg, *Rabson v Judicial Conduct Commissioner* [2017] NZSC 66; *Pinochet* (n 269) at 132.

Such arguments for tolerating less impartiality on the basis of statutory indications or necessity should still be considered in light of any contextual factors that make an impartial decision-maker especially important in the circumstances. Statute may, of course, dictate a lower standard of impartiality than would otherwise be appropriate. However, recall that such statutory abrogation of natural justice requirements will be found only if the statute's text, context and purpose clearly require this – otherwise, judges will supplement the legislation by implying what is necessary to achieve justice.[296]

(8) Variability between and within the Four Types of Situation

Each of the four different types of situation that can give rise to an appearance of bias has a different degree of concern inherently arising from it. But this level of concern also varies in different versions of each situation, and the different situations sometimes blend into each other. Moreover, in each type of situation, the expected standard of impartiality (and perhaps also the level of concern that will suffice to disqualify) depends on the contextual factors: the nature of the decision-maker and the nature of the decision.

(a) Financial Interest in the Outcome

A financial interest in the outcome is a type of situation that gives rise to a high degree of concern. It is never permissible for a judge. As already noted, a direct financial interest may give rise to the separate doctrine of presumptive bias and hence to automatic disqualification.[297] While that doctrine is now in doubt, as noted earlier, it is still true that any form of direct private interest in the matter for decision is inherently improper.

For administrative decision-makers, this type of situation can raise a similarly high level of concern. However, it depends on the details of the interest and on the nature of the decision. In particular, a financial interest is a very different matter if it is not held by the decision-maker personally in his or her private capacity but rather is an interest of the authority *qua* authority. While the latter may still represent a conflict of interests, it is much less inherently concerning than a personal financial interest. There are examples of unsuccessful bias challenges to authorities that had a financial interest *qua* authority.

In *Friends of Turitea*, for instance, the local authority exercised its power to change the nature of a reserve to enable a power company to develop a wind farm on the reserve. The authority had entered into an agreement with the power company under which the authority would receive payments from the company if the project went ahead. In dismissing a bias challenge, the court pointed out that those payments would be for the benefit of the local community and ratepayers, for whom the council was 'in

[296] *Daganayasi v Minster of Immigration* [1980] 2 NZLR 130 (CA) at 141.
[297] *Dimes* (n 268); *Auckland Casino* (n 264).

substance a trustee'.[298] Another way of putting this point is that any financial benefit that will flow to the authority *qua* authority is a legitimate policy consideration that can be weighed among other policy considerations.

In *Enterprise Miramar*, the Court of Appeal did not directly acknowledge the legitimacy of this type of conflict of interest, but a challenge still failed. The council granting consent for a housing development also owned some of the land. The development thus represented a commercial opportunity for the council. The Court considered this conflict acceptable, in part because Parliament had chosen to vest both roles in the council.[299]

Even the lesser form of conflict of interest seen in these cases is acceptable only because the decision at issue is a decision on a large scale, where policy considerations are relevant. At the other end of the spectrum of types of decision, we would not countenance such a conflict of interest in a court of law. For instance, it is hopefully inconceivable, even in this age of user-pays policies, that courts might obtain some of their funding by requiring successful plaintiffs to pay to the court a share of any damages.

(b) A Personal Relationship, or Some Other Personal Stake in the Outcome

A personal relationship (friendly or hostile) with a party gives rise to a high degree of concern. A relationship with another participant in the proceedings, such as a witness or counsel, may also give rise to concern. In this type of situation, there may not be much variation in the standards expected of judges and administrative or even executive decision-makers.[300]

What does vary from case to case is the significance of the relationship, which determines the degree of concern arising from it. Relevant factors here include how close and how current the relationship is, and how closely and significantly the other person is involved in the matter for decision.[301] In *Saxmere*, for instance, the business relationship between Wilson J and counsel for one of the parties was initially found to be insufficient to disqualify the judge.[302] However, that conclusion changed when further evidence emerged to show that at the time of the hearing, the business relationship not only was active but also involved the judge being financially indebted to counsel.[303] In the *Auckland Casino* case, the Court of Appeal was inclined to find apparent bias arising cumulatively from various connections held by members of the Casino Control Authority, and from their conduct at the hearing. The most significant connection was one member's longstanding personal friendship with a director of the

[298] *Friends of Turitea Reserve Society Inc v Palmerston North City Council* [2008] 2 NZLR 661 (HC) at [96], [105].

[299] *Enterprise Miramar* (n 278) at [75]–[77].

[300] Elliott and Varuhas (n 280) at 341.

[301] *Locabail* (n 254) at [25].

[302] *Saxmere* (n 250). For another unsuccessful challenge, this time based on a personal relationship between a judge and a witness, see *Man O'War Station Ltd* (n 277).

[303] *Saxmere* (n 250).

company which held 80 per cent of the shares in Sky Tower Casino Ltd, the successful contender for the casino licence.[304]

The threshold question concerns the requirement for a logical link between the relationship and the feared deviation from impartial decision-making.[305] In *McGrath v Minister of Justice*, such a link was found to be missing.[306] The challenge was to the Minister's decision to extradite Mr McGrath. It relied on the fact that a family friend of the Minister had demonstrated animus towards Mr McGrath on his blog. However, the friend was not a participant in the proceedings, nor was there any evidence to suggest that the Minister shared the family friend's views, or that she even knew about them.

Once the threshold of a logical link is crossed, then the contextual factors concerning the nature of the decision may be relevant to whether the degree of concern arising from the relationship suffices to disqualify the decision-maker. However, personal relationships, once relevant to the decision, should arguably always attract a demanding standard.[307]

(c) Attitudes: Predisposition or Predetermination

Predetermination is a form of predisposition – a complaint about the decision-maker's attitude to the case. What level of predisposition is enough to disqualify a decision-maker varies greatly according to the contextual factors, as we will see.

First, however, there needs to be sufficient evidence of predisposition. The reviewing court's enquiry is not into the decision-maker's subjective state of mind, but into objective evidence that gives rise to a concern about the decision-maker's attitude to the case. That evidence may take the form of statements or conduct indicating a predisposition.

The threshold question once again is whether there is a logical link between the claimed predisposition and the feared deviation from deciding the matter on its merits. That is why allegations of a generalised predisposition based on a personal characteristic such as the decision-maker's religion, ethnic origin, class, gender or age, or due to their previous associations, will rarely, if ever, be enough to disqualify a decision-maker.[308] In *Helow*, a sufficient appearance of predisposition did not even arise from current membership of an association whose journal sometimes published views hostile to people in the position of the complainant, as there was no reason to conclude that the decision-maker shared those views.[309]

The clearest evidence of impermissible predisposition is found in statements by the decision-maker expressing views on the actual matter to be decided. An instance where something slightly less direct sufficed is found in *Zaoui v Greig*.[310] The

[304] *Auckland Casino* (n 264) at 147, 149. The challenge failed, however, due to waiver and because the Court exercised its remedial discretion: ibid at 153.

[305] *Saxmere* (n 250) at [20].

[306] *McGrath* (n 276) at [18]–[22].

[307] A suggestion, ibid, that a 'closed mind' standard was one of the options must be open to serious doubt.

[308] *Locabail* (n 254) at [25].

[309] *Helow v Secretary of State for the Home Department* [2008] UKHL 62, [2008] WLR 2416.

[310] *Zaoui v Greig* HC Auckland CIV-2004-404-317, 31 March 2004.

Inspector-General of Security and Intelligence was found to be disqualified from determining the validity of a security risk certificate that had been issued against Mr Zaoui, a refugee. Confirmation of the certificate would expose Mr Zaoui to deportation. The Court was concerned about statements suggesting a predisposition against Mr Zaoui's case. The Inspector-General had given an interview in which he said that we would not want too many refugees 'coming in on false passports that they have thrown down the loo' and 'perhaps having some association elsewhere'. While this statement included no specific reference to Mr Zaoui's case, it essentially described Mr Zaoui's situation and expressed doubts about allowing someone like that to stay. In combination with other conduct suggesting friendly relations with the Director of Security who had issued the certificate, this was held to the cross the line.

Turning to the standard of impartiality expected of the decision-maker, as noted this varies greatly in this context. Judges must be very careful about statements or conduct that may suggest any directly relevant predispositions. However, the nature of the decision is at least as important as the nature of the decision-maker. Thus, a similarly high standard also applies to administrative decision-makers deciding individual matters with high stakes for the affected individual. That was the case, for instance, in *Zaoui v Greig*,[311] since Mr Zaoui faced deportation if the security risk certificate was upheld. A further reason why impartiality was especially important was that much turned on Mr Zaoui's version of events, and hence on his credibility. Even Ministers – elected politicians – may attract a similarly high standard of impartiality when exercising similar types of power.[312]

At the other end of the spectrum, nothing short of a 'closed mind' will disqualify administrative or executive decision-makers exercising powers on a large scale. In other words, a predisposition here does not disqualify unless it rises to the level of predetermination.

Instances of situations in which the 'closed mind' test for predetermination applies include Cabinet's decision to fast-track approval for a new aluminium smelter in *CREEDNZ*;[313] a local authority's decision to change the designation of a reserve to allow construction of a windfarm in *Friends of Turitea*;[314] and a local authority's decision to fast-track approval for an affordable housing development in *Enterprise Miramar*.[315] At least some lowering of the expected standard of open-mindedness also applies to tribunals that have policy-setting functions. This was held to apply to the Planning Tribunal,[316] the predecessor of the Environment Court.

In such contexts, it is appropriate for decision-makers to bring their policy preferences to the decision, and they may already have expressed support for the project. Complaints of predetermination will thus fail so long as the decision-maker was still

[311] ibid at [46], [87] and [107].

[312] *McGrath* (n 276) at [18]. But note that this case concerned a personal relationship, where arguably the lenient 'closed mind' test is simply not appropriate at all: see n 309 and accompanying text. Extradition decisions may arguably permit a Minister to have predispositions of a policy nature; the Court in this case did not comment on this question.

[313] *CREEDNZ* (n 108).

[314] *Friends of Turitea* (n 298).

[315] *Enterprise Miramar* (n 278).

[316] *Turner v Allison* [1971] NZLR 833 (CA) at 843, 849.

open to persuasion, and genuinely addressed the statutory criteria. This point is sometimes put in different language: it is said that actual bias (in the form of a closed mind) rather than a mere appearance of bias is required in such contexts.

Where the legislation provides for an inquisitorial process, this also affects the expected level of neutrality. The Royal Commission charged with investigating the causes of the miscarriage of justice in the Arthur Allan Thomas case, for instance, was required by its terms of reference and its inquisitorial role to probe police evidence. The level of hostility towards the police witnesses displayed by the Commissioners troubled the Court of Appeal, but was held not to cross the line into impermissible predetermination.[317]

Predetermination overlaps with other grounds of review. A decision-maker with a closed mind will not accord a party a fair hearing. Where submissions are mandatory relevant considerations, a decision-maker with a closed mind will have failed to take these into account.[318] And if the decision-maker's mind is closed because of adherence to a fixed policy, then the rule against fettering applies.

(d) Both Judge and Prosecutor

If the same person is both judge and prosecutor, this inherently gives rise to a high level of concern about lack of impartiality. It is never permissible for a judge.

However, in administrative processes it is common to see versions of this situation – one person or body holding the roles of both decision-maker and opposing party, or the decision-maker lacking independence from the opposing party.[319] This can be appropriate. It always depends on the particular context: the types of administrative decision-makers and types of powers vary in many respects.[320] On the one hand, we should not simply assume that separation of these roles and strict independence is necessary – in many contexts it would represent an inappropriate extension of the adversarial model established in our courts. On the other hand, we should be ready to interrogate structures and methods of administrative decision-making to determine whether they fall short of appropriate standards of impartiality.[321]

The choices made in designing administrative processes respond to a variety of competing objectives. The merits of these choices in light of those objectives are debated in the literature on administrative justice.[322] Courts considering bias challenges to administrative processes would benefit from taking note of that literature.

Often, of course, the decision-making structure in question is provided by statute. Where that is the case, some courts have dismissed bias challenges simply on the

[317] *Re Royal Commission on Thomas Case* [1982] 1 NZLR 252 (CA) at 279–84.

[318] See, eg, *New Zealand Fishing Industry Association Inc v Minister of Agriculture and Fisheries* [1988] 1 NZLR 544 (CA).

[319] Independence is the structural framework that secures the impartiality that is the concern of the bias rule: *Gillies v Secretary of State for Work and Pensions* [2006] UKHL 2, [2006] 1 WLR 781 at [38].

[320] See, generally, Matthew Groves, 'Clarity and Complexity in the Bias Rule' (2020) 44 *Melbourne University Law Review* 565, esp at 570–71, 579–82.

[321] See, eg, *Re Royal Commission on Thomas Case* (n 319) at 273: counsel assisting an inquiry should not take any part in the Commission's deliberations and in drafting its report.

[322] See Chs 13–15.

basis that the structure is provided by statute.[323] However as noted earlier, courts could also read such statutes subject to applicable requirements of impartiality as far as possible,[324] and nowadays they could also make a declaration of inconsistency with section 27 of the Bill of Rights. Even in the context of statutory processes, therefore, what is required to achieve fairness is a live issue for the courts.

In some administrative contexts, the combination of the two roles is quite unobjectionable. This includes cases where authorities are consulting on their own proposals, as they are often required to do by statute. That is also one of the situations in which predispositions are often permissible so long as the decision-maker does not have a closed mind.[325] The reasons why both the combination of roles and the resultant predisposition is permissible include that the combination of the conflicting roles is provided by statute, and the fact that policy decisions on a large scale are involved.[326]

Even where administrative decisions about individuals are concerned, the combination of roles is common and sometimes unobjectionable, particularly for the initial decision on any application by an individual. The bulk of such decisions is made without an oral hearing, and there is no participation by any parties beyond the decision-maker and the applicant.[327] The decision-maker could therefore be said to be acting as both judge and opponent, although it is also at least conceivable that decision-makers in some contexts might be understood as assisting the applicant.[328] Either way, this common type of process is arguably entirely appropriate, at least as long as there is recourse to an appeal or review on the merits that does involve a hearing.

It is also quite common for disciplinary or enforcement action to be taken against an individual on an authority's own motion, or for the same authority to both investigate and decide complaints. This can be described as an inquisitorial process.[329] The detail varies. Sometimes even this type of decision is made entirely on the papers and without involvement of any third party, as for instance with sanctions imposed on social security beneficiaries for breaching their obligations.[330] Sometimes there is an oral hearing, but it still only involves the disciplinary body and the person charged, as with standards committees that investigate and hear complaints against lawyers.[331] Even where the charge is presented by a separate person at the hearing,[332] the disciplinary body

[323] Eg *Rich v Christchurch Girls High School Board of Governors* (No 1) [1974] 1 NZLR 1 (CA) at 8–9; *McGuire v Wellington Standards Committee* (No 1) [2015] NZCA 569 at [25].

[324] See, eg, *Paki v Maori Land Court* [1999] 3 NZLR 700 (HC) at [80]–[84], inserting a procedural safeguard into an inquisitorial statutory process.

[325] *Friends of Turitea* (n 298) at [89]–[110].

[326] See *Enterprise Miramar* (n 278) at [74]–[77]; *Friends of Turitea* (n 298) at [93]–[97].

[327] See Matthew Groves, 'The Rule Against Bias', in HP Lee and Matthew Groves (eds), *Australian Administrative Law: Fundamentals, Principles and Doctrines* (Cambridge, Cambridge University Press, 2007) 316 at 325–26.

[328] On duties to inquire, see Hanna Wilberg, 'Administrative Law' (2010) 1 *New Zealand Law Review* 177 at 202–06; for a dictum suggesting a duty to assist, see *Hall v Director-General of Social Welfare* [1997] NZFLR 902 (HC) at 912.

[329] *McGuire* (n 323) at [25]; *Sharman v New Zealand Association of Counsellors Inc* [2013] NZHC 3553 at [16].

[330] Social Security Act 2018, s 232.

[331] Lawyers and Conveyancers Act 2006, ss 130, 152 and 156.

[332] See, eg, *Paki v Maori Land Court* (n 324) at [80]–[84].

still has a dual role if it has initiated the process, or investigated the matter up to the hearing, or both.

Perhaps the appropriateness of combining the roles of judge and prosecutor in these contexts should be subjected to more scrutiny, given the significance of disciplinary or enforcement decisions for the individuals involved. However, courts have tended to uphold such processes, on the basis that the statute clearly provides for it[333] or that they are an appropriate response to resource constraints.[334] Again, there is usually access to an appeal or review with a more formal hearing, and that has been held to render the overall process fair.[335]

In some contexts, however, courts have required greater separation. *Simes*, for instance, concerned a decision to cancel a lawyer's legal aid provider status. The Court of Appeal held that a Legal Services Agency employee who had been closely involved in investigating complaints about the lawyer should not have been advising the Panel appointed to make the decision.[336]

Even in hearings on appeal from an initial decision, the other side is not always represented. This may again be for reasons of resource constraints. It may also be a part of an enabling process designed to assist unrepresented appellants by avoiding an inequality of arms.[337] Unfortunately, however, the unintended result may be that the hearing body's impartiality is left in doubt. That risk is particularly high where the hearing body finds it necessary to question the appellant in a way that suggests scrutiny of their case rather than assisting them to make that case.[338] A better solution may be for the respondent authority to be represented, but for the representative to be committed to supporting an enabling approach.[339]

A further related issue is that administrative hearing bodies often lack independence. Bodies hearing first instance review applications often lack independence from the authority whose decisions they are reviewing, as with Benefit Review Committees reviewing Work and Income decisions.[340] In prison disciplinary matters, the initial decision process involves a broadly adversarial hearing, but the hearing adjudicator is a Corrections staff member appointed by the prison manager.[341] In other contexts, tribunal members who are not on the staff of the respondent authority may still have potentially conflicting roles, such as where a member of a disability appeal tribunal was also engaged as an independent examining doctor for the respondent agency in other cases.[342] Even external appellate tribunals lack independence from government, to the extent that their members do not have security of tenure.[343]

[333] *McGuire* (n 323) at [25].

[334] *Sharman* (n 329) at [48]–[55].

[335] See *Porter v Magill* (n 252) at [92]–[94].

[336] *Secretary for Justice v Simes* (n 35) at [107]–[108].

[337] See Ch 15.

[338] See Peter Cane, *Administrative Tribunals and Adjudication* (Oxford and Portland, Hart Publishing, 2009) at 242–44. On the risk, see ibid, esp fn 123.

[339] For an example, see Hazel Genn and Yvette Genn, *The Effectiveness of Representation at Tribunals* (Lord Chancellor's Department, 1989) at 160–63.

[340] Social Security Act 2018, Sch 7.

[341] Corrections Act 2004, ss 15 and 133. Hearings by the prison governor passed scrutiny in *R (King) v Secretary of State for Justice* [2012] EWCA Civ 376, [2012] HRLR 17.

[342] A complaint failed in *Gillies* (n 319) at [17]–[27], [30]–[33], [36]–[46].

[343] Groves, 'Clarity and Complexity' (n 320) at 581–82.

(9) Waiver of Bias

The right to object on grounds of bias may be waived. That was one of the grounds on which the bias complaint failed in *Auckland Casino*.[344] Recent instances include the Supreme Court declining to recall its judgment in a defamation case. The reasons amounted to finding that the bias objection had been waived.[345]

Waiver applies to bar a bias complaint if the party bringing that complaint was aware of the facts giving rise to apparent bias at the hearing, and freely chose not to object.[346] The rationales include finality of proceedings, and guarding against tactical use of the bias objection (in the form of the objecting party keeping the objection 'up their sleeve' to use in case the decision goes against them).[347] Arguably, these are valid considerations for legally represented parties, but more difficult to justify where the objecting party was unrepresented at the hearing.[348] Even for a represented party, it can be an 'agonising choice' whether to object during a hearing: if the objection is upheld, it will cause delays and additional cost; if it is dismissed, it may then predispose the judge or decision-maker against the objecting party.[349]

Concerns have been expressed more generally about the tension with the public confidence rationale underlying the bias rule: the parties should not have power to waive a concern that belongs to the public.[350] However, allowing tactical use of the objection may also harm public confidence in the justice system or public administration.[351] The Court of Appeal acknowledged the concern about private waiver of a public interest in *Auckland Casino*. However, it took the view that waiver should be excluded only for blatant bias and for judges in criminal trials, as the public confidence rationale of the bias rule is particularly salient in those contexts.[352] We might also say that the objecting party's choice is particularly 'agonising' in those contexts.

F. A Duty to Give Reasons?

A further question is when decision-makers are required to give reasons for their decisions, as part of delivering that decision.[353] Reason-giving can be seen as an aspect of procedural fairness, or alternatively as part of transparency in government.[354]

[344] *Auckland Casino* (n 264) at 151–53.
[345] *Craig v Williams* [2019] NZSC 60.
[346] *Auckland Casino* (n 264) at 151.
[347] Matthew Groves, 'Waiver of the Rule Against Bias' (2009) 35 *Monash University Law Review* 315 at 320–24; see, eg, *Craig v Williams* (n 345).
[348] Groves, 'Waiver' (n 347) at 338–46.
[349] *Auckland Casino* (n 264) at 151–52.
[350] Bridgette Toy-Cronin, 'Waiver of the Rule Against Bias' (2002) 9 *Auckland University Law Review* 850; Michael Taggart, 'Administrative Law' [2003] *New Zealand Law Review* 99 at 104.
[351] Groves, 'Waiver' (n 347) at 322–24.
[352] *Auckland Casino* (n 264) at 152.
[353] To be distinguished from disclosing a proposed decision for comment prior to making it; and also from affidavits explaining the reasons to the court when the decision has been challenged.
[354] For transparency, see also the Official Information Act 1981 and Local Government Official Information and Meetings Act 1987 (see Ch 2.B(1)), and the duty of candour (Ch 2.C(1)(d)).

The common law has long maintained that there is no general duty to do so, even for judges[355] – resisting calls from commentators.[356] However, more often than not, reasons are required either by the common law or by statute.

The main issues that arise are in what circumstances either statute or the common law requires reasons (section (2)), how much is required by way of reasons in those circumstances (section (3)), and what remedies will be granted for breach of such a requirement (section (4)). We should also note alternative routes by which decision-makers might be required to justify their decisions (section (5)). First, however, we should consider why reasons are considered important (section (1)).

(1) Why should Decision-makers Give Reasons?

Alongside a range of benefits, a requirement to give reasons has some potential downsides. Both the benefits and the downsides vary with the context, and these competing considerations need to be weighed up – as with other aspects of procedural fairness.[357]

The rationales for requiring reasons, as for other aspects of procedural fairness, include a dignity rationale. Respect for persons affected by a decision requires offering them an explanation.[358] Acceptance of a decision also is more likely when it is explained.

A range of further rationales have been discussed in cases like *Singh*,[359] *Lewis v Wilson & Horton*[360] and *Belgiorno-Nettis*.[361] First, the principle of open justice looms large for courts and tribunals, but its equivalent may also extend to administrative decision-makers. Legitimacy and accountability are promoted through openness and accessibility. Second, reasons allow persons affected to see whether the decision has been made in accordance with the law, such as whether mandatory considerations have been given genuine consideration and submissions have been listened to. Third, this, in turn, provides the basis for deciding whether to challenge a decision, and for judicial supervision on review or appeal. Both the right to judicial review in section 27(2) of the Bill of Rights and any applicable appeal right have therefore been held to support a right to reasons adequate for that purpose. Fourth, reasons can also provide guidance for the future for those impacted by the relevant regime. Last, but not least, a reasons requirement imposes a discipline that guards against arbitrariness. The process of

[355] *R v Awatere* [1982] 1 NZLR 644 (CA) at 648–49; *Lewis v Wilson & Horton Ltd* [2000] 3 NZLR 546 (CA) at [75], [83]–[85].

[356] See, eg, Michael Taggart, '*Osmond* in the High Court of Australia: Missed Opportunity' in Michael Taggart (ed), *Judicial Review of Administrative Action in the 1980s* (Auckland, Oxford University Press, 1986) 53; Tim Cochrane, 'A General Public Law Duty to Provide Reasons: Why New Zealand Should Follow the Irish Supreme Court' (2013) 11 *New Zealand Journal of Public and International Law* 517.

[357] Mark Elliott, 'Has the Common Law Duty to Give Reasons Come of Age Yet?' [2011] *Public Law* 56 at 60.

[358] See Sian Elias, 'Administrative Law for "Living People"' (2009) 68 *Cambridge Law Journal* 47 at 64.

[359] *Singh v Chief Executive Officer, Department of Labour* [1999] NZAR 258 (CA) at 262–63 (Keith J).

[360] *Lewis v Wilson & Horton* (n 355) at [76]–[82] (Elias CJ).

[361] *Belgiorno-Nettis v Auckland Unitary Plan Independent Hearings Panel* [2019] NZCA 175, [2019] 3 NZLR 345 at [46]–[50] (Asher J).

marshalling reasons makes it more likely that decisions are indeed made for adequate reasons, and may well change or refine a decision-maker's views.

Potential downsides in some contexts include the administrative burden. Depending on the detail that is required, reason-giving could be unduly time-consuming. There is also concern about over-judicialising administrative processes. For instance, what is required of front-line decision-makers has to take account of the realities of that context.[362] Concerns such as these fall to be balanced in deciding how much is required by way of reasons and when.[363]

(2) When are Reasons Required?

As noted, reasons may be required either by the common law or by statute.

Statutory duties to give reasons are now widespread. They apply not only to statutory appellate tribunals[364] and individual decisions at first instance[365] but also, for instance, to local authorities making policy statements and plans under the Resource Management Act.[366] However, it is also notable that some statutory provisions expressly exclude any obligation to give reasons.[367]

In addition to specific statutory requirements, the Official Information Act 1982 provides a general right of access to reasons for a decision in section 23. However, this applies only on request; thus it depends on the person being aware of the right. There are further limits. The Act does not apply to courts, tribunals and commissions of inquiry.[368] Section 23 applies only to decisions in respect of the requester in their personal capacity. Some of the Act's reasons for withholding information also apply to this right.

The proliferation of statutory duties at least somewhat reduces the practical significance of the question when a duty to give reasons arises at common law.[369] More often, the issue is the one addressed under the next heading – how much is required by way of reasons.

Where the existence of a duty to give reasons does turn on the common law, there is a growing trend towards a presumptive duty.[370] The courts tend to discuss this issue by reference to the rationales discussed above. Generally speaking, reasons will be required in circumstances where those rationales apply and are sufficiently important.

362 For a revealing study, see Jennifer Raso, 'Unity in the Eye of the Beholder? Reasons for Decision in Theory and Practice in the Ontario Works Program' (2020) 70 *University of Toronto Law Journal* 1.

363 Elliott, 'Common Law Duty to Give Reasons' (n 357) at 64; Cochrane, 'A General Public Law Duty to Provide Reasons' (n 356) at 542–45.

364 See, eg, Social Security Act 2018, s 404(1)(b) concerning the Social Security Appeal Authority.

365 See, eg, Immigration Act 2009, ss 27 and 138(4)(b).

366 See, eg, Resource Management Act 1991, sch 1, cl 10(2)(a).

367 See, eg, Immigration Act 2009, s 11(1)(c).

368 Official Information Act 1981, s 2(6).

369 Joanna Bell, 'Reason-Giving in Administrative Law: Where are We and Why have the Courts not Embraced the 'General Common Law Duty to Give Reasons'?' (2019) 82 *Modern Law Review* 983 at 989, 991.

370 *Waikanae Christian Holiday Park Inc v New Zealand Historic Places Trust Maori Heritage Council* [2015] NZCA 23, [2015] NZAR 302 at [70]; also *Discount Brands Ltd v Westfield (New Zealand) Ltd* [2005] NZSC 17, [2005] 2 NZLR 597 (SC) at [56] (Keith J).

The importance of the rationales turns at least in part on the importance of what is at stake,[371] and on other factors relevant to procedural fairness generally, including the statutory context.

Reasons are, for instance, likely to be required for decisions with serious effects on important individual interests, such as liberty.[372] In *Taito*, the Privy Council held in passing that reasons were required when declining legal aid for criminal appeals to the Court of Appeal, both for the initial decision and on review.[373] This was because of the importance of the decision, given that an appeal could not be effectively pursued without aid. Further, without reasons for the initial decision it would be difficult to apply for a review of that decision.

In *Lewis v Wilson & Horton*, reasons were required for a grant of name suppression due to the unusual circumstances.[374] Name suppression impacted the right to freedom of expression, and an effective opportunity to seek judicial review required access to reasons. In particular, however, the problem was that part of the name suppression hearing had been held in chambers. In order to still serve open justice in those circumstances, reasons were essential.

Recent instances of no reasons being required include *Waikanae Christian Holiday Park*,[375] a challenge by an affected landowner to a decision to register some land as a wahi tapu[376] area under the Historic Places Act. The Court considered the usual rationales did not apply. The documentary evidence was sufficient to explain the decision, the council's process had been open, and there was no need for added discipline as it was evident that careful consideration had been given.

Another instance of no reasons being required concerned a decision not to hold a hearing on a fast-track consenting decision in *Te Korowai o Ngāruahine Trust*.[377] The Court relied mainly on the fast-track nature of the statutory process. However, the incidental procedural nature of the impugned decision must also have been relevant. If all such decisions required reasons, that really would be an excessive administrative burden.

The case-by-case judgments in cases like these have been deplored as 'ad hocery', making it too difficult to predict outcomes.[378] On the other hand, there is arguably nothing unusual about courts determining what is required for procedural fairness on a case-by-case basis in light of contextual factors including the particular statutory context.[379] A final point to note is that in some cases, courts take the alternative route of drawing adverse inferences in the absence of reasons, rather than determining whether reasons were required.[380]

[371] See *Ngāti Hurungaterangi v Ngāti Wahiao* [2017] NZCA 429; [2017] 3 NZLR 770 at [63].

[372] See, eg, *R v Secretary of State for the Home Department, ex p Doody* [1994] 1 AC 531 (HL).

[373] *R v Taito* [2003] 3 NZLR 577 (PC) at 599. See similarly the observation in *Legal Services Agency v Minchington* [2003] 1 NZLR 263 (HC) at [10]–[11], and Legal Services Act 2011, s 56(2).

[374] *Lewis v Wilson & Horton* (n 355) at [77]–[78], [86].

[375] *Waikanae Christian Holiday Park* (n 370) at [67]–[74].

[376] Sacred place.

[377] *Te Korowai o Ngāruahine Trust v Hiringa Energy Limited and Balance Agri-Nutrients Limited* [2022] NZHC 2810 at [259]–[266].

[378] Michael Taggart, 'Administrative Law' [2000] *New Zealand Law Review* 439 at 442.

[379] Elliott, 'Common Law Duty to Give Reasons' (n 359) at 66. Bell, 'Reason-Giving in Administrative Law' (n 371) at 1005–06 draws attention to the importance of the statutory framework.

[380] See further below, section (5) of this part.

(3) Content of Duty to Give Reasons

In many cases, some reasons have been given and the issue is whether those reasons are adequate. How much is required varies with the context: the factors discussed under the previous heading are also relevant to this determination. In some contexts, reasons may be abbreviated or may be evident without express reference.[381] Some general points can, however, be stated about the required content of reasons.

Reasons should include findings on material questions of fact, reference to the relevant law, and application of the law to the facts as found.[382] They should also be adequate for serving the rationales noted earlier. They must therefore enable the recipient to understand why the decision was made, and to assess its lawfulness for the purposes of a potential appeal or judicial review application.[383]

Where a decision-maker had submissions to take into account, *Belgiorno-Nettis* held that the reasons needed to address these at least in summary fashion.[384] This does, however, depend on the context.[385]

(4) Consequences of Breach of Duty to Give (Adequate) Reasons

When it comes to remedies for breach of a duty to give reasons, there are two main options. Courts may merely order reasons (or further reasons) to be given, or may quash the decision for failure to do so and remit the matter for reconsideration.

The Court of Appeal in *Belgiorno-Nettis* confirmed that both options are available, and traversed the factors to be balanced.[386] In favour of quashing, there is the concern that a decision made without the discipline of reasons may also be defective in other ways. Furthermore, a court-ordered statement of reasons may represent at best dim recollections and at worst after-the-fact rationalisations. On the other hand, quashing and remitting may impose a significant burden on the authority and sometimes on third parties, for instance because a large-scale consultation may need to be re-run. The extent of that burden in the particular case falls to be weighed against the strength of the concerns just noted. Where the subject-matter of the decision is less important than, for instance, human rights, that may also weigh against imposing the burden of reconsideration.

In *Belgiorno-Nettis*, the planning decision at issue was presumably at the less important end. The Court concluded that on balance an order to give reasons was appropriate.[387] Further defects were unlikely as the process followed by the Panel was thorough and careful. And the Panel, being chaired by a judge, could be trusted

[381] *Lewis v Wilson & Horton* (n 355) at [81].

[382] See *Singh* (n 359) at 263; Official Information Act 1981, s 23(1).

[383] *Lewis v Wilson & Horton* (n 355) at [80]; *Belgiorno-Nettis* (n 361) at [49].

[384] *Belgiorno-Nettis* (n 361) at [65]. See, similarly, *Simes* discussed below at n 392.

[385] See, eg, *Woolworths New Zealand Ltd v Auckland Council* [2023] NZSC 45, [2023] 1 NZLR 113. The High Court decision in that case upheld a reasons challenge, applying *Belgiorno-Nettis*, but the Supreme Court reinstated the decision (barely touching on the reasons point).

[386] *Belgiorno-Nettis* (n 361) at [102]–[110]. See also Elliott (n 359) at 72–74, arguing for quashing.

[387] ibid at [103], [106], [109], [110].

not to adopt after-the-fact rationalisations. If other defects did emerge from the reasons provided, further proceedings could be filed. In *Lewis v Wilson & Horton*, in contrast, the name suppression decision was quashed.[388] The choice of remedies was not addressed, but the decision's impact on freedom of expression would have been relevant.

(5) Alternative Routes: Other Grounds of Review

A significant alternative approach should also be mentioned. Rather than finding a duty to give reasons and granting a remedy for breach of that duty, courts may find that the lack of reasons supports another ground of review. Two grounds in particular may be utilised.

First, in the absence of reasons courts may draw adverse inferences as to the legality of the reasoning.[389] Decision-makers are encouraged to assist the court by filing an affidavit in the proceedings.[390] In the absence of an explanation in the form of either contemporaneous reasons or an affidavit, however, the inference arising from the available evidence may be that the reasoning was unlawful in some respect.[391] Similarly, where reasons have been given, courts have concluded that mandatory considerations that are not sufficiently addressed in those reasons were not genuinely taken into account.[392]

Secondly, rights-based review increasingly demands reasons, promoting a 'culture of justification'.[393] Under section 5 of the New Zealand Bill of Rights Acts, a decision-maker bears an onus of justification for limiting a right.[394] Such justification may still be provided in evidence when a decision is challenged. However, New Zealand courts have increasingly required decision-makers to have considered the question of justification before deciding.[395] Similarly, heightened scrutiny unreasonableness review in cases where rights or other important interests or values are at stake often involves a demand for cogent justification based on adequate evidence.[396]

[388] *Lewis v Wilson & Horton* (n 355) at [87].

[389] See Ch 5.C(3).

[390] *Fiordland Venison Ltd v Minister of Agriculture* [1978] 2 NZLR 341 (CA) at 345–46, 354; *New Zealand Fishing Industry Association Inc v Minister of Agriculture and Fisheries* [1988] 1 NZLR 544 (CA) at 554.

[391] *Fiordland Venison* (n 392) at 346–50, 357; *Zhang v Minister of Immigration* [2020] NZHC 568, [2020] NZAR 201 at [68]–[72]; *Padfield v Minister of Agriculture, Fisheries and Food* [1968] AC 997 (HL) at 1032–33.

[392] *Secretary for Justice v Simes* [2012] NZCA 459, [2012] NZAR 1044 at [58]–[60].

[393] Advocating for this, see, eg, David Dyzenhaus, Murray Hunt and Michael Taggart, 'The Principle of Legality in Administrative Law: Internationalisation as Constitutionalisation' (2001) 1 *Oxford University Commonwealth Law Journal* 5.

[394] *Ministry of Health v Atkinson* [2012] NZCA 184, [2012] 3 NZLR 456 at [163]. See further Ch 6.D.

[395] *Taylor v The Chief Executive of the Department of Corrections* [2015] NZCA 477, [2015] NZAR 1648 at [81]–[93], [101]–[104]; *Wallace v Chief Executive of the Department of Corrections* [2023] NZHC 2248 at [110]–[111].

[396] *Minister of Justice v Kim* [2021] NZSC 57, [2021] 1 NZLR 338 at [41]. See further Ch 7.B.

5

Traditional Grounds of Review: Illegality

This chapter is devoted to illegality as a ground of review. The grounds of review have two aspects, as discussed in more detail in the Introduction and Chapter 2: they represent both instructions to administrators on how (not) to exercise their powers, and instructions to judges on the nature and extent of their supervisory powers. In their first aspect, as instructions to administrators, they are relevant well beyond judicial review proceedings – they should be considered before decisions are made and can be invoked when decisions are challenged by other avenues of recourse. The second aspect is mostly relevant to judicial review proceedings and other judicial proceedings invoking the grounds of review: for instance, we will see that courts will not intervene on the grounds that a decision-maker has given insufficient weight to a mandatory consideration.

Illegality takes many forms. In its broadest sense, illegality or error of law encompasses all grounds of review. That is because a decision is unlawful if any of those grounds are made out. However, this chapter is concerned with illegality as a particular ground of review.

The most basic form of the illegality ground applies to a purported exercise of a power which the decision-maker does not have in law. Usually, the decision-maker will have misinterpreted or overlooked some relevant limit and thus exceeded the scope of an available power. This is covered briefly in the final part of this chapter.

A very significant additional source of limits on the scope of a power nowadays is found in fundamental rights from various sources. These limit the scope of powers because empowering legislation is read subject to such rights unless it clearly abrogates the right. This is discussed in detail in Chapter 6.

The other most common form of the illegality ground, however, does not necessarily involve exceeding the scope of the power at all. Judicial review has developed a range of legality constraints on how discretionary powers may be exercised. These are the focus of this chapter.

There are two broad types of constraint on the exercise of discretion.[1] First, where the law confers a discretion, this must be exercised in each individual case and must be exercised by the appropriate decision-maker. Otherwise, there is an unlawful abdication of discretion. This can take the form of unauthorised delegation, acting under dictation, or fettering of discretion. Secondly, judicial review scrutinises the reasoning that supports an exercise of discretion. Unlawful reasoning renders a decision unlawful even though it was within the scope of a power available to this decision-maker. It can take one of two broad forms: the first involves acting for an improper purpose, taking into account irrelevant considerations, or applying the wrong test; the second is failing to take account of mandatory relevant considerations.

Often it will be open to the decision-maker to make the same decision again, but the law requires them to exercise their judgement and discretion on the correct legal basis. There is, after all, at least a possibility that this will result in a different outcome.

[1] What follows is one of several possible ways of categorising these illegality grounds.

The two broad types of legality constraint on the exercise of discretion are explored in Parts B and C of this chapter, followed by a brief discussion of basic illegality in the form of exceeding the scope of the power in Part D. First, however, Part A introduces debates about administrative discretion.

A. Rules vs Discretion

Legislation that sets up regimes of public administration confers many discretionary powers, leaving choices to the decision-maker. Often, the legislation does this by identifying relevant competing considerations and requiring decision-makers to weigh these in the particular circumstances. As already noted, the forms of illegality discussed in Parts B and C of this chapter represent legal constraints on exercises of such discretion. Underlying all of this, there is a tension between the advantages and disadvantages of rules and discretion. The legal constraints contribute to managing that tension. To understand the illegality grounds, it is helpful to be aware of this underlying tension.

For completeness, we should note that there is a debate in political philosophy as to whether regimes involving administrative discretion are legitimate at all. Objections stem from an economically conservative liberal individualist philosophy that is concerned in particular about broad powers to promulgate delegated legislation. That debate is outlined in Chapter 3.

In this chapter we can take as our starting point that administrative regimes involving extensive discretion have operated in Aotearoa NZ for at least a century now, and are widely accepted as legitimate. The point here is that even on that basis, there remain ever-present questions as to the extent of discretion that is necessary and appropriate in particular contexts and, conversely, the extent of constraint that is appropriate. Focusing on individuated decisions, the advantages and disadvantages of discretion have been much discussed in contexts such as social welfare benefits[2] or school discipline.[3]

On the one hand, discretion is necessary if the modern administrative state is to serve effectively the plethora of public interest objectives that are entrusted to it. No legislation can specify in advance exactly who should receive social security benefits, or allocations of fishing quotas, or clearance for mergers and acquisitions, to name but a few examples. While the rule of law requires government to be subject to law, it also requires that law should not be arbitrary. Any attempt to lay down comprehensive rules governing decision-making in such contexts would inevitably result in arbitrary outcomes in unforeseen cases. This would involve denying justice to the affected individuals. The central benefit of discretion, then, is that it facilitates decision-making responsive to relevant individual circumstances.

[2] See, for example, Robert E Goodin, 'Welfare, Rights and Discretion' (1986) 6 *Oxford Journal of Legal Studies* 232.

[3] See, for example, *M & R v S & Board of Trustees* [2003] NZAR 705 (also known as *M v Syms*; decided in 1990 and reported retrospectively) at 714, 716.

On the other hand, the benefits of rules include that they provide clarity and certainty. This can be important for a range of reasons. For instance, it is important for effective discipline in contexts such as schools and prisons. In other contexts, predictability can help applicants avoid wasting effort on hopeless applications. Rules can furthermore promote justice by avoiding inconsistent decision-making. In the context of social security and other provision of assistance or services, rules promote justice by creating entitlements rather than leaving claimants at the mercy of officials' discretion.[4] Rules are also efficient: they are easier, faster and cheaper to administer and they reduce the difficulty of maintaining control over front-line decision-making.

These advantages and disadvantages of rules and discretion provide the rationale for several features of empowering legislation, administrative practice and judicial review doctrine. The advantages of discretion, of course, provide the rationale for legislation conferring such discretion. They also provide part of the rationale for the judicial review principle against authorities fettering their own discretion – the other part being the constitutional requirement to respect Parliament's choice to confer discretion. Both of these help to explain why courts in judicial review must not control exercises of discretion to the point of usurping that discretion.

It is because of the disadvantages of discretion that legislation should avoid excessively broad conferrals of discretion. Administrative agencies can help address the potential disadvantages of the discretion that legislation does grant by adopting policies to guide their exercise of that discretion and publishing those policies to promote greater predictability.

Judicial review also helps to address the disadvantages of the discretion conferred by legislation. The illegality grounds of review allow courts to respect that discretion at the same time as imposing legal constraints on its exercise. They achieve this by structuring as well as confining the discretion.[5] Courts confine discretion by identifying its express or implied limits (*what* sorts of decisions may be made and by *whom*). They structure discretion (*how* the discretion may be exercised) by scrutinising the decision-maker's reasoning for consistency with the statute.

With this background in mind, the next two parts of this chapter explore the two groups of illegality grounds that concern how discretion may be exercised: unlawful abdication of discretion and unlawful reasoning. The final brief part concerns the legal limits on the scope of discretionary powers.

B. Unlawful Abdication of Discretion

As already noted, where the law confers a discretion, this must be exercised in each individual case by the appropriate decision-maker. Otherwise, there is an unlawful abdication of discretion. The three grounds that may be grouped under this heading are (1) unauthorised delegation; (2) acting under dictation; and (3) the fettering of discretion.

[4] Goodin (n 2).

[5] Peter Cane, *Administrative Law*, 5th edn (Oxford, Clarendon Press, 2011) at 172; KC Davis, *Discretionary Justice: A Preliminary inquiry* (Urbana, University of Illinois Press, 1977).

(1) Unauthorised Delegation

Unauthorised delegation is one form of the designated decision-maker abdicating a discretion granted by statute. At the same time, purported exercise of a power pursuant to an unauthorised delegation could also be understood as a form of basic illegality: the actual decision-maker does not have the power to make the decision.

At common law, the starting point is the maxim that a delegate may not sub-delegate the delegated power.[6] This applies to powers 'delegated' to a specified decision-maker by statute. However, it is merely a presumption of statutory interpretation: it prohibits delegation only in the absence of statutory authority, which may be express or implied.[7] One of the maxim's applications is to delegated legislation: unless authorised by statute, it is unlawful for such legislation to sub-delegate any part of the powers granted by the statute. The issue in this context usually concerns the extent of implied authority to sub-delegate. The maxim also operates to prohibit unauthorised delegation of any other statutory power, as those who are granted such power are considered Parliament's delegates for the purposes of the maxim.

The rationale behind the maxim rests on three connected ideas.[8] First, a designated decision-maker will have been chosen for particular attributes, such as position, expertise, access to information or representation of interests. Secondly, public power may be exercised only in accordance with its terms, which includes a requirement that it is exercised by those who have been specifically authorised. That reflects both the rule of law and Parliamentary sovereignty. Finally, public power should be exercised by those who are accountable for its exercise. This reflects the rule of law and democratic principles. In short, it matters who makes the decision.

Illegality arises if either a purported delegation was outside the scope of available authority to delegate, or the purported exercise of the delegated power was outside the scope of the delegation. An instance of the first is the *Lauren* case, where an animal welfare inspector was found to have acted pursuant to an invalid delegation. The senior official who had purported to delegate his power to the inspector had been authorised to delegate only to members of his own team, and the inspector was not within that class.[9]

The qualifications to the maxim include the principle established in *Carltona*. We will look at this in section (a). We will then look at (b) New Zealand's system of express statutory authorities to delegate, and (c) issues concerning implied power to delegate, which arise particularly in challenges to delegated legislation on grounds of unauthorised sub-delegation. The lesser option of delegating only preparatory work is discussed in section (d).

[6] *Delegatus non potest delegare*.

[7] *Borrowdale v Director-General of Health* [2021] NZCA 520, [2022] 2 NZLR 356 at [175].

[8] ibid at [170], adopting John Willis, 'Delegatus Non Potest Delegare' (1943) 21 *Canadian Bar Review* 257 at 259–60.

[9] *Lauren v Attorney-General* [2012] NZHC 352. The Court exercised its remedial discretion to merely declare the invalidity of the delegation, rather than quashing the inspector's decision.

(a) The Carltona 'Alter Ego' Principle

The *Carltona* principle is an important qualification to the non-delegation maxim.[10] It allows powers granted to government ministers to be devolved to civil servants of suitable seniority within the minister's department, for whom the minister accepts responsibility.[11] The operation of the principle differs from normal delegation, in that the civil servant acts as the minister's 'alter ego', issuing the decision in the minister's name.[12] For that reason, it has been described as more akin to agency than delegation.[13] This principle recognises the reality that ministers cannot personally exercise all of the powers granted to them – we might say the rationale is administrative necessity. The principle has further been justified on the basis that a minister's accountability for the exercise of the powers in question is maintained via the constitutional doctrine of individual ministerial responsibility for the actions of their departments.

The administrative necessity rationale has much less purchase where powers to make generally applicable rules are concerned. Such rules will, of course, be made on the advice of officials, but it seems reasonable in most contexts to expect the designated office holder to approve them personally.

There is some authority for extending the *Carltona* principle beyond ministers to powers granted to other office holders. Courts have considered this appropriate provided the office holder is accountable to a minister, to maintain the link to ministerial responsibility.[14]

The principle may be displaced by statute, expressly or by implication.[15] There is uncertainty around whether it continues to be available as an alternative in contexts where statute has provided for express delegation. I will return to this after outlining the statutory regimes.

(b) A System of Express Statutory Authorities to Delegate

Statute law in New Zealand provides a comprehensive set of express authorities to delegate public powers. The most informal process is provided in section 7 of the Constitution Act 1986, which authorises any minister of the Crown to exercise the powers of any other minister. Similarly, there is a general authority for powers to be exercised by deputies.[16]

Other provisions for delegation require express delegation in writing to particular persons or classes of person, specifying the powers included in the delegation. Schedule 6 of the Public Service Act 2020 provides two sets of authority to delegate.[17]

[10] *Carltona Ltd v Commissioner of Works* [1943] 2 All ER 560 (CA).

[11] See also *R v Secretary of State for the Home Department, ex p Oladehinde* [1991] 1 AC 254 (HL) at 300, 303.

[12] See *Commissioner of Inland Revenue v Chesterfields Preschools Ltd* [2013] NZCA 53, [2013] 2 NZLR 679 at [56]–[57]. The principle therefore does not extend to allowing exercise of ministerial powers by independent statutory officers: *R (Bourgass) v Secretary of State for Justice* [2015] UKSC 54 at [49]–[50].

[13] *Borrowdale* (n 7) at [177]–[178].

[14] *Chesterfields* (n 12) at [58]; *Borrowdale* (n 7) at [178] (both obiter).

[15] See, eg, *R v Adams* [2020] UKSC 19 at [37]–[40]; also *Bourgass* (n 12) at [64].

[16] Legislation Act 2019, s 47.

[17] The predecessor provisions are found in the State Sector Act 1988, ss 28 and 41.

Ministers may delegate to the chief executives of their public service departments, and chief executives may delegate to other public service chief executives, employees or contractors. In each case, the delegate may further subdelegate the power, but only with the prior written approval of the delegator. Both provisions make it clear that the designated power holder remains responsible for the actions of persons acting under the delegation. Similar regimes apply outside public service departments pursuant to other legislation, such as the Crown Entities Act 2004[18] and the Local Government Act 2002.[19] The effect of these regimes is to facilitate delegation, while ensuring that this only occurs in a deliberate fashion and establishing clear and explicit lines of accountability for the exercise of delegated powers.

Such a comprehensive statutory regime providing authority to delegate raises a question as to its impact on the common law *Carltona* principle. The practical need for the principle is removed where statutory authority to delegate is available. Moreover, arguably reliance on such an informal qualification is inconsistent with the formal and structured statutory regime and thus must be considered abrogated by implication. The question has not so far been directly addressed at appellate level in New Zealand.[20] However, the High Court in *Bounty Oil* considered that the *Carltona* principle continues to be available alongside the statutory regime,[21] and other New Zealand cases have proceeded on that assumption.[22]

(c) Issues in Challenges to Delegated Legislation for Unauthorised Sub-delegation

The most difficult issues about unauthorised delegation concern powers granted by delegated legislation. For simplicity, I will here refer to delegated legislation as regulations, although it may go by a variety of other names. Regulations are, of course, made pursuant to power delegated by statute. The rule against sub-delegation thus applies to them: powers conferred by regulations on administrative decision-makers may be challenged on the grounds of unauthorised sub-delegation.[23] In this context, the application of the principles concerning delegation is very much a question of degree.

In the case of statutory powers to make individual decisions, it makes sense to say that they should ordinarily be exercised by the designated decision-maker and should not be delegated without authority. Regulations, however, generally must include provisions empowering others at least to apply the regulations' general rules. Usually, such powers to apply the rules will include some level of discretion. For instance, regulations governing disciplinary hearings under a Corrections Act will need to confer certain powers on officers conducting hearings. In other words, some level of 'sub-delegation' of powers by the regulations is unavoidable and thus must be authorised

[18] Crown Entities Act 2004, ss 73–76A.

[19] Local Government Act 2002, ss 32–32B.

[20] It was left open in *Waikato Regional Airport Ltd v Attorney-General* [2004] 3 NZLR 1 (PC) at [64]; the Court of Appeal had ignored the possibility of *Carltona* applying to remedy the lack of express delegation.

[21] *Bounty Oil & Gas NL v Attorney-General* [2010] NZAR 120 (HC) at [25]–[28].

[22] See, eg, *Chesterfields* (n 12) at [56]–[59]; also *Borrowdale* (n 7) at [178].

[23] See Michael Taggart, 'From "Parliamentary Powers" to Privatization: The Chequered History of Delegated Legislation in the Twentieth Century' (2005) 55 *University of Toronto Law Journal* 575 at 600–03.

by the empowering statute by implication. The issue in each case is not whether that is so, but how much and what kind of 'sub-delegation' of powers is impliedly authorised.

The success of a sub-delegation challenge to regulations therefore involves two interlocking enquiries.[24] First, the scope of the regulation-making power: how much power to 'sub-delegate' can be implied from the terms and context of the empowering statute? Secondly, what is the nature and scope of the powers that are purportedly granted by the impugned regulations?

The older case law on this was bedevilled by categorical distinctions between legislative, judicial and administrative powers. While administrative law has moved away from such categorical approaches, a distinction between individualised decisions and rule-making is relevant in this context. It is more likely that an empowering statute impliedly authorises regulations to grant individualised decision-making power than further rule-making power. However, even grants of individualised decision-making power may amount to unauthorised 'sub-delegation', on the grounds that the powers granted are too broad and therefore the regulations 'delegate' too much. Regulations granting either type of power are the more likely to be authorised, the more they set out criteria constraining the exercise of the power. The broader and more unqualified the grant of power in the regulations, the less likely it will be found authorised.

In *Borrowdale*, a challenge to a pandemic lockdown order on grounds of unauthorised sub-delegation failed partly on that basis. The order made by the Director-General of Health pursuant to powers in the Health Act 1956 required all businesses to close, unless they were essential businesses. It defined essential businesses by reference to a list published on a website by a different government department. The Court of Appeal held that this did not amount to unlawful delegation of too broad a power: guidance in the form of general principles provided by the Director-General to the other department represented sufficient constraint.[25]

In the alternative, the Court held that what happened did not amount to sub-delegation at all. As a matter of fact, the Director-General had retained oversight and sign-off powers over the list. That meant that he had exercised the power of defining essential businesses personally, on the advice of officials in the other department.[26] On that view of the case, it involved delegation only of preparatory work. Issues concerning that different situation are discussed under the next heading.

(d) Delegation Only of Preparatory Work

A different and lesser form of delegation can conveniently be discussed here, because it is necessary to clear up confusion between the two forms. In some cases, what has been delegated is not the power to make the decision, but merely some of the work in preparation for the decision. In particular, such delegated preparatory work may include the tasks of hearing affected parties and of gathering and processing relevant evidence.

[24] For lists of relevant factors, see *Borrowdale* (n 7) at [176]; Colin Aikman, 'Sub-delegation of the Legislative Power' (1960) 3 *Victoria University of Wellington Law Review* 69 at 83–85.

[25] *Borrowdale* [2021] NZCA 520 (n 7) at [187]–[188].

[26] ibid at [177]–[178], [184]–[186].

As with delegation of the power to make the decision, this is a response to the otherwise unrealistic demands on ministers and other decision-makers with extensive statutory powers. Joseph considers this a preferable half-way house solution, because greater accountability is retained if the designated decision-maker decides personally.[27]

The leading case on this lesser form of delegation is *Air Nelson*.[28] Such delegation does not require any particular authority to be lawful: decision-makers have power to regulate their own procedure.[29] However, it engages other requirements, as confirmed in *Air Nelson*. If submissions or evidence on central issues are not reported to the decision-maker in sufficient detail, the decision can be challenged for failure to take into account mandatory relevant considerations[30] or for mistake of fact.[31] If the submissions of parties with a right to be heard are not reported to the decision-maker in sufficient detail, this may also be challenged as a breach of the right to a hearing: the one who decides must hear.[32] The Court in *Air Nelson* preferred the first of these grounds, without dismissing the relevance of the others.[33]

The difficulty with *Air Nelson* is that the reasoning erroneously conflated the two forms of delegation.[34] It did this by discussing *Carltona* in this context, claiming that authority on the lesser form of delegation both reaffirms the *Carltona* principle and circumscribes it.[35] The Court did correctly note that *Carltona* involves officials making the decision in the Minister's name. That needed to be distinguished from the lesser form of delegation at issue in this case, in which the Minister personally makes the decision.[36]

(2) Acting under Dictation

Acting under dictation from someone else is one way to abdicate discretion. Alternatively, like unauthorised delegation, it might also be seen as involving exercise of a power by the wrong person: while the decision is formally made by the designated decision-maker, in substance the power is exercised by the person who is dictating its exercise.

Two brief examples will suffice. A classic example is the Canadian *Roncarelli* case (better known for its ruling on improper purposes). A liquor licensing board exercised its power to cancel Mr Roncarelli's licence, for no other reason than that the Premier

[27] Philip A Joseph, *Joseph on Constitutional and Administrative Law in New Zealand*, 5th edn (Wellington, Thomson Reuters, 2021) at 1049, 1051.

[28] *Air Nelson Ltd v Minister of Transport* [2008] NZCA 26, [2008] NZAR 139.

[29] *Jeffs v New Zealand Dairy Board* [1967] NZLR 1057 (PC) at 1068.

[30] *Minister for Aboriginal Affairs v Peko-Wallsend Ltd* (1986) 66 ALR 229 (HCA) at 30–31, 44–46.

[31] *E v Secretary of State for the Home Department* [2004] EWCA Civ 49, [2004] QB 1044 at [45]–[48], [63], [65].

[32] *Jeffs* (n 29) at 1066–68.

[33] *Air Nelson* (n 28) at [55]; for the list of grounds pleaded, see at [36].

[34] For similar confusion about *Carltona*, see also *Peko-Wallsend* (n 30) at 37–39.

[35] ibid at [47]–[48]. For another difficulty (involving reliance on *Bushell v Secretary of State for the Environment* [1981] AC 75 (HL)), see text at n 135.

[36] See *R (National Association of Health Stores) v Department of Health* [2005] EWCA Civ 154 at [71]–[72].

of Quebec directed it to do so. This was unlawful as it amounted to acting under dictation.[37]

A modern New Zealand example is found in the *Criminal Bar Association* case.[38] Decisions on legal aid applications were entrusted by statute to the Commissioner for Legal Aid – an independent office within the Ministry of Justice. The Commissioner applied an inflexible policy issued by the Secretary for Justice (the head of the Ministry). One complaint about this was that it involved fettering, and we will return to that. It was also inconsistent with the statute which required the Commissioner to act independently. But the relevant point for present purposes is that it amounted to unlawfully acting under dictation from the Secretary.

It is permissible to consider suggestions or submissions made by others, and to accept such a suggestion or submission in the exercise of the decision-maker's discretion. What is unlawful is to fail to exercise that discretion altogether. Here, that line was crossed because of the inflexible terms of the Secretary's policy,[39] as further discussed below.

(3) Fettering Discretion

Fettering of discretion is the final form of unlawfully abdicating discretion. This can occur when decision-makers adopt insufficiently flexible policies, guidelines or practices;[40] or when they give undertakings or enter contracts.[41] For brevity's sake we will consider only the former. Acting under dictation from another person, discussed under the previous heading, could also be considered a form of fettering of discretion.

The rule against fettering by inflexible policy guidelines was confirmed and applied in *Criminal Bar Association*.[42] Decision-makers may adopt policy guidelines: the Court of Appeal acknowledged this is not only administratively convenient but also can advance rule of law values such as certainty and consistency.[43] However, the line between such beneficial guidance and unlawful fettering is crossed when the policy admits of no exceptions or is followed blindly. It is crucial that the decision-maker still decides each case on its merits.[44]

[37] *Roncarelli v Duplessis* [1959] SCR 121 (SCC).

[38] *Criminal Bar Association of New Zealand Inc v Attorney-General* [2013] NZCA 176, [2013] NZAR 1409 at [64]–[104], esp at [92]–[99].

[39] ibid at [90]–[91].

[40] Note that delegated legislation cannot be challenged on this ground: where rule-making is authorised by an Act of Parliament, then it may impose inflexible constraints on exercises of statutory discretion so long as that is within the ambit of the delegated authority: see, eg, *Ankers v Attorney-General* [1995] 2 NZLR 595 (HC) at 599. Only informal policies and guidelines, also known as 'soft law' or tertiary rules, are subject to the rule against fettering.

[41] On the latter, see ACL Davies, 'Ultra Vires Problems in Government Contracts' (2006) 122 *Law Quarterly Review* 98.

[42] *Criminal Bar Association* [2013] NZCA 176 (n 38). The leading English authority is *British Oxygen Co Ltd v Minister of Technology* [1971] AC 610 (HL).

[43] For those reasons, in some contexts there is even a duty to promulgate and publish a policy: see *R (Purdy) v Director of Public Prosecutions* [2009] UKHL 45, [2010] 1 AC 345.

[44] *Criminal Bar Association* (n 38) at [118]–[119].

In *Criminal Bar Association*, a policy specifying fixed fees for various categories of criminal legal aid grants amounted to unlawful fettering. The statute provided a discretionary power to specify a maximum amount available under a particular grant of legal aid. The policy applied such maximum amounts across the board. It did provide for departures from these fixed fees where a case was 'unusually complex' and the fixed fee was 'completely inadequate'. But these narrow tests were made even more demanding by a further requirement that a case must meet at least two of a specified list of eight features. In practice, exceptions had been made in only 0.04% of cases. The problem thus was the extremely limited scope for discretion left by the policy.[45] We can see, then, that fettering does not have to be absolute to be unlawful.[46]

The degree of permissible fettering depends on the circumstances. Practicalities demand adoption of a policy – albeit one that permits of exceptions – in contexts where there is a large number of applications.[47] In some other contexts, however, any amount of policy guidance may be problematic: each case must be assessed directly against statutory criteria.[48] The nature and importance of the subject matter is a relevant factor. Guidance may also be found in the empowering legislation.

The fettering rule overlaps with several other grounds. We have already seen its overlap with acting under dictation. Further, it is often stated in terms that link it to the right to a hearing: decision-makers with discretionary powers must not shut their ears to applications that fall outside the terms of policy guidelines they have adopted.[49] Similarly, failure to consider the merits of the individual case may also be challenged on grounds of bias in the form of predetermination, or on grounds of failure to take into account mandatory relevant considerations.[50]

Before leaving policy guidelines, we should note two more points. First, undue inflexibility is only one way in which a policy can be inconsistent with the empowering legislation. Any other inconsistency, such as with the legislative purpose, will also render the policy and decisions applying the policy unlawful.

Secondly, compliance with published policies is now enforced, in the absence of good reasons for departure from them, on grounds of substantive legitimate expectations or a duty of consistency.[51] There is an apparent tension between the rule against fettering and this newer doctrine. However, this certainly does not reach the point of contradiction: there is nothing inconsistent in the courts insisting both that decision-makers must be ready to make an exception from a policy and that they should not depart from a policy without good reason.[52]

[45] ibid at [121]–[126].

[46] Similarly, see *Financial Services Complaints Ltd v Chief Ombudsman* [2018] NZCA 27, [2018] 2 NZLR 884.

[47] *Criminal Bar Association* (n 38) at [120].

[48] Discussed in *Practical Shooting Institute (NZ) Inc v Commissioner of Police* [1992] 1 NZLR 709 at 718.

[49] See, eg, *Westhaven Shellfish Ltd v Chief Executive of the Ministry of Fisheries* [2002] 2 NZLR 158 (CA) at [39], [45].

[50] For the latter point, see *Criminal Bar Association* (n 38) at [119].

[51] See Ch 7.C and D.

[52] See Michael Taggart, 'Administrative Law' [2000] *New Zealand Law Review* 439 at 444–45.

C. Unlawful Reasoning

Judicial review on grounds of illegality extends to scrutinising the legality of the reasoning that supports an exercise of discretion. Unlawful reasoning will render a decision unlawful even if was within the scope of an available power, and even if the correct decision-maker exercised discretion in relation to the individual case. In other words, it may well be open to the decision-maker to make the same decision again for different reasons, but the law requires them to exercise their judgement and discretion on the correct legal basis. Unlawful reasoning can take two forms: first, acting for an improper purpose, taking into account irrelevant considerations, or applying the wrong test; and secondly failing to take account of mandatory relevant considerations.

Both forms have the same basis: an aspect of the reasoning is inconsistent with the empowering statute. However, they call for differently structured analysis, as one involves wrong reasons and the other missing reasons. These two forms are therefore discussed in turn in sections (1) and (2), followed by a brief section (3) concerning the types of evidence courts use to find the decision-maker's reasons for a decision.

(1) Improper Purposes, Irrelevant Considerations and Wrong Tests

There is no such thing as an unfettered public power: the exercise of even the most broadly expressed discretion is constrained by the purpose for which the power was granted.[53] This principle was affirmed by the Supreme Court in *Unison Networks*:[54]

> A statutory power is subject to limits even if it is conferred in unqualified terms. Parliament must have intended that a broadly framed discretion should always be exercised to promote the policy and objects of the Act. These are ascertained from reading the Act as a whole. The exercise of the power will be invalid if the decision-maker 'so uses his discretion as to thwart or run counter to the policy and objects of the Act'.

The landmark English authority for this principle is *Padfield*.[55] In most cases where this principle is successfully invoked, it operates to render the decision-maker's reasoning unlawful.[56] Alternative versions of the principle that have the same effect involve irrelevant considerations or the wrong test.

The further point established in the leading *Ireland* case is that an additional unauthorised purpose pursued by a decision-maker is improper only if it is inconsistent with the Act.[57] This was also confirmed by a dictum in *Unison Networks*.[58]

[53] However, provisions expressly conferring 'absolute discretion' are surprisingly common, and the courts do not always demur: Hanna Wilberg, 'Interrogating "Absolute Discretion": Are NZ's Parliament and Courts Compromising the Rule of Law?' (2017) 45 *Federal Law Review* 541.

[54] *Unison Networks Ltd v Commerce Commission* [2007] NZSC 74, [2008] 1 NZLR 42 at [53].

[55] *Padfield v Minister of Agriculture, Fisheries and Food* [1968] AC 997 (HL). The quote within the passage quoted above from *Unison* is from *Padfield* at 1030.

[56] For the exception, see section (a) below, and further discussion in Part D.

[57] *Attorney-General v Ireland* [2002] 2 NZLR 220 (CA).

[58] *Unison Networks* (n 54) at [53].

In exploring this principle, this part addresses the following points: (a) the three versions of the principle; (b) how courts determine what are impermissible (improper or irrelevant) reasons; (c) the element of judicial choice involved in that determination; (d) the special case of inherently improper purposes; (e) the tolerance for unauthorised but not improper additional purposes; (f) the materiality test that applies when there are multiple purposes; and (g) an evaluation of the approach to the last two questions.

(a) The Three Versions of the Principle

Closely related to improper purpose as a ground that renders the reasoning unlawful is the ground of taking into account an irrelevant consideration. The leading New Zealand case on the latter is *Fiordland Venison*.[59] Most textbooks treat these two grounds separately, while noting significant overlap between them.[60] However, they are best understood as largely interchangeable. Some challenged reasons are better described as purposes and others as considerations. However, there is no clear line between the two. More importantly, the distinction entails no consequences. Both involve exercising an available power for impermissible reasons, and the test for determining whether either type of reason is permissible is consistency with the statute. They were applied interchangeably, for example, in the leading *Poananga* case.[61] A difference that is sometimes claimed to exist lies in different materiality tests.[62] However, the materiality tests are the same at least in New Zealand, as we will see.[63]

A complaint that the decision-maker applied the wrong test can also function as a version of irrelevant considerations or improper purpose. In *Unison Networks*, the Court noted the 'considerable' overlap between these grounds.[64] This ground was invoked, for instance in *Hawke's Bay Regional Investment Co.*[65]

The one difference is that improper purposes and wrong tests (unlike irrelevant considerations) can also feature in a different role: rather than representing unlawful reasons, in some cases they go to the scope of the power, as discussed further in Part D. below. Where the impugned exercise of the power is not capable of serving the statutory purpose or of meeting the right test, it is outside the scope of the power. However, where the challenge is to the legality of the decision-maker's reasoning, it makes little difference whether the error is described as an improper purpose, an irrelevant consideration or a wrong test.

[59] *Fiordland Venison Ltd v Minister of Agriculture* [1978] 2 NZLR 341 (CA).

[60] See, eg, Joseph, *Constitutional and Administrative Law* (n 27) ch 23; Graham Taylor, *Judicial Review: A New Zealand Perspective,* 4th edn (Wellington, LexisNexis NZ Ltd, 2018) at 811.

[61] *Poananga v State Services Commission* [1985] 2 NZLR 385 (CA).

[62] GDS Taylor, 'Judicial Review of Improper Purposes and Irrelevant Considerations' [1976] *Cambridge Law Journal* 272 at 289–91.

[63] See (f) below.

[64] *Unison Networks* (n 54) at [50], [76]–[77].

[65] *Hawke's Bay Regional Investment Co Ltd v Royal Forest and Bird Protection Society of New Zealand Inc* [2017] NZSC 106, [2017] 1 NZLR 1041.

(b) What Reasons are Improper or Irrelevant is a Question of Statutory Interpretation

The propriety of purposes, relevance of considerations and correctness of tests is a matter of statutory interpretation. That was affirmed in *Unison Networks*.[66]

Some statutes provide detailed and exhaustive criteria. In that context, interpretation is confined to determining the meaning and application of those express criteria. In *Fiordland Venison*, for instance, the statute required a licence for a game meat-packing house to be granted if five specified criteria were satisfied. The absence of residual discretion rendered the list of criteria exhaustive. Considerations outside those criteria were therefore irrelevant. The Minister's reason for denying the licence was that there was no need for a further game-packing house: the existing houses had sufficient capacity. The only statutory criterion that was in issue was whether the issue of a new licence would have a 'significant detrimental effect on the economic operation' of another establishment. That was a very different test from the one the Minister had applied: the Minister had misconstrued the legislation.[67]

Not all expressly listed criteria are exhaustive. Non-exhaustive formulations can take many forms. These include the addition of a final catch-all phrase, and the list being introduced by permissive or inclusive language. The mere absence of any words to indicate that the express criteria are exhaustive also leaves it at least arguable that other matters may be considered.

Where the listed criteria are open-ended rather than exhaustive, other considerations may be permissible. However, the legislative context may still supply constraints on what reasons are relevant or proper. If there is a common theme running through all the express criteria, then a final catch-all phrase may be interpreted as confined to matters of the same nature – although the courts nowadays stress that the *ejusdem generis* principle to that effect is only one possible guide to interpretation.[68] An open-ended list of criteria may also be accompanied by an express overarching test or purpose. Further unlisted reasons are then permissible only if they are consistent with the overarching test.

Both types of argument can be seen in *Wahrlich v Bates*, concerning a denial of legal aid. The statute provided an open-ended list of specific criteria, along with an overarching question as to whether aid was 'desirable in the interests of justice'. On review, the High Court interpreted that final phrase as referring to justice in the individual case, based in part on what it saw as a theme running through the express criteria. On that basis, the decision-maker's reliance on resource constraints was an irrelevant consideration.[69]

Other statutes confer power in broad and apparently unfettered terms. Such a power was at issue, for instance, in *Padfield*. In such cases, the purpose (or the 'policy

[66] *Unison Networks* (n 54) at [53], quoted above.

[67] *Fiordland Venison* (n 59) at 348, 350, 356–57.

[68] RI Carter, *Burrows and Carter Statute Law in New Zealand*, 6th edn (Wellington, LexisNexis NZ Ltd, 2021) at 300, 331. In *Schmuck v Opua Coastal Preservation Inc* [2019] NZSC 118, [2019] 1 NZLR 750, the Supreme Court appears to question the validity of the principle: at [108], [111].

[69] *Wahrlich v Bate* [1990] 3 NZLR 97 (HC). Criminal legal aid is now governed by the Legal Services Act 2011, interpreted in *Marteley v Legal Services Commissioner* [2015] NZSC 127, [2016] 1 NZLR 633.

and objects') of the power must be 'ascertained from reading the Act as a whole'. Any other reasons are then unlawful if they 'run counter to or thwart' that purpose.[70]

Such implied limits on permissible reasons can be simple and obvious. In the old Canadian case of *Roncarelli*, for instance, the liquor licensing statute did not spell out its purpose, nor any criteria for cancelling a liquor licence. However, the court had little difficulty in concluding that a licence holder's practice of posting bail for Jehovah's Witnesses arrested for pamphleteering was irrelevant to the statute's subject matter and was thus an unlawful reason.[71]

Often, however, more detailed examination of the statute and its context is required. Arguments from the scheme of the statute are commonly used to imply constraints on permissible reasons. For instance, in *Poananga*, the applicant was transferred from her employment with the Ministry of Foreign Affairs to another government department pursuant to an administrative transfer power that involved no hearing or right of appeal. The reasons for the transfer included genuine administrative reasons; but they also included a series of disciplinary complaints. The statute separately provided for transfer as a penalty for disciplinary offences, but that was subject to protections in the form of rights to a hearing and to appeal. The Court held that the administrative power could not be exercised where the purposes included discipline, because that would be inconsistent with the scheme of the statute. It would undermine the additional protections intended for those who faced disciplinary complaints.[72]

Another instance is *Hawke's Bay Regional Investment Co.*[73] The impugned decision revoked the 'conservation park' status of land that was wanted for a proposed dam and instead applied that status to another block of land that was offered in exchange. The Supreme Court struck this down on the grounds that the Minister applied the wrong test. The Minister's reason was that the exchange would result in an overall gain of conservation value – applying a test provided by the Act for exchanging 'stewardship land', a less protected category, for other land. The Court held that the use of this test was inconsistent with the scheme of the Act, which was to accord a higher level of protection to conservation land. The implication from that scheme was that 'conservation park' status could be revoked only on the basis that the land had lost the value that originally led to it being given that special status.

(c) Judicial Choice in Statutory Interpretation

Courts tend to have choices in how to interpret the statute in these cases, particularly where purposes and other constraints are a matter of implication. In some cases, they have upheld decisions by interpreting the statutory purpose broadly and generously

[70] *Padfield* (n 55) at 1030.
[71] *Roncarelli v Duplessis* [1959] SCR 121 (SCC) at 140–41. For an alternative reading, see the text at n 81.
[72] *Poananga* (n 61) at 394.
[73] *Hawke's Bay Regional Investment* (n 65).

and declining to imply a limiting purpose,[74] while in other cases a narrower interpretation of the statutory purpose has led to the decision being found unlawful.[75] Much the same point applies to implied mandatory relevant considerations.

Such choices may be guided by an assessment of the appropriate balance between judicial control and administrative autonomy in the particular context.[76] They may also be influenced by judicial value judgments concerning the subject of the decision.[77] Yet in most cases, neither of these types of further considerations is acknowledged: the courts' reasoning is purely in terms of statutory interpretation.

The influence of judicial value judgements is more blatantly obvious in some old decisions reflecting now-outdated values. In *Roberts v Hopwood*, for instance, the defendant local authority had a statutory power to pay its employees such salaries and wages as it 'may see fit'. Its decision to increase wages beyond the rate of inflation and to apply the same minimum pay rate to both men and women was successfully challenged by ratepayers. For the House of Lords, the implicit proper purpose was to pay a fair wage for the work. The authority was motivated instead by 'some eccentric principles of socialist philanthropy' and by a 'feminist ambition to secure equality of the sexes'.[78]

This entertainingly colourful example can easily be mistaken to imply that judicial reliance on value judgements is illegitimate. That is not its point. There is nothing wrong with courts relying on value judgments where that is necessary for resolving issues that require judicial resolution. And there is certainly nothing wrong with the other type of influence: courts evaluating the appropriate balance between judicial control and administrative autonomy in the particular context. Rather, the point is that it would be preferable for courts to acknowledge the room for judgement and to articulate the choices they make rather than pretend that the answers are dictated by the statute. This issue is explored further in Chapter 9.

(d) Inherently Improper Purposes

Aside from the constraints that flow from the particular statute, certain purposes are never proper purposes for the exercise of public powers. This certainly applies to ulterior private purposes. Pursuit of the decision-maker's private gain, friendship or ill will are always impermissible reasons – even fear for the decision-maker's own safety would be an improper reason.[79] Such inherently improper self-interested motives are not found very often, but the improper purpose in *Stratford Racing Club* came at least close. A controlling faction blackballed new membership applications to retain its

[74] See, eg, *Unison Networks* (n 54) at [65]–[72]; *Canterbury Regional Council v Independent Fisheries Ltd* [2012] NZCA 601, [2013] 2 NZLR 57 at [101], [122].

[75] See, eg, *Wahrlich* (n 69).

[76] See Dean R Knight, *Vigilance and Restraint in the Common Law of Judicial Review* (Cambridge, Cambridge University Press, 2018).

[77] See, eg Paul Craig, *Administrative Law*, 9th edn (Sweet & Maxwell, 2021) at [19-001iii] and ch 19.4 and 19.5.

[78] *Roberts v Hopwood* [1925] AC 579 (HL) at 594, and see at 590, 595.

[79] *R (Corner House Research) v Director of the Serious Fraud Office* [2008] UKHL 60, [2009] 1 AC 756 at [53].

control. That was unlawful because it was contrary to the club's objective to grow its membership, but the Court also considered it arguable that it involved bad faith.[80]

In addition, purposes may also be improper by reference to other general principles. In the old Canadian *Roncarelli* case, the plaintiff's restaurant liquor licence was cancelled because of his practice of posting bail for fellow Jehovah's Witnesses who had been arrested for pamphleteering. If this had been a private vendetta, it would have been an even easier case. But Premier Duplessis who was behind the decision probably considered he was acting in the public interest. The reason why this was still inherently improper was that it amounted to punishing Mr Roncarelli for exercising his legal rights.[81]

The improper purpose of private gain includes political gain in the form of electoral advantage, but in this regard a distinction needs to be drawn. Where powers are conferred on politicians, Parliament is usually taken as having accepted that those powers will be exercised in part with an eye to electoral popularity. Therefore, this is not an improper purpose, provided that it is merely an additional reason for a decision that also pursues the statutory purpose. For instance, declaration of a new marine reserve was not rendered unlawful by the Minister's purpose of wooing the electorate just before an election.[82] In contrast, a clear example of an unlawful ulterior purpose of political gain is seen in *Porter v Magill*. The power to sell social housing stock was used in a deliberate attempt to change the composition of the electorate in marginal wards in the governing conservative party's favour: the sales would result in social housing tenants being replaced by home owners, who were expected to be more likely to vote conservative.[83]

An inherently improper purpose may be seen as an exception to the usual statutory basis for this ground. However, we could also say that it is an aspect of the implied purpose of every statutory power that it must be exercised for public purposes.

(e) Tolerance of Unauthorised but not Improper Additional Purposes: Ireland

There is some controversy over the correct legal response where a decision-maker pursues an unauthorised purpose as well as the statutory purpose. We have seen that courts often have a choice as to how broadly or narrowly to define the statutory purposes. On a broader interpretation, an impugned additional purpose may itself be authorised, and the issue does not arise. However, what if the impugned purpose is outside the scope of the statutory purposes as interpreted by the court, and is therefore an unauthorised additional purpose: does that automatically render it improper, and the decision unlawful? The leading authority on this is *Ireland*,[84] which establishes some tolerance for unauthorised purposes: they are improper only if they are inconsistent with the statute or if the statutory purpose is not being pursued as well.

[80] *Stratford Racing Club Inc v Adlam* [2008] NZCA 92, [2008] NZAR 329 at [58].

[81] *Roncarelli v Duplessis* [1959] SCR 121 (SCC) at 141. This was also one of the reasons in *Wheeler v Leicester City Council* [1985] 1 AC 1054 (HL) at 1079–81 (Lord Templeman).

[82] *R (Bancoult No 3) v Secretary of State for Foreign and Commonwealth Affairs* [2018] UKSC 3.

[83] *Porter v Magill* [2001] UKHL 67, [2002] 2 AC 357 (HL). Lord Bingham distinguished this from the permissible type of political purpose.

[84] *Attorney-General v Ireland* [2002] 2 NZLR 220 (CA).

This section outlines this approach and its implications. The related question as to what materiality test applies in cases of multiple purposes is the subject of the next section. Criticisms of *Ireland* are then addressed in the final section of this part. In my view it represents a valid choice between competing values.[85]

Ireland concerned a decision by the Department of Conservation about the management of a historic reserve.[86] The relevant power was to do 'such … things as may be considered necessary for the proper and beneficial management, administration, and control of the reserve with.[87] The problem was that war-time buildings on the reserve were dilapidated and frequently vandalised, and hence had been fenced off. Coincidentally, the Department also needed premises for its regional headquarters. It decided to kill two birds with one stone: renovating the buildings and fitting them out as its regional offices would both improve the management of the reserve and deal with its own administrative needs. The decision therefore had multiple purposes. One of these was unauthorised because it did not benefit the reserve in question.

The improper purpose challenge failed because the Court held that the additional unauthorised purpose of housing department offices was not improper. In short, this was because the statutory purpose was also served, and the additional purpose was not inconsistent with the statutory purpose and did not frustrate it.[88] Indeed, the additional purpose helped facilitate the resource allocation that was necessary for serving the statutory purpose.[89]

The Court's reasoning in support of that finding can be distilled into two requirements for unauthorised but permissible purposes. First, the statutory purpose must be pursued as well.[90] An unauthorised purpose is therefore permissible *only* if it is an *additional* purpose. Secondly, there must be nothing in the legislation to indicate, either expressly or impliedly, that the additional unauthorised purpose is prohibited.[91] Implied prohibition may be found if the unauthorised purpose is inconsistent with the scheme or purpose of the statute or prejudices or frustrates the purpose.[92]

This approach is consistent with *Padfield*. That decision established two directly corresponding requirements: first that discretion 'should be used to promote the policy and objects of the Act', and secondly that it must not be used to 'thwart or run counter to the policy and objects'.[93] The approach has also been approved by the Supreme Court in *Unison Networks*.[94] While that was obiter, the Court of Appeal has taken the view that any revisiting of the approach must now be by the Supreme Court.[95]

[85] The discussion draws on Hanna Wilberg, 'The *Ireland* Principle on Unauthorised but not Improper Purposes: An Exploration and Defence' [2016] *New Zealand Law Review* 95.

[86] North Head or Maungauika in Auckland, depicted on the cover of this book.

[87] Reserves Act 1977, s 58(d).

[88] A further point, not addressed in the decision, is that the Department's interest in housing its offices was still a public interest and therefore did not fall foul of the prohibition on private purposes. That prohibition would be engaged if officials were seeking to gain an office with a view.

[89] *Ireland* (n 84) at [43]–[45].

[90] ibid at [43], [45].

[91] ibid at [43].

[92] ibid; also at [40], [42], [44].

[93] *Padfield* [1968] AC 997 (n 55) at 1030. It is also consistent with *PF Sugrue Ltd v Attorney-General* [2005] UKPC 44, [2006] 3 NZLR 464 at [20], [23]–[24].

[94] *Unison Networks* (n 54) at [53].

[95] *Criminal Bar Association of New Zealand Inc v Attorney-General* [2013] NZCA 176, [2013] NZAR 1409 at [55].

Furthermore, the *Ireland* approach to unauthorised purposes is also consistent with the long-established approach to irrelevant considerations, and thus further aligns these two grounds. Additional unauthorised considerations have always been tolerated and permissible unless either the statute provides an exhaustive list of criteria or the additional consideration is in some other way inconsistent with the statute.[96]

It will be helpful to explore the operation of each of the two *Ireland* requirements a little further, to see how they limit the tolerance for unauthorised purposes

(i) The Statutory Purpose Must be Pursued as Well: Otherwise Outside the Scope of Power

An unauthorised purpose is permissible *only* if it is an *additional* purpose. Since the statutory purpose must be pursued as well,[97] failure to do so renders the decision unlawful even if the unauthorised purpose would have been permissible as an additional purpose.[98] Discretionary powers 'should be used to promote the policy and objects of the Act'.[99] If the challenged purpose is the *sole* purpose, therefore, the test is whether it is *within* the statutory purpose, not merely whether it is *consistent* with the statute.

Where this first *Ireland* requirement is not met, what invalidates the decision is not so much an impropriety of the unauthorised purpose, but the failure to pursue the proper purpose. That can be understood as engaging different grounds of review. It may still represent unlawful reasoning: at least in some circumstances, it could be seen as failure to take into account mandatory relevant considerations. But it also involves exceeding the scope of the power, the more basic form of illegality: if the statutory purpose is not pursued, the power is not available. That ground is discussed further in Part D.

(ii) The Additional Purpose Must not be Inconsistent with the Statute

The second *Ireland* requirement is that the additional purpose must not be expressly or impliedly prohibited. Express prohibition of additional unauthorised purposes may take the form of an exhaustive list of criteria. *Fiordland Venison* is an example.[100] An express purpose could also be stated in terms indicating that it is exhaustive, but this seems uncommon.[101] Finally, an express purpose might be interpreted as being exhaustive by implication. In such contexts, all purposes are required to fit *within* the statutory purposes or criteria.

[96] See section (b) above, in particular, eg, *Fiordland Venison* (n 59); *Wahrlich v Bate* (n 69).

[97] *Ireland* (n 84) at [43], [45] may suggest an even stronger requirement that the purpose be 'achieved' or 'satisfied'. In support of the lesser requirement, see *Unison Networks* (n 54) at [69], [71] and [72].

[98] See also, eg, *R v Secretary of State for Foreign and Commonwealth Affairs ex p World Development Movement Ltd* [1995] 1 WLR 386 (QBD) at 401–3 (accounts of the case that treat the political purpose as necessarily irrelevant or improper are erroneous).

[99] *Padfield* (n 55) at 1030.

[100] *Fiordland Venison* (n 59); discussed above at n 67.

[101] An example may perhaps be found in the Canterbury Earthquake Recovery Act 2011, s 10(1) but the wording 'in accordance with the purposes of the Act' is not unambiguously exhaustive.

The more common basis on which an unauthorised additional purpose will be unlawful, however, is what *Ireland* calls implied prohibition. This will be found where the additional purpose is in some way inconsistent with the statute. It raises the range of statutory interpretation questions discussed earlier. As noted earlier, there tends to be room for judgement in this regard.

It will often be arguable that the addition of a non-statutory purpose thwarts or prejudices pursuit of the statutory purpose.[102] This therefore is a significant limit on the tolerance for unauthorised additional purposes. The thwarting of the statutory purpose is obvious in cases where the additional purpose pulls in the opposite direction. For instance, in *New Zealand Milk Corporation*, the Corporation had a statutory power to grant its contractors exclusive zones for milk delivery. This was under transitional legislation that required continuation of home delivery as a 'vital feature' but was due to expire shortly to give way to a less regulated regime. That power could not be used to institute a new system that was in part designed to facilitate a reduction in home deliveries *before* the expiry of the legislation.[103] But inconsistency with the statutory purpose is by no means confined to such obvious cases. Where the statute requires the decision-maker to balance competing purposes or considerations, any additional unauthorised purpose may affect the balance struck and thus prejudice the pursuit of the statutory purposes.

Alternatively, the inconsistency may not be with the statutory purpose but with the broader scheme of the statute, or with a theme running through express criteria. *Ireland* discussed *Poananga* as an example in which pursuit of an additional unauthorised purpose undermined a statutory scheme of protection for affected interests.[104]

Finally, there is no mention in *Ireland* of the inherently improper purposes discussed earlier,[105] but they must be equally improper even if they are additional purposes.

(f) Materiality Tests in Cases of Multiple Purposes

A question of materiality arises where the challenged decision was made for multiple purposes, not all of which are improper or irrelevant: how material does the improper or irrelevant purpose have to be to invalidate the decision? Another way of thinking about this is that even improper purposes will be tolerated if they are insufficiently material to the decision.

This is an unsettled and confused area of the law. As many as six possible materiality tests have been identified for improper purpose cases, ranging from an enquiry into either the 'true' or the 'dominant' purpose, to a 'but for' test, to the position that the mere presence of an unauthorised or improper purpose always invalidates a decision.[106]

[102] *Ireland* (n 84) at [40], [42]–[44].
[103] *New Zealand Milk Corp Ltd v McDonald* [1993] 2 NZLR 543 at 546, 549.
[104] *Poananga* (n 61); *Ireland* (n 84) at [36] and [43].
[105] See (d) above.
[106] Harry Woolf and others, *De Smith's Judicial Review*, 8th edn (London, Sweet & Maxwell, 2018) at [5-119] ff (this list no longer appears in the 9th edn); Taylor, *Judicial Review* (n 60) at [15.65].

The issue arose in *Ireland*, but unfortunately the decision does not reach any explicit conclusions on the choice of materiality test.[107] The position in New Zealand therefore has to be gathered in the first instance from earlier authority. In addition, we need to consider whether following *Ireland*, the newly recognised distinction between improper purposes and unauthorised but permissible purposes entails any change to the materiality tests.

Prior to *Ireland*, the leading case was *Poananga*,[108] which established a 'but for' test for improper purposes. The effect of this test is not often clearly spelt out, but it is clear from a closer reading of this decision. Recall that a decision to transfer a public servant to another department was found to be unlawful because one of the purposes was disciplinary, and that was an improper purpose in the context. Cooke J noted that the decision would still be lawful if it could be shown that 'but for' the disciplinary purpose, the decision would have been the same. He went on to say that this would apply only if this improper purpose was 'put entirely aside'.[109] Furthermore, the onus is clearly on the defendant. Hence the test amounts to a presumption of materiality.

The materiality test for irrelevant considerations is often discussed separately. An irrelevant consideration invalidates a decision unless the judge is confident that it made no difference to the decision.[110] Like the 'but for' test for improper purposes, that test amounts to a presumption of materiality. The two tests are the same.

Following *Ireland*, the question arises whether this decision has resulted in any change to the materiality test for improper purposes, and also whether any such test applies even to an unauthorised but permissible purpose. Concerning improper purpose in the new narrower sense (excluding unauthorised but permissible purposes), there is nothing in *Ireland* to suggest a departure from the established 'but for' test. This test remains an appropriate basis for tolerating even such truly improper purposes. If a decision-maker can rebut the presumption of materiality and persuade the court that the improper purpose had no material influence on the decision at all, then there can be no objection to letting the decision stand. That view is also consistent with *Poananga*. The additional purpose that invalidated the decision in that case was not only unauthorised but truly improper (although that distinction had not yet been recognised): it cut across the statutory scheme for protecting the interests affected.[111] The 'but for' test was established in this case as the limited basis for tolerating such truly improper purposes. Some cases since *Ireland* have persisted in stating this as the test.[112]

Turning to unauthorised purposes, no materiality test is needed where such a purpose is permissible. However, recall that the first requirement in *Ireland* is that the statutory purpose must also be pursued: an unauthorised purpose is not tolerated if it is the sole purpose. It turns out that one of the old materiality tests is to much the same

[107] It mentions the six possible tests: *Ireland* (n 84) at [39].

[108] *Poananga* (n 61).

[109] ibid at 393–95; see also at 398.

[110] *Poananga* (n 61) at 398 where Somers J analysed the case in terms of irrelevant considerations; *Wahrlich v Bate* (n 69) at 12.

[111] *Poananga* ibid.

[112] See, eg, *Avowal Administrative Attorneys Ltd v District Court at North Shore* [2010] 2 NZLR 794 (HC) at [30].

effect but involves a slight enhancement of this requirement. The 'true' purpose test concerns the materiality not of an additional purpose but of the statutory purpose: the latter must be a 'true' purpose, in the sense that it must not be a mere pretext.[113] Arguably this should still apply as a limit to the tolerance for unauthorised additional purposes. That is essentially what has also been proposed by Kós J as an addition to the *Ireland* requirements. He considered that an additional unauthorised purpose must invalidate a decision if it 'subverts' the statutory purpose in the sense that the statutory purpose is mere 'window-dressing'.[114] That is another way of stating the old 'true' purpose test.

To summarise the position outlined in this section and the previous one, a purpose additional to the statutory purpose is tolerated in New Zealand in two situations. The first is when the additional purpose is merely unauthorised but not improper, and the statutory purpose is also being pursued. Courts may further require the statutory purpose to be a true purpose rather than a mere pretext. The second is when the additional purpose is a truly improper purpose (one that is inconsistent with the empowering Act), but the court is satisfied that the decision would have been the same without ('but for') that additional purpose.

(g) Evaluation of the Ireland *Approach*

The *Ireland* approach has been criticised in some quarters. Philip Joseph has argued that tolerating unauthorised purposes is unprincipled and compromises the rule of law.[115] In my view, however, *Ireland* is perfectly defensible in terms of the rule of law – it simply represents the choice of a weaker version of the relevant rule of law principle than the strong version implied by Joseph's objection.[116]

The relevant rule of law principle is that government must be subject to law. Joseph's position implies that this requires all government action, including the purposes pursued, to be *positively authorised* by law: a very strong version. *Ireland*, on the other hand, is consistent with a weaker version of the same principle: even if government action itself must be positively authorised, the purposes pursued are unlawful only if they are *contrary* to or *inconsistent* with the law, or if the lawful purposes are not being pursued at all.

Competing values and objectives are at play here. The strong version prioritises protecting the liberty of those who are constrained or burdened by exercises of public power. The weaker version gives greater weight to the effective discharge of public authorities' responsibilities under the various administrative regimes of regulation, welfare or public provision. There is no right answer to this: striking the balance comes down to a fundamental value judgement.

[113] *Westminster Corporation v London and North Western Railway Co* [1905] AC 426 (HL) at 432; *R v Governors of Brixton Prison ex parte Soblen* [1963] 2 QB 243.

[114] *Back Country Helicopters Ltd v Minister of Conservation* [2013] 1 NZAR 1474 (HC) at [171].

[115] Joseph, *Constitutional and Administrative Law* (n 27) at 1005–07. See also Dean Knight, 'Importation and Indigeneity: The Quartet in New Zealand Administrative Law' in TT Arvind and others (eds), *Executive Decision-Making and the Courts: Revisiting the Origins of Judicial Review* (Oxford, Hart Publishing, 2019).

[116] Wilberg, 'The *Ireland* Principle' (n 85) Part III.

If *Ireland*'s tolerance of unauthorised purposes is accepted as striking the better balance, a further point of detail may still be open to debate. This concerns the role of the 'dominant' purpose test. *Ireland* must be taken as having rejected this test as a limit on toleration of unauthorised purposes. Accepting such a limit (which may be the position in England) would represent something of a half-way house between the strong and weak version of the rule of law principle. One practical objection was noted in *Ireland*: the 'difficulty for the Courts of speculating about the weight actually given to particular purposes'.[117]

(2) Mandatory Relevant Considerations

Failure to take account of mandatory relevant considerations is the companion ground to irrelevant considerations and improper purposes and takes the obverse form: instead of the inclusion of an impermissible reason, here a required reason is missing. What both types of grounds have in common is that they concern the legality of the decision-maker's reasoning rather than of the outcome. In the case of mandatory relevant considerations, it may well be open to the decision-maker to make the same decision again on the basis that the mandatory consideration is outweighed by other relevant considerations. However, the law requires them to turn their mind to the mandatory consideration and to weigh it in the balance.

This part explores the mandatory relevant consideration ground, addressing the following points: (a) its statutory basis, (b) the qualification that some mandatory considerations are imported from sources external to the empowering statute, (c) the intermediate category of permissible but not mandatory considerations, (d) the need for decision-makers who delegate preparatory work to receive and personally consider an adequate summary of mandatory considerations, (e) that the weight to be accorded to mandatory decisions is for the decision-maker, but genuine consideration must be given to them, and (f) the applicable materiality test.

(a) Statutory Basis of this Ground, Express or Implied

As with irrelevant considerations and improper purposes, the usual basis of this ground is statutory interpretation. A consideration will be mandatory if it is provided as such by the statute either expressly or by implication.

Express statements of matters that must be taken into account are not uncommon in empowering statutes. An example is found in the fisheries legislation that was at issue in *New Zealand Fishing Industry Association*.[118] In deciding on the amount of resource rentals to be paid for fishing quotas, the Minister was expressly directed to have regard to a list of matters, including two potentially competing criteria (trading value of the quota and net returns achieved by quota holders) as well as submissions received from

[117] *Ireland* (n 84) at [39].

[118] *New Zealand Fishing Industry Association Inc v Minister of Agriculture and Fisheries* [1988] 1 NZLR 544 (CA).

the industry. Express mandatory considerations often raise issues concerning their interpretation.[119]

A mandatory relevant consideration derived by implication featured in *Simes*.[120] This was a successful judicial review challenge to a decision to cancel a legal practitioner's listing as an approved provider for clients with legal aid, on grounds including failure to take account of a mandatory relevant consideration. There had previously been an audit of Ms Simes' practice under the same Act. The report from that audit noted three missed court appearances, but commented favourably on ten randomly selected files. This report, including particularly the favourable part of it, was held to be an implied mandatory consideration for a number of reasons: it was prepared under the same Act to address the same issues as the cancellation decision (namely quality and value of services); there was a statutory relationship between audit and cancellation of listing; and the contents of the report were clearly relevant and important to the cancellation decision. In short, the report was relevant to the subject matter of the decision, and its relevance was further supported by implication from the scheme of the Act. There tends to be room for judgement in deciding whether to imply mandatory considerations.

When there is a right to a hearing or a duty to consult, this gives rise to an implication that the resulting submissions are a mandatory relevant consideration.[121] This was affirmed in *Air Nelson*. The airline's challenge to new landing fees set by the Minister succeeded because its submissions had not been adequately conveyed to the Minister.[122]

Where a decision-maker has failed to consider submissions, this can be challenged on several different grounds. The ground which the Court in *Air Nelson* considered most appropriate was failure to take account of a mandatory relevant consideration. But the point had also been put in terms of mistake of fact, abdication of discretion and right to a hearing, and the Court did not dismiss any of these as necessarily inappropriate.[123] In *New Zealand Fishing Industry Association*, a closely related point was also put in terms of bias in the form of predetermination: when a party has a right to be consulted and has made submissions in exercise of that right, then the decision-maker must not have a closed mind when considering those submissions.[124]

(b) Qualification: External Sources of Rights as Mandatory Considerations

There is an important qualification to the statutory basis for mandatory relevant considerations. Those who are subject to decisions may have relevant rights under te Tiriti o Waitangi,[125] international law or the NZ Bill of Rights Act 1990 that are

[119] See, eg, *Auckland Council v CP Group Ltd* [2023] NZSC 53, [2023] 1 NZLR 35 at [62]–[69]; *West Coast ENT Inc v Buller Coal Ltd* [2013] NZSC 87, [2014] 1 NZLR 32.

[120] *Secretary for Justice v Simes* [2012] NZCA 459, [2012] NZAR 1044 at [55].

[121] Sometimes the submissions are expressly listed as a mandatory relevant consideration: see, eg, the legislation at issue in *NZ Fishing Industry Association* (n 118) at 547.

[122] *Air Nelson Ltd v Minister of Transport* [2008] NZAR 139 (CA) at [39]–[56].

[123] ibid at [36], [55].

[124] *NZ Fishing Industry Association* (n 118) at 552, 558–61, 566–67.

[125] The Treaty of Waitangi; the Māori language version is given greater weight, and the convention is to refer to this by the Māori name.

impacted by the decision. An important New Zealand innovation is that one of the range of ways in which all three sources can be given effect is by importing them into statutory powers, where they are relevant, as mandatory relevant considerations.[126] Interpretation of the empowering statute still plays a role in this context, but only as a constraint rather than as the basis for the mandatory consideration: the implication of such externally derived mandatory considerations is available only where that is not inconsistent with the empowering statute.

(c) Not All Relevant Considerations are Mandatory: Some are Merely Permissible

It is important to add that not all relevant considerations are mandatory, as established in *CREEDNZ*.[127] An express list of relevant considerations is mandatory only if it is stated in mandatory terms. Where a relevant consideration is implied, it is a further and separate question whether the statute also clearly implies that the consideration is mandatory. In other words, there is an intermediate category of considerations which are permissible – neither irrelevant nor mandatory: it is up to the decision-maker whether to take these into account.

A related question is whether impliedly mandatory considerations may extend beyond criteria, questions or issues to be addressed, and may include particular facts and evidence going to those questions. There is conflicting authority on this. One authority against it is *Lewis v Wilson & Horton*, a challenge to a name suppression order for an accused. The judge had taken into account the impact on the accused's reputation but was unaware of a relevant fact in that regard. The Court of Appeal dismissed a challenge on that ground: only the question of reputation was mandatory to consider, not the facts going to that question.[128]

Other cases, however, have accepted that particular relevant facts or evidence can be mandatory. For instance, the report that was held to be an implied mandatory consideration in *Simes* is an instance of particular evidence being found to be mandatory.[129] *Quake Outcasts* was a successful challenge to the decision to make lower offers for government buy-outs of uninsured properties in the red zone following the Canterbury earthquakes. The Supreme Court accepted that insurance status was relevant but held it should not have been determinative. Several other relevant facts were mandatory to consider as well, such as that insurance was unavailable for some types of properties, and that the government offer for many insured properties exceeded their insured value.[130]

[126] *Huakina Development Trust v Waikato Valley Authority* [1987] 2 NZLR 188 (HC); *Tavita v Minister of Immigration* [1994] 2 NZLR 257 (CA); *New Health New Zealand Incorporated v Director-General of Health* [2023] NZHC 3183. For further discussion, see Ch 6.

[127] *CREEDNZ v Governor-General* [1981] 1 NZLR 172 (CA) at 183. Adopted for the UK in *In re Findlay* [1985] 1 AC 318 (HL).

[128] *Lewis v Wilson & Horton Ltd* [2000] 3 NZLR 546 (CA) at [90]. Nor did this amount to a reviewable mistake of fact: ibid at [92].

[129] *Simes* (n 120) at [55].

[130] *Quake Outcasts v Minister for Canterbury Earthquake Recovery* [2015] NZSC 27, [2016] 1 NZLR 1 at [152]–[171], [187]–[188].

(d) Decision-makers May Delegate Investigation, but Must Receive Adequate Summary

We have already seen that decision-makers may delegate the process of hearing affected parties, and more generally of gathering and processing relevant evidence, but they must then receive a sufficiently detailed report setting out all the salient points from the evidence and submissions. When that has not happened, the decision may be challenged for failure to take account of mandatory relevant considerations, or alternatively for mistake of fact, or for breach of the right to a hearing or consultation.[131]

The issue, then, is how much information needs to be considered by the decision-maker personally. *Air Nelson*[132] was a successful challenge to a Minister's decision to increase airport landing charges for a regional airport. The Court accepted that there was a duty to consult airlines. Air Nelson's submissions opposing the increase had been received only by officials advising the Minister. The summary prepared for the Minister was insufficient. It omitted all relevant context, including the flaws in an earlier aborted decision and the airline's plans to introduce larger planes which would attract higher charges without any increase in the current rates.

If mandatory considerations can extend to facts and evidence other than submissions, that similarly raises questions as to the level of detail that must be considered by decision-makers personally rather than merely by those advising them. In *CREEDNZ*, the Court of Appeal said that some matters will be 'so obviously material' to a decision that anything short of direct consideration by the decision-maker will be unlawful.[133] The issue was not further discussed in that case. But this dictum has been applied in other cases where facts pleaded as mandatory were held to be too specific to require the Minister's personal attention.[134]

There has been some confusion about this. The requirement to adequately inform decision-makers has been challenged on the ground that the knowledge of officials can simply be imputed to the decision-maker. This argument erroneously invokes a dictum by Lord Diplock in *Bushell* to the effect that the collective knowledge of civil servants in a department is to be treated as the minister's own knowledge.[135] The erroneous use of this dictum in this context goes back to older leading cases such as *CREEDNZ*. But those cases also support the requirement to adequately inform the decision-maker. They invoke the *Bushell* dictum, but subject to the qualification that the crucial considerations must be considered by the decision-maker personally.[136]

In *Air Nelson*, the objection that such personal consideration is not required was rightly rejected.[137] In keeping with the older cases, however, the Court failed to question the relevance of the *Bushell* dictum.[138] For a persuasive explanation as to why

[131] *Air Nelson* (n 122) at [36], [53]; *Peko-Wallsend* (n 30) at 30–31, 44–46; see further, text at nn 29–32.

[132] *Air Nelson* (n 122).

[133] *CREEDNZ* (n 127) at 183.

[134] See *State Housing Action Inc v Minister of Housing* [2016] NZHC 2924, [2017] 2 NZLR 281 at [32]–[52].

[135] *Bushell v Secretary of State for the Environment* [1981] AC 75 (HL) at 95.

[136] *CREEDNZ* (n 127) at 183, 200–01; *NZ Fishing Industry Association* (n 118) at 567.

[137] *Air Nelson* (n 122) at [41]–[54]; see also *Peko-Wallsend* (1986) 66 ALR 229 (HCA) at 30–31.

[138] For another problem, see text at n 35. The reliance on a different dictum from *Bushell* (n135) at 97 is less problematic (but also taken out of context): *Air Nelson* (n 122) at [45], [48], [53].

this is not relevant, we can turn to Sedley LJ in *National Association of Health* Stores. The dictum is properly understood as addressed instead to an aspect of procedural fairness: whether departmental advice received by a minister must be disclosed to affected parties for comment.[139]

The substantive merits of the objection were also addressed by Sedley LJ: the argument was 'unsound in law' and 'antithetical to good government'. It would entail 'either a de facto abdication' by the decision-maker or 'a division of labour in which the person with knowledge decides nothing and the decision is taken by a person without knowledge'.[140] The UK Supreme Court confirmed this point in *Tooth*, albeit the issue arose in a different context: 'There is no principle of collective knowledge within a department.'[141] A Minister may delegate the decision itself, as we have seen. However, where the Minister retains that power and delegates only the preparatory work, then the Minister as decision-maker must be aware of the crux of all submissions and other information going to mandatory considerations.

(e) The Weight is for the Decision-maker, but Genuine Consideration is Required

How mandatory considerations apply in the particular case and how they should be weighed against each other can be highly contentious and very much matters of evaluation. In *New Zealand Fishing Industry Association*,[142] for instance, there was tension between the two mandatory criteria for setting fishing quota resource rentals, trading values and net returns. This was at the heart of the dispute between the industry and the Minister. A rental based on trading values might be significantly higher than one based on net returns. It would not be appropriate for courts in judicial review to take sides in such disputes.

That is why the courts have made it clear that the weight to be assigned to mandatory relevant considerations is entirely a matter for the decision-maker, within the limits of reason.[143] The subject of scrutiny on this ground is confined to whether the consideration in issue is legally mandatory and, if so, whether it has, in fact, been ignored or excluded from consideration.[144] In the *Fishing Industry Association* case, therefore, the fact that the Minister's focus had been very much on trading values did not invalidate the decision. There was just enough evidence to satisfy the Court that net returns had also been taken into account.[145]

[139] *R (National Association of Health Stores) v Department of Health* [2005] EWCA Civ 154 at [33]; see also at [72]. For the same reason, the *Bushell* dictum is also not authority for decision-makers being free to delegate investigation, contrary to Joseph, *Constitutional and Administrative Law* (n 27) at 1048, 1051. *Daganayasi v Minster of Immigration* [1980] 2 NZLR 130 (CA) at 142–43 correctly discussed the *Bushell* dictum on the disclosure issue: see Ch 4.B.(1)(a).

[140] *National Association of Health Stores* (n139) at [26]; see also *Peko-Wallsend* (n 137) at 30–31.

[141] *Revenue and Customs Commissioners v Tooth* [2021] UKSC 17, [2021] 1 WLR 2811 at [70].

[142] *New Zealand Fishing Industry Association* (n 118).

[143] ibid at 522.

[144] For an example of undisputedly mandatory considerations not in fact taken into account, due to misunderstanding the statute, see *Enterprise Miramar Peninsula Inc v Wellington City Council* [2018] NZCA 541, [2019] 2 NZLR 501.

[145] *New Zealand Fishing Industry Association* (n 118) at 557.

The weight accorded to a relevant consideration is reviewed only if it was entirely unreasonable; and if so, the ground of review is *Wednesbury* unreasonableness.[146] For instance, the Supreme Court in *Marteley* struck down a denial of legal aid as unreasonable. The Tribunal's decision had been dominated by its assessment of the appeal as lacking merit. It had given scant attention to other mandatory factors, in particular the seriousness of the charge and the appellant's inability to effectively present his case.[147]

Wrong weight may, however, also amount to applying the wrong test and hence illegality. That will be so if the statute specifies the weight of considerations expressly[148] or by implication, and the decision-maker has failed to understand and apply this. This may provide an alternative explanation of *Marteley*. On the Supreme Court's interpretation of the criminal legal aid provision, the merits of the appeal were relevant but not decisive or even dominant: they had to be weighed against the other listed considerations. To the extent that the Tribunal failed to understand this aspect of the legislation, its decision was affected by illegality.

Finally, the courts have also made it clear that mandatory considerations must be given genuine consideration.[149] Exactly what that means and how it is determined is not very well settled. There is a tension here between courts avoiding merits review on the one hand, and not allowing the reasoning obligation to be satisfied by a mere box-ticking exercise on the other.

An example that falls at the interventionist end of the spectrum in this regard is the application of the genuine consideration requirement in *Simes*, the case concerning cancellation of legal aid provider approval. As we have seen, the predominantly favourable findings in an earlier practice audit report were mandatory considerations. There were only two indications in the written decision that the audit report had been taken into account: the decision mentioned the one negative aspect of the report, and the report was included in a list of matters taken into account. The Court was not satisfied that the favourable parts of the report had been given any genuine consideration. It was necessary for the decision to refer specifically to these parts, to discuss their significance, and to give reasons for discounting them.[150]

This represents a significantly stronger version of the genuine consideration requirement than the version in *New Zealand Fishing Industry Association*.[151] There, the court was prepared to infer from quite slight evidence that some consideration had been given to net returns in setting the resource rental. The approach in *Simes* might be better described as requiring the decision-maker to *demonstrate* that consideration has been given. It is unclear how this approach would work in cases where no reasons have been given at all, given that there is no general duty to give reasons.[152]

[146] *Associated Provincial Picture Houses Ltd v Wednesbury Corporation* [1948] 1 KB 223 (CA); see Chapter 7.A. The shift in grounds is spelt out in *Peko-Wallsend* (n137) at 310; *Tesco Stores Ltd v Secretary of State for the Environment* [1995] 1 WLR 759 (HL) at 764.

[147] *Marteley v Legal Services Commissioner* [2015] NZSC 127, [2016] 1 NZLR 633 at [75]–[77]; this is not expressly put in terms of *Wednesbury* unreasonableness.

[148] See, eg, the express ranking of considerations in s 34(1) of the Housing Accords and Special Housing Areas Act 2013, at issue in *Enterprise Miramar Peninsula* (n 144) at [32]–[59].

[149] *NZ Fishing Industry Association* (n 118) at 552.

[150] *Simes* [2012] NZCA 459 (n 120) at [58]–[63]. See also the obiter dictum in *H (SC 104/2020) v Minister of Immigration* [2021] NZSC 192 at [31] fn 27.

[151] *NZ Fishing Industry Association* (n 118) at 557.

[152] See discussion below at n 162, and in Ch 4.F.

(f) Materiality Test

As with irrelevant considerations and improper purposes, a challenge for failure to take account of a mandatory relevant consideration can fail where the consideration was insufficiently material. However, as with these other grounds, materiality is not a high hurdle. This was affirmed in *Simes*. It is certainly not necessary to show that consideration of the mandatory matter would have led to a different decision. It is sufficient that the matter was clearly important and hence there was a 'realistic prospect' that it might have made a difference.[153] That formulation was sufficient to dispose of this case. When anything turns on it, courts might well be prepared to adopt an even lower threshold formulation. There is no reason why the presumption of materiality that we saw in relation to irrelevant considerations and improper purposes should not apply here. On that approach, failure to take account of a mandatory relevant consideration would invalidate a decision unless the court is satisfied that it could not have made any difference.

(3) What if No Reasons are Given?

The unlawful reasoning grounds presuppose that the decision-maker's reasons are before the court. Yet the law requires decision-makers to give reasons only in some contexts.[154] Decision-makers are encouraged to explain their reasons to the court in judicial review proceedings by filing an affidavit, but this, too, is not a legal obligation.[155] There are, however, fairly extensive obligations under the Official Information Act to give reasons for decisions and to disclose information, both on request,[156] and the courts can order the discovery of relevant documents.[157]

In the absence of a statement of reasons, courts will draw inferences from the documents and the circumstances as to what considerations have been taken into account. The most obvious inference to draw is that the decision-maker's reasons included any reasons that appear in advice which was received and followed by the decision-maker.[158] Further, a decision-maker who declines to give reasons runs the risk of an adverse inference if all of the available information points to a reasoning flaw.[159] However, in at least some cases, the courts have been willing to draw favourable inferences from fairly slight evidence.[160]

This reliance on inferences has its limits. The documentary evidence does not always include a clear statement of advice that was followed, or where such a statement exists it may be complicated by other features of the evidence. In some cases, there may be very little documentary evidence; especially where the Official Information Act does

[153] *Simes* (n 120) at [64]–[65].
[154] See Ch 4.F.
[155] *Fiordland Venison* (n 59) at 345–46; *NZ Fishing Industry Association* (n 118) at 554, 568; *Ririnui v Landcorp Farming Ltd* [2016] NZSC 62, [2016] 1 NZLR 1056 at [105].
[156] Official Information Act 1982, esp ss 5, 12 and 23.
[157] Taylor, *Judicial Review* (n 60) at [10.11]–[10.15].
[158] See, eg, *Fiordland Venison* (n 59) at 347.
[159] See, eg, ibid at 350; *Ririnui* (n155) at [105]. This is sometimes referred to as a duty of candour.
[160] Eg *New Zealand Fishing Industry Association* (n 118) at 555–57, 562, 568.

not apply, such as with private associations. Improper purposes may not be inferred from the mere fact that there is no obvious good reason for a decision.[161]

It is also not clear whether or how a strong requirement of genuine consideration as seen in *Simes*[162] could be applied in a case where no reasons had been stated, and where no clear document setting out the advice given to the decision-maker was available. It is clearly undesirable that decision-makers should find it easier to defend a challenge when they decline to state their reasons. The *Padfield* answer to this objection was that courts will draw inferences where no reasons are given,[163] but that must surely be a less effective basis for enforcing a strong requirement of genuine consideration.

To add to the uncertainty in this area, on the question of affidavits there is also a conflicting line of authority. In *Taylor*, for instance, the Court of Appeal held that decision-makers will not be permitted to explain their reasons in an affidavit. '[T]he general rule is that judicial review proceedings are determined on the basis of the material before the decision-maker at the time of the decision', and decision-makers 'must refrain from descending into ex post facto justification.'[164] This makes sense where the decision-maker is under a justificatory obligation, so that a lack of contemporaneous explanation will rebound against the decision-maker.[165] *Taylor* was such a case: it involved a Bill of Rights Act challenge, where the onus of justification under section 5 is on the Crown.[166] In contexts where there is no such justificatory obligation, judicial scrutiny would be even further compromised by this approach than it already is by the lack of a right to reasons.

D. Outside the Scope of the Power

The most basic form of illegality is acting beyond the scope of the relevant power: making a decision which the legislation relied on does not authorise. The decision-maker will have misinterpreted or overlooked some relevant limit to their power. The limit may take one of three forms. It may be an express limit in the empowering legislation, implied from that legislation, or found in the general law beyond that legislation. Thanks to the latter two forms, the scope of even the most broadly worded powers can sometimes be made subject to some limits.

An example involving the first type of limit would be a school board purporting to expel a student under the age of 16. For students at that age, the legislation only

[161] See Michael Taggart, 'Administrative Law' [2006] *New Zealand Law Review* 75 at 89–91, discussing *Hopper v North Shore Aero Club* [2007] NZAR 354 (CA).

[162] *Simes* [2012] NZCA 459 (n 120) at [58]–[63], discussed above at n 150.

[163] *Padfield* [1968] AC 997 (n 55) at 1032–33.

[164] *Taylor v The Chief Executive of the Department of Corrections* [2015] NZCA 477, [2015] NZAR 1648 at [33]–[39].

[165] This is the general position in Canada, and decision-makers there are generally confined to the contemporaneous record: see Paul Daly, '*Vavilov* and the Culture of Justification in Contemporary Administrative Law' (2021) 100 *Supreme Court Law Review (2d)* 279 at 283–88; discussing *Canada (Minister of Citizenship and Immigration) v Vavilov* 2019 SCC 65, [2019] 4 SCR 653.

[166] See Ch 6.D.

provides for them to be excluded and required to enrol elsewhere – expulsion is available only for older students.[167] The board in such a case would have overlooked or misunderstood this express limit in the empowering legislation.

The second type, implied limits, may flow from the purpose of the legislation or more generally from its scheme and context. As to purpose, a power must be used 'to promote the policy and objects of the Act'.[168] A purported exercise of a power is unlawful if it is not reasonably capable of being regarded as serving those purposes.[169] The scope of some powers is explicitly defined by reference to their purpose.[170] For instance, the scope of compulsory purchase powers is defined by their public purpose: they are not available unless this purpose is pursued, as seen in *Seaton*.[171] Similarly, in *Trans-Tasman Resources* the relevant purpose provision for a power to grant resource consents included one purpose that was held to impose a bottom line, based on its wording and context. If this purpose of protection against material harm could not be achieved, the power was not available.[172] This type of challenge could be brought under the heading of improper purpose, but it concerns the scope of the power rather than the lawfulness of the reasoning. In *Seaton*, the Supreme Court considered that nothing was added by putting this argument in terms of improper purpose.[173]

Broader powers without such an obvious purpose may still be confined by implication from the scheme and context of the legislation. For instance, in *Palestine Solidarity Campaign* the UK Supreme Court held that the Secretary of State's power to issue 'guidance' to local authority pension fund administrators could not be used to prohibit investment policies in the nature of boycotts or divestment. Permissible guidance was limited to *how* to make investment choices, not *what* choices to make. Lord Wilson inferred this limit from a theme running through both the empowering regulations and the provisions of the Act that set out a non-exhaustive list of purposes for which regulations were authorised.[174]

This is also one of the tools available for confining broad powers to make delegated legislation.[175] It may not work if the power is too broad and unconfined. A notorious example is section 11 of the Economic Stabilisation Act 1948, which authorised such regulations as appeared 'necessary or expedient for the general purpose of this Act'. That 'general purpose' according to section 3 was 'to promote the economic stability of New Zealand'. When the Muldoon government in the 1970s and 1980s imposed wage and price freezes and car-less days pursuant to this provision, nearly all attempts at legal challenge failed, due to the great breadth of the statutory purpose.[176]

[167] Education and Training Act 2020, ss 81–83.

[168] *Padfield v Minister of Agriculture, Fisheries and Food* [1968] AC 997 (HL) at 1030.

[169] *New Zealand Drivers' Association v New Zealand Road Carriers* [1982] 1 NZLR 374 (CA) at 388.

[170] See, eg, *Astrazeneca Ltd v Commerce Commission* [2009] NZSC 92, [2010] 1 NZLR 297 at [39].

[171] *Seaton v Minister for Land Information* [2013] NZSC 42, [2013] 3 NZLR 157 at [23], [48] and [71].

[172] *Trans-Tasman Resources v Taranaki-Whanganui Conservation Board* [2021] NZSC 127, [2021] 1 NZLR 801 at [239]–[263], [302], [315]–[317].

[173] *Seaton* (n 171) at [38].

[174] *R (Palestine Solidarity Campaign Ltd) v Secretary of State for Housing, Communities and Local Government* [2020] UKSC 16, [2020] 1 WLR 1774 at [26]–[27], [31].

[175] See, eg, *New Zealand Animal Law Association v Attorney-General* [2020] NZHC 3009 at [139]–[147].

[176] See, eg, *New Zealand Drivers' Association* (n 169); *Brader v MOT* [1981] 1 NZLR 73.

However, courts sometimes find ways of confining very broadly expressed powers by interpreting them in context. For instance, *Reade v Smith* struck down regulations providing for the forced transfer of students to new schools to address overcrowding.[177] The two relevant powers were to make regulations for any purposes considered 'necessary in order to secure the due administration' of the Act, or 'necessary or expedient for avoiding any doubt or difficulty' in the administration of the Act due to any omission or inconsistency in it. Measures pursuant to the latter power were given 'the force of law, anything to the contrary in the principal Act notwithstanding'. That amounted to a so-called 'Henry VIII' clause, providing for delegated legislation to override primary legislation.

The Court held that in construing such an extraordinary provision, it must strive for a restricted interpretation:[178] Parliament cannot have intended to issue a 'blank cheque'. Its restricted interpretation of both powers relied on the scheme and purpose of the legislation, which made attendance at school compulsory but gave a free choice of school, subject only to enrolment limits in force for some schools. It held that that forced transfers could not be considered 'necessary' in that context. The term 'difficulty' was to be interpreted narrowly to mean a difficulty in the nature of a doubt as to the meaning and requirements of the Act.

The third type of limit to the scope of statutory powers, as noted, is found outside the empowering statute. Nowadays the most common version of this is rights-based review. Statutory powers are, as far as possible, read subject to rights protected by Te Tiriti o Waitangi, the Bill of Rights, international law or common law. This is discussed in Chapter 6.

However, this external form of limit also extends beyond such fundamental rights. Relevant provisions in any other statute may have the effect of limiting the scope of an empowering provision: depending on how both provisions are interpreted, exercises of the power inconsistent with the other statute may be unauthorised. This proposition is most familiar in the case of powers to make delegated legislation, where it is known as the repugnancy principle: at least unless expressly authorized, 'subordinate legislation cannot repeal or interfere with the operation of a statute'.[179]

Such a repugnancy argument succeeded on one occasion even in relation to the Economic Stabilisation Act 1948.[180] In *Combined State Unions*, the Court of Appeal found wage freeze regulations pursuant to that Act to be invalid in their application to the state services.[181] The successful ground of challenge was inconsistency with relevant provisions in the State Services Conditions of Employment Act 1977. The regulations could not override the 1977 Act unless the empowering legislation very clearly gave such power. While the power in the 1948 Act was very broad, it did not include any such specific power.[182]

[177] See *Reade v Smith* [1959] NZLR 996 (SC).

[178] For restricted interpretation of Henry VIII clauses, see also *Idea Services v Attorney-General* [2022] NZCA 470 at [24].

[179] *Zaoui v Attorney-General* [2005] 1 NZLR 577 (CA & SC) at [87]; *Powell v May* [1946] KB 330 (KBD).

[180] The ruling was, however, promptly reversed by amendment to the Act.

[181] *Combined State Unions v State Services Co-ordinating Committee* [1982] 1 NZLR 472 (CA).

[182] For more recent instances, see *Taylor v Attorney-General* [2013] NZHC 1659 at [26]–[30]; *Alan Johnston Sawmilling Ltd v Governor-General* [2002] NZAR 129 (HC) at 143.

The rationale for the repugnancy principle lies in the doctrine of Parliamentary sovereignty. Giving effect to Henry VIII clauses is in great tension with that doctrine. Courts will therefore not read rule-making powers that are conferred in broad or general terms as impliedly conferring such power.[183]

[183] *Combined State Unions* (n 181) at 745, 747. For a similar point, see *Ortmann v United States of America* [2020] NZSC 120, [2020] 1 NZLR 475 at [110].

6

Modern Extensions: Rights as Grounds for Review

Judicial review invoking fundamental rights, as affirmed in a number of sources, is one of the major areas of expansion in modern judicial review. The nature and extent of the effect given to such rights, and the method or approach adopted, are unsettled and evolving. That is at least in part because it is a matter of controversy what the approach should be, in light of competing constitutional commitments.

On the one hand, we may consider the fundamental or constitutional nature of these rights to call for a stronger role for the courts, involving more substantive review, in order to ensure protection against abuse of state power.[1] Limits or qualifications on these rights are often permissible, but must be shown to be justified: rights are interests that have a special high priority. Such justifications must be open to scrutiny. If that protection and scrutiny is to be reliable, it needs to be entrusted to an institution independent from executive and administrative government. The legislature may to some extent perform that role, but its role is not to focus on individual cases. It can also threaten the rights of minorities – in Aotearoa especially of Māori.[2] Furthermore, in our system the legislature is controlled by the executive government, hence it lacks independence. For these reasons judicial enforcement of rights is important.

On the other hand, there are at least two constitutional reasons to limit the role of courts in protecting rights. First, in our system of Parliamentary sovereignty, courts cannot enforce rights against legislation. That also means that there are limits to the extent to which courts can invoke rights to limit powers granted by Parliament. Secondly, the general rule is that judges in judicial review must not substitute their view for the value judgements made by primary decision-makers, because judges lack democratic legitimacy and are expected to respect Parliament's allocation of authority to the decision-maker.[3] This raises questions about the appropriate extent of the judicial role in applying rights, and especially in determining whether limits on rights are justified.

In the contest between these competing constitutional commitments, there are no right answers – reasonable people will continue to disagree. For that reason, the approach to the protection of fundamental rights – the methods and intensity of judicial scrutiny – is likely to wax and wane over time and remain unsettled.

[1] Philip A Joseph, *Constitutional and Administrative Law in New Zealand*, 5th edn (Wellington, Brookers, 2021) in ch 12.2 calls this 'constitutional review'.

[2] Claire Charters, 'Responding to Waldron's Defence of Legislatures: Why New Zealand's Parliament Does Not Protect Rights in Hard Cases' [2006] *New Zealand Law Review* 621.

[3] See Ch 3.

The 'righting' of judicial review has had a significant impact on the overall nature and scope of the supervisory jurisdiction.[4] It has expanded the ability to rely on arguments concerning substantive merits. Public authorities must now justify in court, for instance, why different groups are treated differently or why liberties must be constrained. It has also resulted in a revival of challenges to delegated legislation, which can be found to exceed the scope of the empowering provision when it limits rights without sufficiently clear authority in that provision.

Fundamental or constitutional rights are affirmed in a range of sources, and judicial approaches currently vary between those sources. This chapter therefore deals with each of the main sources in turn. For each source, we need to note the nature of the source; what rights are protected by it and the extent to which those rights are subject to limits or qualifications; and then examine the courts' approaches to protecting these rights in judicial review. The sources covered are te Tiriti o Waitangi | the Treaty of Waitangi (Part A), international law (Part B), fundamental common law rights (Part C) and the New Zealand Bill of Rights Act 1990 (Part D). One way of protecting rights from all these sources is by means of rights-consistent interpretation of empowering statutes. We will turn to the approach to this separately at the end of the chapter (Part E).

A. Te Tiriti o Waitangi

Entered in 1840 before the establishment of the British colonial government in Aotearoa, Te Tiriti o Waitangi[5] granted certain powers of government to the British Crown, in return for a guarantee of existing Māori rights.[6] These rights relate to land, natural resources, culture and equal citizenship – and importantly also to authority.[7] The extent of both the Crown's powers of government (kawanatanga) and the authority reserved to Māori (tino rangatiratanga) is unclear. We should also note that the international law rights of indigenous peoples include many similar rights.[8]

Te Tiriti was ignored or dismissed by governments and courts for well over a century but is now recognised as a fundamental constitutional document.[9] As discussed in Chapter 1, obligations under Te Tiriti are constitutional norms that shape our institutions and processes, and compliance with them affects constitutional legitimacy.

[4] See, eg, Sian Elias, 'Righting Administrative Law' in David Dyzenhaus, Murray Hunt and Grant Huscroft (eds), *A Simple Common Lawyer: Essays in Honour of Michael Taggart* (Oxford, Hart Publishing, 2009) 55; David Dyzenhaus, Murray Hunt and Michael Taggart, 'The Principle of Legality in Administrative Law: Internationalisation as Constitutionalisation' (2001) 1 *Oxford University Commonwealth Law Journal* 5.

[5] The Māori name of the Treaty of Waitangi is now used to signify the Māori language version. By virtue of the contra proferentem principle, this version has the greater weight when resolving conflicts between the two language versions: see Waitangi Tribunal, *He Whakaputanga me te Tiriti: The Report on Stage 1 of the Te Paparahi o te Raki Inquiry* (WAI 1040, 2014) at [10.4.1].

[6] For the full English and Māori texts, see the schedule of the Treaty of Waitangi Act 1975.

[7] See Andrew Erueti, 'Conceptualising Indigenous Rights in Aotearoa New Zealand' (2017) 27 *New Zealand Universities Law Review* 715.

[8] United Nations Declaration on the Rights of Indigenous Peoples, 61/295 (13 September 2007) On the effect of international law, see Part B.

[9] See Matthew SR Palmer and Dean R Knight, *The Constitution of New Zealand: A Contextual Analysis* (Hart Publishing, 2022), ch 10.

For a long time, the official understanding of Te Tiriti was that it granted overriding sovereignty over Aotearoa New Zealand to the Crown, subject to an obligation to protect Māori rights.[10] However, the more recent reassessment of Te Tiriti's fundamental exchange by the Waitangi Tribunal[11] is that rangatira[12] who signed Te Tiriti did not cede sovereignty. They granted power to the Crown to govern only its own people, the settlers. They retained a parallel and equal authority over their own people, with the interface between these two authorities to be a matter for ongoing negotiations.[13]

The implications of this newer understanding remain to be worked through. Te Tiriti has been approached for the past 40 years through the development of 'Treaty principles'. The most widely invoked of these are partnership, active protection and the duty of redress for Treaty breaches.[14] These remain broadly appropriate, albeit they need adjusting and expanding. A principle of options, allowing Māori communities to choose their own path, is a notable addition.[15] Against this development, legislation was introduced in 2024 to redefine the principles, stripping out almost all Māori rights.[16] But this is not expected to pass.

Giving full effect to the authority reserved to Māori by Te Tiriti may require a fundamental restructuring of our government institutions and redistribution of powers.[17] Smaller steps towards a more equal partnership and a measure of shared authority have taken the form of co-management of rivers, reserves and national parks,[18] and the devolution of responsibility for social services.[19] The case law may be moving slowly in the direction of some recognition of this dimension.[20]

Another development that derives support from the new understanding of Te Tiriti is the recognition of tikanga – Māori customary law – as forming part of the law of New Zealand.[21] Te Tiriti supports this because the authority and autonomy retained by Māori entails continued force for their law, and includes power to develop that law.[22] Tikanga, in turn, can be a source of rights. Customary title according to tikanga has

[10] See, eg, Waitangi Tribunal, *Muriwhenua Fishing Claim Report* (Wai 22, 1988) at 186–88; *New Zealand Maori Council v Attorney-General* [1987] 1 NZLR 641 (CA) (*Lands* case) at 663, 664, 665–66.

[11] This is the body charged by statute with interpreting Te Tiriti: Treaty of Waitangi Act 1975, s 5(2).

[12] Chiefs or leaders.

[13] Waitangi Tribunal, *He Whakaputanga me te Tiriti* (n 5) at [10.4.2].

[14] See the *Lands* case (n 10) at 664–666; Kevin Hille, Damen Ward and Carwyn Jones, *Treaty Law: Principles of the Treaty of Waitangi in Law and Practice* (Wellington, Thomson Reuters, 2023).

[15] For this and other developments see, eg, Waitangi Tribunal, *Te Mana Whatu Ahuru: Report on the Rohe Pōtae Claims* (Pre-publication Version, Parts I and II, Wai 898, 2018) at 183–85, 189; Waitangi Tribunal, *Hauora: Report on Stage One of the Health Services and Outcomes Kaupapa Inquiry* (Wai 2575, 2019) at 27–36.

[16] Principles of the Treaty of Waitangi Bill 2024 (94–1).

[17] See *The Report of Matike Mai Aotearoa – The Independent Working Group on Constitutional Transformation* (2016). It could not be achieved by the courts: Erueti (n 7) at 742.

[18] See, eg, Te Urewera Act 2014, esp part 2.

[19] See Māmari Stephens, 'Tuhoe-Crown Settlement – A Transforming Dawn? The Service Management Plan' (October 2014) *Māori Law Review*. Available at: www.maorilawreview.co.nz.

[20] See, eg, *Te Pou Matakana Ltd v Attorney-General* [2021] NZHC 2942 at [90]–[101], [115]–[117], [130]–[131], [134]; contrast, eg, *Te Whanau o Waipareira Trust v Attorney-General* [2012] NZHC 3107at [124]–[132].

[21] *Ellis v R (Continuance)* [2022] NZSC 114, [2022] 1 NZLR 239; *Trans-Tasman Resources v Taranaki-Whanganui Conservation Board* [2021] NZSC 127 at [9], [169], [237], [296]–[297], [332].

[22] See Joseph Williams, 'Lex Aotearoa: An Heroic Attempt to Map the Māori Dimension in Modern New Zealand Law' (2013) 21 *Waikato Law Review* 1 at 7, 9; Waitangi Tribunal, *Rohe Pōtae Report* (n 15) at 157, 158, 189; *Trans-Tasman Resources* (n 21) at [154], fn 287; *Ellis* (n 21) at [98], [126], [257].

longer-standing legal recognition.[23] The courts have begun to explore other tikanga-based arguments in judicial review.[24]

Much of the effect of Te Tiriti in our current system is outside the scope of administrative law. Te Tiriti is given effect through settlements negotiated between the Crown and iwi and hapū[25] to remedy past breaches,[26] the Māori seats in Parliament,[27] the status of te reo Māori[28] as an official language,[29] and many other arrangements protecting Māori interests and facilitating Māori participation in government and self-government.

The courts' role is limited, because they have maintained their longstanding position that Te Tiriti does not have legally enforceable effect in its own right. That means not only that, given our system of Parliamentary sovereignty, it does not have enforceable constitutional status.[30] It also means that it is not legally enforceable in its own right at all: like international treaties,[31] it requires incorporation by statute to acquire legal effect.[32]

This position reflects constitutional orthodoxy. However, there are arguments for moving beyond this and according Te Tiriti a special status, qualifying Parliamentary sovereignty, even if the current orthodoxy is maintained in all other contexts. If Te Tiriti represents the only legitimate basis for the establishment of colonial government in 1840, then today's government arrangements continue to lack legitimacy to the extent that they do not honour it.[33] Counter-majoritarian safeguards are needed for this, because Treaty rights are additional rights of a minority that impinge on the short-term interests of the majority. A well-functioning democracy may be expected, by and large, to respect *equal* rights for minorities, as long as there is a sufficiently widespread commitment to the common good; but *additional* rights of a minority are necessarily precarious if they are left to the mercy of the democratic process.[34]

Even as the law currently stands, however, judicial review does play a significant role in giving effect to Te Tiriti (and also to tikanga). This reflects Te Tiriti's fundamental constitutional status. It is found in two different types of context, which we

[23] *A-G v Ngati Apa* [2003] 3 NZLR 643 (CA).

[24] See, eg, *Sweeney v The Prison Manager, Spring Hill Corrections Facility* [2021] NZHC 181, [2021] 2 NZLR 27 at [71], [74]–[77]; and see Chs 4, 10 and 12.

[25] Iwi and hapū are tribes and subtribes.

[26] These are implemented by legislation: see, eg, Ngāi Tahu Claims Settlement Act 1998 and Tūhoe Claims Settlement Act 2014.

[27] Electoral Act 1993, ss 45, 76–79.

[28] The Māori language.

[29] Te Ture mō Te Reo Māori 2016 / Māori Language Act 2016; previously Maori Language Act 1987.

[30] Eg *Lands* case (n 10) at 655.

[31] Or indeed, since it *is* an international treaty: see, eg, Matthew Palmer, *The Treaty of Waitangi in New Zealand's Law and Constitution* (Wellington, Victoria University Press, 2008) at 167; Anna Hood, 'Statehood in Aotearoa New Zealand' in An Hertogen and Anna Hood (eds), *International Law in Aotearoa New Zealand* (New Zealand, Thomson Reuters, 2021.

[32] *Hoani Te Heu Heu Tukino v Aotea District Maori Trust Board* [1941] NZLR 590 (PC).

[33] See Ch 1.F; and see Hanna Wilberg 'Facing Up to the Original Breach of the Treaty' [2007] *New Zealand Law Review* 527.

[34] For similar arguments, see Claire Charters, 'Responding to Waldron's Defence of Legislatures: Why New Zealand's Parliament Does Not Protect Rights in Hard Cases' [2006] *New Zealand Law Review* 621; Max Harris, 'Is New Zealand Law Ready for a Marbury v Madison Moment?' (2021) 25 *New Zealand Universities Law Review* 210 at 230–34.

will consider in turn in this part. The first and obvious one is where Tiriti obligations have been referenced or incorporated in statute as constraints on public powers: it falls to judicial review courts to determine the effect of such provisions (section (1)). The second context is where statutes are silent on Te Tiriti, but Tiriti obligations are relevant to powers being exercised. In such contexts, courts have employed methods that parallel their approach to unincorporated international law (see Part B of this chapter): they have either implied relevant Tiriti obligations as mandatory considerations, or have interpreted statutory powers subject to a presumption of consistency with Te Tiriti (section (2)).

A further issue that arises in treaty litigation is the justiciability of disputes relating to Treaty settlements. Chapter 8 has a section on this.

(1) Effect of Express Statutory References

Many statutes include express reference to 'the principles of the Treaty of Waitangi' in the context of granting public powers. Such provisions are commonly referred to as 'Treaty clauses'. A large proportion of Treaty clauses make Treaty principles an express mandatory consideration, occasionally with mandatory weight. For instance, section 8 of the Resource Management Act 1991 (RMA)[35] makes Treaty principles a mandatory consideration in decision-making concerning natural and physical resources. Instances of mandatory weight are found in section 7(a) of the RMA, which requires 'particular regard' to be had to kaitiakitanga,[36] and section 6(e), which requires decision-makers to 'recognise and provide for … the relationship of Maori and their culture and traditions with their ancestral lands, water, sites, waahi tapu,[37] and other taonga[38]' An alternative approach that is often found in more recent statutes is to include specific requirements intended to give effect to Te Tiriti, such as requiring Māori representation on decision-making bodies and promoting Māori participation in delivery of social services.[39]

Some of the Treaty clauses go further than this. They require all powers conferred by the relevant Acts to be exercised consistently with Treaty principles. The courts have given full effect to such clauses, recognising that they make Treaty principles a substantive constraint on the scope of all powers under those Acts. The *Lands* case concerned the first of these provisions, section 9 of the State-Owned Enterprises Act 1987. The challenge was to the transfer of Crown lands to the state-owned enterprises (SOEs) created by the Act. The Court of Appeal held that section 9 prohibited such transfer, unless a system was first put in place to safeguard the Crown's ability to settle Treaty claims to those lands.[40] Within the scope of the

[35] Slated for repeal at the time of writing.
[36] Guardianship.
[37] Sacred sites.
[38] Things or values that are treasured. For strong use of these provisions, see, eg, *Tauranga Environmental Protection Society Inc v Tauranga City Council* [2021] NZHC 1201; *McGuire v Hastings District Court* [2002] 2 NZLR 577 (PC), [21]–[29].
[39] See, eg, Pae Ora (Healthy Futures) Act 2022, ss 6, 12, 15, 16A, 29–31, 89.
[40] *Lands case* (n 10) at 666.

Act, the Court considered section 9 had the effect of a 'constitutional guarantee'[41] – hence, even this central aspect of the powers apparently conferred by the Act was subject to the section 9 constraint.

Another one of the strong Treaty clauses is section 4 of the Conservation Act 1987, which requires that Act to be interpreted and administered so as to 'give effect to the principles of the Treaty of Waitangi'. In *Ngāi Tai ki Tāmaki v Minister of Conservation*, the Supreme Court emphasised the 'firm obligation' created by these 'imperative terms'; section 4 could not be trumped by competing considerations in the legislation.[42] Ngāi Tai claimed mana whenua[43] over two islands designated as reserves. The Treaty principle of active protection did not necessarily preclude the Minister granting concessions for tourist operations by outsiders. However, it could have that effect in some circumstances and at least entitled Ngāi Tai to some preference. The decisions were unlawful because the Minister's delegate had not correctly understood these obligations.[44]

More recently, strong Treaty clauses have been included in legislation providing for partial privatisation of SOEs engaged in hydroelectric power generation,[45] and for a fast-track consenting process designed to promote economic recovery after the Covid-19 pandemic.[46] In two challenges relying on those clauses, the courts have re-affirmed the strong effect of this form of Treaty clause.[47] However, in both cases the courts concluded that no inconsistency with Te Tiriti had been established.[48]

As reflected in these last three cases, a significant limit on the effect of these strong Treaty clauses is the qualified nature of the principles of the Treaty themselves, as interpreted by the courts. They require only that government take reasonable action by way of active protection and redress for past breaches,[49] balancing Māori interests against other relevant interests.[50] An earlier instance of this is seen in the older *Broadcasting Assets* case.[51]

These qualified requirements also introduce issues as to the role of the reviewing court: what is the standard of review? The obligation is substantive, but in deciding what it requires in the circumstances, courts may decide to accord some latitude to the decision-maker's view. This issue has not yet received much consideration in this context, unlike in relation to the Bill of Rights.

The circumstances of some cases may relieve the courts of the need to consider substantive compliance at all. Where decision-makers have failed to turn their mind to Treaty obligations, or have misunderstood those obligations, the court may instead

[41] ibid at 658.

[42] *Ngāi Tai Ki Tāmaki Tribal Trust v Minister of Conservation* [2018] NZSC 122 at [48], [52], [54], [77].

[43] Power or authority over or of the land.

[44] ibid at paras [69]–[73], [90]–[98].

[45] Section 45Q of the Public Finance Act 1989, inserted in 2012 as part of a new Part 5A providing for the partial privatisation.

[46] COVID-19 Recovery (Fast-track Consenting) Act 2020, s 6 (now repealed).

[47] *New Zealand Maori Council v Attorney-General* [2013] NZSC 6, [2013] 3 NZLR 31 (*Water Rights*) at [52]–[64]; *Greenpeace Aotearoa Inc v Hiringa Energy Ltd* [2023] NZCA 672 at [182]–[185].

[48] ibid: *Mighty River Power* at [134]–[150]; *Hiringa Energy* at [186]–[207].

[49] *Ngāi Tai* (n 42) at [50]–[52], [95]; *Mighty River Power* (n 51) at [88]–[90].

[50] *Hiringa Energy* (n 51) at [203], [207].

[51] *New Zealand Maori Council v Attorney-General* [1994] 1 NZLR 513 (PC) (*Broadcasting Assets*).

employ the traditional approach of remitting the decision for reconsideration. The Supreme Court took that approach, for instance, in the *Ngāi Tai* case.[52]

(2) Implied Mandatory Consideration and Presumption of Consistency with Te Tiriti

Even in the absence of an express Treaty clause, it is well established that Treaty obligations will to some extent constrain the exercise of powers to which they are relevant. The courts will read relevant constraints into the empowering statute, unless the statute cannot be read that way. The courts' approach to rights-consistent interpretation is explored in Part E.

Less certain is the nature of the implied constraint. Are Treaty principles merely an implied mandatory consideration or is there a presumption that powers must be exercised consistently unless the statute clearly authorises infringement?[53] In this regard, the approach to implied protection for Te Tiriti parallels the approach to unincorporated international obligations, discussed in part B of this chapter: the same unacknowledged choice of two different methods features in both contexts.

The mandatory consideration method is the weaker option, as explained further in Part B: it imposes no more than a reasoning process obligation, leaving the discretion substantively unconstrained. In contrast, a presumption of consistency results in a substantive constraint on the scope of the discretion. The latter option (the presumption) is also sometimes put in terms that Te Tiriti may be protected by the principle of legality; that is the usual name of the presumption of consistency with common law rights, as discussed in Part C.

One option the courts could adopt is to consider both methods to be available as appropriate:[54] that is the approach emerging in relation to the Bill of Rights (see Part D). If a decision-maker has failed to consider Treaty principles, the decision can be quashed on that basis. Where the decision-maker has done so, the court will need to consider whether the decision gives adequate effect to those principles.

A number of early cases, such as *Huakina*, treated relevant Treaty obligations as implied mandatory considerations.[55] The well-known *Ngai Tahu* case about whale watching accorded mandatory weight to Treaty obligations,[56] which amounts to a version of substantive constraint. However, the decision is best understood as relying

[52] *Ngāi Tai* (n 42) at [98]–[100].

[53] For discussion of both options, see Hanna Wilberg 'Judicial Remedies for the Original Breach?' [2007] *New Zealand Law Review* 713, 725–734.

[54] *New Zealand Maori Council v Attorney-General* [2007] NZCA 269, [2008] 1 NZLR 318 (*Te Arawa Cross Claim*) at [72]–[74] (obiter) endorsed both options – the first for 'judicial review cases' and the second for 'cases involving statutory interpretation'.

[55] *Huakina Development Trust v Waikato Valley Authority* [1987] 2 NZLR 188 (HC); arguably also *Attorney-General v New Zealand Maori Council* [1991] 2 NZLR 129 (CA) (*Radio Frequencies*) at 135, but cf the sequel in *Attorney-General v New Zealand Maori Council (No 2)* [1991] 2 NZLR 147 (CA) (*Radio Frequencies No 2*).

[56] In *Ngai Tahu Maori Trust Board v Director-General of Conservation* [1995] 3 NZLR 553 (CA), the claimant iwi was held to be entitled to a 'reasonable degree of preference' (at 562) and the Crown's duty to protect the iwi's interests was a 'residual factor of weight' (at 560).

on the strong Treaty clause in section 4 of the Conservation Act – in other words, the Treaty obligation did not need to be implied.[57]

The alternative approach involving a presumption of consistency with Te Tiriti was endorsed in the *Lands* case in an obiter dictum by Cooke P, but only for interpreting ambiguous legislation.[58] On one interpretation, that could mean that the presumption does not constrain discretionary powers.[59] Until relatively recently, there was only High Court authority for an unqualified presumption. In *Barton-Prescott*, the High Court held that where Treaty obligations are relevant to a statutory regime, the provisions of that statute must, as far as possible, be interpreted consistently with the Treaty.[60]

This approach has now received appellate endorsement in *Tukaki*[61] and *Trans-Tasman Resources*.[62] *Tukaki* was an unsuccessful challenge to an extradition decision. The District Court had declined to exercise its discretionary power to determine Mr Tukaki not eligible for extradition to Australia. The statutory test was whether, due to delay and having regard to all the circumstance of the case, it would be unjust or unduly oppressive to surrender him.[63]

Mr Tukaki was Māori and, for the past 17 years since returning from Australia, had established a tikanga-based lifestyle within his iwi. Affirming the presumption of consistency with Te Tiriti,[64] the Court held that the tikanga value of whanaungatanga[65] can be weighed in the interpretation and exercise of this discretion.[66] However, that did not override the statutory threshold requirement of undue oppressiveness, and the Court saw nothing wrong in the Judge's application of that test in this case.

The Court did not spell out why the threshold of undue oppressiveness was not overridden, but this can be seen as flowing both from the limits of the Treaty obligation and from statutory interpretation. First, as we saw earlier, the courts have understood the Treaty obligation of active protection as not absolute: it requires only reasonable action, which allows for balancing against competing objectives. Secondly, even if the Treaty obligation was understood as being stronger, the empowering provision perhaps was not capable of a reading that accommodated such a stronger obligation. That would rebut the presumption of consistency.

In *Trans-Tasman Resources* the Supreme Court applied this common law presumption to an express statutory Treaty clause.[67] The clause made specific but limited

[57] The empowering legislation had no Treaty clause, but it was administered by the Department of Conservation, as provided in Sch 1 to the Conservation Act 1987. That rendered s 4 of the latter Act relevant: *Ngai Tahu* (n 56) at 558. For this explanation of the case, see also *Ngāi Tai ki Tāmaki* (n 42) at [34], [49].

[58] *Lands* case (n 10) at 655–56.

[59] See Part E(2) of this chapter for an explanation.

[60] *Barton-Prescott v Director-General of Social Welfare* [1997] 3 NZLR 179 at 184.

[61] *Tukaki v Commonwealth of Australia* [2018] NZCA 324, [2018] NZAR 1597; also *Urlich v Attorney-General* [2022] NZCA 38, [2022] 2 NZLR 599 at [62]–[63], [75]–[76].

[62] *Trans-Tasman Resources v Taranaki-Whanganui Conservation Board* [2021] NZSC 127, [2021] 1 NZLR 801.

[63] Extradition Act 1999, ss 8(c) and 24(4).

[64] *Tukaki* (n 61) at [35]–[36].

[65] kinship, relationship.

[66] *Tukaki* (n 61) at [38], [40].

[67] *Trans-Tasman Resources* (n 62).

provision for the effect of Te Tiriti, and the Crown argued that this specific provision constrained its effect in the context of the statute concerned. In dismissing that argument, the Court re-iterated that Treaty clauses are to be given broad and generous effect. In addition, it relied on a presumption of consistency.

The main judgment offered two formulations of this presumption. First, 'courts will not easily read statutory language as excluding consideration of Treaty principles if a statute is silent on the question'. Secondly, '[a]n intention to constrain the ability of statutory decision-makers to respect Treaty principles should not be ascribed to Parliament unless that intention is made quite clear'.[68] Williams J's concurring judgment put it this way: 'If Parliament intends to limit or remove the Treaty's effect in or on an Act, this will need to be made quite clear.'[69]

The precise nature of the effect that is presumed here is open to argument. Unlike the strong statement in the concurring judgment, the formulations in the main judgment suggest something less than a full presumption of consistency. Potential qualifications flow from the reference to 'consideration' of the principles in the first formulation and to the 'ability' to respect the principles in the second. As Cooke J pointed out in *Students for Climate Solutions*, this did not amount to saying that decision-makers 'are *obliged* to comply'. However, a full presumption may nevertheless be the overall effect of the judgment.[70] The effect which the Court went on to give to Te Tiriti arguably reflects a requirement of consistency. Cooke J's decision was upheld on appeal, but the Court of Appeal did not comment on these dicta.[71]

Several commentators have taken the view that *Trans-Tasman Resources* adopted a full presumption of consistency.[72] In *Ellis*, Glazebrook J noted that a presumption of consistency is 'generally accepted'.[73]

The impact of the *Trans-Tasman Resources* presumption on express Treaty clauses is also a significant development. On this new approach, the common type of Treaty clause that requires no more than consideration of Treaty principles may also no longer be read as exhausting the effect of Te Tiriti within the relevant regime.

There is much scope for further development and clarification of the approach to Te Tiriti in administrative law. Among the four sources of rights discussed in this chapter, the approach to Te Tiriti is the least developed in the case law and has so far attracted the least academic debate.

[68] ibid at [151].

[69] ibid at [296].

[70] *Students for Climate Solutions Inc v Minister of Energy and Resources* [2022] NZHC 2116, [2022] NZRMA 612 at [90]–[91], emphasis in original.

[71] *Students for Climate Solutions Inc v Minister of Energy and Resources* [2024] NZCA 152; an application for leave to appeal to the Supreme Court was pending at the time of writing.

[72] Natalie Coates 'The Rise of Tikanga Māori and Te Tiriti o Waitangi Jurisprudence' in John Burrows and Jeremy Finn (eds) *Challenge and Change: Judging in Aotearoa New Zealand* (LexisNexis, Wellington, 2022) 65 at 81; Dean R Knight 'New Zealand – Te Tiriti o Waitangi norms, discretionary power and the principle of legality (at last)' [2022] PL 701.

[73] *Ellis* (n 21) at [98].

B. International Law

International law remains an important source of rights in New Zealand despite the enactment of the New Zealand Bill of Rights Act 1990 and other rights-conferring statutes. The Bill of Rights is confined to civil and political rights,[74] and a relatively narrow set of those.[75] Other statutory provisions recognising and protecting rights include, for instance, section 33 of the Education and Training Act 2020 which gives a right to free enrolment and free education at state primary and secondary schools.[76] Whenever such statutes incorporate international law rights, those can be claimed by virtue of that statute. For example, the Convention relating to the Status of Refugees is incorporated in the Immigration Act 2009's regime for determining refugee status. However, there are other rights that can only be claimed as such in reliance on international law, including particularly the rights of children and families.[77] Beyond those two, there has so far been very little litigation in New Zealand relying on economic, social and cultural rights.[78] Such rights claims would also have to rely on international law.[79]

International law also provides an alternative to te Tiriti as a source of Māori rights. The main international law source is the United Nations Declaration on the Rights of Indigenous Peoples.[80]

The starting point, however, is that international treaties are not enforceable in the domestic courts unless they have been incorporated by statute. The traditional dualist doctrine, following the English position,[81] treats international law and domestic law as separate spheres.[82] The only form of international law that does not require

[74] It affirms the rights in the International Covenant on Civil and Political Rights (16 December 1966) (ICCPR).

[75] See part D of this chapter.

[76] For the limits of this right, see *Attorney-General v Daniels* [2003] 2 NZLR 742 (CA).

[77] United Nations Convention on the Rights of the Child (UNCROC), esp art 3; ICCPR, esp arts 17, 23 and 24.

[78] The few instances include *Lawson v Housing New Zealand* [1997] 2 NZLR 474 (HC) (right to adequate standard of living); *Harlen v Ministry of Social Development* [2012] NZHC 669, [2012] NZAR 491 (right to adequate standard of living); *W (CA642/2019) v New Zealand Police* [2021] NZCA 326 (right to work); *Borrowdale v Director-General of Health* [2020] NZHC 2090 (right to health). Further to *Borrowdale*, see text at nn 143–145.

[79] Especially the International Covenant on Economic, Social and Cultural Rights (ICESCR); also International Labour Organisation (ILO) conventions.

[80] United Nations Declaration on the Rights of Indigenous Peoples, 61/295 (13 September 2007). On the courts' approach to this, see Claire Charters, '*Wakatū* in Peripheral Vision: Māori Rights-Based Judicial Review of the Executive and the Courts' Approach to the United Nations Declaration on the Rights of Indigenous Peoples' [2019] *New Zealand Law Review* 85.

[81] *JH Rayner (Mincing Lane) Ltd v Department of Trade and Industry* [1990] 2 AC 418 (HL) (*International Tin Council*) at 476–77, 499–501; *R (Miller) v Secretary of State* [2017] UKSC 5, [2018] AC 61 at [54]–[58]; *R (SC) v Secretary of State for Work and Pensions* [2021] UKSC 26, [2022] AC 223 at [76]–[78].

[82] *Ashby v Minister of Immigration* [1981] 1 NZLR 222 (CA) at 224.

incorporation is customary international law,[83] which is treated as forming part of the common law.[84]

In modern New Zealand law, that dualist doctrine is subject to significant qualifications. Many commentators consider that in light of these, the dualist orthodoxy no longer accurately reflects the law.[85] Unincorporated international obligations are given effect by means of two approaches. First, there is a presumption of consistency that applies in statutory interpretation: statutes are read consistently with relevant international obligations wherever a consistent interpretation is available.[86] Similarly, courts also seek to develop the common law to achieve consistency with international law.[87] Secondly, in the context of administrative law, some cases have adopted the alternative approach of treating relevant international obligations as mandatory relevant considerations.[88] Both these approaches are also used to give further effect to customary international law in the context of statutory powers.[89] The choice between these two alternatives is not usually acknowledged in the cases; how they relate to each other is therefore not addressed either.

This modern New Zealand position can be contrasted with the English approach. There, the presumption is triggered only by ambiguity on the face of the statute, and statutory conferral of a discretion is not considered to represent an ambiguity.[90] However, English courts often achieve the same thing by finding a corresponding common law right that can be given effect via the principle of legality.[91] The lesser constraint of a mandatory relevant consideration has also generally been rejected.[92] In *Friends of the Earth*, however, while holding that international obligations are permissible rather than mandatory considerations, the Supreme Court appeared at least to accept the possibility that an international obligation might be so obviously relevant that no reasonable decision-maker could fail to take it into account.[93]

This Part starts by outlining the reasons for the traditional dualist approach and justifications for the modern qualifications (section (1)). It then examines the effect of the two established methods for giving some effect to international law and the

[83] For explanation, see Matthew SR Palmer and Dean R Knight, *The Constitution of New Zealand: A Contextual Analysis* (Hart Publishing, 2022) at 237–38.

[84] Treasa Dunworth, 'Hidden Anxieties: Customary International Law in New Zealand' (2004) 2 *New Zealand Journal of Public and International Law* 67 at 68–77 surveys the case law, noting it is a little more complex than that.

[85] See Treasa Dunworth, 'International Law in New Zealand Law' in Alberto Costi (ed), *Public International Law: A New Zealand Perspective* (Wellington, LexisNexis, 2020) 597 at 598.

[86] *New Zealand Airline Pilots' Association Inc v Attorney-General* [1997] 3 NZLR 269 (CA) at 289.

[87] *Hosking v Runting* [2005] 1 NZLR 1.

[88] *Tavita v Minister of Immigration* [1994] 2 NZLR 257 (CA) at 265–66.

[89] Treasa Dunworth, 'Sources of International Law in Aotearoa New Zealand' in An Hertogen and Anna Hood (eds), *International Law in Aotearoa New Zealand* (Wellington, Thomson Reuters, 2021) 15 at 22–24.

[90] *R v Secretary of State for the Home Department, ex p Brind* [1991] 1 AC 696 (HL) at 748; *R (Yam) v Central Criminal Court* [2015] UKSC 76, [2016] AC 771.

[91] See David Dyzenhaus, Murray Hunt and Michael Taggart, 'The Principle of Legality in Administrative Law: Internationalisation as Constitutionalisation' (2001) 1 *Oxford University Commonwealth Law Journal* 5 at 18; Jason NE Varuhas, 'The Principle of Legality' [2020] 79 *Cambridge Law Journal* 578 at 580–82.

[92] *Yam* (n 90) at [35]–[36]; but cf *E v Chief Constable of the Royal Ulster Constabulary* [2008] UKHL 66, [2009] 1 AC 536 at [60].

[93] *R (Friends of the Earth Ltd) v Heathrow Airport Ltd* [2020] UKSC 42 at [118]–[119], [122].

difference between them (section (2)), and the state of authority as to which of these two options applies in what contexts (section (3)). It also briefly outlines other possible approaches that are not often discussed in this context (section (4)). The approach to statutory interpretation – whether and when powers are capable of being read subject to the two established forms of international law constraint – is discussed separately later, in Part E of the chapter.

(1) Should Unincorporated International Law be Given Any Effect and Why?

The dualist orthodoxy is underpinned by a constitutional rationale. Entering into treaties is very largely left to executive government – it is part of the modern remnants of the royal prerogative. Parliament has, in more recent times, acquired a limited role. Most treaties must be presented to the House before they are ratified,[94] and Parliament can pass advisory resolutions.[95] If government considers that legislation is required to implement the treaty, by convention that legislation must be passed before the treaty is ratified.[96] However, Parliament's involvement does not extend to requiring its consent. For as long as that remains the case, giving treaties the force of law in New Zealand would be inconsistent with democratic government and Parliamentary sovereignty.[97] It would mean that law made by Parliament might be abrogated by international commitments, and international commitments would apply as law to the people of New Zealand without ever having received the democratic endorsement of their representatives.

On the other hand, however, it is concerning if New Zealand's government is considered free to disregard solemnly adopted international commitments. International law creates 'normative expectations',[98] and should not be reduced to mere 'window-dressing'.[99] Since many modern treaties – notably human rights conventions – provide for the relationship between individuals and states, rather than between states, these expectations concern the domestic sphere.

The modern qualifications to dualism address these concerns at least to some extent. At the same time, arguably they can still be reconciled with Parliamentary sovereignty, as statutes still prevail over international obligations in the event of inconsistency.[100]

Two main arguments may justify the presumption of consistency. First, all branches of government should aim for Aotearoa New Zealand to be a good international citizen, and to observe the rule of law on the international plane.[101] Courts

[94] See Standing Orders of the House of Representatives 2020, SOs 405–408.

[95] Bruce Harris, *New Zealand Constitution: An Analysis in Terms of its Principles* (Wellington, Thomson Reuters, 2018) at 303.

[96] Cabinet Office, *Cabinet Manual 2023* at [5.80].

[97] See *Ortmann v United States of America* [2020] NZSC 120, [2020] 1 NZLR 475 at [110] (obiter), noting that courts would hesitate to find that a statute intended to provide for international treaties to override some of its provisions; *Miller* (n 81) at [57].

[98] Harris (n 95) at 296.

[99] *Tavita* (n 88) at 266.

[100] That is subject to the contentious question concerning the strength of the presumption and what suffices to rebut it: see Part E of this chapter.

[101] See Claudia Geiringer, 'International Law Through the Lens of Zaoui: Where is New Zealand At?' (2006) 17 *Public Law Review* 300 at 313–14; Alice Osman, 'Demanding Attention: The Roles of Unincorporated

share that responsibility,[102] as does Parliament. On that basis, it is part of the courts' proper role to presume that Parliament does not intend to legislate inconsistently with international law obligations. Secondly, where international law protects human rights, those have inherent importance and normative force. Their importance and normative force have an even firmer foundation if the rights in question have also long been recognised by our domestic common law, or if the international instrument in question has been adopted almost universally around the world, or both.[103] Courts should be slow to accept that domestic law fails to comply with such human rights obligations.

The mandatory relevant considerations approach can be understood as a different application of the interpretive presumption: Parliament must have expected the international obligation at least to be taken into account.[104] That allows this approach to be justified on the same basis as the presumption of consistency. The reason for limiting the effect to a mandatory relevant consideration could also be put in these terms: it may be considered more consistent with Parliament's intention to confer a discretionary power. Alternatively, this approach has been presented as an application of the unreasonableness ground of review: some international obligations are in the category of considerations that are so manifestly important in relevant contexts that no reasonable Minister could fail to take them into account.[105]

While this chapter is devoted to rights, it is important to note that human rights are only one of the many subjects of international law. Other parts of international law concern diverse matters such as trade, transport, arbitration, environmental protection and counter-terrorism measures. Whether such other parts of international law should be given qualified effect in the same way is a difficult question. The argument from the inherent importance and normative force of the norms in question has less validity for some non-rights-related international obligations.

Treasa Dunworth has cautioned against an assumption that international law always presents a 'civilising' or 'taming' influence on domestic law.[106] Partly for this reason, Dunworth and others have called for a 'pedigree' approach to the reception of international law, in which the degree of effect given to it depends on the value of the norm, its status at international law and its fit with the domestic system.[107]

Similar factors were considered in the *Airline Pilots Association* case, one of several leading cases in which the presumption of consistency has been invoked outside the context of human rights.[108] The presumption was held *not* to protect international law rules concerning air accident investigations, partly because of their 'relative unimportance'. In that regard, they were contrasted with the international law rules of the air

International Instruments in Judicial Reasoning' [2014] 12 *New Zealand Journal of Public and International Law* 345 at 365–367.

[102] *Tavita* (n 88) at 266, citing the Balliol Statement of 1993 and the Blomfontein Statement of 1993, and further describing the United Nations Human Rights Committee as 'in a sense part of this country's judicial structure'.

[103] Dyzenhaus, Hunt and Taggart (n 91) at 32–33.

[104] See, eg, *Ashby* (n 82) at 226.

[105] See *Tavita* (n 88) at 266; *Ashby* (n 82) at 224–26, citing *CREEDNZ v Governor-General* [1981] 1 NZLR 172 (CA) at 183.

[106] Dunworth, 'International Law in New Zealand Law' (n 82) at 623–24.

[107] ibid at 625.

[108] *Airline Pilots Association* (n 86) at 289–90.

and with fundamental human rights treaties. Inherent importance is thus not confined to human rights norms, but does vary. The importance of the rules of the air can be explained in terms of the international rule of law argument: international air transport would be unreliable and hazardous without such rules and without widespread respect for them. That explanation also applies to *Sellers*, where the presumption was held to protect the freedom of the high seas. The Court emphasised the long-standing presumption in this particular context: legislation regulating maritime matters should be read consistently with the law of the sea if possible.[109] Arbitration is a further area in which the international rule of law is important.[110]

(2) Comparing the Mandatory Consideration and Presumption of Consistency Approaches

The two approaches to implying international law constraints on the exercise of statutory powers have very different effect.[111] A mandatory consideration according to orthodox administrative law doctrine is merely a reasoning process obligation, leaving the discretion substantively unconstrained.[112] Courts increasingly require decision-makers to demonstrate that they genuinely turned their mind to mandatory considerations,[113] but courts do not review the weight accorded to those considerations. Provided the matter has been considered, therefore, the decision-maker may conclude that it is outweighed by competing considerations, and the courts will not intervene unless that weighing exercise was *Wednesbury* unreasonable.[114]

The presumption of consistency approach entails much stronger effect for the unincorporated international obligation: subject to express or implied provision to the contrary, the substantive scope of the statutory power excludes power to do anything that would breach the international obligation. In *Zaoui*, for example, the apparently unqualified statutory power to deport a person who had been assessed as a risk to national security simply could not be exercised if that would breach the international law prohibition on returning a person to a country where they are at risk of being arbitrarily deprived of life or subjected to torture.[115] In contrast, if the international law prohibition had been merely a mandatory relevant consideration, the power to deport could have been exercised freely, provided only that the Ministers could demonstrate that they had genuinely turned their minds to the international obligation.

[109] *Sellers v Maritime Safety Authority* [1999] 2 NZLR 44 (CA) at 57.

[110] The presumption was invoked in *Zurich Australian Insurance Ltd v Cognition Education Ltd* [2014] NZSC 188, [2015] 1 NZLR 383 at [40] in that context.

[111] Claudia Geiringer, '*Tavita* and All That: Confronting the Confusion Surrounding Unincorporated Treaties and Administrative Law' (2004) 21 NZULR 66 at 82–88.

[112] See Ch 5.C.

[113] *Secretary for Justice v Simes* [2012] NZCA 459, [2012] NZAR 1044 at [58]; in relation to international obligations, see *Zhang v Minister of Immigration* [2020] NZHC 568 at [68]–[72]; *H (SC 104/2020) v Minister of Immigration* [2021] NZSC 192 at [31] n 28 (obiter).

[114] *New Zealand Fishing Industry Association Inc v Minister of Agriculture and Fisheries* [1988] 1 NZLR 544 (CA) at 552; in relation to international obligations, see *Harlen* (n 78) at [68].

[115] *Zaoui v Attorney-General (No 2)* [2005] NZSC 38, [2006] 1 NZLR 289 at [64], [90]–[93].

Even the weaker mandatory consideration approach, however, can result in successful challenges where respondents cannot demonstrate that they turned their minds to the relevant international obligations. For instance, if decision-makers had no information on the facts bearing on a relevant obligation, they cannot have taken that obligation into account. Thus where children's best interests are mandatory to consider, the decision-maker must have had information on the decision's effect on the children. Decision-makers have also failed to discharge the reasoning process obligation if they turned their minds to the international obligation but misunderstood its content.[116]

Importantly, both approaches are equally subject to anything to the contrary in the relevant legislation: international law cannot be invoked to contradict or avoid statutory provisions.[117] This is a question of statutory interpretation. Statutes that implement international obligations can raise particularly difficult interpretive questions if they use different terms than the international instrument or implement only part of it. McGrath J in *Helu* emphasised that courts must apply the implementing statute rather than the international text, albeit the statute will still be read as consistently as possible with the international obligation.[118] Whether or not differences and omissions are deliberate can be a difficult question.[119] The approach to rights-consistent interpretation of statutes is further discussed in Part E of this chapter.

The advantages and disadvantages of each approach flow from their different effects. The presumption approach gives the maximum effect to international law that can still be reconciled with Parliamentary sovereignty. That may be seen as desirable for the reasons canvassed earlier. However, it may also raise concerns about incorporating treaties 'by the back door' and hence undermining dualist orthodoxy. The mandatory considerations approach, conversely, may be criticised for giving insufficient effect to international law. By the same token, however, it also weakens the force of the objection from Parliamentary sovereignty. The strength of the arguments on either side depends on the context, such as the nature of the international obligation and the terms and purpose of the statute.

The distinction between the two approaches is complicated by the fact that international obligations can themselves be qualified. This can take two different forms. First, in some cases, the international obligation itself is merely a reasoning process obligation, specifying a matter to be taken into account. In such a case, the difference in the effect disappears: even applying the presumption, decision-makers are still free to decide as they see fit, provided only that the mandatory consideration has demonstrably been considered.

Secondly, the international obligation may be qualified but still substantive: for instance, an obligation to take reasonable steps towards a goal,[120] or to assign priority to a consideration. In such a case, decision-makers merely turning their minds to the

[116] See, eg, *Ye v Minister of Immigration* [2009] NZSC 76, [2010] 1 NZLR 104 at [60]–[61].

[117] *Helu v Immigration and Protection Tribunal* [2015] NZSC 28, [2016] 1 NZLR 298 at [143]–[144].

[118] ibid at [143]–[144]. See also *Trans-Tasman Resources v Taranaki-Whanganui Conservation Board* [2021] NZSC 127 at [99]–[100], [107], [322]–[325].

[119] In *Helu* (n 117), different views of the statute were taken by the majority at [147]–[150] and by the Chief Justice at [71]–[73].

[120] That is a common formulation, eg, in the ICESCR (n 79).

matter in question will not satisfy the international obligation. The effect will therefore once again differ depending on whether a court gives domestic effect to that obligation via the presumption of consistency or the mandatory consideration approach.

Some international obligations are open to differing interpretations in this regard. For instance, article 3 of the UN Convention on the Rights of the Child requires the best interests of the child to be 'a primary consideration' in all actions concerning children. This would seem to assign mandatory weight: a qualified yet substantive obligation. But the Supreme Court in *Ye* denied this substantive aspect, holding that the words of article 3 do not denote how this consideration ranks against others.[121] In summary, the effect of both approaches to giving effect to international law is the same whenever the international obligation itself is no more than a reasoning process obligation. Whether that is so turns on the wording of the international obligation and its interpretation.

(3) Which Approach Applies When?

While the two approaches clearly have a different effect in most cases, unfortunately our case law fails to provide any clear guidance on how to choose between them. Most cases do not acknowledge the choice at all. Even more unhelpfully, in several leading cases it is not clear which of the two approaches is being applied.

One possible answer may be that both are available as appropriate in the circumstances. If the decision-maker has not turned their mind to a relevant obligation, the decision can be struck down on that basis. Otherwise, the court needs to apply the presumption and decide whether the resulting international law constraint has been complied with. Such an approach is emerging in Bill of Rights cases, as we will see in Part D.

The closest we come to guidance is the Supreme Court decision in *Helu*, where McGrath J clearly stated that either of these two approaches may apply to a statutory discretion. However, as to how to choose between them, he merely said that this depends 'on the statute and, in some instances, the nature of international obligation'.[122] What do we make of this?

In the *Airline Pilots Association* case that was cited for this proposition, these points went to whether an international law constraint should be implied at all. The answer was no, both because the statute could not be read subject to the required constraint, and because the relevant international law obligation was insufficiently binding, important, or determinate.[123]

Similar arguments may, however, also be relevant to the choice between the two approaches. Commentators have argued in favour of a 'pedigree' approach to both questions (whether a constraint should be read in, and what kind of constraint) that takes account of the nature and significance of the relevant international obligation

[121] *Ye* (n 116) at [24]–[25].
[122] *Helu* (n 117) at [144], citing *Airline Pilots Association* (n 86) at 289.
[123] *Airline Pilots Association* (n 86) at 289–90.

and its fit with the domestic system.[124] For instance, the stronger effect provided by the presumption of consistency is easier to justify where the right at stake is an absolute right, such as the right against torture. Conversely, where the statute at issue emphasises the breadth of discretion, this may point towards employing the weaker mandatory relevant consideration approach. While these arguments are almost never spelt out in the cases, most cases appear consistent with such an approach.

The leading authorities for the mandatory considerations approach are two cases concerning immigration officers' obligations when deciding on the removal of immigrants with citizen children: *Tavita*[125] and *Puli'uvea*.[126] While the question was, strictly speaking, left open in both, these decisions have been treated as establishing that the international obligations to those children must be taken into account as a mandatory relevant consideration. The decision in *Puli'uvea*, however, can also be interpreted as relying on the presumption of consistency instead.[127]

The same ambiguity is found in two more recent Supreme Court decisions that also concerned the rights of children in the immigration context.[128] In *Ye*, the Court expressly relied on the presumption of consistency at several points.[129] However, the international obligation in question was to consider the interests of children as 'a primary consideration'.[130] Since the Court read that international obligation itself as no more than a mandatory relevant consideration,[131] as already noted, this was one of the cases where both approaches have the same effect: the interests of the children were a mandatory relevant consideration. In *Helu*, the Court again referred to the presumption of consistency.[132] It invoked the international law rights of families and young people to reinforce an express statutory provision mandating consideration of those interests.[133] It is difficult to say which of the approaches this represents. Finally, in a challenge to Immigration Instructions in *H v Minister of Immigration*, the Court accepted (obiter) that the Refugee Convention would have been a mandatory consideration if it had been relevant.[134]

Despite the frequent ambiguity, the constraint in all these cases is only a reasoning process constraint, mandating consideration of the relevant interest. This may, in part, reflect the courts' reluctance to interfere too assertively in immigration decisions.[135] The qualified terms of the international obligation are also clearly a factor. Both points are consistent with the pedigree approach.

[124] Geiringer, '*Tavita*' (n 111) at 102–03; Dunworth, 'International Law in New Zealand Law' (n 82) at 625.
[125] *Tavita* (n 88).
[126] *Puli'uvea v Removal Review Authority* [1996] 3 NZLR 538 (CA).
[127] See Geiringer, '*Tavita*' (n 111) at 92–94, also 85–88.
[128] In addition, see also, eg, *Matua v Minister of Immigration* [2018] NZHC 2078 at [81]–[82]; *Zhang v Minister of Immigration* [2020] NZHC 568.
[129] *Ye* (n 116) at [21], [24]–[25], [31]–[32].
[130] UNCROC (n 77), art 3.
[131] *Ye* (n 116) at [24]–[25].
[132] *Helu* (n 117) at [143]–[144], [207].
[133] ibid at [170]–[176].
[134] *H (SC 104/2020) v Minister of Immigration* [2021] NZSC 192 at [31], fn 27.
[135] The approach has also featured in a social security case: *Harlen* (n 78) at [68]. This is another context in which courts tend to adopt a restrained approach to review.

Authority for the presumption of consistency approach includes the *Airline Pilots Association* case,[136] which also expressly endorsed a version of the pedigree approach. As already discussed, the presumption was held inapplicable on that basis. The alternative approach was not mentioned.

The presumption approach was applied in two leading cases. *Sellers* concerned the power to deny permission for pleasure craft to depart New Zealand ports if their safety equipment was not considered adequate.[137] The Court held that this power could be exercised in relation to foreign-flag-flying craft only to the extent consistent with the international law freedom of the high seas. As that principle stood at the time, that meant the power was essentially never applicable to these foreign craft.[138] In *Zaoui*, as already noted, the Supreme Court also applied the presumption of consistency (citing *Sellers*), this time alongside and in conjunction with the interpretive direction in section 6 of the Bill of Rights.[139]

In both cases, the use of the stronger presumption approach may be explained, at least in part, by the importance of the right at stake – consistently with the pedigree approach. The right against torture, at stake in *Zaoui*, has been held to be absolute.[140] In *Sellers*, the Court emphasised the importance of compliance with international maritime law, and that this importance was clearly recognised in the statute at issue.[141]

Further cases in which the Supreme Court affirmed and applied the presumption are not directly relevant, as they did not involve judicial review of administrative discretion.[142] The mandatory relevant consideration approach was therefore not available as an alternative.

(4) Further Possible Approaches

Two further possible approaches should be mentioned. First, unincorporated international law rights could be invoked to help justify limits on rights affirmed in the Bill of Rights. Social, economic or cultural rights are particularly relevant for this purpose, as they are often in tension with the civil and political rights affirmed in the Bill of Rights. However, this approach is not yet widely used or noted.

One instance of this approach is found in the first instance decision in *Borrowdale*, in the unsuccessful challenge to pandemic lockdown orders that limited freedom of movement, association and assembly. While section 5 justification was conceded in this case, the High Court still invoked the international law right to health[143] in support of a purposive and liberal approach to interpreting the empowering provision.[144]

[136] *Airline Pilots Association* (n 86) at 289.
[137] *Sellers* (n 109).
[138] ibid at 57, 60–62.
[139] *Zaoui* (n 115) at [90]–[93].
[140] *Fitzgerald v R* [2021] NZSC 131, [2021] 1 NZLR 551 at [38], [78], [160], [241].
[141] *Sellers* (n 109) at 57–58.
[142] See *Fitzgerald* (n 140) at [116], [225]–[227], [250]; *Ortmann* (n 97) at [96]; *Zurich* (n 110) at [40].
[143] Preamble to the Constitution of the World Health Organisation; ICESCR (n 79), art 12.
[144] *Borrowdale v Director-General of Health* [2020] NZHC 2090, [2020] 2 NZLR 864 at [36]–[47], [97], [100], [103].

However, the Court of Appeal, while dismissing an appeal, cast some doubt on this argument. It considered that these rights carried less weight because they had not been included in the Bill of Rights.[145]

The point of invoking unincorporated international rights in defending limits on rights in the Bill of Rights is that this lends both legitimacy and weight to the reason for the limit. In *Brooker*, McGrath and Thomas JJ, dissenting, went so far as to consider a competing unincorporated right to be of equal status and weight, rejecting any priority for the right protected by the Bill of Rights in the balancing exercise.[146] Their Honours would have upheld a conviction for a protest action that was challenged on Bill of Rights grounds. They considered that the protest infringed the privacy right of the police officer whose home was targeted by it, and that this privacy right in the circumstances outweighed the protester's freedom of expression. Employing economic, social and cultural rights in this fashion to set against the Bill of Rights' civil and political rights could help redress the focus in our rights jurisprudence on individual and primarily negative rights.

Secondly, the variable intensity approach to the unreasonableness ground of review adopts heightened scrutiny for decisions that impinge on human rights.[147] This is not usually discussed in relation to international law. However, in several of the leading cases on this approach, the rights that triggered heightened scrutiny were unincorporated international law rights.[148] As we will see in the next part, that approach can also be used in combination with a presumption of consistency.

C. Fundamental Common Law Rights

A further source of rights that continues to feature alongside the New Zealand Bill of Rights Act 1990 is the common law. Fundamental common law rights include, for instance, the right of access to the courts,[149] the privilege against self-incrimination[150] and legal professional privilege.[151]

Common law rights are not ordinarily fundamental rights, and it is elementary that they are subject to statute. However, courts have identified certain common law rights as meriting protection against the exercise of public power on the basis that

[145] *Borrowdale v Director-General of Health* [2021] NZCA 520 at [111]–[118].

[146] *Brooker v Police* [2007] NZSC 30, [2007] 3 NZLR 91 at [129], [131]–[134], [210]–[212], [231]–[232]. Thomas J, for that reason, rejected s 5 as the vehicle for the balancing exercise, preferring to treat privacy as an "existing right" acknowledged by s 28 of the Bill of Rights: at [210]–[212].

[147] See Part C(1) of this chapter and Ch 7.B.

[148] *Wolf v Minister of Immigration* [2004] NZAR 414 (HC); *Kim v Minister of Justice of New Zealand* [2019] NZCA 209, [2019] 3 NZLR 173 (the Supreme Court, dismissing an appeal, left open whether heightened scrutiny was appropriate).

[149] *R v Lord Chancellor, ex parte Witham* [1998] QB 575 (HC); *R v Secretary of State for the Home Department, ex parte Simms* [1999] UKHL 33, [2000] 2 AC 115; *R (UNISON) v Lord Chancellor* [2017] UKSC 51, [2017] 3 WLR 409.

[150] *Taylor v New Zealand Poultry Board* [1984] 1 NZLR 394 (CA).

[151] *B v Auckland District Law Society* [2004] 1 NZLR 326 (PC).

they are fundamental.[152] The common law ordinarily protects private legal rights by recognising wrongs and providing remedies. For instance, private law rights of property and privacy are protected by the tort of trespass which allows the right-holder to sue others who infringe those rights. However, such rights can also be claimed against public authorities exercising public powers.[153] In that context, courts have declared it a constitutional principle that these rights constrain the scope or exercise of those public powers.[154] That echoes Dicey's view that the rule of law is served by making public officials subject to the general common law.[155]

Furthermore, the right to natural justice, established by the common law of judicial review, also has that special status and effect, albeit this is not commonly put in terms of constitutionality.[156] Finally, courts have recognised broadly framed constitutional rights, such as the right of access to court, by abstracting from various more specific common law principles or remedies, and by relying on fundamental constitutional principles such as the rule of law.[157] In *Miller (No 2)*, the UK Supreme Court went so far as to recognise the principle of responsible government, which had so far been considered a non-justiciable constitutional convention, as a fundamental common law principle that constrains the scope of public powers.[158] Whether New Zealand courts would follow this is uncertain.

Many of these common law rights are not enshrined in the Bill of Rights. For instance, while the Bill of Rights includes rights to judicial review and to bring or defend proceedings against the Crown in the same way as private proceedings,[159] it does not include a general right of access to the courts. Even where common law rights have been affirmed by the Bill of Rights, such as with the right to natural justice,[160] courts often prefer to rely on the common law as the main source.[161]

Courts have used two different methods for protecting fundamental common law rights by constraining the scope or exercise of public powers. One is to apply heightened scrutiny to decisions that affect such rights.[162] The other is the interpretive presumption of consistency that has become known as the 'principle of legality'.[163] In addition, there are also dicta by some judges that some rights might lie so deep

[152] For discussion of what common law rights are treated as fundamental, see Andrew Burrows, *Thinking about Statutes: Interpretation, Interaction, Improvement (The Hamlyn Lectures 2017)* (Cambridge, Cambridge University Press, 2018) at 69, 71–74; Jason NE Varuhas, 'The Principle of Legality' [2020] 79 *Cambridge Law Journal* 578 at 580–89.

[153] For further discussion, see Chs 10 and 12.

[154] See *Choudry v Attorney-General* [1999] 2 NZLR 582 (CA) at 592–93.

[155] Albert V Dicey, *Introduction to the Law of the Constitution* (Oxford University Press, New York, 2013 (first published 1885)) at 100.

[156] *Daganayasi v Minster of Immigration* [1980] 2 NZLR 130 (CA) at 141; *Cooper v Wandsworth Board of Works* (1863) 14 CBNS 180 at 194.

[157] *Witham* (n 149) at 581–85; *UNISON* (n 149) at [66]–[73], [76]–[82]. In the United Kingdom before the Human Rights Act 1998, courts also treated freedom of expression as a common law right.

[158] *R (Miller) v The Prime Minister* [2019] UKSC 41, [2020] AC 373 (*Miller (No 2)*).

[159] New Zealand Bill of Rights Act 1990, s 27(2) and (3).

[160] Ibid, s 27(1).

[161] See, eg, *Drew v Attorney-General* [2002] 1 NZLR 58 (CA) at [67].

[162] *R v Ministry of Defence, ex parte Smith* [1996] QB 517 (CA).

[163] *Simms* (n 149).

that courts would not enforce legislation abridging them.[164] However, this has never gone beyond dicta.

Once again, as with the choice of methods for giving some effect to Te Tiriti or unincorporated international law obligations, the choice between the two methods is rarely acknowledged. Most often, courts simply apply one or the other of these methods, without any mention of the alternative. It is therefore difficult to know how to choose between these two methods. Arguably, however, they should be applied in combination. This has been accepted in some cases.

This part of the chapter outlines these two methods in turn (sections (1) and (2); it then considers the authorities and arguments for the combined method (section (3)).

(1) Heightened Scrutiny

Heightened scrutiny is well established in the United Kingdom. In New Zealand, there is authority for it, and it is widely used at least at the High Court level, but it remains to be authoritatively adopted by our appellate courts. The state of authority on heightened scrutiny in both jurisdictions will be discussedin the next Chapter.[165] Here, our interest is in understanding its role in protecting fundamental common law rights.

A widely quoted formulation of heightened scrutiny is found in *ex parte Smith*:[166]

> The more substantial the interference with human rights, the more the court will require by way of justification before it is satisfied that the decision is reasonable.

Three points are notable about this formulation. First, heightened scrutiny concerns the reasonableness of the decision. It is generally understood as a variation on the *Wednesbury* unreasonableness ground of judicial review,[167] involving more intensive scrutiny and a lower threshold of intervention. However, sometimes this point is lost sight of.[168]

Secondly, heightened scrutiny is triggered by the fact that an impugned decision interferes with human rights: it is a method for protecting rights. The right at issue in *ex parte Smith* was not a common law right; it was the right to family life and privacy in Article 8 of the European Convention on Human Rights, which at that point was still unincorporated international law. This approach has, however, been treated as the approach for non-statutory rights generally, and especially for common law rights,[169] as well as for other particularly important interests or values.[170]

[164] See, eg, *Taylor v NZ Poultry Board* (n 150) at 398 (Cooke J).

[165] See Ch 7.B.

[166] *ex p Smith* (n 162) at 554.

[167] *Associated Provincial Picture Houses v Wednesbury Corporation* [1948] 1 KB 223 (CA).

[168] In some cases, courts may be considering variable scrutiny to apply to all grounds: eg *Kim v Minister of Justice of New Zealand* [2019] NZCA 209, [2019] 3 NZLR 173 at [45]–[47]. That would be an interesting departure from orthodoxy: see Ch 9.A and C. But it is not at all clear that the courts involved appreciated that point.

[169] See, eg, *Kennedy v Charity Commission* [2014] UKSC 20, [2015] AC 455 at [51]–[52].

[170] Such as, eg, the expectation that Ombudsman recommendations will be accepted: *R (Bradley) v Secretary of State for Work and Pensions* [2008] EWCA Civ 36, [2009] QB 114.

Third and finally, the reasonableness enquiry here focuses on a particular question: the justification for abrogating the rights in question. It therefore performs the same role as the proportionality test that is established for determining the justification of limits on rights under section 5 of the Bill of Rights. This is not as commonly noted as the other two points.[171] What is, however, commonly debated is whether use of the proportionality test itself should be expanded beyond Bill of Rights cases.[172]

Heightened scrutiny at least in Aotearoa New Zealand often involves scrutiny of the cogency of the reasoning or the adequacy of the evidence.[173] Commentators have welcomed this as generating a 'culture of justification' in relation to rights: decision-makers can abrogate rights where they consider this necessary for serving other important objectives, but the courts will require justification and scrutinise that justification.[174]

(2) The Principle of Legality

The 'principle of legality' is a principle of statutory interpretation.[175] Its classic formulation is found in Lord Hoffmann's speech in *Simms*:[176]

> Fundamental rights cannot be overridden by general or ambiguous words. … In the absence of express language or necessary implication to the contrary, the courts … presume that even the most general words were intended to be subject to the basic rights of the individual

It operates much like the presumption of consistency with international law, or like section 6 of the Bill of Rights. It often raises difficult questions as to what counts as 'express language or necessary implication'. Those issues will be explored in Part E of this chapter on rights-consistent statutory interpretation.

This principle is well established by authority in New Zealand.[177] The label 'principle of legality', however, is relatively recent and not universally used: much of the authority on this principle uses different terminology and differently formulated tests. For instance, in *Choudry* the Court of Appeal adopted a narrow reading of a search power due to:[178]

> the important constitutional consideration that at common law every invasion of private property is a trespass and any intended erosion of the protection of the common law should be spelt out in the plainest possible terms.

[171] The 'analogy' is noted in *UNISON* (n 149) at [89].

[172] See Ch 7.B.

[173] See, eg, *Wolf v Minister of Immigration* [2004] NZAR 414 (HC) at [66]–[72]. For further discussion, see Ch 7.B(3).

[174] David Dyzenhaus, Murray Hunt and Michael Taggart 'The Principle of Legality in Administrative Law: Internationalisation as Constitutionalisation' (2001) 1 *Oxford University Commonwealth Law Journal* 2001 at 26–32.

[175] Although in the UK it has recently been held to apply to prerogative powers as well: text at n 193.

[176] *Simms* (n 149) at 131.

[177] See, eg, *Cropp v Judicial Review Committee* [2008] NZSC 46, [2008] 3 NZLR 774 at [27]; *D v New Zealand Police* [2021] NZSC 2, [2021] 1 NZLR 213 at [76].

[178] *Choudry* (n 154) at 592–93.

In *Taylor v New Zealand Poultry Board*, while the Court of Appeal rejected a narrow reading of the power at issue, it accepted this general proposition:[179]

> The common law favours the liberty of the citizen, and, if a Court is not satisfied that a statutory power of questioning was meant to exclude the privilege [against self-incrimination], it is in accordance with the spirit of the common law to allow the privilege.

Both passages effectively invoke the principle of legality, but do not use that name.

Among the rationales for this principle, it is worth noting Lord Hoffmann's reliance in *Simms* on the need to ensure political attention and accountability for the statutory abrogation of rights. He said that 'Parliament must squarely confront what it is doing and accept the political cost.' If general or ambiguous words could override rights, 'there is too great a risk that the full implications of their unqualified meaning may have passed unnoticed in the democratic process'.[180]

(3) Relationship between these Two Approaches

Much of the case law and commentary does not acknowledge that there are two methods for protecting fundamental common law rights, and therefore does not address the relationship between these.[181] Where occasionally the existence of both methods has been acknowledged, they have often been considered to belong to different grounds of review: heightened scrutiny forms part of the irrationality ground, while the principle of legality forms part of illegality. The latter is seen as affording the stronger protection for rights.[182]

Arguably, however, the most appropriate approach combines the two. Such a combined approach corresponds to the approach established for the Bill of Rights.[183] The justification for a rights infringement is first tested by heightened scrutiny. If the rights infringement is found not to be justified, the empowering provision is then read down, invoking the principle of legality. In short, the principle of legality applies subject to allowing justified limits on rights.[184]

There are good reasons for adopting this combined approach. One is that it promotes coherence and consistency, given it corresponds to the approach to the Bill of Rights.[185] More substantively, this approach recognises that justified limits on rights are not rights violations, hence there is no need to avoid them.[186] Conversely, it recognises the importance of scrutinising the justification for limits.[187]

[179] *Taylor v Poultry Board* (n 150) at 402.
[180] *Simms* (n 149) at 131.
[181] For instance, see *ex parte Smith* (n 162) on heightened scrutiny; and *Witham* (n 149) on the principle of legality.
[182] See, eg, John Laws, 'Is the High Court the Guardian of Fundamental Constitutional Rights?' [1993] *Public Law* 59 at 76.
[183] Discussed in Part D of this chapter.
[184] See Hanna Wilberg, 'Common Law Rights Have Justified Limits: Refining the "Principle of Legality"' in Dan Meagher and Matthew Groves (eds), *The Principle of Legality in Australian and New Zealand Law* (Federation Press, 2017) 139. For a more critical view, see Varuhas (n 152) at 592–598, 608–613.
[185] *Four Midwives v Minister for COVID-19 Response* [2021] NZHC 3064, [2022] 2 NZLR 65 at [64].
[186] Wilberg (n 184) at 151–152.
[187] Dyzenhaus, Hunt and Taggart (n 174) at 27.

The possibility of such a combined approach was rarely mentioned until recently. However, it has now been adopted and applied in the High Court by Palmer J in *Four Midwives*.[188]

While this remains to be confirmed by appellate authority in New Zealand, there is significant support for it in United Kingdom case law. First, several leading decisions can be seen as tacitly following this approach. The most notable instances are found in Lord Steyn's speech in *Simms*[189] and Lord Bingham's speech in *Daly*.[190] These contain statements of both methods and apply them in combination. They first engage in detailed scrutiny of the justification for the challenged rule, concluding that the limit on the rights is disproportionate to the legitimate objective pursued. It is only after reaching that conclusion that they then apply the principle of legality to conclude that the rights infringement is not authorised. A more recent instance is found in *UNISON*.[191]

Explicit authority for the combined approach, albeit perhaps obiter, can be found in *Miller (No 2)*. The Supreme Court cited *UNISON* for the following proposition, which amounts to the combined approach:[192]

> Unless the terms of the statute indicate a contrary intention, the courts have set a limit to the lawful exercise of the power by holding that the extent to which the measure impedes or frustrates the operation of the relevant [constitutional] principle must have a reasonable justification.

It applied this proposition in the context of a challenge to the exercise of a prerogative power, holding that it applied to prerogative powers as well as to statutory ones. The impugned exercise of the power to prorogue Parliament was found to be unlawful for infringing constitutional principles, because the infringement was not reasonably justified.[193]

Returning to New Zealand, earlier appellate authority for the combined approach may be found in *Taylor v New Zealand Poultry Board*, albeit the point was not made explicit. We have already seen that the Court of Appeal accepted what amounts to the principle of legality to protect the privilege against self-incrimination. One of the reasons for rejecting the narrow reading of the relevant power that was proposed on this basis amounted to finding the impugned limit on the privilege to be justified. The Court pointed out that this case concerned economic regulation (a statutory egg marketing regime) rather than 'actual invasion of physical liberty', and that it was 'necessary to keep a sense of proportion' in the protection of the privilege.[194]

[188] *Four Midwives* (n 185) at [63]–[64].
[189] *Simms* (n 149) at 128–130.
[190] *R (Daly) v Secretary of Statement for the Home Department* [2001] UKHL 26, [2001] 2 AC 532 at [5], [12], [19]–[21].
[191] *UNISON* (n 149), esp at [79]–[80] and [87]–[89].
[192] *Miller (No 2)* (n 158) at [49].
[193] ibid at [40], [49], [50].
[194] *Taylor v Poultry Board* (n 150) at 402. See also *Melser v Police* [1967] NZLR 437 (CA) at 445.

D. The Bill of Rights

The New Zealand Bill of Rights Act 1990 in Part 2 enshrines most of the civil and political rights found in the main international law instruments – in particular the International Covenant on Civil and Political Rights[195] – and in classic constitutional bills of rights such as in the United States or French constitutions. These include rights to life and security of the person, the right to vote and freedom of expression, non-discrimination and minority rights, and criminal procedure rights.[196] The Bill of Rights further includes the right to natural justice and rights to bring and defend civil proceedings against the Crown (s 27). A notable qualification is that several of the broader rights are represented only in narrow versions.[197] Instead of a general right to privacy and family life,[198] for instance, there is only the right against unreasonable search and seizure in section 21. The right to liberty[199] is represented only by the right not to be arbitrarily arrested or detained (s 22) and other particular liberties such as freedom of expression (s 14); and equality[200] takes the form of freedom from discrimination (s 19). There is no right to property. However, existing rights are expressly saved by section 28.

Justified limits are allowed by section 5: the rights 'may be subject only to such reasonable limits prescribed by law as can be demonstrably justified in a free and democratic society'. This universal limitation clause is the Canadian model.[201] The alternative model is to attach tailor-made limitation clauses to individual rights, as in the European Convention of Human Rights which is incorporated into United Kingdom law by the Human Rights Act 1998.[202]

The rights in the Bill of Rights do not have justiciable supreme law status: section 4 expressly provides that courts cannot invalidate or disapply Acts of Parliament on the grounds of inconsistency with the Bill of Rights. Subject to this, however, courts have been given significant and important powers to protect these rights against abuses by public authorities.

First, the rights bind executive government in the absence of a statutory power to abrogate them. Oddly, this is not spelt out.[203] But it follows from section 3, providing

[195] International Covenant on Civil and Political Rights (16 December 1966) (ICCPR). According to its long title, the New Zealand Bill of Rights Act 1990 (Bill of Rights) affirms New Zealand's commitment to this instrument. See also the Universal Declaration of Human Rights (10 December 1948) (UDHR).

[196] Bill of Rights, ss 8–11, 12, 14, 19–20, 21–26.

[197] See Claudia Geiringer, 'When Constitutional Theories Migrate: A Case Study' (2019) 67 *American Journal of Comparative Law* 281; Claudia Geiringer and Paul Rishworth, 'Magna Carta's Legacy? Ideas of Liberty and Due Process in the New Zealand Bill of Rights Act' [2017] *New Zealand Law Review* 597.

[198] Cf Convention for the Protection of Human Rights and Fundamental Freedoms (4 November 1950) (ECHR), art 8, incorporated into UK law by the Human Rights Act 1998 (UK).

[199] See, eg, Canadian Charter of Rights and Freedoms, pt 1 of the Constitution Act 1982, being Sch B of the Canada Act 1982 (UK), s 7.

[200] See, eg, ibid, s 15.

[201] See, eg, ibid, s 1.

[202] See ECHR, arts 2(2), 4(3), 5(1), 7(2), 8(2), 9(2), 10(2), 11(2). Each limitation clause is in slightly different terms, and some rights have no limitation clause (notably the prohibition of torture, art 3).

[203] In contrast, see the Human Rights Act 1998 (UK), s 6.

that the Bill of Rights 'applies' to all branches of government and to everyone exercising public power. Secondly, where potentially rights-limiting statutory powers are involved, section 6 requires courts to search for a more rights-consistent meaning and adopt such a meaning if available. The rights are thus protected by a statutory presumption of consistency, corresponding to the common law presumptions that protect rights from other sources.[204] Finally, a recent development is that courts now also have power to declare statutory provisions to be inconsistent with the Bill of Rights where no rights-consistent interpretation is available.[205]

In the administrative law context, there are four main sets of issues about the approach to the Bill of Rights. In this Part of the chapter the focus is on the set of issues concerning section 5 – justified limits on rights. The other three sets of issues concern sections 3 and 6 and remedies. The section 3 issues, concerning the bodies and powers to which the Bill of Rights applies, are addressed in Chapter 11. The section 6 issues, concerning the strength of the direction to adopt a rights-consistent meaning when interpreting other enactments, are covered in Part E of this chapter. One major remedies issue, namely when damages are available, is covered in Chapter 12.

On the section 5 issues, the leading decision is the Supreme Court decision in *Hansen*.[206] This settled three questions about section 5. First, its role: section 5 plays a central role in the overall Bill of Rights analysis, and the section 6 interpretive direction is subject to it. Secondly, the test for applying section 5: *Hansen* adopted the proportionality test set out in the Canadian *Oakes* case.[207] Thirdly, the role of the courts in applying section 5: *Hansen* recognised the need for some deference.

However, *Hansen* was a criminal law case. In that context, courts exercise primary jurisdiction. The *Hansen* answers to the three questions about section 5 are not necessarily all appropriate in administrative law. Courts in administrative law exercise a limited supervisory jurisdiction. Furthermore, administrative law cases arise in a wide variety of different decision-making contexts. The scope and intensity of supervision and other features of review vary according to that context. These points are relevant to the questions about section 5.[208] Until recently, it was difficult to find administrative law cases that engaged with section 5 in any detail at all,[209] and there were a bewildering array of different approaches.[210]

When courts have discussed departures from the '*Hansen* approach', unfortunately they have rarely distinguished between the above three questions about section 5.[211]

[204] See Parts A–C of this chapter. The extent to which all these interpretive presumptions attract the same approach is discussed below in Part E.

[205] *Taylor v Attorney-General* [2018] NZSC 104, [2019] 1 NZLR 213; Bill of Rights, ss 7A–7B.

[206] *R v Hansen* [2007] NZSC 7, [2007] 3 NZLR 1.

[207] *R v Oakes* [1986] 1 SCR 103.

[208] See Janet McLean, 'The Impact of the Bill of Rights on Administrative Law Revisited: Rights, Utility, and Administration' [2008] *New Zealand Law Review* 377.

[209] See Claudia Geiringer, 'Sources of Resistance to Proportionality Review of Administrative Power Under the New Zealand Bill of Rights Act' (2013) 11 *New Zealand Journal of Public and International Law* 123.

[210] See Marcelo Rodriguez Ferrere, 'The New Zealand Bill of Rights Act 1990 and Administrative Law: A History of Confusion and Inertia' [2021] *New Zealand Law Review* 71.

[211] See, eg, *D (SC 31/2019) v New Zealand Police* [2021] NZSC 2, [2021] 1 NZLR 213 at [75], [101], [259], fn 361.

Yet these are distinct questions, and it is possible to depart from the *Hansen* approach on one of these and adhere to it on others. The lack of attention to this has caused much unnecessary confusion.

In discussing the current position below,[212] I address the position on each of the three components of the *Hansen* approach, and also on three further points that have been introduced by administrative law cases since *Hansen*. These six points are addressed in the following order: (1) the central role of section 5: it cannot be bypassed, except in relation to certain rights that render it redundant; (2) the test used to apply section 5 is either a structured proportionality test or a more general balancing test, (3) the onus of justification is on the respondent, but courts take care not to set an unrealistic standard of proof; (4) courts accord decision-makers' views on section 5 a measure of respect, depending on context; (5) decision-makers have often been required to satisfy themselves that the limit is justified in terms of section 5 (a form of mandatory relevant consideration approach) and (6) the section 5 justification enquiry is sometimes framed in terms of the unreasonableness ground.

(1) The Central Role of Section 5 in Relation to Section 6

Decision-makers can defend a Bill of Rights challenge by arguing that the impugned limit on the claimed right was justified in terms of section 5. Where such justification is made out, the section 6 direction to search for a rights-consistent meaning is not engaged, because there is no inconsistency with the Bill of Rights. This is the central role of section 5, the first of the three components of the *Hansen* approach.[213] It also follows that where the limit is *not* justified, section 6 requires a search not for the least rights-limiting meaning, but for a meaning that limits the right no more than can be justified in terms of section 5.[214]

This point about the central role of section 5 was put in *Hansen* in terms of a methodology involving a sequence of steps, in which section 5 comes before section 6. Tipping J's six-step version is most commonly cited.[215] Preoccupation with that six-step test has sometimes obscured the real point about the central role of section 5.

The central role of section 5 reflects two fundamental points. The first is that the Bill of Rights protects rights only to the extent that is reasonable in the circumstances.[216]

[212] This discussion draws on Hanna Wilberg, 'Settling the Approach to Section 5 of the Bill of Rights in Administrative Law: Justification, Restraint and Variability' (2021) 19 *New Zealand Journal of Public and International Law* 97.

[213] *Hansen* (n 206) at [58]–[59], [89]–[91], [178]–[192].

[214] *Fitzgerald v R* [2021] NZSC 131, [2021] 1 NZLR 551 at [48], fn 70 (Winkelmann CJ).

[215] *Hansen* (n 206) at [92]; the other statements of the test have fewer steps but are largely the same in substance: see at [60] (Blanchard J), [192] (McGrath J).

[216] See Paul Rishworth, 'Interpreting and Invalidating Enactments Under a Bill of Rights: Three Enquiries in Comparative Perspective' in Rick Bigwood (ed), *The Statute: Making and Meaning* (Wellington, LexisNexis, 2004) 251 at 277.

'Limits can be fundamental too',[217] because 'rights are part of a social order in which they must accommodate the rights of others and the legitimate interests of society as a whole'.[218] The second point, conversely, is that limits on rights must be demonstrably justified as reasonable. The point of the Bill of Rights is to accord special priority to rights, and this is achieved by the requirement of demonstrable justification.

Yet there have been recurring suggestions that section 5 justification could be bypassed. By now, however, there is much administrative law authority rejecting this, except in relation to certain rights that render section 5 redundant. That confirms the approach to the Bill of Rights in administrative law that has been proposed by commentators since the earliest years of the Bill of Rights[219] and has been adopted in the United Kingdom without any debate.[220]

Let us explore four aspects of this position: (a) authority against bypassing section 5 justification and using s 6 to invalidate justified limits; (b) uncertainty around bypassing section 5 justification where impugned limits are clearly authorised regardless of justification; (c) what to make of much-cited dicta in *Hansen* and *D v Police*; and (d) what to make of leading authorities that appear to suggest section 5 could be bypassed.

(a) Authority against Bypassing Section 5 where Limits are Justified

New Health is authority against bypassing section 5 and using s 6 to invalidate limits on rights that are justified. The Supreme Court relied on section 5 justification in dismissing a challenge to fluoridation of drinking water supplies. Fluoridation did engage the section 11 right to refuse medical treatment, but it was a justified limit on this right and therefore there was no reason for the empowering provisions to be read down.[221] However, this decision did not fully clarify the position on the role of section 5 in administrative law cases, as it did not involve a challenge to the exercise of discretion.[222] Furthermore, the Court also maintained that alternative approaches are available, without specifying when that is so.[223]

The question whether section 5 can be bypassed in challenging an exercise of administrative discretion then became very significant in the Covid-19 pandemic. Emergency measures such as lockdowns and vaccine mandates involved severe limits on rights. When they were first imposed, the government had a strong case for a section 5 justification, but it was much more arguable whether the measures were authorised by the statutory powers that were invoked at that time. Those empowering provisions could be read as authorising the measures, but a generous and purposive reading was required to

[217] Andrew Butler and Petra Butler, *The New Zealand Bill of Rights Act: A Commentary*, 2nd edn (Wellington, LexisNexis NZ, 2015), heading above [6.9.8], and see throughout that chapter.

[218] *Hansen* (n 206) at [186] (McGrath J).

[219] Janet McLean, Paul Rishworth and Michael Taggart, 'The Impact of the New Zealand Bill of Rights on Administrative Law' in Legal Research Foundation (ed), *The New Zealand Bill of Rights Act 1990* (Auckland, Legal Research Foundation, 1992) 62.

[220] See, eg, *R (Aguilar Quila) v Secretary of State for the Home Department* [2011] UKSC 45, [2012] 1 AC 621 at [45]–[77].

[221] *New Health NZ Inc v South Taranaki District Council* [2018] NZSC 59, [2018] 1 NZLR 948 at [112]–[145].

[222] ibid at [5], [111], fn 103, [176]. Both majority judgments nevertheless considered that, at least in some cases, s 5 justification does fall to be considered in relation to an exercise of discretion.

[223] ibid at [104], fn 94.

achieve that. Challenges to these measures therefore would succeed if courts could be persuaded to bypass section 5 justification and to go directly to the interpretive direction in section 6. On that basis, courts could adopt a narrow, rights-preserving meaning of the empowering provisions that did not authorise the measures. That was the approach proposed by the applicants in both *Borrowdale* and *Four Midwives*.

The Court of Appeal in *Borrowdale* clearly rejected this approach, holding that the *Hansen* approach was appropriate. This decision was less clear on the relevance of section 5 justification to the interpretation of the empowering provision.[224] However, it did find that the lockdown order was authorised, and supported this interpretation by emphasising the statutory purpose of protecting the 'greater good' in 'times of dire emergency'.[225]

The High Court in *Four Midwives* again rejected bypassing section 5, in the context of a challenge to vaccine mandates for the health care workforce and teachers.[226] Palmer J did spell out the relevance to interpretation: if the limit is justified, then a generous purposive interpretation of the empowering provision is available because the section 6 interpretive direction is not engaged.[227]

A series of further challenges to orders imposing vaccine requirements and to mandatory isolation requirements have also turned on section 5 justification: where justification was made out, challenges have failed; where it was not made out, they have succeeded. These cases include the Court of Appeal decisions in *NZTSOS* on appeal from *Four Midwives*,[228] and in *Four Members of the Armed Forces*.[229] There has been no further suggestion that section 5 should be bypassed.[230] The Supreme Court in *Moncrief-Spittle* also relied on section 5 justification in dismissing a challenge on the grounds of freedom of speech to a decision cancelling a speaking event.[231] These cases should help to end the long-standing uncertainty on the role of section 5 in administrative law cases.

Turning briefly to evaluating this position, the courts' approach in these cases is consistent not only with *Hansen* but also with the fundamental point underpinning it: rights should be protected only to the extent that is reasonable in the circumstances. Against this, it could be argued that while limits on rights may be justified, that should be for Parliament to decide. If Parliament has not authorised limits specifically, it is not for the courts to decide that they are justified.

[224] See Hanna Wilberg, 'Pandemic Litigation Reaffirms Hansen Approach but Also Exposes Two Flaws in Its Formulation' (2022) 30 *New Zealand Universities Law Review* 69 at 73–74.

[225] *Borrowdale v Director-General of Health* [2021] NZCA 520, [2022] 2 NZLR 356 at [155].

[226] *Four Midwives v Minister for COVID-19 Response* [2021] NZHC 3064, [2022] 2 NZLR 65 at [40]–[53].

[227] ibid at [50].

[228] *NZTSOS Inc v Minister for COVID-19 Response* [2024] NZCA 74, [2024] 2 NZLR 624 (the Supreme Court denied leave to appeal).

[229] *Four Members of the Armed Forces v Chief of Defence Force* [2024] NZCA 17, [2024] 3 NZLR 1 (under appeal at time of writing).

[230] For decisions that turned on section 5 justification, see also *GF v Minister of COVID-19 Response* [2021] NZHC 2526, [2022] 2 NZLR 1 at [75]–[94]; *Four Aviation Security Service Employees v Minister of COVD-19 Response* [2021] NZHC 3012, [2022] 2 NZLR 26 at [78]–[127]; *Grounded Kiwis Group Inc v Minister of Health* [2022] NZHC 832, (2022) 13 HRNZ 32 at [251]–[429].

[231] *Moncrief-Spittle v Regional Facilities Auckland Limited* [2022] NZSC 138, [2022] 1 NZLR 459.

The choice between these positions should perhaps be seen as depending on the context, such as the severity of the limit on the right, and conversely the strength and obviousness of the justification for the limit. In most contexts, however, requiring specific statutory authorisation would be too restrictive of government's ability to use statutory powers for purposes beneficial to the public interest, such as safeguarding public health in a pandemic. Parliament may not have foreseen the need for the particular rights-infringing type of measure. It should be enough that the impugned measure serves the purpose for which the power was enacted, can be brought within the terms of the power, and is a justified limit.

(b) Bypassing Section 5 where Limits are Clearly Authorised Regardless?

There is another context in which an issue about bypassing section 5 arises. It involves cases where the statute clearly authorises the limit on the right and cannot be read any other way, regardless of justification. In such cases, courts have sometimes considered section 5 justification to be a moot point and unnecessary to consider.[232]

This approach is in tension with the second of the two fundamental points noted earlier. To respect the priority assigned to rights, courts should insist on limits on rights being demonstrably justified even when they are clearly authorised by the statute.

The approach that avoids this step is now less likely. Because a declaration of inconsistency is now available if a clearly authorised limit is not justified in terms of section 5, the courts are less likely to consider a section 5 analysis unnecessary in such cases.[233] Furthermore, the onus is on defendants to establish section 5 justification.[234] In the claim for a declaration of inconsistency in *Make It 16*, a full section 5 analysis of the age discrimination involved in the voting age of 18 was not possible due to the Crown declining to substantiate the claimed justification. However, rather than bypassing section 5, the Supreme Court responded by declaring that the age discrimination had not been justified.[235]

(c) What to Make of Dicta in Hansen *and* D v Police

Prior to *New Health* and the pandemic cases, there was much uncertainty whether the central role of section 5 applies at all in administrative law cases. One of the reasons was found in dicta in *Hansen* itself. The majority contemplated that its approach might not apply in all types of cases.[236] It declined to overrule *Moonen*, which was then the leading administrative law case on the Bill of Rights and which appeared to deny section 5 its central role.[237]

[232] See eg *Mangawhai Ratepayers and Residents Association Inc v Kaipara District Council* [2015] NZCA 612, [2016] 2 NZLR 437 at [183].

[233] But see *Commissioner of Police v G* [2023] NZCA 93, [2023] 2 NZLR 107 at [156]–[157]. The Court did find that there was no substantive unfairness: ibid at [162]–[168].

[234] *Ministry of Health v Atkinson* [2012] NZCA 184, [2012] 3 NZLR 456.

[235] *Make It 16 Inc v Attorney-General* [2022] NZSC 134, [2022] 1 NZLR 683 at [70], [72].

[236] *Hansen* (n 206) at [61], [93]–[94], [192]. In addition, there was a strong dissent on the role of s 5 by Elias CJ: at [6]–[7], [15]–[24].

[237] *Moonen v Film and Literature Review Board* [2000] 2 NZLR 9 (CA) at [16], [17].

These dicta were re-affirmed in two more recent Supreme Court decisions. In *New Health*, the Court still maintained that alternative approaches remain available, without specifying when that is so.[238] In *D v Police*, most well-known for its assertive rights-consistent interpretation of a retrospectivity provision, a separate challenge concerned the proper approach to a judicial discretion whether to make an order under the legislation. The Court considered that the '*Hansen* methodology' was not appropriate in this context, apparently because discretion was involved.[239]

However, the *Hansen* dicta are best understood as allowing departures only from the six-step test, not from the central role of section 5. This was the view of Palmer J in the *Four Midwives* case: while the six-step test is not essential, the substantive point established in *Hansen* concerns the role of section 5 in relation to section 6. This point *does* apply in all contexts.[240]

What, then, do we make of the departure from *Hansen* in *D v Police*? While the Court did not explicitly engage in a section 5 analysis in this part of the case, it did clearly state that an exercise of the discretion is consistent with the Bill of Rights if the limit on the relevant right is justified.[241] That is entirely consistent with *Hansen* on the role of section 5.[242] There are, then, two alternative explanations of the dictum. One is that this too may be read as departing only from the six-step test. Alternatively, this is an instance of the confusing failure to distinguish between the three questions about section 5 settled in *Hansen*. The aspect of the '*Hansen* methodology' that was rejected here was the *Oakes* proportionality test for applying section 5. We will return to this.[243]

(d) What to Make of Leading Cases Bypassing Section 5

The long-standing uncertainty concerning the role of section 5 was further due to the existence of a string of leading Bill of Rights cases that did not feature a section 5 justification analysis. Several of these – notably *Drew*, *Zaoui* and *Cropp* – concerned challenges to administrative measures. However, these cases were convincingly explained and distinguished in *Borrowdale* and *Four Midwives*.[244] Certain rights render section 5 redundant, and all of these cases involved those rights. We can identify two different versions of this qualification.

First, the formulation of some rights makes reasonable limits part of their definition, and this makes reference to section 5 redundant. One such 'internally qualified' right is the section 21 right to be free from unreasonable search and seizure. The Supreme Court in *Cropp* held that once a search has been found to be 'unreasonable', there is no room left for a section 5 justification.[245] Other internally qualified rights are the right to natural justice in section 27(1), at issue in *Drew*,[246] and the right not to be

[238] *New Health* (n 221) at [104], fn 94.
[239] *D v Police* (n 211) at [100]–[101].
[240] *Four Midwives* (n 226) at [45]–[46], [50], [52].
[241] *D v Police* (n 211) at [100]–[101], [108], [129].
[242] See *Four Midwives* (n 226) at [49].
[243] Section (2) of this part D.
[244] *Borrowdale* (n 225) at [137]–[141]; *Four Midwives* (n 226) at [48].
[245] *Cropp v Judicial Committee* [2008] NZSC 46, [2008] 3 NZLR 774 at [33].
[246] *Drew v Attorney-General* [2002] 1 NZLR 58 (CA) at [67].

subject to 'disproportionately' severe punishment in section 9, at issue in *Fitzgerald*.[247] While some would prefer to retain a role for section 5 even in these contexts,[248] what matters here is that this qualification does not detract from the fundamental point that rights are protected only to the extent that is reasonable.

The second qualification is that a small number of rights are considered absolute, thus leaving no role for section 5. The clearest example is the section 9 right not to be tortured, as affirmed by the Supreme Court in *Fitzgerald*.[249] This was also the right at issue in *Zaoui*, one of the administrative law cases that did not feature a section 5 analysis.[250] Perhaps such absolute rights do qualify the fundamental proposition, but we could also say that there are simply no circumstances in which any limits on these rights are reasonable. Even if this second point does qualify the fundamental proposition, this is very much an exception to the normal rule.

In conclusion, then, the central role of section 5 does apply in the administrative law context. Section 5 cannot be bypassed except where it is redundant because the right at issue either is absolute or includes a balancing test in its definition.

(2) The Test for Section 5 Justified Limits

The basis for justifying a limit on a right under section 5 is that the need to protect the right is outweighed by an important competing objective served by the limit. A test for this is the second component of the *Hansen* approach. *Hansen* adopted the proportionality test from the Canadian *Oakes* case.[251] This is a structured test involving a sequence of questions:

- Does the limit serve a legitimate and sufficiently important objective?
- Is it rationally connected to that objective?
- Does it impair the right no more than is reasonably[252] necessary for serving that objective?
- Is proportional to the importance of the objective?

The third step generally requires consideration of alternative means for serving the objective.[253] At the final step, the factors to be weighed are not very clearly established. A useful approach is to weigh up two pairs of factors.[254] On the one hand, the importance of the right (generally and in the particular context)[255] and the extent of the limit

[247] *Fitzgerald* (n 214) at [78].
[248] Butler and Butler (n 217) chs 6.5 and 6.6.
[249] *Fitzgerald* (n 214) at [38], [78], [160], [241]; see also *Hansen* (n 206) at [65] (obiter).
[250] *Zaoui v Attorney-General (No 2)* [2005] NZSC 38, [2006] 1 NZLR 289.
[251] *Hansen* (n 206) at [64], [79], [103]–[104]; *Oakes* (n 207).
[252] For the 'reasonably' qualification, see *Hansen* (n 206) at [79], [104], [126], [279]; *New Health* (n 221) at [132], [134].
[253] See, eg, *Hansen* (n 206) at [79], [217]–[224]; *NZTSOS* (n 228) at [70]–[76].
[254] Similarly, see *NZTSOS* (n 228) at [81]; *Ministry of Transport v Noort* [1992] 3 NZLR 260 (CA) at 283–84, adopted in *Hansen* (n 206) at [64] (Blanchard J).
[255] See *Hansen* (n 206) at [193]–[199], [225]–[228] (McGrath J).

on the right.[256] On the other hand, the importance of the objective served by the limit and the effectiveness of the limit in serving that objective.

As an alternative to this structured test, courts sometimes adopt a broader balancing approach, simply balancing the importance of protecting the right against the importance of serving the competing objective.[257] Often when courts talk about departing from the *Hansen* approach, they are referring to this choice of tests for section 5. *D v Police* is an example,[258] as already noted.

The Supreme Court in *Moncrief-Spittle* confirmed that the test must be adjusted according to context. A general balancing test may be more appropriate when reviewing the exercise of a discretionary power, as in that case. The Court added that there is 'no immutable rule' and emphasised that a less structured approach 'does not entail a lesser threshold'.[259]

Administrative law cases in which the full structured test has been applied include the Supreme Court's decision in *New Health*,[260] in which the issue concerned the scope of the statutory power. However, they also include most of the challenges to emergency measures for fighting the pandemic, including the Court of Appeal's decision in *NZTSOS*.[261] These were challenges to exercises of discretion, but it may be relevant that they concerned delegated legislation rather than decisions on individual cases.

(3) The Onus of Justification

The onus or burden of showing a limit to be justified rests on the public authority defendant.[262] This is one of the points about section 5 that have been established by cases subsequent to *Hansen*. Discharging the onus requires not only legitimate and sufficient reasons, but also evidence to back up the factual validity of those reasons: evidence that the problem addressed by the limit exists; and evidence of the chosen measure's effectiveness in addressing that problem, compared to the effectiveness of available alternatives.[263] To put this differently, the courts in this context engage in close scrutiny of relevant factual findings and evaluations, demanding a satisfactory evidential foundation – much as in the context of heightened scrutiny reasonableness review.

However, this requirement for evidence to support the justification must have its limits. It is in the nature of public policy decisions that they often have to be made in the absence of conclusive evidence.[264] Evidence may be hard to come by, or there may be much conflicting evidence. Requiring proof on the balance of probabilities may represent a lack of deference to the decision-maker's judgment in resolving the conflicts in the evidence – though the appropriate level of deference does depend on

[256] See *New Health* (n 221) at [135].
[257] See *Taylor v The Chief Executive of the Department of Corrections* [2015] NZCA 477, [2015] NZAR 1648 at [72], [84]; *D v Police* (n 211) at [100]–[101], [108], [129].
[258] *D v Police* (n 211) at [100]–[101].
[259] *Moncrief-Spittle* (n 231) at [87]–[92], quoted passages are at [91].
[260] *New Health* (n 221) at [112].
[261] *NZTSOS* (n 228) at [63]–[83].
[262] *Atkinson* (n 234) at [163].
[263] See, eg, *New Health* (n 221) at [123]–[143].
[264] *Atkinson* (n 234) at [165].

the context. More importantly, it would risk paralysing government in areas where government intervention is needed. The most pressing problems are often also the ones surrounded by the greatest uncertainty.

Atkinson therefore held that decision-makers are justified in proceeding on the basis of applying 'common sense to what is known, even though what is known may be deficient from a scientific point of view'.[265] According to *New Health*, the courts will 'undertake a broad assessment' to determine whether 'the evidence provides a proper basis' for the justification offered.[266] This approach has also been adopted in challenges to pandemic emergency measures, where the 'precautionary principle' has been held to apply.[267] Despite this acknowledged need for realistic limits to what courts demand by way of evidence, there have been cases in which justification has failed for lack of supporting evidence.[268]

(4) Respect, Latitude etc: Limits to the Role of Courts in Relation to Section 5

Determining whether a limit is justified in terms of section 5 involves judgement in weighing up competing and often incommensurable values and interests. It also involves factual findings on risks and benefits based on conflicting evidence, often in the face of inherent uncertainty. The role of the courts in this regard is therefore restricted, especially in the administrative law context. Rather than substituting their own conclusions on these matters, courts accord some respect to the decision-maker's views. Alternative terms for this respect include weight, deference, leeway or latitude. The details of this approach depend on context and are contested.

This is the third component of the *Hansen* approach. Even in the criminal context, the *Hansen* Court considered that section 5 justification is not a question on which courts should simply substitute their own view: a court's function in this regard is rather one of review. The respect or deference in *Hansen* was accorded to Parliament.[269]

In the administrative law context also, respect can be accorded to Parliament where the issue concerns the scope of a statutory power as in *New Health*.[270] More often, however, in this area the section 5 justification issue concerns a rights-limiting exercise of administrative discretion. A court's respect in such a case is accorded to the executive or administrative decision-maker. There is some debate as to when and to what extent respect is appropriate in this context.

Against according any respect or latitude to the decision-maker at all, it has been argued that section 5 sets out a legal test, and questions of law in our system of administrative law are for the courts to determine.[271] To put it slightly differently, by enacting a Bill of Rights, Parliament has entrusted application of that test to the courts.

[265] ibid at [166], adopting the Canadian approach in *RJR-MacDonald Inc v Canada* [1995] 3 SCR 199 at [137].

[266] *New Health* (n 221) at [122], implicitly adopting the respondents' argument based on *Atkinson* (n 234) at [118].

[267] *NZTSOS* (n 228) at [92]–[93].

[268] See, eg, *Grounded Kiwis* (n 230) at [325], [328], [406].

[269] *Hansen* (n 206) at [105]–[119], [207], [211], [222].

[270] *New Health* (n 221) at [114], [121]–[122].

[271] See, eg, *Four Aviation Security Employees* (n 230) at [79], [82]–[83].

The Supreme Court in *Moncrief* rightly dismissed this objection. While 'the extent of reasonable limits is a legal question', 'the application of that legal standard' involves 'mixed questions of fact and law'.[272] On that basis, the supervisory jurisdiction does not extend to courts substituting their judgement on section 5 justification. Even outside the context of rights, courts accord some deference on the application of legal tests where the test leaves room for judgement in its application.[273]

The real issue is how much respect is due and when.[274] Courts certainly must discharge their responsibility to protect rights by scrutinising exercises of power that impact on those rights. At the same time, however, they should pay attention to the extent to which the particular issues of justification in each case attract justiciability concerns on grounds of either institutional capacity or democratic legitimacy.[275]

The Supreme Court in *Moncrief* confirmed that the extent of respect must depend on the context, such as the decision-maker's expertise and the nature of the decision. The Court was not prepared to be 'more definitive' on the point.[276]

The aspect that can be considered beyond dispute is that courts do not resolve scientific disputes. The Supreme Court confirmed this point in *New Health*.[277] In *Moncrief* the Court noted its limitations in undertaking factual inquiries when there has been no cross-examination of deponents.[278] Institutional capacity concerns thus underpin this aspect.

It is somewhat more controversial whether courts also accord respect to decision-makers' judgements on the balance between competing values and interests. However, this too is supported by both principle and the weight of authority. In terms of principle, this aspect reflects concerns about courts' democratic legitimacy. In terms of authority, the Court in *Moncrief* considered some respect may be given to the decision-maker's view of where to strike the balance.[279] In *New Health*, the Supreme Court mentioned the need for respect not only on scientific issues surrounding fluoridation of drinking water but also on 'political issues'.[280] While the discussion focused on the scientific disputes, perhaps that reflects the court's hesitation to be drawn into the political issues. In *Atkinson*, a Ministry of Health funding policy was challenged as discriminatory, and the Court accorded some respect to the Ministry's judgement that the challenged distinction was justified.[281]

The best guide to the appropriate extent of respect is the extent to which the justiciability arguments in favour of respect apply in the particular context. This varies

[272] *Moncrief-Spittle* (n 231) at [84]. See also Grant Huscroft, 'Reasonable Limits on Rights' in Paul Rishworth and Grant Huscroft, *The New Zealand Bill of Rights* (2003) 168 at 192, 194.

[273] See Ch 9.B(1) for discussion of *R v Monopolies and Mergers Commission ex p South Yorkshire Transport Ltd* [1993] 1 WLR 23 (HL); *Vodafone New Zealand Ltd v Telecom New Zealand Ltd* [2011] NZSC 138, [2012] 3 NZLR 153.

[274] The Supreme Court is expected to shed further light on this in the appeal from *Four Members of the Armed Forces* (n 229).

[275] For discussion of these concerns and their relevance to intensity of review, see Ch 8.A.

[276] *Moncrief-Spittle* (n 231) at [85]–[86].

[277] *New Health* (n 221) at [121]–[143]; see also, eg, *Four Aviation Security* (n 230) at [84]–[85]; *Grounded Kiwis* (n 230).

[278] *Moncrief-Spittle* (n 231) at [86].

[279] ibid at [85].

[280] *New Health* (n 221) at [122].

[281] *Atkinson* (n 234) at [172]–[174].

even between different stages of the analysis in the same case. For instance, greater respect is due where democratic legitimacy is most important, such as on matters of social policy.[282] Decisions on gathering restrictions during a pandemic have been considered a paradigm example.[283] Less respect is due where the matter is closer to the court's own expertise, such as the reasonableness of search and seizure and the use of the evidence obtained.[284] Greater respect is also arguably due where Parliament has expressly provided for rights to be limited to some extent, and has entrusted the line drawing to the primary decision-maker's discretion.[285]

(5) Further Requirement: Decision-maker Must be Satisfied that Limit is Justified

In at least some contexts, administrative decision-makers are required to consider the right and be satisfied that the limit they are imposing on it is justified. This reasoning process requirement applies in addition to the courts' substantive scrutiny of the justification for the limit. A challenge may thus succeed on either or both of two bases: first because the decision-maker has not considered justification, and secondly because the court rejects the decision-maker's justification.

This dual constraint applies only in administrative law. It is thus a further point about section 5 that is found in cases other than *Hansen*. It may be seen as related to the decision-maker's onus of justification. There is significant authority for it, but it is still not adopted in all cases.[286] While the Supreme Court has adopted it in two cases, there is a level of ambiguity in both decisions.

The first Supreme Court authority is *Moncrief-Spittle*, where the Court adopted the dual constraint approach in a dictum.[287] Cooke J in the High Court has taken the decision as establishing this point.[288] However, in a footnote, the Supreme Court left open what a court should do where a decision-maker does not engage with the effect of the Bill of Rights.[289] Yet later on, under the heading of unreasonableness, the Court held that the decision-maker was required to consider freedom of expression and to give it a heavy weighting; a requirement that was met on the facts.[290] It is not easy to know what to make of this. In another High Court decision, Radich J has acknowledged uncertainty about what the Court decided in this case.[291]

[282] See, eg, ibid; *NZTSOS* (n 228) at [80].

[283] *Orewa Community Church v Minister for COVID-19 Response* [2022] NZHC 2026, [2022] 3 NZLR 475 at [105]–[106]. This point was not at issue in the unsuccessful appeal.

[284] Eg in *Dotcom v Attorney-General* [2014] NZSC 199, [2015] 1 NZLR 745 at [199]–[201], there was no discussion of deference in this regard.

[285] Eg the powers and functions of the Broadcasting Standards Authority under the Broadcasting Act 1989, ss 13 and 21; and the censorship powers under the Films, Videos and Publications Classification Act 1993.

[286] It was not mentioned, for instance, in *New Health* (n 221) or *Borrowdale* (n 225).

[287] *Moncrief-Spittle* (n 231) at [83]–[84].

[288] *Wallace v Chief Executive of the Department of Corrections* [2023] NZHC 2248 at [65] and [110]–[111]; *New Health New Zealand v The Minister for COVID-19 Response* [2023] NZHC 2647 at [71].

[289] *Moncrief-Spittle* (n 231) at [84].

[290] ibid at [115], [121].

[291] *New Health New Zealand Inc v Director-General of Health* [2023] NZHC 3183, [2024] 2 NZLR 1 at [11], [40]–[41].

The question arose again in the Supreme Court in *A (SC 70/2022) v Minister of Internal Affairs*.[292] Here, the Court applied the dual constraint it had recognised in *Moncrieff-Spittle*. One of the grounds on which the decision to cancel a passport was found unlawful was that the Minister had failed to do address the reasonableness of the limit on rights affected by the decision. This must be considered clear authority for the dual constraint approach.[293]

However, the Court again went on to introduce some confusion. In the next paragraph, it said on the one hand that if the decision was a justified limit, then 'a failure to address the issue would not be fatal to the validity of the decision'; and on the other that this would still not leave the Minister's advisers free not to address the issue.[294] It made no mention of the High Court decisions since *Moncrief* that had debated the effect of that decision.

A series of decisions adopting the dual constraint, mostly at the High Court level, goes back at least 20 years.[295] The earlier cases included several challenges to decisions of the Broadcasting Standards Authority. The High Court found that the Authority could not lawfully uphold complaints without satisfying itself that the resulting limit on freedom of speech was justified.[296] The Court of Appeal has also appeared to adopt the approach, notably in *Taylor* in the context of a decision to decline a prisoner's request for an interview with a journalist. However, again this decision was somewhat ambiguous.[297]

There is little authority against this approach.[298] The uncertainty stems from ambiguous decisions and decisions that make no mention of this approach.

One of the instances where the outcome turned on this approach is found in the High Court's decision in a more recent fluoridation challenge, *New Health New Zealand Inc v Director-General of Health*. The Court found that the Director-General was justified in exercising a power to require fluoridation of drinking water, but he had acted unlawfully in failing to turn his mind to the right to refuse medical treatment. In such circumstances, it may be appropriate to grant a limited remedy in the exercise the remedial discretion.[299] Here, the Director-General was ordered to reconsider, without quashing the decision.[300]

A similar combination of reasoning process and substantive obligations is expressly provided by the statutory bills of rights in the Australian state of Victoria and the Australian Capital Territory.[301] In New Zealand, the COVID-19 Public Health

[292] *A (SC 70/2022) v Minister of Internal Affairs* [2024] NZSC 63, [2024] 1 NZLR 372 at [138]–[139].
[293] The Court acknowledged the other part of the dual constraints, judicial scrutiny of the justification, but considered this unnecessary to address since the decision had already been found unlawful: ibid at [141].
[294] ibid at [140].
[295] For further detail, see Wilberg, 'Settling the Approach' (n 212) at 115–16.
[296] See, eg *Television New Zealand Ltd v Viewers for Television Excellence Inc* [2005] NZAR 1 (HC) at [52].
[297] *Taylor* (CA 2015) (n 257) at [72], [84]–[86], [92]–[93], [101]–[104].
[298] But see doubts expressed in *Smith v New Zealand Parole Board* [2018] NZHC 955 at [40]–[46].
[299] *New Health New Zealand Inc v Director-General of Health* (n 291) at [11], [40]–[41], [48]–[54], [89]–[90], [94]–[98], [104]–[109].
[300] *New Health New Zealand Inc v Director-General of Health* [2024] NZHC 196 (remedies decision).
[301] Human Rights Act 2004 (ACT), s 40B; Charter of Human Rights and Responsibilities 2006 (Vic), s 38(1).

Response Act 2020[302] similarly required the Minister to be satisfied that an Order to be made under the Act was a justified limit on the rights and freedoms in the Bill of Rights.

The dual constraint approach also gains strong implicit support from another novel development. In challenges to pandemic emergency measures, the Court of Appeal has found an ongoing obligation to keep the justification for such rights-limiting delegated legislation under review.[303] This was based on first principles rather than on the statutory obligation that has just been mentioned. The Court took the view that the Bill of Rights speaks to decision-makers, requiring them to act consistently with it both at the time an instrument is made and on a continuing basis.[304]

Turning to evaluation of this approach, there would be strong objections to treating the Bill of Rights as a mere mandatory consideration. It must instead be a substantive constraint on the scope of public powers.[305] The former is too weak: as a mandatory consideration, the Bill of Rights would be merely a factor that must be considered but can be outweighed by competing considerations. As a substantive constraint, in contrast, it means powers cannot be exercised at all in ways that involve unjustified limits on rights.[306]

However, the dual constraint approach is best understood as avoiding this objection. It does not merely treat the Bill of Rights as a mandatory consideration: it is stronger in two respects, and an approach with these two features is a good approach.[307]

The first and obvious difference from a pure mandatory considerations approach is the dual nature of the dual constraints approach. While the decision-maker is required to address the question of justification, that is only one of the two constraints. Even where this requirement has been met, the decision may still be unlawful if the court rejects the decision-maker's justification.

The dual constraints approach, then, adds a further layer of rights protection; it does not take away the protection that flows from the court's scrutiny of the justification. The additional protection of requiring the decision-maker to have engaged with the justification question may be considered especially important in contexts where the courts limit their substantive scrutiny by according significant respect to the decision-maker.[308]

The second difference is a little more subtle. On a common version of this approach, it is not enough for the decision-maker to *consider* section 5 justification: the decision-maker must be *satisfied* or must conclude that the limits on affected rights are justified.

[302] Section 9(1)(ba).

[303] *Free to Be Church Trust v Minister for COVID-19 Response* [2024] NZCA 81, [2024] 2 NZLR 746 at [118]–[127].

[304] ibid at [121].

[305] McLean, Rishworth and Taggart (n 219); *R (SB) v Governors of Denbigh High School* [2006] UKHL 15, [2007] 1 AC 100 at [29]–[31], [68]; *Belfast City Council v Miss Behavin' Ltd* [2007] UKHL 19, [2007] 1 WLR 1420 at [31].

[306] The distinction is explained in Part B(2) of this chapter.

[307] See, further, Claudia Geiringer, 'Process and Outcome in Judicial Review of Public Authority Compatibility with Human Rights: A Comparative Perspective' in Hanna Wilberg and Mark Elliott (eds), *The Scope and Intensity of Substantive Review: Traversing Taggart's Rainbow* (Oxford, Hart Publishing, 2015) 329 at 334–35, 338, 341–43, 356–58, 360.

[308] See Part (4) of this Part D. An alternative safeguard is found in some cases: there is arguably no basis for such respect where the decision-maker did not address justification; see, eg, *Aguilar Quila* (n 220) at [58].

It is thus not lawful to impose the limit if the decision-maker concludes it cannot be justified. This point appears in most formulations of the dual constraints approach,[309] including the formulations adopted by the Supreme Court. The Supreme Court specifically distinguished this from a mere mandatory consideration and instead saw it as following from its view that the Bill or Rights is a substantive constraint.[310]

The Supreme Court's framing points the way to understanding the nature of this constraint. The language of mandatory considerations has been used in some of the cases, and even the Supreme Court still discussed the requirement in terms of the decision-maker addressing the question or turning his mind to it. However, the approach is better understood as involving a different form of the illegality ground: applying the wrong test, due to misunderstanding the law. The decision-maker's legal error is in failing to understand that the empowering legislation is subject to the Bill of Rights and thus authorises only justified limits on rights.[311]

A further and separate objection to requiring decision-makers to engage with section 5 justification is that it may excessively juridify administrative decision-making.[312] This, however, is a concern about the structured *Oakes* proportionality test: that detailed legal test may be inappropriate for at least some administrative decision-makers. This concern can be dealt with by instead requiring decision-makers to apply no more than a general balancing test in some contexts. As we have seen, there is much New Zealand authority for such variation of the test.[313] Indeed, adoption of the balancing test is especially common in cases in which courts require decision-makers to be satisfied that there is good section 5 justification, such as in *Taylor*.[314] Some cases note that there are many different kinds of administrative decision-makers and contexts, and more detailed justificatory reasoning may be expected of some than of others.[315]

There is much to be said for this dual constraint approach. As noted, it is stronger, not weaker, than a simple substantive constraint approach. The choice of different justification tests provides flexibility for dealing with the variability of contexts. A further advantage is that the obligation on decision-makers may promote a culture of justification in public decision-making where rights are engaged.

(6) Query Framing Section 5 Justification in Terms of Unreasonableness Ground

Finally, courts have in some cases framed the section 5 justification enquiry in terms of unreasonableness as a ground of review. In *Moncrief*, the Supreme Court addressed

[309] See eg, *Viewers for Television Excellence* (n 296) at [57]; *Smith v Attorney-General* [2017] NZHC 463, [2017] NZLR 704 at [84], [87]–[88].

[310] *Moncrief-Spittle* (n 231) at [82]–[84]; *A v Minister for Internal Affairs* (n 292) at [138]–[139].

[311] That is unless the relevant provision is not capable of being read subject to the NZBORA pursuant to s 6.

[312] *Denbigh High School* (n 305); Thomas Poole, 'Of Headscarves and Heresies: the Denbigh High School Case and Public Authority Decision-Making under the Human Rights Act' [2005] *Public Law* 685.

[313] See section (2) of this Part D.

[314] *Taylor* (CA 2015) (n 257) at [84]. See also the Broadcasting Standards Authority cases noted in n 295.

[315] See, eg, *Smith v Attorney-General* (n 309) at [80]–[86]; *Smith v New Zealand Parole Board* (n 298) at [40]–[46].

some arguments under this ground in addition to applying the Bill of Rights as a separate ground.[316] In other cases, the Bill of Rights analysis has been framed solely in these terms.[317]

In substance, this approach may not be very different from the usual approach. First, it simply amounts to determining section 5 justification subject to some respect for the decision-maker's judgment, and it usually involves applying the general balancing approach rather than the structured proportionality test.[318] Secondly, it also sometimes involves requiring the decision-maker to determine section 5 justification, in which case it amounts to the dual constraint discussed under the previous heading.[319]

On the usual approach, however, the Bill of Rights is treated as giving rise to a separate ground of review.[320] Alternatively, to the extent that Bill of Rights challenges can be classified within the traditional grounds of review, they are more readily understood as fitting within illegality. The advantage of conceiving of Bill of Rights challenges as distinct is that this triggers consideration of the case law establishing the specific questions to ask in this context.

There is, perhaps, an element of confusion here between two different uses of 'unreasonableness'. As noted, courts determine the section 5 justification question subject to some respect for the decision-maker's judgment. This point may also be put in terms of standards of review:[321] the standard of review for section 5 justification is unreasonableness rather than correctness. However, it does not follow that the relevant ground of review is unreasonableness. While the standard of review on the unreasonableness ground of review, by definition, is unreasonableness, that standard can also apply in the context of other grounds. It applies whenever there is good reason for some deference or respect for the decision-maker's judgement.[322] That is the position in relation to the section 5 justification enquiry in a Bill of Rights challenge.

The concern is that such confusion may potentially lead to some more substantive confusion concerning standards of review. The unreasonableness ground usually applies to the substantive merits – the types of questions that are for the decision-maker and not for the court. That is why the starting point for this ground is the highly deferential standard of review known as *Wednesbury* unreasonableness. In contrast, the starting point for section 5 justification is the judicial responsibility to protect the rights affirmed by the Bill of Rights, albeit subject to appropriate respect for the decision-maker's judgment.

It would be unfortunate if judicial scrutiny of section 5 justification was diminished, in contexts where there is insufficient reason for this, simply by the association

[316] *Moncrief-Spittle* (n 231) at [114]–[131].

[317] See, eg, *Chief Executive of the Department of Corrections v Smith* [2020] NZCA 675. There are hints of this approach also in *Taylor* [2015] NZCA 477 (n 257), see esp at [46], [94], [101].

[318] See *Watson v Chief Executive of the Department of Corrections (No 2)* [2016] NZHC 1996, [2016] NZAR 1264 at [34].

[319] In *Moncrief-Spittle* (n 231), as noted earlier, this was the part of the decision in which the reasoning process obligation was most clearly adopted: at [115], [121].

[320] See, eg, Philip A Joseph, *Constitutional and Administrative Law in New Zealand*, 5th edn (Wellington, Brookers, 2021) at 985.

[321] See Ch 9.

[322] Notably, in applying statutory terms that leave room for judgment in their application: see *South Yorkshire Transport* (n 273); *Vodafone* (n 273) at [50]–[58].

with the unreasonableness ground. Conversely, it would be unfortunate if the more intensive scrutiny that is clearly appropriate for section 5 justification in many contexts was transferred to other contexts in which the deferential *Wednesbury* standard is appropriate.

(7) Summary

The cases on section 5 in administrative law establish the following series of propositions. First, Bill of Rights challenges always turn, at least in part, on section 5 justification, except where the right at issue is one that renders section 5 redundant. A justified limit is never found unlawful on Bill of Rights grounds. And where statute clearly authorises a limit regardless of its justification, section 5 becomes relevant to a possible declaration of inconsistency.

Secondly, the test for justification varies between the structured *Oakes* proportionality test and more general balancing. Thirdly, the onus of justification lies on the respondent. This requires evidence as well as arguments, but courts are alert to the need to make public policy in a context of incomplete and inconclusive evidence. Fourthly, courts accord a measure of respect to the decision-maker's judgement, to varying extents depending on context. Fifthly, there is much authority for requiring decision-makers to satisfy themselves that a limit is justified, as well as requiring the limit to be justified as assessed by the court. Finally, the occasional framing of Bill of Rights challenges in terms of the ground of unreasonableness is potentially problematic.

E. Rights-Consistent Interpretation of Empowering Legislation

All the rights discussed in this chapter are protected by interpretive presumptions of consistency. The protection for Te Tiriti and for international law is expressly framed this way: Parliament is presumed to have legislated consistently with these sources. Protection for other rights is framed differently: the principle of legality states that common law rights can be abrogated only by express words or necessary implication; section 6 of the Bill of Rights requires other enactments to be given a rights-consistent meaning if this can be done. However, both operate in the same way and to the same effect as interpretive presumptions: statutes are read consistently with the right wherever possible.

This final Part of the chapter outlines the approach to these interpretive presumptions: how and to what extent are empowering provisions given rights-consistent meanings? This has usually been addressed for each of the sources of rights in isolation from the others. The tests used differ between the sources, and the presumptions in the past have been applied more strongly for rights from some sources than others. However, it is not clear that there are real and substantive differences, applied consistently, between sources of rights in these regards. This Part discusses rights from all the different sources together; any differences between the sources are addressed where relevant. Cases from contexts other than administrative law are relevant on this issue and will be drawn on in the discussion below: the interpretive issues are generally the same.

Section (1) of this Part outlines two competing commitments that underlie debates about these presumptions. The next three sections examine three possible ways to frame the limits of the interpretive presumptions, and the current position on each of these: (2) a facial ambiguity pre-condition; (3) consistency with normal statutory interpretation; and (4) the express words or necessary implication test. Section (5) explains when even express words can be read down. Finally, the section (6) further considers what accounts for variations in the approach.

(1) Underlying Tension between Competing Commitments

The approach to the interpretive presumptions is a site of contestation between competing constitutional commitments. The established doctrine of Parliamentary sovereignty in Aotearoa New Zealand privileges the decisions of Parliament as a representative institution. This stands in tension with the commitment to fundamental rights and norms, to the extent that this is understood as requiring some counter-majoritarian safeguards. This tension in turn flows from fundamental disagreements about the nature of law, about conceptions of democracy, about the best constitutional balance of power, and about values.[323]

A commitment to at least a measure of counter-majoritarian safeguards justifies strong uses of the interpretive presumptions, to set some form of limits to what Parliament can do. If an unqualified commitment to Parliamentary sovereignty is maintained, in contrast, the presumptions can be justified only on the basis that Parliament must in fact have intended to legislate consistently with the rights.[324] While only judicial invalidation of statute would amount to abandoning Parliamentary sovereignty entirely, strong use of presumptions can obstruct Parliament's ability to pursue its public policy objectives.

Shifts between these commitments are often not openly acknowledged. Because Parliamentary sovereignty is the orthodoxy, it is relatively rare in New Zealand for interpretive presumptions to be justified as counter-majoritarian safeguards. Instead, even when they are used in that way, they are still couched in terms of presumed legislative intent. This adds to the confusion and uncertainty.

In *D v Police*[325] and *Fitzgerald*,[326] the Supreme Court appears to have adopted stronger use of the interpretive presumptions, reflecting a shift away from the commitment to Parliamentary sovereignty. However, arguably *Fitzgerald* turns out to be more orthodox than it appears.

[323] See, generally, Tom Campbell, 'Grounding Theories of Legal Interpretation' in Jeffrey Goldsworthy and Tom Campbell (eds), *Legal Interpretation in Democratic States* (Ashgate Dartmouth, 2002).

[324] Alison L Young, 'Fundamental Common Law Rights and Legislation' in Mark Elliott and Kirsty Hughes (eds), *Common Law Constitutional Rights* (Oxford, Hart Publishing, 2020) 223 labels these two types of justification "normative" and "positive".

[325] *D (SC 31/2019) v New Zealand Police* [2021] NZSC 2, [2021] 1 NZLR 213.

[326] *Fitzgerald v R* [2021] NZSC 131.

It remains to be seen whether a shift is, in fact, occurring.[327] The next three sections explore the current New Zealand position on three possible limits on the use of interpretive presumptions.

(2) No Facial Ambiguity Precondition: Discretion can be Read Down

In the United Kingdom, the reach of the interpretive presumption of consistency with international law is limited: it is available only where a provision is ambiguous on its face.[328] That constraint has been discarded in Aotearoa New Zealand.[329] It has never applied to the principle of legality, which has always been available to read down general provisions as well as ambiguous ones.[330] Nor does it apply to section 6 of the Bill of Rights.[331]

This is of particular relevance in administrative law: it means that interpretive presumptions can be used to read discretionary powers subject to rights.[332] This was confirmed in *Drew*. A broad power to make regulations for the procedure at prison disciplinary hearings was read as not authorising measures that violate the right to natural justice, a common law right affirmed by section 27 of the Bill of Rights.[333]

The facial ambiguity precondition reflected commitment to Parliamentary sovereignty, along with adherence to the old literal approach to statutory interpretation. Judicial respect for Parliament's law on this approach meant adherence to the literal words. That approach, however, has long been discarded in favour of the modern purposive approach.[334] On that approach, ambiguity may be introduced by context and purpose, even where the words do not appear ambiguous on their face.[335] That applies to general words or discretionary powers, and even to apparently clear express words.[336]

(3) Constrained by Normal Principles of Statutory Interpretation?

In the leading *Hansen* case, the Supreme Court required uses of section 6 of the Bill of Rights to be consistent with normal principles of statutory interpretation. A rights-consistent meaning was available only if it was tenable in light of the provision's text,

[327] For further discussion, see Hanna Wilberg, 'Aotearoa New Zealand: Legislators' Understanding as a Constraint on Interpretive Presumptions' in Matthias Klatt (ed), *Constitutionally Conforming Interpretation: Comparative Perspectives* (Oxford, Hart Publishing, 2023) 407, part III.

[328] *R v Secretary of State for the Home Department, ex p Brind* [1991] 1 AC 696 (HL) at 747–48; *R (SG) v Secretary of State for Work and Pensions* [2015] UKSC 16, [2015] 1 WLR 1449 at [15], [137], [239].

[329] See, eg, *Sellers v Maritime Safety Authority* [1999] 2 NZLR 44 (CA).

[330] *R v Secretary of State for the Home Department, ex parte Simms* [2000] 2 AC 115 (HL).

[331] See, eg, *Drew v Attorney-General* [2002] 1 NZLR 58 (CA).

[332] In contrast, this was denied for the UK in *Brind* (n 328).

[333] *Drew* (n 331) at [66]–[68].

[334] See RI Carter, *Burrows and Carter Statute Law in New Zealand*, 6th edn (Wellington, LexisNexis NZ Ltd, 2021) ch 8; New Zealand Law Commission, *A New Interpretation Act to Avoid "Prolixity and Tautology"* (NZLC R17, 1990).

[335] See *Commerce Commission v Fonterra Co-operative Group Ltd* [2007] NZSC 36, [2007] 3 NZLR 767 at [22].

[336] See further below, section (5) of this Part.

context and purpose.[337] This is the first of two usual limits to the use of interpretive presumptions. It has also featured in relation to other presumptions, especially the presumption of consistency with international law.[338]

Hansen rejected the stronger approach established in the United Kingdom.[339] Section 3 of the Human Rights Act 1998 has been held to require a rights-consistent interpretation of other legislation even if that interpretation both departs from the evident legislative intention and is inconsistent with the words, just so long as it is not inconsistent with a fundamental feature of the legislation.[340]

Adherence to normal principles of statutory interpretation entails various limits on the use of interpretive presumptions. One of these is seen in *Hansen*, where Blanchard and Tipping JJ considered it important to respect 'a specific intention relating to an issue plainly within the contemplation of the legislators'.[341] The Court held that a reverse onus provision could not be read down so as to impose only an evidential burden, which would have been more consistent with the presumption of innocence.[342] The argument from specific intention was that case law on the virtually identical predecessor provision had clearly established that it imposed a full legal burden; legislators therefore must have understood the provision accordingly.[343]

Similarly, in *Commissioner of Police v G*, a statutory monitoring regime for offenders deported to New Zealand after release from prison in Australia was held to apply retrospectively to offenders convicted before its enactment. While the legislation was silent on its temporal application, the legislative history clearly showed an intention to apply it to all deportees arriving after its enactment.[344]

Another potential form of implied limit to the use of a presumption may be found where legislation partially incorporates international law or Te Tiriti obligations. In *Helu*, the limited right to enter one's country in the Bill of Rights Act was treated as impliedly excluding the unincorporated aspects of the broader international law right.[345] In *Trans-Tasman Resources*, in contrast, the Supreme Court held that more explicit provision would be required to exclude Tiriti obligations. The common type of Treaty clause that makes specific but limited provision for the effect of Te Tiriti thus does not constrain or exhaust the effect of Te Tiriti in the context of the statute involved.[346]

[337] *R v Hansen* [2007] NZSC 7, [2007] 3 NZLR 1 at [57], [61] (Blanchard J), [149]–[158] (Tipping J), [237]–[252], [258], [290] (McGrath J).

[338] See, eg, *Helu v Immigration and Protection Tribunal* [2015] NZSC 28, [2016] 1 NZLR 298 at [143]–[144]; *New Zealand Airline Pilots' Association Inc v Attorney-General* [1997] 3 NZLR 269 (CA).

[339] *Hansen* (n 337) at [156], [158], [240]–[247].

[340] *Ghaidan v Godin-Mendoza* [2004] UKHL 30, [2004] 2 AC 557 at [30]–[33]. It also must not involve the court devising an entire new scheme: *Bellinger v Bellinger* [2003] UKHL 21; [2003] 2 AC 467.

[341] *Hansen* (n 337) at [61], [156]; but cf at [14] (Elias CJ), [289] (Anderson J). McGrath J did not comment on this point.

[342] ibid at [56], [165]–[166], [255]–[257].

[343] ibid at [53], [55], [99], [156], [166].

[344] *Commissioner of Police v G* [2023] NZCA 93, [2023] 2 NZLR 107 at [140]–[153].

[345] *Helu* (n 338) at [149], [178].

[346] *Trans-Tasman Resources v Taranaki-Whanganui Conservation Board* [2021] NZSC 127, [2021] 1 NZLR 801 at [146]–[151].

Other cases established that a rights-consistent interpretation must not be adopted if it would cut across the legislative purpose.[347] In *Taylor v New Zealand Poultry Board*, for instance, the Court of Appeal recognised an interpretive presumption against abrogating the common law privilege against self-incrimination. However, it found that presumption rebutted, because the purpose of the power to make regulations providing for the producer board to obtain information would be compromised if the power were read subject to this privilege.[348]

All these aspects of the normal statutory interpretation constraint reflect the orthodox commitment to Parliamentary sovereignty. Purposive interpretation reflects judicial respect for Parliament's policy judgments. Reliance on legislative intention is a contested subject.[349] However, it is best understood in this way: First, we need context to make sense of words. Secondly, reliance on legislative intention simply means fixing the relevant context by adopting the perspective of the enacting Parliament.[350] The Court of Appeal has dismissed an objection based on Parliamentary privilege to the use of legislative history for this purpose.[351]

In *Fitzgerald*,[352] a clear majority of the Supreme Court appeared to move away from these normal statutory interpretation constraints, but arguably it did not in substance move far. We need to look both at what was said about the approach, and at what approach the Court actually used to reach its interpretive conclusions.

As to what was said, Winkelman CJ rejected *Hansen* and instead aligned herself with the *Hansen* minority and with the stronger UK approach that had been rejected by the majority.[353] She also rejected reliance on specific intention to rebut the interpretive presumption.[354] The three remaining majority Justices, however, were at pains to insist that their approach was consistent with *Hansen*.[355] Even the Chief Justice still considered that it must be possible to arrive at the rights-consistent meaning '*through the process of interpretation*',[356] and it must not nullify the purpose.[357] Section 4 of the Bill of Rights made clear that the meaning adopted must not amount to disapplying a provision or treating it as impliedly repealed, nor must it cross the line into amendment.[358]

Turning to what approach the Court actually used, the striking feature is that the Court felt able to read down very clear and emphatic language. At issue was a 'three strikes' sentencing provision that clearly required imposition of the maximum term of imprisonment on a third conviction for a relevant offence. This was reinforced by

[347] See, eg, *Arps v New Zealand Police* [2019] NZCA 592, [2020] 2 NZLR 94 at [57]; *Borrowdale* (n 222) at [155].

[348] *Taylor v New Zealand Poultry Board* [1984] 1 NZLR 394 (CA) at 402, 405.

[349] For intention sceptics, see, eg, Andrew Burrows, *Thinking about Statutes: Interpretation, Interaction, Improvement (The Hamlyn Lectures 2017)* (Cambridge, Cambridge University Press, 2018) at 17–18.

[350] See Wilberg (n 327) at 419–22. Contextual interpretation is required by the Legislation Act 2019, s 10(1).

[351] *Commissioner of Police v G* (n 344) at [125]–[139].

[352] *Fitzgerald* (n 326).

[353] ibid at [70]–[72].

[354] ibid at [55], [124].

[355] ibid at [148], [244] (O'Regan and Arnold JJ).

[356] ibid at [59], emphasis in original.

[357] ibid at [67]–[68].

[358] ibid at [50], [60], [66], [68], [73].

the words 'despite any other enactment'. Yet the Court held that this must be read subject to the right against grossly disproportionate punishment in section 9 of the Bill of Rights: where the high threshold of section 9 was crossed, the three strikes provision did not apply.[359] This suggests that normal principles of statutory interpretation no longer constrain the use of the presumption, contrary to the majority's professed adherence to the *Hansen* approach.

However, two features of the approach cast doubt on how far this really departs from normal principles of statutory interpretation: both the purpose and specific intention were relied on in this decision.

Purpose was endorsed by the Chief Justice as a constraint on the use of the interpretive presumption.[360] Applied here, the 'three strikes' regime's purpose was to deter and incapacitate repeat serious offenders. While this required a mandatory and predictable regime, her Honour was satisfied that it did not necessitate sentences for non-serious offenders that are so grossly disproportionate as to be in breach of section 9 of the Bill of Rights.[361] O'Regan and Arnold JJ also found that the rights-consistent meaning did not defeat the purpose, thus implicitly endorsing this constraint, albeit they equated purpose with specific intention.[362]

Turning to specific intention, we have already seen that the Chief Justice rejected this as a constraint. However, it was a central plank of the majority's argument *for* a rights-consistent interpretation, including in the Chief Justice's judgment. Based on Parliamentary debates and on the scheme of the Act, the Court concluded that the 'three strikes' regime's harsh and disproportionate sentences were intended to be reserved for serious violent offending, and were thus not expected to engage the section 9 right.[363] William Young J, dissenting, also relied on the specific intention – drawing the opposite conclusion from the evidence as to what was intended.[364] Either conclusion was plausible on the evidence, as there were ill-thought-through amendments to the Bill during its passage.

The majority's reliance on the rights-consistent specific intention is similar to the *Simms* justification for the principle of legality: rights should not be overridden inadvertently and covertly.[365] It remains to be seen whether the Court would be willing to follow the Chief Justice's dictum and disregard specific intention in a case where it clearly supported a rights-limiting meaning.

There are, however, other leading cases that used interpretive presumptions in ways that are difficult to reconcile with normal principles of statutory interpretation. For instance, in *Sellers* a statutory power to require pleasure craft departing New Zealand ports to carry safety equipment was read subject to the international law freedom

[359] Ibid at [112]–[139], [186]–[231], [247]–[251].

[360] Ibid at [67]–[68], [71]–[72], adopting the UK position. More recent UK authority supporting this approach includes, eg, *R v Waya* [2012] UKSC 51, [2013] 1 AC 294 at [21].

[361] *Fitzgerald* (n 326) at [122]–[123], [135].

[362] ibid at [220]. Their Honours also noted that the provision was not deprived of meaning, as they expected the rights qualification to apply only in rare cases (ibid at [219]).

[363] ibid at [123]–[128], [186]–[204], [250] n 358. For Glazebrook J, this meant that recourse to the presumption was not needed: ibid at [244] and fn 348.

[364] ibid at [326].

[365] *Simms* (n 330) at 131 (Lord Hoffmann).

of the high seas, thereby excluding foreign vessels.[366] This compromised the provision's likely purpose, to avoid unnecessary waste of resources in maritime search and rescue.[367]

Another example is *Zaoui*, concerning a detailed and strict statutory regime requiring the deportation of persons who had been certified to be a risk to the security of New Zealand. The Supreme Court read this subject to the relevant rights in the Bill of Rights and at international law. The power to deport was not available if there were substantial grounds for believing that the person would be in danger of being arbitrarily deprived of life or subjected to torture.[368] The Court ignored numerous indications in the statutory scheme that cast doubt on any such exception.[369]

There are other examples of strong uses of the presumptions protecting international law,[370] the Bill of Rights, and common law rights.[371] It is unclear, then, when and to what extent normal principles of statutory interpretation constrain the use of interpretive presumptions.

(4) Rebutted Only by Express Words or Also by Necessary Implication?

The second of the two usual constraints on the use of interpretive presumptions is the express words or necessary implication test. This is the established test for the principle of legality,[372] and it may also be used in the context of other interpretive presumptions. The presumptions apply to general or ambiguous words, which will not be read as abrogating fundamental rights. Presumptions are rebutted where the rights in question are abrogated by express words or necessary implication.

This test is often applied consistently with normal statutory interpretation – and hence consistently with an unqualified commitment to Parliamentary sovereignty – by adopting a purposive approach to necessary implication. On the other hand, in some cases there is a shift towards a measure of counter-majoritarian safeguards: courts insist on nothing short of express words or adopt a very stringent version of necessary implication.

The commonly cited formulation of the 'necessary implication' test is the following from *Morgan Grenfell*, which sounds very stringent:[373]

> A necessary implication is not the same as a reasonable implication .... A *necessary* implication is one which necessarily follows from the express provisions of the statute construed in their context. It distinguishes between what it would have been sensible or reasonable for

[366] *Sellers* (n 329) at 60–62.

[367] The purpose is noted ibid at 48–49.

[368] *Zaoui v Attorney-General (No 2)* [2005] NZSC 38, [2006] 1 NZLR 289 at [90]–[93].

[369] Claudia Geiringer, 'International Law Through the Lens of *Zaoui*: Where is New Zealand At?' (2006) 17 *Public Law Review* 300 at 317–18.

[370] Eg *Ye v Minister of Immigration* [2009] NZSC 76, [2010] 1 NZLR 104. See Hanna Wilberg, 'Administrative Law' [2010] *New Zealand Law Review* 177 at 193–202.

[371] *R v Poumako* [2000] 2 NZLR 695 (CA) relied on all three; for discussion, see below at n 408.

[372] *Simms* (n 330) at 131; *Cropp v Judicial Committee* [2008] NZSC 46, [2008] 3 NZLR 774 (SC) at [27].

[373] *R (Morgan Grenfell & Co Ltd) v Special Commissioner of Income Tax* [2002] UKHL 21, [2003] 1 AC 563 at [45], emphasis in original.

> Parliament to have included or what Parliament would, if it had thought about it, probably have included and what it is clear that the express language of the statute shows that the statute must have included. A necessary implication is a matter of express language and logic not interpretation.

There is, however, significant authority for a purposive version of this test. The Privy Council in *B v Auckland District Law Society* adopted the *Morgan Grenfell* test but explained it in purposive terms.[374] 'A useful test', it said, is to write in a rights-protecting qualification,[375]

> and ask, not "does that produce a reasonable result?" or "does it impede the statutory purpose [...]?" but "does that produce an inconsistency?" or "does it stultify the statutory purpose?"

The purposive limit established in *Taylor v New Zealand Poultry Board* is also directly relevant.[376] This case would today be decided in terms of the principle of legality. Framed that way, it would have held that the privilege against self-incrimination was abrogated by necessary implication because a rights-consistent reading would defeat the purpose of the provision at issue.

In some other cases, however, courts have insisted on nothing short of express words or have applied the necessary implication test so stringently as to effectively amount to an express words test.

D v Police is an example of the latter.[377] The Supreme Court by a bare majority applied the presumption against retrospective penalties. The Act at issue provided for a post-sentence monitoring regime for child sex offenders. The wording of the provision purporting to apply the regime retrospectively to offenders in D's position was flawed, and the Court held it was not sufficiently clear to displace the presumption against retrospectivity.[378] This rendered the scheme of the Act decidedly odd. Moreover, an intention to make the power available retrospectively clearly appeared from the debates on the Bill. However, for the majority those points were not enough to give rise to a necessary implication.[379] Glazebrook J, dissenting, relied on both points.[380] A further point that might have given rise to a necessary implication was the purpose of protecting children: this would at least be compromised by the rights-consistent interpretation, but that point was not mentioned at all.

Turning to contexts where courts have insisted on nothing short of express words, there are at least three contexts to consider.

First, Laws J in *Witham* took the view that the common law right of access to the courts could only be taken away by express words.[381] However, that is not the accepted

[374] *B v Auckland District Law Society* [2004] 1 NZLR 326 at [58]–[59].
[375] Ibid at [59]. Similarly, see *R (Dolan) v Secretary of State for Health and Social Care* [2020] EWCA Civ 1605; [2021] 1 WLR 2326 at [66], [69]–[71].
[376] *Taylor v NZ Poultry Board* (n 347). See discussion above at n 347.
[377] *D v Police* (n 325).
[378] Ibid at [78].
[379] Ibid at [81].
[380] Ibid esp at [235]–[243]; and see William Young J, dissenting, at [279]–[289].
[381] *R v Lord Chancellor ex p Witham* [1998] QB 575 (DC) at 586.

position on the principle of legality generally. The weight of authority is against it.[382] In New Zealand, the Court of Appeal in *Independent Fisheries* dismissed a submission that only express words could abrogate the right of access to the courts.[383]

Secondly, where full privative clauses are concerned, settled authority protects the right of access to the courts by an especially strict express words requirement. The leading English cases, *Anisminic* and *Privacy International*, concerned provisions that very expressly barred judicial review. The courts refused to give these provisions any effect.[384] New Zealand cases since *Bulk Gas* have adopted the same reasoning for disregarding full privative clauses.[385] We might say that the approach in these cases amounts to insisting that the right to judicial review could be abrogated only if a provision expressly acknowledged the right and authorised infringing it.

Thirdly, there is a line of authority in which certain statutes are designated constitutional statutes. According to the orthodox doctrine of implied repeal, if there is an irreconcilable conflict between two statutes,[386] the later statute prevails to the extent of that conflict. That reflects the later Parliament's 'continuing sovereignty' to make and change law.[387] Laws J in *Thoburn*, however, held that this does not apply where the earlier statute is a constitutional statute: these prevail over later conflicting statutes unless the later statute expressly provides for an override.[388] The examples given included the Human Rights Act 1998 (UK) and other statutes with constitutional subject-matter.[389] This approach is widely considered established in the UK.[390] It is distinguishable from the principle of legality that protects common law rights: it applies only when the protected norm is enshrined in statute.

In New Zealand, authority for recognising constitutional statutes is still somewhat qualified. Reasoning that effectively treated a statutory prohibition on retrospective increases in criminal penalties as a constitutional provision featured in *Pora* but was adopted only by a minority.[391] That case might also be distinguished, because the conflicting earlier and later provisions were in the same statute.[392]

In *D v Police*, the Court did not expressly mention constitutional statutes. However, it relied on the provision against retrospective penalties in section 6 of the Sentencing

[382] Authority for the full test includes *Simms* (n 330) at 131 and *Cropp* (n 372) at [26].

[383] *Canterbury Regional Council v Independent Fisheries Ltd* [2012] NZCA 601, [2013] 2 NZLR 57 at [140], citing *Simms* (n 330).

[384] *Anisminic Ltd v Foreign Compensation Commission* [1969] 2 AC 147 (HL) at 169–171, 207–212; *R (Privacy International) v Investigatory Powers Tribunal* [2019] UKSC 22, [2020] AC 491 at [107]–[111], [161]–[167].

[385] *Bulk Gas Users Group v Attorney-General* [1983] NZLR 129 (CA) at 133, 136. The wording of the clause at issue here was less absolute, but the reasoning would have led to the same result even if the wording had been unqualified: see Ch 8.E(2).

[386] The conflict must be truly irreconcilable. There is a presumption against this: *H v Lord Advocate* [2012] UKSC 24, [2013] 1 AC 413 at [30].

[387] *Ellen Street Estates Ltd v Minister of Health* [1934] 1 KB 590; *R v Pora* [2001] 2 NZLR 37 (CA) at [110].

[388] *Thoburn v Sutherland City Council* [2003] 1 QB 151.

[389] ibid at 186.

[390] Appellate authority is, however, still better considered equivocal. See *H v Lord Advocate* (n 386) at [30]; *R (Buckinghamshire County Council) v The Secretary of State for Transport* [2014] UKSC 3, [2014] 1 WLR 324 at [208]; *R (Miller) v Secretary of State* [2017] UKSC 5, [2018] AC 61 at [66]–[67]; *Privacy International* (n 384) at [120].

[391] *Pora* (n 387) at [54], [56], [119]–[120], [125], [146]–[147], and [156].

[392] As pointed out by Glazebrook J in *D v Police* (n 325) at [178].

Act 2002, which is stated to apply 'despite any other enactment or rule of law', holding that this wording could be overridden only by express provision in a later enactment.[393] Glazebrook J, dissenting, pointed out that this amounted to treating section 6 as a constitutional provision.[394] The majority did not comment.

In *Fitzgerald*, three of the four majority judges expressly relied on the Bill of Rights being a constitutional statute.[395] Yet, inconsistently with this, they also appeared to contemplate that the rights could be abrogated by necessary implication.[396] Winkelman CJ, the fourth majority judge, explicitly held that only express words could rebut the interpretive presumption in section 6 of the Bill of Rights. However, this was only in relation to cases such as this, where the rights infringement was particularly egregious.[397] Her Honour did not mention constitutional statutes.

In conclusion, authority is mixed as to whether interpretive presumptions can be rebutted by necessary implication, and on the stringency of that test. On normal principles of statutory interpretation, rights would be abrogated by necessary implication where a rights-consistent interpretation defeats the statutory purpose.

(5) Express Words can be Read Down if Supported by Context or Purpose

Some confusion about the express words test must be addressed. It is sometimes erroneously thought that reading down express words must amount to exceptionally strong use of interpretive presumptions.[398] The Chief Justice in *Fitzgerald* appeared to take that view.[399]

However, on the modern approach to statutory interpretation, even apparently clear words must be checked against the context and purpose.[400] Reading down express words can thus be consistent with normal statutory interpretation if two criteria are met. Firstly, the reading down must have sufficient support in the provision's context and purpose, and secondly the provision must still be given some meaningful effect.[401]

Uses of interpretive presumptions are exceptionally strong if they disregard these criteria. The cases on full privative clauses, for instance, do involve an exceptionally strong use of interpretive presumptions because they disregard the privative provision entirely. Nor do these cases rely on context or purpose to support the disregard for the express words.

Similarly, in *Poumako*, the Court of Appeal would, if the issue had arisen, have read down an express provision giving retrospective effect to a new mandatory minimum non-parole period, so as to reduce the retrospective effect to a mere 15 days.[402]

[393] ibid at [54].
[394] See ibid at [175].
[395] ibid at [221]–[224], [250] n 361.
[396] ibid at [215] and [218]. See the express discussion of necessary implication in fn 313.
[397] *Fitzgerald* (n 326) at [119].
[398] See, eg, Jason NE Varuhas, 'The Principle of Legality' [2020] 79 *Cambridge Law Journal* 578 at 600–604.
[399] *Fitzgerald* (n 326) at [56].
[400] *Commerce Commission v Fonterra Co-operative Group Ltd* [2007] NZSC 36, [2007] 3 NZLR 767 at [22]; *Shark Experience Ltd v PauaMAC5 Inc* [2019] NZSC 111, [2019] 1 NZLR 791 at [28].
[401] For the second point, see *Fitzgerald* (n 326) at [219] (O'Regan and Arnold JJ).
[402] ibid at [36]–[40].

While the Court did rely on some elements of context, this reading down would have deprived the provision of any meaningful effect.

Fitzgerald is an example of reading down express words that does *not* amount to exceptionally strong use of the interpretive presumption, at least if we accept the Court's factual premises. The Court read down the express requirement to impose the maximum sentence for an offence on a third conviction, by reading it subject to the right against grossly disproportionate sentences. It further read down the words 'despite any other enactment', by reading these as not referring to the Bill of Rights. However, it did so on the basis that this reading did not deprive the provision of meaningful effect;[403] there was evidence that the provision was specifically intended to apply only to serious violent offending;[404] and the narrow reading did not defeat the regime's purpose.[405] Based on these premises (albeit these could be considered doubtful), the decision does not amount to exceptionally strong use.

(6) Why the Difference in Approaches between Cases?

We have seen a great deal of variation in approaches and uncertainty as to the correct approach. In some cases, such as *Hansen* and *Helu*, courts insist that the use of presumptions must remain consistent with normal statutory interpretation. Very arguably, *Fitzgerald* is still consistent with that. Yet in other cases, they make much stronger use of presumptions, amounting to at least a degree of counter-majoritarian safeguard. Examples include the cases on full privative clauses, *Poumako*, *Sellers*, *Zaoui* and *D v Police*.

What accounts for this variability? At least to some extent, it reflects the instability that is due to the underlying tension outlined in section (1) of this Part. But are there any other explanations? Can we identify factors that influence the approach?

One possible explanation is that some of the interpretive presumptions are stronger than others. For instance, Winkelman CJ in *Fitzgerald* considered section 6 of the Bill of Rights to be stronger than the principle of legality.[406] Certainly section 6 has a democratic legitimacy that the other presumptions lack, which could justify stronger use. However, for a time it seemed that the presumption of consistency with international law was stronger than section 6 of the Bill of Rights.[407] Similarly, *D v Police* could be seen as considering the principle of legality to be stronger than section 6 of the Bill of Rights. More generally, the cases simply do not consistently treat some presumptions as stronger than others. Another complication is that many rights are protected by several of these interpretive presumptions.

A second possible explanation is that the approach is changing over time. For instance, *Fitzgerald* could be taken as abandoning *Hansen* and ushering in a stronger approach to section 6 of the Bill of Rights. However, if the approach is changing

[403] *Fitzgerald* (n 326) at [219].
[404] ibid at [123]–[128], [186]–[204], [250] n 358.
[405] ibid at [122]–[123], [135], [220].
[406] ibid at [56]–[57].
[407] See, eg, the contrast between *Sellers* (n 329) and *Hansen* (n 337).

over time, then the change is not all in the same direction: there were stronger uses of section 6 before *Hansen*, such as *Poumako*.[408]

Finally, however, stronger uses of interpretive presumptions can often be explained based on the courts' evaluation of substantive factors in the particular context. The strongest uses of presumptions are often seen in cases involving egregious breaches of especially important rights, or of rights that are considered absolute. In that regard, a degree of assertive use of the presumptions in *Fitzgerald* is of a piece with earlier leading cases such as *Zaoui*[409] and *Poumako*.[410] All majority judgments in *Fitzgerald* emphasised the special strength of the rights argument in that case,[411] and the Chief Justice expressly noted the variability in the use of interpretive presumptions according to such substantive factors.[412] The Court of Appeal in *Commissioner of Police v G* also adopted this approach. In the context of that case, the presumption against retrospectivity was considered weak because no unfairness was involved.[413]

[408] *Poumako* (n 341).
[409] *Zaoui* (n 368).
[410] *Poumako* (n 341).
[411] *Fitzgerald* (n 326) at [116]–[120], [218], [224], [251].
[412] ibid at [59]. Whether *D v Police* (n 325) can be explained on that basis is more doubtful.
[413] *Commissioner of Police v G* (n 344) at [162]–[168].

7

Unreasonableness and Modern Extensions of Substantive Review

Substantive review involves courts engaging with the substantive merits of challenged decisions. In other words, where any aspect of a decision is subject to substantive review, courts consider whether the decision in that regard is a good one in light of relevant (and usually contested and competing) evidence, interests and values. This can be distinguished from the main traditional forms of judicial review, which involve determining the applicable law and ensuring adherence to fair procedure. As we saw in Chapter 6, substantive review is a significant aspect of judicial review on grounds of rights, especially where the issue concerns the justification for limits on rights. Beyond rights-based review, common law grounds involving substantive review have also been expanding and multiplying. That is so at least in the United Kingdom; the extent to which these developments apply in New Zealand remains uncertain. These common law grounds are the subject of this chapter.

Traditionally, the only common law ground of substantive review was irrationality or *Wednesbury* unreasonableness, involving an extremely high threshold of intervention.[1] The modern extensions take broadly three forms. First, the old ground of irrationality or unreasonableness can be applied with varying intensity, so that the threshold of intervention is lowered in some cases. In a variation on this, unreasonableness may also be replaced with a proportionality test in some cases. The remaining two forms involve distinct new grounds rather than merely a modification and extension of the existing substantive ground. The second extension is review for disappointing a substantive legitimate expectation; and the third is review for mistake of fact. Part A of this chapter outlines the traditional ground of *Wednesbury* unreasonableness, and Parts B to D address each of the three extensions of substantive review in turn.

All three forms of expansion are the subject of debate, both as to whether they are desirable at all and as to how far they should be taken. As a result, the law in this area is unstable and unsettled. In this chapter we consider these debates as well as the current state of the law.

What is at stake in these debates? We will return to this question under each heading, but an outline of general concerns is helpful here. On the one hand, the traditional limits of the supervisory jurisdiction reflect respect for Parliament's allocation of powers to the primary decision-maker. They also reflect a pair of justiciability concerns about the suitability of substantive merits questions for judicial determination.[2] The first concern is about the courts' lack of democratic legitimacy. Decisions about contested and competing values and interests ought to be made by elected representatives or by officials who are accountable to those representatives. The second concern is about the courts' institutional capacity. The courts' adversarial procedure generally, and judicial review procedure

[1] *Associated Provincial Picture Houses Ltd v Wednesbury Corporation* [1948] 1 KB 223 (CA).
[2] On justiciability, see Ch 8.A.

especially, is not well suited to determining the merits of contested policy or factual questions.

On the other hand, democratic accountability offers scant protection to individuals whose important interests are affected by decisions. A measure of substantive review may be necessary for ensuring adequate protection from arbitrary exercises of power. Without such protection, the rule of law and individual liberty may be compromised.

A. *Wednesbury* Unreasonableness

Traditionally, the substantive merits of an impugned decision were beyond the reach of judicial review unless a decision crossed the very high threshold of being *Wednesbury* unreasonable. The decision had to be 'so unreasonable that no reasonable authority could ever have come to it' – this required 'something overwhelming' or 'absurd'.[3] It had to be 'outrageous in its defiance of logic or accepted moral standards'.[4] Courts would not intervene on this ground if there was room for reasonable disagreement on the point at issue.

Indeed, for a long time the courts did not even acknowledge that this ground amounted to merits review at all. Instead, it was explained on the basis that a court in such a case has to assume the decision-maker must have laboured under some unidentified misconception as to the law.[5] That fiction was dismissed by Lord Diplock in the *CCSU* case.[6] Since then, irrationality has been recognised as a ground in its own right and it does concern the substantive merits. However, orthodoxy was maintained by confining such merits review to be a last resort in truly extreme cases.

While there is debate and uncertainty concerning the potential lowering of the threshold for intervention in appropriate contexts, it is well established that the high threshold remains applicable in at least some contexts. This was confirmed by the Supreme Court in *CP Group*,[7] dismissing an attempt to depart from the earlier leading case of *Woolworths*.[8] Both cases hold that unreasonableness challenges to local authority decisions on setting rates must cross the high *Wednesbury* threshold. This is a type of decision where the justiciability concerns are especially pertinent and the countervailing considerations are weak.

Given the high threshold, this ground is rarely made out. Furthermore, where a decision is sufficiently questionable to cross this threshold, it will very often also attract review on one of the other grounds. The rare cases where the threshold has been crossed are often in contexts where the court may have felt well placed to assess the merits, and thus tacitly lowered the threshold – as, for instance, in a challenge to a decision upholding a complaint against a lawyer.[9]

[3] *Wednesbury* (n 1) at 229–230.

[4] *Council of Civil Service Unions v Minister for the Civil Service* [1985] 1 AC 374 (HL) (*CCSU*) at 410.

[5] *Edwards (Inspector of Taxes) v Bairstow* [1956] AC 14 (HL) at 36.

[6] *CCSU* (n 4) at 410–11.

[7] *Auckland Council v CP Group Ltd* [2023] NZSC 53, [2023] 1 NZLR 35 at [84]–[98].

[8] *Wellington City Council v Woolworths New Zealand Ltd (No 2)* [1996] 2 NZLR 537 (CA) at 545–47, 552–53.

[9] *Parmenter v Legal Complaints Review Officer* [2021] NZHC 2025 at [39]–[45].

Unreasonableness can be found in either the outcome or the reasoning. While the formulations quoted above suggest the first option, unreasonableness of outcome, there is also much authority for the second. For instance, a decision may be unreasonable where mandatory relevant considerations are given manifestly unreasonable weight.[10]

Confusion can be caused by references to the '*Wednesbury* grounds' in some sources. That phrase usually refers to a broader set of grounds for reviewing exercises of discretion that were referenced in the *Wednesbury* decision. These include unreasonableness but also irrelevant considerations, improper purposes and failing to take into account mandatory relevant considerations.[11]

B. Heightened Scrutiny and Proportionality

English courts have, within the last three decades, developed an approach involving variable intensity of review on the unreasonableness ground. The old high *Wednesbury* threshold is still considered appropriate for some cases, but some other cases attract 'heightened scrutiny': more searching scrutiny on a lower threshold.[12] This applies where the impugned decision impacts on fundamental rights or other very important interests, as discussed in Chapter 6 on fundamental common law rights.[13] In Aotearoa New Zealand, the law on this remains uncertain.

Where rights protected by the Human Rights Act 1998 (UK) or the New Zealand Bill of Rights Act 1990 are engaged, yet another approach applies to scrutinising the justification for limiting those rights, namely a proportionality test – as also discussed in Chapter 6.[14] Whether this test should also be available as a common law ground of review in other contexts has been a matter of speculation and debate in the United Kingdom. Such a development has attracted less attention and little support so far in the New Zealand courts.

This Part of the chapter addresses (1) the state of authority on whether heightened scrutiny is available in New Zealand; (2) what factors would determine its application; (3) what heightened scrutiny means; and (4) whether proportionality should be an alternative ground of review.

(1) State of Authority on Heightened Scrutiny

There are two questions about heightened scrutiny. First, should the intensity of scrutiny on the unreasonableness ground vary, with heightened scrutiny applying in

[10] *New Zealand Fishing Industry Association Inc v Minister of Agriculture and Fisheries* [1988] 1 NZLR 544 (CA) at 552.

[11] *Wednesbury* (n 1) at 228–29.

[12] *R v Ministry of Defence, ex p Smith* [1996] QB 517 (CA); *Kennedy v Charity Commission* [2014] UKSC 20, [2015] AC 455 at [51], [52].

[13] See Ch 6.C.

[14] See Ch 6.D.

appropriate contexts? Secondly, should the high *Wednesbury* threshold for intervention be discarded entirely?

There is significant New Zealand authority for applying heightened scrutiny in appropriate contexts. However, the development still has not been authoritatively adopted at appellate level. What is clear is that the high threshold of *Wednesbury* unreasonableness does continue to apply in appropriate contexts as discussed in part A. Let us look at the authorities.

Heightened scrutiny was first adopted by the High Court in *Wolf*. Wild J stated that the time had come to recognise that the high *Wednesbury* threshold is not appropriate in all contexts, and went on to apply heightened scrutiny.[15] He considered the high threshold inappropriate where rights or other important interests are at stake. The state of authority on the availability of heightened scrutiny, however, is still uncertain two decades later.[16] As we will see, the Court of Appeal has been very slow to commit to any authoritative pronouncement, and the Supreme Court has not yet expressed a view.

Starting with the position at High Court level, heightened scrutiny has been used since *Wolf* in many High Court decisions, but authority at that level remains divided. In recent years, two High Court judges have championed competing positions; both have since been elevated to the Court of Appeal. Palmer J has adopted heightened scrutiny in a number of cases, including in *Hauraki Coromandel Climate Action*, considering that it was appropriate to signal the 'degree of priority of attention and care' required.[17] Cooke J has consistently rejected the idea of variable intensity scrutiny in any context. In *Students for Climate Solutions*, he rejected the heightened scrutiny adopted in the *Hauraki* case, while also rejecting *Wednesbury* in favour of a single unreasonableness test with a lower threshold.[18]

For many years, there was little more than a string of supportive dicta at Court of Appeal level.[19] Two decisions did appear to adopt heightened scrutiny, but neither seems very clear authority on the point. In the little-noted decision in *Pring*, the Court accepted that resource management decisions with the potential of adversely and directly affecting neighbours would be scrutinised 'more carefully and with a less tolerant eye' than the usual standard.[20] However, there was no discussion or citation of authority to support this point; and the challenge did not succeed on this basis. In *Quake Outcasts* the Court applied more intensive reasonableness scrutiny to strike down a decision, citing *Wolf*.[21] But the context was post-earthquake emergency legislation that included an express reasonableness requirement to constrain very exceptional

[15] *Wolf v Minister of Immigration* [2004] NZAR 414 (HC) at [47], [65].

[16] See MB Rodriguez Ferrere, 'An Impasse in New Zealand's Administrative Law: How Did We Get There?' (2017) 28 *Public Law Review* 310.

[17] *Hauraki Coromandel Climate Action Inc v Thames-Coromandel District Council* [2020] NZHC 3228, [2021] 3 NZLR 280 at [49]–[51].

[18] *Students for Climate Solutions Inc v The Minister of Energy and Resources* [2022] NZHC 2116, [2022] NZRMA 612 at [41], [83]. The point was not at issue on appeal.

[19] See, eg, *Pharmaceutical Management Agency Ltd v Roussel Uclaf Australia Pty Ltd* [1998] NZAR 58 (CA) at 66.

[20] *JC Pring v Wanganui District Council* [1999] NZRMA 519, (1999) 5 ELRNZ 464 (CA) at [7].

[21] *Quake Outcasts v Minister of Canterbury Earthquake Recovery* [2017] NZCA 332, [2017] 3 NZLR 486 at [72]–[73], [76]–[77].

powers.[22] The Court did not address whether heightened scrutiny might apply outside that context.

The Supreme Court has, on at least three occasions, declined to weigh in on the availability of heightened scrutiny.[23] In the *Ye* litigation, the Court of Appeal divided on the issue,[24] but the Supreme Court chose to focus solely on the impact of international law.[25]

The *Kim* litigation was a remarkable episode in this saga. It was common ground between the parties that heightened scrutiny did apply to the Minister's decision on Mr Kim's extradition. Both the Court of Appeal and the Supreme Court accepted this agreement and applied heightened scrutiny. However, surprisingly, the Supreme Court held that due to this agreement, the question of whether heightened scrutiny is available in New Zealand law was not before the Court for decision. While the Court of Appeal endorsed the parties' position that it is available (without any substantive reasoning),[26] the Supreme Court expressly left that point open.[27]

When the point arose again in *CP Group*, the Supreme Court did settle one point. We still do not know whether heightened scrutiny is available, but we do know that it does not apply in all cases. *Wednesbury* is not dead: it continues to apply in appropriate contexts. In particular, it applies to local authority decisions on rates – the type of decision at issue in this case.[28]

If heightened scrutiny is available, therefore, it is available only in some cases. Let us turn next to the factors that are relevant to deciding when it may apply.

(2) What Factors would Support Heightened Scrutiny?

In *CP Group*, the Supreme Court re-affirmed the long-standing authority of *Woolworths* for applying the high *Wednesbury* threshold to review of rating decisions. The reasoning in that case remained applicable.[29] The relevant features were the nature of decisions on rates, councils' democratic mandate, and the context of statutory consultation and transparency processes that served to hold councils accountable.[30] Rating decisions are 'often not amenable to right or wrong answers'. They require 'resolution of factual issues, the weighing of competing interests, and competing policy considerations', and 'ultimately require judgment'.[31] As *Woolworths* put it, there are 'constitutional and

[22] ibid at [70]–[73], [77].

[23] See MB Rodriguez Ferrere and Andrew Geddis, 'The Supreme Court, Public Law and Adjudicative Minimalism' in Michael Littlewood and Janet McLean (eds), *The New Zealand Supreme Court: The Second Ten Years* (Wellington, LexisNexis, 2024) 207 at 211–12, 215–18.

[24] *Ye v Minister of Immigration* [2009] 2 NZLR 596 (CA) at [303]; see also at [112], [569]; *Huang v Minister of Immigration* [2008] NZCA 377, [2009] 2 NZLR 700 at [67].

[25] *Ye v Minister of Immigration* [2009] NZSC 76, [2010] 1 NZLR 104.

[26] *Kim v Minister of Justice of New Zealand* [2019] NZCA 209, [2019] 3 NZLR 173 at [45]–[47].

[27] *Minister of Justice v Kim* [2021] NZSC 57, [2021] 1 NZLR 338 at [41], [46], [51].

[28] *Auckland Council v CP Group Ltd* [2023] NZSC 53, [2023] 1 NZLR 35 at [89].

[29] *Wellington City Council v Woolworths New Zealand Ltd (No 2)* [1996] 2 NZLR 537 (CA); *CP Group* (n 28) at [98].

[30] *CP Group* (n 28) at [80]–[98].

[31] ibid at [96].

democratic constraints on judicial involvement' in this area: the complex 'economic, social and political assessments involved' in rating decisions are 'within the customary sphere of those entrusted' with them.[32]

If heightened scrutiny is to be available, it would be in a very different type of context, as exemplified by the *Wolf* case. The challenge was to an immigration tribunal's dismissal of Mr Wolf's appeal against deportation. That appeal relied on humanitarian grounds concerning the impact on his New Zealand children. Wild J held that heightened scrutiny was appropriate because what was at stake was the break-up of a New Zealand family unit, which engaged New Zealand's international human rights law obligations.[33] In other words, heightened scrutiny may apply where rights or other important interests or values are at stake.

Wild J also explained what made this case different from *Woolworths*. This case did not involve 'an elected body' nor decisions on a subject with 'high policy content'. While the tribunal had relevant 'experience/expertise' in this area, the court was equally well placed to apply the relevant tests.[34]

We may note that the factors that are relevant to the level of scrutiny are the same sorts of factors as those used to determine justiciability.[35]

(3) What does Heightened Scrutiny Mean?

Heightened scrutiny, as we have seen, refers to more searching scrutiny on a lower threshold. In two respects, however, it is not always clear what is meant by it.

The first and main point that is not always clear concerns exactly what is involved in heightened scrutiny. The options include at least two: heightened scrutiny may narrow the range of reasonably available outcomes or answers; or it may involve courts demanding more by way of cogent justification for the decision.[36] The New Zealand cases adopting heightened scrutiny tend not to address this choice expressly, but most of them can be seen as adopting versions of the second approach.[37] Occasionally, courts expressly acknowledge taking this approach. In *Hu*, for instance, Palmer J commented that unreasonableness unsurprisingly can be found in the reasons.[38]

In *Wolf*, what was found unreasonable on heightened scrutiny were two defects in the immigration tribunal's reasoning for dismissing the humanitarian circumstances appeal against deportation. One was failure to take proper account of evidence that supported Mr Wolf's claim that the children would suffer.[39] The other concerned an inference from some evidence. Mr Wolf had been using a false name since arriving in

[32] *Woolworths* (n 29) at 546, 553.

[33] ibid at [64]–[66], [72].

[34] *Wolf* (n 15) at [72].

[35] See Ch 8.A.

[36] For the second option, see David Dyzenhaus, Murray Hunt and Michael Taggart, 'The Principle of Legality in Administrative Law: Internationalisation as Constitutionalisation' (2001) 1 *Oxford University Commonwealth Law Journal* 5.

[37] In addition to *Wolf* (n 15) and *Kim* (SC) (n 27) discussed below, this is also the case in *Quake Outcasts* (n 21).

[38] *Hu v Immigration and Protection Tribunal* [2017] NZHC 41, [2017] NZAR 508 at [30]–[31].

[39] *Wolf* (n 15) at [66]–[67].

New Zealand, to help conceal a criminal conviction in Germany. The tribunal drew an adverse inference from the fact that he had never disclosed his true identity and background to his NZ children, concluding that he did not really care much about them. The Court rejected this inference as illogical and unwarranted.[40] Together with a breach of natural justice in the form of failing to warn of an unexpected finding,[41] these flaws added up to a decision that could not pass heightened scrutiny.[42]

We see the same type of approach in *Kim*, where both appellate courts engaged in heightened scrutiny on the basis of the parties' agreement. In the Supreme Court, the question was put as whether the Minister's conclusion on extradition was 'reasonably open on the basis of sufficient and relevant evidence'.[43] The Court proceeded to scrutinise the Minister's reasoning and the evidence on each of the factors that were relevant to the decision. To take just one example, it held that the Minister was wrong in disregarding a particular report as unreliable.

None of the cases state that heightened scrutiny may *only* take this second approach of scrutinising the reasoning process and the cogency of the justification; the fact that this has been often used may just be happenstance. However, it seems likely that courts feel more comfortable in applying intensified scrutiny to the decision-maker's reasoning than directly judging the reasonableness of the outcome on an intensified basis. Scrutiny of reasoning processes is well established as part of traditional illegality review, and hence seems less of a radical expansion of the courts' supervisory powers.

A second sometimes uncertain question about the meaning of heightened scrutiny concerns what ground of review is involved. Heightened scrutiny is usually understood as a variant of the ground of unreasonableness. However, that is not always entirely clear. In some cases, courts appear to contemplate variable scrutiny applying to all grounds of review.[44] That would be a radical departure from orthodoxy, as discussed in Chapter 9. While interesting and arguably welcome, it is not at all clear that the courts appreciated that point in these cases

In some other cases, courts hearing Bill of Rights Act challenges have relied on cases concerning heightened scrutiny.[45] As explained in Chapter 6, the respect which courts accord to decision-makers when it comes to justification for limits on rights in that context is better understood as part of a separate ground of review (illegality or breach of the Bill of Rights as a new ground), rather than as an instance of heightened scrutiny unreasonableness review.

The converse question, however, is one that has been the subject of much debate. Should the test developed for assessing the justification for limits on rights – proportionality – also be used as a ground of review in its own right outside of that context?

[40] ibid at [68].

[41] ibid at [69].

[42] ibid at [72].

[43] *Kim* (SC) (n 27) at [41].

[44] See, eg, *Kim* (CA) (n 26) at [45]–[47].

[45] See esp *Taylor v The Chief Executive of the Department of Corrections* [2015] NZCA 477, [2015] NZAR 1648 at [87]–[91].

(4) Proportionality as a Ground of Review?

Proportionality is the test for justifying limits on rights in terms of section 5 of the Bill of Rights, as we saw in Chapter 6. The test can vary, but the usual form is the so-called *Oakes* test.[46] This asks whether the limit on the right serves a legitimate objective, whether the limit is rationally connected to the objective, whether it represents a reasonably minimal impairment of the right, and whether it is proportional overall.

There has been much academic debate on whether this proportionality test is available as a ground of review outside the context of the Bill of Rights Act or the Human Rights Act (UK). Some have argued that proportionality should function as an alternative to the unreasonableness ground, to be used in appropriate contexts.[47] Some have even argued that it should replace that ground entirely.[48] While the United Kingdom courts have for some time appeared tantalisingly close to accepting that proportionality is available as an alternative to unreasonableness,[49] the New Zealand courts have been much more reluctant in this regard.

The one and only context in which a form of proportionality ground is established is where penalties are being challenged. There is good authority that courts may strike down penalties for being disproportionate.[50] However, that is a simpler question. The form the test takes in that context is not the structured *Oakes* test: the question is quite simply whether the penalty is excessive in relation to what is being punished. Beyond that, to the extent that courts have entertained proportionality complaints at all, they have considered these as simply a form of unreasonableness.[51]

In *Wolf*, the High Court left the question of proportionality as an alternative ground of review open but cast a great deal of doubt on it.[52] The Court of Appeal has also noted that the point remains open.[53] The matter has not moved much beyond that since then.[54]

As to the desirability of adopting proportionality as a ground, let us explore two questions. First, how different is this to heightened scrutiny? Secondly, is it desirable to replace unreasonableness entirely with either of these?

(a) Is there Much Difference between Heightened Scrutiny and Proportionality?

Turning to the first of these, there is a question mark over the significance of the debate about proportionality as a ground of review. Mike Taggart argued persuasively that

[46] The test as set out in *R v Oakes* [1986] 1 SCR 103 was authoritatively adopted for New Zealand in *R v Hansen* [2007] NZSC 7, [2007] 3 NZLR 1 (SC).

[47] See, eg, Jeff A King, 'Proportionality: A Halfway House' [2010] *New Zealand Law Review* 327.

[48] See, eg Paul Craig, *Administrative Law*, 9th edn (London, Sweet & Maxwell, 2021) at Ch 21.5.

[49] See, eg, *Kennedy* [2014] UKSC 20 (n 12) at [54]; *R (Youssef) v Secretary of State for Foreign and Commonwealth Affairs* [2016] UKSC 3, [2016] AC 1457 at [56].

[50] *Institute of Chartered Accountants of NZ v Bevan* [2003] 1 NZLR 154 (CA).

[51] See, eg, *Isaac v Minister of Consumer Affairs* [1990] 2 NZLR 606 (HC).

[52] *Wolf* (n 15) at [26]–[36].

[53] *Bevan* (n 50) at [55].

[54] See, eg, *ANZ Sky Tours Ltd v New Zealand Tourism Board (ta Tourism New Zealand)* [2019] NZHC 925, [2019] NZAR 951 at [131]–[140].

heightened scrutiny amounted to much the same as proportionality.[55] There certainly cannot be much doubt that unreasonableness (even the *Wednesbury* variety), like proportionality, involves the courts assessing the balance struck between competing considerations[56] – notwithstanding a much-quoted dictum of Lord Steyn in *Daly* to the contrary.[57] The advantages of proportionality for its proponents are that it is a structured test, involves more intensive scrutiny, and puts the onus of justification on the defendant.[58] On closer examination, it turns out that heightened scrutiny may share much of these features.

First, heightened scrutiny incorporates significant elements of the structured proportionality test – most notably the enquiry into less rights-infringing alternatives. In *Simms*, for instance, the House of Lords considered that the legitimate objective of prison discipline could have been served by a more limited ban on interviews with journalists: a ban that did not extend to interviews for the purpose of establishing a miscarriage of justice.[59] Conversely, we should note, proportionality is not always a structured test: it can also take the form of a simple unstructured balancing test, as we saw in Chapter 6.

Secondly, while proportionality usually involves more intensive review than *Wednesbury* unreasonableness, clearly heightened scrutiny does too – that is its defining feature. Conversely, we have seen that courts apply proportionality with very significant restraint in some contexts:[60] just as with reasonableness, the intensity of review for proportionality is variable – the test does not entail any particular intensity of review.

Finally, traditional *Wednesbury* unreasonableness clearly put no onus of justification on the defendant, unlike proportionality. It required the plaintiff to demonstrate a relevant flaw. However, heightened scrutiny does – almost by definition – involve a justificatory burden on the defendant.[61] In summary, it is strongly arguable that adoption of proportionality as a ground adds little of substance to heightened scrutiny unreasonableness review.

(b) Should Either of these Replace Unreasonableness Entirely?

The second question is whether either or both of these could or should entirely replace unreasonableness. Of course, the Supreme Court has confirmed that the high threshold of *Wednesbury* unreasonableness continues to apply in some contexts. However, Paul Craig has argued that replacing unreasonableness with proportionality would not necessarily result in discarding such highly deferential review.[62] As already noted, proportionality can be applied with very significant deference. We could have a

[55] Michael Taggart, 'Proportionality, Deference, *Wednesbury*' [2008] *New Zealand Law Review* 423 at 435, 448–449.

[56] See Paul Craig, 'The Nature of Reasonableness Review' [2013] *Current Legal Problems* 1.

[57] *R (Daly) v Secretary of State for the Home Department* [2001] UKHL 26, [2001] 2 AC 532 at [27].

[58] Craig, *Administrative Law* (n 48) at [21-037]–[21-042].

[59] *R v Secretary of State for the Home Department, ex parte Simms* [2000] 2 AC 115 (HL) at 129–30.

[60] See Ch 6.D.

[61] But cf Taggart (n 55) at 465 apparently to the contrary.

[62] Craig, *Administrative Law* (n 48) at [21-037].

spectrum of variable intensity review, all in the form of proportionality. The attractions are the structured nature of the test, and the resulting obligation on the decision-maker to provide a reasoned justification.

There are several objections to this. The first is the point already noted: proportionality itself varies in form, not only in intensity. Even in the Bill of Rights context, its form is adjusted for different contexts. It does not always take the form of the structured *Oakes* test. It is difficult to argue, therefore, that it should do so in other contexts.

Secondly, the structured *Oakes* test is designed to give special priority to a right or other important interest or value. The minimal impairment step of that test means that a right may be limited only where this is necessary as a means for serving a sufficiently important competing objective: no adequate alternative means are available.

This minimal impairment test is not appropriate when nothing is at stake that deserves such priority. In such cases, two consequences follow, as Taggart pointed out.[63] First, the structure of the proportionality test falls away: without the minimal impairment step, the test simply involves balancing competing interests and objectives. It then has little to recommend it over unreasonableness. Secondly, using 'proportionality' as the label for the simple balancing test that is appropriate in cases not involving rights creates a risk. The use of this label may lead courts to approach cases differently and unwittingly adopt a higher intensity of review that is not warranted in such cases.

Taggart and some other authors therefore proposed adopting proportionality only for cases where rights or other important interests or values are at stake and retaining *Wednesbury* unreasonableness in other cases.[64] He argued this would help to structure judicial discretion and promote predictability. Other commentators, however, have rejected such 'bifurcation'.[65]

So far, as we have seen, Aotearoa New Zealand has not adopted either option: there is no clear authority that either heightened scrutiny or proportionality are available at all. As an alternative, similar expansion of substantive scrutiny can also be achieved by adopting new grounds to deal with particular types of complaints. The rights-based grounds of review (Chapter 6) are instances of this. In the United Kingdom, two further new grounds have been adopted, but these again remain uncertain in New Zealand. The remaining two parts of this chapter examine these in turn.

C. Substantive Legitimate Expectations

Is it lawful for a decision-maker to break a promise or undertaking, or to depart from a published policy or established practice? These things may give rise to legitimate

[63] Taggart (n 55) at 478–79.

[64] ibid at 477–78. See also, eg, Mark Elliott, 'From Bifurcation to Calibration: Twin-Track Deference and the Culture of Justification' in Hanna Wilberg and Mark Elliott (eds), *The Scope and Intensity of Substantive Review: Traversing Taggart's Rainbow* (Oxford, Hart Publishing, 2015) 61.

[65] See, eg, Murray Hunt, 'Against Bifurcation' in David Dyzenhaus, Murray Hunt and Grant Huscroft (eds), *A Simple Common Lawyer: Essays in Honour of Michael Taggart* (Oxford, Hart Publishing, 2009) 99; Craig *Administrative Law* (n 48) ch 21.6.

expectations. Arguably, we should be entitled to rely on such expectations. But the extent of their effect is a contested and unsettled question.[66] A resulting procedural obligation is well established: legitimate expectations give rise to a right to a hearing before a decision disappointing them can be taken, as discussed in Chapter 4.[67] The controversial question concerns the substantive effect of a legitimate expectation of a substantive benefit. Such effect is established by modern English cases: it is unlawful to disappoint a legitimate expectation of a substantive benefit unless this is justified by an overriding public interest. In Aotearoa New Zealand, this development has not yet been clearly and fully adopted.

The sections in this Part of the chapter concern (1) the reasons for and against allowing review on this ground, (2) when a legitimate expectation counts as substantive and therefore as more controversial, (3) what gives rise to a substantive legitimate expectation and (4) the extent and nature of the substantive effect that is given to such an expectation and the intensity of review.

(1) The Reasons For and Against Adopting this Ground of Review

The development of this new substantive ground responds to some good and strong reasons. As we will see, an expectation is considered legitimate only if it is a reasonable reaction to an assurance given, or a practice or policy adopted, by the decision-maker. In such circumstances, elementary notions of fairness and trust in public administration require a satisfactory justification from a decision-maker for disappointing the legitimate expectation.[68] Such a requirement promotes good administration, and is conducive to rule of law values of certainty, predictability and avoiding arbitrariness.[69] Where published policies are concerned, we may add that one of the reasons for publishing policies is to give guidance to the public on the criteria and processes that will apply.[70] A 'non-reneging' principle arising from this provides a further good reason for considering that people are entitled to rely on published policies.[71]

However, the new ground is a form of merits review: it goes beyond policing the boundaries of the relevant statutory power and requiring fair procedures and law-abiding reasoning processes. In scrutinising the justification for disappointing a legitimate expectation, a court evaluates the balance struck between competing considerations. As such, this ground engages the fundamental concerns about merits review outlined in the introduction to this chapter: the concerns that this exceeds the constitutional and institutional limits of judicial power on review.

[66] For the debate, see, eg, Alison Young, 'Stuck at a Crossroad? Substantive Legitimate Expectations in English Law' [2021] 80 *Cambridge Law Journal* 179; Matthew Groves and Greg Weeks (eds), *Legitimate Expectations in the Common Law World* (Oxford, Hart Publishing, 2016).

[67] See Ch 4 C.

[68] Christopher Forsyth, 'The Provenance and Protection of Legitimate Expectations' [1988] *CLJ* 238 at 241–245.

[69] See Ch 3.

[70] *In re McFarland* [2004] UKHL 17, [2004] 1 WLR 1289 (HL) at 1299.

[71] See Shona Wilson Stark, 'Non-fettering, Legitimate Expectations and Consistency of Policy: Separate Compartments or Single Principle?' in Jason NE Varuhas and Shona Wilson Stark (eds), *The Frontiers of Public Law* (Oxford, Hart, 2020) 443 at 450, 452.

Having said this, merits review has never been entirely excluded: as we have seen, *Wednesbury* unreasonableness is now recognised as involving merits review, albeit only on an extremely deferential standard. The law has always struck a balance between the desirability of some substantive constraints on exercises of public power and the concerns about merits review. The new ground merely amounts to striking that balance differently, in a specific context where the arguments in favour of constraints are arguably especially strong. Reasonable minds can differ on where the balance should be struck.

There is a further objection that is specific to the new ground: it is in tension with the established rule against fettering discretion. However, properly understood the two principles can be reconciled. According to the rule against fettering, it is unlawful for decision-makers exercising discretion to apply blanket policies.[72] If the enforcement of substantive legitimate expectations required precisely what is prohibited by this rule, then the two could not co-exist. And there are good reasons for maintaining the rule against fettering: discretion should be exercised in a way that is responsive to the circumstances of each individual case, and decision-makers must be free to change any policies they adopt so as to reflect their judgment of what best serves the public interest.

However, direct conflict between the rule against fettering and enforcement of substantive legitimate expectations can be avoided, albeit a tension probably remains. Here we see why the substantive effect given to legitimate expectations cannot be absolute: that would be inconsistent with the rule against fettering. Hence substantive effect takes the qualified form of a requirement that there must be satisfactory justification for disappointing legitimate expectations. If this ground is available, then the combined effect of the two grounds is that decision-makers must always be ready to depart from policies (etc) where there is reason to do so, but at the same time must not depart from them unless they do have a good reason.[73] There is no conflict between these two propositions.

(2) How to Recognise Cases Involving the New Substantive Ground

It is important to distinguish between the new ground of substantive legitimate expectations and the established use of legitimate expectations as part of procedural fairness. Controversy attaches only to the new substantive version. And authority for the procedural effect should not be mistaken as establishing the new version.

In short, the new ground is involved only where both the *content* and the *effect* of the legitimate expectation is substantive. The *content* is substantive if the expectation is of a substantive benefit: for instance, an expectation to keep or to be granted a licence or permit. The *effect* is substantive if the court enforces such a substantive expectation, requiring the decision-maker to grant the expected substantive benefit or not to cancel it.

[72] See Ch 5.B.

[73] Shona Wilson Stark (n 71) at 456–57, 464–65; Michael Taggart, 'Administrative Law' [2000] *New Zealand Law Review* 439 at 444–45.

In contrast, the well-established use of legitimate expectations is to support a right to a hearing or to consultation, as discussed in Chapter 4. Confusion can creep in because the content of the expectation for this purpose can be either procedural (expecting a hearing or consultation) or substantive (expecting a substantive benefit). However, the distinctive point is that the *effect* given is purely procedural: before a legitimate expectation can be disappointed, those who have the expectation are entitled to a hearing or consultation.

The substantive effect that distinguishes the new ground cannot be absolute, requiring the expectation to be satisfied come what may. The effect is always qualified by allowing the decision-maker to disappoint the expectation if there is sufficient justification. But the effect does not count as substantive unless the court evaluates a decisionmaker's reasons for disappointing the expectation and finds the decision unlawful if there is insufficient justification. In reviewing the justification, courts apply varying standards of review, as we will see.

One further option found in the modern cases on substantive legitimate expectations is to treat the expectation as a mandatory relevant consideration. That is an intermediate type of effect: it is neither substantive in the sense that it constrains the scope of legally available outcomes, nor is it procedural in the sense of a mere hearing requirement. This is, however, usually accompanied by scrutiny of the justification for disappointing the expectation, albeit perhaps on a deferential standard. As discussed, that is a form of substantive effect.

(3) What Will Give Rise to a Substantive Legitimate Expectation

The vast majority of attempts to invoke the substantive legitimate expectations ground fail because there was no sufficient basis for a legitimate expectation. It is therefore important to understand what is required under this heading. In short, an expectation counts as legitimate only if it is a reasonable reaction to an assurance given, or a practice or policy adopted, by the decision-maker. Only if an expectation passes this hurdle of being 'legitimate' is it capable of attracting substantive effect. Essentially the same requirement also applies even to the procedural version (though perhaps courts will tend to set the hurdle slightly higher for substantive effect).[74] A mere hope is never enough.

We should note also that the assurance, practice or policy must normally be lawful. Only exceptionally will courts enforce expectations founded on promises, policies or practices which the decision-maker had no power to make.[75]

It may not be necessary to show that the applicants have changed their position to their detriment in reliance on the expectation. That is a requirement in the private law cause of action for estoppel but does not necessarily form part of the requirements for this new ground of judicial review.[76]

[74] Cases on the procedural effect of legitimate expectations are therefore relevant as authority under this heading.

[75] See Paul Craig, *Administrative Law*, 9th edn (London, Sweet & Maxwell, 2021), Ch 22.9–11; Oliver Friend-Smith, 'Should There Be Exceptions to the Rule That Courts Cannot Enforce Ultra Vires Legitimate Expectations?' [2024] *Public Law* 29.

[76] See *Re Finucane* [2019] UKSC 7, [2019] 3 All ER 191 at [72], [158]–[160].

The importance of establishing the basis for a legitimate expectation is reflected in the often-quoted three-step enquiry set out by the Court of Appeal in *Terminals (NZ)*:[77]

(1) 'establish the nature of the commitment' made by way of the promise, practice or policy: an 'ambiguous' promise, policy or practice is unlikely give rise to a legitimate expectation;
(2) 'determine whether the plaintiff's reliance on the promise or practice in question is legitimate' – this turns on whether the reliance was 'reasonable in the context';
(3) 'decide what remedy, if any, should be provided if a legitimate expectation is established'.

The first two of these three stages concern whether there is a sufficient basis for a legitimate expectation. Where the first stage test is passed, a range of factors is relevant to the second stage, whether the reliance was 'reasonable in the context'. We will look at these factors in the next section, as the same factors also determine the nature and extent of the substantive effect once a legitimate expectation is established. In this section, let us consider each of the possible bases in turn: a promise, an established practice, or a policy.[78]

(a) Promise, Undertaking or Assurance

A promise, undertaking or assurance is the most obvious and perhaps strongest basis for a legitimate expectation. However, all depends on the nature and terms of the promise. In order to give rise to a legitimate expectation, it must be an affirmative promise rather than a more tentative indication, and its terms must be unambiguous. Furthermore, even where an unqualified and unambiguous promise has been made, the reasonableness of reliance on it also depends on who made it and in what form and context.

A claim that failed despite invoking an undertaking made directly to the applicant is found in *Terminals (NZ)*, which illustrates both of these points.[79] The claimed expectation was based on a representation made by a customs official concerning the excise duty payable on a certain type of product. For two reasons, this expectation did not cross the hurdle of being legitimate. First, the initial representation was not unambiguous: there was a misunderstanding between the parties as to what the enquiry and the representation related to. Secondly, the only point at which there may have been an unambiguous representation was in a telephone conversation (there was also a written exchange, but that was affected by the ambiguity already noted). The Court held it was not reasonable to rely on a mere telephone conversation as the basis for deciding on a large-scale investment with large fiscal implications in terms of excise duty.[80]

[77] *Comptroller of Customs v Terminals (NZ) Ltd* [2012] NZCA 598, [2014] 2 NZLR 137 at [125]–[127]. There was an appeal, but not on this point.

[78] Note that some commentators propose confining substantive legitimate expectations to the first of these: see, eg, Jason Varuhas, 'In Search of a Doctrine: Mapping the Law of Legitimate Expectations' in Matthew Groves and Greg Weeks (eds), *Legitimate Expectations in the Common Law World* (Oxford, Hart Publishing, 2017) 17.

[79] *Terminals (NZ)* (n 77) at [128]–[132].

[80] Similarly, see also *Hugh Green Ltd v Auckland Council* [2018] NZHC 2916 at [152]–[169].

(b) Established Practice or Existing Benefit

Turning to an established practice as a basis for a legitimate expectation, this perhaps is the most difficult basis to establish. A practice has to be so well-established and well-recognised that it can reasonably be considered to carry with it a commitment to continue the practice.[81]

(c) Policy Guidelines

Administrative policy guidelines can provide the basis for a legitimate expectation. They can raise a range of issues, depending on the circumstances.

Where a relevant published policy remains unchanged, there is both authority and good reason for finding a legitimate expectation that it will be applied according to its terms.[82] This may even extend to cases where the applicant did not know about the policy, but that is more controversial.[83] Arguably, the better basis for intervention in such a case is a distinct, though related, duty of consistency, discussed in Part D below.

More difficult are the cases where a policy on which the applicant has relied has changed. The starting point is that public authorities must be free to change their policies when they consider this to be in the public interest.[84] We can distinguish two basic scenarios. The first is where the relevant policy changed before the applicant submitted an application in reliance on it. Given the premise that policies must be open to change, ordinarily there can be no cause for complaint in this first scenario.

A legitimate expectation of a decision in accordance with an old policy may arise, however, in the second scenario: where an application was lodged in reliance on that old policy before it changed. At the very least, the courts will give that expectation procedural effect: the applicants' right to a hearing will include a right to be notified of the change in policy, so they can amend the application in light of that change.[85]

Beyond that, however, in this scenario there can also be a sufficient basis for a substantive legitimate expectation. A decision inconsistent with the old policy may thus be unlawful unless there is good justification for applying the changed policy. The basis here is detrimental reliance: a legitimate expectation arises where applicants have spent time and effort, and often money, in the reasonable expectation that they had good prospects for success based on the then current policy. Such a claim was entertained in *New Zealand Association for Migration and Investment*, albeit it failed on the facts.[86]

The upshot is that when an authority changes its policy, it may be obliged to adopt transitional provisions that protect the legitimate expectations of persons who have

[81] *R (Davies) v Revenue and Customs Commissioners* [2011] UKSC 47, [2011] 1 WLR 2625 at [49].

[82] *R (Kambadzi) v Secretary of State for the Home Department (Bail for Immigration Detainees intervening)* [2011] UKSC 23, [2011] 1 WLR 1299; *Smith v Attorney-General* [2017] NZHC 136; *Te Pou Matakana Ltd v Attorney-General* [2021] NZHC 2942 at [115]–[116].

[83] *R (Rashid) v Home Secretary* [2005] EWCA Civ 744.

[84] See Ch 5 B.

[85] *Smithkline Beecham (NZ) Ltd v Ministry of Health* [1992] NZAR 357 (HC). For a similar point, see also *Pathan v Secretary of State for the Home Department* [2020] UKSC 41, [2020] 1 WLR 4506.

[86] *New Zealand Association for Migration and Investments Inc v Attorney-General* [2006] NZAR 45 (HC) at [174].

already lodged applications in reliance on the old policy. In *Association for Migration*, the Immigration Service had done so, but the complaint was that the transitional provisions did not reach far enough. To become eligible to apply for permanent residence in the entrepreneur category, applicants first had to obtain a business investor visa and run a business in New Zealand pursuant to that. When the criteria for permanent residence were tightened, transitional provisions protected those who already had a business investor precursor visa. The unsuccessful applicants for judicial review in this case had applied for that precursor visa, spending significant time and money, but had not yet received it. The case illustrates the difficulty of drawing the line. It might have been considered arguable that an application for the business investor visa amounted to sufficient detrimental reliance on the more favourable criteria for permanent residence in the old policy, but this would certainly have represented a rather lengthy transition to the new criteria.

(4) The Nature and Extent of the Substantive Effect

Once a legitimate expectation of a substantive benefit has been established, the question arises whether a court will give some form of substantive effect to such expectations. If so, the nature and extent of any substantive effect can take a range of forms. In this regard, the English cases have gone further than most New Zealand cases.

(a) The English Position

The new ground was established in the United Kingdom by the Court of Appeal in *Coughlan*.[87] The Supreme Court has confirmed it at least in obiter in *Re Finucane*.[88]

In *Coughlan*, substantive effect was applied to the maximum extent.[89] The Court held that it was unlawful to disappoint the legitimate expectation in that case unless that was justified by an overriding public interest. Whether such justification was made out was a question for the court, rather than merely being tested for reasonableness. This amounts to applying a substitutionary standard of review. As the Court was not satisfied with the justification, the decision was quashed.[90]

Miss Coughlan was severely disabled and dependent on full-time nursing care following an accident in 1971. In 1993 she had been persuaded to move from the hospital that then cared for her to Mardon House, a new purpose-built facility for long-term care, under a promise that this would be her home for life. However, the new facility did not work out as planned and, in 1998, the respondent health authority decided to close it and transfer all residents elsewhere. Miss Coughlan successfully challenged this decision on the grounds that it unjustifiably disappointed her legitimate expectation based on the promise that Mardon House would be her home for life. The authority's

[87] *R v North and East Devon Health Authority ex p Coughlan* [2001] QB 213 (CA).

[88] *Re Finucane* (n 76). See also *Paponette v Attorney General of Trinidad and Tobago* [2010] UKPC 32, [2012] 1 AC 1.

[89] *Coughlan* (n 87) at [52]–[60].

[90] ibid at [4], final Conclusions section.

justification was that Mardon House was excessively expensive for the limited services provided there, but the Court did not consider this sufficient to outweigh the promise made to Miss Coughlan.[91]

The Court also outlined the effect of substantive legitimate expectations more generally. The maximum effect seen in this case was not always appropriate: in some cases with different circumstances, the effect of a substantive legitimate expectation would take a somewhat more limited form. While the Court listed 'three possible outcomes' that may apply once a legitimate expectation has been established,[92] the second is not relevant to the present topic, as it involved an expectation that a particular procedure would be followed.[93] Only the first and third involved expectations of substantive benefits. One of these was the maximum effect given to the promise in *Coughlan* itself.

The other possible outcome involved a more limited form of effect: 'the authority is only required to bear in mind its previous policy or other representation, giving it the weight it thinks right, …, before deciding whether to change course. Here the court is confined to reviewing the decision on *Wednesbury* grounds'.[94] This amounted to saying two things: (1) the expectation is a mandatory relevant consideration; and (2) the justification for disappointing the expectation will be reviewed only on the very deferential *Wednesbury* unreasonableness standard.

The Court did not fully explain how to choose between these two possible forms of effect. However, it relied on the following factors to support the choice of maximum effect in this case: the expectation arose from an actual promise (rather than a policy or practice) made in precise and unqualified terms; this promise was made directly to one person or a few people, 'giving it the character of a contract'; it was relied on, and was of great importance to, that individual; and finally, the consequences for the authority were likely to be financial only.[95] In the absence of some of these factors, presumably, the more limited form of effect will be appropriate.

Subsequent cases have affirmed that the nature and extent of substantive effect can take these two different forms, and that it depends on factors such as these. *Bibi* confirmed that a substantive legitimate expectation is a mandatory relevant consideration.[96] *Begbie* clarified that the two types of outcomes identified in *Coughlan* are two ends of a spectrum rather than two 'hermetically sealed' categories.[97] In other words, the intensity with which the justification is reviewed can fall somewhere in between the substitutionary standard adopted in *Coughlan* and a mere *Wednesbury* unreasonableness standard. The Court also further articulated the relevant factors; in particular, decisions lying in the 'macro-political field' are likely to fall at the least intrusive review end of the spectrum.[98]

[91] ibid at [83]–[89].

[92] ibid at [57].

[93] Query the claim in this respect that the 'difficulty of segregating the procedural from the substantive' can make it preferable not to attempt the distinction (ibid at [59]).

[94] ibid at [57].

[95] ibid at [59]–[60], [86].

[96] *R (Bibi) v Newham London Borough Council* [2001] EWCA Civ 607, [2002] 1 WLR 237 at [39]–[59]; adopted and confirmed by the Privy Council in *Paponette* (n 88) at [45]–[47].

[97] *R v Secretary of State for Education and Employment, Ex p Begbie* [2000] 1 WLR 1115 (CA) at 1130.

[98] ibid at 1131.

The Supreme Court in *Finucane* affirmed and applied both of these points from *Begbie*, and confirmed *Coughlan* as the leading case.[99] The Court found that Mrs Finucane did have a legitimate expectation, based on an unambiguous and unqualified undertaking made to her, that a public inquiry would be held into alleged state involvement in her husband's assassination by loyalist militants in Northern Ireland. The challenged decision was not to hold the inquiry in the promised public form, because the promise had been overtaken by political developments. The Court went on to hold that this decision fell into the 'macro-political' area. As a result, the government's justification was readily upheld, with minimal scrutiny.[100]

Finally on the English position, obiter comments in *Nadarajah* proposed testing the justification for disappointing substantive legitimate expectations by means of the proportionality test developed in the context of the Human Rights Act.[101] This has been mentioned with apparent approval by the Supreme Court – most recently in *Finucane*.[102]

(b) The Position in Aotearoa New Zealand

In Aotearoa New Zealand, the position as to the effect of a substantive legitimate expectation remains uncertain and unsettled. An intermediate position has the greatest support. This involves two elements: treating the legitimate expectation as a mandatory relevant consideration and scrutinising the justification for disappointing it on a variable standard of review depending on the context.

However, this is largely based on High Court authority, and authority at that level is very mixed. The Supreme Court has not considered the ground at all, and the main Court of Appeal authority in *Terminals (NZ)* is of limited assistance.[103]

As we saw earlier, the first two stages of the much-cited three-stage test in *Terminals (NZ)* concern the basis for establishing a legitimate expectation (whether of a substantive benefit or a procedure to be followed). Only the third stage concerns the effect to be given to the expectation. The question at this stage is put as 'what remedy, if any, should be provided'.[104] The Court addresses this question only in brief obiter comments, given that the claim in the case failed at the second stage. The Court states that 'relief … of a substantive nature … is rarely, if ever, granted', as this would usurp the public authority's function.[105] What a court may do, short of this, is set out very briefly. Aside from enforcing procedural expectations, which is uncontroversial, '[i]n other cases, the court may direct the decision maker to reconsider the decision in light of the expectation'.[106]

Where does this leave the matter? The final sentence amounts to recognising that legitimate expectations may be mandatory relevant considerations: the *Coughlan* approach is approved at least to that extent. As to scrutiny of the justification for

[99] *Re Finucane* (n 75) at [56].
[100] ibid at [74]–[76].
[101] *R (Nadarajah) v Secretary of State for the Home Department* [2005] EWCA Civ 1363 at [68].
[102] *Re Finucane* (n 88) at [59]; also *Paponette* (n 88) at [38].
[103] *Terminals (NZ)* (n 77).
[104] ibid at [127].
[105] ibid at [154]–[155].
[106] ibid at [155].

disappointing the expectation, however, the discussion is unclear and inconclusive: Will courts do so at least on the highly deferential *Wednesbury* unreasonableness standard? The only possibly relevant passage on this is the statement quoted above about 'relief' of a substantive nature, but that is a very ambiguous statement.

Relief, strictly speaking, is a separate question that arises only after the substantive effect of the representation has been determined. Relief of a substantive nature would mean an order to grant the benefit sought (in this case, the expected lower rate of excise duty). That is indeed exceptional in judicial review.[107] Such exceptional relief was not granted even in *Coughlan*,[108] where the Court gave the substantive legitimate expectation the strongest form of substantive effect. The decision to disappoint the expectation was found unlawful, but the relief granted was only an order to quash the decision, not an order to grant the substantive benefit.

In light of this, it seems likely that the statement about 'relief' was instead intended to address the question of substantive effect. On this reading, the Court of Appeal was casting doubt on whether New Zealand courts would go as far as *Coughlan* in giving substantive effect to an expectation. That still leaves open, however, whether a court might scrutinise the justification for disappointing the expectation at least on a deferential reasonableness standard. *Terminals (NZ)* has nothing to say on that point.

One perhaps related point is established by the Court of Appeal in *Goulding*: a decision about a person cannot be revoked or varied once it has been communicated to that person in final terms.[109]

The remainder of the case law is at the High Court level. Among the very few cases where a sufficient basis was found for a legitimate expectation, some denied any substantive effect at all[110] while others adopted the strongest version of substantive effect,[111] but in both cases with very limited discussion. The early case of *Tay* treated a legitimate expectation as a mandatory relevant consideration.[112] In the vast majority of cases where the ground has been considered, a legitimate expectation of a substantive benefit was not established on the facts, so that the question whether the new ground should be adopted did not strictly arise for decision. Some of these cases have, however, considered in some detail what the outcome would have been if the claimed legitimate expectation had been established.

These detailed obiter discussions represent the most helpful authority. They are found in particular in *New Zealand Association for Migration*[113] and *Hugh Green*.[114] Both decisions accept (1) that a legitimate expectation of a substantive benefit may be a mandatory relevant consideration, and (2) that the justification for disappointing the expectation will be scrutinised on a reasonableness standard, varying in intensity according to the context. While, as noted, authority at High Court level is mixed and

[107] See Ch 10.
[108] *Coughlan* (n 87).
[109] *Goulding v Chief Executive, Ministry of Fisheries* [2004] 3 NZLR 173 (CA).
[110] Eg *GXL Royalties v Minister of Energy* [2009] NZAR 478 (HC) at [50]–[51].
[111] Eg *Aoraki Water Trust v Meridian Energy Ltd* [2005] 2 NZLR 268 (HC).
[112] *Tay v Attorney-General* [1992] 2 NZLR 693 (HC) at 700–05.
[113] *Association for Migration* (n 86).
[114] *Hugh Green* (n 80).

unsettled, *Association for Migration* is one of the cases most often cited with approval at both High Court and Court of Appeal level.

In *Association for Migration*, the challenge was to the application of a changed policy for permanent residence applications that imposed a more stringent language competence requirement.[115] As we saw, the challenge failed at the first hurdle, for lack of a sufficient basis for a legitimate expectation that the old policy would apply. In the alternative, however, even if the expectation was legitimate, the decision to disappoint it was not unlawful on the approach favoured by Randerson J after surveying the English cases.

The New Zealand courts' response to a legitimate expectation of a substantive benefit, his Honour held, would depend on a range of factors, and the intensity of scrutiny of the decision to disappoint the expectation may vary. The range of factors was similar to that identified in *Coughlan*.[116] It included:[117]

> the degree of specificity of the promise; the significance of the consequences to the individual or class concerned …; whether the decision maker has given proper consideration to the position of the affected parties; what provision … has been made to accommodate those affected …; and the nature and strength of any countervailing public interest factors …

As for the intensity of scrutiny, Randerson J outlined two different approaches.[118] One approach was appropriate in cases where 'specific promises are made to an individual or a small class with serious consequences for them'. In such cases, 'particularly close examination' would be called for, with the court being 'astute to ensure the decision maker has conscientiously considered the position of those affected' and 'has sound and logical reasons for reneging on the promises made'. This amounts to saying that the expectation in such cases is a mandatory relevant consideration, and that the justification for disappointing it will be subjected to heightened scrutiny reasonableness review. The other approach was appropriate in cases 'where the policy choices are very much in the macro-political field and there are strong countervailing grounds to support the course adopted'. In such cases, greater latitude was due to the decision-maker, although the lawfulness, fairness and reasonableness of the decision were still for the court to assess.

The facts in this case all fell very much within the second type of case.[119] The Court's application of the second type of approach suggests that even in this type of case, the expectation still is a mandatory relevant consideration: the Court emphasised in dismissing the challenge that the minister had clearly turned her mind to the consequences of the change for those who had commenced the process of applying for the required precursor visa in reliance on the old policy.[120]

In summary, according to *Association for Migration*, a legitimate expectation is always a mandatory relevant consideration. Even if it has been taken into account, a decision to disappoint it may still be struck down as unreasonable. That amounts

[115] *Association for Migration* (n 86).
[116] *Coughlan* (n 87).
[117] *Association for Migration* (n 86) at [157].
[118] ibid at [158].
[119] ibid at [177].
[120] ibid at [176].

to adopting the weaker type of outcome set out in *Coughlan*.[121] Furthermore, the choice of approaches set out here amounts to variable intensity reasonableness review. While the point is not quite spelt out, it seems clear that the choice between these two approaches turns on an assessment of the range of factors set out earlier, and that the two approaches represent two ends of a spectrum.

Randerson J's final comment on the question of approach was that he could never 'envisage a Court directing that a substantive benefit … be granted'.[122] This is an ambiguous and arguably misleading comment, but it has been affirmed in several cases since, including by the Court of Appeal in *Terminals (NZ)*.[123] As explained above in discussing that case, an order to grant a substantive benefit would indeed be highly exceptional, and is not part of the English approach following *Coughlan*. What Randerson J probably meant to say is that New Zealand courts will not go as far as the English courts did in *Coughlan*: they will not substitute their view for that of the decision-maker on the question of justification for disappointing the expectation.

Hugh Green is one of a number of other High Court decisions expressing support in principle for giving some substantive effect to legitimate expectations of a substantive benefit.[124] Unlike most, this case contains both an extended survey of the English and New Zealand case law[125] and discussion of how the principles would have applied in this case if a legitimate expectation had been made out. That discussion affirms both of the points from *Association for Migration*. First, once a legitimate expectation is made out, the question becomes whether there is a satisfactory justification for frustrating it. The intensity of review on that question varies, depending on factors such as how many people are affected by the decision, whether the decision was in the 'macro-political field', and the nature of the public interest at stake.[126] Going beyond *Association for Migration*, the Court also put this question in terms of proportionality.[127] Secondly, if a legitimate expectation had been made out, it would have been a mandatory relevant consideration. A challenge would have succeeded, given that far too limited information on that point was put before the decision-making body.[128]

A rare instance of the High Court giving substantive effect to a legitimate expectation is found in *Hart*, but it is debatable to what extent the content of the expectation was substantive. The Department of Conservation had taken custody of whale bones that had washed up on the beach and were claimed as taonga[129] by two different iwi.[130] It had undertaken to release them only once the two iwi had resolve their dispute about them. It then delivered the taonga to one of the iwi in breach of that undertaking. This

[121] *Coughlan* (n 87) at [57]. See also *Air New Zealand Ltd v Wellington International Airport Ltd* [2009] NZAR 138 (HC) at [61]–[62] (there was an appeal, but not on this point).

[122] *Association for Migration* (n 86) at [159].

[123] *Terminals (NZ)* (n 77); see discussion above at nn 104–108.

[124] *Hugh Green* (n 80). See also, eg, *Oosterveen v Ministry of Business, Innovation and Employment* [2014] NZHC 1709, [2014] NZAR 1091 at [50].

[125] *Hugh Green* (n 80) at [63]–[80].

[126] ibid at [173]–[180].

[127] ibid at [173]. See also *Oosterveen* (n 124).

[128] ibid at [240]–[243].

[129] Treasures.

[130] Tribes.

was unlawful on a number of grounds, including breach of the other iwi's legitimate expectations.[131]

In summary, then, the position that has the greatest support in New Zealand is an intermediate position that combines treating the expectation as a mandatory consideration with variable intensity reasonableness review of the justification for disappointing the expectation. There is much authority for doubting that New Zealand would accept the stronger substantive effect that is available in appropriate contexts in England, in which the court substitutes its view on the justification for disappointing the expectation.

D. A Duty of Consistency?

A further question is whether there is a duty of consistency. This is related to substantive legitimate expectations, but might be recognised as a distinct and separate ground. It might take one or both of two forms: first, a duty to apply a current and relevant policy unless there is good justification for departing from it in the individual case; and secondly, a duty to decide individual cases consistently unless there is good reason for treating them differently. In either case, the potential effect of such a duty would include treating the policy or the previous similar case as a mandatory consideration that must be understood correctly; and scrutinising the justification for departing from the policy or from the treatment in the earlier case on a more or less intensive standard of review. Let us consider each of these two versions of the duty in turn.

(1) Duty to Apply Policy

We noted earlier that the strongest case for a substantive legitimate expectation based on a policy is where published policy has not changed, and where according to its terms it should apply to the applicant. In many cases, the legitimate expectation ground will be all that is needed to compel application of a policy in the absence of good justification for departing from it. What, however, is the position where the policy was not known to the applicant? While the legitimate expectation ground has, on occasion, been stretched to encompass such cases,[132] this requires resort to fiction and artificiality. Obviously, applicants could not actually expect compliance with a policy of which they are unaware.

This highlights that there is an alternative foundation for the duty to apply policy: a duty of consistency. The rationale for this applies regardless of the applicant's awareness of the policy: it is more simply the value of consistency[133] or the principle of

[131] *Hart v Director-General of Conservation* [2023] NZHC 1011, [2023] 3 NZLR 42 at [121]–[124].
[132] *R (Rashid) v Home Secretary* [2005] EWCA Civ 744.
[133] *Mandalia v Secretary of State for the Home Department* [2015] UKSC 59, [2015] 1 WLR 4546 at [29].

equality before the law, which is an aspect of the rule of law.[134] More specifically, we might also say that there is a non-reneging principle: courts should expect public authorities to do as they said they would, unless there is good reason not to do so.[135]

There are some concerns about the legitimacy of informal rule-making in the form of policies.[136] However, policies also have benefits.[137] Where an authority has adopted a policy, the law can enforce some of those benefits. Policies are adopted for the very purpose of promoting consistent decision-making.[138] Due to their generality and impersonal nature they may also counteract possible bias or other irrelevant and arbitrary reasons.[139] Having adopted policies for those purposes, it is a departure from good administration to simply ignore or disregard such policies.

In the United Kingdom, a duty to apply policy unless there is good reason not to do so is well established. It was adopted in a line of appellate level authorities culminating in *Mandalia*.[140] Some commentators have read the Supreme Court's decision in *Gallaher*[141] as casting doubt on this duty,[142] but that is an unlikely reading.[143] *Gallaher* concerned the different version of the duty of consistency discussed in the next section, and did not mention the authorities that establish the duty to apply policy. The Supreme Court has subsequently continued to accept the duty to apply policy, with no mention of this case.[144]

In the special case where a published policy conflicts with an unpublished policy, *Lumba* confirmed that the decision-maker is bound by the published policy (again subject to good reason for departing from it).[145] We might say that the legitimate expectation generated by publication takes priority in this situation.

There is less authority on this point in Aotearoa New Zealand. A duty to apply policy unless there is good reason not to do so has been recognised in a number of cases, but it has not been recognised as providing a distinct ground of review. In *Chiu* the Court of Appeal held that misinterpretation of an applicable policy would usually vitiate a decision on one of a range of grounds, including error of law or frustrating legitimate expectations. It considered unreasonableness to be an appropriate ground in that case.[146]

[134] Tom Bingham, *The Rule of Law* (London, Penguin Books, 2010), Ch 5.

[135] Shona Wilson Stark, 'Non-fettering, Legitimate Expectations and Consistency of Policy: Separate Compartments or Single Principle?' in Jason NE Varuhas and Shona Wilson Stark (eds), *The Frontiers of Public Law* (Oxford, Hart Publishing, 2020) 443 at 450, 452.

[136] See Michael Taggart, 'From 'Parliamentary Powers' to Privatization: The Chequered History of Delegated Legislation in the Twentieth Century' (2005) 55 *University of Toronto Law Journal* 575 at 605.

[137] See also Ch 5.A.

[138] *Pora v Attorney-General* [2017] NZHC 2081, [2017] 3 NZLR 683 at [115], [121], [133(b)].

[139] See also Yoav Dotan, 'Why Administrators should be Bound by their Policies' [1997] 17 *Oxford Journal of Legal Studies* 23 at 28–30.

[140] *Mandalia* (n 133) at [29]–[31].

[141] *R (Gallaher Group Ltd) v Competition and Markets Authority* [2018] UKSC 25, [2019] AC 96.

[142] See, eg, Wilson Stark (n 135) at 453–54.

[143] Hanna Wilberg, 'A Duty of Consistency? The Missing Distinction Between Its Two Forms' (*UK Constitutional Law Blog*, 27 February 2020). Available at: www.ukconstitutionallaw.org.

[144] See, eg, *R (Begum) v Special Immigration Appeals Commission* [2021] UKSC 7, [2021] AC 765 at [124].

[145] *R (Lumba) v Secretary of State for the Home Department* [2011] UKSC 12, [2012] 1 AC 245 at [20], [26].

[146] *Chiu v Minister of Immigration* [1994] 2 NZLR 541 (CA) at 550.

The High Court in three further decisions relied on legitimate expectations as the basis for this duty. In *Smith* and *Taylor*, the Court held that Department of Corrections officials are obliged to apply the Department's internal policies when reviewing a prisoner's security classification.[147] In the *Pora* case on the quantum of ex gratia compensation for miscarriage of justice, the Court held that the interpretation of the guidelines on this was a question of law for the court, and that the guidelines had been misunderstood and misapplied.[148] The basis for relying on the guidelines in this way was that guidelines must be followed and applied unless there is good reason to depart from them.[149]

These cases did not consider the intensity of review that applies to the justification for departing from policy. The complaint was more basic: either that the decision-maker was entirely unaware of the relevant policy, or that it was misinterpreted.

(2) Duty to Decide Individual Cases Consistently?

A duty of consistency might also take the different form of a duty to reach consistent decisions in two or more individual cases. However, this further type of duty is much more controversial, unless it is confined to review on a reasonableness standard.[150] That is because it requires the reviewing court to decide which differences between individual cases should be considered significant and which should be immaterial. Arguably this goes to the heart of the merits of a decision. It is quite different from merely interpreting and applying the rules adopted by the authority for itself, which is the courts' task in the context of the duty to apply policy – that does not require courts to identify their own criteria for comparing the individual cases in question.

In the United Kingdom, the Supreme Court in *Gallaher* unequivocally rejected a standalone duty of consistent treatment of individual cases. Arguments of consistency may be entertained, but only in the context of the ground of unreasonableness.[151]

The position in Aotearoa New Zealand appears to be the same, but we do not yet have the same unequivocal authority. The Supreme Court and, prior to that, the Privy Council have repeatedly treated consistency as going to unreasonableness. That approach can be seen in *Pharmac*[152] and again in *Ririnui* and *CP Group*. In *Ririnui*, the Court upheld a challenge on the ground that inconsistent treatment of two parties was due to a mistake of fact.[153] Inconsistency was treated as an aspect of unreasonableness, and formed at most only part of the reason for upholding the challenge.[154] In

[147] *Smith v Attorney-General* [2017] NZHC 136 at [22]; *Taylor v Chief Executive of the Department of Corrections* (n 45) at [79].

[148] *Pora* (n 138) at [105]–[106].

[149] ibid at [135(a)(ii)], [136].

[150] For the debate, see, eg, Michael Foran, 'The Cornerstone of Our Law: Equality, Consistency and Judicial Review' [2022] 81 *Cambridge Law Journal* 249; Mark Elliott, 'A 'Principle' of Consistency? The Doctrinal Configuration of the Law of Judicial Review' [2018] *Cambridge Law Journal* 444.

[151] *Gallaher* (n 141) at [24]–[26], [50].

[152] *Pharmaceutical Management Agency Ltd v Roussel Uclaf Australia Pty Ltd* [1998] NZAR 58 (CA); *Roussel UCLAF Australia Pty Ltd v Pharmaceutical Management Agency Ltd* [2001] NZAR 476 (PC).

[153] See further Part E.

[154] *Ririnui v Landcorp Farming Ltd* [2016] NZSC 62, [2016] 1 NZLR 1056 at [92]–[97], [98(e)], [143(a)].

CP Group, inconsistency was one of a number of arguments for claiming unreasonableness in a challenge to a targeted rate, and the Court held that the high *Wednesbury* threshold applied in this context. For a successful challenge, the Court held, more than 'simply apparent unfairness' in the treatment of different ratepayers had to be shown.[155] In neither case did the Court mention the possibility that inconsistency might be a separate and distinct ground of review.

Court of Appeal authority is generally to the similar effect.[156] However, in *Financial Services Complaints (No 2)*, the Court of Appeal went further. The grounds for overturning the Ombudsman's decision to deny permission to use the Ombudsman name included failure to identify a valid reason for treating the applicants differently from other parties.[157] Even here, the argument was also put in terms that the decision was unreasonable for this reason.[158] The Court relied on a dictum concerning the principle of equality in *Matadeen v Pointu* that has also been cited by the Supreme Court.[159] But unlike the Supreme Court, it omitted mention of the qualification that followed the dictum. This decision is doubtful as authority for recognising a new free-standing ground.

(3) Summary

In summary, both authority and principle support the first version of a duty of consistency: a duty to apply policy unless there is good reason to depart from it. The second version, however – a duty to treat like cases alike – is best understood as no more than an argument that may establish unreasonableness.

E. Mistake of Fact

What happens if a decision is affected by an incontrovertible mistake of fact: will a court on judicial review intervene to correct this? Traditionally, facts were considered part of the substantive merits and as such were the domain of the decision-maker. Courts would usually intervene only where factual errors reached the level of the findings being perverse,[160] or where findings were not supported by any probative evidence.[161]

One of the emerging extensions of substantive review, however, is a new ground of mistake of fact. Unlike the other two modern extensions, the availability of this ground in New Zealand is now supported by Supreme Court authority: it was

[155] *Auckland Council v CP Group Ltd* [2023] NZSC 53, [2023] 1 NZLR 35 at [116].
[156] See, eg, *Wellington City Council v Minotaur Custodians Ltd* [2017] NZCA 302, [2017] 3 NZLR 464 at [49]–[68].
[157] *Financial Services Complaints Ltd v Chief Ombudsman (No 2)* [2022] NZCA 248, [2022] 2 NZLR 740 at [75], [82].
[158] ibid at [78].
[159] *Matadeen v Pointu* [1999] 1 AC 98 (PC), cited in *Ririnui* (n 154) at [94] and in *Financial Services Complaints* (n 157) at [75].
[160] *Edwards (Inspector of Taxes) v Bairstow* [1956] AC 14 (HL).
[161] *Re Erebus Royal Commission; Air New Zealand Ltd v Mahon* [1983] NZLR 662 (PC).

accepted in *Ririnui*,[162] albeit that decision is unfortunately brief and ambivalent on the point. The ground adopted there is the English ground of review established in the *E* case.[163] The precise parameters of that ground remain uncertain, but the essence is that there has to be a material mistake as to an uncontentious and objectively verifiable fact.

This Part is divided as follows. Section (1) outlines arguments for and against review of factual determinations, section (2) examines the state of authority on mistake of fact as a ground of review, section (3) outlines the test in *E* and how it is best understood so as to meet the objections to this ground, (4) clarifies how a mistake of fact can be an error of law, and section (5) considers the role of the new ground in the context of the broader expansion of substantive review.

(1) Arguments For and Against Mistake of Fact as a Ground of Review

There are strong arguments for judicial intervention to correct incontrovertible mistakes of fact that are material to the decision.[164] A decision-maker who laboured under such a mistake was never in a position to consider the true merits of the case. Justice and fairness for the party subject to the decision therefore require a remedy. An aspect of the public interest is also at stake: the statutory regime will not operate as intended in such a case.

However, the traditional rejection of the ground reflects at least three objections. We will see that these can be avoided by appropriate limits to the new ground. First, there are the constitutional objections to merits review that are relevant to all of the expansions of substantive review and are set out in the introduction to this chapter. Courts must respect Parliament's allocation of authority to the decision-maker, and they lack the appropriate democratic legitimacy and institutional capacity. Secondly, judicial review is not an appropriate procedure for fact-finding.[165] In particular, evidence is usually by affidavit, and cross-examination – a key procedure for helping resolve factual disputes – requires special leave.[166] Third and finally, review of factual determinations may unduly compromise finality in dispute-resolution.[167] A helpful way of understanding the limits of the new ground as established in the English *E* case is as avoiding these objections, as we will see in section (3).

[162] *Ririnui v Landcorp Farming Ltd* [2016] NZSC 62, [2016] 1 NZLR 1056.

[163] *E v Secretary of State for the Home Department* [2004] EWCA Civ 49, [2004] QB 1044.

[164] See, eg, Christopher Forsyth and Emma Dring, 'The Final Frontier: The Emergence of Material Error of Fact as a Ground for Judicial Review' in Christopher Forsyth, Mark Elliott, Swati Jhaveri and others (eds), *Effective Judicial Review: A Cornerstone of Good Governance* (Oxford, Oxford University Press, 2010) 245 at 245–46, 259–60.

[165] See *R v Derbyshire County Council ex parte Noble* [1990] Industrial Case Reports 808 (CA) at 813.

[166] Graham Taylor, *Judicial Review: A New Zealand Perspective*, 4th edn (Wellington, LexisNexis NZ, 2018) at [10.19], [10.26]–[10.29].

[167] See *Shaheen v Secretary of State for the Home Department* [2005] EWCA Civ 1294, [2006] Imm AR 57.

(2) The State of Authority on Mistake of Fact as a Ground of Review

The ground of mistake of fact has been adopted in England and Wales by the Court of Appeal in *E*.[168] In Aotearoa New Zealand, the new ground can be considered to be established by the Supreme Court's decision in *Ririnui v Landcorp*[169] and three Court of Appeal decisions. However, these New Zealand cases all have limited reasoning and provide limited guidance on the scope and limits of the ground. The Supreme Court's decision in *Bryson* is also often cited in this context but is less relevant than is often suggested.[170]

Ririnui adopted and applied the new ground, citing the *E* case.[171] However, the decision is brief and somewhat ambivalent on the point. It concerned the sale by Landcorp Farming Ltd (a state-owned enterprise) of a block of land. The land was subject to a Treaty of Waitangi claim by the applicant's iwi[172] and might therefore have been offered to the iwi on a preferential basis. However, the Office of Treaty Settlements mistakenly advised that the iwi's Treaty claims had all been finally settled. As a result, neither Landcorp nor the relevant Ministers contacted the iwi.

By majority, the Court declared that the mistake rendered these decisions unlawful.[173] But the Court left open the nature of the mistake: was it one of fact or law? While the distinction may in some circumstances be significant for judicial review, it did not matter here: 'Even if it is regarded as a mistake of fact', in the circumstances of this case that would render the decision susceptible to review.[174]

The decision has two limits as authority for mistake of fact as a ground of review.[175] First, the Court's statement on this topic is most likely obiter: the mistake was most likely a mistake of law (overlooking express limits in the coverage of the iwi's existing settlement agreement), in which case the issue did not arise. Secondly and more importantly, the Court heard no argument on the availability of the ground, and its reasoning on this point is exceedingly brief.[176] It alluded to the unsettled legal position and cited the English *E* case in support of the ground, but it gave no reasons at all for adopting the ground. It also did not set out a test for this ground, and its discussion touched on only two of the four parts of the test in *E*.[177]

Three Court of Appeal decisions have also recognised the new ground. The most helpful is *Winton Properties*, although the discussion was again brief.[178] The Court confirmed the existence of the ground, citing *Ririnui*, but again gave no reasons. It noted that the scope of the ground remains unsettled, but set out two sets of limits drawn from the decisions in *Bryson* and *E*. It went on to apply the main requirement

[168] *E* (n 163).
[169] *Ririnui* (n 162).
[170] *Bryson v Three Foot Six Ltd* [2005] NZSC 34, [2005] 3 NZLR 721.
[171] *E* (n 163).
[172] Tribe.
[173] *Ririnui* (n 162) at [74], [76], [97], [98](c) and (e), [110], [138], [143], [147], [152], [194] esp fn 166.
[174] ibid at [54]; William Young J dissented on this point, at fn 166.
[175] Further on both points, see H Wilberg, 'Mistakes about Mistake of Fact: The New Zealand Story' (2017) 28 *Public Law Review* 248, Part IV.
[176] *Ririnui* (n 162) at [53]–[55]; see also at [98](c) and (e), [110], [138], [143], fn 166.
[177] See further section (3).
[178] *Winton Property Investments Ltd v Minister of Finance* [2023] NZCA 368 at [101]–[103].

set out in *E* to find that the complaint in this case did not meet that requirement. We will return to this.

Two earlier Court of Appeal decisions are less helpful. *Taylor v The Chief Executive of the Department of Corrections*[179] was a successful challenge to a refusal of permission for a television interview with prison inmate and serial litigant Arthur Taylor. Among the grounds for setting aside the decision were two factual errors concerning the risk posed by Mr Taylor. However, it is far from clear whether the Court was adopting mistake of fact as an independent ground of review. The Court touched on the unsettled state of the law on this point and on alternative grounds available to deal with complaints about erroneous findings of fact.[180] The mistake of fact complaint was initially treated as an instance of the ground of unreasonableness, and the main ground of challenge was a Bill of Rights Act breach.[181] One likely reading of the decision is that the factual errors were seen as defeating the s 5 justification for the limit on the Bill of Rights Act right, rather giving rise to a separate ground of review.

Finally, mistake of fact was clearly adopted and applied as a ground in *Charter Holdings*. However, the Court gave no reasons for finding the ground available, instead relying on the *Taylor* case as 'clear authority' that the ground is available.[182] As we have just seen, *Taylor* is not very clear authority on the point.

These four decisions are the main New Zealand authorities on the new ground. There has long been a recurring claim that the ground was well established in New Zealand[183] but, prior to *Ririnui*, this claim misrepresented the case law. Two groups of appellate decisions were commonly cited as having established mistake of fact as a ground, but none of these cases supported that claim. In *Daganayasi*[184] and *New Zealand Fishing Industry Association*,[185] Cooke J championed the ground, but this position failed to gain a majority. In *Lewis v Wilson & Horton*,[186] *Squid Fisheries*,[187] and *Air Nelson*,[188] the Court commented on mistake of fact as a ground, but those comments range from non-committal in the second and third, to rejecting the ground in the first of these cases. At High Court level, there was a significant level of support, but authority at that level was uncertain and very much divided. The strongest authority pre-*Ririnui* was found in the Court of Appeal's decision in *Glaxo Group*.[189]

Finally, we need to deal with the Supreme Court's decision in *Bryson* that is often cited in this context.[190] The Court applied the old test in *Edwards v Bairstow*: the

179 *Taylor v Chief Executive of Department of Corrections* [2015] NZCA 477, [2015] NZAR 1648.
180 ibid at [94].
181 ibid at [2], [60]–[91].
182 *Charter Holdings Ltd v Commissioner of Inland Revenue* [2016] NZCA 499, (2016) 27 NZTC 22 at [76]; the full discussion is at [66]–[76].
183 See, eg, H Wade and C Forsyth *Administrative Law*, 11th edn (Oxford University Press, Oxford, 2014) 231.
184 *Daganayasi v Minster of Immigration* [1980] 2 NZLR 130 (CA).
185 *New Zealand Fishing Industry Association Inc v Minister of Agriculture and Fisheries* [1988] 1 NZLR 544 (CA).
186 *Lewis v Wilson & Horton Ltd* [2000] 3 NZLR 546 (CA) at [92]. The decision elsewhere applies the old *Edward v Bairstow* ground (n 160), which is much more limited: at [63]–[73].
187 *Squid Fishery Management Company Ltd v Minister of Fisheries* CA39/04, 13 July 2004 at [104].
188 *Air Nelson Ltd v Minister of Transport* [2008] NZAR 139 (CA) at [52].
189 *Glaxo Group Ltd v Commissioner of Patents* [1991] 3 NZLR 179 (CA) at 181, 164.
190 *Bryson* (n 170).

factual determination in that case could be disturbed only if it was clearly untenable and insupportable.[191] This case has been used as authority for two points. First, some have claimed that it rejected the mistake of fact ground established in *E*.[192] That is incorrect. We will see in the next section that *Bryson* did not concern the type of factual mistake that is recognised as giving rise to review in *E*, and the Court therefore did not mention *E*. It is also worth noting that the Supreme Court in its later decision in *Ririnui* relied on *E*, without mentioning *Bryson*. Secondly, however, *Winton Property* correctly considered *Bryson* to be relevant to the limits of judicial review on grounds of factual error. We will return to this.

(3) Understanding the Test in *E*: When is Mistake of Fact a Ground of Review?

The scope of the new ground is not yet well settled. There is no clear New Zealand statement of a test. However, the English decision in *E* sets out an appropriate test for mistake of fact as a ground of review. It seems likely that this will be followed in New Zealand: *E* was cited in *Ririnui*,[193] and *Winton Property* adopted at least part of its test.[194] According to *E*, the following four criteria must be met:[195]

(1) the decision-maker made a mistake as to an existing fact, including the availability of evidence;
(2) that fact was 'established', that is, 'uncontentious and objectively verifiable';
(3) the claimant could not fairly be held responsible for the error; and
(4) the mistake played a 'material' part in the reasoning, though it need not be decisive.

These criteria represent significant limits on the new ground: the ground does not by any means encompass every challenge to determinations involving facts. In particular, the second requirement means that there must be an incontrovertible mistake. The other side of the coin is that there is no deference to the decision-maker's assessment once these requirements are made out: it is implicit in the decision that the standard of review is correctness, not rationality.

This section explores how these four requirements may work. New Zealand case law provides some indications, but on most questions we only have *E* itself and other English cases to go on. There too, the meaning of the requirements remains to be clarified fully. The requirements are best understood as being designed to avoid the objections to mistake of fact as a ground of review (outlined earlier in section (2)).[196]

[191] *Edwards v Bairstow* (n 160) at 36.
[192] Philip A Joseph, *Constitutional and Administrative Law in New Zealand*, 5th edn (Wellington, Brookers, 2021) at 1062–1065.
[193] *Ririnui* (n 162).
[194] *Winton Property* (n 177) at [103]–[105].
[195] *E* (n 163) at [63], [66]. The Court's reference to 'unfairness' as the outcome has been held not to add anything to the test: *Chalfont v Chiltern District Council* [2014] EWCA Civ 1393 at [100].
[196] Further on this, see Hanna Wilberg, 'Mistake of Fact as a Ground of Review: Distinct and Defensible' in Joe Tomlinson and Anne Carter (eds), *Facts in Public Law Adjudication* (Oxford, Hart Publishing, 2023) 201 at Parts I–IV.

(a) Existing Fact, Including Availability of Evidence

As can be seen, there are two versions of the first requirement. The main version – that the mistake is about an existing fact – is largely self-explanatory: the fact about which the decision-maker was mistaken must have been in existence at the time of the decision. It is not a mistake to be unaware of facts that come into existence only subsequently.[197]

The alternative version calls for some explanation. What is meant by a mistake as to the availability of evidence? Two of the earlier English cases relied on in *E* provide helpful examples. Both could have been decided based on this version of mistake of fact if that ground had existed at the time. In the *Criminal Injury Compensation Board* case, the challenge was to the Board's decision rejecting a compensation claim for an alleged sexual violation.[198] The Board had concluded that there was no evidence to support the claim. Unbeknownst to the Board, however, there was a report by a police doctor who had examined the claimant at the time, which stated that the examination findings were consistent with the alleged violation. The police had omitted to present this evidence. This availability of evidence in support of the claim was a relevant existing fact. The Board was mistaken on this fact.

Similarly, in *Tameside* the challenge was to the Minister's decision that a local council had acted unreasonably in deciding on the timing of a change in the school system.[199] Unreasonable action by a council triggered the Minister's statutory power of intervention. The Minister's conclusion that this requirement was met rested on a belief that there was no professional expert advice which supported the council's decision. In fact, the council did have such supportive expert advice, but the Minister had not been made aware of it. The availability of that advice was an existing fact. The Minister was mistaken on this, and this mistake qualifies under *E*.

(b) Established Fact

The second requirement in *E* is that the fact about which the decision-maker was mistaken must have been 'established', that is, 'uncontentious and objectively verifiable'. This requirement was affirmed and applied by the Court of Appeal in *Winton Properties*.[200] It is closely related to a point found in several earlier New Zealand statements of the ground: it is not a mistake to adopt one of several reasonably open conclusions in relation to the facts.[201] In short, the mistake must be incontrovertible.

[197] The same usually goes for evidence: it must have been available at the time, except in the rare case where new evidence is admissible on appeal, or where a decision-maker has power to reconsider in light of new evidence.

[198] *R v Criminal Injuries Compensation Board ex p A* [1999] 2 AC 330 (HL) (*CICB*) at 342–46, discussed in *E* (n 168) at [45]–[48], [63], [65].

[199] *Secretary of State for Education and Science v Metropolitan Borough Council of Tameside* [1977] AC 1014 (CA and HL) at 1030.

[200] *Winton Properties* (n 177).

[201] See, for example, *New Zealand Fishing Industry Association* (n 185) at 552 (Cooke P).

This requirement, in combination with the first, is best understood as avoiding the objection to merits review. While the facts are traditionally thought to go to the merits, the better view is that only evaluative judgements go to the merits.

In relation to facts, there are two types of evaluative judgements. An alleged mistake meets the second requirement in *E* only if establishing it does not require either type of evaluative judgement. The first type is evaluation of the facts for the purpose of applying an evaluative test. This is excluded by the 'objectively verifiable' requirement.[202] The second type is evaluation of conflicting evidence to make findings of fact. This is excluded by the 'uncontentious' requirement.[203]

The 'uncontentious' part of the requirement also serves to avoid the further objection that judicial review is not a suitable procedure for fact-finding. There is no need for a fact-finding procedure if there is no conflicting evidence.

Some examples will help with understanding these two aspects of the second requirement. Let us take the two aspects in turn.

(i) Not Evaluating the Facts to Apply an Evaluative Legal Test

As just discussed, the 'objectively verifiable' aspect of the second requirement excludes alleged mistakes in evaluating the facts for the purpose of applying an evaluative test. A mistake that meets this aspect of the requirement may involve misunderstanding the evidence, making findings contrary to the evidence, or overlooking or being ignorant of relevant evidence.

An example of a mistake in understanding the evidence – rightly found to qualify as a mistake of fact – is found in the English case of *Haile*.[204] The decision-maker determining an asylum claim confused two different organisations. The claimant in his evidence referred to an organisation called EPRP. The decision-maker mistook this as a reference to a very different organisation called EPRF. On that basis, he considered the evidence not credible. Had he understood that the reference was to the EPRP, then the evidence would have been perfectly credible.

An example of a factual finding overlooking relevant evidence and contrary to that evidence – again rightly held to qualify as a mistake of fact – is found in *Charter Holdings*.[205] This was a successful challenge to Inland Revenue's refusal to amend the plaintiff's tax assessment. A director of the applicant company had failed to claim a tax credit for business losses when filling in the relevant tax return form, and his explanation was that he had misunderstood the form (as opposed to having subsequently invented the losses in question). An Inland Revenue officer disbelieved that explanation because she mistakenly thought that the director had correctly filled in the same form for his personal tax return. In fact, exactly the same incorrect response had been given in that other form.

[202] For a similar interpretation, see Rebecca Williams 'When is an Error not an Error? Reform of Jurisdictional Review of Error of Law and Fact' [2007] PL 793 at 7.

[203] For a similar point, see Michael Kent QC, 'Widening the Scope of Review for Error of Fact' [1999] *Judicial Review* 239.

[204] *R (Haile) v Immigration Appeal Tribunal* [2001] EWCA Civ 663, [2002] INLR 283.

[205] *Charter Holdings* (n 182). See also, eg, *Deliu v Hong* [2012] NZHC 158, [2012] NZAR 209.

A final example is the mistake in *Ririnui*, namely that the iwi had no extant claim to the land at issue.[206] If this was a mistake of fact, then it lay in the decision-makers overlooking the identity of the ancestor from whom the iwi's claim to that land derived. Claims deriving from that ancestor were expressly excluded from the existing settlement of most of the iwi's claims. There was no dispute on who the relevant ancestor was: overlooking this was an incontrovertible mistake.

The type of evaluation that is excluded by this 'objectively verifiable' requirement can be illustrated by the *South Yorkshire Transport* case, albeit no mistake was actually found there.[207] The defendant Commission had exercised its power to intervene in the claimant's merger with another bus company. It had power to do so only on the basis that the services of the merged business covered a 'substantial' part of the United Kingdom, and the challenge was to its conclusion that this test was satisfied.

There was no dispute as to the facts found by the Commission in this regard, such as that the area covered comprised 1.65 per cent of the size of the United Kingdom and contained 3.2 per cent of its population. The challenge was instead to the Commission's conclusion that the facts overall satisfied the 'substantial' test. While that challenge was unsuccessful, the point for our purposes is that the conclusion would not have qualified as a mistake of fact under the test in *E*, even if it had been considered wrong. Instead, any mistake could only have taken one of two forms, as the House of Lords held in that case. One was a legal mistake in interpreting the term 'substantial'. The other was a mistake in evaluating the undisputed facts for the purposes of applying the legal test of 'substantial'. The latter is the type of factual mistake that does not qualify under *E*. Instead, according to this case, courts intervene only if the finding is irrational.

In light of this, we can also see why the New Zealand Supreme Court's decision in *Bryson*[208] cannot be taken as rejecting the ground of mistake of fact as defined in *E*. The issue was of the same kind as the one in *South Yorkshire*: had the Employment Court erred in concluding that Mr Bryson was an 'employee' rather than an independent contractor? This term was defined by a complex evaluative test, requiring a range of criteria to be weighed.[209] There was no dispute about the relevant findings of fact, such as that Mr Bryson had worked full time for a fixed wage for over a year exclusively for this company, that he had received several weeks of training, and that he did not supply his own tools.[210] The claimed error instead concerned the conclusion that these facts satisfied the legal tests defining an 'employee'.

The Supreme Court dismissed that challenge. A challenge could succeed only if the conclusion was entirely untenable and unsupportable, satisfying the *Edwards v Bairstow* test. The question is the significance of this finding. What type of mistake was at issue here? As in *South Yorkshire*, there were only two possible types of error. First, there might have been an error concerning the legal tests. Secondly, if instead there was a mistake concerning facts, it was in evaluating the facts as found, for the purposes of

[206] *Ririnui* (n 162).

[207] *R v Monopolies and Mergers Commission ex p South Yorkshire Transport Ltd* [1993] 1 WLR 23 (HL). See also, eg, *Vodafone New Zealand Ltd v Telecom New Zealand Ltd* [2011] NZSC 138, [2012] 3 NZLR 153.

[208] *Bryson* (n 170).

[209] ibid at [4]–[5].

[210] ibid at [3], [14].

applying the legal test. The alleged factual error here, then, is another example of the type of evaluative judgement that is excluded from the mistake of fact ground by the 'objectively verifiable' part of the test in *E*.

It is therefore unsurprising that the Supreme Court did not contemplate finding a mistake of fact as adopted in *E*. That ground was not available because the second requirement in *E* was not met. That also helps explain why *E* was not cited: if the decision had rejected a leading English decision, one might have expected the Court to say so and to give its reasons for this divergence.

At the same time, *Bryson* indirectly affirms the limits of the mistake of fact ground recognised in *E*. Where the second requirement in *E* is not met because the alleged error concerns evaluation of the facts, then review is available only on the highly deferential rationality standard of review represented by *Bairstow*. That is consistent also with *South Yorkshire*.

Evaluation of the facts is involved in applying the law whenever the law uses broad evaluative terms such as 'substantial', or requires multiple factors to be weighed, as with the test defining 'employee'. However, not all questions of application are evaluative: there are others that are susceptible of simple right and wrong answers. In *Oggi*, for instance, a bylaw imposed different requirements for registration of billboards depending on the date of construction.[211] A mistake in applying that date of construction test would meet the second requirement in *E*.

(ii) Not Evaluating Conflicting Evidence to Find the Facts

We turn next to the other aspect of the second requirement in *E*, requiring the fact to be 'uncontentious'. Recall that this is best understood as excluding evaluation of conflicting evidence. This might involve resolving a conflict between witnesses by assessing their credibility and reliability or resolving a conflict between experts by assessing their expertise.

An example to illustrate this requirement can again be found in *Oggi*, where the mistake concerned the date at which the billboard in question had been constructed.[212] Although this met the one aspect of the 'established fact' requirement (it concerned finding the facts rather than evaluating them), it may not have met the other. The reviewing Court had before it two affidavits that conflicted on the date of construction. It granted leave to permit cross-examination in an attempt to resolve this conflict.[213] However, if the conflict could be resolved only by cross-examination, then the second aspect of the established fact requirement was not met.

A further example of an alleged mistake of fact that had to fail because it did not involve uncontentious facts can be found in the *Climate Science Education Trust* case.[214] The applicant society, devoted to casting doubt on climate change, unsuccessfully

[211] *Oggi Advertising Ltd v Auckland City Council* [2005] NZAR 451 (HC).
[212] ibid.
[213] ibid at [4].
[214] *New Zealand Climate Science Education Trust v National Institute of Water and Atmospheric Research Ltd* [2012] NZHC 2297, [2013] 1 NZLR 75. See also *New Health New Zealand v Minister for COVID-19 Response* [2023] NZHC 2647 at [29]–[36].

challenged a decision to publish reports that showed temperature increases over the past 100 years at several New Zealand weather stations. The mistake of fact complaint alleged errors or flaws in the scientific method. The complaint failed, rightly, because it concerned a matter of scientific debate, and the method adopted by the respondent was tenable and based on credible scientific opinion.

Finally, *Winton Property* also illustrates a version of this aspect. The alleged error there concerned the Overseas Investment Office's assessment of the likely economic benefits of the proposed purchase by an overseas buyer, as compared to a local buyer.[215] Such an assessment of likely future benefits as compared to hypothetical future benefits flowing from an alternative scenario is inherently contentious. It does not concern an established fact.

Turning to examples of cases where this requirement was met, we can refer back to two earlier examples. In *Haile*,[216] the decision-maker misheard the applicant's reference to EPRP as a reference to a very different organisation called EPRF. There was no conflict in the evidence: the problem lay purely in the decision-maker's attention to that evidence. In *Charter Holdings*,[217] the Inland Revenue officer's belief that the company's director had correctly completed the relevant form on another occasion was due to the officer's inadequate attention to the evidence. The form in question was available to her and clearly showed the same incorrect response by the taxpayer.

(iii) Some Final Points on the 'Established Fact' Requirement

It is worth clarifying that, in some cases, mistakes of fact may concern facts or evidence that are quite contentious and yet meet the 'established fact' requirement. That is because the mistake as to an existing fact, the first requirement in *E*, may take the form of ignorance of the availability of relevant evidence. Such ignored evidence may itself be contentious, so long as its availability and relevance is incontrovertible. For instance, in the *Criminal Injury Compensation Board* case, the Board deciding the compensation claim was unaware that a police doctor had reported findings consistent with the claim.[218] On the available evidence as a whole, there was still room for disagreement on whether the violation in fact occurred.[219] But it was indisputable that the doctor's report was available and relevant evidence.

We can now see also how this second requirement in *E* responds to the third objection to mistake of fact as a ground of review. That objection flows from the need for finality in dispute resolution. Re-opening factual determinations is problematic from this perspective. However, where the second requirement in *E* is met, we are dealing with an incontrovertible mistake. The need to correct such a mistake weighs heavily in the balance favour of recourse. Whether it outweighs the need for finality in dispute resolution then depends largely on whether the mistake is sufficiently material. We will return to this, as it is the fourth requirement in *E*. Next, however, we turn to the third requirement.

[215] *Winton Property* (n 177) at [85], [93]; and see the application of the test at [104]–[105].
[216] *Haile* (n 204).
[217] *Charter Holdings* (n 182).
[218] *CICB* (n 197) at 343.
[219] Expressly acknowledged ibid at 343, 346.

(c) Applicant not Responsible

The third requirement of the *E* test is that the applicant could not fairly be held responsible for the error. Unlike the first two requirements in *E*, this requirement was expressly touched on in *Ririnui*, albeit without noting the link to *E*. The Court noted that the error at issue in that case was clearly not the plaintiff's responsibility.[220]

This requirement is largely self-explanatory. Where the mistake takes the form of an erroneous finding of fact, an applicant will likely be responsible for the error if the source of the error is found in evidence adduced by the applicant.[221] Alternatively, where the mistake takes the form of ignorance of the availability of relevant evidence, then the question is whether it was the applicant's responsibility to put that evidence before the decision-maker. This question was addressed in the *Criminal Injuries Compensation Board* case. It may have been possible for the applicant to adduce the missing doctor's report that was consistent with her claim, or at least to mention its existence. However, she had been told police would produce all statements in their possession. As a result, she could not fairly be held responsible for this gap in the evidence.[222]

(d) Materiality

The fourth and final requirement in *E* is that the mistake must be sufficiently material. The formulation in *E* is that the mistake must have played a material part of the decision-maker's reasoning, though it need not be decisive. However, there is diverging authority on the formulation and strength of the materiality test.

In *Ririnui*, the court found the error to be material.[223] The point was put in a range of different ways: the challenged decisions were 'influenced' by the mistake,[224] they were 'based on' it,[225] and the mistake even 'overwhelmed or sidelined any other considerations'.[226] The last two formulations are more demanding than the test in *E*, but they seem best understood as describing how unquestionably material the mistake was on the facts of this case. The passage that is most likely intended as a statement of the test is the first, which refers to the decision being 'influenced' by the mistake.

Some cases set the bar for materiality quite low – effectively adopting a presumption of materiality. In *Haile*, for instance, the mistake was merely one of six reasons for an adverse credibility finding against an asylum claimant. Credibility was a crucial issue. The Court considered that leaving the mistake uncorrected must leave a 'deep sense of injustice', and that the mistake 'cannot confidently be said to have made no ultimate difference to the result'. Some recent appellate authority in New Zealand is consistent with this, holding that a mistake is material if it was 'not inevitable that the same conclusion would have been reached without the error'.[227]

[220] *Ririnui* (n 162) at [53].

[221] As, eg, in *Phelps v First Secretary of State, London Borough of Bromley* [2009] EWCA 1676 (Admin) at [22].

[222] *CICB* (n 197) at 343.

[223] *Ririnui* (n 162) at [53].

[224] ibid at [53], [62], [74].

[225] This formulation was used most frequently: ibid at [55], [76], [97], [98](e), [143].

[226] ibid at [98](e).

[227] *Taylor* (n 179) at [95]–[99]; see also *Charter Holdings* (n 182) at [69]–[69], [75].

On the other hand, the more stringent formulation in *Ririnui*, that the decision is 'based on' the mistake, is supported by some older New Zealand authority.[228]

It may be that the strength of the materiality test should vary between different types of cases. Recall that the objection from the need for finality must be balanced against the need for redress for an incontrovertible mistake. The strength of the need for redress may depend, for instance, on the importance of what is at stake. That may help to explain the low bar in *Haile*, a refugee case. There is also good reason to apply a more stringent materiality test to mistakes in the form of ignorance of the availability of evidence. After all, for most decisions it will be possible to identify some further evidence of some potential relevance that was not before the decision-maker: the evidence cannot possibly include everything of some potential relevance. For this type of mistake, therefore, there must be some realistic limits to when this can invalidate the decision.

(4) How can a Mistake of Fact be an Error of Law?

A source of confusion in this area is courts describing factual errors as errors of law. This terminology is used partly because several of the cases in this area involved administrative law appeals on questions of law, rather than judicial review. But how can a mistake of fact be an error of law? There are two parts to the answer.

First, 'error of law' in the context of administrative law can simply mean reviewable error: any kind of error that constitutes a ground of judicial review. This is the broader one of at least two meanings of 'error of law'. The narrower and more obvious sense corresponds to the illegality ground of review. It comprises misinterpretation of statutes or other law and reasoning errors such as taking account of irrelevant considerations. A mistake of fact that provides a ground of review is an error of law in the broad sense, though not in the narrow one.

The second point to note is that all grounds of judicial review are available in administrative law appeals on questions of law.[229] Therefore, if mistake of fact is a ground of review, it is also a ground for an appeal on a question of law.

(5) How does this Ground Relate to the Broader Expansion of Substantive Review?

The context for the question about mistake of fact as a ground of review has changed greatly in recent decades. Other established grounds of review have long been potentially available to address complaints relating to the facts. For instance, ignoring a relevant fact might give rise to review for failure to take account of a mandatory relevant consideration.[230]

[228] *Glaxo Group* (n 189) at 184. See also, eg, *W v Staffordshire County Council* [2006] EWCA Civ 1676 at [18].
[229] *E* (n 163) at [40]–[42]; *Wolf v Minister of Immigration* [2004] NZAR 414 (HC) at [41]. See also Ch 10.D.
[230] See, eg, *Air Nelson* (n 188).

However, such alternatives have multiplied. There has been a great expansion of substantive review, as discussed in the earlier parts of this chapter and in chapter six on rights-based review. This expansion includes increased scrutiny of factual determinations. In particular, the demand for justification in rights cases and as part of heightened scrutiny has resulted in courts asserting the power to reconsider factual findings. If the decision-maker got relevant facts wrong, for instance as to relevant risks or benefits, that may defeat the justification. We saw that this is a likely explanation of the decision in *Taylor*.[231] Furthermore, in this context courts also scrutinise evaluative judgements on a much more intensive standard of review. Cooke J pointed out this contrast in *New Health v Minister for COVID-19 Response*.[232]

This might reduce the need for the new ground and its significance. However, the new ground is still likely to be needed for correcting incontrovertible mistakes in at least some contexts. These include contexts where no rights are at stake and heightened scrutiny does not apply. They also include cases such as *Haile* where the incontrovertible mistake concerns a single relevant fact that is sufficiently relevant to raise concerns about the decision, but is not so significant as to render the overall decision unreasonable or disproportionate.[233]

[231] *Taylor* (n 179) and accompanying text.
[232] *New Health* (n 214) at [35]. For a correctness standard on both law and facts in this context, see, eg, *R (AAA (Syria)) v Secretary of State for the Home Department* [2023] UKSC 42, [2023] 1 WLR 4433.
[233] *Haile* (n 204).

Part III

The Limits of Judicial Review

8

Availability of Judicial Review

This chapter is concerned with when judicial review is available to challenge a decision or other measure. Other terms for this topic are reviewability or amenability to review. For a variety of reasons, not all public administrative decisions or measures, and not all issues about them, are reviewable.

This is the first of three chapters in Part III of the book on the nature and limits of courts' powers in judicial review and related proceedings. The remaining two chapters concern the framework for calibrating restraint in judicial review (Chapter 9) and the nature and limits of judicial remedies for breaches of administrative law (Chapter 10).

As we saw in Chapter 1, there are two aspects to the principles of judicial review. The first is addressed to administrative decision-makers and comprises norms that govern their exercise of power. The discussion of the grounds of review in Part II of this book focuses on this first aspect. The second aspect is addressed to courts and concerns the nature and limits of the courts' power. We explore that aspect of the principles in this Part III.

We start in this chapter with limits to the availability of judicial review, found both in common law and in statute. The common law has developed two main limits, 'justiciability' and the 'public nature' test, along with others that are less often at issue. Justiciability, discussed in Part A, refers to whether a matter is suitable for judicial determination. Two further related common law limits are outlined in Part B: 'standing', which may restrict who may bring judicial review proceedings, and limits on review of preliminary steps before a substantive decision and of mere reports or advice. The 'public nature' test, the second main limit, restricts judicial review where the public law principles developed in judicial review are not appropriate, because the decision-maker or the decision in question are not of a sufficiently public nature. This is touched on briefly in Part C of this chapter but is discussed in full in Part IV of the book which concerns the relationship between public and private law and power.

Statute is relevant in two respects. First, it is important to appreciate that the Act concerning judicial review, now the Judicial Review Procedure Act 2016, merely provides a simplified procedure and better remedial options. It does not govern the availability of review, as explained in Part D. Secondly, some empowering statutes contain 'privative' or 'ouster' clauses: provisions purporting to exclude or restrict access to judicial review. Part E outlines the different types of privative clauses and the courts' approach to these.

How are these limits given effect? When judicial review is not available for one of these reasons, then an application may be struck out in interlocutory proceedings.[1] Such cases do not reach the stage of filing submissions and evidence concerning the pleaded grounds. However, we will also see that this does not exhaust the effect of most of the limits on judicial review. Where the relevant limit to judicial review does not apply sufficiently clearly or strongly to exclude review entirely, it may still result in the

[1] In the United Kingdom, permission may be refused; but Aotearoa New Zealand does not have a permission requirement.

court limiting the grounds it will entertain, limiting the intensity of review or granting only limited remedies. The limits introduced in this chapter therefore feature also in Chapters 9 and 10.[2]

Limits on accessing judicial review are always contentious. In debates about these limits, judges and commentators invoke competing constitutional and public interest considerations, and their answers reflect value judgments as to the relative weight of these considerations. As a result, the law on these questions cannot simply be determined by logical or doctrinal reasoning; and it rarely stands still for very long.

A. Justiciability

The justiciability test limits the availability of judicial review. A matter is justiciable if it is suitable for judicial determination.[3] If a matter is not justiciable in that sense, that means it is best left to the executive or administrative decision-maker without judicial oversight. It may be subject to political scrutiny involving Parliament and the electorate; or there may be other appropriate forums and modes of accountability. A challenge concerning non-justiciable matters can be struck out before it reaches a full hearing.[4]

Justiciability now usually turns on the subject-matter of the issues raised in a challenge. That is discussed in detail in section (1). There are, however, two special categories of justiciability limit. These are briefly outlined in section (2).

(1) Justiciability Determined by Subject-matter

Justiciability on the modern approach is determined by reference to subject-matter.[5] The first three sections below outline the main features of this modern approach. Section (a) outlines the two main types of justiciability concern – constitutional legitimacy and institutional capacity. Section (b) explains the shift in focus from the source of a power to the subject-matter. Section (c) explains the effect of justiciability concerns. The modern approach, dubbed 'secondary justiciability', employs justiciability concerns in a nuanced fashion, so as to exclude or limit judicial review only on some issues or grounds, rather than declaring entire areas of activity to be 'no-go zones'. The next two sections survey the case law on the two main types of decision affected by justiciability concerns: high policy decisions (Section (d)) and those involving expert judgment (Section (e)). The remaining two sections address two more specific questions. In the past, matters of 'grace and favour' were considered non-justiciable, but the

[2] See also the discussion in Chapters 6 and 7 of the scope and intensity of substantive grounds of review and rights-based review.

[3] See generally BV Harris, 'Judicial Review, Justiciability and the Prerogative of Mercy' (2003) 62 *Cambridge Law Journal* 631.

[4] *Curtis v Minister of Defence* [2002] 2 NZLR 744 (CA) at [29].

[5] Noted in *Ririnui v Landcorp Farming Ltd* [2016] NZSC 62, [2016] 1 NZLR 1056 at [89].

courts have moved away from that view (Section (f)). The non-justiciability of prosecutorial discretion has also been qualified (Section (g)).

(a) Two Types of Justiciability Concern: Constitutional and Institutional

Justiciability concerns take broadly two forms: constitutional concerns about courts' lack of accountability and democratic legitimacy, and concerns about the limits of courts' institutional capacity and competence.[6] Both types of concern fall to be weighed against countervailing concerns about maintaining the rule of law and protecting individuals against abuses of public power, by subjecting the legality of exercises of public power to judicial scrutiny.

We should note that there is some debate as to whether judicial review should be limited on grounds of justiciability at all. This is not universally accepted. A number of accounts simply say very little about it.[7] Others expressly argue for abandoning it. TRS Allan raises fundamental objections from the rule of law and the need to protect against abuse of power.[8] Chris Finn's objection is that justiciability criteria are redundant.[9] The grounds of review incorporate the limits that are needed to avoid judges straying into the merits: review is limited to issues concerning legality and procedure. Those issues are always within the institutional competence and constitutionally legitimate role of judges, regardless of the nature and subject-matter of the impugned decision. We will return to these objections.

Under headings (i) and (ii) below I explain the nature of each of the two types of concern in turn. A central concept that is relevant to both concerns is polycentricity, introduced under heading (iii). Case law illustrating these concerns and concepts is discussed in more detail in sections (d) and (e) below.

(i) Constitutional Legitimacy

Turning first to constitutional legitimacy concerns, the basic principle here is democracy. Judges are not democratically accountable and judicial processes do not involve democratic participation. Courts therefore lack legitimacy to determine matters for which such accountability and participation is appropriate. Leaving such matters to executive government, subject only to Parliamentary oversight, is then an aspect of our separation of powers.[10] The rule of law is a countervailing principle, requiring courts to ensure that government acts within the law. However, it has also been recognised that not all aspects of society need, or indeed should, be governed by law.[11]

[6] See generally Harris, 'Judicial Review, Justiciability' (n 3), esp at 637–43.

[7] Eg Paul Craig, *Administrative Law*, 9th edn (London, Sweet & Maxwell, 2021) refers to justiciability only in two specific contexts: the remedy of a declaration and tort liability: ibid at [26-026] and ch 12.

[8] See TRS Allan, *Constitutional Justice: A Liberal Theory of the Rule of Law* (Oxford, OUP, 2001), ch 6.

[9] Chris Finn, 'The Justiciability of Administrative Decisions: A Redundant Concept?' (2002) 30 *Federal Law Review* 239 at 243–44.

[10] See *Curtis v Minister of Defence* [2002] 2 NZLR 744 (CA) at [22], [26], [28]; Harris 'Judicial Review, Justiciability' (n 3) at 637–39.

[11] See Ch 3.

The types of matters that raise justiciability concerns on these constitutional grounds are matters of politics or high policy. These include matters of defence, national security and international relations.[12] Declaring war or entering a treaty are among the most obvious examples.[13] These matters also more broadly include contested allocations of resources or risks, particularly on a large scale.[14] Examples might include a decision on closing a hospital[15] or on a system of safety regulation. Settlements of Treaty of Waitangi claims also raise such concerns, both because they involve large scale contested resource allocation and because of their high policy nature.[16]

Some cases have considered resource allocation to raise justiciability concerns even where it is on an individual basis rather than on a large scale.[17] That is, however, open to doubt.[18] The better view is that the problem with resource allocation issues lies in polycentricity. This applies primarily to large-scale resource allocation decisions rather than to individual ones.

(ii) Institutional Capacity

The second basis for justiciability concerns relates to institutional capacity and competence. There are three main relevant limits to the courts' institutional capacity and competence, with large overlaps between them: courts need a legal yardstick;[19] courts may lack relevant expertise and access to information;[20] and judicial procedures are not suited to polycentric issues. The third of these, polycentricity, is introduced under the next heading.

The types of matters that may be rendered non-justiciable by these considerations very broadly fall into two groups. In the first group are high policy decisions and contested allocations of resources or risks on a large scale, the types of issues that are also affected by the constitutional legitimacy concern. These are affected by all three limits to the courts' institutional capacity and competence. In the second group are decisions turning on expert judgement – drawing on specialist expertise, such as medical, scientific or academic expertise. These are affected by the courts' first two institutional limits: lack of a legal yardstick and limits of judicial expertise and access to information.

An objection to the concern about expertise is that this need not be a bar to competent judicial resolution of issues: judges regularly use expert evidence to assist in such contexts. It is open to debate whether expert evidence is always a sufficient answer to a lack of judicial expertise, but certainly this option needs to be considered before relying on lack of expertise as a factor against justiciability. This solution does not

[12] *Council of Civil Service Unions v Minister for the Civil Service* [1985] 1 AC 374 (HL) at 418. See, eg, *Curtis* (n 10).

[13] *Blackburn v Attorney-General* [1971] 1 WLR 1037 (CA).

[14] See, eg, *Lawson v Housing New Zealand* [1997] 2 NZLR 474 (HC) at 486–87.

[15] *Napier City v Healthcare Hawke's Bay Ltd* HC Napier CP29/94, 15 December 1994.

[16] See *New Zealand Maori Council v Attorney-General (Te Arawa Cross Claim Case)* [2007] NZCA 269, [2008] 1 NZLR 318 at [83].

[17] See, eg, *Akatere v Attorney-General* [2006] 3 NZLR 705 (HC) at [31], [38].

[18] *Akatere* (ibid) was not followed in *Pora v Attorney-General* [2017] NZHC 2081, [2017] 3 NZLR 683.

[19] *Curtis* (n 10) at [14], [23], [27]–[28]; Harris 'Judicial Review, Justiciability' (n 3) at 643.

[20] *CCSU* (n 12) at 401–07.

help where access to information is restricted for reasons of national security.[21] In that context, however, courts need to consider whether such information can be disclosed to judges without disclosing it to the parties.[22]

(iii) Further on Polycentricity vs Individual Focus

Polycentricity plays a large role in justiciability concerns about high policy decisions and contested allocations of resources or risks on a large scale. We have seen that it is linked to both types of concerns: constitutional legitimacy and institutional capacity. This concept calls for explanation.

An issue is polycentric if the benefits and burdens of resolving it one way or the other are distributed widely, in a complex pattern.[23] Consider the example of a decision whether to close a hospital. The cost savings will benefit other hospitals, other public services, or taxpayers at large. The burden will fall on potential patients who lose access to health services or have to travel further, on staff who lose their positions or have to relocate, and on other services that interact with or depend on the hospital in various ways – for instance, there will probably be an increase in the workload of local general practitioners. Any slight adjustment to the proposal (eg the timing, or the details of where particular services are relocated) will redistribute those benefits and burdens in a complex pattern.

Lon Fuller likened this complex distribution of impacts to pulling on one strand of a spider's web. The pull exerts different amounts of tension at different points in the web; and that distribution of tensions will shift if one of the strands snaps due to the tension.[24]

We will see that polycentricity concerns have more validity in relation to decisions on a large scale. Where a decision instead directly concerns the rights or interests of an individual, polycentricity concerns recede into the background, and that is a factor in favour of justiciability.[25]

The institutional capacity issue is that judicial proceedings are not suited to polycentric issues, because courts' adversarial procedures are designed to deal with bipolar disputes: one party makes a claim and another party resists that claim.[26] Courts make their decisions based on the evidence and arguments put forward by those two parties. Their procedures are not designed to gather, analyse and evaluate information on the various impacts of the available options on a multitude of different groups of people. Courts are therefore not well equipped to make good quality decisions on polycentric issues.[27]

[21] See, eg, *R (Begum) v Special Immigration Appeals Commission* [2021] UKSC 7, [2021] AC 765.
[22] For brief discussion of the 'closed materials procedures' commonly used in this area, see Ch 4.B(3)(g).
[23] Lon L Fuller, 'The Forms and Limits of Adjudication' (1978) 92 *Harvard Law Review* 353 at 394–404.
[24] ibid at 395.
[25] *Pora v Attorney-General* (n 18) at [91].
[26] Fuller (n 23) at 394–404.
[27] See *CCSU* (n 12) at 411.

It is, of course, possible to modify and adapt judicial procedures.[28] The adversarial model has, in fact, been significantly modified in modern times. Third parties (usually representatives of some wider public interest) can now be given leave to intervene, and it is more common for evidence on wider social and economic impacts to be offered and admitted.[29] It remains a matter for debate, however, how much change in this direction is desirable. There are also surely limits to how much they can achieve in terms of equipping the courts to deal with polycentric issues.

Polycentricity is also closely linked to the constitutional concerns about democratic legitimacy. Democratic accountability and democratic participation is desirable for decisions involving contested allocations of resources or risks in polycentric contexts. Since courts lack these credentials, they should hesitate to weigh in on such questions.

The counter argument to the institutional and constitutional concerns about polycentricity is that *all* issues in public law are polycentric.[30] Issues that appear bipolar, because they arise between an authority and an individual, always have wider repercussions. For instance, the funds or resources used to implement a decision in favour of the individual will not be available for others; and the reasoning and outcome will send messages as to permissible policy directions. Furthermore, every court decision becomes a precedent applicable to future cases; and many judicial review decisions determine the interpretation or validity of generally applicable rules in statutes and delegated legislation.

However, there is a difference at least in degree between the polycentricity of an individual decision and that of a large-scale decision such as whether to close a hospital.[31] The more a decision focuses on one individual, the more indirect and the more confined are the polycentric impacts. Conversely, the more general the decision, the larger the range of polycentric impacts and the more they move from the background into a front and centre position. That is why polycentricity concerns arguably render issues non-justiciable only in decisions on a sufficiently large scale. Cases invoking these concerns in relation to individual decisions are open to doubt.

There is also a difference in terms of political accountability as an available alternative to judicial scrutiny. In the case of a large-scale decision, usually made by high-level decision-makers, political accountability is a realistic alternative to legal scrutiny; in the case of an individual decision, this is much less realistic.[32] Courts should pause before using justiciability to deny or limit legal accountability in contexts where alternative forms of accountability or alternative remedies are not realistically available.[33]

[28] For this solution see, eg, John W F Allison, 'The Procedural Reason for Judicial Restraint' [1994] *Public Law* 452.

[29] See, eg, *Lab Tests Auckland Ltd v Auckland District Health Board* [2008] NZCA 385, [2009] 1 NZLR 776 (CA).

[30] Jeff A King, 'The Pervasiveness of Polycentricity' [2008] *Public Law* 101; Finn, 'Justiciability' (n 9) at 243–44.

[31] See, similarly, Daniel Squires and Duncan Fairgrieve, *The Negligence Liability of Public Authorities*, 2nd edn (Oxford, Oxford University Press, 2019) at [2.83]–[2.85]; Jeff A King, 'Justiciability of Resource Allocations' (2007) *Modern Law Review* 197; Fuller (n 23) at 397–98.

[32] See Harris, 'Judicial Review, Justiciability' (n 3) at 635; Squires and Fairgrieve (n 31) at [2.87]–[2.88].

[33] DGT Williams, 'Justiciability and the Control of Discretionary Power' in Michael Taggart (ed), *Judicial Review of Administrative Action in the 1980s* (Auckland, Oxford University Press, 1986) 103 at 121.

Traditionally, standing rules served to confine judicial review to decisions about individuals in most contexts. Polycentricity as a criterion of justiciability was not needed in that context. However, that limit has been largely discarded.[34] This is one of several examples of justiciability becoming more of an issue due to the demise of traditional formal limits to judicial review.

(b) Subject-matter Rather Than Source of Power Determines Justiciability

The source of a power used to be the main basis for justiciability determinations: only statutory powers were subject to judicial review. Review was excluded in particular for exercises of prerogative powers, except to the extent of testing their existence and scope.[35] However, the landmark case of *Council of Civil Service Unions* established that exercises of royal prerogative powers are, at least in principle, subject to judicial review. Their justiciability depends on the subject-matter, just as for other decisions. While their subject-matter often involves high policy matters such as national security, they are not immune from review as a category.[36] This was adopted for New Zealand in *Burt*.[37] It has been consistently affirmed in the case law since then.[38]

This reviewability in principle extends to non-statutory powers generally.[39] Aside from prerogative powers, these may include what Bruce Harris has called the 'third source' power[40] – to do what is not prohibited by law – but the extent of this power is contested.[41] In any event, government does make decisions without a statutory basis, such as determining ex gratia compensation. Such decisions are not rendered non-justiciable by the lack of a statutory basis.[42]

The lack of a statutory basis can, however, constrain the available arguments on review.[43] For instance, *MKD v Minister of Health* dismissed a challenge on grounds of improper purpose to Cabinet's decision to make the paediatric vaccine against COVID-19 available free of charge. One of several reasons was that in the absence of a statutory power, no legal yardstick was available for determining whether that alleged purpose was improper.[44]

[34] See part B(1) of this chapter.

[35] *Case of Proclamations* (1611) 12 Co Rep 74, 77 ER 1352; *Attorney-General v De Keyser's Royal Hotel Ltd* [1920] AC 508 (HL).

[36] *CCSU* (n 12) at 407, 409–11, 416–19.

[37] *Burt v Governor General* [1992] 3 NZLR 672 (CA) at 678.

[38] See, eg, *R (Bancoult) v Secretary of State for Foreign and Commonwealth Affairs (No 2)* [2008] UKHL 61, [2009] 1 AC 453 at [35], [105] concerning prerogative powers to legislate for colonies; *R (Miller) v The Prime Minister* [2019] UKSC 41, [2020] AC 373 at [32], [35].

[39] See also Ch 11 on contractual powers.

[40] Bruce v Harris, 'The "Third Source" of Authority for Government Action' (1992) 109 *Law Quarterly Review* 626.

[41] See, eg, Philip A Joseph, *Constitutional and Administrative Law in New Zealand*, 5th edn (Wellington, Brookers, 2021), ch 19.3.3. *Quake Outcasts v Minister for Canterbury Earthquake Recovery* [2015] NZSC 27, [2016] 1 NZLR 1 at [111]–[112] leaves the point open.

[42] *Pora* (n 18) at [92]–[98]; more ambivalent is *In re McFarland* [2004] UKHL 17, [2004] 1 WLR 1289 (HL).

[43] See, eg, *R (Sandiford) v Secretary of State for Foreign and Commonwealth Affairs* [2014] UKSC 44, [2014] 1 WLR 2697 at [61]–[62], [81].

[44] *MKD v Minister of Health* [2022] NZHC 1997 at [95]–[97].

(c) Shift from Primary to Secondary Justiciability

There has been a further shift. In cases like *CCSU*, justiciability based on subject matter rather than source was applied to types of decisions.[45] As Bruce Harris has pointed out, this resulted in entire subject areas, such as defence, foreign affairs and national security, being declared judicial 'no-go zones'. However, subject-matter justiciability could also be used in a more subtle and nuanced fashion, examining suitability for judicial determination in relation to each particular issue or ground of review. He coined the labels primary and secondary justiciability for these different approaches.[46]

Secondary justiciability is the approach more commonly used today. In *Thomson v Minister of Climate Change Issues*, the High Court affirmed the modern preference for this approach.[47] Where the subject matter raises justiciability concerns, some grounds may not be available at all, because the issues they raise are not suitable for judicial determination. Such exclusion is most likely to apply to the grounds that come closest to review of the merits – notably unreasonableness or irrationality.[48] Alternatively, justiciability concerns may lead to such grounds being employed with even less intensive scrutiny than usual.[49] Furthermore, some other grounds may be deployed in a more limited fashion than usual; for instance, courts may be less willing to imply limits to permissible purposes or considerations.[50] Procedural fairness grounds are the least likely to be affected by justiciability concerns, but the context may lead to procedural fairness having limited content.[51] Finally, justiciability concerns may also affect what remedies courts are prepared to grant.[52]

On this secondary approach, the role of justiciability concerns has changed. They may still determine the availability of judicial review. Where none of the issues raised are justiciable, that still provides a basis for striking out causes of action.[53] However, justiciability concerns can also be seen as contributing to variability in the scope and intensity of review across different grounds of review[54] – the phenomenon that has been explored in detail by Dean Knight.[55] As Mike Taggart put it, non-justiciability and limited scope or intensity of review are part of the same spectrum or 'rainbow' of standards of review.[56] However, this observation about variability in the scope and

[45] *CCSU* (n 12) at 418; see also *Ririnui* (n 5) at [89].

[46] Harris, 'Judicial Review, Justiciability' (n 3) at 644–46.

[47] *Thomson v Minister for Climate Change Issues* [2017] NZHC 733, [2018] 2 NZLR 160 at [104], [134].

[48] See, eg, *CCSU* (n 12) at 441; *Air New Zealand Ltd v Wellington International Airport Ltd* [2009] NZCA 259, [2009] 3 NZLR 713 (CA) at [76].

[49] See, eg, *Auckland Council v CP Group Ltd* [2023] NZSC 53, [2023] 1 NZLR 35 at [62]–[69], [89]–[98].

[50] See, eg, *Unison Networks Ltd v Commerce Commission* [2007] NZSC 74, [2008] 1 NZLR 42 at [55]; *CREEDNZ v Governor-General* [1981] 1 NZLR 172 (CA) at 197–98.

[51] See Ch 4; and see, eg, *Burt* (n 37).

[52] See Ch 10.C.

[53] See, eg, *Curtis* (n 10) at [29].

[54] Further discussed in Chs 6, 7 and 9.

[55] Dean R Knight, *Vigilance and Restraint in the Common Law of Judicial Review* (Cambridge, Cambridge University Press, 2018); on justiciability, see at 99–101, 111, 150–53.

[56] Michael Taggart, 'Proportionality, Deference, *Wednesbury*' [2008] *New Zealand Law Review* 423 at 451–54.

intensity of review is not universally accepted, nor is the role of justiciability concerns in this regard.[57]

If accepted, this modern approach provides an answer to Chris Finn's objection that justiciability criteria are redundant.[58] He argues that the only justiciability criterion we need is that there is a legal yardstick, and that is satisfied whenever a ground of review is made out. It is true that the established grounds of review are designed to confine reviewing courts to their constitutionally appropriate supervisory role. However, on the approach described here, the scope and intensity of scrutiny on each of those grounds may be affected by justiciability concerns.

The secondary justiciability approach can be observed in action in much of the modern case law. We turn now to explore that case law in relation to several types of issues.

(d) High Policy and Contested Allocations of Resources or Risks – Cases

The leading case of *Curtis v Minister of Defence* provides a good illustration of the secondary justiciability approach even in the context of high policy decisions about defence (and also about large-scale contested allocation of resources).[59] On behalf of a group called Save Our Squadrons (SOS), Mr Curtis challenged the Minister's decision to axe the armed combat wing of the air force. The Court of Appeal invoked justiciability concerns in striking out this challenge, but only in relation to one specific issue – several other potential issues were determined against Mr Curtis by applying the law.

Power of control of the defence force is vested in the Minister by the Defence Act 1990. Much of the judgment is devoted to issues of legality in terms of the Act. The Court determined the extent of the legal requirements imposed by that Act, and found that the decision complied with these.[60] The Act was held to require maintenance of three separate armed forces including an air force. Even if it further required each of those forces to be armed – a point that was arguable either way – that requirement was complied with here, because the air force remained armed to some extent. The remaining aircraft all played a combat support role and could be fitted with weapons appropriate to their role.

In light of these findings about legality in terms of the Act, the only remaining issue was whether the level at which the air force was now armed was insufficient. That was the issue which the Court considered 'par excellence a non-justiciable question'.[61] The reasons were twofold. First, the Court's role was limited to determining the lawfulness of the Minister's decision, and the issues must therefore be susceptible of determination by a satisfactory legal yardstick. Secondly, there was no such yardstick: the Act provided no express or implicit guidance on what amounts to being armed at a sufficient level – this was purely a matter of policy and politics. The government is

[57] See, eg, *Osborne v Worksafe New Zealand* [2017] NZCA 11, [2017] 2 NZLR 513 at [35]; Jeff A King, 'Institutional Approaches to Judicial Restraint' (2008) 28 *Oxford Journal of Legal Studies* 409 at 420–22.

[58] Finn, 'Justiciability' (n 9) at 243–44.

[59] *Curtis* (n 10).

[60] ibid at [15]–[21].

[61] ibid at [22], [28].

accountable at the ballot box for decisions on such questions, and it is constitutionally improper for the courts to examine these.[62]

Curtis is an illustration of secondary justiciability, although the Court did not put it in those terms. Only one of several issues was considered non-justiciable – the Court did rule on several other issues.

Other cases also illustrate that even in the context of high policy decisions, some issues can be justiciable. That goes for legality arguments with a sufficiently clear statutory basis, as in *Curtis*. For instance, in *Thomson* discretionary decisions on setting emissions reduction targets as part of climate change policy were held to be potentially justiciable.[63] The Court did not find any reviewable error in a target notified to international bodies pursuant to the Paris Agreement. But it did find that under the Climate Change Response Act 2002, a new report of the Intergovernmental Panel on Climate Change (IPCC) was an implied mandatory consideration in deciding whether to review targets.[64]

A similar point also goes for procedural fairness issues. Issues concerning consultation in particular will often be justiciable despite the decision involving high policy. *Walsh*, for instance, was a successful challenge to a decision by Pharmac not to fund a particular cancer drug[65] – a decision about allocation of resources on a large scale. The statute required Pharmac to consult the public 'when it considers appropriate'. Pharmac applied a policy of not consulting on decisions to decline funding. That was held not to be a valid exercise of the discretion concerning consultation.

Curtis arguably also illustrates how the justiciability of the subject-matter of a decision affects the scope and intensity of review. Whether there is a legal yardstick depends at least in part on whether a court is prepared to employ all of the normally available yardsticks. Grounds of review that might have been relevant to the 'insufficiently armed' challenge in *Curtis* include implied mandatory relevant considerations and irrationality, but none of these were mentioned at all. That may just be because no such grounds were argued. However, it also seems likely that the Court would have been very slow entertain any grounds beyond reliance on the express terms of the statute, given the high policy subject matter.

Challenges to decisions on settling Treaty of Waitangi claims may raise justiciability concerns, both because such decisions involve large scale contested resource allocation and because of their high policy nature. Challenges to negotiators' mandates and to the terms of settlements by dissenting iwi or hapū[66] or by cross-claimants have been dismissed on that basis.[67]

However, the Supreme Court in *Ririnui v Landcorp* cautioned that justiciable issues may still arise in challenges to Treaty-related decisions.[68] A challenge to a decision not to intervene in a sale of Crown land that was subject to a Treaty claim was justiciable

[62] ibid at [14], [22]–[23], [26]–[28].
[63] *Thomson* (n 47) at [133].
[64] ibid at [94].
[65] *Walsh v Pharmaceutical Management Agency* [2010] NZAR 101 (HC).
[66] Tribes or sub-tribes.
[67] See, eg *Manuiriangi v Nga Hapu o Nga Ruahine Iwi Inc* [2011] NZAR 166 (HC) at [33]–[35].
[68] *Ririnui* (n 5) at [89]–[90]; see also *Ngāti Mutunga o Wharekauri Iwi Trust v Minister for Treaty of Waitangi Negotiations* [2019] NZHC 1942 at [24]–[26].

in that case, because the Court considered that justiciable grounds of review had been made out.[69] Where settlements are concerned, once a settlement has been concluded, its interpretation is a justiciable issue.[70]

(e) Expert Judgment – Cases

As noted earlier, challenges to decisions that turn on expert judgment – drawing on specialist expertise such as medical, scientific, commercial or academic expertise – may raise justiciability concerns not on constitutional grounds but on grounds of institutional capacity. Two concerns in that regard are relevant in this context: the lack of a legal yardstick and the limits of judicial expertise.

As to the first concern, while expert judgments often employ established standards, some of those standards will not be legal ones. Their interpretation is then not a question of law on which a court should weigh in, at least not without significant deference. For instance, plagiarism may be defined in a university's statutes or regulations, but the interpretation and application of that definition is arguably largely a matter of academic standards and judgement, as was found in the UK in *Clark v University of Lincolnshire and Humberside*.[71] Courts certainly have considered examination marking to turn on non-justiciable academic standards.[72]

On the other hand, in keeping with the secondary justiciability approach, review may well be available in the same contexts on some grounds. This will be so whenever a legal yardstick can be found for addressing the particular issue. For instance, in *Clark* the challenge to the student's result was allowed to go ahead on the ground that her prospects on a resit had been confined to at best obtaining a third-class degree, when the regulations did not confine the potential outcome of a resit in that way.[73] Procedural fairness challenges have also succeeded in the context of decisions that turned on academic judgement.[74]

Unison Networks Ltd v Commerce Commission may also be considered an example of limited review due to the limited justiciability of standards designed for application by expert judgement. The Commerce Commission was an expert regulator, exercising broadly expressed powers that were designed to achieve expansively expressed economic objectives. The Supreme Court considered that it must have been intended to take into account wide policy considerations.[75] In *Z v Dental Complaints Assessment*

[69] *Ririnui* (n 5) at [98](e).

[70] See, eg, *Te Waka Hi Ika o Te Arawa v Treaty of Waitangi Fisheries Commission* [2002] 2 NZLR 17 (PC); *Thompson v Treaty of Waitangi Fisheries Commission* [2005] 2 NZLR 9 (CA).

[71] *Clark v University of Lincolnshire and Humberside* [2000] 1 WLR 1988 (CA) at [12]; but cf *Bell v Victoria University of Wellington* HC Wellington CIV-2009-485-2634, 8 December 2010.

[72] See obiter dictum in *Norrie v Senate of the University of Auckland* [1984] 1 NZLR 129 (CA) at 139.

[73] *Clark* (n 71) at [9].

[74] See, eg, *R (Persaud) v University of Cambridge* [2001] EWCA Civ 534. A bias challenge was entertained in *Lamb v Massey University* HC Palmerston North CIV 2003-454-336 & 337, 19 October 2004 but failed on the facts.

[75] *Unison Networks* (n 50) at [55]. For a critique, see Edward Willis, 'Economic Law – Analysing Competition Law and Economic Regulation' in Michael Littlewood and Janet McLean (eds), *The Supreme Court: The Second 10 Years* (Wellington, LexisNexis, 2024) 315.

Committee, the Court confirmed that a similar deference is accorded to professional disciplinary bodies within their area of expertise.[76]

Courts certainly will not seek to resolve scientific debates. Where issues turn on such debates, the most a court will do is to determine whether the defendant's position was tenable and based on credible scientific opinion. That was the approach taken by the High Court in *NZ Climate Science Education Trust*, a challenge to the methodology employed in some reports on temperature increases over the past 100 years.[77] The same kind of restraint is due on issues of scientific debate even in the context of challenges pursuant to the New Zealand Bill of Rights Act 1990. The Supreme Court affirmed this in *New Health NZ Inc v South Taranaki District Council*, a challenge to fluoridation of public water supply.[78]

Similar restraint also applies in challenges to clinical medical judgement, as noted in *Shortland v Northland Health*, an unsuccessful challenge to a decision that continuing dialysis would not be in the best interests of the patient concerned.[79]

In relation to commercial judgement, the leading authority for confining review of decisions to extremely limited grounds is *Mercury Energy v Electricity Corp*.[80] Courts are slow to impose public law standards here largely out of respect for private ordering.[81] However, justiciability concerns (lack of legal yardsticks and judicial expertise) may also be a factor.[82]

(f) Move Away from Non-Justiciability for Matters of 'Grace and Favour'

In the past, exercises of the prerogative of mercy and decisions on ex gratia compensation were two types of decision that were considered not amenable to judicial review. That was partly due to the fact that they are not governed by statute. While the source of power no longer determines justiciability, it still may give rise to a lack of a legal yardstick for some grounds of challenge. To that extent review can be somewhat limited even on the modern approach.

Another reason why these decisions were considered non-justiciable is because they are matters of 'grace and favour'. The modern cases have rejected that argument. To some extent the argument was linked to the old requirement that, in order to be reviewable, a decision had to determine a person's rights. On the modern approach to judicial review, it is sufficient that a person's interests are affected: the distinction between rights and privileges no longer determines reviewability.[83] Furthermore, the courts no longer accept that either the prerogative of mercy or ex gratia compensation are matters of 'grace and favour' at all. Instead, in *Burt* and in *Pora* both these powers were considered

[76] *Z v Dental Complaints Assessment Committee* [2008] NZSC 55, [2009] 1 NZLR 1 at [139].

[77] *New Zealand Climate Science Education Trust v National Institute of Water and Atmospheric Research Ltd* [2012] NZHC 2297, [2013] 1 NZLR 75, see eg at [41]–[47].

[78] *New Health NZ Inc v South Taranaki District Council* [2018] NZSC 59, [2018] 1 NZLR 948 at [121]–[122].

[79] *Shortland v Northland Health Ltd* [1998] 1 NZLR 433 (CA) at 442.

[80] *Mercury Energy Ltd v Electricity Corporation of New Zealand Ltd* [1994] 2 NZLR 385 (PC) at 391.

[81] See Ch 11.

[82] See also *Lab Tests Auckland Ltd v Auckland District Health Board* [2008] NZCA 385, [2009] 1 NZLR 776 (CA) at [340].

[83] See Paul Craig, *Administrative Law*, 9th edn (London, Sweet & Maxwell, 2021) at [26-006].

to be safeguards against mistakes that are integral parts of the criminal justice system.[84] Exercises of these powers were therefore in principle amenable to review.

Burt was an unsuccessful challenge on procedural fairness grounds to a refusal to exercise the prerogative of mercy. The Court held that basic principles of procedural fairness applied to this power. However, their scope was limited in this context, given that a person seeking a pardon has already had full hearings at the trial and on appeal and that some requests may lack any merit. The government's established practice complied with those limited requirements. It was not necessary for the independent investigation report to be disclosed for comment before the Minister decided how to advise the Governor-General.[85] This contextual approach is broadly consistent with the standard approach to procedural fairness.[86]

Compensation for miscarriages of justice is available only on an ex gratia basis because of the judicial immunity from tort liability. Challenges to decisions on the amount of such ex gratia compensation have been considered by the High Court in *Akatere* and *Pora*, with diverging results. The Court in *Akatere* would have found this power to be non-justiciable if it had been necessary to decide, but dismissed the challenge on the basis that the grounds were not made out.[87] More recently, *Pora* was a successful challenge: the power was justiciable, and grounds were made out.[88] At least as regards justiciability in principle, *Pora* is more consistent with *Burt* and with the modern approach to justiciability generally.

The successful ground in *Pora* relied on the government's published guidelines for ex gratia compensation. The interpretation of such guidelines has been held to be a question of law for the court.[89] The complaint was that the government's benchmark amounts had not been inflation-adjusted for 16 years. The decision was found to be unlawful because the government had been advised against inflation adjusting based on an erroneous interpretation of the guidelines.[90] It is notable that the relevant legal yardsticks were exploited to the full in this case, perhaps at least partly because the Court did not accept that the ex gratia nature of compensation affects its justiciability.[91]

In *Akatere*, the Court appeared to accept that the resource allocation nature of the decision raised justiciability concerns,[92] but *Pora* did not mention that point. As noted earlier, the better view is that resource allocation raises justiciability concerns only when it is on a large scale.

Challenges to ex gratia compensation claims in other contexts were found non-justicable in both *McLellan* and *XY*. The problem was that no guidelines existed, hence there was no legal yardstick.[93] However, by no means all possible grounds of review

[84] *Burt* (n 37) at 681; *Pora v Attorney-General* (n 18) at [18]–[35], [92]–[96].

[85] *Burt* (n 37) at 681–83.

[86] See Ch 4.

[87] *Akatere* (n 17) at [79].

[88] *Pora* (n 18).

[89] See Ch 7.D(1).

[90] *Pora* (n 18) at [121]–[123], [133]–[137].

[91] ibid at [92]–[98].

[92] *Akatere* (n 17) at [31]; the court adopts the Attorney-General's arguments at [38].

[93] *McLellan v Attorney-General* [2015] NZHC 3218, [2016] NZAR 859 at [57]–[61], [64]–[65]; *XY v Attorney-General* [2016] NZHC 1196, [2016] NZAR 875 at [35].

depend on there being guidelines. Here, for instance, challenges on grounds of the right to a hearing and legitimate expectations were also argued but no breaches were found on the facts.

In summary, then, exercises of these powers are best seen as reviewable on the usual grounds of review. A challenge on grounds of illegality, substantive legitimate expectations or consistency can be brought pursuant to guidelines where they exist, but can otherwise be difficult. Procedural fairness applies, but its requirements may be relatively limited.

(g) Prosecutorial Discretion

Exercises of prosecutorial discretion are a further type of decision that was traditionally considered non-justiciable. The reasons included the high content of judgement and discretion;[94] constitutional concerns not to fuse the roles of judge and prosecutor;[95] a concern to avoid collateral challenges to criminal proceedings (ordinarily, any abuse of process can be dealt with by the criminal trial court);[96] and a concern that courts in civil jurisdiction should not normally deal with criminal matters, as they may deprive those concerned of safeguards provided by the criminal process.[97]

However, there have long been qualifications. In *Hallett (No 2)*, the High Court accepted that courts would intervene to ensure that the discretion is, in fact, exercised: a blanket policy not to prosecute certain types of offences would be unlawful.[98] In *Polynesian Spa Ltd v Osborne*, the Court considered that review might also be available on grounds of bad faith or 'collateral purpose'.[99]

It is now clear that exercises of prosecutorial discretion are, in principle, justiciable. In *Osborne v WorkSafe*, the Court of Appeal unanimously confirmed this, but also held that there are good reasons for judicial restraint in this regard.[100] Courts should be more ready to intervene in decisions *not* to prosecute, because review in that context does not represent a collateral challenge to criminal proceedings – the option of leaving it to the criminal trial court to deal with abuses of process is not available. At least in that type of case, review is available on all the usual grounds. However, grounds such as irrelevant considerations or failure to take account of mandatory considerations were likely to be difficult to make out, due to the width of the discretion. The challenge to WorkSafe's decision to discontinue a prosecution went on to succeed in the Supreme Court.[101]

[94] See dictum in *Fox v Attorney-General* [2002] 3 NZLR 62 (CA) at [31].

[95] *Hallett v Attorney-General (No 2)* [1989] 2 NZLR 96 (HC) at 101; *Fox* (n 94) at [28]–[31].

[96] *Polynesian Spa Ltd v Osborne* [2005] NZAR 408 (HC) at [62], [68].

[97] *Hallett v Attorney-General* [1989] 2 NZLR 87 at 94.

[98] *Hallet (No 2)* (n 95) at 102; citing *R v Metropolitan Police Commissioner ex p Blackburn* [1968] 2 QB 118 (CA).

[99] *Polynesian Spa* (n 96) at [64]. See also *R v Director of Public Prosecutions Ex parte Kebilene* [2000] 2 AC 326.

[100] *Osborne v WorkSafe New Zealand* [2017] NZCA 11, [2017] 2 NZLR 513 at [27]–[53]. This point was not appealed.

[101] *Osborne v WorkSafe New Zealand* [2017] NZSC 175, [2018] 1 NZLR 447 at [72]–[73].

(2) Special Categories of Justiciability Limit

This section addresses two special categories of justiciability limit. One is the non-interference principle concerning Parliament: courts do not rule on the legislative process (section (a)). The other relates to the recent confirmation that tikanga Māori is a source of law. The courts have made it clear that their own role in relation to this source of law is limited (section (b)).

(a) Legislative Process is Non-Justiciable: The Non-Interference Principle

One special category that does still determine justiciability concerns the legislative process: courts have no business interfering in this. It is elementary that legislation cannot be challenged in court: Parliamentary sovereignty does not permit this. That extends to challenges to the validity of legislation on grounds of faulty process.[102] In addition, however, courts also will not entertain challenges to steps taken in the legislative process,[103] or challenges seeking to stop that process.[104] This is the principle of non-interference or comity. It flows from Parliamentary privilege as well as from Parliamentary sovereignty and is affirmed in the Parliamentary Privilege Act 2014.[105]

This non-interference principle extends to decisions taken by the executive government in preparation for introducing legislation. That is where it impacts on judicial review of executive government decisions. While the exclusion is categorical, there is room for argument as to how far this non-justiciability of pre-legislative decisions extends.

This issue has often arisen in challenges to Crown decisions on settlements of Treaty of Waitangi claims, given that such settlements are usually implemented by legislation that simply adopts the terms of the Deed of Settlement.[106] In *Ngāti Whātua Orakei*, the Supreme Court sounded 'a note of caution' about the reach of the non-interference principle.[107] For instance, the timing of the challenged decision may be more relevant than it has been treated in cases like *Milroy*.[108] The rationale for Parliamentary privilege is to protect free speech in the House of Representatives, suggesting a need for a fairly direct temporal link to what occurs in the House.[109]

The applicant iwi sought to challenge proposed settlements with other iwi that affected lands also claimed by the applicant. A strike-out application on grounds of non-justiciability failed for some of these claims. The crucial question in the Court's

[102] *British Railways Board v Pickin* [1974] AC 765 (HL); *Mangawaro Enterprises Ltd v A-G* [1994] 2 NZLR 451; *Ngati Apa Ki Te Waipounamou Trust v R* [2000] 2 NZLR 659.

[103] *Boscawen v Attorney-General* [2009] NZLR 229 (CA).

[104] *Te Runanga o Wharekauri o Rekohu Inc v Attorney-General* [1993] 2 NZLR 301 (CA) at 307–308; *Timaru District Council v The Minister of Local Government* [2023] NZHC 244 at [146]–[167].

[105] For an application, see *The Kiwi Party Inc v Attorney-General* [2020] NZCA 80, [2020] 2 NZLR 224 at [37]–[45].

[106] Eg *Te Runanga o Wharekauri o Rekohu* (n 104) at 308.

[107] *Ngāti Whātua Ōrākei Trust v Attorney-General* [2018] NZSC 84, [2019] 1 NZLR 116. For further discussion of this issue, see Claire Charters, '*Wakatū* in Peripheral Vision: Māori Rights-Based Judicial Review of the Executive and the Courts' Approach to the United Nations Declaration on the Rights of Indigenous Peoples' [2019] *New Zealand Law Review* 85.

[108] *Milroy v Attorney-General* [2005] NZAR 562 (CA).

[109] *Ngāti Whātua Ōrākei* (n 107) at [46]–[47].

view was whether the applicant was claiming justiciable rights, and whether the rights in issue extended beyond the specific rights affected by the legislative proposal.[110] Applying that approach, the Court re-instated four claims for declarations concerning rights of possible relevance beyond the settlement decisions at issue here (which were the decisions to be implemented by legislation).[111] For instance, claims to ahi kā and mana whenua[112] were relevant to the ongoing relationship between Ngāti Whātua Ōrakei and the Crown, and to any future settlements with other iwi that may not necessarily be implemented by legislation.

Similarly, in the earlier case of *Port Nicholson Block Settlement Trust*, the High Court dismissed an objection to a claim for declarations that a proposed settlement with another iwi was inconsistent with the plaintiff's settlement Deed and Act. The non-interference principle did not apply to issues concerning the interpretation of these instruments and rights under them.[113]

Some challenges in the Treaty settlement context will still fall foul of the non-interference principle. Both in *Ngāti Whātua Ōrakei* and subsequently in *Hata*, the courts declined to entertain challenges directly to the lawfulness of a proposed settlement.[114]

(b) Justiciability of Tikanga Māori (and Other Separate Normative Systems)

An issue that has come to the fore across various areas of law in recent years is the status and role of tikanga[115] in our legal system. In *Ellis*,[116] the Supreme Court affirmed a general recognition of tikanga as law in at least two senses. First, tikanga is recognised in the development of the common law where it is relevant.[117] Secondly, tikanga is a separate source of law that shapes and regulates the lives of Māori, independently of its place in state law.[118] Tikanga will continue to evolve, as Māori communities continue to apply and develop it. The common law will recognise tikanga as it stands at the time.[119]

The issue that is relevant to the discussion in this part concerns the courts' role in relation to tikanga. The Supreme Court in *Ellis* emphasised that this role is limited. Since tikanga is a system of law and custom in its own right, the courts have neither the mandate nor the expertise to declare the content of tikanga or to change it.[120] The guarantee of tino rangatiratanga in article two of te Tiriti is relevant here. Tino rangatiratanga includes the right of iwi and hapū to live by their tikanga. It also includes their authority to determine what is tika (right or correct) and to keep developing tikanga

[110] ibid at [34], [48]; see also at [38], [42].
[111] ibid at [50]–[66].
[112] Continued occupation and authority over land.
[113] *Port Nicholson Block Settlement Trust v Attorney-General* [2012] NZHC 3181 at [53]–[64].
[114] *Ngāti Whātua Ōrākei* (n 107) at [3], [65]–[67]; *Hata v Attorney-General* [2023] NZHC 1255 at [44], [50].
[115] Māori customary law.
[116] *Ellis v R* [2022] NZSC 114, [2022] 1 NZLR 239.
[117] ibid at [108]–[110], [171]–[174], [257]–[259].
[118] ibid at [107], [172], [267].
[119] ibid at [111], [123], [270]–[272].
[120] See esp ibid at [270]–[272] (Williams J). Also at [120], [123], [181].

as their own system of law. The courts' obligation is to recognise not only tikanga but also the authority that underpins it.[121]

The resulting limits of the courts' role in relation to tikanga are particularly relevant in the administrative law context. Issues about tikanga arise in administrative law at least where the challenge is to the decision of a Māori authority or of a state authority with a mandate to decide according to tikanga, and where the Crown's obligations to iwi and hapū turn in part on tikanga. Let us consider two cases of this nature in which the courts emphasised the limits of their role. We can note at the outset that the limits to the courts' role in relation to tikanga, unlike other justiciability constraints, have not generally led to claims being struck out.

Wairarapa Moana Ki Pouākani Inc v Mercury NZ Ltd concerned a preliminary determination by the Waitangi Tribunal – a statutory body with an implicit mandate to determine matters in part according to tikanga.[122] The Tribunal had indicated that it was open to making a resumption order (requiring the return of land held by State-Owned Enterprises to claimants) relating to land over which the claimants lacked mana whenua.[123] Cooke J had appeared to hold that this was contrary to tikanga – a surprising step to take. Williams J, writing for the Supreme Court on a leapfrog appeal, rejected that view of the relevant tikanga.[124]

Cooke J more likely understood the Tribunal's decision as asserting that it may disregard tikanga and ruled against that. On the Supreme Court's reading, however, the Tribunal was instead engaging in a nuanced and iterative evaluation of what was tika in the particular context.[125] The Tribunal was 'uniquely placed' to do this.[126] Even on this version of what went wrong in the High Court, it illustrates the pitfalls for courts engaging with tikanga: courts may not only misunderstand tikanga, but also may misunderstand the unfamiliar reasoning processes of tikanga practitioners.

In *Ngāti Whātua Ōrakei (No 4)*, the High Court took pains to avoid overstepping the limits of the judicial role.[127] Before the Court was a dispute between several iwi about mana whenua to the lands comprising central Auckland. The Court was asked to declare the position at tikanga, which was relevant to settlements the iwi was seeking with the Crown. The Court heard extensive evidence from pūkenga (experts in tikanga) and other witnesses. However, it declined to resolve the dispute. It merely recorded the evidence and issued declarations of the position according to each iwi's different tikanga.[128] It also offered assistance to facilitate tikanga-based resolution processes, and to record the outcome of any such process by a declaration.[129]

[121] See Joseph Williams 'Lex Aotearoa: An Heroic Attempt to Map the Māori Dimension in Modern New Zealand Law' (2013) 21 *Waikato Law Review* 1 at 9. This was adopted in *Ellis* (n 116) at [98] (fn 139), [126], [257]; *Trans-Tasman Resources v Taranaki-Whanganui Conservation Board* [2021] NZSC 127, [2021] 1 NZLR 801 at [154] fn 287.

[122] *Wairarapa Moana Ki Pouākani Inc v Mercury NZ Ltd* [2022] NZSC 142, [2022] 1 NZLR 767.

[123] Authority over land.

[124] *Wairarapa Moana* (n 122) at [74]–[84].

[125] ibid at [77]–[85], fn 80.

[126] ibid at [84].

[127] *Ngāti Whātua Ōrākei Trust v Attorney-General (No 4)* [2022] NZHC 843, [2022] 2 NZLR 601.

[128] The main judgment *(No 4)* proposed these declarations and sought further submissions on them. The declarations were then made in *Ngāti Whātua Ōrākei Trust v Attorney-General (No 5)* [2023] NZHC 74.

[129] *Ngāti Whātua Ōrākei (No 4)* (n 127) at [55].

The Court explained why any more definitive declarations would be beyond the limits to the judicial role.[130] Courts paying due regard to tikanga can sometimes play a role: they can, for instance, find and apply undisputed tikanga. Where tikanga is disputed, however, it is for tikanga processes – not for the courts – to resolve that dispute. That is not only because courts lack both expertise and authority to do this, but also because tikanga governs process as well as substance, and determination by a state court is unlikely to be a tika process. Resolution of the differences between the parties here, if desired, is better explored on a marae than in a court. The Court did not rule out that where tikanga-based resolution of disputes about tikanga is not feasible at all, recourse to courts may be appropriate, and may be the modern alternative to resolution by battle. However, the Court was not persuaded that this stage had been reached in this case.

The Court in *Ngāti Whātua Ōrakei (No 4)* could be criticised for failing to fulfil its function of resolving a dispute brought before it. However, if we accept that there are limits to the role of courts in relation to tikanga, the mere fact that one party wants a dispute about tikanga to be resolved by a court is not a sufficient reason for the court to do so.

Arguably, the only situations in which a court is justified in making findings on tikanga are where the tikanga is undisputed; where both parties agree that the court should resolve the dispute; or where resolution is necessary and tikanga-based resolution is truly not possible. Whether the third situation has been reached in a particular case is plainly a difficult judgment to make. There are several examples of the first situation: cases in which courts have relied on undisputed evidence of tikanga in judicial review challenges.[131]

A related point is that there are other separate systems of law or other norms that, unlike tikanga, have not been recognised as part of the law of New Zealand. In relation to these, the role of courts is more limited still. Disputes as to religious doctrine, for instance, will generally not be entertained: they are non-justiciable.[132] Judicial review is available to challenge decisions by religious associations only where the issues concern property or other civil rights or obligations recognised by the general law.

B. Further Related Common Law Limits on Access to Review

In addition to limits arising from justiciability concerns and the public nature requirement, there are at least two further common law limits to the availability of judicial review. These may be considered to be broadly related to justiciability limits but are less

[130] ibid at [29]–[38], [361]–[379], [458]–[464].

[131] See, eg, *Sweeney v The Prison Manager, Spring Hill Corrections Facility* [2021] NZHC 181, [2021] 2 NZLR 27 at [71], [74]–[77]; *Te Pou Matakana Ltd v Attorney-General (No 2)* [2021] NZHC 3319, [2022] 2 NZLR 178 at [108]–[112].

[132] See *Khyentse v Hope* [2007] 1 NZLR 645 (CA) at [36], [37], [50]; *R v Chief Rabbi of the United Hebrew Congregations of Great Britain and the Commonwealth, Ex parte Wachmann* [1992] 1 WLR 1036 (QBD) at 1042–43.

often at issue. They are limits to who has standing to bring judicial review proceedings (section (1)) and limits to seeking judicial review of preliminary determinations or of mere reports (section (2)).

(1) Standing

One requirement limits *who* may bring a judicial review application: only those who have standing may do so. At its most restrictive, standing can be limited to parties whose legal rights or obligations are determined by the impugned measure or decision. Historically, this was the test for *some* of the remedies that are now available through judicial review.

However, standing has been greatly liberalised since the 1980s, following the approach taken around the same time by the English courts. It is no longer necessary to show that an individual right, obligation or even interest is affected by the impugned decision. Individuals or groups can seek judicial review representing the public interest at large or the interests of groups or categories of people.[133]

This approach was established in *Environmental Defence Society v South Pacific Aluminium (No 3)*, where a conservation group was held to have standing to challenge a decision to apply the fast track planning procedure under the National Development Act 1979 to a proposed new smelter.[134] The Court of Appeal cited with approval an influential dictum of Lord Diplock in the *Fleet Street Casuals* case:[135] it would be a 'grave lacuna' in the law if concerned citizens could not seek judicial review of an unlawful exercise of public power to 'vindicate the rule of law'. This was affirmed recently in *Moncrief-Spittle v Regional Facilities Auckland*, where members of the public with a bona fide interest in free speech rights had standing to challenge a decision to cancel an event to which they held tickets, featuring two controversial speakers.[136]

To the extent that standing is still considered, it is addressed in the context of the merits: the applicant's interest is assessed in relation to what is being challenged and on what grounds. Striking out a claim without consideration of the merits would be unusual.[137] But standing has been liberalised to such an extent that in a great proportion of cases where it might once have been an issue, standing is no longer even addressed. For instance, there was no mention of standing limits in *Curtis*, a challenge to the decision by the Minister of Defence to axe the armed wing of the air force.[138]

[133] Peter Cane, 'Standing Up for the Public' [1995] *Public Law* 276 identified distinct categories of liberal standing, but courts have not tended to distinguish between these.

[134] *Environmental Defence Society Inc v South Pacific Aluminium Ltd (No 3)* [1981] 1 NZLR 216 (CA) (*EDS*).

[135] *R v Inland Revenue Commissioners ex p National Federation of Self-Employed and Small Businesses Ltd* [1982] AC 617 (HL) (*Fleet Street Casuals*) at 644; cited in *EDS* (n 134) at 220–21.

[136] *Moncrief-Spittle v Regional Facilities Auckland Ltd* [2021] NZCA 142, [2021] 2 NZLR 795 at [130]–[132]. The Supreme Court in dismissing an appeal did not comment on standing.

[137] *Smith v Attorney-General* [2017] NZHC 1647, [2017] NZAR 1094 at [2]; *Fleet Street Casuals* (n 135) at 631, 636.

[138] *Curtis v Minister of Defence* [2002] 2 NZLR 744 (CA); discussed above at n 59.

However, some potential limits do remain: as Palmer J has put it, while standing has been significantly relaxed, 'it is not so relaxed as to be horizontal'.[139] In the UK, Joanna Bell has reported a resurgence in case law on standing, including some cases in which standing was denied.[140] There does not seem to be a similar increase in cases in Aotearoa NZ. But standing has been declined in some exceptional contexts.

Bell draws a useful distinction between measures 'targeted' at a particular individual and 'non-targeted' ones that operate at a more general level.[141] The liberal approach to standing usually facilitates challenges to non-targeted measures – such as, for instance, in *Curtis*. In addition, it also applies in challenges to resource management decisions such as the *Environmental Defence Society* case. While those may be targeted at an applicant for consent, our law treats a broad range of other affected interests as relevant, and, in that sense, such decisions are similar to non-targeted decisions.

The rare occasions on which New Zealand courts have denied standing have involved challenges by third parties to targeted decisions that are favourable to the targeted individual: in particular, a grant of parole in *McVicar*[142] and a certificate authorising an abortion in *Wall v Livingston*.[143] Since a parole decision turned on individual circumstances, it was held not to engage the kind of public interest that gives rise to liberal standing in other cases.[144] The abortion legislation was held to commit the decision to the medical judgment of the certifying consultants.[145] In both cases, the courts further considered that the statutory scheme indicated strict limits on the types of persons who were to have a role in the relevant decision-making. Granting public interest standing to a third party would cut across that scheme.[146]

In contrast, challenges in the abortion context have been entertained where the challenged measure was a non-targeted one.[147] In the parole context, challenges even to targeted decisions have been entertained provided the applicant was representing a relevant interest.[148]

United Kingdom governments have twice considered reining in liberal standing rules, but on both occasions have accepted advice not to do so.[149] In New Zealand, the topic has not to date attracted this kind of political attention.

[139] *Smith* (n 137) at [2].

[140] Joanna Bell, 'The Resurgence of Standing in Judicial Review' (2024) 44 *Oxford Journal of Legal Studies* 313.

[141] ibid.

[142] *McVicar v New Zealand Parole Board* [2015] NZHC 2153, (2015) 23 PRNZ 21.

[143] *Wall v Livingston* [1982] 1 NZLR 734 (CA).

[144] *McVicar* (n 142) at [47], [50].

[145] *Wall v Livingston* (n 143) at 739.

[146] *McVicar* (n 142) at [48]; *Wall v Livingston* (n 143) at 740.

[147] See, eg, *Right to Life New Zealand Inc v Abortion Supervisory Committee* [2012] NZSC 68, [2012] 3 NZLR 762.

[148] See, eg, *Whanganui District Council v New Zealand Parole Board* [2012] NZHC 2248 at [79]–[84]; *Gilmour v Chief Executive of the Department of Corrections* [2017] NZCA 250.

[149] See Ministry of Justice, *Judicial Review: Proposals for Further Reform* (Cm 8703, September 2013) Part 4; Lord Edward Faulks QC, *The Independent Review of Administrative Law* (CP 407, March 2021) at [4.98].

(2) Preliminary Decisions and Mere Reports

A further question is whether the respondent has done something that qualifies as a decision for the purposes of judicial review. The question arises in relation to preliminary decisions and also mere reports.

Concerning preliminary decisions, the Judicial Review Procedure Act 2016 expressly contemplates review of 'proposed' decisions.[150] However, the Act merely regulates the procedure for judicial review: the availability of review remains a question for the common law.[151] Courts sometimes appear not to appreciate this,[152] but it was affirmed by the Court of Appeal in *Singh*.[153]

If a court takes the view that judicial review is premature, it may exercise the discretion to refuse relief,[154] or it may strike out the application for judicial review at the outset.[155] New Zealand courts are generally very slow to do so. Yet the much-cited decision in *Singh* claims that review of preliminary decisions is exceptional. The position on this is therefore a little uncertain.

The Court of Appeal in *Singh* discussed the approach to the reviewability of preliminary decisions in detail,[156] and the decision is usually cited as the leading case. It held that courts will not usually intervene where the powers that have been exercised at the preliminary stage are unlikely to be influential in the final decision, and where the party who is subject to the decision still has adequate opportunity to address the issues raised.[157] There were 'sound policy reasons' for denying review in such cases, where it is 'most unlikely that the subject's rights will be adversely affected'. Moreover, where there are 'adequate opportunities for appeal or review of the decision ultimately reached', it is not in the public interest to 'trouble' those charged with conducting the preliminary investigation and the courts with applications for judicial review at that preliminary stage.[158] This last point reflects what in England has recently been discussed as a principle of proportionate dispute resolution.[159]

Two instances of judicial review applications being struck out on this basis are *Singh* itself[160] and *Marlborough Aquaculture*.[161] Both cases involved the defendant authority disclosing preliminary views or proposed decisions to the affected party for the purpose of giving that party the opportunity to comment. Crucially, the

[150] The Judicial Review Procedure Act 2016, ss 4 and 11; previously the Judicature Amendment Act 1972, s 4(1).

[151] See Part D.

[152] See, eg, *Zaoui v Attorney-General (No 2)* [2005] 1 NZLR 690 (CA) at [106]–[107].

[153] *Singh v Chief Executive of the Ministry of Business, Innovation and Employment* [2014] NZCA 220, [2014] 3 NZLR 23 at [31]. See also (more clearly) *Mercury NZ Ltd v The Waitangi Tribunal* [2021] NZHC 654 at [19]–[20].

[154] *Zaoui* (n 152).

[155] *Singh* (n 153).

[156] ibid at [38]–[40].

[157] For an application of this point, see also *Trustpower Ltd (formerly Bay Energy) v Electricity Authority* [2016] NZHC 2914, [2016] 2 NZLR 253.

[158] On this last point, see also *Marlborough Aquaculture Ltd v Chief Executive, Ministry of Fisheries* [2003] NZAR 362 (HC) at [21].

[159] *R (Cart) v Upper Tribunal (Public Law Project Intervening)* [2011] UKSC 28, [2012] 1 AC 663 at [51].

[160] *Singh* (n 153).

[161] *Marlborough Aquaculture* (n 158).

proposed decision was explicitly subject to revision in light of further comment and information received in response from the affected party.[162] The courts declined to allow the affected parties to take advantage of such a process by challenging the preliminary decision. In *Marlborough Aquaculture*, this was the main concern: allowing review of such a communication would discourage this type of very beneficial hearing process.[163]

In *Singh*, the Court touched on this procedural fairness point.[164] However, its focus was on the basic test: whether the challenged decision is likely to be influential in the final decision. The letters under challenge in this case were part of an investigation by officials. This was the first of three stages in a statutory process that culminated in a decision by the Minister, and it was clear that the officials remained willing to correct the record. 'Nothing had been done up to that point that could have been influential in a later decision by the Minister.'[165] This basic test for denying review was also met in *A Lawyer v New Zealand Law Society*, where the Court of Appeal exercised its discretion against granting review. The Court's reasoning in this case, however, appears to misunderstand the test.[166]

Turning to cases in which courts did or would intervene, there are a number of situations in which the preliminary decision *is* likely to be influential in the final decision. First, the outcome in a case like *Singh* and *Marlborough Aquaculture* would likely be different if there was bias or predetermination affecting the preliminary investigation stage. In *Marlborough Aquaculture*, the Court acknowledged that there may be situations where the decision-making procedure 'has seriously gone off the rails at an early stage'. It gave 'overt bias' as an 'obvious example'.[167] This would meet the *Singh* criterion that what happened at the preliminary stage *was* likely to be influential in the final decision.

In *Singh* itself, there was an allegation of pre-determination at the investigation stage, but this was dismissed on the facts. The somewhat conclusory terms of the first of two letters sent to Mr Singh did provide some foundation for the allegation. However, the concern was assuaged by the second letter. This made it clear that the officials remained willing to correct the record if Mr Singh supplied further evidence to show that a document he had previously supplied was wrong. The letter offered adequate time for Mr Singh to obtain such evidence.[168]

A second situation where the *Singh* test for intervention may be made out is where the subject of challenge is a formal recommendation to the decision-maker. In *Zhao v New Zealand Law Society*, for example, the challenge was to a recommendation made by interviewers appointed by the Law Society as part of considering Mr Zhao's application to practice on his own account. The High Court found such recommendations

[162] *Singh* (n 153) at [47]; *Marlborough Aquaculture* (n 158) at [23].

[163] *Marlborough Aquaculture* (n 158) at [21].

[164] *Singh* (n 153) at [46].

[165] ibid at [50], and see at [42], [45].

[166] *A Lawyer v New Zealand Law Society* [2021] NZCA 47, [2021] NZAR 138 at [79]–[151]. The Supreme Court declined leave to appeal: *A Lawyer v New Zealand Law Society* [2021] NZSC 75.

[167] *Marlborough Aquaculture* (n 158) at [15].

[168] *Singh* (n 153) at [6]–[7], [9], [26], [47], [51].

to be reviewable, since they are given significant weight by the Law Society in the final decision.[169]

Thirdly, review is also likely to be available in relation to formal interlocutory rulings by the designated decision-making body itself. In *Zaoui (No 2)*, the Inspector-General was carrying out the first ever statutory review of a security risk certificate which, if upheld on this review, would lead to Mr Zaoui's deportation despite his refugee status. To resolve disputes between the parties concerning the applicable law and procedure, the Inspector-General issued what was termed an interlocutory decision. The Court of Appeal dismissed a prematurity objection. Whether or not the ruling was, in fact, a formal interlocutory determination, it was clearly likely to be influential in the Inspector-General's final decision.[170] I will return to this case below to identify further features that favoured review of the interlocutory decision.

Fourthly, even preliminary decisions that explicitly remain subject to revision have been held reviewable where other factors are sufficiently strong. In *Mercury NZ Ltd v The Waitangi Tribunal*, the High Court entertained judicial review of preliminary determinations of the Waitangi Tribunal, even though the determinations expressly remained subject to revision as part of an 'iterative process' of engaging with claimants.[171] The factors supporting review were that the preliminary determinations were made by the designated decision-maker itself; the determinations really were final on the specific points addressed; and there was a lack of authority to guide the exercise of the power at issue.[172] The reviewability point was no longer at issue in the appeal to the Supreme Court, reported as *Wairarapa Moana Ki Pouākani Inc v Mercury*. That Court relied on the determinations' lack of finality in disposing of a different point,[173] but did not comment on the availability of review in light of this.

In all these situations where courts have entertained review of preliminary steps, it could be argued that judicial review should wait until the final decision has been made. The grounds of review at that stage could then still include concerns about earlier stages of the process, along with any other grounds available at that point. Such an approach would be supported by the policy reasons noted in *Singh*: it would avoid burdening decision-makers and courts with challenges at multiple stages in a decision-making process.[174]

However, the New Zealand courts have usually rejected this approach in cases where the preliminary determination was likely to be influential in the final decision, at least where both the interests at stake and the alleged errors are sufficiently significant. In *Zaoui*, for instance, the Inspector-General's interlocutory rulings addressed central issues of natural justice and the relevance of international human rights law in the review of the security risk certificate against Mr Zaoui. The Court of Appeal

[169] *Zhao v New Zealand Law Society* [2012] NZHC 2169, [2012] NZAR 894.

[170] *Zaoui* (n 152) at [12]–[13], [19], [186]; and see more generally at [89], [106]–[107], [183]–[187]. This aspect of the decision was not subject to the appeal in *Zaoui v Attorney-General (No 2)* [2005] NZSC 38, [2006] 1 NZLR 289.

[171] *Mercury NZ v Waitangi Tribunal* (n 153) at [12]–[14], [17]–[18], [32].

[172] ibid at [22]–[32]. See also *New Zealand Air Line Pilots' Association Industrial Union of Workers Inc v Director of Civil Aviation* [2017] NZCA 27 at [44]–[45] (there was an appeal but not on this point).

[173] *Wairarapa Moana Ki Pouākani Inc v Mercury NZ Ltd* [2022] NZSC 142 at [58]–[59], and see at [9], [49]–[50], [56].

[174] *Singh* (n 153) at [39]. The point is acknowledged, but considered outweighed, in *Zaoui* (n 152) at [185]; *Mercury NZ v Waitangi Tribunal* (n 153) at [29].

held that these issues needed to be addressed at the preliminary stage due to a number of features. This was the first such review, and the issues raised were important to 'the structure and scope of the inquiry'. Without 'judicial guidance', 'the whole process … may miscarry'. Furthermore, the consequences would be 'grave', as Mr Zaoui's liberty and convention rights were at stake.[175]

Clearly, *Zaoui* was a strong case for review at the preliminary stage.[176] Review at that stage has, however, also been entertained in other cases where the factors supporting it were not as strong.[177] Qualifying the suggestion in *Singh*, therefore, such review is not entirely 'exceptional'.[178]

Finally, issues about preliminary decisions are also addressed in a separate line of cases, concerning whether the right to a hearing applies at that stage. The test for that purpose is the extent to which the preliminary decision has real consequences for those affected, rather than whether the decision is likely to be influential in the final decision.[179] For instance, a decision to suspend a public servant without pay triggers a right to some form of a hearing on that basis, despite being preliminary to a hearing of disciplinary charges.[180] The availability of review may not be expressly addressed in such cases. If a right to a hearing applies, however, judicial review must be available to claim this right.

What, then, of mere reports? Reports of bodies whose findings do not determine any rights or liabilities, such as commissions of inquiry, used to be subject to judicial review only on a very limited basis.[181] But *Peters v Davison* established that such reports are reviewable on all grounds, where the error 'affects a matter of substance relating to a finding on one of the terms of reference'.[182] This was generally due to the public interest in 'ensuring the integrity of the essential findings of a report in its answers to the terms of reference'. The Court further acknowledged that where there is damage to the reputation of persons concerned in the inquiry, this is as an even stronger reason for intervention.[183] A right to a hearing for the affected person in that situation was one of the longer-standing available grounds – another example of reviewability flowing from the application of this right.[184] Furthermore, preliminary determinations in this context are also, in principle, reviewable.[185]

The question whether the respondent has done something that qualifies as a reviewable decision arose in a more unusual form in *Ririnui v Landcorp*.[186] The applicant iwi challenged not only a decision by Landcorp to sell certain land, but also the decision of relevant Ministers not to intervene on the applicant's behalf. The Ministers' role involved a failure to act, and there was no relevant statutory power that might generate

[175] *Zaoui* (n 152) at [19], [107], [184], [186].
[176] In some respects, *Mercury NZ* (n 153) may have been a similarly strong case: see esp at [30].
[177] See, eg, *Zhao* (n 169).
[178] *Singh* (n 153) at [40]; such a restriction is rejected in *Mercury NZ* (n 153) at [21].
[179] See Ch 4.B(3)(c).
[180] *Birss v Secretary for Justice* [1984] 1 NZLR 513 (CA).
[181] See *Re Erebus Royal Commission; Air New Zealand Ltd v Mahon* [1983] NZLR 662 (PC).
[182] *Peters v Davison* [1999] 2 NZLR 164 (CA) at 189.
[183] ibid at 185, 189. For review on both procedural and other grounds, see also, eg, *Carroll v Auckland Coroner's Court* [2013] NZHC 906, [2013] NZAR 650.
[184] See *Re Erebus* (n 181).
[185] *Peters v Davison* (n 182) at 183 (obiter).
[186] *Ririnui v Landcorp Farming Ltd* [2016] NZSC 62, [2016] 1 NZLR 1056.

a duty to consider acting. However, the Supreme Court held this was a reviewable exercise of power, taking into account that the Ministers did intervene on behalf of another iwi and were free in law to do so.[187]

C. Public Nature

The requirement that the decision and decision-maker be of a sufficiently public nature is the second main common law limit on the availability of judicial review. There is a large and complex body of case law on drawing this line. The issue arises in challenges to decisions of state-owned enterprises and other corporatised or privatised public entities, and of private associations exercising powers over their members or those who wish to join. It also arises in challenges to contracting and other commercial decisions by public authorities.

This issue is of a different nature from justiciability. The issue is not whether courts have a role to play at all. If the body and the decision are not sufficiently public to attract the principles of judicial review, they are still subject to private law constraints and often also to statutes imposing regulation that is enforceable by the courts. The public nature test therefore determines not whether the body and the decision are subject to judicial proceedings, but rather whether the public law constraints comprised in the grounds of judicial review apply *in addition* to all these other constraints.

Furthermore, the issue is also not necessarily about the availability of judicial review proceedings. Even if the conclusion is reached that at least some of the special public law constraints of judicial review should apply, then this does not always result in the courts entertaining judicial review proceedings. Instead, in some cases, courts will entertain proceedings in contract and will imply public law constraints into the relevant contract as implied terms.

This public nature test is usually discussed alongside justiciability as the second main common law limit on judicial review, and that is one appropriate place to think about it. However, as just explained, the test also concerns the interplay between public and private law. For that reason, in this book a chapter discussing this test appears instead in part IV on the relationship between public and private law.

Next, we turn to a question concerning the effect of statutes that is particularly relevant to the common law public nature test.

D. The Judicial Review Procedure Act and its Predecessor

So far, this chapter has been devoted to common law principles determining the availability of judicial review. It is time now to turn to the question whether access to judicial

[187] ibid at [38], [86], [91(a)–(b)], [98(d)].

review is also governed by statute. This Part deals with the first of two questions in this regard.

Judicial review in New Zealand is today most commonly brought under the Judicial Review Procedure Act 2016 (JRPA). Despite its date, this is not new legislation: it is the successor of the Judicature Amendment Act 1972 (JAA), and is expressly intended to merely re-enact that old Act in clearer terms and with a clearer structure, but without changing its effect.[188] I will refer to JAA and JRPA collectively as 'the Act'.

The important point about the Act for the purposes of this chapter is that it does not codify the law of judicial review. It is concerned solely with the procedure and remedies for judicial review, not with the grounds of review nor generally with its availability. The purpose was to simplify the procedure and improve the remedial options.

At common law, there were at least five distinct remedies, which could be grouped into prerogative writs and equitable remedies. These can still be sought by the procedure set out in part 30 of the High Court Rules. Each of these had their own detailed procedural rules and rules as to their availability, presenting endless pitfalls for applicants: a case could fail just because counsel had chosen the wrong remedy.

Very little tends to be said about these specific remedies today, because since 1972 we have had provision in the Act for one single 'application for judicial review',[189] with one set of procedural rules, that gives access to orders in the nature of any of those remedies.[190] The Act has been described as the 'master key' that opens all doors.[191] In addition, it also includes some useful remedial innovations (further adding to flexibility). All these remedial options are discussed in Chapter 10.

However, the Act ended up creating a fresh pair of issues, which are addressed here in turn. The first can be disposed of quickly (section (1)), but the second has caused much confusion (section (2)).

(1) What is the Effect of the Act on Judicial Review of Non-statutory Powers?

First, by virtue of the definition of 'application for judicial review' and 'applicant', now in section 4 of the JRPA,[192] the remedy set out in sections 8 and 16[193] applies only to statutory powers. As we saw earlier in this chapter, at common law the availability of judicial review has long since expanded beyond statutory powers.[194] The Act adopted the traditional restrictive legal position – except, as we will see, that the statutory definition of statutory power is a significantly expanded one in one respect. As a result, the gateway into the Act is narrower than reviewability at common law has become since 1972. The first issue therefore is what happens to judicial review of non-statutory powers such as, in particular, prerogative powers.

[188] Judicial Review Procedure Act 2016, s 3.
[189] Judicature Amendment Act 1972, s 4; now Judicial Review Procedure Act 2016, s 8.
[190] ibid, s 4; now Judicial Review Procedure Act 2016, s 16.
[191] *New Zealand Engineering, Coachbuilding, Aircraft, Motor and Related Trades Industrial Union of Workers v Court of Arbitration* [1973] 2 NZLR 534 (SC) at 535.
[192] Previously JAA 1972, s 3.
[193] Previously ibid, s 4.
[194] See also Ch 11 concerning contractual powers.

The answer has never really been doubted. Judicial review of non-statutory powers is available despite the Act. The limited terms of the Act merely mean that the Act's procedure for review is not available for review of such powers. As we have seen, however, the Act is not the only procedural route into judicial review. The old common law remedies are available by means of the procedure in the High Court Rules, part 30. That route is available for non-statutory powers where the common law tests of reviewability are met. This point was confirmed by the Privy Council in *Mercury Energy*, accepting a concession to this effect.[195]

(2) Does the Act Extend Reviewability of Private Bodies and Decisions Beyond the Common Law Limits?

On the second question, the Act has caused a lot of confusion. The definition of 'statutory power', now in section 5 of the JRPA,[196] is very broad in one odd respect: it includes powers conferred by or under 'the constitution or … rules … of any body corporate'. It is important also to take account of the types of powers listed in subsection (2), which does narrow the definition. Even so, this definition extends to powers that would not be reviewable at common law.

The second issue therefore is whether this expanded definition entails a great extension of the availability of judicial review under the Act, beyond what would be available at common law. In particular, is review under the Act available for decisions of private incorporated bodies (societies or companies) that do not meet the common law 'public nature' test?

'No' is the better answer. There are opposing views on this to be found in the case law and commentary, but the alternative view seems to be due to inattention. The better view is that the Act is concerned solely with procedures and remedial options, as already noted. On this view, the expanded 'statutory power' test merely represents the gateway to the Act's simplified procedures. Judicial review is not available simply by virtue of meeting that test: it is always necessary to clear the hurdle of the common law tests as well.

We should reject the alternative view, found in some sources. On that view, the Act has jurisdiction-conferring effect: judicial review is available in *all* cases in which the test in section 5 of the JRPA is made out, *regardless* of whether the common law test are also made out. Cases adopting that view have allowed judicial review to be used to challenge the exercise of powers conferred by or under the constitutions or rules of commercial companies, incorporated societies, unit titles bodies corporate, and any other incorporated bodies – regardless of whether there was anything public about these bodies or their decisions in terms of their nature or impact.

Instances of courts unreflectively adopting this alternative view include the decision of a five-judge Court of Appeal in *Electoral Commission v Cameron*, finding that the Advertising Standards Complaints Board – an unincorporated board established

[195] *Mercury Energy Ltd v Electricity Corporation of New Zealand Ltd* [1994] 2 NZLR 385 (PC) at 388.
[196] Previously JAA, s 3.

by an incorporated society – was amenable to judicial review. The Court noted that this could arise either from the fact that the Board exercised a public function (one of the relevant common law tests) or from the 'more direct' statutory route.[197] The law on unincorporated societies has been particularly affected by this confusion.[198]

The short point about this alternative jurisdiction-conferring view is that it must be wrong. Mike Taggart described it as a 'fallacy'.[199] The provisions of the Act represent a trap for the unwary. That was particularly true of the old JAA that was less obviously concerned with procedure than the JRPA. The alternative view amounts to falling into that trap. It is easy to conclude that one needs to look no further on seeing that Act regulates judicial review. Even the JRPA can give that impression. It provides in sections 4, 8 and 16 that an application for judicial review is available to challenge exercises of statutory power, defined in section 5. However, the assumption that the common law tests do not apply because they are not expressly saved or referred to is wrong.

The vast majority of cases where the point is addressed more explicitly support the view that the Act has purely procedural effect. These include the Court of Appeal decisions in *Daemar v Gilliand*[200] and in *Hopper*.[201] Dean Knight has provided comprehensive reasons for understanding the Act as having purely procedural effect.[202] These include the following three.

First, a closer reading of section 16 of the JRPA reveals that it only makes available the relief that the applicant would be entitled to in proceedings for one of the common law remedies. The applicant would be entitled to no such relief in a case that does not meet the common law tests of justiciability and public nature, and hence s 16 calls for application of those tests. That was the view taken by Cooke J in *Daemar v Gilliand*.[203]

Secondly, the Act's legislative history makes it clear that there was no intention to change the substance of the law of judicial review: the intention was simply to provide a simplified procedure. As already noted, the JRPA now makes that point in its very title: it is the Judicial Review *Procedure* Act.

Finally, the sheer breadth of the availability of judicial review in relation to purely private decision-making entailed by the alternative jurisdiction-conferring view would represent a very significant change to the substance of judicial review.

[197] *Electoral Commission v Cameron* [1997] 2 NZLR 421 (CA) at 429. See also Velich *v Body Corporate No 164 980* (2005) NZCPR 143 (CA) at [45]–[46]; *Budget Rent A Car Ltd v Auckland Regional Authority* [1985] 2 NZLR 414 (CA) at 418; *New Zealand Stock Exchange v Listed Companies Association Ltd* [1984] 1 NZLR 699 (CA) at 706–07.

[198] See Ch 11.B(4).

[199] Michael Taggart, 'Administrative Law' [2006] *New Zealand Law Review* 75 at 99.

[200] *Daemar v Gilliand* [1981] 1 NZLR 61 (CA) 63–64.

[201] *Hopper v North Shore Aero Club* [2007] NZAR 354 (CA) at [9]. See also, eg, *Sweeney v The Prison Manager, Spring Hill Corrections Facility* [2021] NZHC 181, [2021] 2 NZLR 27 at [47]; *Falun Dafa Association of New Zealand Inc v Auckland Children's Christmas Parade Trust Board* [2009] NZAR 122 (HC) at [24]; *O'Regan v Lousich: Proprietors of Mawhera v Maori Land Court* [1995] 2 NZLR 620 (HC).

[202] Dean Knight, 'Privately Public' (2013) 24 *Public Law Review* 108; see also Marcelo B Rodriguez Ferrere, 'The Inherent Jurisdiction and its Limits' (2013) 13 *Otago Law Review* 107; Michael Taggart, 'State-Owned Enterprises and Social Responsibility: A Contradiction in Terms?' [1993] *NZ Recent Law Review* 343 at 355–56.

[203] *Daemar v Gilliand* (n 200) at 63–64; see also *McGechan on Procedure* (Brookers Online).

E. Privative Clauses

Let us turn to the second of the issues concerning statutes. In addition to the several common law restrictions, some empowering statutes include provisions purporting to exclude or restrict access to judicial review. These are known as privative or ouster clauses. The question is whether courts give effect to such clauses by striking out judicial review applications.

There are two parts to the answer. First, on the orthodox approach, adopted from the United Kingdom, courts effectively refuse to give any effect to privative clauses. Secondly, however, in Aotearoa New Zealand this approach now generally applies only to privative clauses that purport to oust judicial review entirely. I call these full privative clauses. A different approach applies to clauses that merely restrict access to judicial review, which I call partial privative clauses. The courts give effect to partial privative clauses on certain conditions. The exact parameters of when courts will do this remain unsettled and uncertain.

Section (1) of this Part outlines the orthodox approach to full privative clauses. Section (2) identifies two possible qualifications to that approach. Section (3) explores the effect given to partial privative clauses in detail.

(1) Orthodox *Bulk Gas* Approach

The orthodox approach involves effectively disregarding full privative clauses. Ever since the landmark *Bulk Gas Users Group* decision,[204] following *Anisminic Ltd v Foreign Compensation Commission* on this point,[205] courts have invoked a strong interpretive presumption that Parliament could not have intended to exclude judicial review: such an intention would need to be expressed extremely clearly.[206] The Supreme Court in *Fitzgerald* acknowledged that the courts' interpretations of these clauses 'have arguably cut across the apparent legislative purpose, at least on occasion'.[207]

The reasons that courts give for this strong presumption are constitutional and doctrinal. First, it is the constitutional role of the courts to interpret the law and, in particular, to enforce the limits on public powers.[208] This argument amounts to a very strong application of the principle of legality: legislation will not be read as abrogating the right of access to the courts unless it says so exceptionally clearly.[209] In several more recent cases, courts have considered this position to be further reinforced by the New Zealand Bill of Rights Act 1990. Section 27(2) affirms the right to apply for

[204] *Bulk Gas Users Group v Attorney-General* [1983] NZLR 129 (CA).

[205] *Anisminic Ltd v Foreign Compensation Commission* [1969] 2 AC 147 (HL) at 169–71, 207–12.

[206] *Bulk Gas* (n 204) at 133, 136; *H (SC 52/2018) v Refugee and Protection Officer* [2019] NZSC 13, [2019] 1 NZLR 433 at [63]; *R (Privacy International) v Investigatory Powers Tribunal* [2019] UKSC 22, [2020] AC 491 at [37].

[207] *Fitzgerald v R* [2021] NZSC 131, [2021] 1 NZLR 551 at [209].

[208] *Bulk Gas* (n 204) at 133; *Anisminic* (n 205) at 207–08.

[209] *Fitzgerald* (n 207) at [209]; *Privacy International* (n 206) at [100]. See Ch 6.C further on this principle.

judicial review, and section 6 requires statutes to be given a meaning consistent with that right if such a meaning is available.[210]

Secondly, the Court in *Bulk Gas* harked back to an old-fashioned doctrine about jurisdiction.[211] According to *Bulk Gas*, any defect in a decision that gives rise to a ground of review takes the decision-maker outside its jurisdiction. Such a decision is a 'nullity' and cannot be protected by the privative clause. It may be open to Parliament to confer authority on an administrative decision-maker to 'determine questions of law conclusively', but there is a strong presumption against it.[212]

In light of this reasoning, it is doubtful whether the wording of a privative clause purporting to exclude judicial review entirely would ever be found sufficiently clear to be given effect.[213] In the United Kingdom, these doubts culminated in an obiter dictum by a plurality of the Supreme Court in *R (Privacy International) v Investigatory Powers Tribunal*, affirming that any privative clause that offends the rule of law should not be given effect.[214]

There is room for debate as to whether the *Bulk Gas* approach goes too far in disregarding privative clauses entirely. It is convenient to leave that for discussion in Chapter 9.

(2) Two Possible Qualifications

There are two possible qualifications to the above account of the law that have not been widely noted. Neither of these casts any real doubt on the established understanding, but we should note them for completeness.

First, strictly speaking, there may not be binding authority in New Zealand for disregarding full and unqualified privative clauses. The United Kingdom does have such authority. The clause in *Anisminic* was in unqualified terms, and the clause in *Privacy International* went so far as to expressly protect 'decisions as to whether they have jurisdiction'. Both were disregarded. In New Zealand, however, no such clause has come before the courts (with one exception that we will come to).

On closer examination it turns out that the privative clauses at issue in *Bulk Gas* and all other leading New Zealand cases all included the proviso 'except on the ground of lack of jurisdiction' or similar words.[215] Clearly that proviso means that the purported exclusion of judicial review is not unqualified. But the proviso is also open to a stronger interpretation. As we have just seen, according to *Bulk Gas*, a decision-maker lacks

[210] *H (SC 52/2018)* (n 206) at [63]; *Zaoui v Attorney-General (No 2)* [2005] NZSC 38, [2006] 1 NZLR 289 at [101], [105]. The possibility of justified limits in terms of s 5 is not mentioned in these cases; contrast text at n 225.

[211] Further on this, see Ch 9.D.

[212] *Bulk Gas* (n 204) at 133–34, including the quotation from *O'Reilly v Mackman* [1983] 2 AC 237 (HL).

[213] See *New Zealand Drivers' Association v New Zealand Road Carriers* [1982] 1 NZLR 374 (CA) at 390. *Bulk Gas* (n 204) at 133, 136 only 'assumed' that the presumption could be rebutted.

[214] *Privacy International* (n 206) at [144] (Lord Carnwath). A particularly egregious ouster clause in s 2 of the Safety of Rwanda (Asylum and Immigration) Act 2024 is set to be repealed, and thus will not be tested in court.

[215] The clause is quoted, eg, in *Bulk Gas* (n 204) at 132; *Zaoui v Attorney-General (No 2)* [2005] 1 NZLR 690 (CA) at [86].

jurisdiction whenever any ground of review is made out. If 'lack of jurisdiction' is read that way, the proviso expressly allows review on all grounds: such clauses expressly have no privative effect at all. The courts' failure to treat them as excluding judicial review is then entirely unremarkable.

Admittedly that is unlikely to be the intended meaning: it is difficult to see the point of enacting the clauses on this interpretation. But the words are well capable of having this meaning. In *Zaoui*, the Court of Appeal relied on this reading of the proviso as a central part of the reasons for disregarding the privative clause.[216] The argument also featured in passing in *Bulk Gas*.[217] All of this means that there is no New Zealand authority that deals with the effect of a full privative clause.

Having said that, the jurisdictional and constitutional reasoning in *Bulk Gas* effectively makes the wording of the clause irrelevant. The strong presumption against excluding judicial review applies essentially regardless of the wording. That suggests that the approach would be the same, just as in the United Kingdom, for a full and unqualified privative clause – and that is the generally accepted understanding of the New Zealand position.

Turning to the second possible qualification, the courts' hostility to full privative clauses has one stark exception. New Zealand does have one full privative clause, lacking the usual proviso, in section 186(3) of the Immigration Act 2009. This purports to oust judicial review of decisions to deny temporary entry visas to persons outside New Zealand. This has been considered only at High Court level, and the case law is mixed. In some cases, the Court has interpreted the clause highly restrictively but still purported to give it some limited effect.[218]

In other cases, the Court has surprisingly given full effect to this clause. However, those cases do not involve a conscious departure from orthodoxy. In one of them, there is simply no reference to the authorities on privative clauses.[219] In others, this is presented as a special context in which the right to judicial review may not apply in any event.[220] The provision has been justified by reference to the Crown's prerogative to control New Zealand's borders,[221] and on the basis that applicants can always just re-apply.[222] While these arguments are open to debate, the point is that these cases do not signal any more general waning of commitment to the *Bulk Gas* orthodoxy in relation to full privative clauses.

[216] *Zaoui (No 2)* (n 215) at [16], [101], [105], [179] (NB: the privative clause was no longer in issue on the appeal in *Zaoui (No 2)* (SC) (n 210)).

[217] *Bulk Gas* (n 204) at 135, 139.

[218] *Kaur v Ministry of Business, Innovation and Employment* [2015] NZHC 2741 at [27]–[32], [49]–[54]; *Afghan Nationals v The Minister for Immigration* [2021] NZHC 3154, [2022] 2 NZLR 102.

[219] See *Ceramalus v Chief Executive of the Ministry of Business, Innovation and Employment* [2018] NZHC 45 at [17]–[20]. The Supreme Court refused leave for a leapfrog appeal: *Ceramalus v Chief Executive of the Ministry of Business, Innovation and Employment* [2018] NZSC 26 at [11]–[14].

[220] *AD v Chief Executive of the Ministry for Business, Innovation and Employment* [2020] NZHC 1010 at [53].

[221] *Liu v Minister of Immigration* [2015] NZHC 2048 at [6].

[222] *Kaur v Ministry of Business, Innovation and Employment* [2016] NZHC 2595 at [41]–[42].

(3) The *Bulk Gas* Approach does not (Fully) Apply to Partial Privative Clauses

A different approach, however, applies to partial privative clauses: provisions that merely restrict or redirect scrutiny of protected decisions. There are two forms of these. Time limit clauses bar judicial review brought after the expiry of the time limit. Channelling clauses direct challenges into alternative remedial avenues provided by the statute.[223] Modern New Zealand cases have been more ready to give effect to both of these by striking out applications for judicial review.

The approach to partial privative clauses has generally involved two elements, as we will see. First, courts have identified the legislative policy behind the restrictions on access to judicial review in the particular context, often acknowledging the validity of that policy. Secondly, courts have given effect to these clauses to the extent that they were satisfied that this did not deprive those affected by decisions of an effective avenue of recourse.[224]

A few cases, notably *Affco v Employment Court*, have considered partial privative clauses in terms of the right to judicial review in section 27(2) of the Bill of Rights.[225] Unlike the cases on full privative clauses that have relied on Bill of Rights reasoning, these cases take into account not only section 27(2) and section 6, but also the section 5 provision for justified limits. The reasons that courts have accepted for giving effect to partial privative clauses can be put in terms of section 5: if there is good reason for the restrictions and if effective avenues of recourse are available, then the partial privative clause is a justified limit on the right to judicial review. The section 6 interpretive direction to prefer a less restrictive meaning is not reached where that is the case. To date, the Supreme Court has not yet engaged with this line of argument,[226] but it can be considered entirely consistent with the reasoning in leading cases on partial privative clauses.[227]

In addition to the two main types of partial privative clauses outlined above, we also should note the existence of provisions purporting to confer 'absolute discretion', which tend to constrain and discourage review. This section outlines the courts' approach to each of these types of clauses in turn: (a) time limit clauses, (b) channelling clauses and (c) 'absolute discretion' provisions.

(a) Time Limit Clauses

In Aotearoa New Zealand, no time limit applies to judicial review generally. However, time limits on judicial review are not uncommon as part of particular regimes.[228] Such

[223] I adopt this term from Paul Daly, 'Channelling or Excluding Judicial Review of Administrative Action', *Administrative Law Matters* (12 September 2018). Available at: www.administrativelawmatters.com.

[224] See JG Pemberton, 'The Judicial Approach to Privative Provisions in New Zealand' [2015] *New Zealand Law Review* 617.

[225] *Affco New Zealand Ltd v Employment Court* [2017] NZCA 123, (2017) 14 NZELR 349 at [30]–[37].

[226] It declined to express a view on this point in *McGuire v Secretary for Justice* [2018] NZSC 116, [2019] 1 NZLR 335 at [45].

[227] See Luke Sizer, 'Privative Clauses: Parliamentary Intent, Legislative Limits and Other Works of Fiction' (2014) 20 *Auckland University Law Review* 148.

[228] For example, Immigration Act 2009, s 247(1); Te Ture Whenua Maori Act 1993, s 77; Fisheries Act 1996, s 186J; Local Government Act 1974, s 716D.

provisions have generally been considered uncontroversial. A variant of this model is found in provisions that require exercise of statutory appeal or review rights before allowing judicial review, and impose a time limit on the statutory appeal or review. Once that time limit has expired, judicial review also is rendered unavailable.[229] There is long-standing English authority for giving effect to such provisions.[230] New Zealand authority is to the same effect.[231]

Courts have recognised the need for finality as a good reason for such limits, particularly in areas where decisions, once implemented, are very difficult or costly to undo.[232] In *Privacy International*, Lord Carnwath gave such limits as an example of when the rule of law on balance does not require access to judicial review.[233]

In order to be consistent with the usual insistence on effective avenues of recourse, the effect given to such clauses should depend on whether the time allowed is adequate.[234] Perhaps it should also depend on the balance between the need for finality and the importance of the interests affected.

(b) Channelling Clauses

The courts' willingness to give effect to partial privative clauses also extends to channelling clauses, although there is some variation in the judicial response to these. Courts examine these clauses more closely to ensure that the alternative avenues of recourse are adequately effective. They often identify some exceptions to the apparent scope of the privative clause in order to ensure adequate recourse. Where to draw the lines around permissible restrictions and required exceptions remains uncertain. Courts have recognised that there can be good reason to require recourse to statutory avenues of recourse, so long as those avenues are adequate. Those good reasons include the valuable role of statutory avenues in securing administrative justice.[235]

In the United Kingdom, similar reasons have been given for giving effect to clauses that provide appeal or review rights as the exclusive remedy and subject to a time limit.[236] Apart from that, channelling clauses have received limited attention from either commentators or courts in the United Kingdom.[237] This must, however,

[229] See, eg, Legal Services Act 2011, s 83.

[230] *R v Secretary of State for the Environment, ex parte Ostler* [1977] QB 122 (CA). This is still the current position: see Ivan Hare, Catherine M Donnelly and Joanna Bell, *De Smith's Judicial Review*, 9th edn (London, Sweet & Maxwell, 2023) at [4-048].

[231] See, eg, *Wislang v Medical Council of New Zealand* [2002] NZAR 573 (CA); *Cooper v Attorney-General* [1996] 3 NZLR 480 (HC) at 494; *Whangarei District Council v Northern Regional Council* [1996] NZRMA 445 (HC) at 477, albeit contemplated an exception at 476.

[232] *Ostler* (n 230); *Whangarei District Council* (n 231) at 477.

[233] *Privacy International* (n 206) at [133].

[234] See, eg, the 'reasonable time limit' formulation in *Whangarei District Council* (n 231) at 477.

[235] See further Ch 15.

[236] See Mark Elliott, 'Through the Looking-Glass? Ouster Clauses, Statutory Interpretation and the British Constitution' in Chris Hunt, Lorne Neudorf and Micah Rankin (eds), *Legislating Statutory Interpretation: Perspectives from the Common Law World* (Carswell, 2018) 131 at 135; also *Privacy International* (n 206) at [130].

[237] But see *R (A) v Director of Establishments of the Security Service* [2010] 2 AC 1 (SC) at [23] – disapproved in *Privacy International* (n 206) at [109]. And see *Square Meals Frozen Foods Ltd v Dunstable Corporation* [1974] 1 WLR 59 (CA).

be seen in the context of the requirement to exhaust other remedies such as statutory rights of appeal or review before accessing judicial review. This is enforced in the United Kingdom at the preliminary stage of permission for judicial review.[238] The context is different in Aotearoa New Zealand: there is no permission requirement and failure to use other available remedies is merely one factor going to the remedial discretion.[239]

Access to the High Court at some stage and in some form has often been identified as a minimum requirement in the New Zealand cases. Most channelling clauses merely postpone access to the High Court: they either allow access to judicial review after the statutory avenues have been exhausted[240] or provide an appeal on a question of law to the High Court[241] (which is functionally equivalent to judicial review),[242] or both. The exception is the unusual clause in the employment legislation.

That unusual clause protecting the Employment Court has always been given effect. Let us look at that first, and then at *Tannadyce* and other leading authorities for giving effect to channelling clauses. There is some conflicting authority, as we will see next, but this is either reconcilable with the usual approach or otherwise unlikely to prevail. Finally, the Supreme Court's most recent decision in *H (SC 52/2018) v Refugee and Protection Officer* lays renewed emphasis on ensuring recourse to adequate avenues of redress but remains consistent with the approach established in the older leading cases.

(i) Authority for Giving Effect to the Employment Court's Partial Privative Clause

The most well-established effective partial privative clause is the one that protects decisions of the Employment Court, currently section 193 of the Employment Relations Act 2000 (the Act).[243] In a line of cases starting with *New Zealand Rail Ltd v Employment Court* in 1995,[244] the Court of Appeal has consistently given full effect to this provision and its predecessors, despite it being in unusual terms and very restrictive of access to the general courts.

Section 193 restricts judicial review of Employment Court decisions to the ground of lack of jurisdiction, just like the proviso to the common form of privative clause that has always been disregarded. Here, however, lack of jurisdiction is expressly and narrowly defined as limited to three specified senses: 'the narrow and original sense' that the Court had 'no entitlement to enter upon the inquiry';[245] that the Court went beyond the classes of decision or order which it is authorised to make; or that it acted

[238] See *De Smith's* (n 230)at [16-014]–[16-023].
[239] See Ch 10.C.
[240] For example, Immigration Act 2009, s 249(1) and (2); Legal Services Act 2013, s 83; Official Information Act 1982, s 34; Resource Management Act 1991, s 296.
[241] For example, Accident Compensation Act 2001, s 133(5); Social Security Act 2018, s 405.
[242] See Ch 10.D.
[243] A clause in these terms was first introduced in 1977: see *Parker v Silver Fern Farms Ltd* [2011] NZCA 564, [2012] 1 NZLR 256 at [30].
[244] *New Zealand Rail Ltd v Employment Court* [1995] 3 NZLR 179, [1995] 1 ERNZ 603 (CA); *Affco* (n 225); *Parker v Silver Fern Farms* (n 243); and see further decisions cited in *Affco*.
[245] On this 'original sense' of jurisdiction, see further Ch 9.C(1).

in bad faith.[246] Cases have interpreted this as meaning that review is not available on grounds of ordinary error of law[247] or breach of natural justice.[248]

The Act further provides for such judicial review of Employment Court decisions to be heard by the Court of Appeal rather than the High Court.[249] As an alternative, it provides an appeal on a question of law, requiring leave, that also lies directly to the Court of Appeal.[250] Giving effect to these restrictions is the closest our courts have come to abandoning their usual insistence that avenues of recourse must include access to the general courts equivalent to judicial review.

These provisions reflect a longstanding legislative policy of restricting access to the ordinary courts in employment matters. In giving effect to section 193, courts have acknowledged this policy. Even *Bulk Gas* mentioned this policy as an example of considerations that might exceptionally help rebut the presumption against ouster of review.[251] Originally, this policy reflected a concern that the general courts might not be sympathetic to the legislative attempt to address the power imbalances in this field.[252]

The explanation offered more recently in *Affco* was that speedy and informal dispute resolution was important in the context of employment disputes, which involve dynamic relationships requiring good faith.[253] Further, it was relevant that both the Employment Relations Authority and the Employment Court are 'specialist bodies'; and that most parties, by the time they apply for judicial review, will already have had hearings in both of these fora.[254] These arguments from speed, informality and special expertise are administrative justice arguments for alternative avenues of recourse.[255]

(ii) Leading Cases Giving Effect to Other Channelling Clauses

Aside from the employment cases, there are three leading authorities for giving effect to channelling clauses. Like *Affco*, these decisions feature recognition of special expertise and speedy resolution in the statutory avenues of recourse.

An early instance is *Love v Porirua City Council*. The Court of Appeal saw nothing objectionable in a clause that required exercise of a right of appeal to the Planning Tribunal before accessing judicial review. The appeal to the Tribunal was a full appeal on the merits, which represented more effective recourse than judicial review. Moreover, if the matter did still proceed to judicial review, the High Court would benefit from the considered views of the specialist tribunal on the matter.[256]

Ramsay concerned the accident compensation legislation, where the remedial scheme includes review by a specialist body; a full appeal to the District Court; and

[246] In the UK, a similar provision now limits judicial review of decisions by the Upper Tribunal to decline permission for a review application. This has also been given effect: *R (LA (Albania)) v Upper Tribunal* [2023] EWCA Civ 1337, [2024] 1 WLR 1673 at [30]–[36], [48], [51].

[247] *NZ Rail* (n 244) at 607.

[248] *Parker* (n 243) and *Affco* (n 225).

[249] Employment Relations Act 2000, s 213.

[250] ibid s 214.

[251] *Bulk Gas* (n 204) at 133, explaining *South East Asia Fire Bricks Sdn Bhd v Non-Metallic Mineral Products Manufacturing Employees Union* [1981] AC 363 (PC).

[252] See *Samuels v Employment Relations Authority* [2018] NZEmpC 138 at [21].

[253] *Affco* (n 225) at [38].

[254] ibid at [39].

[255] See Ch 15.

[256] *Love v Porirua City Council* [1984] 2 NZLR 308 (CA).

appeals on questions of law, only with leave, to the High Court and Court of Appeal. The privative clause applies 'if a person has a right to apply for review or appeal about a matter'.[257] The Court of Appeal read this as preserving the right to judicial review for any challenge that is not amenable to the statutory appellate process; hence no further exceptions had to be read into the clause. The Court acknowledged the underlying policy of promoting speedy and final resolution of disputes.[258]

The Supreme Court affirmed this approach to channelling clauses in *Tannadyce*, concerning the clause in section 109 of the Tax Administration Act 1994. The Act provides for merits review of tax assessments and taxpayers can choose between the High Court or the Taxation Review Authority as the forum for this review. The Supreme Court emphasised that the 'right of citizens to have matters of legality determined by the High Court' was not impaired by excluding judicial review in favour of this remedy.[259] Moreover, this was a more effective remedy than judicial review, since it could deal with all possible grounds of review as well as the merits. The advantages of this one-stop-shop process further included that it was quicker and more efficient, and that it prevented taxpayers from gaming the system.[260] In other words, there was good reason for the clause and it did not deprive applicants of access to the High Court and adequate recourse. As a result, the Court should give effect to Parliament's purpose: there was no reason to apply the presumption against this.[261]

However, the Court contemplated two rare exceptions to the effect of the clause: where it is not practically possible for the taxpayer to use the statutory process; or where the complaint is about a flaw in the statutory process itself that cannot be addressed by that process, such as an allegation of bias against a member of the Authority.[262] We might summarise these as situations where the statutory process is not available for bringing a valid challenge. There was a strong dissent but only concerning the scope of the exceptions rather than whether the clause should be given effect at all. The dissenters would have allowed judicial review more broadly whenever the statutory process is not adequate or effective, and when judicial review is the better means of providing the judicial scrutiny that is needed in the circumstances.[263] There is room for reasonable disagreement about whether the *Tannadyce* majority's exceptions were too limited.[264]

(iii) Older Conflicting Authority

In contrast, some other cases have disregarded channelling clauses. Most of these are older cases that may be considered to have been superseded by the leading cases discussed above.

The privative clause in *Bulk Gas* itself could, in fact, be understood as a channelling clause, but the Court did not consider whether it should be given effect on that

[257] Accident Compensation Act 1998, s 134(4); the current version is Accident Compensation Act 2001, s 133(5).
[258] *Ramsay v Wellington District Court* [2006] NZAR 136 (CA).
[259] *Tannadyce Investments Ltd v Commissioner of Inland Revenue* [2011] NZSC 158, [2012] 2 NZLR 153 at [67]–[68].
[260] ibid at [54]–[55], [57], [71].
[261] ibid at [70], [72].
[262] ibid at [58]–[59].
[263] ibid, [7], [11]–[17], [24], [35]–[38].
[264] For such a critique, see Andrew Beck, 'Privative Clauses' [2012] *New Zealand Law Journal* 91.

basis. That approach only developed subsequently. Cooke J did note that provision for an appeal right might weaken the presumption against excluding judicial review,[265] but he failed to mention that the legislation provided an appeal to the Commerce Commission.[266] Perhaps he had in mind only appeals directly to the courts. On the modern approach, it would have been relevant to ask whether the statutory avenues provided sufficiently effective avenues of recourse. Similarly, in *O'Regan v Lousich*, the Court applied *Bulk Gas* to disregard a privative clause, with no mention of appeal rights that were available under the statute.[267]

Zaoui (No 2) is the most significant of these older conflicting cases.[268] A security risk certificate had been issued against Mr Zaoui which, if confirmed, required him to be deported despite having refugee status. The certificate was subject to review by the Inspector-General, and then to an appeal on a question of law with a tight time limit of only three days.[269] The Court of Appeal declined to give effect to a privative clause that purported to exclude judicial review of the Inspector-General's decisions.[270] It considered the *Bulk Gas* approach to be appropriate, as reinforced by section 27(2) and section 6 of the Bill of Rights; particularly given the determination's impact on the liberty and security of the person.[271] On that basis, the Court allowed a challenge to a preliminary determination by the Inspector General.

The Crown argued that the statutory appeal should be read as the exclusive remedy, by implication from the statutory emphasis on speed. Only Glazebrook J addressed this argument. She dismissed it in part because the scope of the appeal right was too restricted for it to be the exclusive remedy: in addition to the three-day time limit, it was not available for the challenge to a preliminary determination in this case, and it was also not available to the Crown.[272]

Zaoui may have been overtaken by *Ramsay*[273] and *Tannadyce*.[274] It was not directly overruled; these decisions simply did not mention *Zaoui*. However, the reasons for giving effect to channelling clauses were arguably first developed in these later cases, and do not appear to have been considered as such in *Zaoui*.

On the other hand, however, it may be that *Zaoui* would still be decided the same way today. Glazebrook J's reasoning that the appeal rights were not adequate as an exclusive set of remedies is consistent with later cases. It is also arguable that the context called for a demanding standard of adequacy, given the importance of what was at stake.

Finally, channelling clauses and the leading cases giving effect to them continue to be ignored in some other contexts. Channelling clauses apply to both the Disputes Tribunal[275] and the Tenancy Tribunal.[276] These provide that orders of the tribunals are final and binding, subject to provisions for rehearing by the tribunal, appeals to

[265] *Bulk Gas* (n 204) at 136.
[266] Commerce Act 1975, ss 99, 122.
[267] *O'Regan v Lousich: Proprietors of Mawhera v Maori Land Court* [1995] 2 NZLR 620 (HC).
[268] *Zaoui (No 2)* (n 215) at [16], [101], [105], [179]–[181].
[269] Immigration Act 1987, s 114P.
[270] Inspector-General of Intelligence and Security Act 1996, s 19(9).
[271] *Zaoui (No 2)* (n 215) at [16].
[272] ibid at [92], [102]–[104].
[273] *Ramsay* (n 258).
[274] *Tannadyce* (n 259).
[275] Disputes Tribunal Act 1988, s 23.
[276] Residential Tenancies Act 1986, s 80.

the District Court, and in the case of the Tenancy Tribunal a further appeal on a question of law to the High Court. In judicial review of the Tenancy Tribunal, courts have not mentioned the privative clause at all.[277] They have, however, in some cases acknowledged the need for a restrained approach to judicial review of a tribunal that is designed to provide an 'informal forum' for resolving disputes 'inexpensively and expeditiously'.[278] Judicial review of the Disputes Tribunal is quite common, although again the courts have noted the need for a restrained approach. They have mentioned the privative clause but have not considered whether it might exclude judicial review.[279] This line of cases seems ripe for reconsideration in light of *Ramsay* and *Tannadyce*.

(iv) What to Make of the Supreme Court's Most Recent Decision in *H*

In the Supreme Court's most recent decision on channelling clauses in *H (SC 52/2018) v Refugee and Protection Officer*, it refused to give effect to such a clause in light of the particular circumstances of the case.[280] The decision is best understood as still consistent with the approach in the older leading cases, but placing greater emphasis on the need for the statutory alternative avenues to provide adequate recourse.

H concerned the channelling clause in section 249 of the Immigration Act 2009, which requires unsuccessful refugee claimants to exercise a statutory appeal to the Immigration and Protection Tribunal before seeking leave to apply for judicial review. The Court acknowledged the intention to 'prevent duplicative proceedings', but insisted that it must 'prevent injustice occurring when a statutory process fails'.[281]

The particular situation in this case called for an exception to the clause, for two connected reasons. First, the Refugee and Protection Officer's first instance process was fundamentally flawed: 'there was no consideration of the merits of the claim at all'.[282] The Officer had declined the refugee status claim without interviewing the claimant, after rejecting a medical certificate for non-attendance at the time scheduled for an interview on highly technical grounds.[283] This was a fundamental breach of natural justice and also left the officer unable to properly evaluate the material that had been submitted in support of the claim.[284]

Secondly, the Court did not accept that the statutory appeal to the Tribunal was an appropriate next step in these circumstances. On its reading, the statutory scheme was intended to afford refugee claimants two hearings on the merits: at first instance by the Officer and then on appeal by the Tribunal.[285] The first instance process involved a set of significant safeguards that were not replicated in the appeal process.[286] A fair hearing in the Tribunal would therefore not cure the breach at first instance. Nor did

[277] See, eg, *Catalin v Tenancy Tribunal* [2020] NZHC 1220.

[278] *MacLaren v Tenancy Tribunal* [2022] NZHC 3562 at [19], [37].

[279] See, eg, *Patterson v District Court, Hutt Valley* [2020] NZHC 259 at [13]–[23]; *Evans v Disputes Tribunal at New Plymouth* (2000) 14 PRNZ 183 (HC) at [17]–[23]; *Graeme Martin Contracting Ltd v Disputes Tribunal* [2018] NZCA 328, [2018] NZAR 1636 at [37]–[38].

[280] *H (SC 52/2018)* (n 206).

[281] ibid at [63].

[282] ibid at [64], [77].

[283] The process is outlined at [9]–[15].

[284] ibid at [14].

[285] ibid at [43], [70]–[74].

[286] ibid [41], [67]–[69].

the Tribunal's powers under the Act allow it to remedy this by remitting the matter for reconsideration by the Officer.[287]

The Court did not quite spell out how this analysis satisfied the usual test for refusing to enforce partial privative clauses: it did not quite say why enforcing the clause would deprive the applicant of an effective avenue of recourse. We might have thought that the entitlement to two fair hearings could still be satisfied by judicial review after an appeal and remitting the matter back to the Officer at that stage. However, perhaps such a process would indeed not have amounted to effective avenues of recourse in these circumstances: the additional stages of the process would have imposed an unnecessarily onerous burden on the applicant, and it might also not serve the purpose of avoiding duplication of proceedings.

The main message from *H* is quite consistent with *Tannadyce*.[288] Channelling clauses may be given effect if the statute provides adequate alternative avenues. *Tannadyce* was distinguished on the basis that the appeal process in that case was sufficiently comprehensive to render judicial review unnecessary.[289]

However, *H* perhaps places greater emphasis on the adequacy of the available avenues. It certainly rejects any notion that all partial privative clauses are unproblematic and should be given effect simply by virtue of being partial. We could also see its approach to exceptions as more consistent with the minority than the majority in *Tannadyce*. In *H* it was not enough that statutory avenues were available for the challenge: the Court would have give effect to the clause only if the statutory avenues had offered adequate recourse in the particular circumstances.

(c) Provisions Conferring 'Absolute Discretion'

A different type of statutory attempt to limit judicial review also should be mentioned. Provisions purporting to confer 'absolute discretion' are surprisingly common, following a recent resurgence in enacting these.[290] While they do not purport to restrict access to judicial review, they clearly are intended to discourage and constrain its use. They purport to countermand common law orthodoxy that there is no such thing as an unfettered discretion.[291] Some such clauses merely reinforce limits which the common law might impose in any case – for instance, limits on review of preliminary determinations. Others, however, apply to the exercise of powers that should be subject to supervision. Notably, the Immigration Act 2009 introduced multiple provisions conferring 'absolute discretion'. For instance, s 177 purports to confer 'absolute discretion' in the exercise of a power to cancel a deportation notice for humanitarian reasons. In practice, in many cases this is the only occasion on which humanitarian considerations

[287] ibid [71], [74]. The Act also appeared to preclude the Officer reconsidering his own decision: ibid [17], [29]–[30].

[288] *Tannadyce* (n 259).

[289] *H (SC 52/2018)* (n 206) at [87].

[290] For further discussion, see Hanna Wilberg, 'Interrogating "Absolute Discretion": Are NZ's Parliament and Courts Compromising the Rule of Law?' (2017) 45 *Federal Law Review* 541.

[291] *Padfield v Minister of Agriculture, Fisheries and Food* [1968] AC 997 (HL) at 1030. Procedural fairness requirements also apply to apparently unlimited powers: *Cooper v Wandsworth Board of Works* (1863) 14 CBNS 180 at 194.

such as the interests of an immigrant's children, protected by international law, are taken into account.

Courts might have been expected to interpret the reference to 'absolute discretion' in such contexts as restrictively as possible, possibly to the point of effectively ignoring them – as they do with full privative clauses. In fact, however, the judicial response has been very mixed. The spectrum of responses runs from cases that do involve a highly restrictive reading of such clauses, through to cases that treat such clauses as being effective to impose severe limits on judicial scrutiny.[292] This issue has not to date attracted the attention that is required to promote a more consistent and appropriate approach.

[292] See Wilberg (n 290) at 559–66.

9

A Better Framework for Calibrating Restraint?

Throughout this book we have seen that limits to judicial review form an integral part of the principles of judicial review: these principles include not only instructions to administrators on how to exercise their powers, but also instructions to judges on the limits of their supervisory powers. Judges deciding judicial review cases have addressed this question as to the limits of their power in light of the constitutional and institutional reasons for such limits. They have considered the proper allocation of authority as between themselves and administrative decision-makers. To what extent should they respect decision-makers' authority and Parliament's allocation of that authority to the decision-maker, by exercising judicial restraint?

Two questions in this regard, however, have not received much judicial attention: the limits of review on questions of law, and whether full privative clauses should be given some effect. This chapter is devoted to exploring these two questions. This exploration raises the further question whether we need a different framework for calibrating judicial restraint.

Let us briefly take stock of where we have seen courts engage with the question as to the limits of judicial review, before introducing the two under-explored questions in a little more detail. We saw in Chapter 7 that case law traditionally limited review of the substantive merits to the highly deferential *Wednesbury* unreasonableness ground, citing the limits of courts' constitutional role. More recently in developing substantive review beyond that, such as by providing some protection for substantive legitimate expectations, courts have grappled with the right balance between the need for greater scrutiny on such matters and the continuing need for judicial restraint. In Chapter 6 we saw that in developing rights-based review, courts have again grappled with that balance, especially on questions of justification for limits on rights. Finally, in Chapter 8 we saw that courts have recognised justiciability as a limit on the types of issues and grounds of review they will entertain. The explicit reasons for this are found in the constitutional and institutional reasons for judicial restraint, to be balanced against the constitutional imperative for exercises of public power to be subject to scrutiny.

The first of the two areas where this judicial engagement with the limits of review is very largely absent is on questions of law. Do reviewing courts ever exercise restraint and allow some latitude to administrative decision-makers on questions of law? Should they? These questions are not directly addressed in most of our case law. The discussion of these questions in this chapter thus interrogates what courts are really doing in this regard, as well as asking whether any change is needed.

The orthodoxy is that questions of law are questions for the courts. Courts therefore substitute their view on such questions, but they rarely spell this out or justify this lack of restraint. This chapter raises that justification question. Arguably there can be good reasons in some contexts for judicial restraint on some questions that might be categorised as questions of law.

The second area where we see a complete lack of restraint concerns the judicial treatment of full privative clauses. We saw in Chapter 8 that courts give no effect at all to full privative clauses. Is that consistent with adequate judicial restraint? That may be open to question. Again, courts have not explicitly engaged with this question.

The reason for the judicial blind spot in these two areas is found in the framework that is currently employed for calibrating restraint. This framework is not usually explicit, so we will begin in Part A by spelling it out. The work of Dean Knight identifying a range of different 'schemata' for calibrating restraint is helpful here.[1] We

[1] Dean R Knight, *Vigilance and Restraint in the Common Law of Judicial Review* (Cambridge, Cambridge University Press, 2018).

will further see in Part B that there is, in fact, a fair deal of tacit adjustment of the boundary around questions of law, to enable courts to exercise restraint in appropriate contexts. All this raises the question of whether there is a better framework for restraint: a framework that would allow explicit calibration of restraint on questions of law as well as in other respects. That is the question we will ask in Part C. Finally, these frameworks also have implications for the treatment of privative clauses. We will explore these implications in Part D.

As a starting point, a useful framework for capturing variation in judicial restraint in judicial review is to think in terms of standards and intensity of review.[2] We can identify two main standards of review. The first we can call a correctness or substitutionary standard, as it involves the court determining and substituting the correct answer. This involves no judicial restraint. The second is a rationality standard, which does involve restraint: the court intervenes only if the decision is outside the range of what is rationally defensible. This second standard can be applied with varying degrees of restraint or, to put it differently, the intensity of review on this standard can vary. Less restraint and greater intensity results in a more confined range of what is rationally defensible.

A. The Current Framework and the Standard of Review on Questions of Law

On the current approach in Aotearoa New Zealand and the United Kingdom, as Dean Knight has pointed out, the standard and intensity of review depends on the ground of review.[3] Each of the three traditional grounds of review has its fixed standard of review. The choice of standard for each ground is explained by reference to categories of question: law, fact and discretion. The illegality ground involves questions of law and that entails a correctness standard: these are questions for the court.[4] The same goes for the procedural unfairness ground: what is required for procedural fairness is a question of law for the court.[5] The ground of irrationality or *Wednesbury* unreasonableness applies to questions of fact and to the substance of exercises of discretion. By definition, it involves a rationality standard. *Wednesbury* unreasonableness represents rationality review with extreme restraint and very limited intensity.

This traditional *Wednesbury* ground does not involve any explicit variation in the intensity of rationality review. However, we do see variable intensity in the modern extensions of substantive review, such as when scrutinising the justification for limits on rights or for disappointing substantive legitimate expectations.

[2] See, eg, Tom Hickman, *Public Law after the Human Rights Act* (Oxford, Hart, 2010), ch 4.
[3] See Knight, *Vigilance and Restraint* (n 1) at 129 and generally Ch 3.
[4] See, eg, *Padfield v Minister of Agriculture, Fisheries and Food* [1968] AC 997 (HL) at 1030.
[5] Affirmed in *R (Osborn) v Parole Board* [2013] UKSC 61, [2014] AC 1115 at [65]; see also *Discount Brands Ltd v Westfield (New Zealand) Ltd* [2005] NZSC 17, [2005] 2 NZLR 597 (SC) at [54].

The standard of review in this scheme depends on what aspect of a decision is challenged. If the decision-maker is alleged to have misinterpreted or failed to apply a relevant legal test, then the standard is correctness. If, on the other hand, the complaint is about the substance of an exercise of a statutory discretion or about a factual determination, the standard is the *Wednesbury* version of the rationality standard.

Most of the time, courts and commentators tacitly assume these categories and the corresponding standards of review, as they are built into the established grounds of review. Given this tacit link between grounds and standards of review, discussion of the standard or intensity of review is usually confined to debates about the modern extensions of substantive review, including rights-based review. There are occasional exceptions, where courts appear to contemplate varying the standard of review across all grounds, but these do not seem to be conscious departures from orthodoxy.[6]

The approach is sometimes inaccurately described in terms of reviewable and non-reviewable questions: questions of law are reviewable, while questions of fact and exercises of discretion are not.[7] This terminology harks back to the old jurisdictional doctrine: a framework that has been discarded, as we will see. A more accurate description of the current approach is in terms of grounds and standards of review, as just outlined. Questions of fact and exercises of discretion are reviewable, but traditionally only on the ground of irrationality with its highly deferential *Wednesbury* version of the rationality standard.

Confusion can surround the phrases 'error of law' and 'question of law'. These are used in at least three different senses. In their narrowest and most obvious sense, these phrases correspond to the illegality ground of review. But there are two broader senses. When it is said that all errors of law are reviewable and render a decision ultra vires,[8] that involves using the phrase in its broadest sense: any of the established grounds of review represent errors of law (including irrationality). This also explains why all grounds of review are available on appeals that are limited to questions of law.[9] Finally, when it is said that a correctness standard of review applies to all questions of law, that involves yet another meaning, narrower than the second but still broader than the first: questions of law here include questions as to both the interpretation of the empowering law (usually statute) and the legal requirements (often common law) of fair procedure, but they do not include questions of fact or the exercise of discretion. In short, 'error of law' or 'question of law' may correspond to one, two, or all of the grounds of review.

[6] See, eg, *Kim v Minister of Justice of New Zealand* [2019] NZCA 209, [2019] 3 NZLR 173 at [45]–[47]; and discussion in Ch 7.B(3).

[7] See, eg, Jack Beatson, 'The Scope of Judicial Review for Error of Law' (1984) 4 *Oxford Journal of Legal Studies* 22.

[8] *Peters v Davison* [1999] 2 NZLR 164 (CA) at 201, see also at 180–81.

[9] See Ch 10.D.

B. Variability in the Line-drawing to Fix the Standard of Review

The current framework depends, as we saw, on drawing lines between categories of question: law, fact and discretion. However, the lines between these categories are by no means always obvious: there is often room for judgement and for argument. This part explores how courts have drawn these lines, to reveal tacit variation in the standard and intensity of review on questions that could have been classified as questions of law. Paul Craig, Michael Taggart and Dean Knight have all drawn attention to this tacit variability.[10]

Justiciability considerations may often influence how courts categorise the question before them in such cases. As noted in Chapter 8, this can be understood as part of the modern preference for secondary justiciability, in which complete non-justiciability is merely the far end of a spectrum of varying scope and intensity of review. It is arguably appropriate for courts to adjust the standard of review in response to concerns about constitutional legitimacy and institutional capacity in particular contexts. However, the influence of those concerns is often not acknowledged, at least not as a reason for adjusting the standard of review on questions of law.

Paul Craig offers one way of thinking about the line-drawing exercise.[11] Consider the structure of a typical empowering provision: 'If X, Y and Z, then the decision-maker may do A.' This raises up to four different questions for decision-makers and reviewing courts:

(i) What is the meaning (both explicit and implicit) of X, Y and Z?
(ii) What are the facts relevant to X, Y and Z?
(iii) How do X, Y and Z apply to those facts?
(iv) If X, Y and Z are met, how should the decision-maker exercise their discretion to do A?

Three of these questions seem easy to categorise: (i) is a question of law, (ii) is a question of fact, and (iv) is a question of discretion.

There are three difficulties with the line-drawing, however. This part of the chapter outlines these in turn. First, question (iii) as to applying the legal criteria to the facts is difficult to categorise: it could arguably be in any of the three categories. A related point is that the line between (i) and (iii) is difficult to draw, and might even be illusory: are interpreting and applying the law really two distinct and separate tasks? These two points are the crux of the difficulty with the line between fact and law. We will explore this in section (1) of this Part.

[10] See, eg, Paul Craig, *Administrative Law*, 9th edn (London, Sweet & Maxwell, 2021), Ch 16; Michael Taggart, 'The Contribution of Lord Cooke to Scope of Review Doctrine in Administrative Law: A Comparative Common Law Perspective' in Paul Rishworth (ed), *The Struggle for Simplicity in the Law: Essays in Honour of Lord Cooke of Thorndon* (Wellington, Butterworths, 1997) 189; Knight, *Vigilance and Restraint* (n 1), Ch 4, esp at 82–88, 107–08.

[11] Craig (n 10) at [16-001], [16-005], [16-007].

Secondly, we may ask to what extent question (i) as to the meaning of the criteria is always purely a question of law on which courts should substitute their view. In cases where the X, Y and Z criteria are broad or evaluative, or where courts are asked to imply some of these criteria from the scheme and purpose of the statute, is there not a significant element of discretion involved? We will explore these issues about the line between law and discretion in section (2).

Third and finally, where an exercise of power engages a right in the New Zealand Bill of Rights Act 1990, a proportionality test applies to determine whether the decision imposes more than a justified limit on the right. This is a legal test, but its application very arguably involves a significant element of discretion. Section (3) briefly outlines this issue.

(1) The Line between Law and Fact

In light of the uncertainty about classifying questions of application, it is debatable whether the categorical distinction between law and fact provides a reliable analytical basis for determining the appropriate standard of review.[12] In the case law, we can see doctrinal devices being used to address this uncertainty. However, these still leave room for judgement, and it seems likely that justiciability factors are influential in this context. There is also some recent authority for deliberately manipulating the categorial approach to take account of justiciability factors or considerations of proportionate dispute resolution. Let us look at these points in turn.

The main doctrinal device to deal with the uncertainty about classifying issues of application is to classify these in two different ways, depending on the type of provision at issue. The meaning of a statutory criterion is always a question of law that attracts a correctness standard. In some cases, the same goes for application. As noted in *Bulk Gas Users Group*, application merges into interpretation, and thus attracts the same correctness standard, where the criterion is a 'definitive' or 'ascertainable' test.[13]

In other cases, however, the application of a criterion is a distinct question that will be reviewed on a deferential rationality standard. Courts employ this approach where a criterion is broad or vague enough to leave room for judgment in applying the criterion, even after the court has settled its legal meaning. For instance, in *South Yorkshire Transport Ltd*, the question whether a proposed merger of bus companies would affect a 'substantial' part of the United Kingdom did leave much room for judgment in application.[14] Lord Mustill, for a unanimous House of Lords, determined on a correctness standard that the meaning of the term in this context lay higher up the spectrum of possible meanings than 'not trifling', but not as high up as 'nearly complete'. The respondent Commission's interpretation was consistent with that. He then upheld the Commission's application of that term on the basis that it was within

[12] See Timothy Endicott, 'Questions of Law' (1998) 114 *Law Quarterly Review* 292 at 320; Rebecca Williams, 'When is an Error not an Error? Reform of Jurisdictional Review of Error of Law and Fact' [2007] *Public Law* 793 at 798.

[13] *Bulk Gas Users Group v Attorney-General* [1983] NZLR 129 (CA) at 135, 136.

[14] *R v Monopolies and Mergers Commission ex p South Yorkshire Transport Ltd* [1993] 1 WLR 23 (HL).

the permissible field of judgment.[15] The New Zealand Supreme Court approved and adopted this approach in *Vodafone*.[16]

Aside from the breadth or vagueness of the statutory test, subjective wording also occasionally plays a role in this context. For instance, the statutory criterion may be whether the decision-maker is 'satisfied' of certain matters, or whether those matters are 'in his opinion' made out. Usually, courts pay no attention to such wording. It is irrelevant when the court's focus is on whether the decision-maker correctly understood the statutory criterion.[17] However, subjective wording can support a conclusion that there is room for judgement in the application of the statutory criterion. This too was noted in *Bulk Gas*.[18]

This device has some obvious appeal as a way of dealing with the uncertain classification of application questions: the distinction between terms that leave room for judgement in application and terms that pose a definitive test can be accepted as both real and significant. However, this distinction has limits as a reliable analytical device: there is still plenty of room for judicial choice in its application. Let me explain why.

First, the question of whether there is room for judgement in the application of a particular criterion seems better understood as a matter of degree. Most statutory criteria will leave room for judgement in application at least at their margins.[19] It is, perhaps, not a coincidence that the leading cases in which courts relied on this room for judgement to adopt a rationality standard were cases involving economic regulation by expert bodies – cases that engage justiciability concerns.

Secondly, where there is room for judgment in the application of the statutory criteria, the court still has a choice which of the two aspects to focus on: interpreting the meaning or scrutinising the application. For instance, in *Discount Brands* the Supreme Court divided on this point. This was a successful challenge to a council's decision not to provide public notification of an application for a resource consent.[20] Under the Resource Management Act 1991, the council could decide not to notify if it was satisfied that any adverse effects of the proposal on the environment would be minor, but it first had to be satisfied that it had adequate information to make that decision. The Supreme Court was unanimous in upholding the challenge, but the reasoning diverged. Elias CJ and Keith J focused on interpreting the meaning: they held that the Council had misunderstood the statute and failed to address itself to the relevant question about the adequacy of the information. Blanchard J took the different route of scrutinising the Council's application of that test: the Council could not reasonably have been satisfied that it had adequate information.[21]

The choice as to which aspect to focus on depends, of course, on where the evidence suggests there may be a flaw in the decision, and also on parties' choice of argument. However, in a case like *Discount Brands*, the evidence may lend itself to either argument.

[15] ibid at 28–33.
[16] *Vodafone New Zealand Ltd v Telecom New Zealand Ltd* [2011] NZSC 138, [2012] 3 NZLR 153 at [50]–[58].
[17] See, eg, *Reade v Smith* [1959] NZLR 996 (SC) at 1000–02; *Discount Brands* (n 5) at [5], [28], [55]–[56].
[18] *Bulk Gas* (n 13) at 136.
[19] HLA Hart, *The Concept of Law*, 2nd edn (Clarendon Press, Oxford, 1994) at 124–131.
[20] *Discount Brands* (n 5).
[21] ibid at [5], [25]–[29], [50]–[55], [116], [121]–[125], [148], [150]–[151], [178].

A court may also address both aspects or stages: whether the decision-maker correctly interpreted the meaning of the criterion and whether the decision-maker's application of that criterion was reasonably open. That is what the House of Lords did in *South Yorkshire*. However, where a judge chooses one aspect to focus on, that choice may also be influenced by the judge's view of the appropriate balance between judicial supervision and the decision-maker's autonomy in the circumstances – that is to say, by justiciability factors.

Third, once a court has decided that there is room for judgment in the application of statutory criteria, if it goes on to scrutinise the rationality of that application, it has a further choice as to the intensity of review. The formulation in *South Yorkshire*, adopted for New Zealand in *Vodafone*, was the highly deferential *Edwards v Bairstow* test: the court could intervene only if the decision-maker's conclusion was entirely untenable.[22] In other cases, however, courts have closely scrutinised the application of broad or vague statutory criteria. For instance, Blanchard J in *Discount Brands* considered close scrutiny appropriate because participatory rights were at stake.[23]

Finally, we might also wonder whether meaning and application are *ever* distinct and separate. In those cases where application leaves room for judgement, the same often goes for the meaning, and the two shade into each other. That is well illustrated by the *South Yorkshire* case, where the Court's determination of meaning involved identifying the correct part of the spectrum of possible meanings. If a rationality test is appropriate for reviewing the application in this type of case, then arguably it is equally appropriate for reviewing the decision on the meaning.

In conclusion, the categorical lines between meaning, application and fact are doubtful. The approach developed in *South Yorkshire* helps but still leaves much room for judicial choice. Rather than drawing these lines on the supposed analytical basis, it appears likely that courts often draw them, explicitly or tacitly, based on justiciability factors affecting the desirability of judicial control or respecting the decision-maker's authority. These factors include the importance of what is at stake, the nature of the decision (for instance, its policy content), and the nature of the decision-maker. Where such factors are the real reason for the court's choice of standard of review, it would be more transparent to avoid reliance on the current categorical framework.

There is indeed some authority in the United Kingdom suggesting an explicitly instrumental approach to drawing the line between law and fact in some contexts, guided by factors other than analytical categories. In *Jones v First Tier Tribunal*, Lord Carnwath suggested that an expert tribunal whose jurisdiction is limited to questions of law might adopt a broad view of what counts as a question of law, to enlarge its jurisdiction and enable it to deploy its expertise to best effect.[24] In *Privacy International*, Lord Carnwath considered that courts should determine the availability and scope of judicial review by asking what level of protection is sufficient and proportionate for

[22] *South Yorkshire Transport* (n 14) at 32; *Vodafone* (n 16) at [52]–[53]; *Edwards (Inspector of Taxes) v Bairstow* [1956] AC 14 (HL) at 36.

[23] *Discount Brands* (n 5) at [116], [148]. See also *McGrath v Accident Compensation Corporation* [2011] NZSC 77, [2011] 3 NZLR 733 at [30]–[32], [37]–[44].

[24] *Jones v First Tier Tribunal* [2013] UKSC 19, [2013] 2 AC 48 at [46].

maintaining the rule of law.[25] He went on to suggest that this might sometimes be achieved by categorising questions of application as questions of fact, to be left to the primary decision-maker.[26]

(2) The Line between Law and Discretion: Reasoning Process Grounds

The categorical lines of the orthodox approach are also problematic in relation to the illegality grounds of improper purpose, irrelevant considerations and failure to take account of mandatory relevant considerations. It is usually assumed that these attract a correctness standard on the basis that they involve questions of law.[27] In applying these grounds, however, judges often have a choice as to how far to constrain the decision-maker's discretion.[28]

They can choose more or less constraining interpretations, either by interpreting express criteria or purposes broadly or narrowly or by deciding whether to imply criteria or purposes. A less-constraining interpretation leaves more room for the decision-maker to exercise discretion which is then subject to review only on a deferential rationality standard. A more constraining interpretation provides more scope for the court to control the legality of the decision-maker's reasoning on a correctness standard.

The degree of choice available to a judge in that regard depends on the type of empowering provision. These range from those that provide express and exhaustive lists of criteria and purposes to those that leave nearly everything to implication. The closer the provision is to the latter end of the spectrum, the greater the choice left to the judge. However, even with an express and exhaustive list of criteria, a judge can have choices available if those criteria are expressed in broad or evaluative terms.

Whenever a judge has this type of choice, this could be exercised according to the judge's evaluation of justiciability factors. Is this a context in which the decision-maker should be left with the maximum amount of discretion that can be reconciled with the statute? Or is it rather a context in which the court should exploit all possible bases for implying legal constraints on the decision-maker's reasoning?

Occasionally, courts have explained their choices in these terms. For instance, in *Unison Networks*, the Supreme Court refused to imply a narrow purpose to constrain the Commerce Commission's statutory power. It supported this choice by pointing to the Commission's expertise and to the broad terms of the relevant power, designed to achieve economic objectives which were themselves expansively expressed.[29] Another

[25] *R (Privacy International) v Investigatory Powers Tribunal* [2019] UKSC 22 at [131]–[132]; developing a line of thinking earlier introduced in *R (Cart) v Upper Tribunal (Public Law Project Intervening)* [2011] UKSC 28, [2012] 1 AC 663.

[26] *Privacy International* (n 25) at [134].

[27] See, eg, *Padfield* (n 4) at 1030.

[28] See also Hanna Wilberg, 'Deference on Relevance and Purpose? Wrestling with the Law/Discretion Divide' in Hanna Wilberg and Mark Elliott (eds), *The Scope and Intensity of Substantive Review: Traversing Taggart's Rainbow* (Oxford, Hart Publishing, 2015) 263.

[29] *Unison Networks Ltd v Commerce Commission* [2007] NZSC 74, [2008] 1 NZLR 42 at [55]. For critical comment, see Edward Willis, 'Economic Law – Analysing Competition Law and Economic Regulation'

instance of such an explicit choice is found in *Hawke's Bay Regional Investment Co.* Here the Supreme Court did imply a test for the apparently open-ended power at issue. It distinguished *Unison Networks* in this regard on the basis that the context of ministerial decisions about conservation land was very different to a policy choice made by an expert regulatory body.[30]

Such express reliance on justiciability factors is, however, uncommon in the case law on improper purpose. This type of inquiry is not an established part of the law on the reasoning process grounds.[31] It may be that courts regularly engage in such reasoning, but they rarely do so explicitly. Instead, they usually present their decision whether and to what extent to impose reasoning constraints as a pure exercise of statutory interpretation. The exercise of choice is not acknowledged.

(3) Applying the Law/Discretion Line to the Proportionality Test under Section 5 of the Bill of Rights

The categorical approach is difficult to apply to the proportionality test that is used to determine whether a limit on a right is reasonable and justified under section 5 of the Bill of Rights. The proportionality test asks whether the limit has a legitimate objective, is rationally connected to that objective, does not limit the right more than is reasonably necessary to achieve that objective, and is overall proportionate.[32] Any limit that is not justified on this test is unlawful if the empowering provision can be given a more rights-consistent meaning pursuant to section 6.[33]

The proportionality test thus forms part of the legal criteria that determine the lawfulness of exercises of power. Yet there is real doubt as to whether this test as a whole comprises questions of law, to be reviewed on a correctness standard. Arguably, the balancing required by it involves a significant element of judgement or discretion, which should attract a rationality rather than correctness standard of review.[34] One way of thinking about this is via the approach in *South Yorkshire* and *Vodafone*: the proportionality test is an instance of a legal test that leaves much room for judgement in its application.[35] The application of the test should therefore be reviewed on a rationality standard.

The approach that courts have taken on this point remains highly unsettled, but judicial restraint has featured in a variety of guises, as discussed in Chapter 6.D. Of interest for our present purposes is that categorical reasoning is usually absent from

in Michael Littlewood and Janet McLean (eds), *The Supreme Court: The Second 10 Years* (Wellington, LexisNexis, 2024315.

[30] *Hawke's Bay Regional Investment Co Ltd v Royal Forest and Bird Protection Society of New Zealand Inc* [2017] NZSC 106, [2017] 1 NZLR 1041 at [110].

[31] An exception is found in cases on economic regulators, where this point from *Unison Networks* (n 29) has been regularly relied on: see Willis (n 29).

[32] *R v Oakes* [1986] 1 SCR 103.

[33] *R v Hansen* [2007] NZSC 7, [2007] 3 NZLR 1 (SC); and see Ch 6.D.

[34] See Grant Huscroft, 'Reasonable Limits on Rights' in Paul Rishworth and Grant Huscroft, *The New Zealand Bill of Rights* (2003) 168 at 192, 194.

[35] *South Yorkshire Transport* (n 14); *Vodafone* (n 16).

the cases: this is one area in which questions of judicial restraint are often addressed directly.

An exception is found in some High Court decisions on challenges to delegated legislation imposing restrictions to fight the COVID-19 pandemic. Cooke J rejected judicial restraint on section 5, on the basis that proportionality is a question of law for the court.[36] This is questionable, for the reason set out in the previous paragraph. The Supreme Court in *Moncrief* rightly dismissed this objection. While 'the extent of reasonable limits is a legal question', 'the application of that legal standard' involves 'mixed questions of fact and law'.[37]

C. Questioning the Current Framework: Alternative Perspectives

The established, categories-based framework for the standard of review is arguably problematic for two reasons. First, we have seen that the lines between the categories are not as clear-cut as they may seem. Judges' reliance on analytical categories conceals the weighing of justiciability factors that often plays a role in drawing the line. Arguably that aspect of the reasoning should always be made explicit. That would require an acknowledgement that the standard of review is in fact variable.

Secondly, even with this tacit variability, a further potential problem with the current framework is that it involves a very expansive role for reviewing courts. Whenever a question is classified as a question of law, there is no room for judicial restraint: no room for according some respect to the decision-maker's interpretive judgements. While the courts occasionally avoid this by manipulating the line, it seems likely that they might find reasons for some restraint in a greater proportion of cases if that was a question they asked themselves explicitly.

This position contrasts with some other common law jurisdictions. As we will see, Canada has rejected the categorical approach: whether the challenge concerns law, fact or discretion does not necessarily determine the standard of review. Until recently, that was also the position in the United States. In these jurisdictions, there has been debate on how and to what extent courts should exercise restraint on all types of questions, including questions of statutory interpretation. That debate has been largely foreign to New Zealand and the United Kingdom. I suggest that there may be room for such debate here.[38]

This part of the chapter explores the arguments for and against the established expansive role for courts and the categories-based framework that demands this expansive role. Section (1) outlines the constitutional reasons for the current approach

[36] See, eg, *Four Aviation Security Service Employees v Minister of COVD-19 Response* [2021] NZHC 3012 at [79], [82]–[83].

[37] *Moncrief-Spittle v Regional Facilities Auckland Ltd* [2022] NZSC 138, [2022] 1 NZLR 459 at [84]. See also *Minister of Justice v Kim* [2021] NZSC 57, [2021] 1 NZLR 338 at [42], [49].

[38] For an outline of literature on this, see Hanna Wilberg and Mark Elliott, 'Deference on Questions of Law: A Survey of Taggart's Contribution and Themes in the Wider Literature' in Hanna Wilberg and Mark Elliott (eds), *The Scope and Intensity of Substantive Review: Traversing Michael Taggart's Rainbow* (Oxford, Hart Publishing, 2015) 197.

of insisting on a correctness standard on questions of law, and sketches the history that helps explain the reliance on categories. Section (2) outlines arguments for considering alternatives, while section (3) sketches the experience with alternative models in Canada and the United States.

(1) Explaining and Justifying the Current Framework

(a) Constitutional Arguments for Correctness Review on Questions of Law

A correctness standard of review on questions of law is considered necessary to uphold the rule of law. Cases occasionally spell this out, but the argument is often implicit. Executive government and administrative authorities must observe the limits to their powers and it is the constitutional role of courts to determine what those limits are. It cannot be left to primary decision-makers to determine the limits of their own power.[39] The point can also be put in terms of maintaining Parliamentary sovereignty, in the particular sense of enforcing Parliament's will that powers conferred by statute should be subject to the limits set out in those statutes.[40]

In addition, correctness review on questions of law is also supported by a different aspect of the rule of law: the requirement of consistency and reasonable certainty. From this perspective, it would be problematic if individual decision-makers were allowed to interpret the same provision differently. The final interpretive authority of the general courts, and the precedential force of those courts' interpretive rulings, contributes to maintaining the rule of law in this sense.[41]

(b) History of the Categories-based Framework: The Demise of the Jurisdictional Doctrine

While constitutional principles explain and potentially justify the adoption of a correctness standard of review for questions of law, some history is necessary to explain both the reliance on categories and the occasional inaccurate description of questions of fact and exercises of discretion as as being non-reviewable questions.

Historically, the categories were based on the concept of jurisdiction: the area of authority assigned to the decision-maker. Prior to the landmark *Anisminic* case, only jurisdictional errors – errors about the extent of the available jurisdiction – were reviewable.[42] Decisions affected by such errors were 'nullities'. Errors within jurisdiction, on the other hand, did not provide any grounds for review: they truly were not reviewable, unlike questions of fact or discretion today. A good exposition of this old framework can be found in the dissenting judgment of Lord Morris in *Anisminic*.[43] At

[39] *Bulk Gas* (n 13) at 133; *Anisminic v Foreign Compensation Commission* [1969] 2 AC 147 (HL) at 174, 207–08, cf at 209.

[40] *Anisminic* (n 39) at 208. For an account of this 'parliamentary monopoly' argument, see also Craig (n 10) at [1-004].

[41] *Pearlman v Harrow School* [1979] 1 QB 56 (CA); *Privacy International* (n 25) at [138]–[139].

[42] *Anisminic* (n 39).

[43] See also Knight, *Vigilance and Restraint* (n 3), Ch 2. His label for this approach is 'Scope of Review'.

that time, the justification for this restriction on review was broadly the same as the justification used nowadays for deferential rationality review on matters of fact and discretion.[44]

The concept of jurisdiction was problematic. The theory was that the line was drawn by interpreting the empowering statute. Jurisdictional questions were those which determined decision-makers' authority to enter upon the enquiry: were they the right person at the right time entering the right enquiry? Were any applicable conditions precedent met? For instance, had a local authority exceeded the territorial limits of its jurisdiction? Or had a specialist tribunal purported to exercise jurisdiction over the wrong kind of dispute or subject matter?[45]

In these examples, the jurisdictional limits are obvious and straightforward. However, the line was by no means always so obvious to draw: many questions might be equally validly understood as either defining the scope of the permitted enquiry (hence going to jurisdiction) or as forming part of that enquiry (hence within jurisdiction). Moreover, jurisdiction could also be lost during the enquiry if the decision-maker acted in breach of natural justice or other fundamental common law requirements such as good faith.[46]

As an example of the difficulties in drawing the line, consider *Anisminic* itself. The case concerned the applicant company's eligibility to receive a share of a fixed amount of available compensation. That amount had been paid to the United Kingdom by Egypt after the latter had nationalised many United Kingdom enterprises during the Suez crisis. The dispute was about the interpretation of statutory eligibility criteria. The respondent Commission was charged by statute with distributing that compensation among all eligible companies. The disputed question concerned the interpretation of the eligibility criteria. Was an error in that regard a jurisdictional error or an error within jurisdiction? This was entirely arguable either way. The eligibility criteria might be understood as determining whether the Commission had power to enter the enquiry as to a company's share of the compensation. Alternatively, their interpretation and application might be understood as part of the enquiry entrusted to the Commission.[47]

The demise of this jurisdictional framework started in *Anisminic* but was not complete in New Zealand until *Bulk Gas*[48] and in the United Kingdom until *R v Hull University Visitor ex p Page*.[49] *Anisminic* itself still maintained the distinction between reviewable jurisdictional errors and unreviewable errors within jurisdiction. The novel step it took was to hold that decision-makers who had power to enter upon the enquiry could lose that jurisdiction and commit a jurisdictional error by asking themselves the 'wrong question': it was only once the right questions had been asked that the answers were protected from challenge as being within jurisdiction.[50] That line, however,

[44] See *Anisminic* (n 39) at 181–82.

[45] ibid at 183.

[46] ibid.

[47] Lord Morris, alone in applying the old jurisdictional approach, took the latter view, because the Commission had to be 'satisfied' the eligibility criteria were met: ibid at 184, 194.

[48] *Bulk Gas* (n 13).

[49] *R v Hull University Visitor ex p Page* [1993] AC 682 (HL).

[50] *Anisminic* (n 39) at 171, 210. Lord Reid preferred avoiding the jurisdictional terminology, but did still use the 'nullity' label.

proved even more illusory than the old line: quite arguably, reaching the wrong answer to any question of law involves asking the wrong question, so that nothing remained protected as being within jurisdiction.

The demise of the jurisdictional doctrine flowed from that instability. Henceforth all questions of law were reviewable on the same basis on which jurisdictional errors had been reviewable – on a correctness standard. In *Bulk Gas*, this was put as a strong, possibly irrebuttable presumption that Parliament has not given the administrative decision-maker 'power to determine questions of law conclusively'.[51]

This background explains the current categories-based framework.The current category of questions of law that attract a correctness standard is the successor to the old category of jurisdictional errors, as expanded by *Anisminic* and the cases that followed it. The jurisdictional terminology has been largely abandoned: instead, courts now say that all errors of law are reviewable and render a decision ultra vires.[52] The common law requirements of natural justice were always considered jurisdictional. Hence they are now considered to involve questions of law, and breach of them renders the decision ultra vires. Questions of statutory interpretation were originally jurisdictional only if they concerned power to enter the enquiry, but that was extended first to asking the right questions and then further to all questions of law.

The categories of questions of fact and exercises of discretion were historically considered not reviewable at all (as reflected in the 'not reviewable' formulation that is still used): review was available only if the decision on the facts or exercise of discretion was so indefensible that the court was driven to conclude the decision-maker must have erred in law in some unidentified respect.[53] That fiction has been abandoned in favour of recognising that courts do review such questions for *Wednesbury* unreasonableness or irrationality, which is a ground of review in its own right rather than a form of illegality.[54] This history also helps explain why the 'error of law' and 'question of law' terminology is confusingly used in at least three senses, as noted earlier.

(2) Arguments for Exploring Alternative Frameworks for the Standard of Review

The proposition that questions of law are for courts to determine, in the sense that they must attract the correctness standard of review, has been considered so axiomatic that any suggestion to the contrary tends to appear like heresy.[55] Yet there are several reasons why the possibility of some judicial restraint on questions of law in some contexts is at least worth debating. Some leading commentators, notably Mike Taggart[56] and Paul

[51] *Bulk Gas* (n 13) at 133.

[52] *Peters v Davison* (n 8).

[53] See *Edwards v Bairstow* (n 22).

[54] *Council of Civil Service Unions v Minister for the Civil Service* [1985] 1 AC 374 (HL) at 410–11.

[55] There are, however, very occasional cases entertaining such a suggestion or giving weight to administrative interpretations: see, eg, *Fulcher v Parole Board* (1997) 15 CRNZ 222 (CA) at 245–47 (Thomas J); *Fischer v The Governing Board of JAS-ANZ* [2016] NZHC 378; *Levi Strauss & Co v Kimbyr Investments Ltd* [1994] 1 NZRL 332.

[56] Taggart (n 10); see also John Smillie, 'Judicial Review of Administrative Action – A Pragmatic Approach' (1980) 4 *Otago Law Review* 417.

Craig,[57] have argued for a move in this direction. Dean Knight has also suggested a possible move to variable intensity review within the current grounds.[58] This section outlines some reasons for considering such a move.

As a starting point, in terms of constitutional principles, no-one disputes that courts must respect Parliament's allocation of authority to the designated decision-maker. That flows from Parliamentary sovereignty and the separation of powers, and is the reason for the limited nature of the courts' supervisory jurisdiction.[59] Under the current categories-based framework to standards of review, this is the reason why evaluation of the facts and exercises of discretion are both reviewed only for *Wednesbury* unreasonableness.[60] It is also the reason why some room for judicial restraint still tends to be incorporated into the modern extensions of substantive review.[61] The only question is whether this principle might ever call for some judicial restraint on questions of law as well as on questions of fact or discretion.

Secondly, we saw in Part B that statutory interpretation very often leaves room for judgement. If there is one right answer to such questions, it is only in the sense that one institution has authority to declare what the right answer is. On the current approach, that institution is the courts. Given the point above about respecting the authority of Parliament's designated decision-maker, however, this point does not go without saying.[62]

Thirdly, under the pre-*Anisminic* historical framework, the courts did respect Parliament's allocation of authority to the primary decision-maker on some questions of law. While the jurisdictional doctrine was not a satisfactory basis for drawing the necessary line, the approach suggests that a more balanced allocation of authority between reviewing courts and primary decision-makers might be available, and that this would not necessarily be inconsistent with the rule of law. As Taggart put it, *Bulk Gas* threw out the baby with the bathwater.[63] The current approach represents the most expansive scope of review that has ever existed.

Fourthly, while the modern approach has discarded the jurisdictional doctrine, it turns out that the most problematic aspect of that framework has been retained: its formalist reliance on categories. In drawing the lines between the categories of the current approach, we have seen that courts are often influenced by justiciability considerations. It would be better for such factors to be recognised directly as part of the test for fixing the standard of review, rather than doing this solely by reference to the categories of question.[64]

Fifthly, this is one of the questions on which a shift from a 'red light' towards a 'green light' approach would make a difference. These competing influences on administrative law are introduced in more detail in Chapter 3. The 'red light' influence has tended to dominate in the mainstream. It is characterised by a focus on controlling and

[57] Craig (n 10), Ch 16.10.
[58] Knight, *Vigilance and Restraint* (n 3), Ch 6.
[59] See Ch 3.B.
[60] *Associated Provincial Picture Houses Ltd v Wednesbury Corporation* [1948] 1 KB 223 (CA) at 228, 230–31; *Wellington City Council v Woolworths New Zealand Ltd (No 2)* [1996] 2 NZLR 537 (CA) at 553.
[61] See Chs 6 and 7.
[62] Taggart (n 10) at 203–04.
[63] ibid at 213; see also Craig (n 10) at [16-038].
[64] Taggart (n 10) at 202–03.

constraining public power to protect individuals against abuse, and by a reliance on the general courts for this. The competing 'green light' influence reflects commitment to the social objectives of public administrative regimes. It seeks to deploy administrative law as a means for promoting those objectives, as much as for preventing abuse.[65]

A move towards varying the intensity of review on questions of law is one of the proposals associated, especially in Canada, with the green light influence. Instead of the extreme 'centralism' of the modern United Kingdom and New Zealand approach, we should make room for greater 'pluralism'.[66] Pluralism in this context means a range of avenues of redress; sharing of interpretive authority; and diversity of interpretation depending on context.[67] In a pluralist framework, the advantages and disadvantages of the general courts and specialist alternative avenues can be weighed up in deciding on the allocation of powers between them. Since facilitating effective and accurate implementation of regulatory schemes is a central objective, the agency charged with administering the scheme may well be better qualified to determine the best interpretation than a generalist court. Specialist expertise and experience are on this view relevant factors in allocating interpretive authority.

Sixthly, versions of such a more pluralist framework have, in fact, been adopted in Canada and (until recently) the United States: this is not merely a theoretical possibility.[68] The development and features of these alternative approaches are outlined in the next section.

Finally, the impact of a move away from a correctness standard of review on questions of law must not be overstated. One objection has been that this would allow decision-makers to act in blatant disregard of the limits of their powers. The Commerce Commission might claim to determine refugee status claims.[69] The answer is that nothing of the sort is proposed. Even if judicial restraint is to extend to all questions of law, that would still involve review on a rationality standard, not no review at all. On that approach, any blatant disregard of legal limits would almost certainly still be struck down on review.

(3) Experience with Alternative Approaches in Canada and the United States

What might an alternative framework for calibrating judicial restraint, including on questions of law, look like? The experience in the United States and Canada furnishes several possibilities. Similar options are suggested by the considerations that can be seen to tacitly underlie the variation of the standard of review in United Kingdom and New Zealand case law.

In the United States, *Chevron* established that courts should substitute their interpretation of statutes only if they find that Congress had a specific intention on the

[65] Carol Harlow and Richard Rawlings, *Law and Administration*, 4th edn (Cambridge, Cambridge University Press, 2022).

[66] See Taggart (n 10) at 212–13, discussing Canadian sources.

[67] See Wilberg and Elliott, 'Deference on Questions of Law' (n 38) at 201–03.

[68] See Taggart (n 10) at 204–12; Craig (n 10) at [16-040]–[16-041].

[69] Or, as English authors like to put it, a rent may be set for the Albert Hall as a furnished tenancy.

precise question at issue. Otherwise, courts should uphold interpretations that are within the range of reasonable interpretations.[70] Judicial restraint thus turned on the clarity and specificity of the relevant statutory provision. This approach was subject to much debate, and was qualified in various ways.[71] After forty years, it has now controversially been abandoned.[72]

Some of the variability seen in United Kingdom and New Zealand cases turns on similar statutory interpretation reasoning.[73] In particular, we have seen that a rationality standard is used to review the application, although not the meaning, of broad or vague statutory criteria.[74] Similarly, courts in some cases have declined to imply constraining purposes into broadly worded empowering provisions.[75]

In Canada, the possibility of judicial restraint (or deference, as it is known there) on questions of law was established in *Canadian Union of Public Employees Local 963 v New Brunswick Liquor Corporation* (*CUPE*).[76] Reasonableness is the presumptive standard of review for questions of law as much as for other types of question, on the current approach established in *Vavilov*,[77] and has been the default standard since *Dunsmuir*.[78] The Canadian approach has been unstable: the Supreme Court has intervened on several occasions to reframe it.[79] However, on all of the approaches adopted since 1979, a reasonableness standard of review has extended to many or most questions of law.

The Canadian approach used to require a contextual balancing of four factors to determine whether the standard of review was reasonableness or correctness.[80] Those factors were: (1) whether there is a privative clause or, conversely, a right of appeal; (2) the expertise of the decision-maker relative to the court; (3) the purpose of the statute as a whole and the provision in particular; and (4) the nature of the issue: did it concern law or fact, or was it a mixed question? The fourth factor is notable. The contextual balancing approach did not discard consideration of the type of question involved as irrelevant, it merely reduced this consideration from categorical and determinative to one factor to be balanced against others.

Similar factors have also appeared to influence the line-drawing in United Kingdom and New Zealand cases. In a few cases, privative clauses have been relied on as legislative indications that judicial review should be restrained.[81] More generally, a range of justiciability factors have tacitly influenced the line-drawing, as we have seen.

[70] *Chevron USA Inc v NRDC* 467 US 837 (1984).

[71] See esp *United States v Mead Corp*, 533 US 218 (2001).

[72] *Loper Bright Enterprises* v *Raimondo*, 603 US 369 (2024), 144 S Ct 2244. For comment see, eg, Cass R Sunstein, 'The Consequences of Loper Bright' (1 July 2024) Harvard Public Law Working Paper No 24–29. Available at: https://ssrn.com/abstract=4881501.

[73] For comparative analysis, see Bree Huntley, 'Judicial Review of Administrative Interpretations: Lessons for New Zealand from the United States?' (2015) 26 *New Zealand Universities Law Review* 791.

[74] *South Yorkshire Transport* (n 14); *Vodafone* (n 16).

[75] *Unison Networks* (n 29).

[76] *Canadian Union of Public Employees Local 963 v New Brunswick Liquor Corporation* (1979) 2 SCR 227.

[77] *Canada (Minister of Citizenship and Immigration) v Vavilov* 2019 SCC 65, [2019] 4 SCR 653.

[78] *Dunsmuir v New Brunswick* [2008] SCC 9, [2008] 1 SCR 190.

[79] See Paul Daly, 'The Supreme Court of Canada's Administrative Law Trilogy' [2020] *Public Law* 408.

[80] See *Pushpanathan v Canada (Minister of Citizenship and Immigration* [1998] 1 SCR 982 at [29]–[37]; also *Dunsmuir* (n 78) at [52]–[55], [64].

[81] See below, Part D, n 101.

In Canada, contextual balancing has now been discarded in favour of a presumptive reasonableness standard for all questions, subject to an exception for three types of question that attract a correctness standard (namely, constitutional questions, questions of general importance to the legal system as a whole, and the demarcation of jurisdiction between different tribunals).[82] The rationale for these exceptions is that the rule of law requires courts to ensure correct and consistent answers to these types of question. A further exceptional category – true questions of jurisdiction[83] – has now been discarded.[84]

The idea that these categories are exceptional resonates with arguments that have featured in United Kingdom and New Zealand case and statute law on privative clauses, as we will see. If, therefore, judicial restraint was available on questions of law in these jurisdictions, courts may still be less inclined to adopt such restraint on these types of questions.

The Canadian experience alerts us to two potential difficulties. The first concerns the choice between contextual balancing and a categorical approach. Canada adopted a contextual balancing approach in recognition that the lines between categories of question are never clear cut. However, since standards of review for all types of question were variable according to those contextual factors, much litigation time and energy was expended on fixing a standard of review in each case. That is why Canada has abandoned the contextual balancing approach in favour of a presumption subject to exceptional categories. However, the return to fixing the standard of review by reference to categories of question may risk a return to formalist reasoning that conceals more substantive reasons. There is no ready answer to this dilemma.

The second difficulty concerns the grounds of review. Since the grounds no longer determine the standard of review in Canada, there has been a strong move away from relying on those grounds at all. The resulting lack of doctrinal structure is problematic. The grounds, after all, serve as standards to guide administrators as well as determining the limits to the courts' supervisory jurisdiction.[85] However, there seems to be no reason in principle why a system of variable standards and intensity of review could not be accommodated within the structure of the grounds.[86]

D. Debate on the Approach to Privative Clauses

As we saw in Chapter 8, the courts' current approach to full privative clauses, established in *Bulk Gas*, is to give them no effect.[87] Just as there is room for doubt whether a correctness standard should continue to apply to all questions of law, so also there is room for doubt about this approach to privative clauses. The two issues are linked by

[82] *Vavilov* (n 77) at [53]. A different approach also applies where the statute provides for an appeal: at [49].
[83] *Dunsmuir* (n 78) at [59].
[84] *Vavilov* (n 77) at [67].
[85] Knight, *Vigilance and Restraint* (n 3) at 24, 129–45, 196–97, 253.
[86] ibid at 256–57; Wilberg, 'Deference on Relevance and Purpose?' (n 28) at 293–94.
[87] *Bulk Gas* (n 13).

the fact that both originate in the old jurisdictional framework, as we will see. Section (1) of this part outlines this historical background as well as the reasons for the current approach, while section (2) explores alternative perspectives.

(1) Background and Reasons for the *Bulk Gas* Approach

(a) History of this Approach: The Jurisdictional Framework

The origins of the *Bulk Gas* approach to privative clauses are found in the old jurisdictional framework that was discarded in *Anisminic* and the cases following it. Recall that on the pre-*Anisminic* approach and also on the approach in *Anisminic* itself while it lasted, availability of review depended on whether a question went to jurisdiction or arose within jurisdiction: review was available for the former but not the latter. Privative clauses, on this approach, could not protect decisions affected by jurisdictional errors, because such decisions were seen as 'nullities': not decisions at all. For errors within jurisdiction, they were not needed, since such errors were, in any event, not reviewable on this approach. Privative clauses did, however, have effect in relation to an exceptional category of error within jurisdiction, namely errors on the face of the record. This was a term of art with a complex and contested meaning. Suffice it to note that this rendered some errors of law reviewable even though they were within jurisdiction. This was the one type of challenge that was precluded by a privative clause.[88]

Although courts have discarded the old jurisdictional framework, *Bulk Gas* oddly retained the concepts of jurisdiction and nullity in terms of the consequences they had for privative clauses. However, the terminology has shifted: instead of jurisdiction, the language of error of law or ultra vires is usually preferred now.[89] On the modern approach, all grounds of review involve errors of law, and errors of law in this broad sense are the modern equivalent of jurisdictional errors. According to *Bulk Gas*, that means that decisions affected by such errors cannot be protected by privative clauses. They are nullities rather than decisions, and hence outside the scope of a clause expressed to protect decisions.[90] The effect is that the concept of jurisdiction has lost its role in limiting review, but it retains its role in justifying disregard of privative clauses. All of this is subject to the possibility that Parliament might confer on a decision-maker power 'to determine' questions of law 'conclusively'. Parliament, being sovereign, has power to do so, but there is a strong and possibly irrebuttable presumption against it.[91]

(b) Reasons for Disregarding Privative Clauses

The modern constitutional reason for this strong or even irrebuttable presumption is that it is the constitutional role of courts to interpret the law and to enforce the

[88] *Anisminic* (n 39) at 182 (Lord Morris, dissenting, setting out the old approach).

[89] See, eg, *O'Regan v Lousich: Proprietors of Mawhera v Maori Land Court* [1995] 2 NZLR 620 (HC) at 626–27.

[90] *Bulk Gas* (n 13) at 134–35, including the quotation from *O'Reilly v Mackman* [1982] 3 All ER 1124 at 1129–33; see also *Anisminic* (n 39) at 170.

[91] *Bulk Gas* (n 13) at 133, 136.

legal limits on public powers.[92] This amounts to invoking the rule of law,[93] although neither *Bulk Gas* nor *Anisminic* expressly use that language.[94] Consistently with Dicey's account,[95] courts have understood the rule of law as requiring that the exercise of public powers must be subject to the supervision of the general courts of superior jurisdiction (the High Court and above).[96] In Aotearoa New Zealand, courts have considered this position to be further reinforced by section 27(2) of the Bill of Rights, which affirms the right to apply for judicial review.[97]

Older cases relied on two further arguments to avoid giving effect to privative clauses. One is the nullity reasoning already noted. The other is that a statute containing a privative clause presents a court with an internal conflict: on the one hand, the statute confers only limited power on a decision-maker, yet on the other hand, the privative clause purports to prevent controls to enforce those limits. The courts can only give effect to one or the other of these conflicting features and, given their commitment to the rule of law, they will give effect to the limits of the power.[98] In the United Kingdom, this argument was resurrected in Lord Sumption's dissent in *Privacy International*.[99]

(2) Alternative Perspectives on Privative Clauses

As discussed in Chapter 8, while courts ignore full privative clauses, they do give effect to partial privative clauses – clauses that restrict or exclude judicial review in favour of statutory avenues of recourse – on certain conditions. This approach to partial privative clauses can be seen as executive-minded abdication of courts' responsibility to maintain the rule of law. It has been criticised on that basis.[100]

However, alternative perspectives are available to support this approach to partial privative clauses. Those same alternative perspectives could arguably also support giving some limited effect to full privative clauses. One form that such limited effect might take is to count the presence of a privative clause as a factor in favour of a more restrained standard of review. This has been suggested very occasionally in the United Kingdom and New Zealand cases.[101] As we have seen, it was the approach in Canada until recently.[102]

[92] ibid at 133; *Anisminic* (n 39) at 207–08.

[93] See Legislation Design and Advisory Committee, *Legislation Guidelines* (Wellington, 2021) at [28.2].

[94] But see, eg, *Tannadyce Investments Ltd v Commissioner of Inland Revenue* [2011] NZSC 158, [2012] 2 NZLR 153 at [3] (McGrath J, dissenting).

[95] AV Dicey, *Introduction to the Study of the Law of the Constitution* (New York, Oxford University Press, 2013 (first published 1885)), Ch IV.

[96] See *Privacy International* (n 25) at [139].

[97] *H (SC 52/2018) v Refugee and Protection Officer* [2019] NZSC 13, [2019] 1 NZLR 433 at [63].

[98] *Anisminic* (n 39) at 208 (Lord Wilberforce).

[99] *Privacy International* (n 25) at [210].

[100] Eg Andrew Beck, 'Accident Compensation and the Supreme Court' [2012] *New Zealand Law Journal* 161.

[101] See, eg, *Anisminic* (n 39) at 207; *Fulcher v Parole Board* (1997) 15 CRNZ 222 (CA) at 247, 259–60; *Graeme Martin Contracting Ltd v Disputes Tribunal* [2018] NZCA 328, [2018] NZAR 1636 at [38].

[102] *Dunsmuir* (n 78) at [52], [64]; but cf now *Vavilov* (n 77) at [30], [39]. The approach continues to apply in British Columbia by virtue of statute: s 58(2)(a) of the Administrative Tribunals Act 2004 (BC).

Sections (a) and (b) below outline relevant alternative perspectives offered by constitutional principles and history respectively. The most thoroughly different perspective, however, is gained by shifting away from the mainstream red light perspective and viewing the issue through a green light lens, as discussed in section (c).

(a) Constitutional Principles

Constitutional arguments are available to support giving effect at least to partial privative clauses. First, there are limits to how much judicial review the rule of law demands. This can be seen by reference to United Kingdom jurisprudence.

In the United Kingdom, an established common law principle requires exhaustion of other remedies before accessing judicial review. This has evidently been considered consistent with the rule of law. If that is correct, then the New Zealand approach of giving effect to partial privative clauses that require recourse to statutory avenues of recourse before accessing the courts is equally consistent.

Further, in *Privacy International*, the United Kingdom Supreme Court expressly accepted that the rule of law does not require unlimited access to judicial review.[103] The plurality judgment of Lord Carnwath favoured a contextual balancing approach to determine what degree and type of scrutiny amounts to sufficient and proportionate protection for the rule of law in each particular context. A minimum requirement was access to the general courts at least for legal questions of general significance.[104] The New Zealand case law giving effect to partial privative clauses is defensible on that basis. The statutory remedial schemes usually include access to the general courts, at least by way of an appeal on questions of law, and the cases have generally insisted on such access as a condition of giving effect to privative clauses.[105]

These rule of law arguments do not justify giving full effect to full privative clauses. But they could justify giving some more limited effect to such clauses, such as by recognising them as a factor in favour of a restrained standard of review.

Secondly, the most obvious constitutional argument in favour of giving effect to privative clauses concerns Parliamentary sovereignty. This requires judges to give effect to Parliament's legislation, which should include privative clauses. Courts have recognised as much in relation to partial privative clauses[106] but, in principle, it applies to full ones too.

The counter-argument, defending the courts' approach of ignoring full privative clauses, is that this is simply an application of the principle of legality.[107] Courts require very clear and explicit words before they accept that legislation was intended to infringe fundamental common law rights.[108] Privative clauses are therefore read, as far

[103] See Hanna Wilberg, 'The Limits of the Rule of Law's Demands: Where *Privacy International* Abandons *Anisminic*', *UK Constitutional Law Blog* (11 September 2019).

[104] *Privacy International* (n 25) at [112], [127]–[139]; drawing on *R (Cart) v Upper Tribunal (Public Law Project Intervening)* [2011] UKSC 28, [2012] 1 AC 663.

[105] See *Tannadyce* (n 94) at [67]–[68]. See also *R (LA (Albania)) v Upper Tribunal* [2023] EWCA Civ 1337, [2024] 1 WLR 1673 at [31], [48], [51].

[106] ibid at [70], [72].

[107] For this link, see *Fitzgerald v R* [2021] NZSC 131, [2021] 1 NZLR 551 at [209]; *Privacy International* (n 25) at [100].

[108] *R v Secretary of State for the Home Department, ex parte Simms* [2000] 2 AC 115 (HL).

as possible, as not abrogating the right of access to the courts. Much the same argument can be made in terms of the Bill of Rights. Section 6 requires an interpretation that is consistent, as far as possible, with the section 27(2) right to judicial review. Therefore, a privative clause will not be read as excluding judicial review where that could not be justified in terms of section 5, unless no more rights-consistent meaning is available pursuant to section 6.

Yet arguably the use of the principle of legality or section 6 of the Bill of Rights is consistent with Parliamentary sovereignty only if the legislation is still given some effect and and is given a meaning that it can plausibly bear. The Supreme Court in *Hansen* established that section 6 of the Bill of Rights supports only reasonably available rights-consistent meanings.[109] Whether that approach has been qualified by the more recent decisions in *Fitzgerald*[110] and *D (SC 31/2019) v New Zealand Police*[111] is open to debate.[112] Arguably, these decisions adopted rights-consistent interpretations that cut across the statutory purpose. However, even on that reading, these cases still do not go as far as the *Bulk Gas* presumption: that entails giving no effect at all to the clear words of full privative clauses.[113]

(b) Old Jurisdictional Framework

The two old arguments in favour of disregarding privative clauses both aim to show that such disregard qualifies as legitimate statutory interpretation, contrary to the concern raised in the previous paragraph. However, both arguments are now open to question.

The first of these old arguments is the nullity argument that was oddly retained in *Bulk Gas*: since a purported decision affected by error of law is a nullity, it does not count as a decision for the purposes of a privative clause.[114] There are at least three reasons to doubt whether this is still a good argument.[115]

First, nullity reasoning has generally gone out of favour in modern New Zealand case law.[116] Decisions affected by error of law are, nevertheless, decisions unless and until they have been quashed on judicial review.[117] This modern approach was affirmed by the Supreme Court in *Ortmann*, rejecting a nullity objection in a different context.[118] Unfortunately, in a footnote the Court declined to comment on the contrary approach taken in a few cases concerning privative clauses.[119] However, these

[109] *Hansen* (n 33).

[110] *Fitzgerald* (n 107).

[111] *D (SC 31/2019) v New Zealand Police* [2021] NZSC 2, [2021] 1 NZLR 213.

[112] For further discussion, see Ch 6.E.

[113] Though recall that the NZ cases have not, in fact, involved clauses with absolute and unqualified wording: Ch 8.E.

[114] See above, text at n 90.

[115] For the first two of these, see Josh Pemberton, 'The Judicial Approach to Privative Provisions in New Zealand' [2015] *New Zealand Law Review* 617 at 644–45.

[116] See, eg, *Martin v Ryan* [1990] 2 NZLR 209 (HC) at 235–37.

[117] See Ch 10.A.

[118] *Ortmann v United States of America* [2020] NZSC 120, [2020] 1 NZLR 475 at [533]–[535].

[119] ibid at fn 609, citing *Malhi v Auckland Co-Operative Taxi Society Ltd* [2014] NZHC 2814, [2015] NZLR 552 at [36]–[39]; *Kaur v Ministry of Business, Innovation and Employment* [2012] NZHC 3563 at [71].

cases are first instance decisions, are against the weight of authority and are not fully reasoned. There is no good reason why this argument should be entertained in the context of a privative clause when it is rejected in other contexts.

Secondly, reliance on the nullity argument in the context of full privative clauses is difficult to reconcile with the modern approach to partial privative clauses.[120] If valid, the logic of this argument would apply equally to partial privative clauses: although their protection is more limited, they still protect 'decisions'. Yet in the partial privative clause case of *Love v Porirua*, the Court of Appeal gave short shrift to the nullity objection. A decision affected by error of law could not be considered legally non-existent. It had sufficient existence to be the subject of a statutory appeal and of the partial privative clause's protection against review before appeal.[121] The more recent cases giving effect to partial privative clauses simply do not mention the nullity objection. All of this casts doubt on the courts' adherence to this argument generally.

Finally, the disregard of privative clauses based on nullity reasoning was easier to defend as involving statutory interpretation on the historical version of the jurisdictional framework than it is on the modern version. That is because the nullity reasoning then still left the privative clause some scope for operation: as outlined earlier, review for errors of law 'on the face of the record' was excluded by a privative clause. Contrast this with the modern version, where full privative clauses are entirely deprived of any effect. That is difficult to present as statutory interpretation.

The second old argument that seeks to present disregard of privative clauses as legitimate statutory interpretation is the internal conflict argument: a privative clause excluding judicial scrutiny contradicts the provisions in the statute that grant powers subject to limits. In light of the rule of law principle, the conflict must be resolved in favour of judicial enforcement of the limits.[122] This is open to question, because it turns on a questionable assumption that limits on powers are meaningless unless they can be enforced by the general courts. Doubts about this are further explored in the next section.

(c) Red vs Green Light

The distinction between red and green light influences is again relevant here. While reliance on the general courts to control exercises of public power is a hallmark of the red light influence, the green light influence instead favours specialist tribunals and other alternative avenues of recourse. It views these as providing better access to justice for affected individuals, and as more likely to promote the regimes' social objectives.

Our system of administrative law today bears a distinct imprint of the green light influence, but the common law of judicial review has been slow to accommodate features supported by that influence. Partial privative clauses, and the courts' approach to these, are one area where both statute and common law do show this influence.

Many administrative or regulatory regimes created by statutes to pursue social and other public interest goals reflect green light thinking in that they include provisions

[120] See Ch 8.E.

[121] *Love v Porirua* [1984] 2 NZLR 308 (CA) at 311.

[122] See above, text at nn 98–99.

for internal review and specialist tribunals. These provisions are often accompanied by partial privative clauses: provisions requiring the statutory avenues to be accessed first or even making them the sole available avenue of recourse.

Where these partial privative clauses are concerned, the green light influence extends to the common law of judicial review. As we saw in Chapter 8, the respect accorded to these clauses is due in part to the courts recognising that statutory avenues for redress of grievances can be preferable to judicial review. That is a green light argument. However, the insistence on access to the High Court in some form and at some stage still reflects the red light influence.

Beyond that, the green light influence has so far had little perceptible impact on the common law of judicial review in New Zealand or the United Kingdom. It would support at least some effect being given to full privative clauses as well. One option for giving them limited effect would be to treat them as a factor in favour of a restrained standard of review. If that approach is to apply in relation to all grounds of review, that presupposes a move to a 'pluralist' framework of varying intensity review on questions of law. As we saw in Part C, such a move is also supported by green light arguments.

10

The Limits of Judicial Remedies

When grounds for judicial review have been established against a challenged decision or measure, what remedies are available in the courts and under what circumstances will these be granted? Among the characteristic features of remedies in judicial review are their limits. First, the nature of the remedies is limited: they do not generally include courts ordering the favourable outcome that is ultimately desired by an applicant for review. Secondly, courts have a discretion to decline remedies even when grounds have been made out. These limits reflect the supervisory nature of the courts' role in this area and the competing public interests engaged by judicial review.

The nature and extent of judicial remedies is one of the more uncertain parts of administrative law. There are many difficult issues, but too often courts dispose of these with little explicit discussion. That leaves those issues to be explored by commentators, but they too have not paid enough attention to this area.[1]

This chapter includes discussion of judicial remedies beyond judicial review. In relation to judicial review proceedings, Part B explores the nature of the available remedies, and Part C the discretion whether to award remedies in judicial review and the factors relevant to that discretion. In addition, Part D concerns appeals to courts on questions of law and Part E collateral challenges. First, however, Part A introduces a theoretical or conceptual question concerning the effect of invalidity that often features in treatments of remedies.

A. Theories of Invalidity – Not the Most Helpful Lens

One way of thinking about judicial remedies in administrative law is to see the issues as turning on a theoretical or conceptual question: What is the effect in law of an unlawful decision? This approach is common particularly in the United Kingdom but is also occasionally seen in Aotearoa New Zealand. The trouble is that there is much controversy and uncertainty on the answer to this question and on its implications for remedies. Moreover, it is doubtful whether this is an appropriate basis for resolving issues about remedies at all.

An alternative lens, and arguably the better way of thinking about remedies, is to recognise that issues about remedies engage a range of competing aspects of the public interest. On any unsettled issue, it is necessary to identify the relevant aspects of the public interest and to make a judgement as to their relative weight. In this chapter, I explore arguments from both of these approaches.

A brief introduction to the debate about theories of invalidity will be helpful by way of background. The choice very broadly is between two possible theories as to the effect of an unlawful decision. One is the traditional absolute theory of invalidity, associated with *Anisminic* and its jurisdictional doctrine discussed in Chapter 9.[2] On this theory an unlawful decision is void ab initio or a nullity: it never has any legal effect. The other is the retrospective invalidation theory that was preferred by Mike Taggart,[3]

[1] See Joanna Bell, 'Remedies in Judicial Review: Confronting an Intellectual Blindspot' [2022] *Public Law* 200.

[2] Amnon Rubinstein, *Jurisdiction and Illegality* (Clarendon Press, Oxford, 1964); *Anisminic Ltd v Foreign Compensation Commission* [1969] 2 AC 147 (HL) per Lord Reid and Lord Pearce.

[3] Michael Taggart, 'Rival Theories of Invalidity in Administrative Law: Some Practical and Theoretical Consequences' in Michael Taggart (ed) *Judicial Review of Administrative Action in the 1980s* (1986) 70.

and was also adopted by Fisher J in *Martin v Ryan*.[4] On this theory, an unlawful decision is voidable. It may become void from the start, but that will only happen when a court of competent jurisdiction exercises its power to quash the decision retrospectively. Until then, it is valid and effective.

There are several variations on these theories. In Sir William Wade's version, an unlawful decision is legally void ab initio but is *treated* as valid unless and until a court of competent jurisdiction exercises its power to quash the decision. It therefore may be void for one purpose and valid for another.[5] In Christopher Forsyth's version, the factual existence of an unlawful and hence void decision can support valid exercises of power by a 'second actor'. It does so in contexts where that second actor has power to act validly regardless of whether the first decision is valid.[6]

Proponents of these theories have sought to provide one coherent theory that could explain all aspects. However, not everyone agrees that this is either possible or desirable. David Feldman has instead argued that remedies respond to a range of competing principles that must be weighed up in particular contexts.[7] Similarly, Joanna Bell has argued that the consequences of legal errors depend on the context, and administrative law issues arise in a great variety of different contexts.[8]

Aotearoa New Zealand's courts since at least the 1980s have been less inclined to rely on theories of invalidity than their UK counterparts. When they do, they usually adopt a position that corresponds to either Taggart's or Wade's theory: an unlawful decision is valid unless and until it is quashed retrospectively by a court of competent jurisdiction, or at least is treated as valid until that point.[9] The Supreme Court in *Ortmann* affirmed this position.[10] That is in contrast to the United Kingdom, where the 'void *ab initio*' option has often been invoked.[11] Even there, it has been questioned in dicta by the Supreme Court in *Majera*.[12] Occasionally, however, the New Zealand courts, too, adopt the 'void *ab initio*' position;[13] or adopt positions on remedial questions that are more consistent with that position.

When theories of invalidity are invoked, a recurring idea is that different types of error have categorically different effects: only sufficiently fundamental errors render a decision void ab initio, while other errors render it merely voidable. This was one characteristic aspect of the old jurisdictional doctrine that has been abandoned since

[4] *Martin v Ryan* [1990] 2 NZLR 209 (HC) at 235–37.

[5] HWR Wade, 'Unlawful Administrative Action: Void or Voidable' (1967) 83 *LQR* 499; (1968) 84 *LQR* 95 (two parts).

[6] Christopher Forsyth, '"The Metaphysic of Nullity": Invalidity, Conceptual Reasoning and the Rule of Law' in Christopher Forsyth and Ivan Hare (eds), *The Golden Metwand and the Crooked Cord* (Oxford, Oxford University Press, 1998) 141.

[7] David Feldman 'Error of Law and Flawed Administrative Acts' (2014) 73 CLJ 275.

[8] Joanna Bell, *The Anatomy of Administrative Law* (Oxford, Hart Publishing, 2020), Ch 7.

[9] Eg *Martin v Ryan* (n 4) at 235–41; *Love v Porirua City Council* [1984] 2 NZLR 308 (CA) at 311.

[10] *Ortmann v United States of America* [2020] NZSC 120, [2020] 1 NZLR 475 at [535]. However, the Court left open the approach to this question in the context of privative clauses: see ibid, fn 609.

[11] See, eg, *Ahmed v Her Majesty's Treasury* [2010] UKSC 2 and 5, [2010] 2 AC 534 at 690; *R (Miller) v The Prime Minister* [2019] UKSC 41, [2020] AC 373 at [69].

[12] *R (Majera (formerly SM (Rwanda)) v Secretary of State for the Home Department (Bail for Immigration Detainees intervening)* [2021] UKSC 46, [2022] AC 461 at [27]–[41].

[13] See, for instance, the High Court cases discussed in JG Pemberton, 'The Judicial Approach to Privative Provisions in New Zealand' [2015] *New Zealand Law Review* 617 at 642–44.

Anisminic:[14] errors within jurisdiction rendered a decision merely voidable, while jurisdictional errors (which meant the decision was outside or without jurisdiction) rendered it void *ab initio*. While modern doctrine has rejected such categorical distinctions, the notion that the most fundamental errors must deprive a decision of any effect, while other errors may have lesser effect, keeps rearing its head.[15]

If we must adopt a theory of invalidity, then some version of the retrospective invalidation theory is clearly preferable to the absolute theory in terms of its fit with the established New Zealand law on remedies as discussed in this chapter. For instance, the remedial discretion would be difficult to explain if the unlawful decision already lacked any effect before a court chooses a remedy. Similarly, if unlawful decisions were void ab initio, then in strict theory there could be no appeal from such decisions; no form of privative clause could protect such decisions;[16] and a decision could not remain in force pending reconsideration.[17]

One aspect of the law, however, is more difficult to reconcile with retrospective invalidation.[18] Collateral challenges involve invoking the grounds of judicial review in proceedings other than judicial review.[19] Such challenges are available at least in some circumstances. They appear to turn on an assumption that unlawful decisions or rules are automatically void by virtue of being unlawful. Otherwise, without prior judicial review proceedings, the invalidity of a decision could not be relied on in proceedings other than judicial review. As such, collateral challenges do not fit with Taggart's retrospective invalidation theory. They are, however, still potentially consistent with Wade's theory according to which unlawful decisions are merely *treated* as effective.

These issues involving theories of invalidity recur in the case law and commentary. It is therefore necessary to have some understanding of them. However, as noted, more substantive public interest considerations are the better basis for determining what the law should be in this area.

B. What Remedies are Available in Judicial Review

(1) The Limited Nature of the Remedies, and Reasons for these Limits

One of the characteristic features of judicial review is found in the limits on the remedies available. These limits reflect the limited, supervisory, role of the courts in judicial

[14] See Ch 9.C(1)(b).

[15] See, eg, the dissent in *R (Privacy International) v Investigatory Powers Tribunal* [2019] UKSC 22 at [197], [199], [203], [211] *New Zealand Employers Federation Inc v National Union of Public Employees* [2002] 2 NZLR 54 (CA) at [112]. For discussion, see also Janet McLean, 'Roadblocks, Restraint and Remedies: The Idea of Progress in Administrative Law' in Grant Huscroft and Michael Taggart (eds), *Inside and Outside Canadian Administrative Law: Essays in Honour of David Mullan* (Toronto, University of Toronto Press, 2006) 211.

[16] See Ch 8.E on this.

[17] Judicial Review Procedure Act 2016 (JRPA), s 17.

[18] Taggart, 'Rival Theories of Invalidity' (n 3) at 92–93.

[19] See Part E of this chapter.

review. As explained in Chapters 1.D and 3.B, it is not for the reviewing court to decide what the correct or best decision would have been. Rather, the court's role is to ensure that decisions are made within the legal limits of the relevant powers, and are arrived at by lawful procedure and lawful reasoning.

Remedies therefore do not involve the reviewing court substituting its own conclusion on the correct or best decision and ordering that outcome. For that type of remedy, aggrieved parties usually need to turn to tribunals or other statutory avenues of recourse.[20] Instead, the usual remedy in judicial review is to quash the decision, and often to send it back ('remit' it) for reconsideration, or to declare it unlawful. This is further discussed in the next section. The effect of quashing and remitting is that a legally flawed decision is not allowed to stand, and that a fresh decision can be made without the relevant flaw. Often – at least where the flaw lay in the procedure or the reasoning – it will be open to the decision-maker to arrive at the same decision again. However, there is always at least a chance that lawful procedure and reasoning the second time around will lead to a different conclusion. Either way, the point is that the conclusion to reach is a matter for the decision-maker, not for the reviewing court.

Judicial review remedies also do not include damages for loss caused by an unlawful decision.[21] The only exception is found in discretionary damages for breach of the New Zealand Bill of Rights Act 1990; we will return to this. Aside from this, damages are available for loss caused by unlawful decisions only where, in addition to making out grounds for review, the applicant can also make out a private law cause of action such as a tort.[22] Many decisions that are legally flawed do not give rise to a private law claim.

A further characteristic of judicial review remedies is that they are discretionary rather than available as of right. Part C of this Chapter deals with the reasons for this and how it works.

(2) Range of Final Remedies and their Sources

The modern application for judicial review is a proceeding provided by the Judicial Review Procedure Act 2016[23] or, alternatively, under Part 30 of the High Court Rules 2016. However, both the availability of such proceedings and the remedies available in them derive from common law.[24] The Act provides that, on an application for review, the court may grant relief in the nature of any one or more of five listed common law remedies.[25] The High Court Rules designate the same five remedies as 'extraordinary remedies' and provide for an application for any one or more of these remedies.[26]

[20] See Chs 2.C.(1) and 15.

[21] *Minister of Fisheries v Pranfield Holdings Ltd* [2008] 3 NZLR 649 (CA) at [75], [84], [98]–[130].

[22] See Ch 12.

[23] This Act in substance re-enacted the Judicature Amendment Act 1972 (JAA), while updating and simplifying the wording and structure.

[24] See Ch 8.D.

[25] JRPA, ss 8 and 16(1) (previously JAA, ss 4 and 9).

[26] High Court Rules 2016 (HCR), rr 30.2 and 30.3.

The first three of these remedies are known as prerogative remedies or prerogative writs. They are mandamus, prohibition and certiorari. The remaining two have been labelled equitable remedies. They are declarations[27] and injunctions. At common law, each individual remedy had its own distinct rules and requirements as to its availability, standing to apply for it and so on. But the point of the statutory procedure is to do away with that complexity: orders in the nature of all of these remedies are available on the same conditions. The only difference between them lies in what they achieve.

Mandamus is an order to perform a duty. An injunction can achieve the same thing if it is a mandatory injunction. The usual form of mandamus is an order to consider a matter according to law: it is the order used when a decision is remitted for reconsideration. Only exceptionally will a court issue mandamus to order a particular outcome; we will return to this.[28] Prohibition is self-explanatory: it achieves the same as an injunction to refrain from doing something (a negative injunction). Certiorari is the order used to quash an unlawful decision: it deprives the decision of legal force. Finally, a declaration is an authoritative judicial statement of the legal answer to a question at issue. The most common form of declaration in the judicial review context is to simply declare a decision, or some aspect of the decision or of the process, to be unlawful. A declaration can also be more specific: it can declare any point of law relevant to the proceedings. The difference between a declaration and quashing is explored in the next section.

The most commonly granted remedies are as follows. Courts will either grant certiorari to quash a decision, often accompanied by mandamus or a mandatory injunction to consider the matter according to law, or a declaration that the decision or some aspect of it is unlawful.

Damages are available as a public law remedy, without making out a private law cause of action, only for breach of the Bill of Rights Act.[29] The Act itself makes no provision for remedies. The damages remedy was established in *Baigent's case*.[30] It is one of a range of remedies for breach of the Act, which also include all of the usual judicial review remedies and exclusion of evidence in criminal proceedings. Courts have a discretion as to remedies under the Act. Damages will be granted in the exercise of that discretion only if other remedies are unavailable or do not adequately vindicate the right.[31] Where judicial review remedies are available, courts usually consider those to be adequate. But there are instances of *Baigent* damages exceptionally being awarded in this context.[32]

The remedies available against the 'Crown' are subject to a further limit. Section 17 of the Crown Proceedings Act 1950 provides that no injunction may be granted against the Crown, and declaratory relief is to be used instead. The scope of this immunity remains uncertain.[33] In most contexts, the 'Crown' includes the central executive

[27] Also available under the Declaratory Judgments Act 1908.

[28] See section (4) of this part of the chapter.

[29] See further Ch 12.B(3).

[30] *Simpson v Attorney-General* [1994] 3 NZLR 667 (CA) (*Baigent's case*).

[31] ibid; *Taunoa v Attorney-General* [2007] NZSC 70, [2008] 1 NZLR 429 at [253]–[259].

[32] See *X and Y v Chief Executive of Oranga Tamariki* [2022] NZCA 622, [2022] 2 NZLR 261 at [82]–[99].

[33] See Philip A Joseph, *Constitutional and Administrative Law in New Zealand*, 5th edn (Wellington, Brookers, 2021) at [18.5.3].

government: ministers and departments. However, *M v Home Office* is generally understood to establish that the Crown immunity against injunctions applies only to the Sovereign and His Representative, the Governor-General.[34] In any event, the immunity lacks significant practical effect, given the principle that public authorities are expected to comply with the law without any need for coercive orders.[35]

(3) Uncertainty as to the Difference between Quashing and Declaration

The usual remedy, as we saw, is either to quash the decision (certiorari) or to declare it unlawful. But what is the difference? One view is that there is no real difference: Graham Taylor states that the two remedies are 'practically fused'.[36] This view has much to commend it. However, it has become common for courts to choose a declaration on the basis that it is a more limited remedy.[37] It is unclear exactly how or in what respects they consider a declaration to be a more limited remedy.

One clear point is that a declaration is not a coercive order.[38] Seeking a declaration is therefore a less adversarial approach.[39] There are also some situations where a declaration is obviously more appropriate than quashing, such as where the challenged measure is spent but a declaration will still serve to vindicate the rule of law.[40]

A declaration does not change the effect or consequences of a decision – it merely declares its legal status.[41] The effect of a declaration therefore depends on the effect of a decision being unlawful – but that is itself a contentious question, as we saw in Part A of this chapter. If an unlawful decision was void ab initio, then declaring a decision to be unlawful would reveal and confirm its pre-existing lack of legal effect. That view remains common in the United Kingdom.[42] On the usual New Zealand approach, however, an unlawful decision has legal effect, or at least is treated as having legal effect, unless and until it is quashed. On this view, an unlawful decision retains this effect if the court issues only a declaration rather than quashing it. That is at first sight a very significant difference, apparently making the declaration a much weaker remedy. However, the significance of the difference is much reduced by a further principle, already mentioned: public authorities are expected to comply with the law without any

[34] *M v Home Office* [1994] 1 AC 377 (HL); *Bennet v Superintendent, Rimutaka Prison* [2002] 1 NZLR 616 (CA).

[35] The Rt Hon Woolf and Jeremy Woolf, *Zamir & Woolf: The Declaratory Judgment*, 4th edn (London, Sweet & Maxwell, 2011) at 7.

[36] Graham Taylor, *Judicial Review: A New Zealand Perspective*, 4th edn (Wellington, LexisNexis NZ, 2018) at [5.04].

[37] On increased use of declarations generally, see Dean R Knight, 'Declaratory Remedies in Judicial Review and the Prudential Exercise of Power' (Public Law Conference, Ottawa, 2–5 July 2024). Available on SSRN.

[38] *McGechan on Procedure* (online looseleaf ed, Thomson Reuters) at [HR30.2.06(2)].

[39] *Zamir & Woolf* (n 35) at 5.

[40] See, eg, *Borrowdale v Director-General of Health* [2020] NZHC 2090 at [280]–[292]. There was an appeal, but not on this point.

[41] *Zamir & Woolf* (n 35) at 1, 7–8.

[42] See, eg, *R (Miller) v The Prime Minister* [2019] UKSC 41, [2020] AC 373 at [69].

need for coercive orders.[43] Therefore, when a decision has been declared unlawful we can expect that it will not be implemented or relied on.

That leaves one potential practical difference between a declaration and quashing. On the 'effective unless quashed' view that is established in New Zealand, it may be that a declaration does not affect actions taken in reliance on the unlawful decision *before* the decision was declared unlawful in judicial review. Courts often appear to proceed on this assumption.[44] In other words, it may be that an appropriately worded declaration operates prospectively only, although the matter is not usually put that way.[45] But this point cannot safely be considered settled – the competing view that a declaration merely confirms an unlawful decision's voidness still has some currency even in New Zealand.

Even on the usual 'effective until quashed' view, the effect of a declaration may depend on its wording. In *Martin v Ryan*, for instance, the remedies included a declaration that the impugned orders had been 'nullities from their inception' – clearly that declaration was intended to have retrospective effect.[46] The declaration granted in *Middledorp*, in contrast, deliberately avoided wording that would equate to quashing.[47] This ability to adjust the wording makes the declaration a flexible remedy.

What types of action in reliance on an impugned decision or measure might be protected by limiting the remedy to a declaration with prospective effect? One example is a contract that has been entered into with a third party in reliance on the impugned decision. Courts wanting to protect that third party have other options, such as declining to grant any remedy. This was the option considered in *Martin v Ryan* for this purpose.[48] In *Ririnui*, however, the Supreme Court sought to protect the third party by granting only a declaration that the impugned decision was unlawful. In declining to require reconsideration that might lead to setting aside the contract, it took the view that the contract was unaffected by the declaration.[49]

Another significant example of a type of action that the courts may seek to protect is action taken pursuant to delegated legislation before it is successfully challenged. It may be that courts can avoid overturning all such past action simply by refusing to quash the delegated legislation and instead adopting an appropriately worded declaration. For instance, in some cases courts have sought to achieve this by merely declaring that the defendant had failed to comply with the duty to consult before promulgating the legislation (rather than that the legislation was unlawful).[50]

[43] *Commerce Commission v Fletcher Challenge Ltd* [1989] 2 NZLR 554 (HC) at 610.

[44] See, eg, *Ririnui v Landcorp Farming Ltd* [2016] NZSC 62, [2016] 1 NZLR 1056 at [189]–[192]; *Middledorp v Avondale Jockey Club Inc* [2020] NZCA 13 at [49].

[45] On the possibility of prospective invalidation see *Martin v Ryan* (n 4) at 238–40. Declarations are not mentioned.

[46] ibid at 244.

[47] *Middledorp* (n 44) at [49].

[48] *Martin v Ryan* (n 4) at 242–44.

[49] *Ririnui* (n 44) at [189]–[192], cf at [139]–[142] (note, however, that the Court presented the choice as being between declaring the decision unlawful or setting aside the contract – there was no mention of setting aside the decision).

[50] See, eg, *R v Secretary of State for Social Services, ex parte Association of Metropolitan Authorities* [1986] 1 WLR 1 (QBD) at 15.

(4) Exceptional Situations when Substitutionary Remedies are Available

Mandamus or a mandatory injunction might at first sight appear to be a substitutionary remedy, contrary to what was said earlier about the limited nature of remedies in judicial review. Could mandamus not be used to order a particular outcome; for instance, to grant a licence? There are in fact occasional cases where such orders are made, but they are exceptional and potentially controversial. This is not what mandamus normally means.

The key to understanding both why mandamus is not normally substitutionary, and when the exception applies, is to recall that mandamus is an order to perform a *duty*. The vast majority of judicial review challenges concern the exercise of *discretion*; or, where they concern the application of rules, the decision-maker has room for evaluative judgement. The only relevant legal duty in such contexts is to exercise that discretion or judgement according to law. That is the duty enforced by mandamus in the usual type of case: as already noted, mandamus takes the form of an order to consider the matter according to law.

The exceptional case allowing a substitutionary order, then, is where the law imposes a duty to reach a particular conclusion: in other words, where the decision-maker does *not* have a discretion nor room for judgement. A straightforward example would be if a clearly qualified voter was turned away. Mandamus should issue to require that she be allowed to vote. Usually, however, even when the law imposes a duty, the application to the facts is not as clear-cut as with qualification to vote: it usually leaves some room for judgement. In such contexts, a substitutionary order may still be available, but this is more controversial. The court first has to conclude that in light of the law and the evidence, only one conclusion was tenable. Some further supporting factors are also usually needed to persuade a court to make an exceptional substitutionary order.

This was the basis of the exceptional substitutionary remedies in both *Fiordland Venison*[51] and *Financial Services Complaints Ltd v Chief Ombudsman*.[52] In *Fiordland Venison*, the empowering provision required the Minister to grant a licence if satisfied that five criteria were met. This amounted to imposing a duty, but one that depended on the decision-maker's judgement as to how the criteria applied to the facts. It was common ground that four of the five criteria were satisfied, but there was no such concession as to the fifth. The successful ground of review was that an irrelevant consideration had been taken into account – one outside of the five exhaustive criteria. Ordinarily, that would leave it open to the decision-maker on reconsideration to come to the same conclusion. However, in considering the remedy, the Court took the view that there was no evidence on which a reasonable decision-maker could find the fifth criterion not satisfied.

[51] *Fiordland Venison Ltd v Minister of Agriculture* [1978] 2 NZLR 341 (CA) at 352–53.

[52] *Financial Services Complaints Ltd v Chief Ombudsman* [2022] NZCA 248, [2022] 2 NZLR 740. For helpful discussion of the test, see also *Te Pou Matakana Ltd v Attorney-General (No 2)* [2021] NZHC 3319, [2022] 2 NZLR 178 at [175]–[176].

Similarly in *Financial Services Complaints Ltd*, all criteria in the relevant guidelines favoured granting approval for the plaintiff to use the Ombudsman name, with just one possible exception. That possible exception was the question of whether use of the name might cause confusion. However, the Court dismissed the Ombudsman's finding that the name might cause confusion, on the ground that this had no rational foundation in evidence. Approval was therefore the only lawfully available decision.[53]

In both cases, the grant of the exceptional remedy was further supported by the unfairness of requiring the applicant to submit to a fresh decision after very significant delays.[54] In *Financial Services Complaints Ltd*, a further consideration was a concern that impartial reconsideration seemed impractical after the original decision by the Chief Ombudsman had been struck down for predetermination.[55]

Aside from explicitly mandatory orders, quashing a decision without remitting it for reconsideration can sometimes also have substitutionary effect. This is the case if the impugned decision imposed a disadvantage such as ordering deportation or cancelling a licence, and if the decision-maker's power under the relevant legislation is spent. In such a case, quashing the decision removes the disadvantage, and declining to remit for reconsideration deprives the decision-maker of the opportunity to make the same decision again. Courts have granted this form of effectively substitutionary remedy for reasons similar to those discussed above. Examples include *Wolf*[56] and *Lewis v Wilson & Horton*.[57] Finally, we will see that interim remedies in some circumstances also have substitutionary effect.

(5) Statutory Option in Section 17 Adds Flexibility

In addition to providing for remedies in the nature of the various common law remedies discussed above, the Judicial Review Procedure Act 2016 includes some additions and modifications of the common law around these remedies. Among these, section 17 allows a reviewing court to remit a decision for reconsideration *without* quashing it: the impugned decision continues in effect unless and until the decision-maker revokes it on reconsideration.[58] This increases remedial flexibility, similar to the use of declarations.[59] Where quashing a decision or measure would be unduly disruptive in the period pending reconsideration, a court may require the decision-maker to remedy flaws without first quashing the decision.[60]

[53] *Financial Services Complaints Ltd* (n 52) at [54]–[75], [92]–[96].
[54] ibid at [107]; *Fiordland Venison* (n 551) at 350.
[55] *Financial Services Complaints Ltd* (n 52) at [98]–[106].
[56] *Wolf v Minister of Immigration* [2004] NZAR 414 (HC) at [73]–[78].
[57] *Lewis v Wilson & Horton Ltd* [2000] 3 NZLR 546 (CA) at [66], [73], [97].
[58] Previously JAA, ss 4(5) and (6).
[59] *Air Nelson Ltd v Minister of Transport* [2008] NZAR 139 (CA) at [74] confirms that the factors guiding the remedial discretion (see Part C of this chapter) are relevant to the s 17 power.
[60] See, eg, *Ngāi Tai Ki Tāmaki Tribal Trust v Minister of Conservation* [2018] NZSC 122, [2019] 1 NZLR 368 at [102]–[104], [108].

(6) Interim Remedies

Finally, it is important to note the availability of interim relief where this is 'necessary … to preserve the position of the applicant'.[61] Provided that the challenge has some prospect of success, this may be granted particularly where the applicant's position would be irretrievably changed by implementing the impugned position before a full hearing of the judicial review application. Conversely, the court also weighs the impact on the public interest if interim relief were granted but the challenge ultimately failed.[62]

For instance, in *Ngā Kaitiaki Tuku Iho*, interim relief was refused in a challenge to the provisional approval of a Covid-19 vaccine, despite finding an arguable case that the relevant power was not available. This was partly because the illegality was considered to be of limited substantive significance (the risks of the vaccine had been fully assessed), and also because the public health repercussions of granting interim relief were 'too great, by some considerable margin'.[63]

Interim relief usually requires implementation of the impugned decision to be delayed. However, difficult judgements are called for where this is not practically possible. A common example is where the impugned decision is to deny participation in an event, and the event cannot wait for the full judicial review hearing.[64] In such cases, interim relief will effectively determine the final outcome. Indeed, this is a special situation in which expressly substitutionary relief is often granted: for instance, an order to allow the applicant to participate in the event.[65] While that is strictly unorthodox and controversial, even interim relief in the usual negative terms will have the effect of a substitutionary remedy in this situation. To stay with the example of participation in an event that cannot be delayed, a defendant who has been ordered not to implement a decision to deny participation has only two options: to allow participation or to cancel the event entirely. The latter will rarely be the preferred option for either party and sometimes will not be possible or in a defendant's power at all. The option taken therefore will be to allow participation. In short, this is a situation in which effectively substitutionary relief is the only relief that can be given.

If possible, it is preferable in such cases to schedule an urgent full hearing. Where that is not possible, courts will look more closely at the strength of the applicant's case before granting interim relief.[66]

[61] JRPA, s 15 (previously JAA, s 8). See also HCR, r 30.4.

[62] The approach is set out in *Carlton & United Breweries Ltd v Minister of Customs* [1986] 1 NZLR 423 (CA) at 430–31; *Minister of Fisheries v Anton Trawling Co Ltd* [2007] NZSC 7, (2007) 18 PRNZ 754 at [3], [8].

[63] *Ngā Kaitiaki Tuku Iho Medical Action Society Inc v The Minister of Health* [2021] NZHC 1107, [2021] NZAR 173 at [75].

[64] Eg *Dunne v CanWest TVWorks Ltd* [2005] NZAR 577 (HC) (pre-election leader's debate); *Watson v Department of Corrections* [2012] NZHC 3542 (family funeral).

[65] That was the form of relief granted in the cases cited in n 64. It is not available under the terms of JRPA, s 15, but may be granted under the HCR instead.

[66] *Kennedy v Boyle* [2015] NZHC 536 at [22].

C. The Remedial Discretion in Judicial Review

When a court has found grounds of review to be made out, it still has a discretion concerning remedies. It may decline to grant any remedy or may grant a limited remedy. This common law discretion is affirmed and continued by section 18 of the Judicial Review Procedure Act 2016.[67]

The remedial discretion can be explained on the basis that the public interest served by judicial review has many facets. Competing aspects of the public interest fall to be weighed in the circumstances of each case. In many contexts, the most important public interests are in upholding the rule of law and protecting individuals from unlawful uses of power, and remedies are granted on that basis. In other contexts, however, these may be partly outweighed by competing public interests, such as avoiding undue disruption to public administration and protecting third party reliance on official decisions. Giving due weight to such competing considerations may call for some or even all remedies to be refused.

Remedial restraint can also be seen as part of the range of available responses to justiciability concerns.[68] Where the matters at issue call for the sort of democratic legitimacy or institutional capacity that the courts lack, courts may decline to intervene at all. Alternatively, however, they may intervene on a more restrained basis in some respect – that is what is referred to as secondary justiciability. One option in this regard is remedial restraint: granting only limited remedies.[69]

Before we explore the factors that may weigh for and against granting a remedy in sections (2) and (3) of this part, section (1) outlines uncertainty in the case law about the breadth of the remedial discretion.

(1) Breadth of Remedial Discretion

There is some divergence in the authorities on the breadth of the remedial discretion. One line of authority, including the Supreme Court decision in *Ririnui*, adopts a strong presumption in favour of relief.[70] For the Court of Appeal in *Air Nelson Ltd v Minister of Transport* also, the 'starting point' was that an applicant who has made out grounds of review is entitled to relief, at least if there is 'substantial prejudice'. A court needs 'extremely strong reasons' to refuse a remedy.[71]

[67] Previously JAA, s 4(3).

[68] See Ch 8.A.

[69] See John Caldwell, 'Judicial Review: The Fading of Remedial Discretion?' (2009) 23 *New Zealand Universities Law Review* 489; Edward Clark, 'Vigilance, Restraint, and Legitimacy: Explaining the Stubborn Persistence of Remedial Discretion in New Zealand Judicial Review' (Public Law Conference, Ottawa, 2–5 July 2024).

[70] *Ririnui* (n 44) at [112] and [147].

[71] *Air Nelson Ltd v Minister of Transport* (n 59) at [60]–[61].

Another line of Court of Appeal authority has cast doubt on this presumption, calling for a more 'nuanced' approach.[72] Perhaps this is no longer good law since the presumption was adopted in the more recent Supreme Court authority of *Ririnui*. However, the Supreme Court made no reference to this competing line of authority.

In my view, there is less of a conflict than appears – although perhaps the discretion is not embraced with equal enthusiasm by all judges. The presumption is never said to be in favour of granting *all* available remedies regardless of the circumstances. The 'nuance' called for in the apparently competing line of authority may well be achieved, consistently with the presumption, by limiting remedies to a declaration in cases where there are factors weighing against relief. That is what the Supreme Court did in *Ririnui*, after all.[73] The presumption in favour of relief was a presumption that *some* relief should be available, such as at least a declaration. Willingness to exercise the discretion also varies according to the circumstances of each case, such as the nature of the decision and the decision-maker. The discretion is more likely to be deployed in contexts that call for limited review.[74]

(2) Factors in Favour of Granting a Remedy

The strength of the public interest in granting remedies depends on the circumstances. The main relevant factors are the gravity of the defect, the strength and importance of the applicant's interest, and to what extent any affected third parties who would be protected by exercising the discretion share responsibility for the defect.[75] We will see examples of each of these factors under the next heading.

The strength and importance of the applicant's interest depends on the particular facts, as we will see, and on whether fundamental rights or other important values are at stake. Where Treaty of Waitangi rights in land will be irretrievably lost, for instance, that should be a strong factor in favour of relief. It is open to doubt whether the Supreme Court fully appreciated the strength of this factor in declining full relief in *Ririnui*.[76] In recent cases, tikanga[77] values have also been taken into account in this context. In *Sweeney*, for instance, a declaration was granted to vindicate the applicant's mana,[78] in circumstances where events had rendered quashing and reconsideration inappropriate.[79]

[72] *Rees v Firth* [2012] 1 NZLR 408 (CA) at [48].

[73] *Ririnui* (n 48) at [148]–[149], [189]–[192].

[74] See *Rees v Firth* (n 71) at [22], [27].

[75] See, eg, *Martin v Ryan* (n 4) at 242–43.

[76] *Ririnui* (n 48) at [43], [149], [189]–[192]; cf the dissent at [132]–[141]. See Hanna Wilberg, 'Administrative Law' [2016] *New Zealand Law Review* 571 at 581–83.

[77] Māori customary law.

[78] Dignity and status.

[79] *Sweeney v The Prison Manager, Spring Hill Corrections Facility* [2021] NZHC 181, [2021] 2 NZLR 27 at [74]–[77].

(3) Factors against Granting a Remedy, and the Balancing Exercise

This section explores how the above considerations interact with factors weighing against granting a remedy. The main relevant factors are (a) prejudice to third parties who have relied on the impugned decision, (b) undue disruption of public administration, and (c) mootness. Also relevant are (d) delay in bringing proceedings, as well as (e) the availability of other remedies. But these will generally only lead to refusal of a remedy in combination with one or more of the other factors. A further factor is (f) where there has been a fair hearing and a lawful decision on an appeal: this may count against relief in relation to the original decision, on the basis that the appeal has 'cured' the defect in the original decision. Finally, a very problematic factor that sometimes plays some part is (g) the futility of a remedy in the sense that the outcome would necessarily be the same even after lawful reconsideration.

(a) Prejudice to Third Parties

Third parties will suffer prejudice due to judicial review remedies where they have spent money or otherwise changed their position in reliance on the impugned decision. For instance, a third party that had been awarded a casino licence had commenced construction of the premises;[80] a third party that had been awarded a contract for laboratory services had set up its operations;[81] and third parties that had purchased disputed farm land had spent money on stock and chattels.[82] As discussed earlier, the prejudice to third parties may be avoided by limiting relief to a declaration that the decision was unlawful, which leaves transactions entered into in reliance on the decision unaffected.[83] It could also be avoided by declining to grant relief altogether.

However, limiting or excluding remedies comes at a cost to the applicant. It is appropriate only where the prejudice to third parties outweighs competing factors. The central competing factors are the gravity of the defects in the decision and the strength and importance of the applicant's interest. For instance, in *Martin v Ryan*, the applicant faced losing the farm he had worked for much of his life, pursuant to an order that had been made in fundamental breach of natural justice. These factors weighed heavily in favour of quashing the decision despite the prejudice to the third-party purchasers.[84]

Alongside those central factors, the relative merits of the applicant and the third parties are relevant in this type of case. Most importantly, prejudice to the third party is the less likely to limit a remedy the more clearly the third party was warned about the likely challenge.[85] Conversely, this is also where delay becomes relevant: if the prejudice to the third party could have been reduced by the applicant bringing proceedings

[80] *Auckland Casino Ltd v Casino Control Authority* [1995] 1 NZLR 142 (CA).

[81] *Diagnostic Medlab Ltd v Auckland District Health Board* [2007] 2 NZLR 832 (HC); the issue did not arise on appeal.

[82] Eg *Ririnui* (n 48); *Martin v Ryan* (n 4).

[83] That was the solution in *Ririnui* (n 48).

[84] *Martin v Ryan* (n 4) at 243.

[85] See, eg, ibid. Cf *Ririnui* (n 48) at [189]–[192], where the warning was considered inadequate.

more promptly, that may weigh against a remedy.[86] Furthermore, the court may also take into account whether the applicant bears any responsibility for contributing to the defect in the decision.[87]

(b) Undue Disruption of Public Administration

Disruption of public administration is a somewhat more controversial factor. Generally, rule of law concerns weigh heavily in favour of invalidating unlawful exercises of public power, and any administrative inconvenience is the necessary price to pay. However, in relatively extreme situations this factor can weigh in favour of a limited remedy that avoids undoing a large number of decisions, particularly where other factors also support this.

The most obvious examples involve crisis responses. For instance, if the statutory notices providing for the COVID-19 pandemic lockdowns in 2020 had been found ultra vires the empowering statute,[88] the Court would likely have given careful consideration to the impact of invalidating those notices. Similarly, where a decision not to disclose individual vaccination information to Māori health providers was found unlawful, the Court only granted limited remedies to avoid wasting valuable time and resources for both sides, in the context of urgent efforts to increase vaccination rates.[89] An earlier example, *Bailey v Christchurch City Council*, concerned an aspect of the Canterbury earthquakes recovery effort. In deciding to install a new wastewater system in the Baileys' neighbourhood, the council had failed adequately to consult residents. However, the challenge was brought 10 months later, by which time installation of the new system was well under way, and up to $1.7 m had been spent. Quashing the decision at that point would also have greatly prejudiced other residents. The combination of these factors persuaded the Court to limit the remedy.[90] It required the Council to reconsider the decision after consulting the Baileys, but it did not quash the decision nor require consultation with all those affected.[91]

Aside from crisis contexts, this factor is also relevant more generally in challenges to delegated legislation. Where a measure has been in force for some time before being found defective, a court may limit the remedy to a declaration in limited terms that do not affect earlier decisions pursuant to the measure.[92]

(c) Mootness

Courts may decline a remedy on grounds of mootness: events have moved on, and there is no longer a live controversy between the parties. Where this applies, however,

[86] Eg *Auckland Casino* (n 79); see further below under (d).
[87] See *Martin v Ryan* (n 4) where little such responsibility was found.
[88] They were upheld in *Borrowdale v Director-General of Health* [2021] NZCA 520, [2022] 2 NZLR 356.
[89] *Te Pou Matakana Ltd v Attorney-General (No 2)* (n 51) at [187]–[179].
[90] Using JRPA, s 17.
[91] *Bailey v Christchurch City Council* [2013] NZHC 1933, [2013] 3 NZLR 679 at [81]–[86].
[92] See, eg, *R v Secretary of State for Social Services, ex parte Association of Metropolitan Authorities* [1986] 1 WLR 1 (QBD).

often the proceedings will be struck out before a full hearing, rather than relying on the remedial discretion once grounds have been made out.[93]

There are also exceptions. Even where a matter is moot, a court may still hear it and grant remedies if the issue remains of significant public importance.[94] For instance, in *Skerret-White*, the Court of Appeal found that the Waitangi Tribunal has jurisdiction to issue summons to Ministers. While the inquiry about proposed legislation in which this issue arose had already been completed urgently due to pressure from the government, a formal ruling on this issue was still appropriate because it was of continuing public importance to settle the point. However, no further orders were made.[95] A similar approach was taken in *Nixon v Chief Executive of the Ministry of Social Development* where a challenge based on defects in a standard form used by the Ministry of Social Development had been settled before hearing. The Court still ruled on the issue concerning the form, as this remained live for other cases.[96]

(d) Delay

The longer a challenge is delayed, the greater the prospect that overturning the decision will cause undue disruption to public administration or prejudice to third parties. In the United Kingdom, judicial review is subject to a three-month time limit largely for that reason.[97] In New Zealand, no time limit applies to judicial review generally, but some statutory regimes impose such limits.[98] In all other contexts, this issue is dealt with purely by means of the remedial discretion.

While delay can be a strong factor against relief, its significance is always assessed in terms of its impact on the interests affected. Even a fairly lengthy delay, such as one year, will not stand in the way of relief where it has no significant impact. In *Air Nelson*, for instance, the one-year delay in challenging airport landing charges was no problem for two reasons. First, it was explained by the fact that the applicant had been pursuing other remedies, and secondly it did not cause any prejudice to anyone.[99] In contrast, in *Bailey*, a ten-month delay in challenging a decision on a new waste water system led the court to grant only a limited remedy, because quashing the decision would have disrupted works already well under way.[100] In a situation like this, even quite a short delay may lead to a remedy being declined, at least provided the applicant was aware that major works would commence promptly in reliance on the decision.[101]

[93] See, eg, *Te Whakakitenga O Waikato Inc v Martin* [2016] NZCA 548, [2017] NZAR 173.

[94] See, eg, *Electoral Commission v Cameron* [1997] 2 NZLR 421 (CA).

[95] *Skerret-White v Minister for Children* [2024] NZCA 160 at [118]–[124].

[96] *Nixon v Chief Executive of the Ministry of Social Development* [2017] NZHC 1807 at [23]–[24]. The Court proceeded to find the Ministry's process lawful.

[97] Civil Procedure Rules 1998, r 54.5.

[98] Eg the Immigration Act 2009 has several such time limits.

[99] *Air Nelson Ltd v Minister of Transport* (n 59).

[100] *Bailey* (n 91).

[101] Eg *Auckland Casino* (n 79), where the delay was only a month and a half, and included the Christmas shutdown period.

(e) Availability of an Appeal

Appeal rights can often be preferable to judicial review: if the right is to a full appeal then it extends to challenging the merits rather than merely the legality of the decision; furthermore, the forum for the appeal may be a specialist tribunal. In the United Kingdom, for that reason and to avoid overloading judicial review courts, as a general rule appeal rights must be exhausted before judicial review is available.[102]

In New Zealand, in contrast, the Act expressly allows judicial review applications even if an appeal is also available.[103] Further, the Supreme Court has held that it is no abuse of process to pursue judicial review and appeal proceedings in parallel.[104] However, an appeal is relevant to the remedial discretion: where an available appeal right is the more appropriate remedy, a reviewing court may exercise its discretion to require that appeal right to be exercised first.[105]

While there is no general requirement to exhaust appeal rights, some particular statutory regimes do include provisions requiring an appeal right to be exercised first (or even substituting an appeal right for judicial review). These are generally considered to be forms of privative clause (we may call them partial privative clauses) and are discussed in Chapter 8.E in that context. In brief, courts tend to give effect to such requirements so long as they do not deprive applicants of effective avenues of redress.

(f) Defect has been 'Cured' by Appeal

A different issue arises when an appeal right has already been exercised, but without success. If judicial review is sought after that, there is then an issue whether this is still available to challenge the original decision or is confined to the decision on appeal. The original decision could no longer be challenged if the appeal hearing had 'cured' the defect in that decision. This possibility applies especially to procedural unfairness challenges: if the applicant has received a fair hearing on the appeal, the unfairness at first instance could be considered cured. But this may also apply to other types of defects.

We will see that on the modern New Zealand position, such curative effect is no more than a factor in the remedial discretion. But what are the circumstances in which an appeal has any such curative effect?

On that question, *Calvin v Carr* is still the leading decision.[106] It held that there is a spectrum of contexts, ranging from contexts where the applicant has a right to nothing less than two fair hearings, to contexts where an unfair first hearing can safely be regarded as superseded by a fair re-hearing. It set out a non-exhaustive list of factors for determining the approach in contexts that lay between those two ends of the spectrum. By implication, similar factors are relevant to determining where on the spectrum any particular case falls. An appeal hearing may not serve to cure defects at the first hearing if one or more of the following three factors apply: the defect is too

[102] See Ivan Hare, Catherine M Donnelly and Joanna Bell, *De Smith's Judicial Review*, 9th edn (London, Sweet & Maxwell, 2023) at [16-014]–[16-023].
[103] JRPA, s 16(3)(a) (previously JAA, s 4(1)).
[104] *Ortmann v United States of America* [2020] NZSC 120, [2020] 1 NZLR 475 at [567]–[590].
[105] *Fraser v State Services Commission* [1984] 1 NZLR 116 (CA) at 123, 128.
[106] *Calvin v Carr* [1980] AC 574 (PC) at 592–93.

flagrant; the consequences are too severe; and the appeal process is not a sufficiently full and independent rehearing. As to the third factor, *Secretary for Justice v Simes* confirms that to have any curative effect, an appeal must be a full re-hearing, approaching the matter afresh.[107]

As to the form of any curative effect, the traditional answer adopted from the United Kingdom was that in the right circumstances the curative effect is absolute: judicial review of the original decision is no longer available.[108] In New Zealand, however, the better view now appears to be that an appeal hearing that has a curative effect is merely a strong factor supporting a discretionary denial of remedies in relation to the original decision. The court's focus, consistent with the approach to the remedial discretion generally, is on whether the appeal has, in substance, removed the prejudice to the applicant.[109]

(g) Futility and Inconsequential Errors – The Most Controversial Factor

The most controversial of the factors against granting remedies is futility in the sense that the outcome will inevitably be the same following any reconsideration. Reliance on this has often been rejected.[110] The main reason is that decision-makers should be under an obligation to exercise their powers lawfully even when the outcome is inevitable: denying a remedy in such cases would send the message that getting the answer right is all that matters. Further reasons against relying on this factor apply in some contexts. In cases involving breach of the right to a hearing, it is arguably impossible to know what the outcome would be if this flaw was remedied: the whole point of the right to a hearing is that the person subject to the decision may have relevant information to share that is otherwise not available to the decision-maker.[111] In cases involving reasoning process errors, it is not for the court to decide what the outcome should have been. Nor can the court readily determine the outcome the authority itself would have reached on lawful reconsideration, as judicial review does not usually elicit evidence on this point.[112]

Despite all this, futility in this sense has occasionally been relied on as part of the reasons for limiting or denying remedies.[113] But usually there will be other additional strong reasons involved. In *Rajan v Minister of Immigration*, for instance, the Court considered it unnecessary to come to a final conclusion on the lawfulness of the impugned decision because the matter had not been fully argued and two parallel proceedings were pending on the matter.[114] In *Moir v IHC New Zealand Inc*, the Court declined a remedy for an ACC reviewer's defective refusal to admit evidence. Aside

[107] *Secretary for Justice v Simes* [2012] NZCA 459, [2012] NZAR 1044 at [109]–[111].

[108] *Calvin v Carr* (n 106) at 596.

[109] *Simes* (n 107) at [109]; *Nicholls v Registrar of the Court of Appeal* [1998] 2 NZLR 385 (CA) at 435–37 (obiter). *Reid v Rowley* [1977] 2 NZLR 472 (CA) at 478–84 seems best read as already signalling this move.

[110] See, eg, *Survey Nelson Ltd v Maritime New Zealand* [2010] NZCA 629 (leave to appeal was refused: [2011] NZSC 61). *Rajan v Minister of Immigration* [1996] 3 NZLR 543 (CA) stated courts should hesitate.

[111] See *R v Taito* [2003] 3 NZLR 577 (PC) at [19], making this point in a different context.

[112] Joanna Bell, 'Remedies in Judicial Review' (n 1) at 208–11.

[113] Eg *Stininato v New Zealand Boxing Association Inc* [1978] 1 NZLR 1 (CA) at 8–9, 29; *GXL Realties Ltd v Minister of Energy for New Zealand* [2010] NZCA 185 at [67].

[114] *Rajan* (n 109) at 552.

from considering that reconsideration would make no difference, the Court was also concerned about excessive delays caused by the applicant and her lawyer, and pointed out that she still had a right of appeal on the merits from the reviewer's substantive decision.[115]

The United Kingdom in 2015 controversially introduced an express statutory requirement to refuse a quashing remedy if it is highly likely that the decision would be the same regardless of the defect.[116] However, research has shown that this provision has been applied exceedingly rarely.[117]

A less controversial provision is found in the Judicial Review Procedure Act 2016. Section 19 expressly provides for a discretion to refuse relief for 'a defect in form or a technical irregularity' that has not led to 'a substantial wrong or miscarriage of justice'.[118] This provision has been very rarely used. A good example of its appropriate use is found in *Northland Regional Council v Rogan*. The Local Government Act 2002 required rates-setting resolutions to specify a due date for rates, and the impugned resolution failed to do so. However, a date had in fact been set by other means, and that date was duly included in rates notices sent to ratepayers. The Court applied section 19, holding that the error was technical and caused no prejudice or disadvantage.[119]

D. Limited Appeals from Administrative Authorities to the Courts

An important alternative to judicial review, for anyone wishing to enforce administrative law, is recourse to statutory appeals. Unlike judicial review, which forms part of the inherent jurisdiction of the High Court, appeals are available only where they are provided by statute. Appeals from administrative decision-makers include appeals to specialist tribunals, which commonly are appeals on the merits. Those are further discussed in Chapters 2 and 15.

In this chapter, we look at appeals from administrative authorities' decisions to the general courts. These are often appeals from internal review decisions or specialist tribunals rather than directly from the original decision. They are usually limited to questions of law.[120] Such appeals on questions of law are also available from tribunals such as the Tenancy Tribunal that consider party-to-party disputes about the application of regulatory regimes at first instance.[121]

[115] *Moir v IHC New Zealand Inc* [2019] NZCA 92 at [48]–[50].
[116] Senior Courts Act 1981, s 31(2A).
[117] Bell, 'Remedies in Judicial Review' (n 1) at 207–08.
[118] Previously JAA, s 5.
[119] *Northland Regional Council v Rogan* [2018] NZCA 63, [2018] NZAR 507 (leave to appeal was refused: [2018] NZSC 69).
[120] See, eg, Accident Compensation Act 2001, s 162; Social Security Act 2018, s 405; Legal Services Act 2011, s 59.
[121] See, eg, Residential Tenancies Act 1986, s 119.

The grounds on which this type of limited appeal can be brought are essentially the same as the grounds of judicial review.[122] A significant part of the High Court's supervisory jurisdiction in administrative law takes the form of these limited appeals. Many leading administrative law cases arose in that context. Some of them expressly noted this equivalence in the grounds; for instance, the *Wolf* case on variable intensity reasonableness review,[123] and the English case of *E v Secretary of State for the Home Department* on mistake of fact as a ground of review.[124] Such cases are good authority in judicial review cases and vice versa.

Less-common types of limited appeals to the courts include appeals 'as if' the impugned decision 'had been made in the exercise of a discretion'.[125] This is understood as allowing somewhat wider scope than judicial review: the court may intervene not only for errors in law – that is, on all grounds of review – but also because the decision is 'plainly wrong'.[126] Limits on appeals can also take the form of procedural constraints, such as a leave requirement,[127] or allowing an appeal only by way of a case stated by the body appealed from.[128]

Let us turn finally to the remedies available in such appeals. These obviously depend on the provisions of the particular statute. Commonly, the statutory remedies include the judicial review remedies of quashing the decision and remitting the matter to the authority or tribunal below.[129]

Often, however, the remedies also include broader options. These include, for instance, power for the appellate court to make 'such other orders as it sees fit'.[130] Some statutes go further and give the appellate court the same remedial powers as the merits tribunal below:[131] a power to 'confirm, modify or reverse' the original decision.[132] Versions of both of these formulations are included in the High Court Rules[133] which apply to many other administrative law appeals.[134]

In considering such broader remedial options, it must be remembered that the scope of the appeal is limited. The apparent breadth of the remedial power is best understood as constrained by the limited scope of the appeal, hence it does not extend to entering the merits. However, such broad powers do appear to authorise substitutionary remedies on a broader basis than judicial review.

[122] Marcelo Rodriguez Ferrere, 'The Functional Convergence of Appeal and Judicial Review' [2016] *New Zealand Law Review* 157.

[123] See *Wolf v Minister of Immigration* [2004] NZAR 414 (HC) at [41].

[124] See *E v Secretary of State for the Home Department* [2004] EWCA Civ 49, [2004] QB 1044 at [40]–[43], [50].

[125] See, eg, Broadcasting Act 1989, s 18(4).

[126] See, eg, *Television New Zealand v West* [2011] 3 NZLR 825 (HC) at [11]; *Shotover Gorge Jet Boats v Jamieson* [1987] 1 NZLR 437 (CA) at 439.

[127] See, eg, Immigration Act 2009, s 245(1).

[128] See, eg, Social Security Act 2018, s 405.

[129] See, Immigration Act 2009, s 245(4); District Courts Act 2016, s 128(1)(b) and (3) which apply to ACC appeals to the High Court by virtue of the Accident Compensation Act 2001, s 162.

[130] Immigration Act 2009, s 245(4).

[131] Social Security Act 2018, s 408.

[132] Social Security Regulations 2018, reg 254.

[133] HCR, r 20.19(1)(a) and (c).

[134] See, eg, Legal Services Act 2011, s 59.

E. Collateral Challenge

Collateral challenges are a potentially controversial remedial option, and the law on them is uncertain and unsettled. It is well established that they are available in some cases, but it is also clear that there are limits. The difficulty is where to draw the line. I will start by (1) explaining what collateral challenges are, and will then (2) clarify the issue and (3) outline what is at stake normatively, before (4) outlining the state of authority.

(1) What is Collateral Challenge?

Collateral challenge involves relying on the grounds of judicial review to challenge the validity of an exercise of administrative power (a decision or a rule) in proceedings other than judicial review or appeal. This can be done in a range of different scenarios. Invalidity can be claimed as a defence to proceedings brought by the state or by an authority that rely on a decision or rule. Those proceedings can be a criminal prosecution for breach of a rule or a civil action to enforce it. Invalidity can also be claimed on the offensive, so to speak, to support a private law claim in tort or restitution against a public official.[135]

An example of defending a criminal prosecution by means of a collateral challenge is found in *Sellers*.[136] Mr Sellers successfully defended a prosecution for breach of minimum safety requirements for yachts departing New Zealand, on the grounds that those requirements exceeded the available powers. The fact that this was a collateral challenge is not mentioned in the judgment.

Collateral challenges in defence to civil proceedings may be found in proceedings brought by an authority to recover a debt that is due pursuant to a decision or rule. For instance, landing charges set by airport authorities have repeatedly been challenged by airlines. This has usually taken the form of judicial review,[137] but an airline may also be able to defend the recovery proceedings on the grounds that the charges are invalid.[138]

Turning to the use in support of private law claims, let us start with tort claims against public officials purporting to exercise statutory powers. A collateral challenge is needed to defeat the official's defence of statutory authority in such a case. For instance, in *Cooper v Wandsworth Board of Works*, a trespass claim succeeded because the defendant had exercised its statutory power to demolish premises in breach of natural justice.[139] In restitution claims against public authorities, a successful collateral challenge can

[135] For more on this last option, see Ch 12.

[136] *Sellers v Maritime Safety Authority* [1999] 2 NZLR 44 (CA).

[137] See, eg, *Air Nelson Ltd v Minister of Transport* (n 59).

[138] *Dunedin Airport Ltd v Mt Cook Group Ltd* HC Dunedin CP 34/96, 10 October 1996; but cf discussion below at n 163.

[139] *Cooper v Wandsworth Board of Works* (1863) 14 CB NS 180, 143 ER 414 (Comm Pleas). For a modern NZ instance, see *Ardern v Rodney District Council* HC Auckland M735/96, 2 October 1997.

establish that a payment demanded by a public authority was not legally due, thus giving rise to a claim for restitution of the payment.[140]

A further possible context is an application for habeas corpus, requiring the authority to release a person from detention unless it can show legal justification for the detention. Such justification could, in principle, be defeated by making out grounds of judicial review. However, the general rule is that where detention is challenged based on grounds of review, that must be done directly by means of judicial review proceedings.[141]

(2) Clarifying the Issue as to its Availability

When it comes to the availability of collateral challenge, we should be clear what is and is not in dispute. The contentious question concerns the appropriate type of proceeding for establishing the invalidity of the relevant exercise of power. There is no doubt that the invalidity of a decision can be relevant to the sort of proceedings outlined in the previous part, once that invalidity has been determined in judicial review proceedings. For instance, a court will not entertain debt proceedings for local authority rates where those rates have been struck down in judicial review.[142] Where judicial review proceedings testing the validity of a relevant decision or rule have not yet been brought or determined, a court can stay other proceedings until that has happened.[143] A collateral challenge is different: it involves asking the court to determine the question of invalidity in those other proceedings, without first seeking judicial review in separate proceedings. The issue is when the courts will permit this procedural move.

Theories of invalidity could pose a problem for collateral challenges, as we saw in Part A. However, courts do allow these challenges in some cases, and they rarely worry about theories of invalidity in this context. A more relevant question is what is at stake normatively.

(3) What is at Stake? Normative Arguments For and Against

Competing normative arguments for and against collateral challenge fall to be weighed against each other, and may apply differently in different contexts. Normative arguments in favour of collateral challenges concern the rule of law and access to justice. The rule of law argument is particularly strong in the context of a criminal prosecution for breach of an invalid rule: no-one should be convicted without a valid legal basis.[144] While a prosecution could always be stayed to allow separate judicial review proceedings, requiring use of that avenue would raise access to justice issues, as not all

[140] See, eg, *Waikato Regional Airport Ltd v Attorney-General* [2004] 3 NZLR 1 (PC).

[141] *Manuel v Superintendent of Hawkes Bay Regional Prison* [2005] 1 NZLR 161 (CA).

[142] *Rogan v Kaipara District Council* [2017] NZHC 2329 at [8], [24]. The case was appealed but not on this point.

[143] *Reid v Rowley* [1977] 2 NZLR 472 (CA) at 483; *Moore v Police* [2010] NZAR 406 (HC) at [29].

[144] *Boddington v British Transport Police* [1999] 2 AC 143 (HL) at 153, 173; *Siemer v Solicitor-General* [2013] NZSC 68, [2013] 3 NZLR 441 at [65] (Elias CJ dissenting).

defendants would be able to afford it.[145] The Supreme Court has suggested in obiter that this concern may be weaker in New Zealand than in the United Kingdom, as judicial review is more accessible in New Zealand.[146] However, the affordability concern applies with equal force. On the basis of these two arguments, the House of Lords held in *Boddington* that collateral challenges should, as a rule, be available in criminal proceedings.[147] Yet we will see that New Zealand courts have recognised many exceptions to this.

There is a range of countervailing normative arguments against collateral challenges. One relevant aspect of the rule of law ideal applies to society rather than government: it requires most people to follow the law without enforcement.[148] From this perspective, a concern about allowing collateral challenge in criminal proceedings is the message this implies: people who have doubts about the validity of a rule may break that rule and wait to be prosecuted.[149] Furthermore, any resulting increased need for enforcement action may also be seen as wasteful of public resources, and may unduly compromise pursuit of the public interest served by the regime.[150] This point also applies in the context of proceedings to recover debts arising from official charges. Indeed, in the context of recovery of local authority rates, Parliament has expressly excluded collateral challenges.[151] These concerns are also reflected in the general presumption of validity of delegated legislation:[152] public authorities are entitled to enforce such legislation unless and until it has been found invalid.[153]

There is room for reasonable disagreement on the relative weight of these arguments for and against defensive collateral challenge. The balance also depends on the particular circumstances. For instance, all else being equal, the argument against collateral challenge is stronger in the case of a defendant who has deliberately flouted a rule than one who was unaware of it.

There are also concerns about collateral challenges undermining features of judicial review that serve the wider public interest and the constitutional limits of judicial review. Dean Knight has explored these concerns and possible solutions.[154] One concern is that in a collateral challenge, unlike in judicial review, there is no remedial discretion.[155] However, *Brady v Northland Regional Council* proposed that courts should decide whether to allow a collateral challenge based on the likelihood of the decision being quashed in judicial review, taking account of the remedial discretion.[156]

[145] *Boddington* ibid at 173–75.
[146] *Siemer* (n 145) at [206], fn 255. Presumably the Court had in mind the lack of a leave requirement and time limit.
[147] *Boddington* (n 144).
[148] Brian Z Tamanaha, 'A Concise Guide to the Rule of Law' in Gianluigi Palombella and Neil Walker (eds), *Relocating the Rule of Law* (Oxford, Hart Publishing, 2008) 3 at 6, 10–11.
[149] See *R v Bird* [2019] 1 SCR 409 (SCC) at [27]–[28], [38].
[150] See *Harwood v Thames Coromandel District Council* [2008] NZAR 518 (HC) at [29].
[151] Local Government (Rating) Act 2002, s 60.
[152] *Harness Racing New Zealand v Kotzikas* [2005] NZAR 268 (CA) at [62].
[153] *Hoffmann-La Roche & Co AG v Secretary of State for Trade and Industry* [1975] AC 295 (HL).
[154] Dean Knight, 'Ameliorating the Collateral Damage Caused by Collateral Attack in Administrative Law' (2006) 4 *New Zealand Journal of Public and International Law* 117 at 130–46.
[155] ibid at 138–40.
[156] *Brady v Northland Regional Council* [2008] NZAR 505 (HC) at [45], [47].

Further, the remedy in a successful collateral challenge is usually of a substitutionary nature: damages are awarded or a conviction is avoided on the basis that the decision or rule is invalid. In contrast, the usual remedy in judicial review – reflecting the supervisory nature of the court's role – is to remit the matter for reconsideration. As a result, judicial review may ultimately result in the same outcome. Knight proposed adjusting collateral challenge accordingly: courts hearing such challenges should, once they find a decision to be unlawful, order a stay of proceedings and remit the matter for reconsideration.[157]

In tort claims, this point is relevant to the measure of damages, at least if reconsideration is no longer practicable. Should damages be awarded for the full loss, on the basis that there was no power to make the challenged decision or rule, or should they be reduced for the contingency that the decision might have been the same on reconsideration? There is diverging authority on this point, which is further explored in Chapter 12.[158]

Finally, concerns about collateral challenges include the fact that judges of the District Court, where many of the relevant proceedings are brought, lack familiarity with the grounds of judicial review. However, the significance of this point has been doubted.[159] The concern could, if necessary, be addressed by transferring proceedings to the High Court.[160]

(4) The State of Authority: When and to What Extent is Collateral Challenge Available?

Collateral challenge is available at least in some contexts. Indeed, its availability in the context of private law claims against public officials is not usually disputed.[161]

Its use as a defence to criminal prosecutions or civil proceedings brought by public authorities is more controversial. Appellate level authority in New Zealand on this use of collateral challenge is largely limited to dicta. Cooke J in *Reid v Rowley* cast doubt on its appropriateness.[162] Similarly, in one of the cases about airport landing charges, the Court of Appeal doubted whether an authority's summary judgment application can be defeated by a collateral challenge.[163] However, dicta in *Sugrue*[164] and *Siemer*[165] start from the assumption that collateral challenge is available by way of defence in

[157] Knight (n 154) at 145.

[158] *Roberts v Rodney District Council* [2001] 2 NZLR 402 (HC) at [47]; *R (Lumba) v Secretary of State for the Home Department* [2011] UKSC 12, [2012] 1 AC 245.

[159] *Boddington* (n 143) at 220, 228; Knight (n 154) at 140–41.

[160] *Chapman v Police* [2023] NZHC 1435 at [23].

[161] For discussion of cases, see Ch 12.B(1).

[162] *Reid v Rowley* (n 143) at 483.

[163] *Air New Zealand Ltd v Wellington International Airport Ltd* [2009] NZCA 259, [2009] 3 NZLR 713 (CA) at [81]–[87].

[164] *PF Sugrue Ltd v Attorney-General* [2004] 1 NZLR 207 (CA) at [47]–[49]. The Privy Council on appeal did not address this point.

[165] *Siemer* (n 143) at [65], [206], fn 255, [208].

some contexts. In *Sellers*[166] and *Taylor v Poultry Board*,[167] the Court of Appeal entertained such collateral challenges without any discussion of the point. The weight of appellate dicta is in favour of at least some availability. In some cases, the Court of Appeal has refused to entertain such a collateral challenge, but that has been presented as an exception to the 'general principle' that such challenges are available.[168]

At High Court level, collateral challenges have been allowed in many criminal cases.[169] There is much recent authority for a general principle of availability that can be displaced by the particular circumstances. A range of factors may contribute to rendering collateral challenge unavailable.

Often the question turns on the terms of the relevant statute. Collateral challenge may be excluded expressly, as with rates,[170] or by implication from the context. For instance, in *Harwood v Thames Coromandel District Council* it was held that enforcement of the dog registration regime would be unduly compromised if a prosecution for failure to register could be defended on the basis that the registration fee was unreasonable.[171]

The availability of other avenues of recourse and other avenues for accountability and participation may also count against collateral challenge to general rules.[172]

Another obstacle is where the authority responsible for the impugned measure is not a party to the proceedings and could not be joined as a party. That may compromise a proper defence of the measure, particularly if the challenge requires a detailed examination of the decision-making process. For instance, in *Grueber* the court declined to entertain a collateral challenge, on grounds of inadequate consultation, to the imposition of road toll charges. The main reason was that the Minister responsible for imposing that charge was not a party, and the agency bringing the prosecution was not well placed to defend the process followed by the Minister.[173] In contrast, no such difficulty arose in *K v New Zealand Police*, given that the challenge turned simply on a question as to the interpretation of the relevant Act.[174]

Finally, it has been considered relevant whether the issue as to validity is sufficiently central to the case that is before the court: where it is relevant only very indirectly, that counts against entertaining a collateral challenge.[175] *Harwood* is an example: the validity of the registration fee was not sufficiently directly relevant to the charge of failing to register.[176]

[166] *Sellers* (n 135).
[167] *Taylor v NZ Poultry Board* [1984] 1 NZLR 394 (CA); the challenge failed on the merits.
[168] See, eg, *Vortac New Zealand Ltd v R* [2021] NZCA 200 at [36]–[42].
[169] See, eg, *K v New Zealand Police* [2021] NZHC 3539; *Whichman v Department of Corrections* [2013] NZHC 3075; *Reade v Smith* [1959] NZLR 996 (SC).
[170] See n 151.
[171] *Harwood* (n 150) at [29].
[172] ibid; *Grueber v New Zealand Transport Agency (No 2)* [2014] NZHC 2924, [2015] NZAR 54 at [27].
[173] *Grueber* (n 172) at [27]. See also, eg, *Manuel* (n 141) at [30], [49].
[174] *K v New Zealand Police* (n 169) at [13]–[14].
[175] *Brady* (n 156) at [45], [46].
[176] *Harwood* (n 150) at [28]–[29]. See also *Stanton v New Zealand Police* [2016] NZCA 561 at [7]–]10]. In contrast, this factor favoured the availability of a collateral challenge in *K v New Zealand Police* (n 169) at [13]–[14].

Part IV

Public and Private

11

Public Law and Private Power: The Public Nature Test

How do we decide whether a decision and a decision-maker are of a sufficiently public nature to be subject to judicial review or more generally to public law constraints? Or, to put it the other way, how far do public law constraints reach into decision-making of a partly private nature or by partly private bodies? That is the question explored in this chapter.

This is the first of two chapters in Part IV of this book concerning the public-private boundary. This boundary concerns the uncertain interface between public and private law, and the extent to which the law treats public and private power differently. The two chapters in Part IV approach this boundary from both directions. The present chapter explores how far public law norms extend into the private sphere: how private can a decision or a decision-maker be and still attract all or some of the public law constraints comprised in the grounds of judicial review and the Bill of Rights? This is followed by Chapter 12, which explores the application of private law obligations and constraints to public officials and authorities exercising public powers.

The 'public nature' question explored in this chapter is a common issue due to the extensive move to privatisation and corporatisation since the 1980s.[1] That move started with the introduction of state-owned enterprises to take on functions such as electricity generation that had been the responsibility of government departments.[2] As we will see, since then, many previously public entities and functions have been shifted outside of the core public sector – extending even to functions like the operation of prisons. Within the public sector, private contracting methods are often used, not just for purchasing supplies such as stationery, but also, for instance, for procuring the delivery of social services and for assessing eligibility for such services. Is provision of social services by private companies under contract, or by privatised or corporatised public entities, sufficiently public to warrant judicial review or other public law constraints? For instance, take Kāinga Ora (previously known as Housing New Zealand), a corporatised public entity charged with providing social housing to those who cannot afford to access housing in the private market.[3] Are its decisions on entering or terminating tenancy agreements sufficiently public to be amenable to judicial review?

The public law constraints at issue include not only the constraints comprised in the common law grounds of judicial review but also the New Zealand Bill of Rights Act 1990. The Act's own application provision, section 3, provides that it applies only to acts done by the three branches of government and by anyone performing a 'public function, power, or duty' conferred or imposed by law. The Supreme Court in *Moncrief-Spittle* affirmed that the analysis required by section 3 is very similar to the public nature test for judicial review but is not necessarily the same.[4]

The 'public nature' test is usually presented as a test for the availability of judicial review.[5] However, a closer look at the case law reveals a broader role for this test. It is better understood as a test for determining whether and to what extent public law

[1] For discussion, see, eg, Michael Taggart (ed), *The Province of Administrative Law* (Oxford, Hart Publishing, 1997).

[2] State-owned Enterprises Act 1986.

[3] Established by the Kāinga Ora–Homes and Communities Act 2019, s 9 as a Crown entity for the purposes of the Crown Entities Act 2004. The predecessor was the Housing Corporation Act 1974, s 3.

[4] *Moncrief-Spittle v Regional Facilities Auckland Ltd* [2022] NZSC 138, [2022] 1 NZLR 459 at [49].

[5] On that basis, it belongs in Ch 8. It is covered there briefly in Part C.

constraints apply to a decision. This is a better framing of the question addressed by this test for two reasons.

First, the function of the 'public nature' test is different from that of the justiciability test (whether the matter is suitable for judicial determination) that goes to the availability of judicial review on a given issue.[6] Unlike justiciability, the public nature test does not address whether courts have a role to play. If a body or a decision are not sufficiently public to be subject to public law constraints, they are still subject to private law constraints and often also to statutes imposing regulation, both enforceable by the courts. What the public nature test determines is rather the range of types of constraint that courts should apply to the decision: whether the public law constraints comprised in the grounds of judicial review and the Bill of Rights should apply *in addition* to private law and statutory constraints. As the Privy Council said in *Mercury Energy*:[7] 'Judicial Review was invented to secure that decisions are made by a public body according to law even if the decision does not otherwise involve an actionable wrong.'

Secondly, where public law constraints do apply, they represent norms applicable to the decision-maker in question regardless of any proceedings to enforce them. Further, the type of proceeding that can be used to enforce them is not limited to judicial review. Other public law avenues of recourse may be used. Importantly, these constraints are also sometimes given effect through private law proceedings. When bodies exercising public powers are sued in tort, for instance, the defence of statutory authority is available, and this may be defeated by invoking the grounds of judicial review.[8] When such bodies are sued in contract, courts may import public law constraints by means of implied terms.[9] The public law constraints that can thus be imposed by means of private law proceedings include both the common law grounds of review and the rights protected by the Bill of Rights.[10]

The terminology relating to the 'public nature' issue is unsettled. 'Justiciability' is sometimes used in a broad sense, including not only the issues concerning suitability for judicial determination that are discussed in Chapter 8.A, but also the public nature test discussed in this chapter.[11] 'Jurisdiction' is another alternative term,[12] presumably referring to jurisdiction to entertain the particular type of proceeding (an application for judicial review). However, both terms are potentially misleading, as they may suggest that a lack of public nature entails that courts have no role or power in relation to the body and decision in question. As we have just seen, that is not so. For clarity, it is preferable to confine justiciability to its narrower sense, and to avoid the term jurisdiction in this context.

There has been a shift in approach to the 'public nature' issue. Just as the approach to justiciability has shifted from focusing on the source of a power to considering the

[6] See Ch 8.A.

[7] *Mercury Energy Ltd v Electricity Corporation of New Zealand Ltd* [1994] 2 NZLR 385 (PC) at 388.

[8] See, eg, *Cooper v Wandsworth Board of Works* (1863) 14 CBNS 180; for details, see Ch 12.

[9] See, eg, *Peters v Collinge* [1993] 2 NZLR 554; for details, see text at nn 69, 214–217.

[10] But recall that the test for the application of the latter may be slightly different: see n 4 and accompanying text.

[11] See, eg, *Te Whakakitenga O Waikato Inc v Martin* [2016] NZCA 548, [2017] NZAR 173 at [18]–[22].

[12] Eg Jenny Cassie and Dean Knight, 'The Scope of Judicial Review: Who and What May be Reviewed' in *NZLS Intensive: Administrative Law* (Wellington, New Zealand Law Society, 2008) 63 at 63, 67, 69–77.

nature of the subject-matter, the approach to the public nature question has shifted from focusing on the institutional nature of a body and the source of its powers to considering the nature of the decision-making function at issue. Yet the institutional nature of the body continues to be one of the factors that help to determine whether the decision is of a sufficiently public nature.

In this chapter, we start by exploring in Part A what might be meant by 'public nature' generally. Issues concerning 'public nature' can be divided broadly into two versions (noting that many cases involve both versions), which we explore in turn in parts B and C. The first arises from the private or partly private nature of the body, while the second arises from the fact that the body (often a clearly public body) is engaging in an activity of a private or commercial nature, most often contracting. Each part considers the approach taken in the case law to its version of the issue and also the competing reasons at play. Why might we want to expose partly private bodies or decisions to public law constraints and, conversely, why might we hesitate to do so?

A. What is Public? Reasons and Indicia

As Peter Cane has pointed out, functions and powers do not come labelled 'public', and public nature is not an observable quality like 'redness'.[13] Nor can we simply assume that any private element should exclude public law controls. Privatisation or the use of private law methods may be intended to take the functions or powers involved outside of public law controls. However, the purpose may also be to achieve other benefits such as greater efficiency, which are not necessarily inconsistent with continued application of public law controls.[14] Either way, courts must judge for themselves what bodies and decisions should be subject to public law constraints and to what extent.

The courts have used a variety of indicators of public nature. While these can be useful, Cane suggests we should not lose sight of the underlying value judgements. Classification of a body or decision as public reflects a judgement that there are good reasons to subject it to public law constraints.[15]

The notion of 'public' for this purpose is best understood as having several different aspects. There are several different reasons for imposing public law constraints. These reasons tend to be invoked as indicia of public nature: where they are engaged, the bodies or decisions at issue have been held to be sufficiently public in nature to attract public law constraints. Each of these indicia may apply in somewhat different circumstances, and each may call for the application of different parts of the arsenal of public law constraints.[16] They are not mutually exclusive: several of them may be engaged in the same case. A particular body or decision thus may be open to challenge on some grounds of judicial review but not others. Overall, public nature is a question

[13] Peter Cane, *Administrative Law*, 5th edn (Oxford, Oxford University Press, 2011) 8–9.

[14] ibid at 15–15, 401–02.

[15] ibid at 8–9, also 271–72.

[16] See Janet McLean, 'Convergence in Public and Private Law Doctrines – the Case of Public Contracts' [2016] *New Zealand Law Review* 5.

of degree. In contexts where individual indicia are weak, or where only some of them apply, only limited versions of the grounds of review may apply, as we will see.

By way of context and contrast, let us start by sketching the nature of private law constraints. Private law generally respects and protects private individual autonomy and freedom of choice. It intervenes primarily for two purposes: first, to enforce consensual arrangements (eg contract) and second, to provide redress where one party's autonomy has been invaded by another party, causing loss or harm (eg tort). In contrast, the public law constraints comprised in the common law grounds of review and the Bill of Rights impose greater limits on the respondent's autonomy and freedom of choice.

What, then, are some of the various reasons for insisting on such further constraints? What types of function or power call for some or all these special public law constraints? Why are private law constraints not enough in relation to these types of function or power?

First, perhaps the most important reason is that public power involves unilateral power – as Cane puts it, public authorities have a monopoly on legitimate coercion.[17] Public officials such as police, immigration officers and social workers have powers to order people to do or not to do certain things, to detain them, expel them, take their children, etc. People need protection against abuse or arbitrary exercise of such unilateral powers. We may say that, without such protection, subjects have no liberty. Arbitrary use of such power, and unfettered discretion in its uses, offends the rule of law.[18]

This need for protection from unilateral power is brought into sharp relief when we note that even in disputes between two private parties, both statute and case law impose constraints equivalent to public law constraints in certain contexts where defendants are exercising unilateral powers. Employment law is the most obvious of several examples, and we will return to this.[19]

A variant of the first reason for public law constraints is that public power may involve a monopoly over certain activities and services.[20] As with the first reason, people need protection against abuse of such power. Again, this need for protection is also reflected in legal controls on purely private parties that wield monopoly power.

A further reason featured heavily in the history of judicial review, and retains some influence today. Historically, judicial review developed as supervision of inferior tribunals. The test for reviewability generally, and for the application of the principles of natural justice in particular, was whether the power was of a judicial or quasi-judicial nature.[21] This test was met by the 'domestic' tribunals of private associations as much as by public tribunals. Natural justice requirements have therefore been applied to

[17] Cane (n 13) at 7.

[18] Martin Krygier, 'What's the Point of the Rule of Law?' [2019] 67 *Buffalo Law Review* 743 at 760 ff.

[19] See text at nn 126, 129.

[20] Colin D Campbell, 'Monopoly Power as Public Power for the Purposes of Judicial Review' (2009) 125 *Law Quarterly Review* 49.

[21] Janet McLean, 'Public Function Tests: Bringing Back the State?' in David Dyzenhaus, Murray Hunt and Grant Huscroft (eds), *A Simple Common Lawyer: Essays in Honour of Mike Taggart* (Oxford, Hart Publishing, 2008) 185 at 195.

private associations for a long time, and that approach continues today. Reliance on a 'public' test to determine the scope of judicial review is of recent provenance. Historically, the 'public' category attracted privileges and immunities rather than special constraints.[22]

Traditionally, the 'quasi-judicial' categorisation applied to a power to interfere with an individual's legal rights or status, or impose penalties or sanctions.[23] The relevant rights historically were understood to include rights of office and of membership in associations as well as property rights.[24] A crucial distinction was between applying specific rules or standards and exercising an unfettered discretion: the former was judicial but the latter was not. For instance, therefore, a right to a hearing applied to dismissal for cause but not where a position was held at pleasure.[25]

The 'quasi-judicial' test has a much-reduced role today.[26] The modern approach is greatly simplified in cases where the challenge concerns a clearly public and unilateral power. In such contexts, the main test for the application of natural justice requirements is whether the decision focuses on an individual. As Cooke J pointed out in *Daganayasi*, where it does, this calls for a procedure that ensures individual circumstances can be fairly assessed.[27]

Where private respondents are concerned, however, it remains relevant to ask why the respondent's choice should be constrained by natural justice requirements or other public law constraints. Aspects of the old quasi-judicial test may remain relevant to this.[28] It may be relevant whether the respondents are exercising the power to interfere with an established right or status, or whether what is at stake is for the respondents to grant or deny as they see fit. One way of determining this may be whether the decision involves applying specific rules or standards, as in the case of dismissal for cause as distinct from holding a position at pleasure. To what extent the interest at stake warrants legal protection may also be relevant.

A further different reason for public law constraints is that public officials exercising public powers are 'uniquely devoid of legitimate self-interests':[29] public powers are granted for the sole purpose of serving the public interest.[30] Constraints must therefore exist to ensure that the exercise of such powers is not influenced by any private interest, fear or favour, nor by other ulterior ends of any kind.[31]

[22] Janet McLean, *Searching for the State in British Legal Thought: Competing Conceptions of the Public Sphere* (Cambridge, Cambridge University Press, 2012) ch 5.

[23] *Ridge v Baldwin* [1964] AC 40 (HL) at 68–72; *Durayappah v Fernando* [1967] 2 AC 337 (PC) at 349.

[24] David Mullan, 'Administrative Law at the Margins' in Michael Taggart (ed), *The Province of Administrative Law* (n 1) 134 at 138.

[25] *Ridge v Baldwin* (n 23) at 65–66; see also *Durayappah* at 351 on whether incompetence is a sufficiently specific charge to attract the right.

[26] See further Ch 4.B(4).

[27] *Daganayasi v Minster of Immigration* [1980] 2 NZLR 130 (CA) at 143, 144.

[28] See, eg, *Royal Australasian College of Surgeons v Phipps* [1999] 3 NZLR 1 (CA) at 12, 14–15, applying *Durayappah* (n 23); see also text at nn 82–83.

[29] Mark Elliott, 'Judicial Review's Scope, Foundations and Purposes: Joining the Dots' [2012] *New Zealand Law Review* 75 at 79.

[30] See also Taggart, 'Province of Administrative Law Determined' (n 1) at 5.

[31] See McLean 'Convergence' (n 16): the focus in public law is on corruption in a broad sense.

Again, such lack of legitimate self-interest is not unique to public officials. It also applies to trustees and other fiduciaries and entails similar constraints in that context.[32] The analogy with private trust is one of the oldest arguments for constraints on public power.[33] It may help explain why receipt of public funding is treated as a factor in favour of reviewability.[34]

A further reason is that the power in question has significant public consequences – a significant impact on significant public interests.[35] Unlike with the trust argument, this reason for constraints turns on the effect of the power rather than on its basis. Note further how this argument also differs from the unilateral power argument: the impact that matters for that argument is on the subject of the decision, whereas here the relevant impact is on the public interest.

Finally, another different reason for public law constraints is found in the old source-based approach to reviewability, treating all statutory powers as amenable to review. We might say a basic justification for this is simply that an Act of Parliament is a public source of power. Furthermore, possession of statutory powers can also be seen as entailing judicial scrutiny to ensure those powers are exercised within their statutory limits and faithful to their statutory purpose. Even if that is accepted, however, it does not necessarily entail application of the full set of public law constraints.[36]

The old approach does linger on in a tendency to assume that statutory powers are automatically amenable to review.[37] Relatedly, the old institutional approach still exerts a lot of influence in the United Kingdom, where extensions of a 'governmental' power test determine reviewability in some contexts.[38]

As noted, all these reasons can be seen reflected in the indicia of public nature that courts have used in the cases. Courts often rely on just one or other of these indicia, without noting the range available or discussing their choice.

In the Bill of Rights context, however, the established approach to the public function test in section 3(b) involves reference to a long (but still non-exhaustive) list of indicia first set out in *Ransfield*.[39] The listed indicia may be summarised as follows:

- whether the entity is publicly owned or exists for profit;
- whether the source of the power in question is statutory;
- the extent of governmental control over the entity;

[32] For the similarity between the obligations of trustees and of public administrative decision-makers, see, eg, *New Zealand Māori Council v Foulkes* [2014] NZHC 1777, [2015] NZAR 1441 at [62]–[64].

[33] See Stuart Anderson, 'Public Law' in William Cornish, Stuart Anderson, Ray Cocks and others (eds), *The Oxford History of the Laws of England* (Oxford, Oxford University Press, 2010) at 367–68. For modern instances of the argument, see, eg, Evan Fox-Decent, *Sovereignty's Promise: The State as Fiduciary* (Oxford, Oxford University Press, 2011).

[34] Eg *Moncrief-Spittle* (n 4) at [51], [109].

[35] Eg *Reay v Attorney-General* [2019] NZCA 475; further see text at n 79.

[36] Elliott, 'Judicial Review's Scope' (n 29) at 83–86: as the sole criterion this would be both under- and overinclusive.

[37] This may be encouraged by the Judicial Review Procedure 2016 (and its predecessor, the Judicature Amendment Act 1972), which provides for judicial review of 'statutory powers'. However, that Act does not determine amenability to review; it merely regulates procedure and remedies: see Ch 8.D.

[38] See Part B(4) of this chapter.

[39] *Ransfield v The Radio Network Ltd* [2005] 1 NZLR 233 (HC).

- whether the function is publicly funded;
- whether the function involves the entity standing in the shoes of government;
- whether the power is exercised in the public interest (as distinct from just being of benefit to the public);
- whether it involves coercive power, monopolistic power, or affects people's rights, powers, or privileges; and
- whether the entity is democratically accountable.

The Supreme Court in *Moncrief-Spittle* approved the use of this list. It emphasised the need for an overall evaluation of how closely the function or power is connected to or identifies with governmental powers and responsibilities.[40]

The next two parts of this chapter are devoted to exploring the case law on the two versions of the issue about public nature: first, when are functions exercised by (quasi-)private bodies sufficiently public in nature to attract public law constraints; and secondly, when are activities of a private or commercial nature, such as contracting, sufficiently public.

B. (Quasi-) Private Bodies Exercising Public Functions

As already noted, there has been a shift in approach, away from an institutional approach focusing on the institutional nature of a body and on the source of a power, and towards a more functional approach to the public nature question. Increasingly the approach has been to look to the particular challenged decision and ask whether this was an exercise of a public power or performance of a public function. A body may be institutionally private in some or most respects yet have some functions or powers that should be subject to public law constraints. In recent times, New Zealand courts have been far more willing to extend public law constraints beyond institutionally governmental bodies than their English counterparts.

Whether public law constraints should apply is a matter of weighing the need for protection from arbitrary power against competing interests and values. Section (1) of this Part outlines the nature of those competing interests and values. The remaining sections discuss the case law on a range of different types of quasi-private bodies: (2) corporatised arm's-length public bodies, (3) private regulatory bodies, (4) private associations and (5) other private bodies.

(1) Why Public Law Constraints do not Generally Apply to Private Bodies

Public law constraints, when applied to public powers, safeguard the individual liberty and autonomy of those who are subject to those powers, as we have seen. If those same constraints were applied to private persons, however, they would

[40] *Moncrief-Spittle* (n 4) at [39]–[42], [46]–[47].

represent constraints on those persons' individual liberty and autonomy.[41] It would be oppressive for the courts to sit in judgment on whether I have chosen my dinner guests for improper purposes. Perhaps the same goes for a company's choice of suppliers. Where membership of associations is at issue, the right to freedom of association is engaged.[42]

Flowing from these rights are arguments for respecting private social ordering. Consensual arrangements generally are appropriately governed by private law, without additional public law constraints.[43] Private associations, in particular, may adopt their own sets of rules governing their affairs, and these are best interpreted and administered by those empowered by the rules themselves to do so.[44] These arguments also invoke the merits of a measure of legal or normative pluralism.[45]

The perennial question is where to draw the line between decision-makers whose liberty and autonomy must be respected by leaving them free of public law constraints, and decision-makers who must be subjected to such constraints in order to safeguard others' liberty and autonomy. Where contractual relationships are concerned, it has been argued that we need to distinguish between the use of contract 'as an instrument of economic exchange', and its use 'as an instrument of governmental or non-governmental organisation and regulation'.[46]

(2) Types of Bodies: Corporatised Arm's-length Public Bodies

It is well established that partial privatisation of public bodies does not automatically take them outside public law controls. Bodies such as state-owned enterprises or council-controlled organisations that have been given corporate form and put at arm's length from Ministers or local authorities are still institutionally public in the significant senses that they are publicly owned, created by statute, and subject to some measure of public control. In the leading *Mercury Energy* decision, the Privy Council established that such bodies are at least in principle subject to judicial review.[47] That approach has been maintained since.[48]

The application of public law constraints to such bodies depends on the particular function or power being exercised. In *Mercury Energy*, commercial contracting decisions were held to be subject to review on only a very limited basis.[49] However, those limits did not

[41] For a similar point, see Laws J in *R v Somerset County Council, ex p Fewings* [1995] 1 All ER 513 (DC) at 524.

[42] But see *Stratford Racing Club Inc v Adlam* [2008] NZCA 92, [2008] NZAR 329 at [58]–[60], where this argument was dismissed on questionable grounds.

[43] Paul Daly, *Understanding Administrative Law in the Common Law World* (Oxford, Oxford University Press, 2021) at 215–16.

[44] See, eg, *R v Hull University Visitor ex p Page* [1993] AC 682 (HL).

[45] Julia Black, 'Constitutionalising Self Regulation' (1996) 59 *Modern Law Review* 24 at 31–32, 38–39.

[46] ibid at 40–42. See also Terence Daintith, 'The Techniques of Government' in Jeffrey Jowell and Dawn Oliver (eds), *The Changing Constitution*, 3rd edn (Oxford, Oxford University Press, 1994) 209.

[47] *Mercury Energy Ltd v Electricity Corporation of New Zealand Ltd* [1994] 2 NZLR 385 (PC) at 388.

[48] See *Moncrief-Spittle v Regional Facilities Auckland Ltd* [2022] NZSC 138, [2022] 1 NZLR 459 at [108]–[109]; *Ririnui v Landcorp Farming Ltd* [2016] NZSC 62, [2016] 1 NZLR 1056 at [70]–[71], [147].

[49] *Mercury Energy* (n 47) at 391.

apply to less purely commercial contracting decisions in *Ririnui*[50] and *Moncrief-Spittle*.[51] Nor did they apply to a decision by a 'Crown Health Enterprise' to downgrade a local hospital.[52] The same focus on the particular function at issue also applies when the application of the Bill of Rights is at issue.[53] These cases are discussed further in Part C(6), concerning the application of public law constraints to contracting decisions.

(3) Types of Bodies: Private Regulatory Bodies

(a) Statutory Regulatory Powers

Private associations may be endowed with statutory powers of a regulatory or disciplinary kind. This is often the case with professional associations and also with some sports-governing bodies. Courts tend to assume with little or no discussion that such powers attract public law constraints.[54]

(b) Contractors Exercising Regulatory Powers

The same assumption tends to be made where the statutory powers of public authorities are exercised by contractors.[55] For instance, contract prisons under the Corrections Act[56] clearly exercise public powers that are subject to public law constraints.[57] Concerning the Bill of Rights Act, section 176(1) of the Corrections Act 2004 expressly provides that acts of contract prisons are 'deemed' to be acts of the executive branch of government, so that the Bill of Rights applies by virtue of its section 3(a).

Other examples include contractors for the Ministry of Health carrying out needs assessments to determine eligibility for paid family care for adults with disabilities[58] and contractors for ACC conducting statutory reviews of ACC decisions on eligibility and cover.[59] All these have been held to be subject to judicial review.

(c) De Facto Regulatory Powers

The established category of private regulatory bodies amenable to judicial review is wider than discussed so far, however: it extends to powers that are neither statutory nor

[50] *Ririnui* (n 48): see discussion at n 199 below.

[51] *Moncrief-Spittle* (n 48) see discussion at n 203 below.

[52] *Napier City v Healthcare Hawke's Bay Ltd* HC Napier CP29/94, 15 December 1994.

[53] *Moncrief-Spittle* (n 48) at [40]–[41], [47].

[54] See, eg, *Cropp v Judicial Committee* [2008] NZSC 46, [2008] 3 NZLR 774 at [5]; *Orlov v New Zealand Law Society* [2013] NZCA 230, [2013] 3 NZLR 562; *Kamal v Restructuring Insolvency and Turnaround Association of New Zealand* [2021] NZCA 514.

[55] More on this below, Part C(5) of this chapter. For discussion of delegation by contract, see ACL Davies, *The Public Law of Government Contracts* (2008), Ch 8.

[56] Corrections Act 2004, s 199AA.

[57] See, eg, *Burke v Serco New Zealand Ltd* [2019] NZHC 1951. See also *McGreevy v Chief Executive of Department of Corrections* [2018] NZHC 2006 concerning a contractor engaged to help implement conditions of release imposed by the Parole Board.

[58] *Chamberlain v Minister of Health* [2018] NZCA 8, [2018] 2 NZLR 771 at [65].

[59] *Moir v IHC New Zealand Inc* [2019] NZCA 92 at [8].

delegated but merely de facto powers. That was established in the landmark *Datafin* case,[60] and adopted for New Zealand in *Cameron*.[61] In both cases, judicial review was held to be available against bodies created by an industry to regulate itself (that is, to make rules for the industry and to adjudicate on the application of those rules):[62] the Panel of Take-overs and Mergers in *Datafin*, and the Advertising Standards Authority in *Cameron*.

These bodies lacked any statutory foundation, although their existence and role was recognised in relevant legislation. However, they exercised de facto unilateral powers of regulation. This was because all industry participants treated their rules and their decisions as binding (no-one would deal with parties that refused to submit to their jurisdiction). Their rules therefore controlled all relevant activity in the industry, extending at least in some respects beyond those who had chosen to submit to their jurisdiction. Thus, submission to their jurisdiction was not voluntary in any meaningful sense. Further significant factors were the magnitude of the powers, the fact that the interest at stake is the ability to make a livelihood, and the unavailability of private law remedies.

The position of the Panel in *Datafin* had two further features that have subsequently been treated in the United Kingdom, but not generally in New Zealand, as necessary for finding a public element. First, 'but for' the Panel's existence, government itself would have regulated in this field: the government had expressly acknowledged that. Moreover, European Union law required such regulation and, in other countries, this was carried out by government. Secondly, breach of the Panel's code could trigger statutory penalties. Taken together with the first point, that meant that the Panel was integrated into a broader governmental framework for the regulation of financial activity. This element of integration is even more obvious in other cases where the private entity's role within the governmental scheme of regulation is expressly arranged by contract with a government agency.[63] In one or both of these senses, United Kingdom courts require powers exercised by private entities to be 'governmental' in order to attract judicial review.[64]

These cases also illustrate a different point. Review tends to be more restrained and limited in scope at the margins of justiciability.[65] That applied in these cases due to the lack of a statutory or other legal framework. In *Datafin*, the Court doubted whether there could be any basis for holding the rules to be ultra vires, and took a restrained approach to reviewing the Panel's application of its rules and exercise of its discretion.[66] In the result, the challenge failed. While in *Cameron* the challenge succeeded, the ground of review was the most basic form of illegality – lack of power to rule on the subject-matter in question.[67]

[60] *R v Panel of Take-overs and Mergers, ex parte Datafin Plc* [1987] QB 815 (CA).

[61] *Electoral Commission v Cameron* [1997] 2 NZLR 421 (CA).

[62] For a definition of regulatory powers in the context of private associations, see Black 'Constitutionalising Self-Government' (n 45) at 27, and for instances of such powers, see ibid at 54–55.

[63] See, eg, *Low Volume Vehicle Technical Association Inc v Brett* [2019] NZCA 67, [2019] 2 NZLR 808 at [23] where reviewability of the regulatory functions was common ground (for details of the Association's position, see at [4], [18]).

[64] *R v Disciplinary Committee of the Jockey Club ex p Aga Khan* [1993] 1 WLR 909 (CA) at 923–24.

[65] See Ch 8.A.

[66] *Datafin* (n 60) at 841–44.

[67] *Cameron* (n 61).

(4) Types of Bodies: Private Associations

Incorporated private associations are now regulated by the Incorporated Societies Act 2022. This provides its own set of constraints and requirements, as well as internal dispute resolution and civil proceedings for court orders. The previous Act did not make provisions for these matters. A significant body of common law therefore developed. The continuing role of this body of law remains to be seen. It certainly continues to apply to unincorporated societies.

The law on judicial review of private associations in Aotearoa New Zealand has been unsettled and controversial. Access to judicial review is much more liberal than in the United Kingdom, where courts have insisted on the strict 'governmental' power test derived from *Datafin*,[68] discussed earlier. In New Zealand, reviewability extends well beyond private regulatory bodies.

In addition to judicial review, there is the option of proceeding in contract. In claims against private associations by their members, the association's rules are treated as a contract between the association and each member. When there are features calling for public law constraints, those can be read into the contract as implied terms.[69] Contract proceedings have been considered the preferred route for challenging private associations.[70]

In the United Kingdom, the picture is complicated by the insistence on procedural exclusivity between public and private law proceedings.[71] It seems fair to say, however, that the narrowed availability of judicial review has been significantly offset by allowing public law complaints to be raised in private law proceedings in contract or for a declaration instead.[72]

One reason for allowing judicial review that has featured in some New Zealand cases must be rejected as erroneous. Review under the Judicial Review Procedure Act 2016 is available in relation to 'statutory powers' and, as defined in that Act, these include the powers of any body corporate under its rules or constitution.[73] That extended definition, of course, extends to incorporated societies' exercise of their powers. If the 'statutory power' test was the sole condition of reviewability, then all decisions of incorporated societies would be reviewable. In several cases the court took that view or appeared to proceed on that assumption.[74] As discussed in Chapter 8.D, however, the Act must be understood as merely providing a streamlined procedure for the pre-existing inherent jurisdiction of judicial review. Therefore the Act's 'statutory power'

[68] *Aga Khan* (n 64); Black (n 45) at 35–37, 42–43.

[69] *Peters v Collinge* [1993] 2 NZLR 554 at 557, 566–67.

[70] *Hopper v North Shore Aero Club* [2007] NZAR 354 (CA) at [11].

[71] *O'Reilly v Mackman* [1983] 2 AC 237 (HL).

[72] See, eg, *Bradley v Jockey Club* [2004] EWHC 2164 (QB), affirmed [2005] EWCA Civ 1056; *Flaherty v National Greyhound Racing* [2005] EWCA Civ 1117. Where there is no contract and no other alternative remedy, courts may perhaps be more ready to allow judicial review: *R v Disciplinary Committee of the Jockey Club ex p Aga Khan* [1993] 1 WLR 909 (CA) at 924 (obiter).

[73] Judicial Review Procedure Act 2016 (JRPA), ss 4, 8, 16; previously Judicature Amendment Act 1972, s 4 (JAA).

[74] Eg *Stratford Racing Club Inc v Adlam* [2008] NZCA 92, [2008] NZAR 329 as interpreted in Dean Knight, 'Privately Public' (2013) 24 *Public Law Review* 108 at 109; *Royal Australasian College of Surgeons v Phipps* [1999] 3 NZLR 1 (CA) at 12, 14–15.

test does not expand the scope of that jurisdiction: the common law public nature test still must be satisfied as well.[75] In any event, the liberal availability of judicial review of private associations pre-dates the expanded statutory definition of 'statutory power';[76] thus there must be other reasons for it.

We can identify various types of decision made by private associations. The available reasons for imposing public law constraints arguably depend to a significant extent on the type of decision. Let us look at decisions (a) concerning regulation and discipline, (b) concerning membership, office and assets, (c) with significant public interest implications, (d) about ordinary operation and internal management, and (e) governed by tikanga or religious doctrine. Finally, section (f) outlines the relevant provisions of the Incorporated Societies Act 2022.

(a) Regulation and Discipline

In *Hopper*, the Court of Appeal held that public law constraints generally apply (preferably by way of contractual proceedings) to three types of decisions by private associations: those concerning discipline, membership, and licences or rights to make a living.[77] Indeed the first and last of these three – powers of regulation and discipline in relation to professions or occupations – have generally been assumed to be sufficiently public in New Zealand.[78]

Such powers have been held reviewable even when they do not involve the sort of de facto unilateral power seen in *Datafin*. However, other reasons for constraint featured in those cases.

In *Reay*, a decision of the Institution of Professional Engineers was found amenable to review. The Institution had no overall responsibility for maintaining professional standards in engineering – it had authority only over its members (and membership was not compulsory).[79] Yet reviewability was not disputed, and there was no mention of *Datafin*.

The brief discussion of reviewability focused instead on the public consequences of the power: the Court of Appeal accepted that the powers had significance for the public interest in safety.[80] This focus was not surprising in this case. The challenge was to a decision to *discontinue* disciplinary proceedings, rather than to the outcome of such proceedings. The applicant for review was not the engineer in question but the Attorney-General, representing the public interest in safety that would be served by disciplinary proceedings.

In *Phipps*, the challenge was brought by a surgeon, to a report of an investigation into medical malpractice by the College of Surgeons. The College was not exercising

[75] Conversely, review of unincorporated societies' decisions is not available under the Act, as it does not meet the 'statutory power' test. This can therefore only be brought under the High Court Rules.

[76] See John Caldwell, 'Judicial Review of Sports Bodies in New Zealand' in Elizabeth Twoomey (ed), *Keeping the Score: Essays in Law and Sport* (Centre for Commercial & Corporate Law, Christchurch, 2005) 43. See, eg, *Swan v Massey University Students' Association* [1972] NZLR 985 (HC) (predating the 1977 amendment that introduced the expanded definition of 'statutory power').

[77] *Hopper* (n 70) at [11].

[78] See *Cropp* (n 54) at [5]; *Orlov* (n 54).

[79] *Reay v Attorney-General* [2019] NZCA 475 at [40].

[80] ibid at [39] and fn 45.

regulatory powers in its own right but was engaged by an employing health agency to investigate. The Court mentioned the public nature test in passing.[81] But the focus was on the circumstances in which the principles of natural justice are applicable – this is one of the cases in which that has effectively been treated as the test for reviewability.[82]

The factors that supported the application of natural justice engaged aspects of the old 'quasi-judicial' test discussed in Part A. above. When the College investigates an individual surgeon's practice at the request of a healthcare agency, accurate findings and appropriate recommendations are essential to the object of the exercise; the report has major significance for the surgeon's employment and professional reputation; the investigation requires factual findings and judgments about how the surgeon's practice measures up to accepted standards; and there are serious consequences for the surgeon.[83]

(b) Decisions on Membership, Offices and Assets

The remaining item in the *Hopper* list of decisions that are subject to public law constraints is decisions concerning membership.[84] Certainly courts commonly entertain judicial review challenges to the expulsion of members.[85] That is the classic case in which application of the old 'quasi-judicial' test leads to the conclusion that natural justice applies and proceedings must therefore be available: expulsion interferes with existing contractual rights and usually involves application of the association's agreed rules.

Controversially, however, the Court of Appeal in *Stratford Racing Club* went further than that. The club's decision to reject a raft of new membership applications was successfully challenged by judicial review. Although the dictum about membership decisions in *Hopper* relates specifically to contractual proceedings, which are available only to existing members, the Court in *Stratford* treated it as equally applicable to this case. While contract is generally the preferred route for challenging decisions of private associations, the Court considered judicial review should always be available as an alternative: especially to non-members who had no alternative, but also to members.[86] The successful ground of review was improper purpose or even bad faith: perpetuating control of the club by a faction, contrary to the club's objectives which included growing the membership.[87]

The objection was that the committee had absolute discretion as to whom to accept as new members. This implicitly reflected the old 'quasi-judicial' test: no existing rights were involved and there were no applicable rules. The Court rejected this argument, invoking a version of the trust analogy: as 'steward of the assets' held by the society

[81] *Phipps* (CA) (n 74) at 11. On appeal to the Privy Council, reviewability was no longer at issue.
[82] ibid at 12.
[83] ibid at 12, 14–15; citing *Durayappah v Fernando* [1967] 2 AC 337 (PC).
[84] *Hopper* (n 70) at [11].
[85] See, eg, *Gibson v New Zealand Search and Rescue Dogs Inc* [2012] NZHC 1320, [2012] NZAR 699; *Pritchard v Evans* [2014] NZHC 3150, [2014] NZAR 370; *Church v Commerce Club of Auckland* [2006] NZAR 494 (HC).
[86] *Stratford Racing Club* (n 74) at [53]–[56].
[87] ibid at [58].

the committee was constrained to exercise its powers 'in the best interests of the club and for proper purposes'.[88]

Stratford is not necessarily good authority for entertaining challenges by disappointed membership applicants.[89] The applicant for review here was a club member who had engaged in a membership drive to help oust the faction that controlled the committee. He might well have argued that his implied rights as a member were affected, gaining strength from the fact that the invalidating improper purpose here came close to bad faith.[90]

Similar to membership, decisions about the appointment or removal of an association's officers have also frequently been subjected to public law constraints.[91] Some cases may suggest that such decisions are reviewable only where they have a disciplinary flavour.[92] However, that would not explain all the cases, and the Court of Appeal has rejected it as a requirement.[93] The better view is that, just as with decisions on membership, such decisions attract public law constraints because they interfere with existing contractual rights and involve application of the association's agreed rules.

Another type of decision that has been held subject to public law constraints is a decision to dispose of assets.[94] This may be explained by the trust analogy.

All these types of decisions could now be the subject of proceedings brought by members under the Incorporated Societies Act 2022, discussed in section (f) below.

(c) Significant Public Interest Impact

In some cases, decisions of private associations have been held subject to public law constraints due to their significant public consequences. We have already seen that this argument is pertinent in a challenge to a failure to pursue disciplinary proceedings in areas such as engineering that engage public safety, as in *Reay*. On this basis, the Attorney-General had standing to bring judicial review proceedings.[95]

A famous example is found in *Finnigan*, where the Court of Appeal declined to strike out a challenge to the NZ Rugby Football Union's decision to send an All Blacks team to tour Apartheid-era South Africa.[96] The Court dealt with reviewability in terms of standing (an issue arising from the claimant's lack of a contractual relationship

[88] ibid at [57]–[58].

[89] For a critique, see Peter Watts, 'The Tort of Refusing to Contract?' (2008) 14 *New Zealand Business Law Quarterly* 69.

[90] Incorporated societies' vulnerability to oppressive conduct by minorities was noted in *Porima v Te Kauhanganui o Waikato Inc* [2001] 1 NZLR 472 (HC) at [81].

[91] See, eg, *Middledorp v Avondale Jockey Club Inc* [2020] NZCA 13 at [9]; *Stratford Racing Club* (n 74) at [79]; *Swan* (n 76); *Porima* (n 90).

[92] See, eg, *Porima* (n 90) at [82].

[93] *Te Whakakitenga O Waikato Inc v Martin* [2016] NZCA 548, [2017] NZAR 173 at [21]–[22], [25], [28].

[94] See, eg, *Stratford Racing Club* (n 74) at [16]–[27].

[95] *Attorney-General v Institution of Professional Engineers New Zealand Inc* [2018] NZHC 3211, [2019] 2 NZLR 731 at [63]–[73]; this point was not appealed and was accepted by the Court of Appeal in *Reay* (n 79) at [39].

[96] *Finnigan v New Zealand Rugby Football Union Inc (No 1)* [1985] 2 NZLR 159 (CA). The litigation was then effectively determined by the grant of an interim injunction (*Finnigan v New Zealand Rugby Football Union Inc (No 2)* [1985] 2 NZLR 181 (HC)), and the Privy Council subsequently declined leave to appeal the standing decision, because it had become academic (*Finnigan v New Zealand Rugby Football Union Inc (No 3)* [1985] 2 NZLR 190 (PC)).

directly with the union) rather than whether the decision was of a sufficiently public nature. It did, however, rely on the public importance of the decision, which it saw as arising from rugby's status as a national sport and from the decision's impact on New Zealand's international reputation.[97]

More often, however, reference to the need for 'public consequences' or a 'public interest component' is simply a synonym for the public nature test.[98] When it is used in that way and without reference to other indicia, it provides limited, if any, guidance.

(d) Ordinary Operation and Internal Management

Decisions that fall outside of the types of decisions discussed so far will often not be reviewable.[99] For instance, review is not normally available against sporting associations to challenge the on-field decisions of referees or umpires.[100]

Decisions about the ordinary operation or activities of a society are also unlikely to be subject to public law constraints. An example is the unsuccessful challenge in *Hopper*. It concerned a decision by a club operating an airfield, declining permission to a member to base his aircraft there. Although amenability to review was ultimately left open, the Court considered the decision not to be 'quasi-public'.[101] It appeared to be applying the long-standing 'reticence to interfere with matters of internal management or regulation'.[102]

In addition, an 'internal management rule' derived from company law has also featured in the cases.[103] This seems best understood as limiting the permissible types of complaint rather than the reviewable types of decision. It precludes review – or perhaps only relief – for complaints about an irregularity in the governance of a society that could be cured by resolution of a simple majority of members.[104]

(e) Decisions Governed by Tikanga or Religious Doctrine

In some contexts, the courts have recognised the desirability of respecting a measure of pluralism when decisions are governed by other normative orders.[105] They will not entertain disputes involving religious doctrine – review of religious associations is usually available only where it concerns property or other civil rights or obligations.[106]

[97] *Finnigan (No 1)* (n 96) at 179.

[98] See, eg, *Phipps* (CA) (n 74) at 11; *Cullen v Pa'u* [2023] NZHC 3782 at [42]–[49].

[99] *Hopper* (n 70) at [11].

[100] Rowan Armstrong 'The Whistle Has Blown … Game Over … Or is it Really? Challenging the Decisions of Sports Governing Bodies in New Zealand' (2008) 14 Canta LR 65 at 78.

[101] *Hopper* (n 70) at [12].

[102] ibid at [10]; this passage may involve confusion between the internal management rule (discussed next) and the non-reviewability of day-to-day operational decisions.

[103] *Finnigan (No 1)* (n 96) at 178 cast some doubt on the application of this rule to private associations (passim), but that has not been mentioned in any of the more recent cases.

[104] For a detailed explanation, see *Barrett v Te Runanga O Ngati Pu Inc* [2002] NZAR 296 (HC) at [27]–[29]. See also *Swan* (n 76) at 988–90.

[105] In the UK, see, eg, *R v Hull University Visitor ex p Page* [1993] AC 682 (HL) at 699, 704; *R v Chief Rabbi of the United Hebrew Congregations of Great Britain and the Commonwealth, Ex parte Wachmann* [1992] 1 WLR 1036 (QBD).

[106] See, eg, *Khyentse v Hope* [2007] 1 NZLR 645 (CA) at [36], [37], [50]; *Khan v Ahmed and Hawke's Bay Mosque and Islamic Centre Trust (Inc)* [2008] NZAR 686 (HC) at [55]. *Rohit v Daya* [2023] NZCA 649 unusually entertained a challenge to the appointment of a religious society's leader.

This might also be considered relevant in the case of iwi[107] governance entities charged with administering iwi resources after the settlement of historical Treaty of Waitangi claims. Such entities take legal forms recognised by the general law of New Zealand, such as incorporated societies. Arguably, however, they should be recognised as instruments of Māori self-governance and thus governed by Māori tikanga.[108] Questions then arise as to the proper role of the courts. In other contexts, it has been held that while courts can find and apply undisputed tikanga, where tikanga is disputed it is for tikanga processes to resolve that dispute.[109] That approach seems appropriate in the present context too.[110] Yet, challenges to the decisions of such bodies have frequently been subjected to the courts' supervisory jurisdiction without any mention of such arguments for restraint,[111] and at least sometimes without attention to tikanga.[112]

(f) The Incorporated Societies Act 2022

The new Act requires societies to adopt procedures for internal resolution of disputes.[113] In addition, it provides for civil proceedings for court orders to enforce a society's constitution and the duties imposed by the Act on officers, and to deal with action that is oppressive, unfairly discriminatory, or unfairly prejudicial to a member.[114]

It is possible that in proceedings under the Act, the courts will still imply public law constraints into societies' constitutions. However, the Act itself provides similar constraints. It requires constitutions and their dispute resolution procedures to comply with natural justice, and the duties it imposes on officers correspond to most other types of public law constraint.[115] There may therefore be limited need or justification for implying further constraints.

Proceedings under the Act are available to members, former members, officers and the society itself.[116] In exceptional circumstances, the Registrar of Incorporated Societies may also apply. Disappointed applicants for membership are still confined to judicial review as the only possibly available avenue. As in *Stratford*,[117] however, existing members could challenge a decision not to admit new members, and it seems that proceedings under the Act could be available for this.

[107] tribal.

[108] customary law.

[109] See Ch 8.A(2)(b).

[110] See Gina Hefferan, 'Post-Settlement Dispute Resolution: Time to Tread Lightly Ko Ngaa Take Ture Maori' (2004) 10 *Auckland University Law Review* 212 at 213, 226–27, 228–29. For reluctance to adjudicate directly on matters of tikanga see, eg, *Rewiti v Maori Women's Welfare League Inc* [2018] NZHC 2713 at [9]. But cf *Tamaki v Māori Women's Welfare League Inc* [2011] NZAR 605 (HC) at [6]–[8], [55]–[59], [68], [70]–[71].

[111] See, eg, *Whakakitenga* (n 93) at [18]–[22]; *Porima* (n 90); *Barrett* (n 104).

[112] Mikayla McKenzie Dempsey, 'Hearing the Māori Voice: The Case for Proper Implementation of Tikanga and Treaty Principles in Natural Justice Analysis' (2021) 27 *Auckland University Law Review* 55 at 62.

[113] Incorporated Societies Act 2022, ss 26, 39–44.

[114] ibid, ss 129–142.

[115] ibid, ss 39, 54–56.

[116] ibid, ss 129–142.

[117] *Stratford Racing Club* (n 74).

(5) Other Private Bodies

Even private companies can sometimes be subject to public law constraints, as can other types of private entities. Public law constraints or constraints that mirror them may be imposed by case law or statute. They may be applied by means of judicial review or, alternatively, by means of statutory regulation or private law proceedings. Explicitly or implicitly, decisions to apply such constraints by any of these means tend to reflect one or more of the reasons discussed in part A. above. We fail to appreciate the full reach of public law constraints if we do not notice such instances.

Three areas are notable: (a) judicial review proceedings against private entities when they impinge on public concerns; (b) statutory regulation of private entities imposing constraints that mirror public law constraints; and (c) contract proceedings involving implied terms that mirror public law constraints.

(a) Judicial Review when Private Entities Impinge on Public Concerns

There is a line of cases concerning televised pre-election leaders' debates. The High Court has repeatedly entertained judicial review of the television companies' selection of the political party leaders to be included in these debates, starting with *Dunne*.[118] The decision challenged in each case was the exclusion of the leaders of some minor parties. This was held to be of significant public importance and impact. The Court in *Dunne* stated that leaders' debates are an important part of the information available to voters. Thus they affect the right to vote, voters' right to receive information and, potentially, the outcome of the election.[119] The Court also noted further indicia as relevant (but not sufficient in itself): the television station in question was a public free-to-air broadcaster, it had statutory obligations under the Broadcasting Act, and there was no alternative avenue for challenging this decision.[120]

This line of argument has, however, been confined to leaders' debates. Regular television news coverage, even in relation to elections, was held not amenable to review on this basis in *Mangu*.[121] *Ransfield* held that commercial radio is not subject to the Bill of Rights simply because its decisions affect free speech or because it operates under a public licence.[122] The impact on a public concern must be more direct and significant.

The issue about impact on public concerns arose in a different context in *Falun Dafa*. A decision on who could participate in Auckland city's Christmas parade was held not amenable to review on that basis. The decision-maker was a charitable trust set up by a private company, with no statutory powers. The applicant group had been excluded because it was considered political. The Court applied something like the governmental power test that limits the reviewability of private associations in the United Kingdom. While the event was supported by the Council granting a permit, closing streets and

[118] *Dunne v CanWest TVWorks Ltd* [2005] NZAR 577 (HC); *Craig v MediaWorks Ltd* [2014] NZHC 1875, [2014] NZAR 973; *Morgan v Television New Zealand Ltd* [2017] NZHC 2178.

[119] *Dunne* (n 118) at [34].

[120] ibid at [29]–[30], [35].

[121] *Mangu v Television New Zealand Ltd* [2006] NZAR 299 (HC).

[122] *Ransfield v The Radio Network Ltd* [2005] 1 NZLR 233 (HC).

granting some funding, that did not render decisions on it public. Nor did the fact that the event was for the benefit of the public and occurred in a public place.[123] In explaining why the Bill of Rights also did not apply, the Court further considered that the trust was not exercising powers that are governmental in any sense and had no coercive powers.[124]

An alternative perspective on *Falun Dafa* might have been that it engaged the trust analogy, one of the reasons for imposing public law contraints. The public funding and closure of central city roads might be argued to carry with it some obligation to serve the public interest, which could have supported review at least on limited grounds. The decision can, perhaps, be contrasted with the *Moncrief-Spittle* case discussed later.[125]

(b) Statutory Regulation of Private Entities Mirroring Public Law Constraints

Constraints that are very similar to those of public law are imposed on private entities by statutory regulation in several contexts. Primarily, such constraints are found in statutes regulating private relationships and transactions such as employment, reflecting recognition of the power imbalance.[126] The existence of monopoly power in the private sector is also recognised and reflected in statutory regulation of such power.[127]

(c) Contractual Implied Terms Mirroring Public Law Constraints

The common law has been slower to develop constraints similar to public law constraints in relation to private entities. In some limited contexts, however, it has developed special controls to protect against de facto unilateral or coercive powers. These include special common law duties imposed on suppliers of essential services known as 'common callings', 'businesses affected with a public interest' and 'prime necessities'.[128]

Common law protections mirroring public law constraints also include implied terms in types of contracts that are considered 'relational' rather than 'transactional'.[129] Perhaps the most well established are implied terms in employment contracts, such as terms of trust and confidence. Other relational contracts include, for instance, those for independent contractors. A 'good faith' term may be implied into such contracts, calling for fidelity to the agreed common purpose and consistency with the other party's justified expectations.[130]

[123] *Falun Dafa Association of New Zealand Inc v Auckland Children's Christmas Parade Trust Board* [2009] NZAR 122 (HC) at [36].

[124] ibid at [43]–[44].

[125] *Moncrief-Spittle* (n 48); see text at n 204.

[126] Employment Relations Act 2000; see, eg, s 4(1A)(c).

[127] Commerce Act 1986.

[128] See Michael Taggart, 'Public Utilities and Public Law' in Philip A Joseph (ed), *Essays on the Constitution* (Wellington, Brooker's, 1995); *Vector Ltd v Transpower New Zealand Ltd* [1999] 3 NZLR 646 (CA); *Sky City Auckland Ltd v Wu* [2002] 3 NZLR 621 (CA).

[129] Victoria Heine KC, 'Obligations of Good Faith and Contractual Discretion' in *Commercial Case Law Update* (New Zealand Law Society, June 2024) 1; Simon Schofield, *New Zealand Employment Law Guide 2024* (Walters Kluwer), ch 3.

[130] See *Devonport Borough Council v Robbins* [1979] 1 NZLR 1 (CA); *Heli Holdings Ltd v The Helicopter Line Ltd* [2016] NZHC 976.

Implied terms mirroring public law constraints have further been found where a contract confers a 'genuine unilateral discretion' on one party – to be distinguished from an 'absolute discretion' that allows the party to choose between options as they please.[131] The distinction is a matter of contractual interpretation. The implied term constraining genuine unilateral discretion can vary in content.[132] At a minimum, it prohibits exercises of the discretion that are arbitrary, capricious, in bad faith or unreasonable in the *Wednesbury* sense. However, it has also been held to extend to other grounds of review, such as prohibiting irrelevant considerations and requiring attention to mandatory considerations[133] or requiring a fair hearing.[134] The reasoning supporting such implied terms is similar to the old 'quasi-judicial' test for finding natural justice applicable to certain decisions by private associations.[135]

C. Contracting and Other Commercial Decisions by (Quasi-)Public Bodies

When public bodies enter contracts, or exercise contractual powers such as termination, they are operating in the realm of private law. However, modern government uses contracts for a wide range of purposes, some of which have a distinct public law aspect. For instance, licences often take the form of contracts but still represent regulation. More importantly, public services and functions are contracted out, ranging from medical laboratory services and social services to running prisons. Having said that, we also need to note that not all contracting by government has such special public character: procurement of stationery is the classic example of government contracting that may be purely a matter of private law. The question is when public law constraints apply.

The traditional rule was that decisions about contracting and exercises of contractual power were not subject to judicial review. However, *Webster* established that the contractual basis of a power is not determinative of its amenability to review: a decision to terminate a licence for a boatshed on the public foreshore was amenable to review, even though the licence took the form of a contract and termination was therefore an exercise of a contractual power.[136] Once again, therefore, the issue is whether the particular contractual decision-making has a sufficiently public nature to warrant imposition of public law constraints.

[131] *C&S Kelly v Earthquake Commission* [2015] NZHC 1690 at [75]; *Woolley v Fonterra Co-op* [2023] NZCA 266, [2023] 3 NZLR 405 at [88].

[132] See Stephen Kós, 'Constraints on the Exercise of Contractual Powers' (2011) 42 *Victoria University of Wellington Law Review* 17.

[133] *Braganza v BP Shipping Ltd* [2015] UKSC 17, [2015] Industrial Case Reports 449 at [18]–[30], [52]–[53], [102]–[103].

[134] *Olsen Consulting Ltd v Goodman Fielder NZ Ltd* HC Auckland CIV-2011-404-5622, 23 November 2011.

[135] See parts A. and B.(4)(a)-(b) above. Kós (n 132) at 26–27 also notes an analogy with trustees' duties.

[136] *Webster v Auckland Harbour Board* [1983] NZLR 646 (CA); and [1987] 2 NZLR 129 (CA).

In this part, I start by outlining some of the main reasons why contracting powers are often considered beyond public law constraints (section (1)). I then sketch the ways in which imposition of public law constraints is not an all or nothing question (section (2)), outline what I consider to be the minimum public law constraints for any public contracting (section (3)), and clarify the issues arising from contracting out (section (4)). Finally, I discuss the case law on two types of challenges to contractual decision-making: challenges by users or subjects of contracted-out services or functions (section (5)) and challenges by (would-be) contractors or commercial contract partners (section (6)).

(1) Why Public Law Constraints are Often Inappropriate for Contractual Decision-making

What is it about contractual decision-making that has often been thought to make public law constraints inappropriate even when the actor is a public authority? The essential point is the primacy of consensual ordering, as already noted in relation to decisions of private bodies. Where two parties have chosen to accept a set of mutual rights and obligations, private law is generally concerned with interpreting and enforcing those consensually adopted rights and obligations. The idea that such consensual ordering should have primacy derives from liberal political theory, which conceives of contract as a realm of individual freedom from state interference.[137]

Secondly, according to the influential Diceyan legacy, equality before the law as a central aspect of the rule of law requires that government officials be subject to the same law as private persons administered in the ordinary courts.[138] This provides one of the explanations for insisting that the primacy of consensual ordering must apply to contracting even by public authorities.[139]

Finally, where legislation allows or even requires public authorities to enter the market, imposing public law constraints in that context would put them at a competitive disadvantage[140] and would compromise their bargaining position.[141]

We will return to these arguments in discussing the cases. None of these reasons justify outright rejection of public law constraints in all contexts. On the better view, the issue is how to draw the line between contexts in which the primacy of consensual ordering should be respected on the one hand, and contexts in which that is outweighed by the need for public law constraints on the other hand. Furthermore, these are not two sharply delineated categories; that is the point of the next section.

[137] Janet McLean, 'For a Law of Public Contract Per Se: An Intervention from Liberal Contract Theory' (2019) 39 *Oxford Journal of Legal Studies* 856.

[138] Albert V Dicey, *Introduction to the Law of the Constitution* (New York, Oxford University Press, 2013 (first published 1885)) at 100.

[139] See McLean (n 137) at 3, 16–17.

[140] *Lawson v Housing New Zealand* [1997] 2 NZLR 474 (HC) at 485.

[141] *Lab Tests Auckland Ltd v Auckland District Health Board* [2008] NZCA 385, [2009] 1 NZLR 776 at [88].

(2) Not All or Nothing

We have already noted that the application of public law constraints is not an all or nothing matter: public nature is a matter of degree and public law constraints accordingly apply to a greater or lesser extent. This point also applies to contracting decisions by government. Where a decision is only marginally public in nature, a limited set of constraints may apply. The options range from applying the full set of public law constraints comprised in the grounds of judicial review, to only a narrow set of grounds, to no public law constraints at all.

Mercury Energy established review on limited grounds as the standard solution for review of commercial contracting decisions by (quasi)public bodies. It held that such decisions by state-owned enterprises are unlikely to be reviewed except on the strictly limited grounds of 'fraud, corruption or bad faith'.[142] *Lab Tests* confirms that this excludes ordinary procedural grounds such as apparent bias and the right to a hearing or to consultation.[143]

Any of these options may be adopted via either contractual or judicial review proceedings, as with challenges to private associations by their members. In contractual proceedings, public law constraints can be implied into the contract.[144] This option can be available even where the challenge is to a decision *not* to contract with the plaintiff, as we will see in the section on procurement.[145]

(3) Are Public Contractual Decisions Ever Free from Public Law Constraints?

Often it seems to be assumed that there must be some kinds of contractual decisions that are so private or commercial in nature that they do not attract even the narrow *Mercury Energy* grounds of review. What, for instance, of a contract to purchase stationery for a government department? In *Mercury Energy* itself, one of the reasons for considering decisions of state-owned enterprises to be reviewable in principle was that decisions made by them in the public interest may adversely affect the rights and liabilities of private individuals without affording them any redress.[146] That suggests that the body needs to be exercising some form of unilateral power, which appears to be absent in the stationery example. It may have been an allusion to Electricorp's monopoly supplier position which did, arguably, give it some de facto unilateral power.

However, a test of unilateral power has not usually been applied to the reviewability of contractual decisions. Instead, in several cases, it has been common ground that at least the narrow *Mercury Energy* grounds applied – suggesting that these are the minimum form of public law constraint for all contractual decisions by public bodies.[147]

[142] *Mercury Energy Ltd v Electricity Corporation of NZ Ltd* [1994] 2 NZLR 385 (PC) at 391.

[143] *Lab Tests* (n 141).

[144] See, eg, *Mercury Energy* (n 142) at 388, where both contractual and judicial review causes of action were pleaded.

[145] Section (6)(b) of this Part C.

[146] *Mercury Energy* (n 142) at 388.

[147] See, eg, *Lab Tests* (n 141). This assumption was described as an unusual one that should not be treated as authoritative in a concurring judgment: ibid, [360]–[361]. However, the same assumption is again seen in *Attorney-General v Problem Gambling Foundation Inc* [2016] NZCA 609, [2017] 2 NZLR 470.

There is indeed good reason for this,[148] although this is not usually explained.[149] Minimum standards of probity must attach to anyone holding public office, and to any decision making use of public resources. Such minimum standards are encapsulated in the *Mercury Energy* grounds: fraud, corruption or bad faith cannot be acceptable in the use of public resources by public officials even for the most mundane transactions. We might say that the analogy with trust powers is the operative reason here.

Indeed, arguably the minimum grounds of review must be wider than a strict reading of *Mercury Energy* grounds, in two respects. First, it must always be unlawful for public officials to use public resources for inherently improper non-public purposes such as private self-interest, favour or ill will – which could also alternatively be described as actual bias. This is supported by the trust analogy. Properly interpreted, the *Mercury Energy* grounds of corruption or bad faith already encompass this ground.

Arguably, the category of inherently improper purposes includes public officials using their control of public resources to punish people for exercising their legal rights.[150] For instance, in the English case of *Trafford*, a council's decision as landlord to terminate a commercial lease was successfully challenged in judicial review on this kind of improper purpose ground. The lessee was a solicitor and was engaged in bringing personal injury claims against the council. This was part of her lawful business, but the council was punishing her for this.[151] Similarly it would surely be an inherently improper purpose for a public authority to reject a tender, if the reason was that the tenderer had been publicly critical of government policies or initiatives.[152]

Secondly, a further minimum ground of review is breach of the Bill of Rights. Where the respondent is part of the executive branch of government,[153] and hence within section 3(a) of the Act, then the nature of the function or power does not matter: the Act applies to *all* 'acts done' by the executive branch.[154] This must be correct, although there is 'little appreciation' of this point.[155] Recent authority apparently to the contrary must be considered per incuriam.[156] We may say that whenever rights are engaged by a decision of the executive branch, the decision is public by virtue of that impact. For instance, where procurement contracts contain gagging clauses

[148] See McLean, 'For a Public Law of Contract (n 137).

[149] *The State of Mauritius v The (Mauritius) CT Power Ltd* [2019] UKPC 27 at [43] insists on minimum public law standards without explanation.

[150] *Wheeler v Leicester City Council* [1985] 1 AC 1054 (HL) at 1080–81; *Roncarelli v Duplessis* [1959] SCR 121 (SCC) at 141.

[151] *Trafford v Blackpool Borough Council* [2014] EWHC 85 (Admin), [2014] 2 All ER 947 at [71].

[152] For this example, see Janet McLean, 'Convergence in Public and Private Law Doctrines – the Case of Public Contracts' [2016] New Zealand Law Review 5 at 19.

[153] The meaning of the 'executive' is an underexplored question in New Zealand: Andrew Butler and Petra Butler, *The New Zealand Bill of Rights: A Commentary,* 2nd edn (Wellington, LexisNexis NZ, 2015) at [5.5.1]–[5.5.6].

[154] ibid at [5.3.3]; Paul Rishworth and Grant Huscroft, *The New Zealand Bill of Rights* (2003) at 89. In the United Kingdom, this distinction is well established: *Aston Cantlow and Wilmcote with Billesley Parochial Church Council v Wallbank* [2004] 1 AC 546 (HL) at [5]–[12].

[155] Butler and Butler (n 153) at [5.5.1].

[156] *Turner v Te Whatu Ora – Health New Zealand, Wairarapa* [2024] NZCA 203. All three points offered in support misrepresent or misunderstand the sources.

purporting to restrain criticism of government policies,[157] this should be open to challenge on grounds of freedom of expression even if the context is highly commercial. The commercial context may in some cases contribute to justifying the limit on the right, but it does not render the Bill of Rights inapplicable.

Rights under Te Tiriti o Waitangi may have a similar effect, rendering any government decision impacting on them public by virtue of that impact. That is one way of reading the reasoning on the public nature question in *Ririnui*, discussed below.[158]

Since these grounds represent the minimum grounds, the courts' choice in challenges to contractual decisions is usually between such limited review and more extensive review on some or all of the usual grounds.

(4) Clarifying the Issues Arising from Contracting Out

Public lawyers' essential concern about contracting out is that it will compromise public law constraints on previously public functions.[159] What is not always appreciated, however, is that contracting out creates a 'triangle' of relationships, and hence three types of potential public law challenges, as noted by Anne Davies.[160] These are challenges by a contractor or would-be contractor against the public authority; by users or subjects of contracted-out services or functions against contractors or corporatised public providers; and by those users or subjects against the public authority that has let the contract. These different relationships and challenges raise different issues concerning public law constraints. The concern about compromising otherwise applicable public law constraints is relevant only to challenges by users or subjects of contracted-out services or functions, either against the public authority or against the contractor or corporatised public provider.

The focus in the United Kingdom case law and commentary has been on one of these two, namely challenges by users against contractors, usually in relation to social services such as aged care or social housing. The United Kingdom courts have been criticised for their caution in imposing public law constraints in this area.[161] Less attention has been devoted to holding the contracting authority itself responsible via judicial review for the functions it has delegated by contract.[162] This may well be considered the better route, or at least a useful additional route, although it will not necessarily be straightforward. The public authority should be held accountable for the terms of the contract and for monitoring its performance.[163]

In Aotearoa New Zealand, there has not been a focus on either of these possible challenges available to users or subjects of contracted-out services or functions.

[157] For this example, see McLean 'For a Public Law of Contract' (n 137) at 14.

[158] *Ririnui v Landcorp Farming Ltd* 2016] NZSC 62, [2016] 1 NZLR 1056, discussed at n 200.

[159] See, eg, Mark Freedland, 'Government by Contract and Public Law' [1994] *Public Law* 86 at 100–02.

[160] ACL Davies, 'The "Contracting State" and the Public/Private Divide' in JN Varuhas and S Wilson Stark (eds), *The Frontiers of Public Law* (Oxford, Hart Publishing, 2020) 335 at 343.

[161] ibid at 335–36.

[162] ibid at 336, 343–46.

[163] Janet McLean, *Searching for the State in British Legal Thought: Competing Conceptions of the Public Sphere* (Cambridge, Cambridge University Press, 2012) at 302.

Instead, in both case law and commentary on public contracting, debates tend to focus on challenges against public authorities by contractors, would-be contractors, or commercial contracting parties more generally. The extent to which such challenges should be allowed to invoke public law constraints is a valid topic of debate. But this is a different debate from the one mentioned at the start of this section. Failing to allow such challenges does not result in a loss of public law constraints that would have applied to public functions had they not been contracted out.

In the remaining two sections of this Part, I will outline and evaluate the case law first on challenges by users or subjects of contracted-out services or functions (Part 5) and then on challenges by (would-be) contractors and other commercial contracting parties (Part 6).

(5) Challenges by Users or Subjects of Contracted-out Services or Functions

The New Zealand case law does include some claims by users or subjects of contracted-out services or functions.[164] However, most of those claims concern contracted-out functions of a quite obviously public nature, such as prison management (unilateral and coercive powers),[165] and ACC review hearings (tribunals).[166] In those cases amenability to review tends to be assumed without discussion, as we have already seen.[167]

Such challenges are entertained against either the public authority or the contractor or both. In *Chamberlain*, the Court of Appeal explained why the Minister was responsible for a contractor carrying out statutory needs assessments: the Minister had delegated his powers by contract and remained responsible for their exercise.[168] The same delegation analysis also entails understanding the contractor's power as governmental and hence public and reviewable.[169] Where the challenge is to the rules or processes put in place by the public authority, that authority must be the defendant.[170] So far, it seems there is, in fact, little cause for worry about loss of public law constraints due to contracting out.

The under-explored question in New Zealand concerns users' ability to invoke public law constraints in challenging the contracted-out provision of a social service such as social housing or rest home care. Even when provided by public or quasi-public (corporatised) bodies themselves, such as Kāinga Ora providing social housing, such services can potentially be seen as a private activity.

The most distinctively public aspect is providing such services on a subsidised or free basis, pursuant to statute, for those who need them but cannot afford to pay for them. However, the statute often separates out the assessment of need and of eligibility for public funding, as well as the provision of that funding, from the provision of the

164 See, eg, *Royal Australasian College of Surgeons v Phipps* [1999] 3 NZLR 1 (CA), discussed at nn 81–83.
165 *Burke v Serco New Zealand Ltd* [2019] NZHC 1951.
166 *Moir v IHC New Zealand Inc* [2019] NZCA 92.
167 See discussion at nn 55–59.
168 *Chamberlain v Minister of Health* [2018] NZCA 8, [2018] 2 NZLR 771 at [65], [85]. For explanation, see ACL Davies, *The Public Law of Government Contracts* (2008), Ch 8.
169 See, eg, *Burke* (n 165) at [3].
170 ibid at [83]–[85].

service. Both for social housing with subsidised income-related rent and for subsidised or fully funded rest home care, the Ministry of Social Development (MSD) has the power to assess eligibility.[171] Another Ministry provides the subsidy for income-related rents.[172] For rest home care, the needs assessment and the funding is the responsibility of Health New Zealand,[173] but the assessment is contracted out.[174] Functions of this nature have been found amenable to judicial review even when contracted out.[175] They may also be subject to an appeal to the Social Security Appeal Authority.[176]

What, then, about the provider? This type of arrangement tends to promote a perception of the provider as private in nature. Continuing with social housing as a case study, the main provider is Kāinga Ora, and its role is solely to provide accommodation. It enters into contracts with the tenants. Rental accommodation is, of course, also available in the private market. All these features may suggest that the provision of the service is a private activity. Where such a function is contracted out to private providers, as with rest home care, that merely adds to the sense of the activity as private.

In the case of social housing, the statute appears to confirm that this is the intention. It provides that Kāinga Ora's power to allocate housing and to review placements does not limit its rights 'as a landlord under the Residential Tenancies Act 1986, including its rights to terminate a tenancy in accordance with that Act'.[177]

Yet Kāinga Ora does exercise significant unilateral power, given that accommodation is an essential need and only limited alternatives are available to social housing applicants.[178] There are long waiting lists for social housing. Many who have been assessed as in need and eligible therefore cannot access the service. Kāinga Ora makes its own decisions about allocating this scarce resource. This includes, for instance, blacklisting some who are in need and otherwise eligible because they have been evicted for disruptive behaviour.[179]

One public law avenue is available, acknowledging this significant power: Kāinga Ora is subject to the Ombudsman jurisdiction.[180] Other accessible avenues for claiming public law constraints are regrettably lacking. There used to be an appeal to a specialist tribunal, but this has been omitted from the current legislation. There is provision for appeals to the Social Security Appeal Authority, but only against MSD's decisions on eligibility: this does not extend to Kāinga Ora's decisions allocating accommodation.[181] The main avenue of challenge for tenancy decisions therefore is the Tenancy Tribunal. However, it is not clear whether that Tribunal has jurisdiction to entertain public law

[171] Public and Community Housing Management Act 1992 (PCHM Act), ss 72, 85, 101, 107; Residential Care and Disability Support Services Act 2018 (RCDSS Act), s 33.

[172] PCHM Act, ss 85, 98, 137A; and see Ministry of Housing and Urban Development. Available at: www.hud.govt.nz/funding-and-support/income-related-rent-subsidy.

[173] Pae Ora (Healthy Futures) Act 2022, s 14.

[174] See New Zealand Needs Assessment Service Coordination Association. Available at: www.nznasca.co.nz.

[175] See, eg, *Chamberlain* (n 168), concerning a needs assessment for paid family care.

[176] PCHM Act 1992, ss 132–134.

[177] ibid s 75.

[178] See Marcelo Rodriguez Ferrere and Katherine Lee, 'Housing New Zealand and the Residential Tenancies Act 1986' [2018] *New Zealand Law Journal* 342.

[179] Disruptive Behaviour Policy (POL-355). Available at: www.kaingaora.govt.nz.

[180] Ombudsmen Act 1975, sch 1, part 2.

[181] PCHM Act 1992, ss 132–134.

arguments. The High Court in *Scott* held that matters under the social housing legislation could not be raised in the Tribunal.[182]

Given the strong argument for applying public law constraints, one can only hope that judicial review would be available if a social housing tenant attempted such a challenge. The decision in *Scott* is not helpful: the Court appeared to accept that the social housing landlord's rights and obligations were no different from those of a private landlord.[183]

In *Lawson*, the High Court held that review of a Housing New Zealand decision was available only on the limited *Mercury Energy* grounds. However, the challenge there was to a high-level policy decision:to increase all rents to market rents. The Court held this was a 'purely commercial decision'.[184] Subjecting it to full judicial review would put Housing New Zealand at a 'competitive disadvantage' with private landlords. The Court was, though, inclined to find the Bill of Rights to be applicable.[185]

Lawson could be distinguished today, as it reflects the heavy emphasis on commercial objectives in the legislation at the time. Under the current legislation, Kāinga Ora has social objectives[186] and is obliged to charge income-related rents to tenants assessed as eligible by MSD.[187] In any event, a judicial review challenge to an individual allocation decision would arguably be quite a different matter.

In the United Kingdom, if public authorities themselves provide social services, judicial review challenges are more readily available than in New Zealand, and there is a significant body of case law. That is at least partly due to quite different legal settings. English law provides several relevant rights and obligations that can provide grounds for challenges, which do not exist in New Zealand. First, United Kingdom public authorities are at least sometimes under relevant statutory duties, such as to provide housing to eligible persons in need.[188] Secondly, the European Convention right to respect for home and family life is invoked when people are evicted from their homes.[189] Thirdly, case law has recognised the enforceability of substantive legitimate expectations, which have been used to challenge interference with a person's home.[190]

However, where contracted-out provision is concerned, United Kingdom case law severely restricts the availability of public law constraints. The cases are not all easy to reconcile but, in essence, it is necessary to show that a contractor exercises some form of coercive power or power to determine entitlements. This may apply where the

[182] *Scott v Housing New Zealand Corporation* [2015] NZHC 1401, [2015] 3 NZLR 816 at [33]. *Winther v Housing Corporation of New Zealand* [2010] NZCA 601, [2011] 1 NZLR 825 held that the Tribunal had no jurisdiction in discrimination complaints; but those can be brought in the Human Rights Review Tribunal.

[183] *Scott* (n 182) at [63]–[70].

[184] *Lawson v Housing New Zealand* [1997] 2 NZLR 474 (HC) at 485.

[185] ibid at 493, following *Federated Farmers of New Zealand (Inc) v New Zealand Post Ltd* [1990–92] 3 NZBORR 339 (HC) at 394–95.

[186] Kāinga Ora–Homes and Communities Act 2019, ss 12 and 14.

[187] Public and Community Housing Management Act 1992, s 72.

[188] Housing Act 1996 (UK), s 189B. Contrast New Zealand, where the legislation expressly denies any such obligation: PCHM Act 1992, ss 76, 97.

[189] European Convention for the Protection of Human Rights and Fundamental Freedoms (1950) 213 UNTS 221, art 8, incorporated into UK law by the Human Rights Act 1998 (UK). The New Zealand Bill of Rights Act 1990 does not have an equivalent right.

[190] *R v North and East Devon Health Authority ex p Coughlan* [2001] QB 213 (CA). In New Zealand, this ground of review is not fully recognised: see Ch 7.C.

contractor itself is subject to some statutory duty, breach of which can be challenged by judicial review,[191] or where a contractor has the power to determine who receives the publicly subsidised service.[192]

(6) Challenges by (Would-Be) Contractors or Commercial Contract Parties

Let us turn finally to challenges by contractors, would-be contractors, or commercial contract parties more generally – the type of challenge on which New Zealand case law and commentary has tended to focus. Some English commentators have argued that availability of review should be the default position, with no need for a special public law element.[193] Others consider that review should be denied entirely at least in some contexts. The usual position in New Zealand is limited review on only the narrow *Mercury Energy* grounds.[194] The position concerning Bill of Rights challenges has been addressed by the Supreme Court in *Moncrief-Spittle*.[195]

Let us look at two groups of cases: (a) those on commercial contracting generally and (b) those on procurement.

(a) Leading Cases on Commercial Contracting

The classic example of a situation attracting only limited review is found in the leading case of *Mercury Energy*. The impugned decision there was a decision by Electricorp, the state-owned enterprise generating and supplying bulk electricity nationwide, to terminate its contract to supply electricity to the Auckland retailer, after attempts to agree on the future price of supply had failed. The Privy Council held that decisions about entering or terminating a 'commercial contract to supply goods or services' were a matter for Electricorp, subject only to accountability to shareholding ministers and to judicial control to ensure the decision was made according to law.[196] The applicable law, it seems, was limited to the minimal grounds of 'fraud, corruption or bad faith';[197] the Board did not accept that anything in the Act constrained the power beyond this.[198] In what circumstances further public law constraints might apply was not fully explained.

In *Ririnui*, in contrast, the decision by a state-owned enterprise to sell surplus land without offering it to the claimant's iwi was fully reviewable.[199] The Supreme Court

[191] *R v Servite Houses, ex p Goldsmith* (2001) 33 HLR 35 (QB); *R (A) v Partnerships in Care Ltd* [2002] EWHC 529 (Admin), [2002] 1 WLR 2610.

[192] *Poplar Housing & Regeneration Community Association Ltd v Donoghue* [2001] EWCA Civ 595, [2002] QB 48; *YL v Birmingham City Council* [2007] UKHL 27, [2008] 1 AC 95; cf *R (Weaver) v London & Quadrant Housing Trust* [2009] EWCA Civ 587, [2010] 1 WLR 363.

[193] Sue Arrowsmith 'Judicial Review and the Contractual Powers of Public Authorities' (1990) 106 LQR 277; SH Bailey, 'Judicial Review of Contracting Decisions' [2007] *Public Law* 444. Note, however, that both authors address public contracting in a broader sense.

[194] *Mercury Energy* (n 142).

[195] *Moncrief-Spittle v Regional Facilities Auckland Ltd* [2022] NZSC 138, [2022] 1 NZLR 459.

[196] *Mercury Energy* (n 142) at 390–91.

[197] Recently affirmed in *The State of Mauritius v The (Mauritius) CT Power Ltd* [2019] UKPC 27 at [66].

[198] *Mercury Energy* (n 142) at 391.

[199] *Ririnui v Landcorp Farming Ltd* [2016] NZSC 62, [2016] 1 NZLR 1056 at [43], [65], [70]–[74].

affirmed that the choice between minimal or full constraints turns on whether there is a sufficient public interest dimension, which may be found even in otherwise commercial contracting. In this case, the disposal of surplus land might be considered a commercial matter. However, the necessary public interest dimension was supplied by the fact that Treaty of Waitangi obligations were engaged. A Treaty claim to the land by the claimant's iwi was pending at the relevant time, and the sale to a third party would render it much more difficult to seek the return of the land.[200] The decision-makers were under an express statutory obligation to exercise their powers consistently with the Treaty.[201] Absent this Treaty dimension, as the Court seemed to acknowledge, the sale would have attracted only limited review on *Mercury Energy* grounds. The Court of Appeal has treated *Ririnui* as exceptional.[202]

Finally, *Moncrief-Spittle* is the leading case on applying the 'public function, power or duty' test in section 3(b) of the Bill of Rights to commercial contracting.[203] A decision by Regional Facilities Auckland Ltd (RFAL), a council-controlled organisation, to cancel a contract for use of a venue managed by RFAL was held to satisfy the test. The contract was for an event featuring two controversial 'alt right' speakers, and the cancellation was due to health and safety concerns arising from anticipated protests against the event.

As already noted, the Supreme Court adopted the *Ransfield* approach to the section 3(b) test.[204] This involves using a non-exhaustive range of indicia to evaluate overall whether the particular power or function is 'governmental'. In this case, the indicia overwhelmingly pointed towards the Bill of Rights applying to RFAL's decision to cancel the speaking event.[205]

RFAL was wholly council-owned, not for profit and received some public funding. It was subject to governance by the Council, which had set the policy framework for the power exercised by RFAL. It had functions and responsibilities under the legislation. The venue was held by a charitable trust, and both the trust and the venue were managed by RFAL on behalf of Auckland Council. In managing the venue, RFAL stood in the shoes of the Council, providing a service intended for the social well-being of the community. Promoting social well-being was one of the Council's statutory responsibilities, and RFAL was an important means by which the Council discharged this responsibility. The venue was publicly owned property used for expressive activity. Being publicly owned was not determinative but was relevant. While RFAL had no obligation to make venues available for any particular purpose, 'the wider context cannot be ignored'. Part of the Council's general powers of competence was the traditional role of councils in providing venues for debate and discussion (the 'town hall'), and RFAL's role was to assist the Council in that – even though the venue here was not the town hall as such. While the decision concerned a commercial contract, which might count against application of the Bill of Rights, this was not determinative.

[200] The Waitangi Tribunal may order the Crown to resume land sold by SOEs and needed for a Treaty claim, but this had never been used at that point.

[201] State-Owned Enterprises Act 1986, s 9.

[202] *Problem Gambling Foundation* (n 147) at [46].

[203] *Moncrief-Spittle* (n 195).

[204] ibid at [39]–[48]; *Ransfield v The Radio Network Ltd* [2005] 1 NZLR 233 (HC) see discussion above at n 39.

[205] ibid at [50]–[59].

(b) Procurement Cases

In relation to procurement decisions, limited review appears to be settling in as the norm. This goes at least for the initial decision, often by tender, but also for decisions on review and renewal of contracts. Although the High Court has occasionally allowed full review,[206] such rulings have been overturned whenever they have been appealed, with the Court of Appeal insisting on limited review.[207] In *Lab Tests*, the incumbent provider of medical laboratory services in Auckland unsuccessfully challenged the award of the contract to a new provider; review was confined to the *Mercury Energy* grounds.[208] Another incumbent provider, this time a charity, met the same fate in relation to the Ministry of Health's contract for problem gambling services in *Problem Gambling Foundation*. Further decisions that have been found subject only to limited review include tendering or otherwise contracting for social services for Māori communities,[209] school bus services[210] and new vessels for the navy.[211]

Proceedings in contract are potentially available as an alternative, but the public law constraints that are implied into the contract have also been strictly limited. When a tendering process is used for procurement, this can give rise to a so-called process contract or preliminary contract: the call for tenders represents a contractual offer to deal with responses in accordance with the process set out there, and this offer is then accepted by every party who submits a tender. A duty to act fairly and in good faith, and to treat all tenderers equally, has been implied into such a contract.[212] This implied term can be seen as a version of minimum public law constraint.[213]

It is not clear whether in the case of public authorities, further public law constraints may sometimes be implied into the process contract. The Privy Council in *Pratt Contractors* held that the implied term does not *as such* impose the full set of constraints comprised in the grounds of judicial review.[214] While that does not preclude implication of some public law constraints beyond the minimum in particular contexts, in this case apparent bias and a right to a hearing were rejected as inappropriate in the context.[215] Whether there is a process contract at all depends on the terms of the tender; in *Problem Gambling Foundation* the terms were held to exclude such a contract.[216]

Turning to the reasons for such limited constraints, the statutory scheme and context has been considered relevant in determining whether a contracting power

[206] *Diagnostic Medlab Ltd v Auckland District Health Board* [2007] 2 NZLR 832 (HC); *Problem Gambling Foundation of New Zealand v Attorney-General* [2015] NZHC 1701; *Telco Technology Services Ltd v Ministry of Education* [2014] NZHC 213.

[207] *Lab Tests* (n 141); *Problem Gambling Foundation* (n 147).

[208] *Lab Tests* ibid at [91].

[209] *Te Whanau o Waipareira Trust v Attorney-General* [2012] NZHC 3107; *Te Tai Tokerau MAPO Trust v Chief Executive of the Ministry of Health* HC Whangarei CIV-2010-488-307, 5 August 2011.

[210] *Bayline Group Ltd v Secretary for Education* [2007] NZAR 747 (HC).

[211] *Schelde Marinebouw BV v Attorney-General* [2005] NZAR 356 (HC).

[212] *Pratt Contractors Ltd v Transit New Zealand* [2003] UKPC 83, [2005] 2 NZLR 433. For hesitation about the process contract approach, see *South Waikato District Council v Roading and Asphalt Ltd* [2013] NZCA 566 at [49].

[213] See McLean, 'Convergence' (n 152) at 10.

[214] *Pratt* (n 212) at [46]–[47].

[215] ibid at [47]–[48].

[216] *Problem Gambling Foundation* (n 147) at [10].

is of a sufficiently public nature to attract public law constraints. In particular, the courts have relied on statutory requirements to act commercially as indicating that the power lacked public nature.[217] A potential objection is that, as noted earlier, the object of such a requirement may be to achieve efficiency rather than to exclude public law obligations.

A more particular reason for limiting review in procurement cases, relied on in several cases starting with *Lab Tests*, is that procurement involves public authorities dealing with private enterprises who are often hard-nosed commercial operators. It would be contrary to the public interest to put public authorities on the back foot by imposing extensive public law obligations on them.[218] Similarly, in *Problem Gambling Foundation* the mere fact that the authority was engaged in procurement was held to be a strong indicator that its decisions in that context were commercial. Integrity and competence in public contracting were important, but could be assured via other avenues such as the Ombudsman and the Auditor General.[219]

All of this raises the question whether procurement decisions will ever be subject to public law constraints beyond the limited *Mercury Energy* grounds. Let me mention three possible arguments calling for greater constraints in some contexts.

First, the Court of Appeal in *Problem Gambling Foundation* held that commercial decisions could exceptionally be subject to full review. However, this was only in cases like *Ririnui* where the challenge raised issues directly relevant to the public interest in question and where the challenger's interests were aligned with that public interest. The Court accepted that the provision of health services always has public interest implications. But a challenge by 'a disappointed commercial party' was not aligned with that public interest; it was instead founded simply on 'disappointment of its own private interests'.[220]

This line of argument from *Ririnui* could, however, have been taken a little further. In the procurement context, the public interest in the service in question can be relevant, since the choice of provider and the terms offered by that provider may affect the quantity and quality of that service. Where that is the case, it may in some contexts trigger a statutory consultation requirement.[221] Relying on such impact to support imposition of public law constraints would be a version of the public impact argument that also provides the basis for public law constraints in some of the cases on private bodies.[222]

If this type of public interest argument is the reason for considering that more than minimal public law constraints are needed, then the most appropriate applicants for review are users of the service who will be affected by the choice of provider. Hence, as noted in *Problem Gambling Foundation*, the public interest dimension is arguably irrelevant in a challenge by a disappointed contractor pursuing that contractor's private interests, which are potentially in tension with the public interest.

[217] *Lab Tests* (n 141) at [58], [60], [77], [87].
[218] Ibid at [88]; *New Zealand Private Hospitals Association – Auckland Branch (Inc) v Northern Regional Health Authority* HC Auckland CP440/94, 7 December 1994.
[219] *Problem Gambling Foundation* (n 147) at [50].
[220] Ibid at [42]–[45], [47], [53].
[221] Such an obligation was at issue in *Lab Tests* (n 141), but it did not apply on the facts: at [332].
[222] See text at nn 95, 97, 119.

However, the challenge in *Problem Gambling Foundation* arguably met the requirement based on *Ririnui*. The High Court decision offered a basis for finding that the interests of a charity devoted to combating problem gambling were sufficiently aligned with the public interest in effective problem gambling services.[223] While the point was arguable either way, the Court of Appeal's out-of-hand dismissal of that possibility is a little surprising.[224] It is also, furthermore, open to question whether competitive contracting should be used at all when engaging non-profit organisations to provide public services. McLean has pointed out the destructive effects of such arrangements on the non-profit sector.[225]

Secondly, *Ririnui* held that the necessary public interest dimension is present when Treaty of Waitangi obligations are engaged by the contracting decision. This may apply in the procurement context and may cast some doubt on a line of High Court decisions in which decisions on contracting for social services with Māori organisations has been held subject to only limited review.[226] Provision of social services for Māori communities by Māori organisations can be seen as a form of self-government that promotes the tino rangatiratanga guaranteed by article two of the Treaty. It can also represent redress for the social harm caused by past Treaty breaches. Even if this Treaty dimension is not as strong as that in *Ririnui*, it is still arguable that a challenge based on it should be available in the procurement context.

Finally, remember that where the respondent forms part of the executive branch of government, the Bill of Rights applies to all its acts by virtue of section 3(a) of that Act. That is potentially relevant in the procurement context, since the rights in the Act can be claimed by legal persons.[227] However, while such claims are available, success may not be common: limits on potentially relevant rights such as freedom of speech may be easier to justify in relation to legal persons.[228] Still, if a non-profit organisation could establish that it was denied renewal of a social services contract because it had criticised government policies, it could presumably invoke freedom of expression to challenge that decision.

[223] *Problem Gambling Foundation* HC (n 206) at [88]–[89], [101].
[224] *Problem Gambling Foundation* CA (n 147) at [42]–[46].
[225] McLean 'Convergence' (n 152) at 19–21.
[226] *Te Whanau o Waipareira* (n 211); *Te Tai Tokerau MAPO Trust* (n 211).
[227] New Zealand Bill of Rights Act 1990, s 29.
[228] Butler and Butler (n 153) at [5.11.7].

12

Private Law and Public Power: Public Authorities' Liability in Damages

Administrative law proceedings are concerned with *decisions* made in the exercise of public powers: their legality and sometimes their correctness. This focus on decisions is reflected in the available remedies. In judicial review, courts quash unlawful decisions and remit them for reconsideration or declare them unlawful. In merits review, tribunals substitute correct or preferable decisions for wrong or suboptimal decisions.

But can public officials and authorities also be liable to pay damages for loss caused by the exercise – or failure to exercise – public powers, or for infringing rights? If so, when and on what basis? That is the question explored in this chapter.

Answering this question generally requires recourse to private law because, in our system, the sort of obligations and constraints that result in damages liability for causing loss or infringing rights are found in private law. The only exception is that the judge-made remedies for breach of the New Zealand Bill of Rights Act 1990 include damages for rights breaches in some circumstances.[1] We might also add that the remedial actions which the Ombudsmen can recommend include ex gratia compensation. In all other contexts, we need to ask whether and how private law obligations and constraints apply to public officials and authorities exercising public powers.

Answers to this question are frequently uncertain and unsettled, because they engage the interface between public and private law. These two broad areas of law involve different frames of reference and different values. At their interface, the relationship between them tends to be uncertain and highly contested.

Part IV of this book, containing the present chapter, approaches this interface from both directions. While the present chapter explores the application of private law to those exercising public powers, the preceding Chapter 11 explores how far public law reaches into the private sphere: how private can a decision or a decision-maker be and still attract public law constraints?

The topic of this chapter, the applicability of private law obligations to public officials and authorities, is a large and complex topic that cannot be comprehensively addressed in this book. This chapter offers a selective window into the topic by focusing on the law of torts. Some of the torts discussed – especially trespass – can also be conceptualised as part of land law and property law. Aspects of how the law of contract interfaces with public powers are addressed in Chapter 11. The law of restitution is touched on in passing in this chapter.

The discussion of tort law in this chapter focuses on what is special about the liability of public authorities. For further explanations of the relevant general principles and concepts of tort law, readers should consult torts textbooks.[2] Three introductory points about tort law may be mentioned by way of background here.

First, we should note that tort liability usually attaches to individuals – in the present context, individual officials. Entities such as public authorities can also be sued, but usually this takes the form of vicarious liability: if a tort is committed by an employee, then the entity shares that individual's liability on a joint and several liability basis. That means a plaintiff may sue either the individual or the entity (or both) to recover the full loss. Unsettled issues concern the question how far vicarious liability extends beyond employment relationships.[3]

Secondly, in Aotearoa New Zealand, a large part of common law tort liability is replaced by the accident compensation scheme (known as ACC).[4] This unique regime provides compensation on a no-fault basis for all personal injury caused by accident, and in turn bars claims for damages for personal injury against those responsible for accidents.[5] Exceptions to the ACC bar have been recognised for some types of claim that are not available under the scheme, as we will see.

[1] *Simpson v Attorney-General* [1994] 3 NZLR 667 (CA) (*Baigent's* case).
[2] Stephen Todd et al, *The Law of Torts in New Zealand* (9th edn, Wellington, Brookers, 2023).
[3] ibid ch 21.
[4] Accident Compensation Act 2001; see Todd et al (n 2) ch 2.
[5] Section 317 of the Act.

The final introductory point concerns the purpose and objectives of tort liability.[6] Very broadly, we could identify two main purposes. On the one hand, tort liability provides redress to victims, restoring them as far as is possible to their pre-tort position by compensating them for loss or harm. On the other hand, it holds wrongdoers responsible and perhaps has a deterrent effect, providing incentives to avoid conduct that may harm others. The deterrent objective is more debatable and contentious, particularly in light of the role of insurance and the increasing scope of vicarious liability.

In the case of public authority defendants, additional objectives are in play. First, liability can be viewed as a form of governmental accountability. Secondly, it can serve to vindicate rights. The rights that are vindicated include those affirmed by the Bill of Rights or by international human rights instruments. However, that is not all. The intentional torts protect private law rights of property, privacy and liberty. In claims against public officials, these rights take on constitutional significance. That is why they are protected by an approach that amounts to applying the so-called principle of legality:[7] statutory powers are not read as abrogating those rights unless the statute spells this out 'in the plainest terms'.[8] The right to natural justice is a further common law right that prevails over statute unless it is expressly abrogated or would frustrate the purposes of the statute.[9] This too can be enforced by tort proceedings, as we will see. Indeed, this type of tort proceeding used to be one of the main ways of holding public authorities accountable in the courts.[10]

In considering questions about the damages liability of public authorities, two settled orthodoxies are the starting points and make up a large part of the answer. The unsettled issues cluster around these orthodoxies. This chapter first introduces the two orthodoxies (Part A), and then explores the uncertain scope of the qualifications to each of them in turn (Parts B and C).

A. Two Orthodoxies are the Starting Point

The first settled orthodoxy is that there is no such thing as administrative law damages: decision-makers are not liable in administrative law for loss caused by decisions that are unlawful on the grounds of judicial review.[11] For instance, administrative law does not provide a damages remedy for the loss of income suffered by an applicant who was denied a fishing licence for an improper purpose.[12] Liability can flow only if the claimant can make out a relevant private law cause of action.

To put this in perspective, it is important to note that damages liability is not always needed to put applicants in the position they would have been in but for the unlawful decision. Where an applicant has been unlawfully denied a financial benefit to which they were entitled, such as accident compensation or a social security benefit, the

[6] See Todd (n 2), Ch 1.4.

[7] See Ch 6.C for this principle.

[8] *Choudry v Attorney-General* [1999] 2 NZLR 582 (CA) at 592–93.

[9] *Daganayasi v Minster of Immigration* [1980] 2 NZLR 130 (CA).

[10] See also, eg, *Ashby v White* (1703) 2 Ld Raym 938, 92 ER 126 (KB).

[11] *X (Minors) v Bedfordshire County Council* [1995] 2 AC 633 (HL) at 730; *Minister of Fisheries v Pranfield* [2008] 3 NZLR 649 (CA) at [84].

[12] *Pranfield* ibid (n 11).

relevant authority will pay that benefit in arrears from the date on which it should have been granted.[13] The reason is that authorities are expected to comply with the law. The issue concerning damages liability is significant for all claims that cannot be addressed by this solution.

The qualifications to the first orthodoxy are explored in Part B. Damages claims are potentially available for loss caused by exercsises of power that are unlawful in administrative law terms, provided certain further requirements – usually, but not always, requirements of a private law cause of action – are met. We will consider several types of claim.

The second settled orthodoxy is that public officials exercising public power are subject to the same liability in the private law of torts as private citizens would be in comparable circumstances. This is Dicey's equality principle: the ordinary law applies to all.[14]

The qualifications to this second orthodoxy are explored in Part C of this chapter. There are a number of areas where the liability of public officials is either restricted or expanded by comparison with private defendants. Special restrictions reflect recognition of the public interest served by exercises of public power. Special expansion of liability reflects recognition of officials' special powers and responsibilities.

B. Liability for Loss Caused by Unlawful Exercise of Public Powers

Can a public official or authority be held liable in damages for infringements of fundamental rights or for loss caused by exercises of public powers that are unlawful on administrative law grounds? The starting point, as we have seen, is the orthodoxy that there is no such thing as administrative law damages. While there are several heads of liability that do provide damages for such claims, each of these turns on making out some further element.

These are explored in this part of the chapter. Section (1) explains that exercises of public power can give rise to liability in the intentional torts unless the official or authority can make out the defence of statutory authority. That defence may be defeated by showing that the exercise of the power was unlawful. Nuisance and restitution claims against public officials involve a similar analysis. Section (2) outlines Misfeasance in a public office: a special public law tort, consisting of the unlawful exercise of a public power with 'malice'. Section (3) concerns damages as a remedy for breach of the Bill of Rights Act. This is a discretionary remedy, granted only where other remedies are not adequate. Section (4) discussed the tort of breach of statutory duty. This is available only if the official was under a duty rather than exercising a discretionary power. Section (5) records that the courts have almost always refused to recognise a tort of negligently unlawful exercise of public power. Finally, section (6) asks whether damages should be introduced as a remedy in administrative law.

[13] However, claimants are not compensated for consequential losses in this situation.

[14] Albert V Dicey, *Introduction to the Law of the Constitution* (New York, Oxford University Press, 2013 (first published 1885)) at 100.

(1) Intentional Torts and the Defence of Statutory Authority

Some exercises of statutory power by public officials or authorities would amount to torts if they were not authorised by statute. This applies to powers involving physical interference with persons or property which engages the intentional torts. Liability exists in such cases if the defence of statutory authority fails. For instance, officers carrying out an unauthorised search without the person's consent commit trespass.[15] Unauthorised arrests or detention amount to false imprisonment.[16] At common law, the torts of assault and battery would be available where authorities kill or injure people without lawful authority. In New Zealand, however, such claims could be brought only where one of the exceptions to the ACC bar is available.

The intentional torts are actionable per se, that is without establishing any concrete loss: damages are awarded for interference with the protected interests in liberty, property and privacy. Liability is moreover strict, in the sense that it is not necessary to show that the defendant failed to take due care. It is enough to show that the defendant deliberately did the act without the plaintiff's consent.[17]

Lawful justification is a defence, but it requires authority in positive law. This may sometimes be found in the common law but usually is found in statute. Common law examples include constables' power to arrest for an imminent breach of the peace. The requirement of imminence tends to be applied strictly.[18]

Statutory authority is also interpreted strictly. As already noted, the common law rights protected by the intentional torts have constitutional significance in claims against public officials. The principle of legality therefore requires statutory authority to interfere with those rights to be explicit and unambiguous. Otherwise, the purported exercise of the power is unlawful on grounds of exceeding the scope of the statutory power, and the defence fails. For instance, in *Choudry* the liberty and property rights affected by a search prevailed over the statutory power, because the statute did not explicitly and unambiguously authorise invasions of those rights.[19]

The defence of statutory authority may also be defeated by invoking other grounds of judicial review. Such use of the grounds of review in support of tort proceedings is known as a 'collateral challenge'.[20] A classic example is *Cooper v Wandsworth Board of Works*. The Board was liable in trespass for exercising its power to demolish a house under construction. It had this power under building bylaws because the builder had failed to give notice to the Board before commencing construction. Yet the defence of statutory authority was held to be defeated by the Board's breach of the builder's right to a hearing.[21]

In old cases, such as *Cooper*, such tort liability followed automatically from establishing a ground of review to defeat the defence of statutory authority. However, this seems inconsistent with the nature of remedies in judicial review. In judicial

[15] *Entick v Carrington* (1765) 2 Wils KB 275, 95 ER 807 (KB); *Choudry* (n 8).

[16] *Blundell v Attorney-General* [1968] NZLR 341 (CA) at 354.

[17] Todd (n 2) at 115, 529.

[18] See, eg, *R (Laporte) v Chief Constable of Gloucestershire Constabulary* [2006] UKHL 55, [2007] 2 AC 105.

[19] *Choudry* (n 8) at 592–93.

[20] See Ch 10.E.

[21] *Cooper v Wandsworth Board of Works* (1863) 14 CBNS 180, 143 ER 414 (Comm Pleas).

review proceedings directly challenging the lawfulness of the exercise of power, the usual remedy involves the decision being quashed and remitted for reconsideration. Following such a remedy, it is often open to the decision-maker to make the same decision again. Alternatively, where it is too late to change the decision, it is open to a court to exercise the remedial discretion and decline to quash the decision at all. If a tort action was later brought in either of these circumstances, the defence of statutory authority would arguably remain available. Perhaps in *Cooper* the remedial discretion would have been exercised to quash without remitting for reconsideration, thus negating the statutory authority. However, the issue was not discussed: liability was simply assumed to follow from establishing that the statutory authority was exercised in breach of judicial review principles.

Some more recent cases have raised issues about this old approach. Arguably, statutory authority is automatically defeated only where the purported exercise was outside the scope of the statutory power, as in *Choudry*, because the statute is not clear enough to authorise otherwise tortious action.[22] Where, instead, the ground of challenge is that there was an unlawful exercise of an available power, for instance an exercise in breach of natural justice, the law is less clear. Alternative approaches could include declining to allow such collateral challenges at all; staying proceedings once a ground of review is made out and remitting the matter for reconsideration before assessing damages;[23] or adjusting the measure of damages to take account of the contingency.

In *Sugrue* the issue was raised but not decided. The plaintiffs unsuccessfully sued in trespass for the seizure of their helicopter. One issue was whether the defendant's statutory authority was vitiated by improper purpose. The Crown argued against entertaining such a collateral challenge. However, it was unnecessary to decide this point.[24] The claim failed in any event because the impugned purpose was held not improper.[25]

Roberts v Rodney District Council is a modern New Zealand instance of a trespass claim based on a collateral challenge being upheld in full. A local authority was held liable in trespass for constructing a sewer pipe across the plaintiff's land without first giving the plaintiff notice and an opportunity to object, as required by statute.[26] In assessing damages, the Court rejected the Council's argument that these should be reduced because it could have achieved the same result after giving the required notice.[27]

In *Lumba*, in contrast, the United Kingdom Supreme Court controversially qualified the old approach. The plaintiff sued in false imprisonment. He was detained in breach of a duty to apply published policy unless there are good reasons not to follow it. However, the Court was satisfied that the plaintiff would have been detained regardless, even if the published policy had been applied. Should his claim still succeed,

[22] *Choudry* (n 8).

[23] See Dean Knight, 'Ameliorating the Collateral Damage Caused by Collateral Attack in Administrative Law' (2006) 4 *New Zealand Journal of Public and International Law* 117 at 145.

[24] *PF Sugrue Ltd v Attorney-General* [2004] 1 NZLR 207 (CA) at [46]–[49].

[25] ibid at [49]–[58]. On appeal, the Privy Council upheld the finding on improper purpose: *PF Sugrue Ltd v Attorney-General* [2005] UKPC 44, [2006] 3 NZLR 464 at [24]. It did not address the availability of collateral challenge.

[26] *Ardern v Rodney District Council* HC Auckland M735/96, 2 October 1997.

[27] The damages issue was dealt with in a separate judgment (under a different name): *Roberts v Rodney District Council* [2001] 2 NZLR 402 (HC) at [47].

and to what extent? The Court allowed the collateral challenge and held that liability for false imprisonment was made out. Establishing the tort did not depend on a causal link between the unlawfulness and the detention.[28] However, the quantum of damage did depend on the causal effect of the unlawfulness: the plaintiff should be put back in the position he would have been in but for the unlawfulness. He therefore received only nominal damages, since he would have been detained with or without the unlawfulness.[29]

The best approach to this issue is very much open to debate.[30] First, it is open to doubt whether the rulings on the two separate points in *Lumba* can be reconciled. If the causal effect of the unlawfulness matters for the quantum of damages, it is not clear why it should not matter for establishing the tort, and vice versa.

Secondly, there is room for debate on whether liability should be restricted. One argument in favour of both finding the tort established and awarding full damages is that the reliance on causal effect is inconsistent with the intentional torts being actionable per se: their purpose is to vindicate the rights to liberty, property and privacy. Only lawful exercise of statutory authority should be a defence to that.[31] If, on the other hand, liability is to be restricted, one alternative method is to treat statutory authority as defeated only where the power is not available at all, or only where the error is sufficiently fundamental.[32] However, such categorical distinctions have been considered troublesome.[33] A further alternative method is to determine the consequences of invalid exercise of power on a case-by-case basis, balancing a range of relevant considerations, interests and values.[34]

The final point to note about the intentional torts is that they are available to remedy unlawful exercises of power only where the exercise of power took the form of a physical interference with the plaintiff's person or property. If the Board of Works in *Cooper* had merely ordered work on the house to cease, there would be no claim in trespass. Yet there might still be a loss. Another common occurrence is unlawful refusal of a licence that is required for some commercial activity such as fishing. By the time the unlawfulness is established, much income will have been lost. However, such facts do not give rise to a claim in any of the intentional torts, since there is no physical interference with person or property.[35]

There are some other heads of damages claims that involve a similar analysis when invoked against public officials exercising public powers. These include claims for restitution. Plaintiffs who have paid money demanded by a public authority pursuant to

[28] *R (Lumba) v Secretary of State for the Home Department* [2011] UKSC 12, [2012] 1 AC 245 at [64]–[72], [88], [175], [195], [207], [238]–[243], [251].

[29] ibid at [95]–[101], [169], [222], [233], [236], [253]–[256], [335], [342], [361]. See also *Lewis v Australian Capital Territory* [2020] HCA 26.

[30] *Lumba* (ibid) has been rejected in Ireland: *GE v Commissioner of An Garda Siochána* [2022] IESC 51.

[31] See *Lumba* (n 28) per Lord Brown; Jason NE Varuhas, 'The Concept of "Vindication" in the Law of Torts: Rights, Interests and Damages' (2014) 34 *Oxford Journal of Legal Studies* 253.

[32] See *Lumba* (n 28) per Lord Brown, Lord Rodger, Lord Walker.

[33] See, eg, *R (Cart) v Upper Tribunal (Public Law Project Intervening)* [2011] UKSC 28, [2012] 1 AC 663 at [40], [111].

[34] See David Feldman, 'Error of Law and Flawed Administrative Acts' (2014) 73 *Cambridge Law Journal* 275.

[35] The economic torts may, however, be available in some circumstances.

statutory powers are entitled to restitution if they can show that the demand was not authorised by those powers and was therefore unlawful.[36] As with intentional torts, issues arise as to the appropriate response in cases where the demand is challenged as an unlawful exercise of an available power. In *Waikato Regional Airport*, the Privy Council held that biosecurity charges imposed on the airport were unlawful on two grounds: failure to take into account a statutory criterion of equity and taking into account irrelevant considerations.[37] It was unclear whether a further ground was that the equity criterion was simply not satisfied. The Privy Council ordered restitution of the charges.[38] Unlike the Court of Appeal,[39] it did not consider the judicial review remedial discretion. Nor did it consider whether the invalidity was sufficient to give rise to a right to restitution.[40]

(2) Misfeasance in a Public Office

So far, we have seen that public officials are not liable for loss simply because it was caused by an unlawful exercise of public power. Nor are intentional torts available where the loss was caused by nothing more than an unlawful order and the plaintiff's compliance with that order: physical interference is required. Public officials may, however, be liable for such loss in the tort of Misfeasance in a Public Office.[41] This is the only exclusively 'public' tort: the only one that is confined in its application to public officials purporting to exercise public powers.[42] In addition to an unlawful exercise of public power causing loss,[43] the elements of this tort include an essential mental element: the official must have been acting with 'malice'.

Malice for this purpose can take one of two forms. The essence of the tort is a lack of good faith in the purported exercise of public power. That is the guiding principle in defining both forms of malice.[44]

The first form is known as 'targeted' malice. It involves an intention to harm the plaintiff; a state of mind that is also described as spite or ill will. This is the more obvious sense of malice, but it is only rarely established by the evidence. A famous example is the Premier of Quebec requiring the liquor licensing commission to cancel the liquor licence for Mr Roncarelli's restaurant to punish him for his support for the activities of Jehovah's witnesses.[45]

[36] *Woolwich Equitable Building Society v Inland Revenue Commissioners* [1993] AC 70 (HL).

[37] *Waikato Regional Airport Ltd v Attorney-General* [2004] 3 NZLR 1 (PC) at [59], [64]–[74].

[38] ibid at [76]–[84].

[39] *Waikato Regional Airport Ltd v Attorney-General* [2002] 3 NZLR 433 (CA) at [139]–[140].

[40] For discussion, see Janet McLean, 'Roadblocks, Restraint and Remedies: The Idea of Progress in Administrative Law' in Grant Huscroft and Michael Taggart (eds), *Inside and Outside Canadian Administrative Law: Essays in Honour of David Mullan* (Toronto, University of Toronto Press, 2006) 211.

[41] See also Erika Chamberlain, *Misfeasance in a Public Office* (Toronto, Thomson Reuters, 2016).

[42] On who counts as a public official, see *Commissioner of Inland Revenue v Chesterfields Preschools Ltd* [2013] NZCA 53, [2013] 2 NZLR 679 at [70]–[82]; *Clayton v Currie* [2013] 1 NZLR 263.

[43] The tort is not actionable per se: *Watkins v Secretary of State for the Home Department* [2006] UKHL 17, [2006] 2 AC 395.

[44] *Three Rivers District Council v Governor and Company of the Bank of England (No 3)* [2003] 2 AC 1 (HL) at 190, 191; *Minister of Fisheries v Pranfield Holdings Ltd* [2008] 3 NZLR 649 (CA) at [118], [121].

[45] *Roncarelli v Duplessis* [1959] SCR 121. The liability here was under provisions of the Quebec Civil Code that were equivalent to the tort of Misfeasance in a Public Office.

The second, alternative and extended form of malice requires a specific level of awareness of two points: that the purported exercise of power was unlawful and that it would probably cause harm.[46] The required level of awareness is either actual knowledge or reckless indifference in a subjective sense. The test for subjective recklessness combines subjective and objective elements: it requires a subjective belief or suspicion as to the unlawfulness or the probable harm, and then failure to take honest and reasonable steps to ascertain the position.[47] Where this combination is present, the official has displayed a 'conscious disregard' for the plaintiff's interests,[48] and was not engaged in an 'honest attempt to perform the functions of a public office'.[49] This does happen, but even this extended form of malice is not often made out.

One of the few successful claims is found in the English *Bourgoin* case.[50] The defendant Minister had revoked import licences for French turkey producers, for the purpose of protecting English producers – which was unlawful under EU law. The Minister was liable because he knew both that this purpose was unlawful and that the decision would harm the French producers. Such actual knowledge on both points is likely to be rare.

The version that is more likely to be satisfied is subjective recklessness, but the two main appellate decisions in New Zealand have adopted relatively demanding approaches to this requirement. The issue in *Pranfield* concerned subjective recklessness as to legality, and the Court held that awareness of legal uncertainty did not suffice.[51] An official in the Ministry of Agriculture and Fisheries had turned down an application for a fishing licence in reliance on an internal policy, despite being aware of a disagreement between different regional offices as to the legality of that policy. Rather than seeking legal advice to resolve the disagreement, he had come to a positive conclusion in his own mind that the policy was not only in the public interest but also lawful. The Court considered that this state of mind did not satisfy the requirement of a belief or suspicion that the policy was unlawful. Therefore the requirement to take honest and reasonable steps to ascertain the position – such as by taking legal advice – was not triggered. The official's conduct was not inconsistent with an honest attempt to perform the functions of the office.[52] This was a finely balanced point that could have been decided either way.

In *Garret*, the contentious issue concerned subjective recklessness as to probable harm. The plaintiff had complained to the police about being raped by a constable. She sued the police not for the rape but for the failure to investigate her complaint. The officer who received the complaint knowingly breached his duty to investigate. He therefore satisfied the 'malice' requirement in relation to the unlawfulness of his

[46] This form was first established in *Bourgoin SA v Minister of Agriculture, Fisheries and Food* [1986] QB 716 (CA).

[47] This subjective recklessness version was established in *Three Rivers* (n 44). It was adopted in *Garrett v Attorney-General* [1997] 2 NZLR 332 (CA) (relying on the High Court decision in *Three Rivers*) and *Pranfield* (n 44).

[48] *Garrett* ibid at 349.

[49] *Pranfield* (n 44) at [118] and [121], quoting and adopting the formulation from *Northern Territory of Australia v Mengel* (1995) 185 CLR 307 at 357.

[50] *Bourgoin* (n 46).

[51] *Pranfield* (n 44) at [98]–[130].

[52] ibid at [118] and [121].

action. As regards the requirement of at least subjective recklessness as to probable harm, however, the Court held that the evidence must establish conscious awareness that concrete loss is likely to result.[53] The plaintiff did plead such concrete loss: losing her job and having to move and sell her home at a loss because of rumours, fuelled by police inaction, that she had made false allegations of rape. However, there was no evidence that the officer appreciated the likelihood of this sort of loss.[54]

The exact implications of this decision are a little uncertain. The jury had apparently rejected allegations of a deliberate cover-up. It had even rejected allegations that the officer realised his breach of duty was at the plaintiff's expense – concluding instead that he thought he was acting in accordance with a request from her not to pursue the complaint.[55] We may wonder whether the Court would still have required awareness of likely concrete loss if the jury had accepted one or both of those allegations of bad faith against the officer.

A further crucial question is what kind of evidence will suffice to establish the subjective state of mind that is needed for a finding of subjective recklessness (belief or suspicion as to unlawfulness or likely harm). Direct evidence of this is likely to be rare. Where decision-makers give evidence, courts can assess the credibility of their denials of this state of mind. Aside from that, the question is when courts should infer such a state of mind from circumstantial evidence. Suppose a decision-maker was presented with much credible information suggesting unlawfulness or likely harm but nevertheless claims to have held a conviction to the contrary. Can the court infer that the decision-maker did, in fact, appreciate the risk of unlawfulness or of harm, so as to trigger the obligation to make reasonable enquiries?[56] This question appears pertinent to the outcome in the *Daisley* case that is pending before the Supreme Court at the time of writing.[57] Perhaps the decision will throw some light on it.

(3) *Baigent* Damages for Breach of the Bill of Rights

A further situation in which public officials may be liable in damages for unlawful exercise of their powers is where the unlawfulness takes the form of breach of the New Zealand Bill of Rights Act 1990. The Act has no provision on remedies; the consequences of breach were left to the courts to determine. The courts have generally employed existing remedies, such as allowing judicial review on grounds of breach of the Act and, in criminal cases, excluding evidence obtained in breach of the Act.

In *Baigent*, the Court of Appeal decided that damages should be available as a further remedy for breach of the Bill of Rights Act.[58] As a public law remedy, the claim lies directly against the Crown (rather than against individual officials as in the case of torts) and the remedy is discretionary. Damages will be awarded only if no other remedy is adequate and effective in the circumstances.

[53] *Garret* (n 47) at 349–352.
[54] Recall that the tort is not actionable per se.
[55] *Garret* (n 47) at 343, 351–352.
[56] See, eg, *Whangarei District Council v Daisley* [2024] NZCA 161 at [166]–[178], [183].
[57] Leave was granted: *Whangarei District Council v Daisley* [2024] NZSC 123.
[58] *Simpson v Attorney-General* [1994] 3 NZLR 667 (CA) *(Baigent's case)*.

The leading case on the exercise of this discretion and on the quantum of damages is *Taunoa*, where prisoners received modest damages for inhumane treatment in breach of section 23(5) of the Act.[59] The purpose of damages in this context is different from private law damages: it is to vindicate the right and deter breaches. The adequacy of other remedies depends on whether they sufficiently serve those purposes. Damages may be unnecessary or inappropriate if other remedies are adequate, and also if a breach is minor or if a private law cause of action such as a tort claim provides adequate compensation.[60] In *Taunoa* itself, damages were necessary for vindication because of the importance of the right and the severity of the breach.[61]

The quantum of damage should be moderate and should not normally approach the level of damages in tort. However, it must be enough to provide an incentive to comply in future and must not be so small as to be derisory or trivialise the breach.[62] The approach in *Taunoa* has been criticised by some commentators,[63] but is consistent with the approach in the United Kingdom.[64]

The rights that may be at issue in a claim concerning a decision pursuant to a public power include rights such as freedom of expression (s 14), freedom from discrimination (s 19) or the right to natural justice (s 27(1)). The usual remedy for such a claim is a judicial review remedy. In most cases, quashing the decision will be effective and adequate, as it removes the breach. This has been considered to be the case especially for breaches of the right to natural justice.[65]

In the leading *Combined Beneficiaries Union Inc v Auckland City COGS Committee* case, the Court of Appeal declined to award damages for breach of section 27(1). The defendant's failure to give notice of a change in policy had deprived the plaintiff society of the opportunity to participate in an annual round of grant applications. The Court left open whether damages are ever available for breach of section 27(1) but set out minimum requirements that would need to be met.[66] Damages were unlikely to be required for vindication in cases where an order to reconsider was available and effective. Even where reconsideration was no longer possible and judicial review could therefore offer no more than a declaration, some further reason was needed to award damages. That might take the form of an affront to a claimant's dignity or intrusion into their personal integrity. The breach would have to be of such 'constitutional significance and seriousness that it would shock the public conscience.'[67]

Damages were, however, awarded for breach of s 27(1) in *X and Y v Oranga Tamariki*. The Court of Appeal distinguished *Combined Beneficiaries Union Inc* as involving 'trivial' breaches.[68] Damages were considered appropriate in this case due to the gravity

[59] *Taunoa v Attorney-General* [2007] NZSC 70, [2008] 1 NZLR 429 (SC).

[60] ibid at [253]–[261].

[61] ibid at [267]–[268].

[62] ibid at [258]–[260], [262]–[265].

[63] Jason NE Varuhas, 'The Development of the Damages Remedy under the New Zealand Bill of Rights Act 1990: From Torts to Administrative Law' [2016] *New Zealand Law Review* 213.

[64] *R (Greenfield) v Secretary of State for the Home Department* [2005] UKHL 14, [2005] 1 WLR 673.

[65] *Taunoa* (n 59) at [261] (obiter).

[66] *Combined Beneficiaries Union Inc v Auckland City COGS Committee* [2008] NZCA 423, [2009] 2 NZLR 56 at [65]–[70].

[67] ibid at [70].

[68] *X and Y v Chief Executive of Oranga Tamariki* [2022] NZCA 622, [2022] 2 NZLR 261 at [88].

of the breaches and the severity of their consequences for the appellants. Mrs X and Mr Y were a couple who became approved caregivers for four young boys with high and complex needs. Although the placement was initially positive, the children were removed from the couple's care following a complaint that Mrs X had hit one of the children. The children later made further complaints of more serious abuse against both Mrs X and Mr Y.[69]

When interviewing Mrs X about the complaints, Oranga Tamariki initially failed to disclose the further complaints. Furthermore, it appeared to regard Mrs X and Mr Y as one unit and failed to interview Mr Y at all. Mrs X was given seven days to respond to a draft investigation report, and her request for further time was denied. There was no urgent need to secure the children's safety, as they had already been removed.[70] Oranga Tamariki's report concluded that the children had likely been physically and emotionally abused, and recommended the immediate revocation of Mr Y and Mrs X's caregiver status.[71]

The Court considered that the case met the high threshold for damages set in *Combined Beneficiaries Union Inc.* The breaches involved a clear affront to dignity, as both Mrs X and Mr Y were labelled likely child abusers. These were allegations of criminality, made in a small community, by an organisation that had actively sought their assistance to house the children. The breach of Mr Y's natural justice rights was particularly egregious. In Mrs X's case, it was the serious consequences of the breach that heightened the need for vindication. She was a counsellor and the process affected her ability to work and harmed her mana.[72]

This case, then, confirms that *Baigent* damages are available for breaches of natural justice on the same basis as for other rights. They will be awarded if removing the breach by quashing the decision does not amount to sufficient vindication of the right.

(4) Other Torts: Breach of Statutory Duty?

A further tort that might potentially be available for holding public officials liable for loss caused by unlawful exercise of their powers is breach of statutory duty. This is a tort in its own right. However, the scope for this is at best very limited. There are two difficulties with its use in this context.

The first difficulty is that liability in this tort requires more than breach of a statutory duty causing loss.[73] The court must further be satisfied that Parliament intended to confer a private right of action for breach of the duty. Indicators of such an intention include that the duty is for the benefit of a limited class of persons and that there are no other remedies provided for its breach. Duties imposed on public authorities are very rarely held to satisfy this test.[74]

[69] ibid at [67], [71].
[70] ibid at [75], [77], [94]–[95].
[71] ibid at [74].
[72] ibid at [82]–[83], [93]–[94], [96], [98]–[99]. Mana (a Māori concept) may be translated as status or dignity.
[73] See *Pranfield* (n 44) at [68].
[74] See, eg, *O'Rourke v Camden London Borough Council* [1998] AC 188 (HL); *Cook v Housing New Zealand Corporation* [2017] NZHC 1781 at [31]–[33]; *Ellis v Counties Manukau District Health Board* [2007] 1 NZLR 196 (HC).

The second difficulty with this tort is more fundamental. The tort applies only where the statute imposes a duty. The statutory powers of public officials are usually discretionary. *Pranfield* confirms that the tort of breach of statutory duty is not available where the loss was caused by the exercise of such a discretionary power. While it could be said that public authorities are under a duty to exercise their statutory powers lawfully, that duty does not qualify as a statutory duty for the purposes of this tort.[75] The tort is therefore available only where statute imposes a duty rather than conferring a discretion. Furthermore, the duty must be a concrete duty to take a specified action on specified conditions. More 'aspirational' duties to take steps towards achieving specified goals again are unlikely to qualify.[76]

(5) Other Torts: Negligently Unlawful Exercise of Power?

Let us turn finally to negligence. This tort is, of course, available in appropriate cases for harm caused by public officials or authorities, as discussed in some detail in Part C of this chapter. The question here is a very specific one: can officials be liable in negligence for loss caused by exercises of their powers that are unlawful in administrative law terms, on the basis that they are under a duty of care to make decisions lawfully? For instance, where an official has caused loss by a decision taken for an improper purpose, can the official be held liable for negligently failing to appreciate that the purpose was not permissible?

Such claims are brought from time to time, but they very rarely succeed. In two High Court decisions where such a claim did succeed, the Court did not advert to the relevant authorities against it. The old case of *Craig v East Coast Bays* awarded damages for loss of a chance after the defendant council negligently breached the plaintiffs' statutory right to be notified and to have an opportunity to object to a development that obstructed their view.[77] The Court of Appeal has doubted the authority of that case in obiter comments.[78]

Recently, the High Court in *Daisley* found the defendant council liable for its officers' negligence in failing to realise that the plaintiff's quarrying activities were authorised by an existing resource consent. As a result, the officers had taken unlawful enforcement action to stop those activities.[79] This ruling on negligence was not appealed.[80] It may be easier to succeed in a claim for negligent maladministration rather than for a negligently unlawful decision. *Daisey* could be interpreted in that way. Another instance is *Te Ua*, where a claim for negligent destruction of relevant files was considered arguable.[81]

[75] *Pranfield* (n 44) at [54], [70], [75].

[76] See also *Cook* (n 75) at [34].

[77] *Craig v East Coast Bays City Council* [1986] 1 NZLR 99 (CA).

[78] *Bella Vista Resort Ltd v Western Bay of Plenty District Council* [2007] NZCA 33, [2007] 3 NZLR 429 esp at [69]–[75], also at [86].

[79] *Daisley v Whangarei District Council* [2022] NZHC 1372.

[80] In the Court of Appeal, the Council admitted negligence but appealed on limitations issues: *Daisley* (CA) (n 56) at [9]–[10] and [57]. The issues on which the Supreme Court granted leave included liability in negligence, but presumably that refers to the limitations issue: *Daisley* (SC) (n 57).

[81] *Te Ua v Secretary for War Pensions* [2014] NZHC 1476 at [187].

A duty of care to make decisions lawfully has *not* been found in cases where the novelty of the claim was recognised. The Privy Council in *Takaro* and other older leading cases left the issue open but cast severe doubt on the existence of a duty of care in this type of case.[82] It was not necessary to decide because, in any event, there was no breach.[83] Several more recent cases have found no duty of care. For instance, in *Morrison*, the council was not liable in negligence for misconstruing its district plan in rejecting the plaintiff's planning application.[84]

A range of policy reasons are given in the cases for rejecting such a duty of care. Some of these may be questionable, but others reflect well-established principles. First, imposing such liability for negligently misconstruing statutory powers would essentially amount to awarding administrative law damages, circumventing the established rule that there is no damages liability for loss caused by unlawful exercise of public powers.[85] We might add that it would also circumvent the 'malice' requirement that limits liability for Misfeasance in a Public Office. Secondly, it has been held that where the empowering statute provides an appeal, superimposing a common law duty of care would cut across the statutory scheme.[86] This concern is most persuasive where the statute imposes time limits on public law remedies including judicial review, and the negligence action would circumvent those limits.[87] In the absence of such statutory time limits or other statutory restrictions on remedies, this argument may be more doubtful. Thirdly, given that an unlawful decision can be overturned on appeal or judicial review, it has been said that there is no great need for damages, as the only remaining detriment is delay in obtaining the lawful decision.[88] However, that delay may have caused loss.[89] One response has been that this can often be avoided by applying for interim relief.[90] Fourthly, a floodgates argument has also been invoked,[91] but usually such concerns only carry weight in combination with significant other factors.

Fifthly, there are justiciability concerns: the reasonableness of an exercise of a discretionary public power or of the authority's interpretation of the empowering legislation is 'hardly susceptible to an application of the negligence standard'.[92] At most, the courts might intervene where the decision crossed the high threshold of being *Wednesbury* unreasonable, but the appropriateness of using that concept in a private law claim has been doubted.[93] This objection does not apply where the impugned

[82] *Takaro Properties Ltd v Rowling* [1987] 2 NZLR 700 (PC) at 708–709; *Dunlop v Woollahra Municipal Council* [1982] AC 158 (HL) at 171.

[83] *Takaro* ibid at 717–718.

[84] *Morrison v Upper Hutt City Council* [1998] 2 NZLR 331 (CA). See also *Pranfield* (n 44) at [89]–[98]; *Bella Vista* (n 78).

[85] *Morrison* ibid at 338.

[86] ibid. Also *Ransfield v Chief Executive of the Ministry of Social Development* [2018] NZHC 434 at [21]–[24].

[87] But cf *Te Ua* (n 81) at [180], concerned simply about duplication of proceedings.

[88] *Takaro* (n 82) at 709–10; *Te Ua* (n 81) at [178]–[179].

[89] Even where an entitlement is fulfilled by back payments after a successful challenge, there may be consequential losses: see *Ransfield v MSD* (n 86) at [19]–[20], [24].

[90] *Harris v Evans* [1998] 1 WLR 1285 (CA) at 1298.

[91] *Morrison* (n 84) at 338.

[92] ibid.

[93] ibid; and see *Attorney-General v Body Corporate No 200200* [*Sacramento*] [2007] 1 NZLR 95 (CA) at [47]–[49]; *Barrett v Enfield London Borough Council* [2001] 2 AC 550 (HL) at 571–572, 586.

decision has already been quashed on appeal or judicial review. However, some of the other concerns still apply in that context.

Sixthly, courts have taken the view that unlawful exercise of powers would rarely be negligent: 'anybody, even a Judge, can be capable of misconstruing a statute' and, when this occurs, 'it can be severely criticised without attracting the epithet "negligent"'.[94] This was a fair point in the context of that case, but there are cases concerning more obvious and egregious errors – as, for instance, in *Daisley*.

A seventh point is the proof of loss problem discussed in the next section.

Finally, imposing a duty of care might result in 'overkill'. For instance, it might encourage excessive resort to legal advice which would cause unnecessary delays in decision-making.[95] It might also discourage the exercise of regulatory enforcement powers.[96]

(6) Should Administrative Law Damages be Introduced?

We have seen that public authorities are sometimes liable for loss caused by the unlawful exercise of their powers, where relevant additional requirements are met. However, there is a significant gap in this liability where none of the established causes of action are available: where intentional torts do not apply because loss is not caused by direct physical interference but rather by a decision such as denial of a licence; the malice test for Misfeasance is not made out; there is no breach of the Bill of Rights that might attract *Baigent* damages; and there either was no statutory duty or the duty was not intended for the benefit of individuals.

The question is whether a more general administrative law damages remedy should be created to close this gap. The case for such a new remedy has been made on many occasions,[97] but there is much room for disagreement about whether this would be a good step to take. Much also depends on the details of the proposal.[98] Liability for loss caused by the exercise of public powers might also be created on a novel basis that is slightly different than simply that the exercise of power was unlawful in administrative law terms.[99]

Arguments against administrative law damages include that public law duties are owed to the public at large rather than to private individuals;[100] and that the large sums of money required are better spent on providing public services than on compensating those who have been harmed by unlawful decisions. On the other hand, however, it is arguable that the cases in which authorities are liable to private individuals in the

[94] *Takaro* (n 82) at 710.

[95] ibid; *Bella Vista* (n 78) at [55]–[59], but cf at [71]. This concern was also relied on in a different context in *Attorney-General v Strathboss Kiwifruit Ltd* [2020] NZCA 98, [2020] 3 NZLR 247 at [266]–[269].

[96] *Trent Strategic Health Authority v Jain* [2009] UKHL 4, [2009] 1 AC 853 at [28]; *Harris v Evans* (n 90) at 1298, 1301.

[97] See, eg, Law Commission (England and Wales), *Administrative Redress: Public Bodies and the Citizen* (2008) at [4.96]–[4.196]; Michael Fordham, 'Monetary Awards in Judicial Review' [2009] *Public Law* 1; Peter Cane, 'Damages in Public Law' (1999) 9 *Otago Law Review* 489.

[98] See Sue Arrowsmith, *Civil Liability and Public Authorities* (1992) at 238.

[99] See, eg, Tom Cornford, *Towards a Public Law of Torts* (Aldershot, Ashgate Publishing, 2008); David Cohen and J C Smith, 'Entitlement and the Body Politic: Rethinking Negligence in Public Law' (1986) 64 *Canadian Bar Review* 1.

[100] This is implied, eg, in *Takaro* (n 82) at 710.

intentional torts are not necessarily more deserving of compensation than the cases in which those torts are not available. For instance, intentional torts protect property rights but not livelihoods, yet arguably the latter are at least as important as the former.

Finally, the problem addressed in *Lumba* in the context of an intentional tort claim applies also to this possible new remedy. In this context, it is usually described as a problem with 'proof of loss' or 'causation'. The unlawfulness of a decision does not necessarily entail entitlement to a favourable decision: rather, the decision-maker usually retains a discretion. If the same decision could have been made lawfully, then any loss caused by the original decision was arguably not wrongfully caused. A solution to this problem would need to be found for the new remedy, but that is the case with most heads of damages discussed in this part. A number of possible solutions have been proposed.[101]

C. Qualifications to the Equality Principle

The starting point for the private law liability of public authorities is Dicey's equality principle: the ordinary law applies to all.[102] In many respects, this is the case. Dicey had in mind liability in the intentional torts such as trespass and false imprisonment. In that context the equality principle is largely unchallenged, though we will see that there are one or two potential qualifications – especially the much greater availability of the defence of statutory authority.

Beyond that, however, qualifications to the equality principle abound. These often give rise to unsettled issues. Some qualifications restrict liability and others expand it. Restrictions on liability reflect recognition of the public interest served by exercises of public power. Expanded liability reflects recognition that public officials and authorities have special powers and responsibilities.

This part of the chapter offers the following: (1) a brief overview of areas of special expanded liability; (2) an outline of special restrictions to liability in the form of the defence of statutory authority and special immunities; (3) an exploration of the negligence liability of public authorities, outlining special considerations that both restrict and expand such liability; and (4) discussion of the bar to common law damages actions found in the accident compensation legislation. Two of the exceptions to the ACC bar are more readily available in claims against public officials, or are available only in such claims, resulting in special expanded liability.

(1) Special Expanded Liability

At least two of the forms of liability discussed in Part A above represent special public authority liability. This applies to Misfeasance, which is a special tort applicable only to public officials. *Baigent* damages too are available only against public authorities.

[101] See, eg, Arrowsmith (n 98) at 237.

[102] Albert V Dicey, *Introduction to the Law of the Constitution* (New York, Oxford University Press, 2013 (first published 1885)) at 100.

Further instances of special expanded liability are identified below in section (3) concerning negligence liability.

(2) Special Restrictions on Liability

Special limits on the liability of public authorities include (a) the defence of statutory authority, (b) common law immunities and (c) statutory immunities. Further instances of special restrictions on liability are identified below in section (3) concerning negligence liability.

(a) Intentional Torts and the Defence of Statutory Authority

As discussed in Part A above, public officials are liable in the intentional torts in the same way as a private person. However, the defence of statutory authority[103] is relevant primarily in claims against public officials and authorities. While it is, in principle, available to any defendant, most relevant statutory powers are powers of public officials and authorities.

(b) Common Law Immunities

Public authorities' liability is furthermore subject to special immunities both at common law and under statute. Starting with common law immunities, there are two of these: Crown immunity and judicial immunity. Let us take these two in turn.

At common law, the equality principle applied only to individual officials – they were liable like a private person. The Crown, however, enjoyed absolute immunity: the position was that the King can do no wrong, and furthermore the King cannot be impleaded in the King's courts. In practice, the Crown would 'stand behind' its officials and pay damages awarded against them, but it was not legally obliged to do so.

This immunity was very largely removed by the Crown Proceedings Act 1950,[104] but the full extent of this is uncertain. What is clear is that the Crown is vicariously liable for the torts of its 'servants and agents'. That is provided in section 6(1)(a). The effect of individual statutory immunities is discussed further below.

The unsettled question is how far the Crown can be liable in tort directly and in its own right, rather than vicariously for its individual officials. Arguably such liability is needed.[105] But unless the Act provides for such liability, it remains excluded by the old common law Crown immunity.

The Act does expressly provide in section 6(1)(b) and (c) and section 6(2) for the Crown to be directly liable to its employees, in its capacity as occupier of land, and for breach of statutory duties. What is not clearly provided for is more general direct

[103] See text at nn 18–21.

[104] The earliest predecessor was the Crown Redress Act 1877. A new Act has been recommended: Law Commission, *The Crown in Court: A Review of the Crown Proceedings Act and National Security Information in Proceedings* (NZLC R135, December 2015), ch 4.

[105] Stuart Anderson, ''Grave Injustice', 'Despotic Privilege': The Insecure Foundations of Crown Liability for Torts in New Zealand' (2009) 12 *Otago Law Review* 1.

Crown liability in tort on an institutional or systemic basis: for instance liability in negligence for loss caused by a government department's inadequate systems and processes.[106] Section 3(2) confers a right to enforce specified types of claims by civil proceedings against the Crown, but, per paragraph (b), this extends to tort claims only where 'the Crown is liable in tort under this Act' – thus it seems the operative provision is section 6. Also relevant is the right to bring civil proceedings against the Crown 'in the same way as civil proceedings between individuals', affirmed by section 27(3) of the Bill of Rights Act: the Crown Proceedings Act should be interpreted consistently with that if it can be.

While the Supreme Court in *Couch (No 2)* left the question open,[107] the Court of Appeal in *Strathboss* accepted the conclusion in several other sources that direct liability is not available.[108]

Turning to judicial immunity, at common law, judges of the High Court and of the appellate courts have a broad immunity from liability.[109] The rationale is to protect judicial independence and impartiality, as well as the finality and binding force of judicial orders. Statute has extended this immunity to District Court Judges.[110] *Chapman* established that the judicial immunity extends to protecting the Crown against *Baigent* damages for judicial breaches of the Bill of Rights Act.[111] As a result of these immunities, unlawful detention pursuant to a judicial order can be compensated only on an ex gratia basis[112] – despite the international law right to compensation.[113]

The related point that is directly relevant to administrative law is that statutory protections apply to officials executing judicial orders such as warrants or sentences. Individual officials usually have either an immunity[114] or statutory authority that extends to good faith or reasonable execution of invalid warrants.[115] The Crown's vicarious liability is also expressly excluded.[116]

(c) Statutory Immunities

The Public Service Act 2004 in section 104 provides a broad immunity for all public service employees and chief executives in the discharge *or intended* discharge of their

[106] There are also doctrinal difficulties with such a claim. However, these can arguably be overcome: see Madeleine Hay, 'Systemic Negligence and Direct Crown Liability: Conceptualising Issues of Justiciability, Proximity and Breach' (2019) 25 *Auckland University Law Review* 57.

[107] *Couch v Attorney-General (No 2)* [2010] NZSC 27, [2010] 3 NZLR 149 at [71], [173] fn 264.

[108] *Attorney-General v Strathboss Kiwifruit Ltd* [2020] NZCA 98, [2020] 3 NZLR 247 at [83]–[109], relying among other sources on Anderson (n 105) at 3–4 and the Law Commission (2015) (n 104) at [3.8].

[109] *Sirros v Moore* [1975] 1 QB 118 (CA); *Gazley v Lord Cooke of Thorndon* [1999] 2 NZLR 668 (CA).

[110] District Courts Act 2016, s 23. Previously District Courts Act 1947, s 119 (as amended in 2004, after *Harvey v Derrick* [1995] 1 NZLR 314 (CA)).

[111] *Attorney-General v Chapman* [2011] NZSC 110, [2012] 1 NZLR 462.

[112] See *Pora v Attorney-General* [2017] NZHC 2081, [2017] 3 NZLR 683 for discussion of the ex gratia scheme for miscarriages of justice.

[113] International Covenant on Civil and Political Rights 999 UNTS 171 (opened for signature 16 December 1966, entered into force 23 March 1976). On the need for at least ex gratia compensation, see *Attorney-General v Fitzgerald* [2024] NZCA 419 at [135]–[139] (under appeal at the time of writing).

[114] Policing Act 2008, s 44; Search and Surveillance Act 2012, s 165.

[115] Crimes Act 1961, s 27 and definition of 'justified' in s 2.

[116] Crown Proceedings Act 1950, s 6(5).

responsibilities, duties, functions and powers. The only condition is good faith.[117] The public service comprises central government agencies such as departments and ministries.[118] Unusually, by virtue of section 6(4A) of the Crown Proceedings Act this individual immunity does not affect the Crown's vicarious liability: the Crown can still be sued.

In addition, a great many empowering statutes provide some form of immunity for actions taken in excess of the powers they confer.[119] The conditions vary: for some, only good faith or the absence of gross negligence is required, whereas others require reasonable cause[120] or reasonable care. Such immunities also exclude the Crown's vicarious liability, as expressly provided in the proviso to section 6(1) and in section 6(4) of the Crown Proceedings Act.[121] For instance, in *Strathboss*, officials in the Ministry of Agriculture and Fisheries were held to be protected by a statutory immunity from a negligence claim for allowing the import of a devastating kiwifruit pathogen.[122] However, despite the Court also finding that the claim would have failed in any case, the Crown settled the claim before an appeal could be heard.

The justification for immunities is open to debate.[123] On the one hand, the reasons for enacting them are similar to the courts' reasons for restricting liability in negligence or the availability of *Baigent* damages.[124] Liability might discourage the exercise of public powers (particularly enforcement powers) or, more generally, distort officials' reasoning in this regard; indeed it might discourage people from taking public office at all. Paying damages and conducting litigation can also be seen as diverting public resources from more productive uses, given that accountability is available through public law remedies. On the other hand, immunities can be criticised for departing from the equality principle, and for reducing both officials' accountability and the redress available to those harmed. The justification for an immunity will vary according to its context and scope. Immunities may be seen as especially problematic where those affected by exercises of power are vulnerable.[125] It is also important to note the limits of an official's exposure: in the absence of an immunity, the official may be sued but may be indemnified by the public authority employer.[126]

Where protection is desired, legislators have a choice between conferring immunities or instead adjusting the scope of the statutory authority.[127] Authority can be expressed to extend to mistaken or otherwise faulty exercises of a power on condition of good faith, reasonable cause or care, or similar. In that case, no immunity is needed. Such extended authority protects the official not only from liability but also from public law remedies.

[117] The predecessor was s 86 of the State Sector Act 1988, which was in essentially the same terms as the current provision since an amendment in 2013.

[118] Public Service Act 2004, ss 5 and 10.

[119] For example, Biosecurity Act 1993, s 163; Civil Defence Emergency Management Act 2002, s 110; Mental Health (Compulsory Assessment and Treatment) Act 1992, s 99A. For a survey, see Law Commission, *Crown Liability and Judicial Immunity: A Response to Baigent's Case and Harvey v Derrick* (NZLC R 37, 1997), Appendix C and Ch 5.

[120] *Strathboss* (n 108) at [137]–[140] held that this is different from reasonable care.

[121] Confirmed ibid at [147]; *Couch (No 2)* (n 107) at [176].

[122] *Strathboss* (n 108) at [112]–[147].

[123] See Law Commission (2015) (n 104) at [3.68]–[3.88].

[124] A connection noted in *Ernst v Alberta Energy Regulator* 2017 SCC 1 at [42]–[49], [51]–[55].

[125] *B v Crown Health Financing Agency* [2009] NZSC 97, [2010] 1 NZLR 338 at [71].

[126] See Law Commission (2015) (n 104) at [3.61]–[3.62]; Public Finance Act 1989, ss 65ZC and 65ZD.

[127] See Law Commission (1997) (n 119) at [128]–[131].

(3) Negligence: Some Special Restrictions and Some Expanded Liability?

When it comes to the tort of negligence, the starting point is that public officials are liable in the same way as private persons – consistent with the equality principle.[128] That is the case particularly where direct infliction of physical injury or damage is concerned. For instance, a public official will generally be liable for negligent driving in the same way as a private person.

However, the special powers and responsibilities of public authorities do give rise to arguments for restriction or expansion of liability in this context too. Negligence liability for omissions or failure to protect has arguably been imposed on public officials and authorities in circumstances where private defendants would not be liable (section (a) below). Conversely, negligence liability is sometimes doubted or denied for reasons that are special to public authorities or at least apply to them to a greater extent. These include policy concerns about defensive practice and consistency with statute (section (b)) and the problem with respecting public authority discretion (section (c)).

The cause of action in negligence has four elements: a duty of care, breach of that duty by falling below the required standard of care, the breach caused the loss and the loss is not too remote.[129] The main element at issue in all of the contexts discussed below is the first: the duty of care. New Zealand courts conduct the duty of care enquiry by reference to two broad enquiries: whether foreseeable loss has been caused within a relationship between the parties that was sufficiently proximate; and whether there are wider policy considerations external to that relationship that either support a duty of care or provide reasons against such a duty.[130]

(a) Omissions and Failure to Protect

As a general rule, liability in negligence does not extend to omissions. A duty of care does not require positive action for the benefit of others. A classic example is that there is no legal duty to shout a warning to a stranger who is about to walk over a cliff. This rule applies also to public officials, and very often defeats claims about public officials' failure to use their powers to protect a plaintiff. However, there are exceptions to this omissions rule, where one of a number of special tests is satisfied. Some of those special tests are most likely to be satisfied in the case of public officials, at least in Aotearoa New Zealand, due to officials' special powers and responsibilities. This may result in special expanded liability.

The omissions rule is engaged whenever the primary cause of the loss or damage was someone or something else, and the claim against the defendants is that they failed to protect or rescue the plaintiff.[131] In the walking-over-the-cliff example, for instance, the primary cause of the harm is the victim's own carelessness. The problem is the same even if the defendant's conduct is not a pure omission, so long as the complaint is that

[128] See, eg, *Robinson v Chief Constable of West Yorkshire Police* [2018] UKSC 4, [2018] AC 736.

[129] See further Todd (n 2) at 155–56.

[130] *North Shore City Council v Attorney-General* [*The Grange*] [2012] NZSC 49, [2012] 3 NZLR 341 at [156]–[161].

[131] See *N v Poole Borough Council* [2019] UKSC 25, [2019] 2 WLR 1478 at [28]; Hanna Wilberg, 'In Defence of the Omissions Rule in Public Authority Negligence Claims' (2011) 19 *Torts Law Journal* 159 at 169.

they failed to protect against harm that was directly caused by someone or something else. In *Strathboss*, for instance, the claim concerned the importation of kiwi-fruit pollen carrying a devastating vine disease. The defendant biosecurity officials engaged in positive conduct in granting the import permit. However, the complaint was that they failed to use their powers to protect growers: they should have refused a permit or imposed appropriate conditions. This was best understood as engaging the omissions rule. The Court of Appeal's decision is ambivalent and confusing on this point. On the one hand, it stated that the omissions rule was not engaged, but on the other hand it did apply one of the tests that apply when that rule is engaged.[132]

In terms of the two-stage test for a duty of care, the problem with liability for omissions or failure to protect concerns proximity in the first instance: what is it about the relationship between the parties that might require the defendant to take care to positively protect or rescue the plaintiff? However, this is closely interdependent with policy issues concerning when and why it is fair and reasonable to impose such a duty. The special tests that are used for exceptional liability for failure to protect tend to form part of the enquiry into both proximity and policy.

There are several such special tests.[133] Only one of these needs to be satisfied to support a duty of care. One test is whether the defendant has assumed responsibility for the relevant risk, and the plaintiff's foreseeable and reasonable reliance on the defendant has resulted in the loss or damage.[134] A second test is whether the defendant has created a risk or danger for the plaintiff which was then foreseeably activated by someone or something else,[135] or whether the defendant has made things worse.[136] A third test is whether the defendant had control over the risk or danger or over the person or thing causing it, and the plaintiffs were foreseeably at special risk from this.[137] In all of these tests, a further question may be whether the plaintiffs could reasonably have protected themselves.

These tests can be satisfied in claims against both private defendants and public officials.[138] What is special about public officials is that they are much more likely than private defendants to satisfy the third test: in several New Zealand cases, courts have found that a public official defendant had control over the risk or danger due to their relevant statutory powers.[139]

This is an area where New Zealand law has diverged from the United Kingdom. There, courts have set their face against using statutory powers as part of the foundation

[132] *Strathboss* (n 108) at [229]–[239].

[133] See Wilberg (n 131) at 170–75; Stelios Tofaris and Sandy Steele, 'Negligence Liability for Omissions and the Police' (2016) 75 *Cambridge Law Journal* 128 at 128.

[134] Eg *Stansbie v Troman* [1948] 2 KB 48 (CA).

[135] That is one explanation of the liability in *Home Office v Dorset Yacht Co Ltd* [1970] AC 1004 (HL). Also *McCarthy v Wellington City Council* [1966] NZLR 481 (CA).

[136] Eg *Capital & Counties Plc v Hampshire County Council* [1997] QB 1004 (CA). This includes 'interfering' with action someone else would have taken to protect against the danger: *Tindall v Chief Constable of Thames Valley Police* [2024] UKSC 33 at [56].

[137] Eg *Dorset Yacht* (n 135) at 1039, 1055, 1063–70.

[138] For a successful claim against a private defendant, see, eg, *Stansbie v Troman* (n 134).

[139] For the central role of legislation in this enquiry see, eg, *The Grange* (n 130) at [224]; *Body Corporate 207624 v North Shore City Council [Spencer on Byron]* [2012] NZSC 83, [2013] 2 NZLR 297 at [29]; *Strathboss* (n 108) at [154].

for a duty of care.[140] In a claim for failure to protect, a duty of care will be found only if the officials have done something to make matters worse,[141] or if they have chosen to do something that amounts to taking control or assuming responsibility.[142]

The most well-established area of liability in New Zealand concerns defective buildings. Old cases concerned defective foundations. More recently, there has been a very large volume of litigation arising from the 'leaky building' crisis: for much of the 1990s and 2000s, new methods of construction and lax controls resulted in great numbers of new residential buildings not being weathertight and requiring expensive remediation. Local authority officials charged with enforcing building standards are liable to owners and subsequent purchasers when they fail to prevent such defective buildings being erected.[143]

In the older leading case of *Hamlin*, this was based on an argument based on control and 'general reliance'. That was a variant of the first special proximity test, assumption of responsibility. There was an established and reasonable general practice in New Zealand whereby purchasers of homes, knowing that councils had control over building projects, relied on councils to have enforced the relevant standards.[144] It was not common to obtain building inspections that might alert them to defects.

An argument based more squarely on control was substituted, however, when the Supreme Court in *Spencer on Byron* extended councils' liability to include commercial buildings.[145] Reliance was no longer accepted as playing any central role. Rather, councils pursuant to legislation exercise control over construction to ensure compliance with the building code. There is a close, almost contractual relationship with the owner, who pays a fee for the service. Loss to subsequent owners is also 'eminently foreseeable'. A system in which owners and subsequent purchasers had to obtain further inspections in addition to those done by the council would be wasteful and inefficient. Todd has further emphasised the direct link with a known affected class that only ever comprises one potential plaintiff: the owner of the building at the time the damage appears.[146]

This liability for defective buildings has been said to be sui generis.[147] However, public officials have been held potentially liable for failing to protect plaintiffs in diverse other situations as well.

The leading case is *Couch*.[148] The Supreme Court considered it arguable that a probation officer owed a duty of care to Ms Couch who was attacked by an offender released on parole under the officer's supervision. Note that in New Zealand, such a

[140] *Stovin v Wise* [1996] AC 923 (HL) at 952; *Gorringe v Calderdale Metropolitan Borough Council* [2004] UKHL 15, [2004] 1 WLR 1057 at [32], [38]; *Poole Borough Council* (n 131) at [65], [72]–[73].

[141] *Capital & Counties* (n 136); *Tindall v Chief Constable of Thames Valley Police* [2024] UKSC 33 at [56]–[62].

[142] See, eg, *Michael v Chief Constable of South Wales Police* [2015] UKSC 2, [2015] AC 1732 at [99]; *Tindall* ibid at [75]–[76], [82]–[84].

[143] This liability does not extend to the central government regulator, the Building Industry Authority: *The Grange* (n 130).

[144] *Invercargill City Council v Hamlin* [1996] 1 NZLR 513 (PC) at 519; affirmed in *North Shore City Council v Body Corporate 188529* [*Sunset Terraces*] [2010] NZSC 158, [2011] 2 NZLR 289 at [48], [50], [61]. Contrast *Murphy v Brentwood District Council* [1991] 1 AC 398 (HL).

[145] *Spencer on Byron* (n 139)at [27]–[28], [32]–[33], [38], [190]–[191], [199], [201].

[146] Todd (n 2) at 346.

[147] *Attorney-General v Carter* [2003] 2 NZLR 160 (CA) at [35].

[148] *Couch v Attorney-General* [2008] NZSC 45, [2008] 3 NZLR 725.

claim for personal injury could succeed only for exemplary damages, since claims for compensatory damages for personal injury are barred by the accident compensation legislation. This issue is discussed under its own heading below.

The test in *Couch* requires two special relationships.[149] First, the that the defendant had control over the wrongdoer: 'sufficient power and ability' to control the wrongdoer so as to prevent the harm. Secondly, that the defendant should have known that the plaintiff individually or as a member of an identifiable class was at a 'distinct and special risk' of the relevant kind of harm from the wrongdoer. The risk must be distinct in the sense of 'clearly apparent', and special in the sense that the plaintiff's circumstances rendered them 'particularly vulnerable' to harm of this kind from the wrongdoer.

In *Couch*, the probation officer had allowed the parolee to work at the Returned Service Association club rooms. The parolee burgled those club rooms for cash, and in the process attacked Ms Couch who also worked there. On a strike-out application, the Court held that the test of distinct and special risk could be met on the basis that the parolee posed a known risk of gratuitous violence, and that he was known to have a need for cash to feed his alcohol addiction. Allowing him to work at a club where he knew the security arrangements for cash holdings put his fellow employees at special risk.[150] The control test could be met due to the probation officer's statutory powers over the parolee, since these included power to approve his place of work.[151] The case was remitted to the High Court, but settled before trial.

A further leading case is *Strathboss*. The Court of Appeal applied the *Couch* test of control and special risk to a claim against biosecurity officials for allowing importation of kiwifruit pollen carrying a devastating vine disease. The Court ultimately rejected a duty of care on policy grounds,[152] but it found proximity established based on the *Couch* test.[153] First, while the biosecurity officials did not have physical control over the importer or the contaminated consignment, they did have the legal power to deny a permit or impose conditions. Secondly, kiwi-fruit growers were not simply part of the general population: they were a class specifically at risk from the pathogen. The officials knew that the pollen would be used in kiwi-fruit orchards, which are highly concentrated geographically, and that the disease, once introduced, would be difficult to contain.

Let us consider each of the two required special relationships a little further. First, to understand the part of the test requiring the plaintiff to be foreseeably at 'distinct and special risk', it is useful to contrast *Couch* and *Strathboss* with the older English *Hill* case.[154] In that case, Jaqueline Hill was killed by a serial murderer who was only identified subsequently. The House of Lords found that police owed no duty of care to protect her. The proximity test for a duty of care was not satisfied, essentially because she was not foreseeably at special risk. All young women in the affected part of England

[149] ibid at [82], [85], [112].
[150] ibid at [124].
[151] The Court simply noted that this was 'possible': ibid at [84].
[152] On one of these, see below under heading (b).
[153] *Strathboss* (n 108) at [223], [230]–[231], [237]–[239].
[154] *Hill v Chief Constable of West Yorkshire* [1989] AC 53 (HL).

were equally at risk from the murderer, and this was far too large and general a class to result in a special relationship.

How does this fit with *Strathboss*, where kiwi-fruit growers were held to be a class at special risk? The difference is that the risk from the pathogen in that case was likely to materialise for most members of that class: each of them was an individual at special risk. In *Hill*, in contrast, only one or a handful of the class at risk would actually fall victim. None of them therefore was an individual at special risk.

Secondly, in all the New Zealand cases discussed above, the application of the control test for the duty of care turns on the defendant's statutory powers. The defendants did not have physical control over the person or thing that directly caused the harm to the plaintiffs, but their statutory powers could have been used to prevent that harm.[155] The existence of the relevant statutory power satisfies the 'control' part of the test for a duty of care. The breach then takes the form of failure to exercise that power with due care in the circumstance. These are essential steps in the reasoning and they are much less likely to be present in a claim against a private defendant. That is to say, these cases may be considered to involve expanded liability for public officials.

There is room for debate on the best approach to this type of claim. On the one hand, the United Kingdom courts in the more recent cases have rejected liability in cases like those discussed above. As already noted, they take the view that public officials should not be subject to special liability based on their special statutory powers.[156]

Some commentators have raised concerns about New Zealand's different approach, particularly in relation to defective buildings,[157] and especially the extension to include commercial buildings.[158] More generally, Jane Stapleton has demonstrated the disproportionate liability that can result from holding public officials liable for failing to protect against harm caused by third parties.[159] The third party is the primary culprit – the public official is causally peripheral. Yet, if the public official owes a duty of care, then both are jointly and severally liable for the entire loss. Public authorities are attractive defendants due to their deep pockets – the primary culprit will often not be worth suing. Finally, public authorities' extensive statutory powers of intervention mean that, for a great proportion of all losses, part of the blame can be placed on an authority. This concern has been borne out in New Zealand's experience with the leaky building crisis. Local authorities have borne a share of the losses that is greatly disproportionate to any reasonable assessment of their share in the responsibility for the defects.[160]

[155] *The Grange* (n 130) at [177].

[156] See text at n 140.

[157] See, eg, Allan Beever, 'How to Save the Law of Negligence from the New Zealand Way' in Michael Littlewood and Janet McLean (eds), *The Supreme Court: The Second 10 Years* (Wellington, LexisNexis, 2024) 297.

[158] For concerns, see Todd (n 2) at 353–54.

[159] Jane Stapleton, 'Duty of Care: Peripheral Parties and Alternative Opportunities for Deterrence' (1995) 111 *Law Quarterly Review* 301 at 310–14.

[160] *Mount Albert Borough Council v Johnson* [1979] 2 NZLR 234 (CA) attributed 80 per cent of the responsibility to the building development company and 20 per cent to the Council. Todd (n 2) at 354 fn 262 notes this seems to be the generally accepted split. Yet often the council is the only available and solvent defendant.

Other than denying a duty of care or taking away the statutory responsibility on which it is founded,[161] one solution to this would be to adjust the rules of joint and several liability.[162] Another solution follows from the logic of Stapleton's argument: we can avoid liability for the most causally peripheral defendants simply by maintaining the requirement of special risk to an identifiable individual or class. Finding a duty of care to the large class in *Strathboss* is defensible for the reasons explained earlier. In relation to Jaqueline Hill, in contrast, the police were truly causally peripheral due to the lack of foreseeable special risk to her.

On the other hand, some commentators and judges have taken the view that the liability of public officials for omissions or failure to protect should be much less restricted, given their special position and responsibilities. Mark Aronson has pointed out that most of the usual reasons against liability for omissions do not apply to public authorities.[163] Those inapplicable reasons include concern about infringing individual liberty and autonomy by requiring people to take positive action for others' benefit, the cost of such affirmative duties, and the 'why me' objection to singling out the defendant from among all those who might have helped. However, Aronson then pointed out another reason for restricting liability that is similar to Stapleton's argument: unrestrained liability in cases like this would amount to a 'tort tax'. In other words, it would result in most wrongful losses being compensated out of taxes (public funds).

In *Couch*, Elias CJ similarly pointed out that public authorities have no liberty and no right to be selfish. The 'why me' objection is not available to them.[164] On that basis, Elias CJ would have rejected the requirement of special risk to an identifiable class. She would have recognised a duty of care based on general reliance in contexts where members of the public are dependent on public authorities because the risks are too large and complex for individuals to guard against, and where Parliament has recognised this dependence by charging public authorities with guarding against those risks.[165]

Similar special liability might also be found where negligent misstatement is concerned: public officials may be especially exposed to such liability. The basis for this form of liability is that the statement was made in circumstances where the plaintiffs reasonably and foreseeably relied on it to their detriment.[166] It may be said that public officials are particularly likely to be approached as sources of authoritative advice on matters within their area of responsibility. For instance, when an intending purchaser of real estate applies for a Land Information Memorandum from the Council, they foreseeably and reasonably rely on Council officers for the accuracy and completeness of the information provided. The officers will be liable if the purchasers suffer loss as a result.[167]

[161] Hon Chris Penk, 'Trusted building professionals able to self-certify' (29 October 2024), available at www.beehive.govt.nz. See also Building Amendment Act 2012, s 17 – not yet in force.

[162] This was explored in Law Commission, *Review of Joint and Several Liability* (NZLC IP32, 2012), but largely rejected in Law Commission, *Liability of Multiple Defendants* (NZLC R132, 2014).

[163] Mark Aronson, 'Government Liability in Negligence' (2008) 32 *Melbourne University Law Review* 44 at 68–69.

[164] *Couch* (n 148) at [56]–[58].

[165] ibid at [64]–[67].

[166] *Hedley Byrne v Heller* [1964] AC 465 (HL).

[167] *Marlborough District Council v Altimarloch Joint Venture Ltd* [2012] NZSC 11, [2012] 2 NZLR 726.

(b) Policy Concerns about Defensive Practice

The second stage of the duty of care enquiry concerns policy considerations external to the relationship between the particular parties before the court.[168] At that stage, there are two types of concern that have particular salience in claims against public officials for loss arising from the exercise of their powers or the failure to exercise those powers. They are concerns about engendering defensive practice in the future exercise of such powers, and about consistency with relevant statute law. Reliance on these concerns can result in special restrictions on liability of public officials. Let me address these two in turn.

Defensive practice is a label for the feared impact of a duty of care on the future behaviour of officials: the spectre of liability may interfere with or inhibit desirable activities in the exercise of public powers. This is a controversial reason for denying liability, and its status in New Zealand is unsettled. However, versions of this concern have been relied on to deny a duty of care in leading cases, including in New Zealand. It is sometimes said to give rise to a blanket immunity for certain public defendants such as police, but is better understood as a potential policy factor against imposing a duty.

The classic source is the old English *Hill* case, rejecting a duty of care owed by the police to the victim of a serial murderer. In addition to the lack of proximity discussed earlier, Lord Keith relied on this policy consideration. Rather than providing an incentive to take due care, imposition of a duty of care might lead the police to carry out their investigative functions with 'a detrimentally defensive frame of mind'.[169] Similarly, in the New Zealand case of *Takaro* one of the reasons why the Privy Council rejected a duty of care to exercise regulatory powers lawfully was a 'danger of overkill'. Officials might respond by always insisting on legal advice before taking decisions, causing unnecessary delay in many cases.[170]

A further version of the concern is that a duty of care would conflict with the authority's primary duties. This was decisive in dismissing claims against child protection agencies by parents wrongly suspected of abuse in *D v East Berkshire*[171] and in *B v Attorney-General*.[172] A duty owed to the parents would conflict with the primary purpose of the statutory powers, which was to protect the welfare and safety of children. The same sort of reasoning is also found in the context of health and safety regulation of businesses. For instance, regulation of nursing homes is meant to protect residents, and safety regulation of other businesses is meant to protect customers. Exercise of the statutory powers for those purposes might be inhibited if regulated businesses could sue for loss due to unnecessary or unlawful intervention.[173]

The empirical validity of the concern – that is, whether the feared effect is in fact likely – has been a matter of controversy.[174] The concern was memorably dismissed

[168] *The Grange* (n 130) at [149], [156], [160].

[169] *Hill* (n 154) at 63.

[170] *Takaro Properties Ltd v Rowling* [1987] 2 NZLR 700 (PC) at 710.

[171] *D v East Berkshire Community Health NHS Trust* [2005] UKHL 23, [2005] 2 AC 373 at [85]–[90], [129]–[132].

[172] *B v Attorney-General of New Zealand* [2003] UKPC 61, [2004] 3 NZLR 145. See also *Sullivan v Moody* [2001] HCA 59, (2001) 207 CLR 562; *Sly Apps Secure Treatment Centre v BD* 2007 SCC 38, [2007] 3 SCR 83.

[173] *Jain v Trent Strategic Health Authority* [2007] EWCA Civ 1186, [2008] QB 246 at [88], [92], [95]–[96], [146], [148]; *Harris v Evans* [1998] 1 WLR 1285 (CA) at 1298, 1301.

[174] Law Commission (England and Wales), *Administrative Redress: Public Bodies and the Citizen* (2008) at [6.18], [6.39]; also *Michael* (n 142) at [121]. But cf *Robinson v Chief Constable of West Yorkshire Police* (128) at [112] (Lord Hughes).

by Lord Reid in the *Dorset Yacht* case on the basis that 'Her Majesty's servants are made of sterner stuff'.[175] However, it must be noted that the deterrence argument that is often invoked in support of liability suffers from the same lack of empirical evidence.[176] There are several other objections. If we accept that public officials may be deterred from their duties, then this may well result even without liability, due to the threat of disciplinary action or negative media coverage.[177] And fundamentally, engendering more care and caution in the exercise of public functions is surely not a bad thing.[178]

In the UK, the defensive practice concern has been dismissed in at least some contexts. Notably, a duty of care on child protection agencies will no longer be rejected on the grounds that this would disrupt those agencies' 'extraordinarily delicate' task.[179] In *Poole Borough Council* and in subsequent cases, the Supreme Court considered public authorities should instead be subject to the same general principles of tort liability as private defendants, except where such a duty would be inconsistent with the scheme of empowering legislation.[180]

In other contexts, however, such as in claims against police, the concern appears to be alive and well. In *Van Colle*, for instance, a claim against police for failing to protect a person against a very specific individual threat from an identified offender was struck out. The reason lay in the 'principle of public policy' from *Hill*: imposing a duty of care on the police would lead to 'defensive policing'.[181]

The New Zealand Supreme Court in *Couch* left the status of the concern uncertain, but rightly rejected the notion that it gives rise to a blanket immunity. The Crown argued that a duty of care to victims of crimes committed by parolees might conflict with the probation service's primary statutory objective of promoting rehabilitation of offenders. The Court declined to strike out the claim on that basis: the appropriate balance between public safety and rehabilitation could only be determined in light of all the relevant facts.[182]

The Court of Appeal in *Strathboss* placed some reliance on the concern as 'an additional telling consideration' – one of multiple reasons for striking out the claim. If the biosecurity service at the border owed a duty of care to producers harmed by an introduced pathogen, this might lead the service to conduct a formal risk analysis for every import request, bringing trade to a standstill. The Court quoted with approval from Lord Toulson in *Michael* commenting that such reprioritisation due to the risk of being sued was hardly in the public interest.[183]

The best view is that the validity and strength of the concern have to be evaluated in the context of each case. As *Couch* made clear, there is no blanket immunity arising

[175] *Dorset Yacht* (n 135) at 1033.

[176] See *Michael* (n 142) at [121].

[177] ibid.

[178] See, eg, *Hill v Hamilton-Wentworth Regional Police Services Board* 2007 SCC 41, [2007] 3 SCR 129 at [43], [56]; *Phelps v Hillingdon London Borough Council* [2001] 2 AC 619 (HL) at 672.

[179] For this concern, see *X (Minors) v Bedfordshire County Council* [1995] 2 AC 633 (HL) at 750.

[180] *N v Poole Borough Council* (n 131) at [74]–[75].

[181] *Van Colle v Chief Constable of Hertfordshire Police* [2008] UKHL 50, [2009] 1 AC 225 at [78]; this point concerned a separate case called *Smith* which was heard jointly with *Van Colle*.

[182] *Couch* (n 148) at [128]–[130].

[183] *Strathboss* (n 108) at [266]–[269], quoting from *Michael* (n 142) at [121]–[122].

from this policy concern: it is one consideration to be weighed in the duty inquiry.[184] Let me mention two particular points relating to this evaluative exercise.

First, the degree of proximity in the particular case is relevant to the validity and strength of the defensive practice concern. This point may be hinted at in several decisions, including *Couch*.[185] It is also supported by Jane Stapleton. As she argues, the defensive practice concern is most readily accepted as a valid concern in contexts where a duty of care saddles a causally peripheral public official defendant with manifestly disproportionate liability.[186] Being causally peripheral is a form of lack of proximity.

Secondly, there is a good argument that the conflict of duties version of the concern, seen in the child protection and safety regulation cases, is generally stronger and more valid than other versions of the concern.[187] The feared inhibition or distortion in these cases is of a very specific nature. The empowering statute privileges or prioritises one of the interests affected by the officials' exercise of power as paramount: the safety of children, nursing home residents or the public must prevail over the competing interests of parents or of regulated businesses. If in doubt, the official should intervene. Yet a duty of care owed to suspected parents or to the regulated businesses would provide a reason to hesitate: the risk of liability for unwarranted intervention might discourage the pursuit of the primary public duty. For that reason, such a duty of care would run directly contrary to the primary public duty.

This concern is stronger because it avoids the objection that more care is surely a good thing. Usually, there is room for reasonable disagreement on this point. However, where taking care not to intervene unnecessarily conflicts with a primary public duty, it clearly is not a good thing.

It may be objected in the child protection cases that the interests of parents and children are identical: both want their family life protected and children to be safe.[188] The point, however, specifically concerns the interests of parents who are suspected of abuse. Their interest is against intervention, regardless whether the suspicion is well founded.[189] If they can sue to protect that interest, then this provides a reason for the official to hesitate, contrary to the duty to intervene if in doubt.

In many contexts, it is debatable whether the relevant public duty is as one-sided as I have described, so as to require the official to intervene if in doubt. This is probably appropriate in the context of child protection, but is more debatable, for instance, in the case of safety regulators. Arguably the latter are instead expected to balance the interests of safety against the competing interests of the regulated business in each case. If that is the case, then the policy concern is weaker: a duty of care would not directly conflict with a primary public duty but might still distort the balancing of

[184] See also, eg, Mandy Shircore, 'Police Liability for Negligent Investigations: When Will a Duty of Care Arise?' (2006) 11 *Deakin Law Review* 33, esp at 40–42, 57.

[185] *Couch* (n 148) at [128]–[130]; see also *Robinson* (n 174) at [53], [69(1)].

[186] Stapleton (n 159) at 314.

[187] See Hanna Wilberg, 'Defensive Practice or Conflict of Duties? Policy Concerns in Public Authority Negligence Claims' (2010) 126 *Law Quarterly Review* 420 at 423–31, 437–40; Duncan Fairgrieve and Daniel Squires, *The Negligence Liability of Public Authorities*, 2nd edn (Oxford, Oxford University Press, 2019) at [4.50], [4.108]–[4.110].

[188] *D v East Berkshire* (n 171) at [37], [43]–[44] (dissent). For a similar objection in relation to police, see *Hill v Hamilton-Wentworth* (n 178) at [40]–[41].

[189] *D v East Berkshire* ibid at [71], [88]–[89], [126].

interests undertaken by the official. That seems the best view also of the probation service's duty to promote rehabilitation, which was invoked by the Crown in *Couch*.

Both the strong conflict concern and the weaker concern about distorting the balancing exercise have a large overlap with the concern about inconsistency with statute. That is the second type of concern that often arises in claims against public officials and can result in special restrictions on liability. Let us turn to this now.

The conflict of duties concern is a good example of this concern. In most cases, the relevant public duties arise from statute. If a duty of care would conflict with those public duties or distort their proper discharge, then that duty is inconsistent with the statute. That is a further reason for considering these concerns to be valid and weighty.

Inconsistency with statute is a problem as it compromises the coherence of the legal system, just as inconsistency with the rules governing other forms of liability would do. Perhaps more importantly, inconsistency with statute is also a constitutional concern. For courts to develop the common law in a way that cuts across or undermines statutes conflicts with Parliamentary sovereignty.[190]

One further example of this concern is the decision in *Sacramento* that the central government Building Industry Authority owes no duty of care to building owners or local authorities in discharging its regulatory functions. One of the main reasons for this decision was that the Building Act 1991 envisages a very light-touch regulatory regime. Imposing a duty of care would be inconsistent with that.[191]

(c) The Problem with Public Authority Discretion

Much of what public officials do involves exercising discretionary powers. When things go wrong, the exercise of such powers may be challenged in a negligence action. Issues then arise as to how best to avoid constitutionally inappropriate merits review of the exercise of discretion. This can result in special restrictions on liability.

In many negligence cases the public official's discretion is merely in the background and has no relevance. We do not need to worry about the discretion, for instance, when a probation officer crashes her car on the way to an appointment with a parolee, or when a food safety inspector breaks some crockery while inspecting a restaurant.

In some claims, however, the discretion *is* relevant, because the negligence complaint is *about* its exercise. For instance, a claim against a probation officer may be for harm done by a parolee. The allegation may be that the harm could have been prevented by a more careful exercise of the officer's discretionary powers to enforce parole conditions: for instance, she should not have allowed the parolee to take a particular job that foreseeably created the opportunity for the harm. That was the claim in *Couch*.[192]

[190] Fairgrieve and Squires (n 187) at [4.108]–[4.110] put the constitutional argument in terms of separation of powers.

[191] *Attorney-General v Body Corporate No 200200 [Sacramento]* [2007] 1 NZLR 95 (CA) at [62], [80]–[81], [93]. When the Supreme Court affirmed the lack of duty in *The Grange* (n 130), its reasoning focused on proximity rather than policy concerns.

[192] Or at least it was one possible version of the claim. It was not clear whether the allegation was negligence by the individual officer or negligent systems operated by the probation service: *Couch* (n 148) at [128]. The latter claim would, of course, also concern exercises of discretion.

That is the type of claim that raises constitutional concerns about the limits of the courts' role. Arguably liability should be imposed only if the exercise of discretion was unlawful in administrative law terms. Such a limit addresses two connected constitutional concerns.

First, there can be no liability 'for doing that which Parliament has authorised'.[193] If the exercise of the discretionary power is not vitiated by administrative law unlawfulness, it should not give rise to liability. This could be put in terms of the defence of statutory authority,[194] although that is not commonly mentioned in this context. A possible objection to this first concern is that negligence in the exercise of the power should be enough to render it unlawful and unauthorised. However, that is where the second concern comes in.

The second constitutional concern is that courts engage in inappropriate merits review if they judge the lawfulness of an exercise of discretion by reference to the private law test of negligence.[195] Merits review is constitutionally inappropriate because Parliament has entrusted discretion to balance the relevant competing public and private interests to the defendant official.[196] For instance, a probation officer is entrusted with the discretion as to how and when to enforce parole conditions, which involves striking a balance between the competing public interests in the parolee's rehabilitation and in minimising the risk the parolee may pose to the public. The legitimate role of the courts is limited to a supervisory role, ensuring that the discretion is exercised in accordance with law.

That is why in judicial review proceedings, unreasonableness is a ground of review only on an extremely deferential standard of review. It must cross the high threshold of *Wednesbury* unreasonableness: the decision is so outrageous that Parliament cannot have intended to authorise it.[197] Heightened scrutiny – lowering that threshold – may apply where fundamental rights or especially important interests or values are at stake.[198] However, in many contexts in which negligence claims may be brought, that qualification is at best of doubtful application.

In contrast, the test for breach of the standard of care in negligence incorporates no such deferential stance on the part of the courts. It is for the court to determine on the evidence whether a reasonable person in the defendant's position would have appreciated the risk of harm arising from the impugned conduct, and whether a reasonable person would have acted as the defendant did in the face of that risk. The second question requires the court to balance competing factors: on the one hand, the social value of the impugned conduct and the burden involved in taking better precautions; and on the other hand, the degree of the risk and the severity of the potential harm.[199] Defendants are not entitled to any judicial deference for their judgements in this context.

[193] *X v Bedfordshire County Council* (n 179) at 736.

[194] See text at nn 18–21.

[195] *Dorset Yacht Co* (n 135) at 1067–68.

[196] See Chs 1.D, 3.B.

[197] *Associated Provincial Picture Houses Ltd v Wednesbury Corporation* [1948] 1 KB 223 (CA).

[198] The qualification was recognised in *Wolf v Minister of Immigration* [2004] NZAR 414 (HC) at [47], but has not yet received the imprimatur of the Supreme Court: see Ch 7.

[199] *Overseas Tankship (UK) Ltd v The Miller Steamship Co Pty* [1967] 1 AC 617 (PC) *(The Wagon Mound (No 2))*; *Bolton v Stone* [1950] AC 850 (HL).

Unqualified application of this private law standard of care to a public official's exercise of a discretionary power would amount to constitutionally inappropriate merits review.[200] That is largely uncontroversial.[201] The more contentious question is what approach is best suited for avoiding this. Should the public law test of unreasonableness be inserted into the negligence enquiry in such cases, and if so at what stage? We will get to this question after the next point.

A further issue concerns justiciability. In some contexts, the reasonableness of a public official's exercise of a discretionary power is not suitable for judicial determination even on the high threshold of *Wednesbury* unreasonableness. This non-justiciability is most likely to apply to high-level policy decisions on the allocation of risks or of scarce resources.[202] It might apply, for instance, in a claim for harm done by a parolee if no fault can be proved against the individual probation officer. In that situation, an alternative target of attack might be a decision by probation service management or Ministers about the resourcing of the service, about staff training, or other such high-level policy decisions.

The potential non-justiciability of the reasonableness of such high-level policy decisions is due to two overlapping reasons.[203] First, the courts lack democratic legitimacy for making decisions on necessary trade-offs between competing interests.[204] Secondly, they lack institutional competence and capacity for making good decisions on such trade-offs.[205]

Judicial review case law has moved away from considering entire decisions to be non-justiciable. For instance, we would not say that a decision about resourcing the probation service is non-justiciable for all purposes. Rather, on the modern 'secondary justiciability' approach, suitability for judicial determination is assessed in relation to each individual issue or ground of review.[206] Where there is some relevant legal standard, judicial review may well be available on grounds of illegality even for such a high-level policy decision.[207] However, given that the unreasonableness ground engages the merits, the application of this ground is most likely to be non-justiciable in relation to a high-level policy decision.[208] It is, therefore, entirely consistent with modern judicial review principles to consider negligence complaints about such high-level policy decisions to be non-justiciable. The remaining question then once again is where to accommodate this in the negligence enquiry, and we will turn to this shortly.

The negligence case law has deployed a distinction between policy decisions and operational decisions in this context. There has been much debate and confusion as to the nature and role of this distinction, and whether it is helpful at all.[209] However, it is best understood as going to the justiciability of the question whether the decision

[200] See Tom Hickman, *Public Law after the Human Rights Act* (Oxford, Hart, 2010) at 205–06, 209–11.

[201] But cf Stephen Bailey, 'Public authority liability in negligence: the continued search for coherence' (2006) 26 *Legal Studies* 155 at 165–66.

[202] *Takaro* (n 170) at 709.

[203] See Ch 8.A(1)(a).

[204] *Curtis v Minister of Defence* [2002] 2 NZLR 744 (CA) at [22], [26], [28].

[205] ibid at [14], [23], [27]–[28]; *Council of Civil Service Unions v Minister for the Civil Service* [1985] 1 AC 374 (HL) at 401–07.

[206] See Ch 8.A(1)(c).

[207] See, eg, *Curtis* (n 204) at [15]–[21], examining compliance with the Defence Act 1990.

[208] *Council of Civil Service Unions* (n 205) at 411.

[209] See, eg, SH Bailey and MJ Bowman, 'The Policy/Operational Dichotomy – A Cuckoo in the Nest' [1986] *Cambridge Law Journal* 430.

is reasonable. Operational and policy decisions are best understood as the ends of a spectrum of types of decision. The closer a decision lies to the policy end of the spectrum, the less likely it is that the reasonableness of that decision is a justiciable question.[210]

What approach to the negligence enquiry, then, best deals with these concerns arising from negligence claims about the exercise of public authority discretion? Two competing approaches are found in the English cases. The New Zealand cases have not yet fully engaged with the issues but appear to be following the more recent English approach.

The older English approach was set out in *X (Minors) v Bedfordshire County Council*,[211] drawing on *Dorset Yacht*[212] and *Takaro*.[213] It involved inserting two preliminary hurdles into the duty of care enquiry. One was the justiciability test: the reasonableness of the impugned exercise of discretion must be a justiciable question. The policy/operational distinction was employed to help determine justiciability. The second hurdle was the public law test: the impugned exercise of discretion must be *Wednesbury* unreasonable and therefore outside the ambit of the discretion. If both hurdles were passed, then the court would proceed to apply the normal duty test and the normal tests for the other elements of the cause of action in negligence.

This approach was rejected in *Barrett*.[214] The House of Lords abandoned the second of the two preliminary hurdles, considering it inappropriate to insert the public law test of unreasonableness into the duty enquiry for negligence claims.[215] It did still maintain the justiciability test as a preliminary hurdle. Once that test is passed, a court will now proceed directly to the normal test for negligence.

The concern about inappropriate merits review on this approach is addressed as part of the breach question rather than the duty question. Where the challenge is to a public official's exercise of discretion, the defendant may invoke the principle in *Bolam*.[216] *Bolam* concerned alleged negligence in the course of professional practice, where the court is reliant on expert evidence to fix the appropriate standard of care. According to *Bolam*, a professional defendant will not be negligent if what she did is supported by a respectable and responsible body of professional opinion, even if it is a minority opinion, so long as there is a rational and logical basis for that opinion.[217]

Courts are also careful not to judge defendants with the benefit of hindsight. Applying this principle, courts will be slow to find a probation or police officer negligent. A further modification to the normal breach enquiry can also apply in this

[210] *Takaro* (n 170) at 709; *X v Bedfordshire County Council* (n 179) at 738; *Barrett v Enfield London Borough Council* [2001] 2 AC 550 (HL) at 571.

[211] *X v Bedfordshire County Council* (n 179) at 737–38.

[212] *Dorset Yacht Co* (n 135) at 1031, 1067–68.

[213] *Takaro* (n 170) at 709.

[214] *Barrett* (n 210) at 571–573. For discussion, see Paul Craig and Duncan Fairgrieve, '*Barrett*, Negligence and Discretionary Powers' [1999] *Public Law* 626.

[215] See also *Robinson* (n 174) at [38].

[216] *Barrett* (n 210) at 572.

[217] *Bolam v Friern Hospital* [1957] 1 WLR 582; *Bolitho v City of Hackney* [1997] 3 WLR 1151 (HL); *Edward Wong Finance Co Ltd v Johnson, Stokes & Master* [1984] AC 296 (PC).

context. Where professionals have to make difficult judgements in high pressure situations, courts will not impose an unrealistically demanding standard of care: not every error of judgement in such a context will amount to breach. That applies, for instance, to police officers seeking to arrest a fleeing suspect.[218]

Many commentators welcomed this shift in approach.[219] We can probably agree that the concern about merits review can be addressed just as readily at the breach stage as at the duty stage of the negligence enquiry. Indeed, since it is a concern about the appropriateness of the negligence approach to breach, that is arguably the best stage to address it.

However, there is room for doubt whether the two modifications to the standard of care enquiry adequately address the concern about merits review. The modifications ensure that public officials are not held to unrealistic standards and give officials the benefit of the doubt in circumstances of scientific uncertainty. However, that is not the same as ensuring judicial respect for the authority of the designated decision-maker to strike the balance between competing values or interests, which is the point of the high *Wednesbury* threshold for intervention on grounds of unreasonableness. Arguably, that public law test should still be applied, albeit now at the breach stage.

The New Zealand cases have not yet fully engaged with these issues. The Supreme Court in *Couch* did not address them. In the only passages that might be read as alluding to these issues in passing, the Court took the view that it did not have enough facts on the strike-out application.[220] In *Sacramento*, the Court of Appeal adopted *Barrett*'s rejection of inserting the public law reasonableness test into the duty enquiry, but said nothing about how this was relevant to the issues in the case.[221]

In *Strathboss* the Court of Appeal tacitly adopted an approach corresponding to the *Barrett* approach. The claim against biosecurity officials for granting an import permit to a shipment carrying a devastating kiwi-fruit pathogen failed for other reasons. However, the Court dismissed objections relating to the officials' discretion at both the duty and breach stages. At the duty stage, it dismissed a justiciability objection, finding that the risk assessment required by the prescribed process was a 'technical decision' that did not involve public policy or political considerations.[222] At the breach stage, it accepted that there was a choice between carrying out a formal risk assessment or an informal one, and that this may have involved judgements on policy considerations. However, the real issue was whether the informal assessment that had been chosen had been carried out with due care. The evidence was that it had not: the officials had failed to gain a sufficient understanding of the proposed import and its implications. This was an actionable error since it concerned an operational decision.[223] It is open

[218] *Robinson* (n 128) at [75], [121].
[219] See SH Bailey and MJ Bowman, 'Public Authority Negligence Revisited' (2000) 59 *Cambridge Law Journal* 85.
[220] *Couch* (n 148) at [35]–[36], [128].
[221] *Sacramento* (n 191) at [47]–[49].
[222] *Strathboss* (n 108) at [188].
[223] ibid at [340]–[348].

to debate whether the policy/operational distinction was the relevant test at the breach stage of the analysis.

(4) Special Expansion: Greater Scope for Exceptions to the ACC Bar

As we saw, the accident compensation legislation bars all claims at common law for damages for personal injury,[224] subject to some exceptions for claims that are not sufficiently covered by the scheme. We will see in this section that one of these exceptions applies only to claims against public officials, and another one is more readily available against public officials than against other defendants. This greater scope for exceptions may be seen as an instance of special expanded tort liability for officials.

The ACC scheme serves the objective of restoring victims of accidents by providing compensation for lost earnings and covering the cost of medical treatment and rehabilitiation. It is widely accepted that the scheme is more effective and beneficial for this purpose than the 'lottery' of tort liability.[225]

The ACC bar on damages claims is the quid pro quo for cover under the scheme – the exchange has been labelled a 'social contract'.[226] It does, however, have the effect of removing any deterrent or incentive effect that tort law may have on those engaged in potentially risky activities – such deterrence has to be achieved by regulation instead. Tort claims that serve accountability as much as compensation include claims for sexual assaults, especially when committed in institutions. Those, too, are excluded because ACC provides cover for mental injury caused by such criminal acts.[227]

In relation to public authorities, this is perhaps more significant than in relation to private entities. We noted in the introduction that tort law can serve the objectives of holding government accountable and vindicating rights. Due to the ACC bar, tort liability is no longer available for these purposes in contexts where public officials cause personal injury. For instance, victims of assault by police or prison officers can no longer turn to the law of torts.

Except where one of the exceptions to the ACC bar applies, accountability and vindication need to be sought elsewhere. The alternatives include public law accountability avenues such as disciplinary proceedings, the Independent Police Conduct Authority or public inquiries, and criminal proceedings. They also include private prosecutions, which are rare.[228]

Case law has established three exceptions to the bar. All involve claims that are not sufficiently covered by the ACC scheme itself to be barred by it. The scope of all three is at least somewhat uncertain and unsettled. First, since ACC provides compensation, it does not bar claims for exemplary damages that are awarded to punish defendants

[224] Accident Compensation Act 2001, s 317.

[225] PS Atiyah, *The Damages Lottery* (Oxford, Hart Publishing, 1997).

[226] *Roper v Taylor* [2023] NZSC 49, [2023] 1 NZLR 1 at [34], [69].

[227] See, eg, ibid. This cannot be circumvented by claiming damages for other aspects of conduct that contributed to the mental injury, such as false imprisonment: ibid at [57]–[71]. Contrast *S v Attorney-General* [2003] 3 NZLR 450 (CA), where the abuse occurred before the ACC legislation first came into force.

[228] See, eg, *Wallace v Abbott* (2002) 19 CRNZ 585 (HC).

rather than compensate plaintiffs.[229] Secondly, it does not bar claims for certain categories of mental injury that are not covered by the scheme. In particular, this includes mental injury that is caused by witnessing personal injury suffered by others.[230] Such claims, however, face stringent requirements at common law.[231] Finally, it also does not bar claims for affront to rights under the New Zealand Bill of Rights Act 1990, even where the action giving rise to the claim also caused personal injury. However, the damages must not be quantified so as to provide compensation for the personal injury.[232]

The first and third of these exceptions are directly relevant to the availability of damages claims against public authorities for the purposes of accountability and vindication. The third exception applies solely in this context, since the Bill of Rights only applies to exercises of public power. The first exception involving exemplary damages is of broader application but is of particular significance in the context of public power. The limits of this remedy therefore also have a special impact in this context. Let us explore both of these points about exemplary damages a little further.

In the case law on exemplary damages, addressing abuse of public power has been identified as an especially appropriate role for these damages. Their availability generally is a contested issue, as their punitive purpose can be seen as out of place in the private law of torts.[233] However, the House of Lords in *Rookes v Barnard* identified three limited situations where exemplary damages are appropriate. One of these was oppressive, arbitrary or unconstitutional action by public officials.[234] While New Zealand courts have not accepted that the remedy is limited to these situations,[235] the remedy may still be seen as especially appropriate in this context.

The test for awarding exemplary damages is outrageous or flagrant wrongdoing, displaying a 'contumelious disregard' for the plaintiff's rights.[236] Whenever it is arguable that this test is made out, a claim for personal injury can be brought against a public official to exact accountability and vindication.

In short, then, exemplary damages may be used to hold public authorities to account in extreme cases of official wrongdoing. Damages claims against public authorities that would otherwise be barred by the ACC legislation are available where they serve this purpose. Other rules governing the availability of exemplary damages are therefore especially significant in this context.

On the one hand, the availability of exemplary damages in Aotearoa New Zealand extends beyond intentional torts to include negligence cases. The Supreme Court in *Couch (No 2)* established a test of subjective recklessness for this.[237] As a result, they

[229] *Donselaar v Donselaar* [1982] 1 NZLR 97 (CA). This is now enshrined in the Accident Compensation Act 2001, s 319.

[230] *Queenstown Lakes District Council v Palmer* [1999] 1 NZLR 549 (CA). The exception is where this occurs at work, since the scheme includes cover for this: see *Roper v Taylor* (n 226).

[231] *Van Soest v Residual Health Management Unit* [2000] 1 NZLR 179 (CA).

[232] *Wilding v Attorney-General* [2003] 3 NZLR 787 (CA) at [16].

[233] See, eg, Alan Beever, 'The Future of Exemplary Damages in New Zealand' (2010) 24 *New Zealand Universities Law Review* 197.

[234] *Rookes v Barnard* [1964] AC 1129 (HL) at 1226.

[235] *Taylor v Beere* [1982] 1 NZLR 81 (CA) at 95.

[236] ibid at 90, 93; *Donselaar* (n 229) at 115.

[237] *Couch (No 2)* [2010] NZSC 27 (n 108) at [178]–[179]; overruling a different test established in *A v Bottrill* [2003] 2 NZLR 721 (PC).

may, for instance, be available in a claim for failure to protect against harm – as in that case. This is a type of claim not reached by the intentional torts.

On the other hand, there are at least two significant limits to the availability of exemplary damages in New Zealand. The first is a clear and significant limit. It is, however, also very difficult to justify.[238] The Law Reform Act 1936 in section 3(2) provides that exemplary damages cannot be claimed on behalf of a deceased plaintiff. As a result, claims can be brought when public officials injure a person (or fail to protect them against injury), but not when that person has died of their injuries. This is surely a perverse outcome. It is in particular tension with Māori tikanga concerning mana (status and dignity): the Supreme Court has determined a similar issue on the basis that the importance of a person's mana is not diminished by their death.[239] On that basis, a remedy designed to provide accountability and vindication is needed just as much after the victim's death.

Secondly, two questions concerning institutional liability remain unsettled. It is clear that individual officials can be liable for exemplary damages if they are at fault and satisfy the test. Whether the vicarious liability of the official's employing authority extends to this remedy, however, is both unsettled[240] and controversial.[241] But it does appear that the authority can be liable by attribution if the official at fault can be shown to have been acting on behalf of the authority.[242] Further, where no individual was at fault but faulty systems were to blame, it is possible that an authority may be directly liable for systemic negligence. Whether exemplary damages are available in that type of claim is again uncertain: can an organisation display the required subjective recklessness?[243]

[238] See Madeleine Hay, 'Should Claims for Exemplary Damages Survive Death?' (2022) 28 *Auckland University Law Review* 165.

[239] *Ellis v R* [2022] NZSC 114, [2022] 1 NZLR 239. See Hay ibid at 181–83.

[240] It was left open in *Couch (No 2)* (n 108) at [158]; *S v Attorney-General* (n 227) at [93]. However, vicarious liability has been accepted in several High Court decisions: see, eg, *Murray v Gebbie* [2009] NZAR 630 (HC).

[241] See, eg, Stephen Todd, 'Vicarious Liability, Personal Liability and Exemplary Damages' in Simone Degeling, James Edelman and James Goudkamp (eds), *Torts in Commercial Law* (Sydney, Thomson Reuters, 2011) 409 at 447.

[242] *Couch (No 2)* (n 108) at [159]–[160]; *S v Attorney-General* (n 227) at [92].

[243] *Couch* ibid at [157]–[161], see also [24], [65].

Part V

Administrative Justice

13

Introduction to Administrative Justice

A. Administrative Regimes, their Design and Evaluation

As outlined in Chapter 2, public administration involves an extensive set of distinct administrative regimes, such as environmental and competition regulation, regulation of professions, censorship, corrections, local government, social security, health, education, legal aid, taxation, and immigration. Each of these has its own substantive rules and its own institutions, guidelines and procedures for making rules and decisions. Today, nearly all such regimes also include their own remedial regimes, operating alongside judicial review as alternative remedial options. These comprise a mix of specialist and generalist, internal and external bodies, all charged with resolving complaints, grievances and disputes about administrative decisions. Collectively, all these regimes for making and challenging decisions can be referred to as the administrative justice system.

This system and the various regimes within it are the subject of a burgeoning literature on the topic of administrative justice.[1] One of the main tasks taken up by this literature is to contribute to designing and evaluating the administrative justice system as a whole, or particular regimes within it. Some of this literature takes the form of normative work, analysing and debating the objectives to be pursued and the principles to be applied: what makes such systems just, or allows them to deliver justice? The

[1] For a survey, see Simon Halliday and Colin Scott, 'Administrative Justice' in Peter Cane and Herbert M Kritzer (eds), *The Oxford Handbook of Empirical Legal Research* (Oxford, Oxford University Press, 2010) 469. For in-depth explorations, see Michael Adler (ed), *Administrative Justice in Context* (Oxford, Hart Publishing, 2010); Marc Hertogh, Richard Kirkham, Robert Thomas and Joe Tomlinson (eds), *The Oxford Handbook of Administrative Justice* (Oxford, Oxford University Press, 2021) (see the helpful preface).

other main aspect of this literature is empirical work that explores the operation of administrative regimes in practice and the experiences of individuals interacting with them. One of the purposes of the empirical work is to provide a better basis for the normative work.

This introductory chapter and Chapters 14 and 15 are devoted to exploring these aspects of administrative justice. They outline the themes and debates in the administrative justice literature concerning the design and evaluation of regimes and systems. They explore how these themes and debates apply to the administrative justice system in Aotearoa New Zealand and to the regimes that make up that system.

The rise of an extensive system of administrative justice, and of the literature on the topic, is closely connected with the 'green light' influence in administrative law. As we saw in Chapter 3, the competing 'red light' influence promotes a focus on external control of executive power, on negative rules constraining power, and on the courts as providing this control and constraint. The green light influence diverges from that approach on all three points: it leads to greater faith in the internal regulation of administrative systems, a focus on correct implementation of each regime's positive rules and on promoting its policy objectives, and preference for specialist administrative tribunals rather than the general courts for external controls. The literature surveyed in the next two chapters tends to feature scholars of that bent. They have been the main contributors to the administrative justice literature and have been instrumental in promoting the development and expansion of the administrative justice system.

The focus in much of this literature is on areas of administrative activity that involve vulnerable groups with limited resources or power, such as social security applicants or immigrants. The quality of first instance decisions and the availability of more accessible avenues of recourse are especially important for people in these groups, as they are less likely to be able to access judicial review and less likely to complain at all.

There are at least three audiences for this work. The first and main audience comprises policy-makers and others engaged in law reform, designing new systems or reviewing existing ones. Secondly, judges deciding judicial review applications can be assisted by a sophisticated understanding of the strengths and weaknesses of different parts of the administrative justice system, especially to inform decisions they make about the scope and intensity of judicial review. Thirdly, this work can assist lawyers and other advocates to make informed choices about where to target advocacy and what remedies to pursue.

B. An Administrative Justice Framework

Several sets of objectives and considerations apply in designing and evaluating regimes for making and reviewing administrative rules and decisions. Many of these are at least potentially in tension with each other. Normative debates about administrative justice are best understood as debates about the necessary trade-offs.

The main objectives of administrative justice as commonly discussed in the literature may be summarised as follows:[2]

(1) Get it right the first time – both in terms of outcome and in terms of procedure and reasoning.
(2) Put errors right with minimal difficulty for the affected person.
(3) Learn from errors.

These three objectives primarily concern individual justice: they focus on the interests of the individual affected by administrative decisions. In addition, protecting these individual interests also serves to promote a set of secondary public interests. First, we all want to live under a system that treats individuals justly – there is a public interest in having such a system. Secondly, a system that does so also gains legitimacy which, in turn, allows it to serve other relevant aspects of the public interest more effectively.

However, there is also a potential tension between individual justice and other aspects of the public interest. What counts as getting it 'right' or as 'errors' turns both on what an individual should receive, and on what is required to serve the social goals served by the relevant regime. For instance, individuals should be granted fishing licences in certain circumstances. But the point of having a system of fishing licences is to limit the number and scope of licences available, to protect fish stocks from excessive exploitation. The 'right' decision on a fishing licence is one that is right from both perspectives.

The two perspectives are not always in tension or competition: for instance, if the social objective of the social security system is to alleviate or prevent poverty and hardship, then both that social objective and individual justice are served by the grant of assistance to an individual. However, modern social security systems also have among their objectives to contain the cost of alleviating hardship and to ensure there are incentives for people to find and retain work.[3] Those create an element of tension with the individual interests affected: the public interest in this respect is served by making grants only to those who meet the relevant restrictive criteria.

There is also an issue about the cost of the system and the resources required for it. The above administrative justice objectives include limiting the cost and burden imposed on the individual seeking just treatment. But there is also a public interest in containing the cost and burden of the system's operation. This is, again, at least potentially in tension with individual justice.

Some parts of the administrative justice literature are firmly focused on individual justice. Other work, however, also reflects the green light focus on the implementation of each regime's positive rules and on promoting its social objectives.[4] While those

[2] See Tom Mullen, 'A Holistic Approach to Administrative Justice?' in Michael Adler (ed), *Administrative Justice in Context* (Oxford, Hart Publishing, 2010) 383 at 386; summarising the objectives set out in the White Paper *Transforming Public Services: Complaints, Redress and Tribunals* (Cm 6243, 2004) at [1.5] and [1.7].

[3] See Welfare Expert Advisory Group, *Whakamana Tāngata: Restoring Dignity to Social Security in New Zealand* (February 2019) at 95.

[4] See, eg, Jerry Mashaw, *Bureaucratic Justice: Managing Social Security Disability Claims* (New Haven, Yale University Press, 1983).

social objectives include assistance for individuals, they also include objectives that are in tension with individual interests.

Administrative justice literature of this broader type would set at least two potentially competing public-interest objectives alongside the three individual-focused objectives listed above:

(4) Conserve public resources.
(5) Serve the social goals of the particular regime.

On such broader accounts, a balance needs to be struck between these competing sets of objectives, calling for highly contestable value judgements.

Such trade-offs are clearly part of the practice of public administration and dispute resolution in the real world. That helps explain why the design and operation of regimes is a matter of ongoing contestation and never seems optimal from any particular perspective.

The question is whether the competing public interest objectives listed above are also valid aspects of the normative framework, and whether the trade-offs can therefore be justified normatively. Legal scholars often tend to assume that such trade-offs are to be regretted, even if they are practically unavoidable, as compromising justice.

The alternative possibility, suggested by a broader green light perspective, is to adopt a broader model of justice. This was argued notably by Jerry Mashaw. He proposed the recognition of 'bureaucratic justice', finding justice in the appropriate balance between these competing objectives. The aim of administrative justice on this view is the 'effective pursuit of collective ends without inordinately sacrificing individualistic or democratic ideals'.[5]

A final set of considerations that are brought to bear in debates about the design and evaluation of administrative regimes are constitutional principles, such as the rule of law and separation of powers. In engaging with such arguments, it is important to remember that the content and meaning of these principles is itself highly contestable.[6]

C. Outline of this Part of the Book

The remaining two chapters in this Part V of the book are framed as addressing the three objectives of administrative justice in the individual sense. Chapter 14 explores how front-line decision-making systems can best serve the first and third objectives. Chapter 15 discusses how remedial regimes can best serve the second objective. Throughout, we will return to the potentially competing public interest objectives, and to the relevance of constitutional principles.

[5] ibid at 222. See also Robert Thomas, *Administrative Justice and Asylum Appeals: A Study of Tribunal Adjudication* (Oxford, Hart Publishing, 2011) at 1.

[6] See Ch 3.B.

14

Front-line Decision-making: Getting it Right and Learning from Errors

Lawyers and legal scholars tend to focus on dispute and grievance resolution, and that focus can also be observed in the administrative justice literature. Much of that literature is concerned with the second objective of administrative justice – putting errors right – and hence with the design and evaluation of remedial regimes. Yet the first objective – getting it right the first time – is the most important in practice. Of the millions of decisions made at first instance, only a small fraction are ever challenged, even using internal review.[1] Studies carried out in other jurisdictions show that the vast majority of people who are concerned that a decision may be flawed do not complain,[2] for a wide variety of reasons.[3] Furthermore, even where people do complain and even where this results in errors being put right, those errors still cause hardship in the interim, as well as taking up time and effort and causing stress.

Efforts to promote administrative justice therefore need to include attention to front-line decision-making: how to ensure good quality decision-making (accuracy and fairness) at this point. That needs to be grounded in an understanding of how front-line decision-making works in practice.

[1] For instance, the Ministry of Social Development (MSD) makes around 8 million reviewable decisions a year, of which around 4,700 – less than 0.06% – are subject to a formal request for a review of decision, the first level of challenge: MSD response to Official Information Act 1982 OIA request, 'Guidelines and processes in place to learn from Benefit Review Committee, Social Security Appeal Authority', 1 July 2022. Available at: www.msd.govt.nz.

[2] Terence G Ison, 'Administrative Justice: Is it Such a Good Idea?' in Michael Harris and Martin Partington (eds), *Administrative Justice in the 21st Century* (Oxford, Hart Publishing, 1999) at 22–24.

[3] See, eg, David Cowan and Simon Halliday, *The Appeal of Internal Review: Law, Administrative Justice, and the (Non-)Emergence of Disputes* (Oxford, Hart Publishing, 2003) Ch 5; Vicki Lens, 'Administrative Justice in Public Welfare Bureaucracies: When Citizens (Don't) Complain' (2007) 39 *Administration & Society* 382.

There is, however, a potential link between the first and second objectives of administrative justice. This is via the third objective – learning from errors. Some of the literature that deals with the first objective does so in terms of the impact that remedial regimes have on front-line decision-making, and hence via consideration of the second and third objective.[4] When errors have been identified by remedial regimes, when and how do administrators learn from those errors, to get it right next time?

This chapter explores this indirect route first (Part A), before turning to consider direct methods for promoting good front-line decision-making (Part B).

A. Learning from Errors: The Impact of Grievance Resolution on the Front Line

In considering the impact of grievance resolution for learning at the front line, the basic point is that findings of error will not automatically filter through to the front line. Front-line decision-makers usually are not lawyers. In most contexts, they apply internal guidelines and checklists rather than directly applying the relevant legislation, let alone applying case law from courts or tribunals. This is the case particularly in regimes that involve very large numbers of day-to-day decisions, such as social security. It is therefore only once findings of error have been converted into revisions to the guidelines and checklists that there is any prospect of future decisions avoiding the same errors as a result.[5] The point also applies especially in contexts where front-line decision-making is being automated. Such systems will not take account of court or tribunal decisions unless they are updated in light of those decisions. Whether, and how quickly and accurately, this occurs is a matter of internal management, which brings us back to mechanisms designed directly in pursuit of the first objective. Agencies need to have systems in place for this.[6]

A spectacular example of such systems failing, partly because they were not sufficiently robust and partly because officials were not complying in good faith, is the Australian 'Robodebt' scandal. The agency administering social security benefits adopted an automated system for establishing supposed overpayments and sending out demands for repayment. The system averaged income over time. This was found unlawful in several first instance decisions of the Australian Administrative Tribunal, but no action was taken to reconsider that system until it was challenged in the Federal Court.[7]

[4] This is only one of a variety of purposes of impact studies: see Peter Cane, 'Understanding Judicial Review and Its Impact' in Marc Hertogh and Simon Halliday (eds), *Judicial Review and Bureaucratic Impact* (Cambridge, Cambridge University Press, 2004) 15.

[5] See GDS Taylor, 'May Judicial Review Become a Backwater?' in Michael Taggart (ed), *Judicial Review of Administrative Action in the 1980s: Problems and Prospects* (Auckland, Oxford University Press, 1986) 152 at 153–54.

[6] Ministry of Business, Innovation and Employment, Government Centre for Dispute Resolution, *Best practice guidance on dispute resolution*. Available at: www.mbie.govt.nz; *Tribunals for Users: One System, One Service. Report of the Review of Tribunals chaired by Sir Andrew Leggatt* (March 2001) (Leggatt Report) at [9.16]–[9.18].

[7] *Royal Commission into the Robodebt Scheme: Report Volume 1* (Commonwealth of Australia, 2022) ch 20. Further on this scheme, see discussion below at n 63.

Many of the studies on the impact of remedial regimes on front-line decision-making concern judicial review.[8] Judicial review has a standard-setting function that can be considered at least as important as its dispute-resolution function: the grounds of review represent instructions to administrators on how (not) to exercise their powers.[9] The studies test the extent to which those judge-made norms do influence administrative decision-making in practice. Consistent with what has just been said, they have found that such an impact is highly contingent.

The norms found in the grounds of judicial review are certainly translated into practice at a high level of generality and in the long term: well-established norms such as those relating to procedural fairness are often reflected in empowering legislation[10] and in the internal guidelines of administrative agencies.[11] But even this reception of relevant high-level guidance from judicial review principles is limited by specialist lawyers' tendency to think in silos: legal analysis of a particular regime often includes limited reference to general principles of judicial review. It tends to ignore cases that develop these principles but are concerned with different regimes. This has also not been helped by the fact that, in New Zealand, few of the authors writing on administrative law had expertise in particular administrative regimes.[12]

As to whether agencies learn from judicial review outcomes in challenges to their own decisions and practices, a study by Simon Halliday found that the extent to which this happens depends on three broad factors. They are individual officials' conscientiousness and competence concerning the law, the agency's commitment to lawfulness, and the extent to which the law is clear.[13] It will be noted that the first two of these factors depend on the agency's internal management. As noted earlier, there is little prospect of front-line decision-making being impacted unless and until guidelines and checklists are amended.

There can be a long time lag between a court decision identifying a clear and significant flaw in current practice and any change to that practice. An example is the Department of Work and Income's response to *Ruka*.[14] The Court of Appeal in that case found significant problems with the test that the Department had been applying to determine whether a beneficiary is in a de facto relationship and hence not entitled to sole parent support or single person rates for other benefits. Yet an investigation four years later found that the vast majority of cases had still been determined using the old, flawed test.[15] The Department had reservations about *Ruka* and had been

[8] See, eg, Simon Halliday, *Judicial Review and Compliance with Administrative Law* (Oxford, Hart Publishing, 2004); Marc Hertogh and Simon Halliday (eds), *Judicial Review and Bureaucratic Impact: International and Interdisciplinary Perspectives* (Cambridge, Cambridge University Press, 2004).

[9] See Chs 1.D and 2.B(1).

[10] This is promoted by the Legislation Design and Advisory Committee, *Legislation Guidelines* (2021 edition). Available at: http://www.ldac.org.nz/.

[11] See also the general guidance to the public service on the standards set by judicial review: Crown Law, *Te Poutārahi: The Judge Over Your Shoulder*, 3rd edn (Wellington, 2019).

[12] This is, perhaps, changing now, given Dean Knight's expertise in local government law, Marcelo Rodriguez Ferrere's in animal law, Ed Willis' in competition law and my own work on social security law.

[13] Halliday, *Judicial Review and Compliance* (n 8).

[14] *Ruka v Department of Social Welfare* [1997] 1 NZLR 154 (CA).

[15] Frances Joychild, *Report to the Minister for Social Services: Review of Department of Work and Income Implementation of the Court of Appeal Decision Ruka v Department of Social Welfare* [1997] 1 NZLR 154

pursuing a legislative amendment to overturn it (which ultimately failed).[16] However, it ought to have implemented the decision in the meantime. The Ministry of Social Development now has a dedicated Appeals Committee that considers all tribunal and court rulings against its decisions. The Committee's task is to determine whether to appeal or whether to revise guidelines in accordance with the ruling.[17]

What about the impact of other avenues of recourse? Concerning the Regulations Review Committee, the main issue is whether recommendations are accepted by government. They often are.[18] Once changes to delegated legislation have been made in response to the Committee's recommendations (or by means of the Parliamentary disallowance procedures – an exceedingly rare occurrence), the impact should be a more clear-cut matter than litigation outcomes. Such changes would hopefully be translated promptly into practice.

Where merits review tribunals are concerned, a further issue is the extent to which their decisions are even considered binding on the respondent authority beyond the particular case. The answer is surprisingly unclear and unsettled.[19] It is often said that tribunal decisions do not create binding precedent. However, even if this is correct, the effect in practice is greatly reduced because tribunal decisions are at least treated as persuasive and influential.[20] Still, there are instances where authorities refuse to change their practice in response to tribunal rulings.[21] While this also occurs in response to judicial review, as we have seen, at least in that context the legal obligation to comply is clear. Whether there is a similar legal obligation to implement tribunal rulings is a significant question that deserves further attention.

The arguments offered against according precedent status to a merits tribunal's decisions include that the function of merits review is to determine the correct or preferable decision in the individual case, not to generate precedents.[22] Furthermore, this function is said to be administrative rather than judicial, and it would offend the non-fettering principle for an administrative decision-maker to treat previous decisions as precedents.[23]

These arguments seem to be open to various objections. At least they need to be qualified in one respect. We should arguably distinguish between two aspects of merits

(June 2001), see esp at 40–44; see also John Hughes, 'Battered Woman's Syndrome and "Independence" as Factors in Establishing Conjugal Status in Social Security Law' (1999) 7 *Waikato Law Review* 104 at 126–29.

[16] Joychild ibid at 31, 44.

[17] Kim Morton and others, *Access to Justice for Beneficiaries: A Community Law Response* (Community Law Canterbury, October 2014) at 109; MSD response to OIA request, 1 July 2022 (n 1).

[18] Dean Knight and Edward Clark, *Regulations Review Committee Digest*, 7th edn (Wellington, New Zealand Centre for Public Law, 2020).

[19] See Trevor Buck, 'Precedent in Tribunals and the Development of Principles' (2006) 25 *Civil Justice Quarterly* 458; also Greg Weeks, *Soft Law and Public Authorities: Remedies and Reform* (Oxford, Hart Publishing, 2016), chs 2 and 4.

[20] See, eg, MSD response to OIA request, 1 July 2022 (n 1).

[21] See, eg, Māmari Stephens, *Social Security and Welfare Law in Aotearoa New Zealand* (Wellington, Thomson Reuters, 2019) at 409–410.

[22] Peter Cane, *Administrative Tribunals and Adjudication* (Oxford, Hart Publishing, 2009) at 195–196 reports that this is how the Australian Administrative Appeals Tribunal (AAT) was understood, see also at 185; MSD response to OIA request, 1 July 2022 (n 1) takes this view in relation to BRC decisions.

[23] Leggatt Report (n 6) at [6.17]–[6.19]; HWR Wade and Christopher Forsyth, *Administrative Law*, 11th edn (Oxford, OUP, 2014) at 272.

tribunals' decisions: interpretation of the law and determinations as to how discretionary powers are best exercised in the circumstances. The arguments just outlined are best understood as applying only to merits review, which is the latter aspect.

Some decisions by merits tribunals also include the former aspect, at least where external tribunals with legally qualified members are concerned: their determination of the correct outcome in the case at hand is sometimes based on a finding that the respondent authority has misinterpreted the law, or has adopted a policy that is inconsistent with the law.[24] The arguments about merits review arguably do not apply to this aspect. Interpretation of the law does not involve the kind of discretion that must not be fettered. On the contrary, a tribunal should strive to interpret the law correctly and consistently across cases.

Whether a tribunal has any authority to settle the correct interpretation of the law is a different issue. It has been argued that tribunals, being administrative decision-makers, cannot have the power to determine questions of law conclusively.[25] This objection too is problematic. It is doubtful whether tribunals should be categorised as purely administrative, and also whether such a categorisation of their function should be determinative as to the nature of their authority. Even if we were to accept both points, however, the argument would still fail. Tribunals' interpretations of the law are almost invariably subject to being overruled (by judicial review or appeals to the general courts). Therefore, their interpretations of the law are not conclusive. But that is not inconsistent with having precedent force unless and until they are overruled.

Interpretations of the law by an independent and legally qualified tribunal arguably should be treated as binding on that basis.[26] It seems highly desirable that tribunals should have this function of improving the authorities' understanding and interpretation of the law. There is at least some support for that in New Zealand case law.[27] Some tribunals, such as the United Kingdom's Upper Tribunal, do explicitly have this function.[28]

If decisions of any kind are to be precedents, however, there are resource implications. For this purpose, decisions need to include written reasons, and the decisions and reasons need to be disseminated both internally and publicly. Dissemination of tribunal decisions will amount to information overload unless it is done selectively.[29] A system is needed for this.[30] Effective internal dissemination, as noted, needs to include revisions to the guidelines.

The Ombudsman and internal review are often considered to have better prospects than judicial review of having an impact on future practice. The Ombudsman can go

[24] See, eg, *An appeal against a decision of a Benefits Review Committee* [2019] NZSSAA 13 at [14]–[48]; *An appeal against a decision of a Benefits Review Committee* [2015] NZSSAA 102.

[25] Cane, *Administrative Tribunals* (n 22) at 195–96.

[26] This is distinct from the controversial question whether a reviewing court should accord any deference to a tribunal's interpretation of its legislation.

[27] See, eg, *Worrall v Chief Executive Department of Work and Income* [2001] NZAR 761 at [18], albeit the Court did not note the distinction suggested here.

[28] Cane, *Administrative Tribunals* (n 22) at 195–96, 199.

[29] See Jerry Mashaw, 'The Management Side of Due Process: Some Theoretical and Litigation Notes on the Assurance of Accuracy, Fairness, and Timeliness in the Adjudication of Social Welfare Claims' (1973–1974) 59 *Cornell Law Review* 772 at 785–87; Leggatt Report (n 6) at [6.24]–[6.26].

[30] See Ch 2.B.

beyond addressing the particular grievance and make explicit recommendations for improvements to systems.[31] In addition, the process followed by the Ombudsman for resolving complaints is investigative and collaborative, engaging in exchanges with officials in the agency that is the subject of the complaint.[32] At least potentially, this can be a learning and reflective process for those officials, and can result in recommendations that are more responsive to the realities of administration.[33]

Internal review could also have good prospects of having an impact on future practice, at least in theory. It involves the agency confronting its own errors, so it should involve learning. The evidence is, however, limited and somewhat equivocal. A United Kingdom study of homelessness decision-making reported that authorities perceived internal review as improving the quality of first instance decision-making.[34] The authors considered that this benefit is much more likely to flow from internal than external review.[35] However, the study had limits: it did not show whether that perception was accurate, nor whether it would be replicated in contexts involving larger organisations than the small local units that decide homelessness applications.[36]

A final question about the impact of both internal and external review concerns the impact that the mere availability of review has on the quality of decision-making. This could go either way. On the one hand, knowing that a decision may be subjected to review may provide an incentive to get it right. This may be enhanced where the decision-maker has a duty to give reasons, which will then be scrutinised on review. On the other hand, it could also provide an excuse for putting limited effort into decisions and instead relying on review to deal with any problems.[37] Decision-making systems may also be designed on that basis. That is highly problematic, given the low rate of challenge that we noted earlier.

B. Direct Methods for Improving Front-line Decision-making

What, then, are effective direct methods for improving accuracy and fair procedure in front-line decision-making, given that learning from errors identified by remedial avenues at best plays a contributory role? Commentary that engages directly with this

[31] Pursuant to of the Ombudsmen Act 1975, s 22(3). See Robert Thomas, 'The English Local Government and Social Care Ombudsman: Systemic Administrative Justice and Bureaucratisation (Part I)' [2023] *Public Law* 240 and '(Part II)' [2023] *Public Law* 424.

[32] See Chs 2 and 15. Where the collaborative approach is taken too far, however, it can compromise the scrutiny function: see *Royal Commission into the Robodebt Scheme* (n 7) ch 21.

[33] Marc Hertogh, 'Coercion, Co-operation, and Control: Understanding the Policy Impact of Administrative Courts and the Ombudsman in the Netherlands' (2001) 23 *Law and Policy* 47 (while discussing a very different legal system, the Ombudsman institution seems broadly similar to ours). For a more cautious assessment, see Chris Gill, 'What Can Government Learn from the Ombudsman?' in Marc Hertogh and Richard Kirkham (eds), *Research Handbook on the Ombudsman* (Cheltenham, Edward Elgar Publishing, 2018) 298.

[34] David Cowan et al, 'Reconsidering Mandatory Reconsideration' [2017] *Public Law* 215 at 224–225, 226.

[35] ibid at 231.

[36] ibid at 233, 234.

[37] Cane, *Administrative Tribunals* (n 22) at 265.

question identifies a wide range of internal management matters.[38] These include good design of the internal guidelines that have already been discussed.[39] They also include adequate resourcing and procedures so as to provide decision-makers with adequate time and information; recruitment of an appropriately skilled and diverse workforce; computer programmes to structure and facilitate decision-making; appropriate training and promotion of a public service culture; and monitoring and auditing.[40]

Jerry Mashaw in his influential study of the disability insurance program in the United States noted the tension between the benefits of internal managerial control and the desirability of responsiveness to clients. He defended internal bureaucratic justice as a valid form of justice, not to be displaced by external accountability. His proposed measures for improving such internal accountability included more extensive and systematic monitoring.[41] In another study he argued that effective monitoring requires regular review of a random sample of individual files, collation of data from such reviews and other sources, and analysis of such data to identify patterns that provide the basis for improvements to systems, manuals and training.[42]

An agency's internal culture is also important, as Fisher and Shapiro argue in a study focusing on expert administrative rule-making and policy-making.[43] They discuss the role of formal internal norms such as guidelines and informal norms found in an organisation's culture, as well as the role of discursive processes. Formal internal norms facilitate accountability by means of managers checking compliance. Informal internal norms – such as mission orientation, a sense of public service and professionalism – if successfully inculcated, promote voluntary compliance with an agency's goals and public purposes. Fisher and Shapiro acknowledge this does not always work but argue we should not underestimate its potential effectiveness. Finally, discursive processes involve contestation and testing of different experts' contributions by each other.

Internal culture can be influenced by internal management, as well as by the tone set by the government of the day. For instance, the report on the 'Robodebt' scandal, mentioned earlier, noted that the Minister's publicly stated 'welfare cop' approach was part of the relevant background.[44] Institutional incentives may help; for instance, Leggatt proposed incentivising good front-line decision-making by allocating the cost of tribunals to departments in proportion to appeal numbers.[45] But crude incentives may have unintended consequences.

[38] For a survey, see Richard Martin, 'Administrative Decision-Making on the Frontline' in Marc Hertogh, Richard Kirkham, Robert Thomas and Joe Tomlinson (eds), *The Oxford Handbook of Administrative Justice* (Oxford, Oxford University Press, 2021) 3 at 14–15.

[39] KC Davis, *Discretionary Justice: A Preliminary Inquiry* (Urbana, University of Illinois Press, 1977).

[40] For discussion of proposals, see, eg, Robert Thomas and Joe Tomlinson, 'Mapping Current Issues in Administrative Justice: Austerity and the 'More Bureaucratic Rationality' Approach' (2017) 39 *Journal of Social Welfare and Family Law* 380 at 381–389.

[41] Jerry Mashaw, *Bureaucratic Justice: Managing Social Security Disability Claims* (New Haven, Yale University Press, 1983).

[42] Mashaw, 'Management Side of Due Process' (n 29) at 791–804. See also Joychild (n 15) at 70–71.

[43] Elizabeth Fisher and Sidney A Shapiro, *Administrative Competence: Reimagining Administrative Law* (Cambridge, Cambridge University Press, 2020) ch 3.

[44] *Royal Commission into the Robodebt Scheme* (n 7) at 28, 70.

[45] Leggatt Report (n 6) at [5.31]–[5.32].

Arm's-length regulation is also widely used.[46] In the case of contracted-out decision making, this distance is built in, and accountability poses special challenges.[47] Systemic problems and possible solutions can also be identified by external investigations, such as those of the Ombudsmen, Auditor-General or public inquiries.[48]

In deciding what can be achieved and what means may be effective, it is essential to understand the realities of front-line decision-making. Literature on public administration sheds light on the limited influence of law at this point. At least in administrative policy-making, a range of different types of expertise and competence play a legitimate and crucial role.[49] Studies of street-level bureaucracy pioneered by Lipsky have explored the variety of pressures under which front-line officials work, and the barriers to effectively controlling their work.[50] Other studies have explored the role of front-line decision-makers' own beliefs, attitudes and values.[51] For instance, Maynard-Moody and Musheno described how bureaucrats apply, bend or ignore rules to support decisions that are at least partly based on their own moral evaluation of clients.[52] Officials' human emotions can also play a role, such as a fear of being "duped" by applicants.[53]

Furthermore, efforts to build internal systems that promote quality decision-making have always been in tension with a desire for thrift and efficiency in public services. As noted in the previous chapter, that competing objective can be conceived of either as compromising administrative justice, or as a valid part of a broader model of administrative justice. In recent decades, this countervailing force has taken two particular forms: the New Public Management movement and the trend towards automated decision-making.

First, the New Public Management movement has brought a shift away from 'compliance' monitoring for accuracy and fair procedures, and towards 'performance' monitoring against targets and standards.[54] There has also been a move towards service rationing and routinisation.[55] This form of control tends to emphasise monetary savings and accountability for the use of taxpayer resources, rather than quality from the perspective of those subject to the decisions. For example, a New Zealand report found that benefit fraud investigators were subject to weak checks on the accuracy and fairness of their work, and instead had targets and incentives for establishing large amounts of overpayments that could then be recovered as debts.[56] If such a managerial

[46] See Christopher Hood et al, *Regulation Inside Government: Waste-Watchers, Quality Police, and Sleazebusters* (Oxford, Oxford University Press, 1999).

[47] For discussion, see the themed analysis section in issue 2 of *Public Law* for 2023.

[48] See Ch 2.C.

[49] Fisher and Shapiro (n 43) ch 2.

[50] David Lipsky, *Street Level Bureaucracy: Dilemmas of the Individual in Public Services* (New York, Russel Sage Foundation, 1980).

[51] For a survey, see Martin (n 38) at 10–12.

[52] Steven Maynard-Moody and Michael Musheno, *Cops, Teachers and Counselors: Stories from the Front Lines of Public Service* (Ann Arbor, University of Michigan Press, 2003).

[53] Simon Halliday, 'Administrative Justice and Street-Level Emotions: Cultures of Denial in Entitlement Decision-Making' [2021] *Public Law* 727.

[54] Hood (n 46), ch 1.

[55] See, eg, Martin (n 38) at 12–13.

[56] Joychild (n 15) at 48–54, 57–59.

model[57] gives little weight to justice for the affected individual, it may be more difficult to consider it a model of administrative justice.[58]

Secondly, a related potentially countervailing force is the growing use of computerisation and automated decision-making, increasingly using artificial intelligence and machine-learning.[59] This may have potential for improving decision-making. Beyond the obvious efficiency gains, automated decision-making might, for instance, help eliminate human biases in decision-making. However, it is far more likely that biases will have been built into the algorithms and into the data sets used to train them.[60] Concerningly, this will often be difficult to detect, given the lack of transparency in such systems.[61] A further risk is that where human discretion is too tightly confined by a computerised system, this may just lead officials to learn how to 'trick the system'.[62]

The efficiency and inflexibility of automated decision-making may also increase the harm done by an unlawful policy. A notorious example is the 'Robodebt' scandal mentioned earlier. Hundreds of thousands of social welfare recipients were sent automated notices requiring repayment of debts due to supposed overpayments, calculated by a computerised data-matching system. The main problem did not lie in the algorithms used – rather, the illegality was found in the policy which they were set up to implement.[63] However, implementation by human officials might have reached fewer people, and even some greater measure of human involvement might have allowed some application of judgement that could have softened the scheme's impact.[64]

A tempting efficiency tool is to use automated decision-making for first-instance decisions, and then invite applications for review by human officials. Recall, however, that the vast majority of people who have doubts about official decisions do not challenge them. If the internal review requires an application, therefore, most of the doubtful decisions by automated decisions will remain undetected. At a minimum, human intervention needs to be on a routine random sampling basis.[65] Tomlinson has argued that the precautionary principle should apply in the development and implementation of automated decision-making systems.[66]

A much preferable approach would see individual decisions fully automated only where they are in favour of individuals; adverse decisions should always involve human

[57] Michael Adler, 'Understanding and Analysing Administrative Justice', in Michael Adler (ed), *Administrative Justice in Context* (Oxford, Hart Publishing, 2010) at 149.

[58] See Cane, *Administrative Tribunals* (n 22) at 215–16.

[59] See, generally, Carol Harlow and Rick Rawlings, *Law and Administration*, 4th ed (Cambridge, Cambridge University Press) at 248–54.

[60] Michèle Finck, 'Automated Decision-Making and Administrative Law' in Peter Cane et al (eds), *The Oxford Handbook of Comparative Administrative Law* (Oxford, Oxford University Press, 2021) 657 at 659, 663–68, 671–72.

[61] This lack of transparency may be inherent in artificial intelligence and thus unavoidable: Greg Adamson, 'Explainable Artificial Intelligence (XAI): A Reason to Believe?' (2022) 37 *Law in Context* 23.

[62] Jennifer Raso, 'Displacement as Regulation: New Regulatory Technologies and Front-Line Decision-Making in Ontario Works' (2017) 32 *Canadian Journal of Law and Society* 75 at 86.

[63] See Yee-Fui Ng and Stephen Gray, 'Disadvantage and the Automated Decision' (2022) 43 *Adelaide Law Review* 641 at 647–50.

[64] See, generally, *Royal Commission into the Robodebt Scheme* (n 7) ch 17. For the potential benefit of human intervention, see also Raso (n 62).

[65] See Ng and Gray (n 63) at 688–76.

[66] Joe Tomlinson, 'Justice in Automated Administration' (2020) 40 *Oxford Journal of Legal Studies* 708 at 733.

intervention before they are finalised. Reportedly, this approach was adopted by the Accident Compensation Corporation.[67] Unfortunately, however, human intervention in either scenario may be compromised by 'automation bias': the assumption that the computer cannot be wrong.[68] A stark illustration of this phenomenon is found in the Post Office 'Horizon' scandal in the United Kingdom, involving faulty accounting software that appeared to show financial losses in many local branches. Challenges to the validity of those accounting records fell on deaf ears, even in the context of criminal proceedings where some of those in charge of branches were wrongly convicted of theft.[69]

A different influence on the quality of front-line decision-making should finally be mentioned. Aside from matters of internal management and regulation, the design of the regime itself also plays a role. A perennial question is the best mix or balance between rules and discretion.[70] Too much discretion puts people at the mercy of individual officials, and risks errors by busy front-line officials. Too little risks arbitrary outcomes in situations not contemplated by the rules and, furthermore, invites evasion of the rules.

Another design question concerns the nature of the regime's substantive rules. In social security, for instance, a tightly targeted, conditional and parsimonious regime such as our current social security regime[71] is much more likely to lead to errors than a more generous regime offering broad entitlements.[72]

[67] Joy Liddicoat et al, 'The Use of Algorithms in the New Zealand Public Sector' [2019] *New Zealand Law Journal* 26.

[68] Harlow and Rawlings (n 59) at 252.

[69] The faults in the system were eventually established in litigation for damages: *Bates v Post Office Ltd (Judgment No 6, 'Horizon')* [2019] EWHC 3408 (QB); see also Harlow and Rawlings (n 59) at 461–463.

[70] See, eg, Robert E Goodin, 'Welfare, Rights and Discretion' (1986) 6 *Oxford Journal of Legal Studies* 232; Harlow and Rawlings (n 59) at 232–34. See further Ch 5.A.

[71] Social Security Act 2018. See Jane Higgins, 'From Welfare to Workfare' in Jonathan Boston, Susan St John and Paul C Dalziel (eds), *Redesigning the Welfare State in New Zealand* (Oxford University Press, 1999) 260.

[72] The 'rule of generosity' proposed to this end by Goodin (n 70) at 259–61 would go even further.

15

Remedial Regimes: Putting Errors Right

This chapter explores administrative justice debates relating to administrative law remedial avenues.[1] This involves three questions: what objectives and principles should guide the design and evaluation of remedial avenues, what are the relevant variable

[1] A version of this chapter also appears in Stephen Thomson, Matthew Groves and Greg Weeks, *Administrative Tribunals in the Common Law World* (Oxford, Hart Publishing, 2024), ch 8.

features of remedial avenues, and what are the advantages and disadvantages of those features in light of the objectives and principles? The discussion draws on the administrative literature[2] and applies it to the remedial avenues that form part of the administrative justice system in Aotearoa New Zealand.[3]

These avenues are diverse.[4] Most specialist administrative regimes include their own remedial regimes, comprising internal review procedures within agencies, specialist tribunals such as the Immigration and Protection Tribunal or the Social Security Appeal Authority, and appeals to the general courts. Non-judicial avenues further include the generalist Ombudsman and Parliamentary avenues such as the Regulations Review Committee. They also include tribunals with a more general jurisdiction. The Human Rights Review Tribunal (HRRT) and the Waitangi Tribunal specialise in particular types of complaints but hear such complaints in relation to any part of government (and in the case of the HRRT, in relation to private defendants as well). Finally, the avenues include judicial review and other judicial proceedings. Most authorities and agencies that form part of public administration are subject to review or appeal via a number of such avenues.

The focus in this chapter is on avenues for challenging decisions or rules. It does not deal in any detail with another type of complaint that is also important: complaints about the way people are treated rather than about the decisions reached. These are sometimes called 'service' complaints. They may be, for instance, about delays, lack of respect, or failing to respect and accommodate a person's culture. Judicial review generally does not address such complaints (with the possible exception of some types of delay). Dealing with these is therefore another important role of the wider administrative justice system. They can be addressed by the Ombudsman, and most administrative regimes also have an internal system for dealing with this type of complaint. Often, internal systems distinguish between challenges to decisions and complaints about treatment, providing separate dedicated avenues for the latter.[5] That has been criticised as unnecessarily confusing for complainants, impeding accessibility.[6]

Part A of this chapter sets out a framework of relevant considerations and of relevant variable features to assess. That framework centres around three criteria: effectiveness, accessibility and trustworthiness. Parts B to D address each of these criteria in turn.

[2] See also Ch 13. For a survey of the literature, see Simon Halliday and Colin Scott, 'Administrative Justice' in P Cane and H M Kritzer (eds), *The Oxford Handbook of Empirical Legal Research* (Oxford, Oxford University Press, 2010) 469.

[3] Best practice guides for the design of remedial regimes include: Ministry of Justice, *Tribunal Guidance – Choosing the right decision-making body – Equipping tribunals to operate effectively* (2015), available at www.justice.govt.nz/tribunals; Government Centre for Dispute Resolution, *Best practice guidance on dispute resolution*, available at www.mbie.govt.nz; Legislation Design and Advisory Committee, *Legislation Guidelines* (2021 edition). Available at: www.ldac.org.nz, ch 28.

[4] See Ch 2.C(1) for a survey.

[5] See, eg, Work and Income, *Making a Complaint*. Available at: www.workandincome.govt.nz/about-work-and-income/complaints.

[6] Mihiata Pirini, 'The Citizen and Administrative Justice: Reforming Complaint Management in New Zealand' (2010) 8 *New Zealand Journal of Public and International Law* 239 at 250–52.

A. A Framework for Assessing Remedial Avenues

Recall that the administrative justice project explored in this part of the book is to evaluate administrative regimes and contribute to the design of new ones. This chapter explores that project in relation to remedial avenues, of which New Zealand has a wide range.

In order to contribute to evaluating and designing remedial avenues, we need to start by identifying relevant points of difference between the available options. Remedial avenues have several variable features. To guide the selection of features to adopt, we also need to identify the relevant objectives, criteria reflecting those objectives, and other relevant considerations. These various sets of considerations are at least potentially in tension, calling for trade-offs.[7]

The *variable features* of remedial avenues include the following:[8]

- scope of scrutiny: full merits review or supervisory review of legality;
- type of remedies available:
  - substitution of decision or quashing and remitting
  - binding determinations or non-binding recommendations
- expertise or experience, in at least three senses:
  - specialist legal knowledge or experience
  - expertise or experience in the subject area, such as medical expertise
  - representation of relevant interests
- degree of independence and impartiality;
- type of procedure: adversarial or an alternative form (inquisitorial, investigative, active, enabling);
- degree of formality in other respects;
- speed of resolution;
- funding and resourcing;
- public awareness and understanding of the avenue; and
- legal representation: whether it is allowed and whether it is funded (legal aid).

The relevant *objective* of administrative justice in this context is to put errors right with minimal difficulty for the affected person.[9] This flows from the first objective of administrative justice, to get it right the first time around: if public administration has failed in that responsibility, the onus is on it to minimise the impact of that failure. The question is what types of remedial regimes best serve this objective.

[7] For similar analysis, see Robert Thomas, *Administrative Justice and Asylum Appeals: A Study of Tribunal Adjudication* (Oxford, Hart Publishing, 2011) at 12–15.

[8] For similar lists of characteristics, see Tom Mullen, 'A Holistic Approach to Administrative Justice?' in Michael Adler (ed), *Administrative Justice in Context* (Oxford, Hart Publishing, 2010) 383 at 386–87, 396.

[9] For the three main objectives of administrative justice, see Ch 13; White Paper, *Transforming Public Services: Complaints Redress and Tribunals* (Cm 6243, 2004) at [1.5] and [1.7].

In answering this question, the literature tends to focus on accessibility. In this regard, the administrative justice literature overlaps with the wider literature on access to justice. However, accessibility alone does not achieve the objective of putting errors right. Other distinct criteria are also reflected in commentators' assessments of different remedial options.

A fuller set of administrative justice *criteria* includes whether an avenue is –

- effective at putting errors right;
- accessible (lacking barriers to entry and use); and
- trustworthy (likely to give the complainant a fair go, both actually and as perceived by potential complainants).

Accessibility is especially important for the disadvantaged or vulnerable. The other two criteria are important for all who wish to challenge administrative decisions.

Each of the variable features listed above can be seen as relevant to one or more of these criteria. Effectiveness at putting errors right depends on the scope of scrutiny and the types of remedies available, expertise or experience, and speed of resolution. Accessibility depends on the formality of the procedures, funding and resourcing, and public awareness, as well as again on speed. Trustworthiness depends on independence and fair hearings.

There are tensions between these criteria. For instance, some features that make a remedial avenue accessible may compromise trustworthiness or effective error correction. In particular, trustworthiness is commonly associated with observance of natural justice, while accessibility is often promoted by informal procedures that may compromise some aspects of natural justice.[10]

Further potentially competing objectives in assessing a remedial system also include wider *public interest objectives*. As discussed in Chapter 13, these may be conceived of as potentially competing with Administrative Justice, or as forming part of a broader conception of Administrative Justice. The relevant public interest objectives here include the two general ones that were also mentioned in Chapter 13, and a third one that is specific to dispute resolution:

- promote the social goals of the particular regime;
- conserve public resources; and
- proportionate dispute resolution.[11]

The proportionality objective serves both individual justice and competing public interests, and it overlaps with the other two public interest objectives. One aspect of proportionality is to avoid adisproportionate commitment of public resources. Another aspect is to avoid a proliferation of proceedings and to ensure an appropriate measure of finality. The latter can serve both public and individual interests. It can serve the former

[10] Law Commission, *Tribunals in New Zealand* (NZLC IP 6, Wellington, New Zealand, 2008) at [6.4], also at [9.6].

[11] White Paper (n 9) at [1.7]: 'the process for putting things right … must be proportionate – that is, there should be no disproportionate barriers to users in terms of cost, speed or complexity, but misconceived or trivial complaints should be identified and rooted out quickly' and see ibid, part 2.

by preventing well-resourced litigants gaming the system and thereby obstructing pursuit of the regime's social goals. That was part of the Supreme Court's reasoning in giving effect to a provision that ousts judicial review in favour of the tax regime's statutory redress procedures in *Tannadyce*.[12] It The individual interests of the applicant and any affected third parties can be served by an appropriate degree of finality since vulnerable applicants, in particular, need their dispute to be resolved by a minimum of proceedings. Finally, an appropriate degree of finality is also an integral aspect of the rule of law.[13]

A further set of considerations that are brought to bear in these debates are *constitutional principles*. The rule of law and the separation of powers are often invoked in arguments about remedial avenues. Again, these considerations can be in tension with other considerations. In engaging with such arguments, it is important to remember that the content and meaning of these principles is itself highly contestable.[14]

Trade-offs are unavoidable in light of the tensions between the various sets of relevant considerations. We should strive for creative solutions that reduce the conflicts as far as possible and achieve good results on most criteria. However, tensions will remain. There is much room for debate about the best balance, and which criteria should be prioritised.

Evaluating the judicial avenues of recourse against the above three administrative justice criteria reveals the reasons why the administrative justice literature has promoted alternative avenues of recourse. The judicial avenues have significant weaknesses and drawbacks in terms of two of the three criteria: their effectiveness in putting errors right, and accessibility. They therefore need to be accompanied by other avenues that make up for these shortcomings. What is the best avenue or combination of avenues for each administrative regime is a much more difficult question to answer, given the need for contestable trade-offs.

The remaining parts of this chapter address the three administrative justice criteria in turn: B. Effectiveness at putting errors right, C. Accessibility and D. Trustworthiness. The discussion in each part assesses the performance of judicial review against the relevant criterion, then gives an overview of how the relevant features of alternative avenues operate in practice, and outlines debates concerning the advantages and disadvantages of each feature in light of the competing objectives and criteria, including the competing public interest objectives and the relevant constitutional principles.

B. Effectiveness at Putting Errors Right

Four sets of variable features are relevant to whether an avenue of recourse is effective at putting errors right: (1) the scope of scrutiny and whether substitutionary remedies are available, (2) expertise or experience, (3) whether binding rulings are available, and

[12] *Tannadyce Investments Ltd v Commissioner of Inland Revenue* [2011] NZSC 158, [2012] 2 NZLR 153 at [71].

[13] Timothy Endicott, 'The Impossibility of the Rule of Law' (1999) 19 *Oxford Journal of Legal Studies* 1.

[14] See Ch 3.B.

(4) speed of resolution. Non-judicial avenues tend to have significant advantages over judicial review when assessed against the effectiveness criterion.

(1) Scope of Scrutiny and Availability of Substitutionary Remedies: Merits Review

Merits review has two closely related features: the scope of scrutiny extends to the substantive merits of the decision, and the available remedies include substitution of the correct or preferable decision.[15] At least prima facie, merits review with these two features makes for the most effective error correction: all types of error can be fully put right.[16]

Merits review is a central feature of almost all the non-judicial avenues of recourse and is one of the main features that distinguish them from judicial ones. It is exceptional for a first appeal from an administrative decision to be a limited appeal.[17]

The precise scope of merits review can vary. Provisions for merits review often lack specificity and are open to interpretation. The power of a merits review body is at least the same as that of a court hearing a general appeal,[18] but it usually goes further both in terms of procedure and substantive power.[19]

One of the more explicit provisions for merits review is found in the Ombudsman Act.[20] The grounds of intervention include that the impugned decision was 'unreasonable, unjust, oppressive' and that it was 'wrong'.[21] In practice, at least in recent years it appears that Ombudsmen have often preferred to couch their findings in terms more similar to judicial review than merits review.[22] But the wider powers are available under the Act.[23]

Specialist review or appeal bodies and tribunals – both internal and external – also usually have merits review powers, and legislation provides for this in a variety of ways. The process may be described as review or appeal. The body may be directed to consider the matter afresh ('de novo').[24] It may be said to stand in the shoes of the primary decision-maker,[25] and may be provided with 'all the duties, functions and

[15] The 'correct or preferable' formulation is used in relation to the Australian Administrative Appeals Tribunal (AAT): see *Shi v Migration Agents' Registration Authority* (2008) 235 CLR 286 at [140] (Kiefel J).

[16] See *Love v Porirua City Council* [1984] 2 NZLR 308 (CA) at 310.

[17] Examples include Legal Services Act 2011, s 52.

[18] On which, see *Austin, Nichols & Co Inc v Stichting Lodestar* [2007] NZSC 103, [2008] 2 NZLR 141.

[19] See Graham Taylor, *Judicial Review: A New Zealand Perspective*, 4th edn (Wellington, LexisNexis NZ, 2018) at [4.05]–[4.06].

[20] Contrast the United Kingdom model, where the Ombudsman is limited to intervention for 'maladministration': Parliamentary Commissioner Act 1967, s 5(1).

[21] Ombudsmen Act 1975, s 22(1) (b) and (d).

[22] See, eg, Ron Paterson, *Investigation into SSC conduct of MFAT leaks inquiry* (Ombudsman opinion, June 2016). A similar tendency has been observed in the Australian Ombudsman's practice: Peter Cane, *Administrative Tribunals and Adjudication* (Oxford and Portland, Hart Publishing, 2009) at 262.

[23] See GDS Taylor, 'May Judicial Review Become a Backwater?' in Michael Taggart (ed), *Judicial Review of Administrative Action in the 1980s: Problems and Prospects* (Auckland, Oxford University Press, 1986) 152 at 173; Kenneth Keith, 'The Ombudsman and "Wrong" Decisions' (1971) 4 *New Zealand Universities Law Review* 361.

[24] See, eg, Accident Compensation Act 2001, s 155(2); Social Security Regulations 2018, reg 253(1).

[25] That is usually said of the Australian Administrative Tribunal: see Cane (n 22) at 145. See similarly, eg, concerning Benefits Review Committees: *Arbuthnot v Chief Executive of the Department of Work and Income* [2007] NZSC 55, [2008] 1 NZLR 13 at [19].

powers of the original decision-maker'.[26] Such provisions indicate that there is no onus on the appellant to show that the original decision was wrong, unlike in a general appeal.[27] This is even clearer where it is provided that the review body must determine the matter without regard to the first instance decision.[28] There may be provision for hearing further and new evidence, which makes it clear that developments since the time of the original decision are relevant. Sometimes, merits review is signalled simply by provision for substitutionary remedies: the review body may confirm, cancel or vary the impugned decision.[29]

In summary, the fullest form of merits review gives the reviewing body full power to consider all relevant law, facts and evidence at the time of its decision, and to reach what it considers to be the correct or preferable decision.

In contrast, the judicial avenues are generally limited to supervisory review of legality and procedure, and to remedies of quashing decisions and remitting them for reconsideration. That goes for both judicial review and appeals on questions of law, which are the usual form of appeal to the general courts in this context.[30]

In evaluating the advantages and disadvantages of merits review compared with limited supervisory review, two questions need to be addressed. First, whether merits review also deals with the types of complaint that are the focus of judicial review, about unlawful reasoning or unfair procedure, and whether it should. Second, why merits review is necessary for effective error correction, and how it relates to competing objectives and considerations.

(a) Does Merits Review Extend to Intervention on the Grounds of Judicial Review? Should it?

The nature of merits review is a greatly understudied topic.[31] A point that is particularly unsettled is whether merits review also deals with the types of complaints that are the focus of judicial review: complaints concerning unlawful reasoning (such as irrelevant considerations) or unfair procedure.[32] Whether it should do so is also unclear.

The Ombudsman's jurisdiction is broad and flexible: it clearly does extend to finding procedural or reasoning process flaws. The issue concerns the jurisdiction of merits review tribunals.

[26] See, eg, Social Security Act 2018, s 401; Trade Marks Act 2002, s 173(b); Tax Administration Act 1994, ss 135(1)(b) and s 138P(1)(b). On the last of these, see *Tannadyce* (n 12) at [50], [54], [55], [57].

[27] Cf *Austin* (n 18) at [4], [13].

[28] Films, Videos and Publications Classification Act 1993, s 52(2). Similarly, see Accident Compensation Act 2001, s 145(1)(a).

[29] See, eg, Social Security Regulations 2018, regs 247(2) and 254(1); Tax Administration Act 1994, ss 135(1)(a) and 138P(1)(b); Trade Marks Act 2002, s 173(a). For more explicit provision, see the Accident Compensation Act 2001: s 145(1)(b) expressly refers to the 'substantive merits', while substitutionary review is provided for in ss 145(3)–(4) and 161.

[30] See, eg, Social Security Act 2018, s 405; Accident Compensation Act 2001, s 162; Immigration Act 2009, s 245. For exceptions where general courts hear merits appeals from administrative authorities see, eg, Accident Compensation Act 2001, ss 149–161; Tax Administration Act 1994, Part 8A; Trade Marks Act 1953, s 27(6) and (7) and Trade Marks Act 2002, ss 170–173.

[31] One of the few instances of in-depth consideration is Cane, *Administrative Tribunals* (n 22), ch 5. Cane's take on merits review has, however, been controversial in Australia, as he acknowledges in the chapter.

[32] See ibid at 149–169.

The significance is that merits review may turn out not to be a comprehensive avenue of recourse if these types of error can only be addressed by judicial review. That further depends, however, on how we conceive of effective error correction, and that is itself a contestable question. Even if an inability to address these types of errors does represent a disadvantage, it may still be justified by competing considerations.

Let us consider first what counts as effective error correction. If an unlawful reasoning process or unfair procedure has led to a decision that is not sound in substance, merits review can substitute a better decision. Arguably that is sufficient for correcting the error. Perhaps, however, the review body should also record the reasoning or process error that contributed to the decision-maker reaching the wrong decision. Conversely, if the decision is sound in substance, on merits review it will usually be upheld even if it was affected by a reasoning or procedural error. In that case, that error may not be corrected at all. However, the review body could still declare that error in its decision.

The legal position on this question in Aotearoa New Zealand is not clear. Support can be found both for and against merits review bodies having power to address reasoning or procedural errors by any of these means, in addition to determining the best outcome. Of course, it may depend on the particular powers of each review body. The Supreme Court in *Tannadyce* interpreted the merits review provisions in the tax regime as including power to adjudicate on any claimed ground of error whatsoever, as well as to determine the correct outcome.[33] It did not elaborate on what this would look like.

Where reasoning process errors are concerned, what is clear is that most merits review bodies can reach the best decision for any reasons they consider relevant and appropriate – they do not need to rely on the original decision-maker's reasons.[34] Conversely, it is also clear that a successful applicant cannot appeal against the reasons for a decision.[35] The question is only whether, in an appeal by an unsuccessful party, a merits review body can, in addition to determining the best outcome, examine the original decision-maker's reasoning process and declare any errors it finds. *Tannadyce* seems to indicate that the answer, at least in some contexts, is yes.

Where procedural unfairness is concerned, the Court of Appeal in *Ramsay* appears to suggest in obiter that merits review bodies cannot always address this.[36] At least on some occasions, however, merits review bodies have recorded breaches of natural justice in their decisions. For instance, the Social Security Appeal Authority did so in a challenge to Benefits Review Committees (BRCs) adopting a practice of deciding some review applications on the papers and identifying their members only by pseudonyms. The purpose of this practice was to protect members from clients who were assessed as disruptive and potentially violent, but the Authority did not accept that this concern justified such an 'alarming' practice.[37]

[33] *Tannadyce* (n 12) at [54]–[57]. Perhaps indicating an opposite view is *Austin, Nichols* (n 18) at [5], commenting that a court hearing a general appeal is not required to pay explicit attention to the reasons of the body appealed from. This was, however, addressed to a different issue: the point was to reject any requirement of deference to those reasons.

[34] *Arbuthnot* (n 25) at [16]–[17].

[35] ibid at [25].

[36] See *Ramsay v Wellington District Court* [2006] NZAR 136 (CA) at [32]. It is not clear whether the doubts about the availability of a natural justice challenge relate to the District Court's merits review jurisdiction, or rather to appeals on questions of law at the next stage of the process.

[37] *An appeal against a decision of a Benefits Review Committee* [2015] NZSSAA 102 at [25]–[32].

What, then, should the position be? The ability to declare errors of reasoning or procedure is important at least in cases where such errors are likely to be repeated unless and until the tribunal declares them erroneous. One of the functions of appeals is to supervise the authority being appealed from (which may be a primary decision-maker or a first instance review body).[38] The problem with BRC members hiding behind pseudonyms is an extreme example of the problematic practices or policies that may creep in when there is a lack of legal supervision of public decision-making regimes. If this supervision could not be provided by merits review, then merits review arguably would not be a fully effective means of correcting errors.

A further question concerns remedies. The usual remedy granted by merits review tribunals is to substitute the decision that in their view should have been made: the correct or preferable decision. When, if ever, can and should they instead remit a decision to the original decision-maker – the usual remedy in judicial review? Some merits review tribunals are expressly provided with that option.[39] The question then is under what circumstances it is appropriate for them to deploy that option.

It could be used in response to reasoning or process errors. However, this would be unnecessary and inappropriate if the hearing and reasoning carried out by the merits review body has repaired and hence cured any procedural or reasoning process defect in the original decision.[40] Whether this is so may depend on the nature of the defect and on the procedures of the merits review body. The question was addressed by the Supreme Court in *H (SC 52/2018) v Refugee and Protection Officer*, albeit for a different purpose.[41] A merits appeal to a tribunal was available in that case. The Court held that such an appeal would not cure a fundamental breach of natural justice in the original decision.[42] This was at least in part because the first instance decision-making process included statutory safeguards that were missing from the tribunal's process.

In other contexts, however, lawful reasoning and procedure by the merits tribunal can cure the defect in the first instance decision.[43] In such cases, it is arguably inappropriate for that merits review tribunal to remit the decisions to the first instance decision-maker: determination of the substantive issue by the tribunal is a more expeditious way of arriving at the same outcome.[44]

(b) How Merits Review Relates to the Relevant Competing Objectives and Considerations

The second question is why merits review is crucial for the administrative justice objective of putting errors right, and how it relates to competing public interest objectives and constitutional considerations.

The administrative justice criterion of effectiveness at putting errors right requires at least one opportunity to have the merits reviewed in the context of most administrative

[38] Law Commission, *Tribunals* (n 10) at [8.2].

[39] See, eg, Social Security Regulations 2018, reg 254(3) and (4). Contrast, eg, Immigration Act 2009, s 198(3).

[40] Cane, *Administrative Tribunals* (n 22) at 150, 151. See also Taylor, *Judicial Review* (n 19) at [4.05].

[41] The issue was whether to give effect to a partial privative clause: see Ch 8.E.

[42] *H (SC 52/2018) v Refugee and Protection Officer* [2019] NZSC 13, [2019] 1 NZLR 433 at [43], [67]–[70], [74], [78].

[43] On curing generally, see *Nicholls v Registrar of the Court of Appeal* [1998] 2 NZLR 385 (CA) at 435–437.

[44] See *Tannadyce* (n 12) at [55]; *Ramsay* (n 36) at [31]. See also *Ortmann v United States of America* [2020] NZSC 120, [2020] 1 NZLR 475 at [546]–[547].

regimes.[45] Errors obviously do happen. They are especially likely in areas where there is a high volume of front-line decisions,[46] and where front-line decisions are made by a truncated process involving limited opportunity for exchange between the decision-maker and the person affected. Without a full opportunity to challenge such errors, individuals would have to live with unjust decisions and administrative regimes would fail to fully achieve their social purposes. Merits review is therefore important for administrative justice, both in the narrower individual sense and in the broader public interest sense.

The individual justice aspect is recognised and reflected in a number of sources. The Regulations Review Committee may raise concerns about delegated legislation on a number of grounds. One of these is that the delegated legislation unduly makes peoples' rights and liberties dependent on administrative decisions that are not subject to review on their merits by an independent tribunal.[47] A similar complaint is available under the European Convention on Human Rights: Article 6(1) provides a right to merits review in relation to many types of administrative decisions.[48]

Errors may still persist after one or two opportunities to revisit the merits. At that point, however, competing considerations become significant. The arguments for further instances of merits review tend to be outweighed by concerns about finality and about proportionate allocation of resources.[49] It must also be noted that each further review opportunity is also a further opportunity for error.

Turning to constitutional principles, there are potential separation of powers concerns about merits review tribunals, but these are sometimes overstated. In other jurisdictions, there have been extensive debates about whether such tribunals are judicial or administrative (executive) in nature.[50] If those two functions are seen as strictly separate and distinct, then merits review is an oxymoron: the exercise of public power is an executive or administrative function, while resolving disputes, including grievances against government, is a judicial function. Yet merits review can be both.

However, the strict separation of branches of government with distinct and mutually exclusive functions, as insisted on in some jurisdictions such as Australia, is not the version of the principle that operates in the UK or Aotearoa NZ.[51] The sharp dichotomy between functions is illusory – for instance, applying general norms to individual cases is both an executive and a judicial function.[52]

The substantive concern underlying separation of powers is to avoid concentrations of power and conflicts of interests that risk abuse of power, and to promote

[45] Law Commission, *Tribunals* (n 10) ch 8.

[46] Cane, *Administrative Tribunals* (n 22) at 179, 228.

[47] Standing Orders of the House of Representatives 2020, SO 327(2)(d).

[48] See *Tsfayo v United Kingdom* (2009) 48 EHRR 18; and more generally Harry Woolf and others, *De Smith's Judicial Review*, 8th edn (London, Sweet & Maxwell, 2018) at [8-049]–[8-051], [10-088]–[10-098].

[49] See Law Commission, *Tribunals* (n 10) at [8.4].

[50] Cane, *Administrative Tribunals* (n 22) ch 2 charts the history of the debate; ch 1 notes that in the UK, tribunals are increasingly treated as judicial, while in Australia, the Constitution requires them to be classified as administrative.

[51] See Law Commission, *Tribunals* (n 10) at [2.8], [2.14]. See also Ceri Warnock, 'Environment and the Law: The Normative Force of Context and Constitutional Challenges' (2020) 32 *Journal of Environmental Law* 365 at 385–86; Cane, *Administrative Tribunals* (n 22) at 13–14, 32.

[52] Cane ibid at 106–07.

integrity by appropriate constraints and checks on exercises of power.[53] Rather than presenting it as a constitutional puzzle, then, the problem with merits tribunals can be restated in terms of a choice of forms of accountability. On the one hand, since the decisions of merits review tribunals direct and shape the administration of the relevant regime, arguably they ought to be subject to bureaucratic supervision that feeds into political accountability. On the other hand, since they play an important role in holding authorities to account, arguably they ought to be independent from the authorities whose decisions they supervise. Independence goes to trustworthiness, one of the administrative justice criteria. Which of these two options is to prevail ultimately comes down to a contestable value judgement, but it also depends on the nature of the tribunal's jurisdiction.

For instance, a lack of political accountability matters most obviously where a merits tribunal has power to deal with the merits of general rules (either administrative guidelines or delegated legislation).[54] The NZ Environment Court, unusually, does have a merits review jurisdiction in relation to statutory instruments of a broad policy nature.[55] The lack of political accountability in that context has been considered problematic. It therefore calls for other appropriate checks and constraints, such as, in this case, procedures involving wide participation.[56] Most merits tribunals, such as the Social Security Appeal Authority, deal primarily with individual decisions. In that context, the need for and appropriateness of political accountability is questionable.

(2) Expertise or Experience

The next feature to consider is the expertise or experience offered by a remedial avenue, and how this is relevant to effective error correction. This section first outlines different types of expertise and experience and which remedial avenues offer these. It then explores reasons for and against having expert or specialist remedial avenues.

In Aotearoa NZ most non-judicial avenues are set up to ensure some form of specialised expertise or experience. The main exception are the Ombudsmen, whose jurisdiction is a generalist one. However, they do specialise in complaints against public administration. The judicial avenues for challenging administrative decisions, in contrast, are entirely generalist. They deal with all parts of the public administration. They also deal with all other types of disputes: there is no specialist administrative court.

Specialised expertise or experience is found in all review bodies that form part of a particular regime.[57] Internal review bodies have specialised experience by virtue of being internal, but special expertise or experience is also a feature of external tribunals such as the Social Security Appeal Authority or the Immigration and Protection

[53] Warnock 'Environment and the Law' (n 51) at 386; Cane ibid at 15, 32.

[54] Tribunals hearing complaints about individual decisions may also have to deal with complaints about general rules, but they only decide whether or to what extent the rule should apply in the individual case, or whether it is consistent with empowering legislation.

[55] Discussed by Warnock (n 51).

[56] See ibid at 379–88.

[57] See, generally, Law Commission, *Tribunals* (n 10), ch 4.

Tribunal. Given the specialised nature of such tribunals' jurisdictions, their members will receive training and build up expertise in that legal regime and experience with its practical operation.[58]

In addition, some review bodies include non-legal expert members. For instance, Medical Boards under the Social Security Act are composed entirely of medical practitioners and persons with qualifications or experience in vocational training and rehabilitation.[59] When hearing Accident Compensation appeals, a District Court Judge may appoint an 'assessor' with relevant expert knowledge if the appeal involves 'matters of a professional, technical or specialised nature'. The Assessor sits with the Court as extra member, but the Judge alone determines the appeal.[60]

There is also sometimes an element of interest representation. In cases dealing with refugee status, the Immigration and Protection Tribunal includes a representative of the United Nations High Commissioner for Refugees as an ex officio member.[61] Members of the Film and Literature Board of Review are chosen by several Ministers, including the Minister for Women's Affairs, having regard to ensuring that the Board includes 'persons with knowledge of, or experience in, the different aspects of matters likely to come before the Board'.[62]

An example of explicit interest representation used to be found in social security tribunals in the United Kingdom. National insurance tribunals, for instance, included an employers' representative and an employees' representative alongside a legally qualified chairperson.[63] Subsequently, however, the nature of the interests represented was rendered much more obscure by appointing them from a single list of persons with 'knowledge or experience of the conditions in the area' and 'representative of persons working or living in the area'.[64]

The latter model appears to have been copied for Benefits Review Committees in New Zealand. Alongside two Ministry employees, each Committee includes a person appointed 'to represent … the community's interests'.[65] The community's interests, however, include the competing interests of containing public expenditure and meeting the needs of social security beneficiaries. It is not clear what interest is meant to be represented. Rather than interest representation, the purpose of such a provision may be better understood as providing a measure of independence from the Ministry and promoting informality and hence accessibility.[66]

[58] For instance, members of the Social Security Appeal Authority are not required to have any particular qualifications (see Social Security Act, s 401 and sch 8), but they do acquire specialist experience in the social security regime.

[59] Social Security Act 2018, sch 9, cl 1(2).

[60] Accident Compensation Act 2001, ss 157–158.

[61] Immigration Act 2009, s 219(1)(c).

[62] Films, Videos and Publications Classification Act 1993, s 93(2) and (5).

[63] For another example, see the Social Security and Child Support (Decisions and Appeals) Regulations 1999 (SI 1999/001) (UK), regs 1 and 36(6) and sch 2, para 5: disability appeal tribunals included a member experienced in the needs of disabled persons, either in a professional or voluntary capacity or due to personal experience.

[64] See Nick Wikeley and Richard Young, 'The Marginalisation of Lay Members in Social Security Appeal Tribunals' (1992) 14 *Journal of Social Welfare and Family Law* 127 at 132–33.

[65] Social Security Act 2018, sch 7, cl 2.

[66] See Kathleen Bell, 'Social Security Tribunals – A General Perspective' (1982) 33 *Northern Ireland Legal Quarterly* 132 at 21–23.

Legal qualifications are a further type of expertise. Some remedial bodies do not require such qualifications at all. External appeal or review bodies do usually require at least one legally qualified member,[67] and the chair or president usually must be legally qualified.[68]

Turning to the advantages and disadvantages of expertise, the chief advantage of expertise or experience is that it equips a tribunal to handle merits review, thus enabling effective error correction. Expert or experienced tribunal members are better placed to determine the correct or preferable decision in the circumstances.[69] They are less likely to misunderstand the regime or its social goals and the context in which it operates, or to be misled by questionable arguments or evidence.[70] In addition to producing better decisions, specialised experience also makes a tribunal more efficient, as it does not need time to familiarise itself with the regime before it can address the issues arising.[71]

This advantage is particularly marked for tribunals that are expected to adopt an 'enabling' approach to assist unrepresented applicants. This is the case for many administrative tribunals, as we will see.[72] Expertise or specialised experience equips the tribunal to more readily identify relevant law and evidence for itself, and therefore to assist claimants in that regard.[73] By facilitating such an enabling approach without compromising the quality of decision, expertise or experience also contributes indirectly to accessibility.

The most commonly noted disadvantage is that expert or specialised tribunals can be less independent.[74] This can come about in several ways. One is that appointment of expert members may be facilitated by involving the authority whose decisions they review.[75] Moreover, some specialist tribunals are administered by those authorities, and ease of interaction with that authority may assist tribunal members in building and maintaining their expertise.[76] Further, expert members have sometimes held dual roles, being engaged in other cases as expert advisers to the respondent authority.[77] Finally, even where such institutional links are avoided, there may be a risk of 'agency

[67] A remarkable exception is the Social Security Appeal Authority: Social Security Act 2018, sch 8, cl 1. However, in practice, the chairperson and deputy chairperson have, for many years, been lawyers, and it has been reported that the Ministry of Social Development's policy specifies this as highly desirable: Kim Morton et al, *Access to Justice for Beneficiaries: A Community Law Response* (Community Law, Canterbury, 2014) at 110.

[68] For example, Films, Videos and Publications Classification Act 1993, s 93(4).

[69] See, generally, Stephen H Legomsky, *Specialized Justice* (Oxford, Clarendon Press, 1990) at 8–13.

[70] This point is distinct from an expectation that specialist tribunals will be more *committed* to the social goals than the general courts – that is a more contingent effect.

[71] Legomsky (n 69) at 17. Query the doubts about this in Cane (n 22) at 125.

[72] See Part C(1) below.

[73] See Samantha Green and Lorne Sossin, 'Administrative Justice and Innovation: Beyond the Adversarial/Inquisitorial Dichotomy' in LA Jacobs and S Baglay (eds), *The Nature of Inquisitorial Processes in Administrative Regimes: Global Perspectives* (Farnham, Surrey, Ashgate, 2013) 71 at 73, 90–91.

[74] ibid at 108. Note, however, that some NZ cases that make this point are discussing a level of predetermination in tribunals with a policy function, such as the Planning Tribunal: see, eg, *Turner v Allison* [1971] NZLR 833 (CA) at 843, 849.

[75] Green and Sossin (n 73) at 99.

[76] Law Commission, *Tribunals* (n 10) at [5.23]–[5.24].

[77] In *Gillies v Secretary of State for Work and Pensions* [2006] UKHL 2, [2006] 1 WLR 781 at [17]–[27], [30]–[33], [36]–[46], a bias challenge on that ground was dismissed. It is at least arguable that greater independence might have been desirable.

capture': a specialist tribunal that deals solely with decisions of one particular agency may develop too close a relationship with that agency.[78]

Where independence is diminished by such features, trustworthiness is affected. That is another administrative justice criterion. The relevance of independence to this criterion is further discussed below. Lack of independence also raises constitutional concerns about the separation of powers and the rule of law: concerns about accountability and checks and balances.[79] However, expertise and specialisation can still be achieved without most of these features that compromise independence. Loss of independence is therefore not a necessary corollary.

A further potential disadvantage is the fragmentation of the administrative justice system that results from a proliferation of specialist tribunals. This jungle[80] can make it difficult for claimants to access review and appeal rights. However, this could be addressed by providing navigational assistance at the entry point.[81]

The concern may also be about a lack of coherent development of general principles.[82] This can be addressed by integrating specialist tribunals into an overall system that includes appeals on questions of law to generalist courts or tribunals.[83] Such proposals have not yet been actioned in Aotearoa NZ, although most regimes include an appeal to the High Court on questions of law.

In any event, not everyone considers the development of pockets of 'local law' to be a disadvantage.[84] A measure of pluralism is welcomed by scholars who favour a 'functional' approach to administrative law, which recognises the different goals served and the different contexts of different administrative regimes.[85]

(3) Binding Rulings or Only Recommendations

Turning finally to the power to make binding rulings, this may seem to be a basic requirement for effectively putting errors right. Nearly all avenues do involve this power. There are, however, exceptions: notably, both the Ombudsmen and the Waitangi Tribunal have power only to make recommendations. At least in the case of the Ombudsman, the effect is not as purely disadvantageous as it might first appear.

[78] Taylor, 'May Judicial Review Become a Backwater?' (n 23) at 168–69.

[79] This was Dicey's reason for insisting on general courts rather than specialist tribunals for controlling exercises of public power: Albert V Dicey, *Introduction to the Law of the Constitution* 8th edn (London, Macmillan and Co) (first published 1885) at 198.

[80] Carol Harlow and Richard Rawlings, *Law and Administration*, 3rd edn (Cambridge, Cambridge University Press, 2009) ch 10 title (the word has been dropped in the current 4th edn).

[81] Pirini (n 6) at 257, 259–60 proposes a one-stop-shop. A power to refer applicants on to the appropriate avenue without further application could be another solution: Taylor, 'Backwater' (n 23) at 176–77.

[82] *R (Cart) v Upper Tribunal (Public Law Project Intervening)* [2011] UKSC 28, [2012] 1 AC 663 at [42]–[44] expressed a concern about specialist tribunals developing 'local law'.

[83] See, eg, the UK system under the Tribunals, Courts and Enforcement Act 2007, broadly following the recommendations of *Tribunals for Users: One System, One Service. Report of the Review of Tribunals chaired by Sir Andrew Leggatt* (March 2001) (Leggatt Report).

[84] See generally Robin Creyke, 'Australian Tribunals: Impact of Amalgamation' (2020) 26 *Australian Journal of Administrative Law* 206.

[85] See, eg, Harry W Arthurs, 'Rethinking Administrative Law: A Slightly Dicey Business' (1979) 17 *Osgoode Hall Law Journal* 1, esp at 29, 32–33, 41. See more generally ch 2.

Although the Ombudsmen lack power to make binding rulings, there is a strong expectation that their recommendations will be accepted, and a consistent practice of doing so. In fact, the majority of complaints that are found to have substance are resolved without formal recommendations.[86] This is largely due to the high standing of the Ombudsmen. Ultimately, they also have the significant sanction of public exposure at their disposal. If they are not satisfied with an agency's response, they may draw the attention of Parliament and the public to the matter.[87]

The success of Ombudsmen's interventions is also helped by their approach of working collaboratively with the government agencies concerned. This approach is actually facilitated in part by the very flexibility inherent in their power being recommendatory.[88] The ability to resolve matters informally also advances speed and accessibility. However, the collaborative style does also carry a risk that scrutiny may be compromised.[89]

Finally, the recommendatory nature of the jurisdiction also renders a wider range of remedies appropriate. For instance, apologies are perhaps more appropriately recommended than ordered. Damages awards against public authorities relating to the discharge of discretionary functions can potentially raise justiciability concerns when ordered by the courts;[90] a non-binding recommendation, in contrast, leaves the final responsibility for the resource allocation with the authority concerned. The Ombudsman also may call for changes to primary legislation;[91] thanks to the recommendatory nature of the jurisdiction, Parliamentary sovereignty is not infringed by this.

(4) Speed

As the old adage has it, justice delayed is justice denied. In terms of the objectives and criteria of administrative justice, delay in disposing of a successful challenge diminishes the effectiveness of putting the error right: the person has had to wait too long for the favourable outcome and, in some contexts, there can be irreversible loss. Delay in holding hearings furthermore impairs accessibility. Speed is therefore relevant to two of the criteria of administrative justice. Alternative avenues are usually intended

[86] Both points are confirmed by several Annual Reports. For acceptance of almost all recommendations see, for instance, Office of the Ombudsmen, *Report of the Ombudsmen for the year ended 30 June 2007* [2007] AJHR A.3 at 22, and similarly the Reports for 2006 and 2010. Office of the Ombudsmen, *Report of the Ombudsmen for the year ended 30 June 2008* [2008] AJHR A.3 at 24 notes that one single recommendation had not yet been fully accepted. The more recent reports do not appear to report on this point. All reports show that the majority of complaints that were found to have substance were resolved without formal recommendations. See also Taylor, 'Backwater' (n 23) at 173: in the first 23 years up to 1986, only seven of a total of 2,760 formal recommendations were rejected.

[87] Ombudsmen Act 1975, ss 22(4) and 23.

[88] See Mai Chen, 'New Zealand's Ombudsman Legislation: The Need for Amendments After Almost 50 Years' (2010) 41 *Victoria University of Wellington Law Review* 723 at 731–39.

[89] See *Royal Commission into the Robodebt Scheme: Report Volume 1* (Commonwealth of Australia, 2022) at 583–85, 599.

[90] See Ch 12.C.(3)(c).

[91] Ombudsmen Act 1975, ss 22(1)(b) and 22(3)(e).

to have advantages over judicial review in this regard, but those advantages are not always realised in practice.

Judicial review is supposed to be relatively simple and prompt,[92] in comparison with other litigation, thanks to procedural features such as receiving evidence ordinarily by affidavit.[93] But the formality of High Court proceedings and the complexity of the law still make it a lengthy process in most cases.

One of the purposes of more informal procedures in non-judicial alternative avenues is to promote speedier resolution than in the courts. However, this can be achieved only if these avenues are adequately resourced.[94] Furthermore, non-judicial procedures are often investigative in nature, to aid accessibility.[95] That calls for additional resources: the more investigative the procedures, the more impossible it is for an avenue to function effectively and with due despatch unless it has the required resources. Regrettably, unacceptable delays, apparently due at least in part to lack of resourcing, are common in some of our alternative remedial avenues.[96]

In addition to proper resourcing, remedial avenues need to adopt systems that will facilitate effective use of their resources and hence speedy resolutions.[97] This can be promoted by the legislative design of those avenues, but also by appropriate monitoring and incentives.[98] Arguably time limits for resolution of complaints should be a feature of most avenues, but these are often absent.[99] The Accident Compensation Act 2001 does impose a time limit for scheduling a hearing, which is enforced by deeming a favourable decision to have been issued if that time is exceeded.[100] Such a provision would be beneficial in other regimes. A time limit for issuing a decision after hearing could also be imposed and enforced in the same way.

One way of promoting speedy resolution of complaints or challenges is to provide early informal interventions. These can take the form of an initial internal review,[101] early neutral evaluation,[102] or both.[103] Such informal interventions can resolve a significant proportion of complaints quickly and informally.

To serve the purpose of speedy resolution, however, these initial procedures must offer truly informal resolution.[104] They should ideally require no formal application

[92] See, eg, *Attorney-General v Dotcom* [2013] NZCA 43, [2013] 2 NZLR 213 at [39]–[40].

[93] See *Roussel Uclaf Australia Pty Ltd v Pharmaceutical Management Agency Ltd* [1997] 1 NZLR 650 at 656–658.

[94] See, eg, Law Commission, *Tribunals* (n 10) at [9.10], [9.11], [9.16], [9.17].

[95] Further discussed below, in Part C of this chapter.

[96] For instance, I have seen instances where Benefits Review Committees under the Social Security Act 2018 took six months to schedule hearings for challenges to decisions about temporary hardship support. For delays in ACC reviews, see Miriam R Dean, *Independent Review of the Acclaim Otago (Inc) July 2015 Report into Accident Compensation Dispute Resolution Processes* (May 2016) at 27.

[97] See, eg, Leggatt Report (n 83) at [8.4]–[8.6] on case management in tribunals.

[98] Law Commission, *Tribunals* (n 10) at [9.7] calls for monitoring and reporting obligations.

[99] Eg there are no legislated timeframes for Benefits Review Committee or Social Security Appeal Authority hearings.

[100] Accident Compensation Act 2001, s 146.

[101] See Law Commission, *Tribunals* (n 10) at [9.29]–[9.34]; Leggatt Report (n 83) at [9.6]–[9.8].

[102] Michael Adler, 'Tribunal Reform: Proportionate Dispute Resolution and the Pursuit of Administrative Justice' (2006) 69 *Modern Law Review* 958 at 976–77.

[103] An offer of mediation is another option – that is the practice adopted by ACC.

[104] Also, there should be no more than one level of internal review: Law Commission, *Tribunals* (n 10) at [9.33].

but rather should be conducted in response to an applicant raising concerns about a decision, or as a preliminary procedure when an applicant files an appeal with an external tribunal. It may also be advantageous if they do not involve any type of oral hearing, although that can be argued either way.

This type of informal intervention is available without any special statutory authority: all statutory powers can be exercised again to correct an error or omission in an earlier exercise.[105] Examples are found in the social security and ACC regimes: informal internal reviews are carried out as a preliminary procedure whenever a formal review application is filed.[106]

However, both regimes additionally include internal review tribunals created by statute that do not operate in such a beneficial fashion. The legislated first instance review by a BRC is essentially internal[107] and fairly informal. However, it requires complainants to apply for it,[108] the application very rarely succeeds unless the complainant attends a hearing or sends a representative,[109] and it can involve very significant delays. Similar points can be made about first instance reviews under the Accident Compensation Act 2001.[110]

Where recourse to such a formalised internal procedure is made a compulsory step before accessing external review, as is the case with BRCs[111] and ACC reviews,[112] the effect is the opposite of promoting speedy resolution. Complainants are required to invest time and effort in this internal review (which has low success rates),[113] delaying access to a more trustworthy external tribunal. If such compulsory internal review avenues are nevertheless to be used, enforceable time limits are especially important.

C. Accessibility

The main features that may make for a good avenue on the criterion of accessibility are (1) informal and enabling procedure, (2) adequate funding and resources, and (3) public awareness of the remedial avenue. Speed, discussed under the previous heading, is also relevant here.

[105] Legislation Act 2019, s 46.

[106] See 'Reviews and Appeals' in the online *Manuals and Procedures*, available at www.workandincome.got.nz/map/Income-support/core-policy. On ACC, see the Dean report (n 96) at 9, 34.

[107] On its lack of independence, see below at n 176.

[108] Social Security Act 2018, s 391.

[109] Morton, *Access to Justice* (n 67) at 98.

[110] Accident Compensation Act 2001, ss 134–135; and see Acclaim Otago (Inc), *Understanding the Problem: An Analysis of ACC Appeals Processes to Identify Barriers to Access to Justice for Injured New Zealanders* (9 July 2015) at [144].

[111] Social Security Act 2018, s 395.

[112] Accident Compensation Act 2001, ss 133(5) and 149.

[113] In social security matters, higher success rates have been reported for the informal administrative review (around one-third) than for the Benefits Review Committee hearing that follows (around 10%): Morton, *Access to Justice* (n 67) at 86, 99 (these percentages are for complete success; a further proportion of cases result in the decision being varied at both stages).

There is also an issue about online systems employed by remedial avenues. These can promote accessibility by reducing the effort required for finding information or engaging with the tribunal. However, where online systems replace in-person services, this compromises access for applicants who lack the skills or technology to engage online.

Judicial review scores poorly on most of these aspects of accessibility, with the exception of public awareness. Non-judicial avenues have the potential to offer much greater accessibility than courts, and that is one of the main reasons for establishing them.[114] However, that potential is not always realised in practice. Alongside lacking political will, the reasons for this also include disagreement on priorities and trade-offs between competing objectives.

(1) Informal Procedure and Departures from the Adversarial Model

Informality can take the form of a departure from the adversarial procedure used in the courts. Adversarial procedure involves two parties competing before a neutral umpire. Alternatives to the adversarial model are variously described as inquisitorial, investigative, active, and enabling.[115] These labels lack a clear and settled meaning. One important aspect of a less adversarial procedure is relaxation of rules of evidence: helpful material may be put in evidence without strict rules. Informality can also mean a lack of formal protocols as to attire, venue, language and other conduct, and a lack of complex rules governing the documents to be filed and the order of proceedings.

Judicial review procedure is formal and adversarial. The initiative is with the parties: it is their responsibility to bring evidence before the court, test the evidence brought by the other side, identify the relevant law and put forward arguments as to how it applies. The court then assesses that evidence and those arguments to determine the dispute. Strict and formal procedural rules apply. There are strict limits on admissible evidence. The formality of proceedings also serves to emphasise the court's independence and authority. As a result, legal representation is almost indispensable to have prospects of success, and adequate funding for this is lacking.[116]

The procedure of the Ombudsmen, in contrast, is at the most informal end of the spectrum. There are no hearings, and hence no formalities. Instead, the Ombudsmen carry out an investigation. Rather than acting as a neutral umpire, they take the initiative in seeking answers to complaints.

Most tribunals are also provided with a measure of procedural flexibility.[117] Some departure from the adversarial model is a common feature. For instance, they may

[114] See Law Commission, *Tribunals* (n 10) at [2.27]–[2.28], [2.41]–[2.43], [3.1]–[3.2]; *Chief Executive of the Ministry of Social Development v Genet* [2016] NZHC 2541 at [18]–[19], [26].

[115] See, eg, Law Commission, *Tribunals* (n 10) at [6.16]–[6.20]; Green and Sossin (n 73) 71; N Bedford and R Creyke, *Inquisitorial Processes in Australian Tribunals* (The Australasian Institute of Judicial Administration, 2006).

[116] Justice Helen Winkelmann, 'Access to Justice – Who Needs Lawyers?' (2014) 13 *Otago Law Review* 229 at 235–39.

[117] See Law Commission, *Tribunals* (n 10) at [6.1]–[6.22].

admit helpful material, regardless of whether it would be admissible as evidence in a court of law.[118]

Their procedures often include an element of enabling approach – in other words, providing some assistance to applicants or appellants in making their case.[119] A measure of investigative or enabling initiative is commonly adopted by tribunals that are empowered to regulate their own procedure;[120] some tribunals are expressly required or empowered to take such approaches.[121] They will usually explain the process to applicants and answer questions about it.[122] They may take an active part in identifying issues and missing evidence;[123] they will usually be ready to identify relevant law that may have been missed by the parties; some will make their own factual enquiries; and they may engage in questioning the parties and witnesses. Some tribunals are specifically empowered to take some of these steps, such as to seek further information.[124] Conversely, the original decision-making authority is often under an obligation to assist the tribunal with information.[125] Beyond informal procedures, some tribunals are also required to focus on the substantive merits and to disregard legal technicalities.[126]

The advantages of these types of informal, non-adversarial procedures include that they may render legal or other representation less necessary. That, in turn, would be one way of dealing with the cost barrier to accessibility. It might also serve the public interest in reducing demands on public resources and might be part of proportionate dispute resolution.

However, there are concerns that, in many contexts, even with an enabling approach, unrepresented complainants do not tend to fare well.[127] Lack of representation may thus compromise the achievements of the other two administrative justice criteria: effective error correction and trustworthiness. We will return to this under the trustworthiness heading.

A common objection to an enabling or investigative approach is that it threatens the neutrality and impartiality that is essential for an adjudicative body.[128] When

[118] See, eg, Social Security Regulations 2018, reg 253(6); Accident Compensation Act 2001 ss 141(4) and 156(1).

[119] For details of the enabling model, see, eg, Green and Sossin (n 73) at 73, 83–84; Leggatt Report (n 83) at [7.5].

[120] For examples of such a power, see Immigration Act 2009, s 222(4); Social Security Act 2018, s 403(1) and sch 8, cl 10D.

[121] See, eg, Immigration Act 2009, s 218(2); Accident Compensation Act 2001, s 140(e). Investigative powers can also be achieved by providing that the Commissions of Inquiry Act 2008 applies (see, eg, Social Security Act 2018, sch 8, cl 12): s 4C of that Act provides such powers.

[122] The Social Security Appeal Authority (SSAA) provides an opportunity for this by way of a pre-hearing telephone conference: see 'Overview – Hearing Process', available for download under 'What happens next' from the 'Social Security' section of the Ministry of Justice Tribunals website. Available at: www.justice.govt.nz/tribunals/social-security-appeal-authority.

[123] In the SSAA, the pre-hearing telephone conference is also used for this: ibid.

[124] See, eg, Immigration Act 2009, ss 228–229.

[125] See, eg, ibid; Social Security Regulations 2018, reg 249.

[126] See, eg, the Human Rights Review Tribunal: Human Rights Act 1993, s 105.

[127] See, eg Morton, *Access to Justice* (n 67) at 100–01, 104, 106, 113–15, 117; Ken MacKinnon, 'Redefining the Facts – Marginalising the Claimant?' in Robin Creyke (ed), *Tribunals in the Common Law World* (Annandale, NSW, The Federation Press, 2008) at 122.

[128] See, eg, Adrian Zuckerman, 'No Justice Without Lawyers – The Myth of an Inquisitorial Solution' (2014) 33 *Civil Justice Quarterly* 355 at 357–63; Winkelmann, 'Access to Justice' (n 116) at 237–38, 241 (the

raised by the respondent authority, this cannot usually be a valid objection. At least in contexts such as social security and ACC, there is an integral imbalance of power[129] and a resulting need for levelling the playing field.[130] Courts in Aotearoa NZ have acknowledged the appropriateness of departures from the adversarial model in such contexts.[131] However, complainants may have a valid concern about trustworthiness where an enabling approach is relied on to replace legal representation. As already noted, we will return to the issue of representation under that heading.

(2) Cost and Resourcing

Cost is a further accessibility issue on which alternative avenues have at least potential advantages over judicial ones. The cost of judicial review includes court fees that start from around $2,700 for a simple one-day hearing.[132] These can be waived on grounds of hardship, but only for those on truly low incomes.[133] Legal representation is likely to add $20,000 to $30,000 in a simple case, and vastly more in complex cases.[134] While legal aid is available for this, it is limited. The fixed rates of aid are often considered inadequate to cover the work required; and eligibility is so limited that many who cannot afford legal representation are nevertheless excluded.[135] Furthermore, civil legal aid is paid as a loan that must normally be repaid.[136] While exceptions are again available on grounds of serious financial hardship,[137] anecdotally it appears that awareness of these exceptions is limited.

In the absence of legal aid, the only assistance with covering legal fees for judicial review claimants is an award of costs.[138] This will usually follow a successful claim. However, awards only cover a proportion of the actual costs. More importantly, all depends on success. If the claim fails, the usual outcome is an award of costs against the claimant, further adding to the cost of the proceeding. Exceptions are made only rarely when the court is satisfied that there was a strong public interest in bringing the case. The risk of an adverse costs award significantly adds to the cost barrier.

first passage relates to courts, but in the later passage the comments are said to apply also to tribunals with inquisitorial approaches).

[129] See Law Commission, *Tribunals* (n 10) at [6.16].

[130] Green and Sossin (n 73) at 92.

[131] See, eg, *Genet* (114) at [14]–[16]. See also *Claydon v Attorney-General* [2004] NZAR 16 (CA) at [66] (concerning the employment tribunal).

[132] See High Court Fees Regulations 2013, sch 1. Winkelmann, 'Access to Justice' (n 116) at 233 calculates fees at $6,700 for a straight-forward one-day proceeding, but fees are lower for judicial review proceedings.

[133] High Court Fees Regulations 2013, regs 18–19.

[134] Up-to-date published information on this is hard to find; this estimate is based on a personal communication from a practising lawyer.

[135] Winkelmann, 'Access to Justice' (n 116) at 234; Bridgette Toy-Cronin, 'Keeping Up Appearances: Accessing New Zealand's Civil Courts as a Litigant in Person' (PhD, University of Otago 2015) at 88–91, 101–02. For the thresholds, see the Legal Services Regulations 2011, reg 5. Both the eligibility and the rates were increased in 2022 but remain low.

[136] Legal Services Act 2011, ss 18 and 21. Interest is payable on unpaid legal aid debts under s 40, although there was a plan to repeal this.

[137] Legal Services Act 2011, ss 42–43.

[138] High Court Rules, r 14.2(1)(a) and (d), r 14.7(e).

Reducing cost barriers to accessibility is one of the purposes of alternative remedial avenues. Cost can be addressed directly by public funding.[139] Unlike courts, the Ombudsmen and some tribunals do not charge fees. The Ombudsmen are allocated funding from Parliament to cover salaries and administrative expenses.[140] Tribunals may be funded by the Ministry of Justice, by the Crown,[141] or by the respondent authority.[142] There are also provisions in some regimes requiring a respondent authority to cover the expenses of the applicant's attendance at a hearing, regardless of outcome.[143]

To the extent that representation is considered necessary, public funding for it takes a variety of forms. One is legal aid.[144] This is sometimes available for legal representation in tribunals and also for pre-hearing legal advice. As already noted civil legal aid is usually a repayable loan, but the debt can be waived on grounds of financial hardship. Community Law Centres are directly funded to provide pre-hearing advice, but generally not to offer representation.[145] Lay advocates are permitted in some tribunals,[146] and can always be used for pre-hearing advice. Public funding is sometimes available for organisations offering lay advocacy, but it is very limited.[147]

Rules for the award of costs can also be adjusted to help address cost barriers. In some tribunals, for instance, costs may be awarded even to unsuccessful complainants, and good faith complainants are protected against adverse cost awards.[148] Costs awards have also been made available for lay advocates providing representation or pre-hearing advice, even where they otherwise offer their services for free.[149]

There is little doubt that funding advocacy and advice promotes administrative justice. The difficulty is simply that such funding is very limited. This reflects the competing public interest in containing the cost of redress systems, and the lack of political will to prioritise the needs of vulnerable groups who lack a strong voice.

(3) Public Awareness and Understanding of Avenues of Redress

The best remedial avenues will be of little use if people aggrieved at decisions are not aware of them, what they do and how to access them. This is the one aspect of accessibility where the judicial avenues currently have an advantage. Most people know that grievances about government can be taken to court. However, only limited accessibility

[139] See generally Law Commission, *Tribunals* (n 10) at [3.5]–[3.10], [3.20]–[3.21], [7.37]–[7.41], table 2.

[140] Ombudsmen Act 1975, s 31.

[141] See, eg, the Social Security Appeal Authority: see Social Security Act 2018, sch 8, cll 6–7.

[142] See, eg, ACC reviewers: Accident Compensation Act, s 137.

[143] See, eg, Social Security Regulations 2018, reg 251.

[144] Legal Services Act 2011, ss 7(1)(e)(v), (g), (i)–(j), 7(5)(f)–(g), 12(1), 18, 21, 42–43.

[145] According to Morton, *Access to Justice* (n 67), the Ministry of Justice in 2013 reduced funding for legal representation, preferring a focus on early resolution. More recent budgets have included funding for a pro bono clearing house, available at https://tearature.co.nz/about/.

[146] See, eg, Social Security Regulations 2018, reg 252(b) (for appeals to the SSAA); Accident Compensation Act 2001, s 142 (for first instance reviews).

[147] On ACC, see Dean report (n 96) at 54–55. For social security, see Morton, *Access to Justice* (n 67) at 143; Law Commission, *Tribunals* (n 10) at [6.39]. The total funding available through the CSF is $300,000 (excl GST) per year: MSD answer to question under the Official Information Act 1982, dated 11 July 2022.

[148] See, eg, Social Security Regulations 2018, reg 255(2); Accident Compensation Act 2001, s 148(2).

[149] *Genet* (n 114).

follows from that: most people do not know enough about courts or the law to access courts effectively without a lawyer.

Tribunals tend to be less well known. Much could be done to improve public awareness and understanding of them.[150] Awareness of the Ombudsman similarly could be improved at least among some groups.[151]

There needs to be a duty on public authorities to advise applicants of their review and appeal rights.[152] Some legislation does impose such duties, but there are significant gaps.[153] In addition, the Ombudsman and the various tribunals need to publish guides on how to access them, and there is room for improvement in that regard. A further proposal, already touched on, is to tame the confusing 'jungle' of different avenues of redress.

Arguably, it is also necessary to go beyond providing written information. Kathleen Bell's study of social security tribunals in the UK in the 1970s found that many claimants struggled with the written information provided, and would have been greatly assisted if they had the opportunity to ask questions or seek advice.[154] An example of doing this, albeit at a fairly late stage of the process, is the Social Security Appeals Authority's practice of scheduling a pre-hearing telephone conference at which questions can be answered.[155]

Finally, it is important that all tribunals have a system for selecting and publishing their significant decisions. Claimants and their advocates need to be able to look up what they can expect of a tribunal. Again, there are significant gaps in this regard.

D. Trustworthiness

The trustworthiness of an avenue of recourse may be assessed at least partly in terms of its compliance with the administrative law principles of natural justice or procedural fairness: (1) its independence and impartiality, and (2) whether it affords complainants a fair hearing in the circumstances.

[150] See Law Commission, *Tribunals* (n 10) at [3.11]–[3.13], [3.18], [3.22]–[3.25]; Morton, *Access to Justice* (n 67) at 60–61.

[151] A nationwide survey in 2012 found that while nearly 70% of the public were aware of the Ombudsmen, this dropped to 22% for those under 30: Office of the Ombudsmen, *Report of the Ombudsmen for the year ended 30 June 2012* [2012] AJHR A3 at 65.

[152] Law Commission, *Tribunals* (n 10) at [3.12]. Though notification by the primary decision-maker may be perceived as casting doubt on the independence of the review body: see, eg, a quote in Gráinne McKeever, 'A Ladder of Legal Participation for Tribunal Users' [2013] *Public Law* 575 at 585.

[153] For example, the Social Security Act 2018 imposes such a duty only in relation to some specific types of decisions: see ss 106, 252(2)(h). It is, however, MSD's usual practice to include such advice in all decision letters: Māmari Stephens, *Social Security and Welfare Law in Aotearoa New Zealand* (Wellington, Thomson Reuters, 2019) at 391.

[154] Kathleen Bell et al, 'National Insurance Local Tribunals: A Research Study – Part II' (1975) 4 *Journal of Social Policy* 1 at 2–4.

[155] See 'Overview – Hearing Process', available for download under 'What happens next' from the 'Social Security' section of the Ministry of Justice website for Tribunals,. available at www.justice.govt.nz/tribunals/social-security-appeal-authority.

This is the one criterion on which judicial avenues score highly, at least in theory. Their crucial feature in this regard is judges' independence from executive government and administrative authorities. In addition, court procedures are also designed to afford a claimant a scrupulously fair hearing, in accordance with the principles of natural justice.

The difficulty for the alternative avenues is that features designed to promote accessibility and effectiveness at putting errors right can compromise independence and other aspects of natural justice. There is much room for debate as to the optimal compromise.

In striking this balance, it is important to remember that the administrative law principles of procedural fairness are highly flexible and context sensitive.[156] The perceived tensions with other administrative justice features are unnecessarily exaggerated if we start from an assumption that all tribunals must adopt procedures modelled on courts.

(1) Independence

Concerns about independence are among the main issues with tribunals.[157] For courts, in contrast, independence is one of their main strengths. Judicial independence is assured by non-political appointments, security of tenure – judges can be removed from office before the compulsory retirement age only for misconduct or incapacity, and only by Parliament – and guaranteed salary,[158] and judicial immunity from suit.[159] The qualification is that judges are part of an elite and tend to be from privileged backgrounds, which may affect the perception of their impartiality and hence their trustworthiness in the eyes of vulnerable litigants from disadvantaged or minority backgrounds.[160]

The most independent among the non-judicial avenues are the Ombudsmen. They are appointed by the Governor-General and are designated officers of Parliament, thus avoiding any suggestion of accountability to executive government.[161] However, even here concerns have been raised. Parliament is, of course, to a large extent controlled by the executive in our system. Furthermore, Ombudsmen are appointed for a fixed term with the possibility of renewal. They may perhaps worry about being denied renewal should they perform their role too assertively; this was allegedly behind the non-renewal of Nadja Tollemache's appointment in 1992.[162] A separate potential

[156] *Daganayasi v Minster of Immigration* [1980] 2 NZLR 130 (CA) at 140–41; *Drew v Attorney-General* [2002] 2 NZLR 58 (CA). See ch 4.

[157] See, eg, Ron Ellis, *Unjust by Design: Canada's Administrative Justice System* (Vancouver, UBC Press, 2013); Matthew Groves and Greg Weeks, 'Tribunal Justice and Politics in Australia: The Rise and Fall of the Administrative Appeals Tribunal' (2023) 97 *Australian Law Journal* 278.

[158] Constitution Act 1986, ss 23 and 24.

[159] *Gazley v Lord Cooke of Thorndon* [1999] 2 NZLR 668 (CA); *Attorney-General v Chapman* [2011] NZSC 110, [2012] 1 NZLR 462.

[160] See Dame Helen Winkelmann, 'What Right Do We Have? Securing Judicial Legitimacy in Changing Times' [2020] *New Zealand Law Review* 175 at 178.

[161] Ombudsmen Act 1975, s 3.

[162] Chen, 'New Zealand's Ombudsman' (n 88) at 751.

concern is that the Ombudsmen's collaborative style of investigation may occasionally compromise the scrutiny they bring to bear.[163]

Turning to tribunals, a lack of independence is often thought to be inherent in the nature of merits review. The agency appealed from is charged with implementing a regime's policy. A merits review tribunal on appeal decides what the decision should have been; as such it too is engaged in implementing the regime's policy. Therefore, it is thought the tribunal cannot be independent from the agency under appeal. This common line of thinking is, however, open to doubt, as Robert Thomas has argued.[164] First, all adjudication – including adjudication by the courts – involves an element of policy implementation: there is no sharp dividing line. Secondly, it is perfectly possible for the agency and the tribunal both to be charged with implementing the same policy according to the same legal standards, but for the tribunal to do so independently of the agency.

Apart from this, a tribunal's independence depends on its structural features. The concern about lack of security of tenure, noted above in relation to the Ombudsman, is at least as strong for most tribunals, even the external ones.[165] Tribunal members are usually appointed for a renewable fixed term of up to five years.[166] The Law Commission reported a consensus against tribunal members' appointments being permanent, up to retirement age, as for judges.[167] It is not necessarily clear why. One alternative is to have a long fixed term with no renewal – the Auditor-General, for instance, is appointed for a single term of seven years.[168] If the present system is maintained for tribunals, then the minimum safeguard should be to expressly allow non-renewal only on limited prescribed grounds.[169]

A vivid illustration of the dangers of lack of independence is the recent fate of the Australian Administrative Tribunal (AAT). Concern over a barrage of partisan appointments has led to such a crisis of legitimacy for that long-standing and highly regarded body that it has been disestablished and replaced by a new body. Groves and Weeks suggest that an apparent concrete effect of the lack of independence can be seen in several AAT decisions upholding the notorious Robodebt scheme[170] that has since been found to be clearly illegal; and in the non-reappointment of one of the few members who did find that scheme to be illegal.[171]

However, external tribunals are at least relatively independent from the department or other body whose decisions they review. Appointment tends to be by the Governor General on the recommendation either of the relevant Minister[172] or of the Minister of

[163] *Royal Commission into the Robodebt Scheme* (n 89) at 583–85, 599.

[164] Thomas, *Administrative Justice and Asylum Appeals* (n 7) at 4–11.

[165] See Law Commission, *Tribunals* (n 10) Ch 5 and also Ch 4.

[166] See, eg, Legal Services Act 2011, sch 3, cl 1; Immigration Act 2009, sch 2, cl 1; Taxation Review Authorities Act 1994, s 6(1); Social Security Act 2018, sch 8, cl 2.

[167] Law Commission, *Tribunals* (n 10) at 5.19, 5.21.

[168] Public Audit Act 2001, sch 3, cl 1.

[169] See Leggatt Report (n 83) at [7.7].

[170] See Ch 14.

[171] See Matthew Groves and Greg Weeks, 'Tribunal Justice and Politics' (n 157) at 289. Cf *Royal Commission into the Robodebt Scheme* (n 89) at 658: there was evidence that the member was not reappointed after finding the scheme illegal, but not enough evidence to infer a link.

[172] See, eg, Legal Services Act 2011, s 64(1).

Justice,[173] often after consultation with the other Minister.[174] Administrative support tends to be the responsibility of the Ministry of Justice, and salaries are paid by the Crown.[175]

For internal review tribunals, in contrast, even that independence from the department under review is missing. Consider, for example, the BRCs provided by the Social Security Act 2018.[176] Two members of each panel of three are Ministry of Social Development employees appointed by the Chief Executive, albeit they must have no prior involvement in the case. The third member is appointed by the Minister of Social Development to represent the community's interest. That third member has little more independence than the employees: the person holds office on such terms as the Minister sees fit.

The ACC regime features a peculiar attempt at independence. The Act requires first instance review applications to be made to the Corporation and requires it to 'engage' independent reviewers.[177] The Corporation has sought to achieve that independence by contracting out to a private entity.[178] It is difficult to see how this results in greater independence, given that the entity has an interest in retaining its contract with ACC.[179]

How much of a concern is the lack of independence seen in some of these remedial avenues? The question is whether it can be justified by reference to competing objectives or criteria. In relation to external tribunals, there is a potential argument for some qualifications to independence. That is not because of the need for specialisation – as already noted, this can be achieved without significantly compromising independence.[180] However, it may be considered important for a merits review tribunal to exhibit some commitment to the social goals of the particular regime. Such commitment may be promoted by a measure of political or bureaucratic supervision. This might perhaps be facilitated by reduced security of tenure: it could be argued that government should be free to appoint new tribunal members after any significant change in the policy and goals of a scheme. However, this would be a controversial argument, and certainly a controversial method. The mainstream position tends to be that we expect neutrality from administrative tribunals with a merits review jurisdiction, no less than from other adjudicative bodies. It is not at all clear, therefore, that this type of argument has played any role in the rejection of security of tenure for NZ's administrative tribunals.

Turning to internal review, while lack of any real independence is inherent in this, it has at least two potential advantages. One possible advantage of a truly internal

[173] See, eg, Taxation Review Authorities Act 1994, s 5(4).

[174] See, eg, Immigration Act 2009, s 219(3): the chair of the Immigration and Protection Tribunal is appointed on the advice of the Attorney-General, after consultation with both Ministers: s 219(2); see, eg, Social Security Act 2018, sch 8, cl 1(2).

[175] See www.justice.govt.nz/tribunals for a list of tribunals administered by the Ministry of Justice (only some of these are administrative tribunals).

[176] Social Security Act 2018, sch 7, cl 2, 3 and 6.

[177] Accident Compensation Act 2001, ss 133–134, 137–139.

[178] See www.fairwayresolution.com.

[179] For concerns, see the Dean report (n 96) at 25, 28–29.

[180] See Part B(2) above.

review is that those involved in that review can learn from the errors they uncover.[181] Secondly, internal reviews can also be beneficial in terms of their speed, accessibility and effectiveness at putting errors right. This second advantage applies *if* internal review deals quickly and informally with more obvious errors, without putting any additional burden on complainants. Internal review of that nature is better categorised as part of the agency's internal quality management systems than as part of the remedial regime.[182]

As noted earlier, however, several internal review tribunals do not operate in such a beneficial way.[183] They do put significant additional burdens on complainants. At the same time, complainants often experience them as failing to give proper consideration to review applications and as rubber stamping the decisions under review.[184]

It is highly problematic if recourse to such formalised internal procedures is made a compulsory step before accessing external tribunals, as is the case with BRCs and ACC reviewers.[185] If the compulsory first instance body is not trusted due to its lack of independence,[186] then complaints may not be made at all. Those who do complain will be too dispirited to apply for a further level of review afterwards.[187] In the UK, for instance, a dramatic drop in numbers of social security appeals was tentatively attributed to the introduction of mandatory internal reconsideration.[188]

(2) Right to a Hearing

As noted, the principles of procedural fairness are context-dependent, and a balance needs to be struck between these and competing administrative justice considerations. However, there are many aspects of the right to a hearing that need not and should not be compromised in tribunals. These include the right to adequate notice, and to disclosure of adverse material for comment. Where informality and procedural flexibility result in muddled proceedings that infringe these rights, administrative justice is no longer served either, because the applicant has not had an effective opportunity to challenge the decision in question.[189]

[181] See David Cowan et al, 'Reconsidering Mandatory Reconsideration' [2017] *Public Law* 215 at 224–25, 226, 231.

[182] For the tension between these competing categorisations, see Carol Harlow and Richard Rawlings, *Law and Administration*, 4th edn (Cambridge, Cambridge University Press, 2022) at 552–53. Benefits Review Committees, according to the Supreme Court, are not judicial authorities but rather stand in the shoes of the primary decision-maker: *Arbuthnot* (n 25) at [28].

[183] Part B(4) above.

[184] See Morton, *Access to Justice* (n 67) at 90, 104; Acclaim (n 110) at paras 150–51.

[185] Social Security Act 2018, s 395; Accident Compensation Act 2001, ss 133(5) and 149.

[186] The lack of trust may be justified: much higher success rates have been reported for the informal administrative review than for Benefits Review Committees: see n 113.

[187] Acclaim Otago (n 110) at para 134; Pirini (n 6) at 253.

[188] Mullen, 'Access to Justice' (n 8) at 119–22; see also Paul Gray, *The Second Independent Review of the Personal Independence Payment Assessment* (HMSO, March 2017) at 45.

[189] ACC review hearings have reportedly been affected by problems of this nature: see Acclaim Otago (n 110) at paras 150–51.

Among the questions that do call for balancing and compromise are whether there should be an oral hearing and whether legal representation should be allowed. An example of a context in which an oral hearing is arguably not desirable is first instance internal review, as noted under the previous heading. In exceptional contexts, proportionate dispute resolution may even favour external tribunals disposing of matters on the papers.[190]

Most tribunals usually hold oral hearings but have a discretion to dispose of matters on the papers.[191] This should be used with great caution. In contexts such as social security, there is much evidence that appeals have better prospects when the appellant attends. Holding a hearing therefore promotes effectiveness at putting errors right. Yet it is common for applicants not to attend hearings and for reviews therefore to be effectively disposed of on the papers.[192]

The question of representation is a very difficult one, because it involves acute tensions between the three administrative justice criteria. It should be noted that representation in many tribunals may take the form of lay representation as well as legal representation,[193] and experienced lay representatives can sometimes be better than lawyers who do not understand the regime in question.[194] However, in areas involving disadvantaged or vulnerable complainants, it is very common for applicants not to be represented at all.[195] That is at least partly because, as we have seen, funding for representation is very limited.[196]

In the administrative justice literature, it has often been assumed that representation is less necessary in tribunals, due to their informal procedures and enabling approaches.[197] The main arguments for seeking to render representation unnecessary in this way concern accessibility: it would remove the need to find a representative, as well as the potential cost barrier.

At the same time, part of the attraction for policy makers undoubtedly is the saving to the public purse. That objective is, however, in clear tension with accessibility. A truly enabling approach that promotes effective error correction without representation is impossible without significant resourcing. Tribunal members must have the expertise and the time to examine the evidence and research the law in order to identify issues, evidence and arguments for themselves.

The NZ commentary tends to assume that representation is necessary for a fair hearing,[198] reflecting the trustworthiness concern. Yet judicial review case law recognises no general right to legal representation as part of a fair hearing. According to *Drew*, whether representation is required at an administrative hearing depends on a range of

[190] An instance where this is arguably appropriate is found in the Films, Videos and Publications Classification Act 1993, s 53.

[191] See, eg, Social Security Act 2018, sch 8, cl 10A.

[192] See Morton, *Access to Justice* (n 67) at 98.

[193] This is permitted, for instance, in the Social Security Appeal Authority (Social Security) Regulations 2018, reg 252(b)) and in ACC reviews (Accident Compensation Act 2001, s 142).

[194] See, eg, Hazel Genn and Yvette Genn, *The Effectiveness of Representation at Tribunals* (Lord Chancellor's Department, 1989) chs 2, 3 and 6.

[195] See, eg, Morton (n 67) at 114; Acclaim Otago (n 110) at [417].

[196] See Part C(2) above.

[197] As noted in Cane (n 22) at 252.

[198] See, eg, Acclaim Otago (n 110).

factors including the nature of the body, the importance of the interests at stake and whether representation is necessary for an effective hearing in the circumstances.[199]

That last factor in *Drew* engages the third of the administrative justice criteria: effectiveness at putting errors right. This can be a strong reason for representation. In many contexts, unrepresented applicants may struggle to marshal the evidence and legal arguments required to win a meritorious case. This is a concern, for instance, in ACC reviews that turn on medical expert evidence.[200]

It is true that this concern may also be addressed by means other than representation, such as by an enabling approach. That alone, however, will not be sufficient in all contexts. This is partly because assistance at the hearing or even at a pre-hearing conference comes too late in the process.[201] More fundamentally, while a tribunal can assist complainants to some extent, its position prevents it being single-mindedly devoted to the complainant's case in the way that a representative would be.[202] Furthermore, where a tribunal takes an active role in identifying and eliciting relevant evidence, its questioning of the complainant may end up being perceived as cross-examination.[203] For all these reasons, it will often be necessary to have good pre-hearing advice as well as a tribunal with an enabling approach, as the minimum required for an effective hearing in the absence of representation.[204]

If these are the minimum requirements, that greatly reduces the ability to contain the cost to the public purse by avoiding representation. An enabling approach and pre-hearing advice both depend on adequate resourcing.

The chief example of an alternative remedial body that appears to operate generally successfully without representation is the Ombudsman. That works because the approach is fully investigatory and there are no hearings. However, the effectiveness of this approach could also be compromised by inadequate resourcing. Furthermore, pre-complaint advice may still help even in this context. In particular, such advice may reduce the risk that a meritorious complaint could be assessed at the preliminary stage as not requiring investigation, or as being outside jurisdiction.

E. Summary

From an administrative justice perspective, non-judicial avenues such as the Ombudsmen and tribunals serve the objective of putting errors right with the minimum difficulty for the affected person. Their main advantages over the judicial avenues in that regard, at least potentially, are their greater effectiveness at correcting errors

[199] *Drew* (n 156) at [45]–[66], [70]–[75], [79]. The lists of factors are at [64] and [71].

[200] See MacKinnon, 'Redefining the Facts' (n 127).

[201] ibid at 137.

[202] Zuckerman, 'No Justice Without Lawyers' (n 128) at 367–69, 371.

[203] Cane, *Administrative Tribunals* (n 22) at 242 (fn 123), 243.

[204] Some overseas studies have found that unrepresented claimants can have a good success rates, but only with pre-hearing advice: see Genn and Genn (n 194) chs 2–3; Michael Adler, 'Self-Representation, Just Outcomes and Fair Procedures in Tribunal Hearings: Some Inferences from Recently Completed Research' (Senior Presidents Conference for Tribunal Judges, 20 May 2009) at 5. See also MacKinnon, 'Redefining the Facts' (n 127) at 138.

and greater accessibility. However, tribunals can have weaknesses in terms of trustworthiness. Two further sets of considerations also influence the design, operation and evaluation of tribunals. First, there are the broader public interest objectives of proportionate dispute resolution, conserving public resources and promoting the social goals of the particular regime. Secondly, constitutional principles must be considered.

Administrative tribunals in Aotearoa NZ do achieve the desired greater effectiveness at putting errors right, through offering merits review by specialist or specialised tribunals. A question deserving of more attention is whether merits review can address complaints about unlawful reasoning processes or unfair procedures. Constitutional concerns about separation of powers and independence in relation to specialisation and merits review feature in overseas literature but have not carried much weight here. A further advantage of specialised tribunals is that they are more likely to understand the social goals of the regime in which they operate.

The Ombudsmen also make a very significant contribution to effective error correction. Their recommendatory jurisdiction extends not only to the merits of decisions but also to other forms of maladministration. They can recommend a wide range of remedies.

However, realising the alternative avenues' potential for greater accessibility is a significant challenge. Speedy resolution is often compromised through inadequate resourcing and problematic design. Compulsory recourse to formalised internal review is a particular design problem impacting on speed. Informal and enabling procedures are widely used in Aotearoa NZ. But without representation or at least good pre-hearing advice (again a resourcing issue), true accessibility remains to be achieved. There are also issues with public awareness and understanding of tribunals.

Trustworthiness due to independence is an area of further weakness for tribunals. The problems can be minimised by appropriate design, but NZ tribunals have a long way to go in this regard. External tribunals could be made more independent, and internal review with its inherent lack of independence too often functions as a barrier to accessing external tribunals.

Index